THE
SHAFTESBURY PAPERS

South Carolina Historical Society

TEMPUS

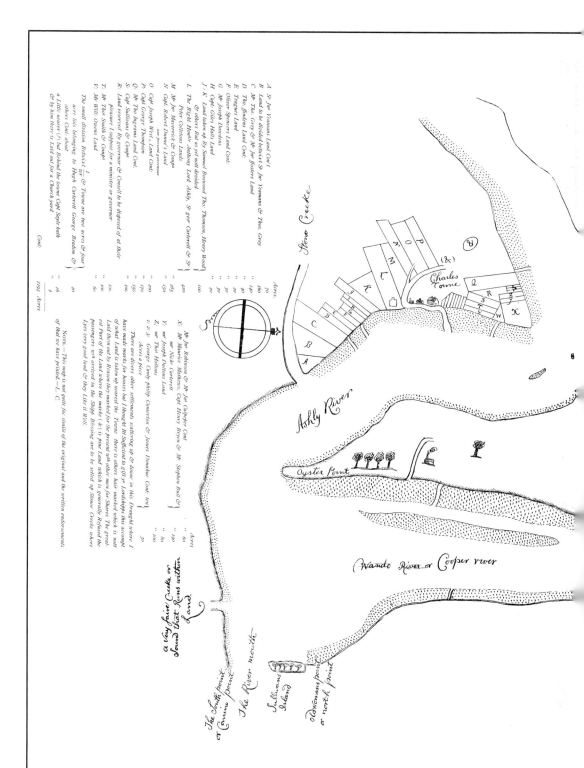

A. Sr Jno Yeamans Land Con'l — 70
B. Land to be divided betwixt Sr Jno Yeamans & Thos. Grey — 160
C. Mr Tho. Grey & Mr Jno fosters Land — 140
D. Tho. findines Land Cont: — 40
E. Teagues Land — 20
F. Oliver Spencers Land Cont: — 20
G. Mr Joseph Dowdens — 30
H. Capt Giles Halls Land — 20
J:-K. Land taken up By Samuel Boxwood Tho. Thomson, Henry Wood & others but as yet not devided — 100
L. The Right Honbl Anthony Lord Ashly, Sr geor Carteret & Sr Peter Collitons Lands — 420
M. Mr Jno Mavericke & Compa — 285
N. Capt Robert Dunne's Land — 150
   one present governor
O. Capt Joseph West, Land Cont: — 200
P. Capt George Thompson — 170
Q. Mr Tho Ingrams Land Cont. — 150
R. Land reserved By governor & Consell to be disposed of at their pleasure I suppose for a minister or governor — 10c
S. Capt Sullivans & Compa — 10c
T. Mr Thos Smith & Compa — 10c
V. Mr Will: Owens Land — 60

The small division Betwixt 1/nr & Towne are two acres & four acres lots belonging to Hugh Carterett George Beadon & others Cont: about — 20

a Little weaver (^) but behind the Same Capt Sayle hath & by him there is Laid out for a Church yard — 16/4

Cont: — 2194 Acres

Acres
X. Mr Robinson & Mr Jno Culpeper Cont — 60
Y. Mr Maurice Mathews, Capt Henry Bryen & Mr Stephen Bull & — 190
   Mr Nicho Carterett
Z. Mr Joseph Daltons Land — 80
   Mr Thos Hollowe — 100
1:2:3: George Canty philip Comerton & James Donahoe Cont: ten — 30

Acres a piece

There are divers other settlements scattering up & downe in this Draught where I have made marks for houses but I thought Itt Sufficient to giff yr Lordshipps this accompt of what Land is taken up neerest the Towne there is others hair marked which is most Land them out by Reason they marked for the present yth other men for Shares The greatest Part of the Land where the marke (&) is pine Land which is generally Refused the passengers yth arrived in the Shipp Blessing are to be setled up Stonoe Creeke where Lyes very good land & they Like it Well.

NOTE.—This map is not quite fac simile of the original and the written endorsements of that we have printed.—L. C.

Stono Creeke

Charles Towne

Ashly River

Oyster Point

Wando River or Cooper river

Sullivans Island

Bowmans point or north point

The Stuff point or Conins point

The River mouth

a very faire Creeke or Sound that Runs within Land

This map detailing the Charleston area originally appeared as a foldout in the 1897 publication.

The Line marked with Red is the bounds betwixte the lands & marshes the prickes within the red Line Signify the marshes betwixt the Land & River and iff any Black lines run through the marsh they notify Creeks & where is any prickes within ye Red lines to Landward there are marshes, there are without question many more marshes & Swampes within Land & small Creeks Running through marshes some to the Land & many Spreding them Selves In the marshes before they Come to Land then I have yett seene or Can now give a discription off the marshes are all over growne with a high flagg or Reed & appears at a distance like a greene meddow, up Wando River there is some Riseing Land & small mountains within, but I have seen none such in Ashly River. I forbear to mention any thing of the Soundings or doings of Rivers Because I am informed ye Lordshipps have already Received the same from others I could not yett possibly gett the use of a boate to informe myselfe any thing off the Coming out of the River & therefore can Say nothing to itt.

A Broad Reddy Creeke that Runs many miles into the County

Ittiwan Creeke

The opening of Ittiwan River

This Branch of the River spends its selfe in A marsh

Scale of five English myles

1 2 3 4 5

First Published 1897

Published by:
Tempus Publishing, Inc.
2 Cumberland Street
Charleston, SC 29401

Typesetting and originaition by Tempus Publishing, Inc.
Printed and bound in Great Britain

Library of Congress Data: Applied for.
ISBN 0-7385-0343-6

Published in association with:
South Carolina Historical Society
Fireproof Building
100 Meeting Street
Charleston, SC 29401

PREFACE TO THE REPRINT
Robert M. Weir

No one did more than the first Earl of Shaftesbury to ensure the success of English settlement in South Carolina, and no single source provides better insight into the process than the volume being reissued here. Since its 1897 publication in the Collections of the South Carolina Historical Society, volume five, The Shaftesbury Papers has been the richest and most conveniently used compendium of materials about South Carolina during the crucial founding years when Shaftesbury was most actively involved with the colony. Unfortunately, however, the volume has long been out of print, and historians have frequently had to rely on substitutes. Thus the author of a fine modern biography of Shaftesbury notes that his papers "relating to Carolina were published" in the society's Collections but that "the most important [items] are summarized in C.S.P. Col. [Calender of State Papers, Colonial], and since these volumes are more easily accessible I have referred to them where the summaries are adequate."[1] But what may be sufficient for one purpose may be inadequate for another. Having all—or nearly all—the extant documents in their entirety obviously serves a much wider range of inquiry.

That said, one notes with some surprise that the letters printed in this volume represent most of the surviving materials written by Shaftesbury during the latter part of his life. The explanation seems to be threefold. First and foremost, he was an extremely busy man, involved in a multitude of affairs, who frequently employed others to generate documents for him. Secondly, some of the affairs in which he was involved were politically dangerous. Thus he, or someone close to him, may well have destroyed many of the more sensitive items. And, finally, Carolina was important enough to him that he devoted much of his discretionary time during the 1670s to it.[2]

Anthony Ashley Cooper, Lord Shaftesbury, was born at Wimborne St. Giles, Dorsetshire, in 1621. During the English Civil War he sided first with King Charles I and then with Parliament. As a member of that body, he eventually headed a group of republicans and Presbyterians who opposed the Lord Protector Oliver Cromwell. No one, Cromwell is supposed to have said, "was so difficult to manage as the little man with three names." Indeed, by 1660 Shaftesbury, who had come to support restoration of the monarch, was one of those who invited Charles II to resume the throne. He became a member of the royal Privy Council and in 1672 Earl of Shaftesbury and Lord Chancellor. Within a few years, however, he fell from grace with the king for opposing a Catholic succession to the monarchy. In 1682 Shaftesbury fled to Holland where he died the following year.[3]

That someone so heavily involved in high politics became deeply committed to a colonizing venture may seem puzzling at first. But the Restoration period was one in which Englishmen displayed considerable interest in the colonies. Under Charles II they founded or acquired New York, New Jersey, and Pennsylvania as well as North and South Carolina. Furthermore, at one time Shaftesbury himself owned shares of a plantation in Barbados and a ship plying the "Guinea Trade." He also served on various committees of the Privy Council that dealt with plantation affairs, including one appointed to draw up a plan of government for Jamaica, which had been captured from Spain in 1655.[4] It was therefore in character for him to become one of eight prominent figures who sought a grant from Charles II to the land on the southeastern coast of North America between Virginia and Spanish Florida. Being indebted to several of these men politically as well as monetarily, the king complied, and in 1663 they became the Lords Proprietors of Carolina. During the next few years, Charles II enlarged the grant; reconnoitering expeditions filed glowing reports about the region; and several groups from New England and Barbados made unsuccessful attempts to settle it. Meanwhile, Lord Ashley mainly went about his other business.

Beginning in 1669, however, he assumed a much more active role among the proprietors. At their meeting on April 26, he persuaded them to help finance another attempt to settle the area. They agreed that each would contribute £500 sterling, and perhaps more if necessary. Ashley then recruited settlers in England, bought and supplied three vessels, and with John Locke drafted the Fundamental Constitutions of Carolina, an extensive, carefully thought-out but somewhat Utopian plan for the social and institutional development of the colony. Not yet the famous philosopher that he was to become, Locke was then acting as secretary to the Proprietors. Equally important, he was also Ashley's personal physician and, as such, in June 1668 had supervised a major operation on his patient's abscessed liver. Thereafter, Ashley carried a permanent silver drain in his abdomen reminding him of his mortality and what he owed to Locke.[5]

Whether Ashley's increased commitment to the Carolina project was the result of his narrow escape from death is an intriguing question that will probably never receive a definitive answer. Doubtless other considerations partly account for the difference in his behavior during the early and late 1660s. From 1665 to 1667 the English were at war with the Dutch; in 1665 the plague ravaged London; and in 1666 the Great Fire destroyed much of the city. These were formidable distractions. Furthermore, the Proprietors initially assumed that others could succeed in settling Carolina without much help from them. By the late 1660s it had become all too clear that this assumption was erroneous. Moreover, shortly after the crown's grant of Carolina to the Proprietors in 1663, the Privy Council had stipulated that similar documents should henceforth contain a clause voiding them if no settlement had been made within a specified period of time. The second Carolina charter omitted the stipulation (but did include trade concessions with an expiration date). In sum, the crown's position on the matter was clear. Still, the fact that Ashley's greater personal involvement with Carolina quickly followed a personal crisis suggests that there might also have been a connection between the two. So, perhaps, do some of the more idealistic features of the Fundamental Constitutions. Earlier writers such as Sir Thomas Moore and James Harrington could describe an imaginary Utopia or Oceana, but Shaftesbury had the opportunity to make Carolina a reality. That he termed it his "Darling" and committed much time and emotional energy to the project makes one suspect that he saw the colony as his ticket to immortality. The record of his activities in this volume suggests that the Ashley and Cooper Rivers emptying into the sea at Charleston are in fact appropriately named.[6]

Certainly the documents assembled here provide an incomparable record, not only of Shaftesbury's efforts but also those of hundreds of others who eventually made Carolina a viable enterprise. Historians, genealogists, and others inquirers have therefore found the work a real mine of information. General histories from David Duncan Wallace, The History of South Carolina (1934) to Walter B. Edgar, South Carolina: A History (1998) have relied on it. So too have numerous specialized studies: take for example, Lawrence S. Rowland, Alexander Moore, and George C. Rogers, Jr., The History of Beaufort County, South Carolina (1996); M. Eugene Sirmans, Colonial South Carolina: A Political History, 1663-1763 (1966); Converse D. Clowse, Economic Beginnings in Colonial South Carolina, 1670-1730 (1971); Peter A. Coclanis, Shadow of a Dream: Economic Life and Death in the South Carolina Low Country, 1670-1920; Peter H. Wood, Black Majority: Negroes in Colonial South Carolina From 1670 through the Stono Rebellion (1974); Chapman J. Milling, Red Carolinians (1940); and James H. Merrell, The Indians' New World: Catawbas and Their Neighbors from European Contact through the Era of Removal (1989), to name only a few. What is significant about even this abbreviated list in the present context is that it contains works published over a considerable period of time covering a wide range of subjects. In short, The Shaftesbury Papers has been—and will continue to be—a vade mecum, an indispensable companion, to historians and others as they explore the early history of the Carolinas, doubtless in ways not yet foreseen, widening the boundaries of the discipline as they proceed. By making The Shaftesbury Papers conveniently available in this edition the South Carolina Historical Society therefore performs a real service.

---

[1] Kenneth Harold Dobson Haley, The First Earl of Shaftesbury (Oxford: Clarendon Press, 1968), 239, n. 2.

[2] Ibid., 235, 253.

[3] Ibid., passim; the quotation comes from Dictionary of National Biography, s.v. "Cooper, Anthony Ashley," eds. Leslie Stephen and Sidney Lee (London: Elder and Co., 1885-1901).

[4] Haley, First Earl of Shaftesbury, 230-231; Acts of the Privy Council of England: Colonial Series, Vol.I, A.D. 1613-1680, eds. W. L. Grant and James Munro (Hereford: Anthony Brothers, for H.M. Stationary Office, 1908), 313.

[5] See below, 91-93; M. Eugene Sirmans, Colonial South Carolina: A Political History, 1663-1763 (Chapel Hill, N.C.: University of North Carolina Press for the Institute of Early American History and Culture at Williamsburg, V.A., 1966), 7.

[6] Acts of the Privy Council, 369; Mattie Erma Edwards Parker, ed., North Carolina Charters and Constitutions, 1578-1678 (Raleigh, N.C.: Carolina Charter Tercentenary Commission, 1963), 97-98; Robert M. Weir, Colonial South Carolina—A History (Millwood, N.Y.: KTO Press, 1983; reprint Columbia, S.C.: USC Press, 1997), 53.

INTRODUCTION TO THE REPRINT
Charles H. Lesser

Langdon Cheves' 1897 edition of "The Shaftesbury Papers" originally appeared in volume five of the Collections of the South Carolina Historical Society. It contains most of the surviving documentation for the beginning of the first permanent English settlement in South Carolina. After more than a century, this feat of antiquarian scholarship still supplies a rich saga of a fledgling colony. Three men were responsible for the publication of the book: an English archivist, a New South mayor, and a scion of South Carolina's lowcountry rice-planting aristocracy. Langdon Cheves, the lowcountry aristocrat in this story, turned the efforts of the other two men into this book. The history of the book's creation helps readers to understand Cheves' sometimes cryptic practices and to make allowance for the ways in which it is incomplete.

The core of the materials printed here is a spectacular cache of manuscripts that Anthony Ashley Cooper (first Earl of Shaftesbury) and John Locke accumulated while Shaftesbury was managing the Carolina Proprietors' affairs and Locke was secretary to that joint enterprise. Shaftesbury and Locke inherited a few documents from Sir John Colleton's earlier management of the proprietorship, but the bulk of this archive dates from early 1669 through mid 1675. It begins when Shaftesbury convinced the other proprietors to send English settlers to their foundering colonial enterprise and runs through that settlement's harrowing first years. The nearly 100 manuscripts in this cache include Shaftesbury's letter book of both incoming and outgoing Carolina correspondence from February 17, 1670, to June 14, 1675; a revised draft of the Fundamental Constitutions for the colony; an astonishingly complete corpus of original financial accounts, passenger and crew lists, reports, letters, and maps from the founding expedition and first year of the settlement; and five sets of abstracts of Carolina papers, 1670-1672, which Locke prepared for the earl. These abstracts include summaries of numerous additional letters that are no longer extant. For example, the abstract of one missing letter relays the charge that the colony's first surveyor, Florence O'Sullivan, was an "Ill natured buggerer of children."[1]

These original documents chronicling South Carolina's founding are now at the British Public Record Office in Kew. Until 1871 they remained at Wimborne St. Giles in Dorset, the ancestral home of the Earls of Shaftesbury. The first earl was born there at his maternal grandfather's house in 1621. He left his Carolina share to his grandson who became the third earl and a noted philosopher. The philosopher's great-grandson, the seventh earl of Shaftesbury, was a reformer and philanthropist known as "the poor man's friend." The seventh earl gave his family's papers to the nation in 1871.

W. Noel Sainsbury, the English archivist in this story, processed these papers as they came in to the Public Record Office. Sainsbury had joined the State Paper Office in London as a temporary clerk at age twenty-two in 1848. He devoted his entire professional life to the Public Record Office, which absorbed the State Paper Office in 1854. Sainsbury was a senior clerk there when the seventh earl donated his family's papers in 1871.[2] Over the next decade, Sainsbury arranged and described the great family archive emerging from the Shaftesbury muniment room at St. Giles House. He explained his work and listed the collection in five detailed reports, dated from 1871 to 1881, which the Public Record Office included as supplements to its annual reports.[3]

The seventh earl's gift began with a 1427 deed and ran through the papers of the fourth earl. Sainsbury placed the papers in twelve sections, which were subsequently divided into fifty numbered bundles. Section IX (which became bundle 48) contains the core of this book, "Letters and Papers relating to Carolina and the First Settlement on Ashley River." Section VIII (bundle 47) has "Locke's Letters and Papers," most of which do not relate directly to the proprietorship. Sainsbury arranged the items within the sections in chronological order.[4] The 157-page Carolina letter book became item 55 in bundle 48, thus explaining the frequency of "Bdle. 48, No. 55" in Cheves' careful annotation of his sources. The original Shaftesbury Papers at the Public Record Office still are arranged in Sainsbury's order with these bundle and item numbers, and the South Carolina Department of Archives and History has microfilm of the bundles most relevant to the colony's history.[5]

Sainsbury considered the Shaftesbury Papers the richest documentation for first settlement of any of the American colonies.[6] By 1871 when he began working with these papers, he already had close ties to American historians and an established reputation as a supplier of London transcripts and abstracts for their work. In 1855 George Bancroft already considered Sainsbury, then not yet thirty years old, "the most inquisitive and sagacious" of all the agents from whom he obtained copies. William James Rivers, South Carolina's pioneering historian of the colony's earliest years, was married to a cousin of Bancroft, and he, too, had acquired transcripts from Sainsbury in the 1850s.[7]

Instead of passing into the custody of later managers and secretaries of the proprietorship, this cache of documents for South Carolina's beginning had remained with the Shaftesbury family archive. John Locke gave up his duties with the proprietary board when he went to France in 1675. That departure, coupled with the tumult and exile that marked the end of the first Earl of Shaftesbury's life, may explain why this rich hoard covering only a few years remained at Wimborne St. Giles.[8] Other records of the joint colonial enterprise followed a more regular path to the last secretary of the proprietorship (Richard Shelton), to the Board of Trade, to the State Paper Office, and finally to the Public Record Office. An entry book in which the Lords Proprietors first began keeping their records in 1663 (cited by Cheves as "Col. Ent. Book, 20") contains additional important material for South Carolina's founding. William James Rivers published transcriptions of many of the most relevant documents in that entry book in his A Sketch of the History of South Carolina to the Close of the Proprietary Government by the Revolution of 1719 with an Appendix Containing Many Valuable Documents Hitherto Unpublished in 1856.[9] The City of Charleston's incorporation centennial in 1883 spurred the state's acquisition of transcripts of the newly available and much richer Shaftesbury Papers and ultimately led to the publication of this edition.

In 1883 William Ashmead Courtenay began serving his second term as Charleston's mayor. Courtenay was more of an advocate of New South measures than many other Charlestonians and a passionate promoter of the city's rich history. An aggressive businessman involved with the management of steamship lines, Courtenay later opened a cotton mill at Newry in Oconee County, S.C. In 1881 "from the vantage point of difficulties surmounted, and with a bright future opening to our view, in the recovered energy of our people, and with their industries reviving and extending," Courtenay began publishing city Year Books recounting his careful fiscal management and substantial municipal improvements. From the first, these Year Books contained extensive supplements of historical materials.[10]

In early May 1883 a special committee of the city's aldermen recommended asking Mayor Courtenay to deliver the centennial address in August. In accepting the invitation, he pointed to the "long neglect" of Charleston's history and suggested that the city make "small annual appropriations" for "the collection of data, the selection of material." The size of that task, he claimed, was beyond the capabilities of "private enterprise." Courtenay himself was a great collector of historical materials. Either as a personal measure or in anticipation of city council action, he already had contracted with W. Noel Sainsbury for transcripts of at least some of the Shaftesbury Papers. Before the year was out, Sainsbury provided the city with copies of all of the South Carolina materials in bundle 48 at a cost of £77.11.0. Mayor Courtenay made use of some of these materials in his August address, but fourteen years would elapse before Cheves' edition appeared in the fifth and last volume of the Collections of the South Carolina Historical Society.[11]

Founded in 1855, the South Carolina Historical Society published three volumes of Collections before suspending its activities at the beginning of the Civil War in 1861. The majority of the pages in those three volumes (1857, 1858, 1859) had their origins in none other than W. Noel Sainsbury, "the Society's agent" in providing a "List and Abstract of Papers in the State Paper Office, London, Relating to South-Carolina."[12]

The society reactivated in 1875. In late 1884 or the first days of 1885, Mayor Courtenay and the Charleston City Council offered the society "about 1000 sheets of Manuscript" transcripts of the Shaftesbury Papers and an annual appropriation "for the three ensuing years 1885, 1886, 1887" to assist "in publishing the same." Langdon Cheves, Joseph W. Barnwell, and J. J. Pringle Smith made up a committee to plan this as well as a backlog of other promised publications. Cheves had been among the most active of those who had reactivated the society. Barnwell and Smith also were leading lights in historical matters at the time, but there were other close ties among the men. Barnwell was married to Cheves' sister Harriott, and Pringle Smith was Cheves' uncle by marriage.[13] After an initial effort toward speedy publication of the Shaftesbury Papers, progress lagged. For many years the committee let Cheves treat the project as his personal avocation until Courtenay again stepped in and prodded their eventual publication.

Langdon Cheves (1848-1940) was the grandson of two wealthy rice plantation barons, Langdon Cheves (1776-1857, of Bank of the United States fame) and Henry Augustus Middleton (1793-1887). His uncle Langdon Cheves (1814-1863), a signer of the South Carolina Ordinance of Secession, was killed in 1863 at Battery Wagner, which he helped design as a captain of engineers. At age sixteen, Cheves himself briefly served as a volunteer aide-de-camp in the engineers at the war's end before graduating with high honors from the College of Charleston in 1871.[14] He worked for a short time in railroad construction in Georgia after graduation, but soon returned to Charleston to study law. Lawyer, plantation owner, historian, and genealogist, Cheves lived on South Bay Street (later renamed South Battery) near his grandfather Middleton's town house for most of his long life and spent parts of the summer and fall at his summer home in Flat Rock, North Carolina. He had just completed making a copy of the Christ Church Parish register for the Historical Society when the society acquired the Shaftesbury Papers. In late 1885 "worked on Shaftesbury Papers" became a common entry in his diary.[15]

Cheves and the Historical Society anticipated prompt publication. Before the year was out, Cheves notified the city that the society had raised the required matching funds and collected the $300 appropriated by the city for the year 1885.[16] The massive earthquake of 1886 and other untoward events then intervened. No further city appropriations for the project were forthcoming. Although as late as 1889 Cheves still said that he hoped to begin publication "this fall at the latest," longer delays set in.[17] The delays were fortunate, however, for they made a more complete and thorough book possible.

In the 1880s Cheves was still planting rice on his family's Delta Plantation, one of the largest on the South Carolina side of the Savannah River. Delta had enabled his grandfather Cheves to amply support and endow a large family.[18] It made a $395 profit in 1885, but consistently

showed a loss thereafter. In 1887 Louis H. Haskell, Cheves' plantation
manager, was unsure whether Cheves was "going to plant another year,"
but he continued for a few more years.[19] Cheves' grandfather Middleton
died at age 93 in 1887 in a temporary residence on South Bay, his
townhouse at No. 68 still not repaired from the shattering it took in the
1886 earthquake. Cheves took the most active role among three executors
of a vast estate that included large rice plantations and property in
Charleston and Newport, Rhode Island.[20] For years to come, Cheves was
heavily involved with this disputed and drawn-out estate settlement in
addition to managing his law practice and his and his widowed mother's
investments. There may well have been some truth in his 1889
explanation of "nothing but want of time" for the delay in publication of
the Shaftesbury Papers.[21]

Langdon Cheves, however, was a perfectionist and clearly enjoyed his
prolonged work toward amplifying, annotating, and editing the
Shaftesbury Papers. During these years he also assisted the New England
Historic Genealogical Society with publications that touched on early
South Carolina families. Even his recreational rowing in the evening and
on Sundays would eventually benefit his explanatory footnotes on
seventeenth-century encounters with the lowcountry landscape.[22] Cheves
knew the Charleston area and its earliest history in ways that few persons
have since.

In 1887 Cheves negotiated with William Ellis Jones of Richmond to print
both the Shaftesbury Papers and the "Report of the Committee Appointed
by the General Assembly of South Carolina in 1740, on the St. Augustine
Expedition." Cheves liked Jones' recent work on the Official Letters of
Alexander Spotswood for the Virginia Historical Society.[23] The St.
Augustine report, edited by Cheves' uncle J. J. Pringle Smith, was a smaller
editorial project that long had been in the society's backlog. Later that year,
a Charleston printer handled the St. Augustine report, allowing the society
to bind and issue volume four of its Collections in 1888 after a lapse of
nearly three decades.[24] Langdon Cheves published a profusely annotated
edition of George Chicken's "Journal of the March of the Carolinians into
the Cherokee Mountains in the Yemassee Indian War, 1715-16" in the
Charleston Year Book for 1894, but he and his Virginia printer did not issue
"The Shaftesbury Papers" in volume five of the Collections until 1897.

Former mayor Courtenay eventually forced Cheves to finish the long-
delayed publication. In 1891 a distinguished group of gentlemen headed
by Courtenay gave the Historical Society the ten large volumes of the
recently completed Colonial Records of North Carolina. Courtenay then
led the Historical Society in a statewide campaign that established a Public
Record Commission charged with producing a similar publication for
South Carolina. The Public Record Commission, the predecessor agency
to today's Department of Archives and History, hired Sainsbury to supply
its Public Record Office transcripts. Headed ex officio by a parsimonious

secretary of state, the commission instructed Sainsbury to omit both the Shaftesbury Papers and documents already published in either Rivers' 1856 volume or the Colonial Records of North Carolina.[25]

By 1895 Courtenay was a resident of his own mill town of Newry and a leading member of the Public Record Commission. He called the commission's attention to the mass of unpublished Shaftesbury Papers and secured a resolution authorizing him to request that the Historical Society turn over the transcripts.[26] The Historical Society decided to reject Courtenay's request and proceed with publishing the papers itself. The society appointed Henry Augustus Middleton Smith, Langdon Cheves' first cousin and another of the best antiquarian scholars of the day, to fill the vacancy on the Publications Committee caused by the death of Smith's father, J. J. Pringle Smith, and "empowered" the committee "to take the necessary steps for an early publication of said papers." The society, hoping to work "in consultation with the State Public Record Commission," appointed Courtenay "as an additional member on said Committee." Courtenay, who was used to getting his own way, resigned his membership in the Historical Society in a huff.[27]

The society requested a full report from Cheves on his progress, which showed he had done a great deal of work. Some of this work would not have been possible when the project started in 1885. Perhaps of most importance, W. Noel Sainsbury's great Calendar of State Papers, Colonial Series, America and West Indies reached the period 1669-1674 in 1889. Cheves had purchased that volume and its predecessor for his own library and now was allowed to borrow the Historical Society's recently acquired copy of the first volume of the Colonial Records of North Carolina, partly printed from transcripts also supplied by Sainsbury.[28] These volumes significantly supplemented the earlier publications that Cheves carefully mined and compared, most notably the documents printed by William James Rivers in 1856 and the Sainsbury abstracts in the first three volumes of the Historical Society's own Collections.

Cheves had the sharp eye and strong memory that make a good editor. In a day before photocopies and microfilm, he was dependent on the accuracy of handwritten transcripts. Sainsbury had not personally made the Shaftesbury transcripts in 1883, but all of them had been checked, "a considerable portion of them" by Sainsbury himself.[29] Sainsbury included his own extensive abstracts and excerpts of the Shaftesbury Papers in the Calendar of State Papers. This allowed Cheves to further check the accuracy of the transcripts, which he sent off to Richmond to be set in type and which he insisted be followed "verbatim et literatum." The modern reader puzzling over the tiny, difficult handwriting of the originals on the microfilm can marvel at what was accomplished in printing these manuscripts. In at least one case, Cheves inserted an accurate, corrected reading in brackets based on his sense of the text alone, for the problem text was not reproduced in the Calendar of State Papers.

Cheves was able to use the first volume of The Colonial Records of North Carolina and the Calendar of State Papers to supplement the documents from the proprietors' first entry book that Rivers had printed. Cheves' priority was printing full texts of the Shaftesbury Papers themselves, but he was also determined to include at least excerpts or abstracts of every relevant document he could find. Rivers also had printed portions of the colony's Journal of the Grand Council, but further pages of the journal recently had been found misbound in another volume. Cheves therefore used three separate sources for council minutes: Rivers (which he did not reprint in full), a manuscript copy made in 1851 during John Sitgraves Green's efforts to preserve the state's colonial records, and the newly discovered pages that had been missing when Green did his work. He also used Green's transcript for his texts of the earliest Miscellaneous Records of the Secretary of the Province.[30] The only surviving pre-1676 records in South Carolina that Cheves did not use are the Warrants for Land, leading him to mistakenly think that the "one lusty negro man" brought by Henry Brayne was the "first negro mentioned in Carolina."[31]

Cheves' meticulous annotation takes a little getting used to. For one thing, he saved space with abbreviations that are not always immediately intelligible to modern eyes. Charles Town sometimes became simply "C. T." in his notes, which often go on to discuss items later in the document than the call down number that brought the reader's eye to the foot of the page. The genealogist's abbreviation "d.s.p." (for "died without issue") appears without explanation, and the Statutes at Large are cited as simply "A. A.," perhaps for Acts of Assembly. At the foot of the page of errata that his careful checking forced him to add at the very last, Cheves also added specific page numbers for sources that his notes had cited only in a more general way. Cheves did a great deal of work in the early deed books and probate records, but the probate volumes now bear different designations than they did in his day.[32]

A few closely related additional sources for the period covered by this book have surfaced since 1897. The most significant is a twenty-page Carolina notebook kept by John Locke while he was secretary to the proprietorship. This little book includes notations of bills ordered to be paid, March 2-April 20, 1671; minutes for eight meetings of the proprietors, 1672-1675; and extracts of seven lost 1674 letters that provide valuable details about the still struggling settlement. One of these explained that "single men" in the colony were apt to run away because they "Desire women." The notebook is a part of the main body of Locke's papers, which the Bodleian Library at Oxford purchased in 1948. Photocopies or microfilm of the notebook are available at the South Carolina Department of Archives and History and at both the Southern Historical Collection at the University of North Carolina and the North Carolina Division of Archives and History. A few related letters to Locke about proprietary affairs have been published.[33] The William L. Clements Library at the University of Michigan recently purchased an additional manuscript account of the 1667 Sandford exploratory expedition written by Lieut. Joseph Woory.

Cheves paid particular attention to what he thought was the "First set of the Constitutions for the Government of Carolina; by John Locke." Sainsbury had placed a manuscript book containing this text in what became bundle 47 ("Locke's Letters and Papers") and printed the text in full complete with cancellations and interlineations in his first report on the Shaftesbury Papers. In the nineteenth century John Locke was commonly believed to be the author of the Fundamental Constitutions. For Sainsbury, the fact that the much-amended manuscript was in Locke's hand proved the attribution. Even though Cheves' printer said that he would have to charge $2 extra per page to depict the amendments, Cheves got the authorization of his Publications Committee and insisted that this item be printed "just as Mr. Sainsbury has it." Anthony Ashley Cooper is now believed to have had a more central role in writing the Fundamental Constitutions, and this text is now known to be Locke's inscription of one stage of amendments to an earlier version sent over with the first settlers.[34]

Cheves' fussing with type faces for the Fundamental Constitutions was typical of his attention to detail as he carefully checked and corrected the proofs that William Ellis Jones sent to him at Flat Rock and Charleston in late 1896 and early 1897.[35] Cheves also prepared the superb index. He was determined to include everything he could before his 1675 cut-off date and to get everything right.

Cheves' edition of South Carolina's earliest records resembles an earlier monument of antiquarian scholarship, J. H. Lefroy's Memorials of the Discovery and Early Settlement of the Bermudas or Somers Islands, 1511-1687. Cheves' own volume was nearly complete when he discovered Lefroy, forcing him to add unindexed extra pages with duplicative page numbers to the front matter and additional notes placed on the page before the index. Indentured servants made up a considerable proportion of the settlers in the first fleet. In January and February 1670, the Carolina made a forced stop of six weeks in Bermuda after a violent storm. Proclamations Cheves found in Lefroy threatened arrest, lengthened terms of servitude, and "condigne punishment," if the settlers did not reassemble so that the ship could depart. These proclamations did not cast a flattering light on the beginnings of his beloved Charleston, but relevant they were, and so he included them.

In October 1897 the other two members of the Publications Committee (Cheves' brother-in-law and his cousin) at last reported that the 500 copies of volume five of the Collections of the South Carolina Historical Society were ready for distribution. Cheves himself modestly did not sign the report. In addition to "The Shaftesbury Papers," the volume included an eighteen-page 1880 address by Joseph W. Barnwell that is omitted here. Barnwell and H. A. M. Smith made clear that they were "not entitled to any credit for the high character of the work." The committee, with Cheves included, had advanced the society $244.30 to meet the society's shortfall against the printer's $855.25 bill. Heavy usage of the volume's increasingly brittle pages over the last century have proven the committee right in their judgment that Cheves' "time expended upon the volume, covering many years, has been well expended."[36]

---

[1] Abstract of missing letter from Maurice Mathews, below, 248. Sullivan's Island, S.C., is named for O'Sullivan.

[2] W. Noel Sainsbury sketch in the Dictionary of National Biography; John D. Cantwell, The Public Record Office, 1838-1958 (London: Her Majesty's Stationery Office, 1991), 169, 193-94, 573.

[3] Sainsbury's five reports annotated with the bundle and item numbers that already were in use before Cheves published this edition are available in List and Index Society, Vol. 70, Public Record Office, Gifts and Deposits, Supplementary List (London: List and Index Society for subscribers, 1971), 81-156. The Shaftesbury Papers are now classified as PRO 30.

[4] Because the papers did not all come in to the Public Record Office at the same time, later installments had to be interfiled with documents received earlier. The 106 Carolina items in bundle 48 (a few of which date after 1675) came in in two batches and were listed in the 1871 and 1873 reports.

[5] In addition to bundles 47 and 48, bundle 49, "Documents about Jamaica, Barbados, The Bahamas, and Foreign Plantations."

[6] W. Noel Sainsbury, Nov. 3, 1883, to Mayor William Ashmead Courtenay, Scrapbook of Sainsbury Correspondence and Other Materials Relating to Obtaining Transcripts in England, 1883-1895, Courtenay Collection, Charleston Library Society (hereafter cited as CLS). This volume is available on South Carolina Historical Society microfiche 51-556 (5 fiches).

[7] George Bancroft, Aug. 9, 1855, to William James Rivers, William James Rivers Papers, South Caroliniana Library, University of South Carolina. Charles H. Lesser, South Carolina Begins: The Records of a Proprietary Colony, 1663-1721 (Columbia, S.C.: The South Carolina Department of Archives and History, 1995), 60-61.

[8] Some of the papers could be considered Shaftesbury's own as "husband" of the funds and manager under the 1669 agreement between the proprietors to fund a settlement. Distinctions between personal and institutional papers were not always clear in the seventeenth century.

[9] William James Rivers, A Sketch of the History of South Carolina to the Close of the Proprietary Government by the Revolution of 1719 with an Appendix Containing Many Valuable Documents Hitherto Unpublished (Charleston, S.C.: McCarter & Co., 1856; reprinted, Spartanburg, S.C.: The Reprint Co., 1972), 335-69, 387-91. Rivers cited the first entry book as "S. P. O. [State Paper Office]

North Carolina. B. T. [Board of Trade], Vol. 2"; it is now classed as CO5/286. For a more extensive treatment of the later administration of the proprietorship and their records, see Lesser, South Carolina Begins, 42-60.

[10] "Mayor Courtenay's Annual Review," Year Book—1880. City of Charleston (Charleston, S.C.: The News and Courier Book Presses for the City of Charleston, 1881), 1; Gail Moore Morrison, "'I Shall Not Pass This Way Again'; The Contributions of William Ashmead Courtenay," ed. David Moltke-Hansen, Art in the Lives of South Carolinians: Nineteenth-Century Chapters (Charleston, S.C.: Carolina Art Association, 1979).

[11] Year Book—1883. City of Charleston (Charleston, S.C.: The News and Courier Book Presses for the City of Charleston, 1884), 325-28, 359; W. Noel Sainsbury to Courtenay, May 21, 1883, and Nov. 17, 1883, Sainsbury Scrapbook, CLS. The May 21 letter is the first in the scrapbook, but it clearly postdates the beginning of the correspondence on the acquisition of the Shaftesbury Papers transcripts. Some arrangements had been made at least as early as April 28, the date of a letter from Courtenay cited in the May 21 letter. The Nov. 11 letter announced shipment of the final parcel of transcripts.

[12] The Introduction to the 1859 volume noted that "abstracts are still coming from the Society's agent and matter sufficient to fill a [further] volume is now on hand," but completion of the project and the proposed index were casualties of the war. The remaining abstracts do not survive.

[13] Minutes of the South Carolina Historical Society, January 13, 1885, 59-60, and undated report of the committee on three following unnumbered pages, South Carolina Historical Society, Charleston (hereafter cited as SCHS); obituary notice of Langdon Cheves, South Carolina Historical and Genealogical Magazine 41 (1940), 96-97 (hereafter cited as SCHM); Cheves Genealogical Table in Richard S. Lounsbury, ed., Louisa S. McCord: Political and Social Essays (Charlottesville, V.A., and London: University Press of Virginia, 1995), 46-47; Langdon Cheves, "Middleton of South Carolina," SCHM 1 (1900), 258-59.

[14] John Amasa May and Joan Reynolds Faunt, South Carolina Secedes (Columbia, S.C.: The University of South Carolina Press, 1960), 128; Timothy Eugene Bradshaw, Jr., Battery Wagner: The Siege, The Men Who Fought, and The Casualties (Columbia, S.C.: Palmetto Historical Works, 1993), 5, 122; Index Card for Langdon Cheves as Volunteer Aide-de-Camp, Reel 84, National Archives Microcopy 253, Consolidated Index to Compiled Service Records of Confederate Soldiers, 1861-1865.

[15] The presentation of the copy of the parish register is also in the Historical Society minutes for Jan. 13, 1885. The diary, 1882-1892, is classed at 12/109/2 in the large collection of his papers at the South Carolina Historical Society. Langdon Cheves' father, Charles Manly Cheves, died at age 30 in 1855, when Cheves was still only a young boy.

[16] Langdon Cheves, on behalf of Arthur Mazyck, Treasurer of the South Carolina Historical Society, to Mayor W. A. Courtenay, December 23, 1885, Letter Book of Langdon Cheves, 1885-1887, Cheves Papers, SCHS. "Transactions of the City Treasury," Year Book—1885. City of Charleston (Charleston, S.C.: The

News and Courier Book Presses for the City of Charleston, 1886), 6.

[17] Langdon Cheves, Charleston, June 12, 1889, to R. A. Brock, Esq., Richmond, Letter Book, 1888-1890, Cheves Papers, SCHS.

[18] Archie Vernon Huff, Jr., Langdon Cheves of South Carolina (Columbia, S.C.: University of South Carolina Press for the South Carolina Tricentennial Commission, 1977), 156, 175-76.

[19] Copies of reports on Delta Plantation rice profits and losses, 1885-1889, filed with 1887 items; Louis H. Haskell, Nov. 6, 1887, Savannah, to Cheves; and correspondence of Haskell, passim, Cheves Papers, SCHS.

[20] Cheves, "Middleton of South Carolina," 258-59, and Cheves Papers, SCHS, passim. The other executors were Henry C. Cheves and Henry Augustus Middleton Smith.

[21] Cheves, June 18, 1889, to Brock, Letter Book, 1888-1890, Cheves Papers, SCHS.

[22] His diary frequently mentions rowing as well as fishing and swimming.

[23] Langdon Cheves on behalf of the Committee on Publication, Charleston, April 18, 1887, to Wm. Ellis Jones, Richmond, with proposals for printing, and subsequent letters from Cheves to Jones of May 4, Sept. 17, and Sept. 23, 1887, Letter Book, 1885-1887, Cheves Papers, SCHS. Cheves' correspondent R. A. Brock edited the Spotswood Papers. See also a letter to Brock, May 4, 1887, Cheves Papers, SCHS. The September letters were from Flat Rock. Initially "several" Charleston printers were also invited to submit bids.

[24] Minutes of the South Carolina Historical Society, May 19, 1888, 74-75, SCHS. Volume four also contains a variety of addresses read to the society (one printed as long ago as 1876) and a memoir of Christopher Gadsden.

[25] Minutes of the South Carolina Historical Society, June 23, Oct. 3, and Dec. 1, 1891, 84-93, SCHS; Lesser, South Carolina Begins, 64-68.

[26] Minutes of the Public Record Commission, January 16, 1895, South Carolina Department of Archives and History. A few of the transcripts had been published in the 1885 and 1886 Charleston Year Books. For the details, see Lesser, South Carolina Begins, 100, n. 101.

[27] Minutes of the South Carolina Historical Society, Feb. 5 and May 22, 1895, 107-8, SCHS.

[28] Ibid., May 22 and June 10, 1895, 108-9, SCHS.

[29] Sainsbury to Courtenay, Nov. 17, 1883, Sainsbury Scrapbook, CLS.

[30] In 1851 the then-known pages of the Journal of the Grand Council and the earliest records of the Secretary of the Province were bound together. The transcript made by Green (which Cheves cites simply as C.J.) includes texts of a few documents that were lost before the earliest secretary's records were published. Thus Cheves includes a few documents here (from the Green transcript) that do not appear in Alexander S. Salley, Jr., ed., Records of the Secretary of the Province and the Register of the Province of South Carolina, 1671-1675 (Columbia, S.C.: The Historical Commission of South Carolina, 1944). See Lesser, South Carolina Begins, 420-422. All surviving council minutes from this period are included in Alexander S. Salley, Jr., ed., Journal of the Grand

Council of South Carolina, August 25, 1671-June 24, 1680 (Columbia, S.C.: The Historical Commission of South Carolina, 1907).

[31] See page 215. Governor Sayle brought a slave family with him on the Carolina with the first settlers. A. S. Salley, Jr., and R. Nicholas Olsberg, eds., Warrants for Lands in South Carolina, 1672-1711 (Columbia, S.C.: University of South Carolina Press, 1973), 52-53.

[32] See Lesser, South Carolina Begins, 285-397. Cheves, who was in a position to know, confirms that "the unbroken series of original wills was here before the war, but they were all burned at Columbia." Cheves, Charleston, Feb. 17, 1886, to [illegible], 1885-1887 Letter Book, SCHS. As only a few researchers ever have, Cheves used the index to the bundles of destroyed wills and inventories in a sophisticated way.

[33] The Lovelace Collection of Locke Papers is treated in more detail in Lesser, South Carolina Begins, 40-42. Accounts and agreements beginning in 1674 between the first Earl of Shaftesbury and Henry Woodward and Andrew Percival for the management of the earl's own seigniory and his trade with the Indians and the Spanish are also now available. They are described in Lesser, South Carolina Begins, 36-38.

[34] Langdon Cheves, Charleston, Nov. 26, 1896, to William Ellis Jones, Richmond, Letterbook, 1895-1897, Cheves Papers, SCHS; Mattie Erma E. Parker, "The First Fundamental Constitutions of Carolina," SCHM 71 (1970), 78-85.

[35] There are twenty-six letters to Jones in this period in the 1895-1897 letter book. Cheves Papers, SCHS.

[36] Oct. 15, 1897, report of "The Committee on publication of the 'Shaftesbury Papers' and other papers directed by the Society to be published," Minutes of the South Carolina Historical Society, 115-116, SCHS. The society had only $610.95: $300 from the City of Charleston, "a small balance . . . from an appropriation by the State of South Carolina after the publication of Volume IV," and the remainder from "the annual subscriptions of the members of the Society."

ERRATA.

Page 9, read *T*, not *F*, Southampton.

Page 12,[1] read *and 1664*, not *1664 and*.

Page 48, last line, read *sounds*, not *bounds*.

Page 52,[1] quotation begins "*of the seditious;*" &c., read *Hewatt*, not *Henct;* April *19*, not *26*. See pages *390, 452*.

Page 88,[1] read *Sandwich*, not *Pandwicke*.

Page 103, line 10, read *Lieutnt*, not *Lieutnts*.

Page 137, top line, read *17th*, not *7th*, August.

Page 143,[1] *Charles*, not *Chester*, town.

Page 156, line 9, read "to your Lordshipps £500 venter."

Page 171,[1] quotation begins "*to stir, &c.*

Page 186,[1] read Lord *Ashley*, not *Dudley*.

Page 189, line 24, read *kays*, not *bays*.

Page 208,[1] read *Ambergris*.

Page 235, line 5-6, read *malassas*, not *masassar;* 235,[1] *Captain*, not *Sir* P. Carteret. See 262.

Page 241, lines 4-5, omit words *for the future, &c., better,* wrongly repeated.

Page 246, line 6, read *damnified*.

Page 249, *Country* should follow *fruitful*, on line 1'.

Page 280,[2] page *209*, not *207*.

Page 313, line 26, read *advantageous*.

Page 347,[1] for *bottom page 48* read *page 352*.

Page 352,[1] read *1671*, not *1761*.

Page 358,[2] read *Pendarvis*.

Page 380,[1] *Vauquillin*.

Page 385, transpose last line 385 and top line 386.

Page 423,[2] read *page 414*, not *413*.

Page 426, line 12, read *Mr. Marshall*, not *Mr. Mathews*.

Page 427,[2] read *page 413*, not *412*.

Page 434,[1] read *Danson*, not *Dawson*.

Page 455, line 25, omit *C* before *Craven*.

AUTHORITIES CITED.

Adair, Jas., 201, 309; Ash, Tho., 308, 358, 377, &c.; Carroll, B. R., 89, 382; Ch'n Yr. Bk., 338-9, 341, 394; Coxe's Ca., 7; Hewatt, Alex., 4, 52, 407, &c.; Johnson's Dic., 147, 201; Le Froy, Hist. Berm'a, 476; Logan, J. H., 428; Lucas, Eliza, 377; Murray's Dic., 259; Mesne Con. Office, 134, &c.; Mills' Stat., 457; N. E. Reg'r, 171; Oldmixon, 324, 377; Probate Ct., 338;' Pub. Rec. Office, 3, 117, 427; Purry, Col., 377; Ramsey, Da., 407, Record Com'n, S. C., 407. Rivers, W. J., 3, 57, 65, 253 *et pas;* Sainsbury, W. N., 307; Savage's Dic., 89; Secretary's Office, 331, &c.; Sieur S. map, 420.

THE

SHAFTESBURY PAPERS

AND OTHER RECORDS

RELATING TO

CAROLINA

AND THE FIRST SETTLEMENT ON ASHLEY RIVER
PRIOR TO THE YEAR 1676.

PUBLISHED BY THE

SOUTH CAROLINA HISTORICAL SOCIETY,

PREPARED FOR PUBLICATION BY

LANGDON CHEVES, Esq.,

A MEMBER.

SOUTH CAROLINA
RECORDS.

SIR ROBERT HEATH'S PATENT 5 CHARLES 1ST [30 OCT: 1629.]

Charles by the Grace of God of England &c. our^e l^{res} patents &c. made to Sir Robert Heath Knight our Atturney Generall bearing date at Westminster 30 october in the 5th year of our reigne &c. tract from the Ocean on the east & soe west as far as the Continent extends & all islands "within the degrees of 31 & 36 of Northerne latitude" &c. and erect the said Region & Isles into a Province & name the same Carolina &c. [*Shaf. Pap. Bdle.* 48, No. 1] *Printed N. C. Records*, Vol. 1, page 5.[1]

EARLY VOYAGES TO CAROLINA.

"Capt: Wm. Sayle of Summers Islands having been lately in England had procured an ordinance of Parliament for planting the Bahamas Islands (now called Eleutheria) in the mouth of the Gulf of Florida & wanting means to carry it on, had obtained of divers parliament men and others in London to undertake the work   *   *   they furnished him with a Ship and all provisions

---

[1] Grant [Oct. 30, 1629] to Sir Robert Heath attorney general of a territory in America betwixt 31 & 36 degrees of North Latitude, not inhabited by the subjects of any Christian King, but partly inhabited by barbarous men who have not any knowledge of the Devine Diety, Sir Robert Heath being about to lead thither a large & plentiful Colony &c. grants all that River of St. Matthew on the South side & of Passamagno on the north side &c. [Pat. Roll 5 Car. I, No. 5] *Am. & W. I.* ⅔ 151.

Nothing was done under this patent; it lapsed and was forfeited for non-user—see page 8. For memorandum of papers in the Public Record Office relating to proposed settlements in Carolina under it by the Baron de Sancé, 1628, 1630, and by George, Lord Berkley, Samuel Vassall, and others, 1630. See *River's S. C.*, page 326; *S. C. Hist. Cols.*, 2, page 200.

&c. and some few persons embarked with him and sailed to the Summers islands * * But on the way to Eleutheria one Capt. Butler a young man who came in the ship from England made use of his liberty to disturb all the Company * * when they arrived at one of the Eleutheria Islands and were intended to settle, he made such a Faction as enforced Captain Sayle to remove to another island & being near the harbour the ship struck & was cast away.   The persons were all saved save one but all their provisions & goods were lost, so as they were forced (for divers months) to lie in the open air & to feed upon such fruits & wild creatures as the island afforded.   But finding their strength to decay & no hope of any relief, Captain Sayle took a shallop & eight men & with such provisions as they could get & set sail, hoping to attain either the Summers Islands or Virginia or New England; and so it pleased the Lord to favor them, that in nine days they arrived in Virginia, their provisions all spent &c.   Those of the Church relieved them & furnished them with a bark & provisions to return to relieve their company left in Eleutheria.''   [*Winthrop's History New England,* 2, page 335] *Rivers S. C.,* page 386.[1]

Capt: Sayle * * leaving Providence sailed along the coast of Carolina where he observed several large navigable rivers and a flat country covered with woods.   He attempted to go ashore in his boat, but seeing some savages on the bank of the River he was obliged to drop his design.   *Hewit S. C. Car. Col.,* I, page 8.

About 1660 Wm. Hilton sailed along the coast to Cape Fear and entered and explored Charles River.

THE FIRST CHARTER

Granted by King Charles the II to Edward earl of Clarendon &c.

----

[1] 1665? Since I petitioned for these islands which was six years ago * * Capt: Sayle and others obtained a patent, went to an island he called Illutheria, where his ship was wrecked but his people saved.   '' I saw him after his escape in a small boat of 3 tons, recovering Virginia, where he procured a pinnace of near 25 tons, with which he carried relief to those he left on the islands '' * * But understood from said Sayle afterwards that none of them knew the place or were ever there before &c. [Gen'l Desc'n Bermudas and Bahamas] *Am. & W. I.,* ⅔ 1110.

Lords Proprietors of Carolina, march 20, 166⅔. *Printed Stat. S. C.*, I, pages 22, 31. *N. C. Records*, I, page 21.[1]

FIRST MEETING OF THE PROPRIETORS.

Saterday May 23rd, 1663.

Present.

The Lord Duke of Albemarle	My Lord Craven
My Lord Berkeley	My Lord Ashley
Mr. Vice Chamberline	Sr Jno. Colleton.

Ordered—1. That ―――― Lepreyrie be Ingeneir & Surveyo^r for Carrolina.

2. That he be allowed until some other way be found for his subsistance twenty shillings weekly to be paid him by Sir Jno. Colleton.

3. That Sir Jno. Colleton be paid from each respective Propryator 25£ to be by him disburst as he shall receave ord^r from the Major parte of the Propryators.

4. That there be reserved in every setlem^t for ye Propryators the quantity of 20000 Acres in such place or places as they or there Agents shall see fitt to take up and that the same be bounded & leyed out for them in ye beginning of each Setlement.

5. That in each Setlement the Court howses & howses for publique meetings be setled on the land & taken up & leyed out for the Propryators.

6. That mapps be printed of the Province and some declaration drawne to invyte the planters with the conditions before mentioned & both published. [*P. R. O. Col. Ent. Bk.*, Vol. 20, page 1.] *N. C.*, I, 33.

SIR JOHN COLLETON TO DUKE OF ALBEMARLE[2] 10 JUNE 1663.

May it please your Grace, There are divers people that desire to settle and plant in his Maj: Province of Carolina under the patent granted to your Grace and others but that there is another like to that Province started by one Mr. Mariot, steward

---

[1] For some account of the Lords Proprietors see *River's S. C.*, page 63.

[2] General George Monk, the restorer of the Monarchy, one of the Lords Proprietors and Palatine of Carolina, died 1670.

to the Duke of Norfolk, grounded on a patent granted in the yeare 1629 now above thirty foure years to Sir Robert Heath and by him assigned to the Ancestors of the now Duke of Norfolk wch patent relates to certaine Articles to bee performed on the part of Sir Robert Heath, the patent is recorded, but the Articles appeere not in the records but the said Mr. Mariot (who lives in Chancery Lane at the next door to the Harrowe) pretends he has the patent and articles which being in force and not declined or made voide will certainly hinder that publique worke which is intended by the settlement and planting of Carolina, for the persons that at present designe thither expect liberty of conscience and without that will not goe, wch by the patent to Sr Robert Heath cannot bee granted them and they cannot settle under the patent least the other gentlemen shall give them trouble or disturbance, So that there is a necessity of the present removall of that obstacle which is humblie left to the consideracon of yor Grace and the other noble persons concern'd.

Yo^r Grace's most humble servant,

JNO. COLLETON.[1]

Cockpitt, 10 June 1663.

[*Col. Papers*, Vol. 17, No. 39.]   *N. C. Rec.*, I, page 34.

STATE OF THE CASE OF THE DUKE OF NORFOLK'S PRETENSIONS TO CAROLINA [inclosed in above letter].

The 13th of 8^{ber} in ye 5th year of King Charles the First was granted to Sir Robert Heath the reagion or Province of Carrolina leying within the latitude of 31 and 36 inclusive upon the condition y^t ye said Sr Robert Heath or his assignes plant ye s^d Province according to such Articles or Instructions as his then Majesty had given him under his sign Manuell & privie Signett signed by his Secretary of State bearing date with the grant afores^d.

Mr. Samuell Vassell had as he pretends an Assignem^t from Sr Robt. Heath for a tearme not yet expyred for ye lattitude of 31

[1]Another Lord Proprietor.   Born 1608; fought for the King, raised a regiment and expended £40,000 in his service; retired to Barbadoes, where he acquired large estates, but returning at the Restoration was made a Baronet.   He married Katherine, daughter of William Amy, of Exon.   Died 1666.

& 33 and ye heires of S[r] Richard Greenefeild[1] for ye remayneing part being 34, 35 & 36 who say they never heard of any pretence by Mr. Howard or any of his Ancestors untill within these three monthes, neither hath Mr. Howard shewn any pattent or grant for ye same but pretends by discourse abroad y[t] ye pattent to S[r] Robert Heath[2] was taken in trust by s[d] Heath for some of his Ancestors. Mr. Howard shews no right nor the Artickles or Instructions by w[ch] he was to plant although often sent for by Mr. Atturney Gen[ll] to Mr. Merriott Mr. Howards Sollissiter.

Neither hath S[r] Robt. Heath, Mr. Howard or any of his Ancestors Mr. Rich. Greenefeild or Mr. Vassell or any of their Assignes planted any part of this Province, there being about 35 years past since ye grant.

Severall persons have a desire to plant in ye s[d] Province under the pattent granted by his now Maj. to my Lord High Chancellor, ye Duke of Albemarle & others but refusing to plant under the pattent to Sir Robt. Heath & forbare to plant under the latter untill ye first be made voyde least when they have planted they shall receave trouble by ye first pattent by meanes whereof the settlement of that hopeful collony wil be lost. It is therefore to be humbly desired y[t] his Maj. wil be graciously pleased by an Act of Councell to resume ye pattent to S[r] Robt. Heath & all Grants from it because they have not planted nor doe not shew ye Artickles or Instructions mencioned in s[d] pattent whereby ye settlem[t] may goe forward whylst many people have stronge desires to it w[ch] will otherwayse dye and hardly be revyved againe.

FROM LONDON, AUGUST 1663. AT A MEETING OF
ADVENTURERS ABOUT CAPE FAYRE.

London, Thursday, August the 6th 1663.
At a meeting of several persons, who have, with several others

---

[1] Sir Richard Grenville. See also Coxe's Carolana.

[2] Memoranda by Lord Ashley, 1671? Sir Robert Heath's patent of Carolina is dated 30th October, 5 Car., I. The articles to which it refers of the same date in the Signet Office. If it refers to text, is not extant, makes the patent void. Several references in the patent to the Instructions. The consideration, the propagating the Gospel *industria et impensis suis*, the honor and profit of the King. There are both articles and Instructions. The first of the date of these presents, the other of a letter to be signed. [*S. P. IX*, B'dle 69.] *A. & W. I.*, ₰ 391.

of New England, subscribed themselves as adventurers for the carrying on a plantation in Charles River on the coast of Florida.

1. Whereas a paper in the name of the Right honorable the Earl of Clarendon &c. to whom the whole coast of Florida hath been lately granted &c. hath been sent down to the said adventurers &c.   *   *   *

3. That as they were invited at first to be subscribers to the said plantation of Charles River, by several persons of New England so the great motive that did principally induce them &c. was &c. that the said New Englanders, had an equitable title to the harbor and soil of the said river together with the lands adjacent; and that though many others of quality had long before indeed sailed upon the coast of Florida, & had settled & had taken possession of some other part of that large and vast country, yet that the said New Englanders, and they only, were the first that did ever, *bona fide*, set foot in that particular harbor and that did find out the entrance and discovery of the said river   *   *   *

At present the undertaking of the plantation of Charles River lieth under some obloquy, that hath given a check to it, some that were sent from New England thither, in order to the carrying on the said settlement, being come back again without so much as sitting down upon it; &c.   *N. C. Rec.*, Vol. I, pages 36–39.

———

AT THE COURT AT WHITEHALL THE 12[th] DAY OF AUGUST 1663.

His Ma[tie] this day taking into Consideracon the State & p[r]sent Condicon of the Province or Region called Carolina in America & his Grant of the same by his Letters patents under the Great Seale of England, to the Right Hono[ble] the Lord High Chancellor of England, George Duke of Albemarle, William Lord Craven, John Lord Berkeley, Anthony Lord Ashley Chancellor of the Excheqr[r] Sr George Carteret Kn[t] Vice Chamberlain of his Ma[ties] Household S[r] William Berkeley, & S[r] John Colladon Kn[ts]. And upon Informacon that all p[r]tenders to former Grants of the said Province, haveing been sumoned (according to former Orders of this Board) to bring or send to his Ma[ties] Attorney Generall such Letters patents, Writings, or other Evidences as they or any of them had, setting forth their p[r]tended

Titles thereunto, yet none of them have appeared, or discovered any such p^rtensions, or Claymes. And forasmuch as no English Whatsoever have, by Vertue of any such Grants hitherto planted in the said Province, by which neglect, such Letters patents (if any were) are become voyd; His Matie by & with the advice of his Councell doth Order, And it is hereby Ordered: That his Maties said Attorney Generall forthwith proced either by Inquisition, or by scire facias in the revoking all former Letters patents, & Grants of the said Province, or any other legall way whereby to make & declare them voyd. And that from henceforwards, when any like Grant of any Forreigne plantacon shall be p^rpared to passe his Maties Great Seale, a Clause be inserted, That if within a certain number of yeares, No plantacon be made & performed, the said Grant shall become void. And it is further Ordered, That the said Lord Chancellor, Duke of Albemarle, & other the before named Patentees, do proceed in the planting of the said Province of Carolina, & that in Order thereunto, they receive all Countenance, favour & protection from this Board: And that from henceforwards no person or persons whatsoever do p^rsume to goe into the said province or molest or disturbe the said Grantees, or any Persons by them or any of them trusted or imployed, upon p^rtence of any former Grant whatsoever, as they or any of them do tender, this his Maties Comand & will answer the contrary at their perills:

Clarendon C		Albemarle
	F: Southampton	
Berkshire	St: Alban	Bath
Gilb: London	Sandwich	W: Compton
Tho: Wentworth	Middleton	Henry Bennet
Cha: Berkeley	Will: Morice	Richard Browne.

[*P. R. O. Shaftesbury Papers*, Section IX, Bundle 48, No. 2.]

1663? THE GREAT SEAL of the Lords Proprietors of Carolina with the Inscription *Magnum Sigillum Carolinæ Dominorum* & motto *Domitus cultoribus orbis*. On the reverse are the Coats of Arms of the eight Lords Proprietors named in above order in Council. [*S. P.*, Sec. IX, No. 105.] For copy seal and signatures, see *Ch'n Year Book, 1883*, page 356, L. C.

PROPOSEALLS OF SEVERALL GENTLEMEN OF BARBADOES.

August this 12th 1663.

Severall gentlemen and persons of good quality in this Island
being very sensible of the great loss and sad disappoyntment
that might redownd to the English nation in Generall as well as to
many particular persons y' ingaiged and intended to ingaige in
the settlement of an English plantation in that goodly land of
Florida by the eivill report bruited thereof, by those sent from
New England to setle at Cape Faire contrary to what Mr. William Hinton[1] and the rest with him sent to discover that coast
did and doe affirme thereof, and having greate confidence in the
said Hinton's fidellity and honest indeavowrs therein, have out
of an earnest desire and confident persuasion of a happy settlement for our English nation in those parts, now againe hired and
sent the above said Mr. Hinton with his ship Adventure and
twenty two men well fitted and victualled for 7 months for discovery of that coast southwards from Cape Faire as far as 31
degrees north latitude: in which design of discovery there are
and will be above 2 hundred gentlemen and amongst them many
persons of good quallity in this Island, whoe are and wilbe at a
considerable charge therein.

The said Adventurers doe earnestly with all Humillity desire
and request that those Noble undertakers whoe have lately obtayned a charter of the Province of Carrolina from his Royall
Maj^{tie} wilbe pleased with as much convenient speede as may be
to send them an exemplification of there said Charter under the
broade seale of England fully recited; and together therewith
and by vertew of the said charter to impower and authorize the
aforesaid Adventurers or such of them as the said Grantees shall
judge fitt to nominate togeather with the rest of there Assotiates
and freinds, them there heires and assignes to take up and purchase of the natives such certine tract or tracts of Lands as they
and such as they shall send theither to setle may or shall finde
fitt for the accommodation of themselves and of there freinds
there, in the forme and manner of a County or Corporation, not

---

[1] Hilton had been sent by the Barbadoes planters to explore Carolina
and had visited Charles river before the New Englanders went there.
On their evil report he was now sent to explore Port Royal.

exceeding or about the quantity of thirty or thirty two myles square, or one thousand square myles which they desire may be called the Corporation of the Barbados Adventures, and that the said tract or tracts of land, County or Corporation, they desire may be granted and confirmed to them and there Assotiates, and to theire heires and assignes for eaver, in full, free and ample manner and with the same power, priviledges, jurisdictions and Immunityes as the aforesaid Province is granted to them by his Majestie.   And if any more or other rents, acknowledgements or services be or shalbe desired, expected or required then the proportion of what is by them the said pattentes or first undertakers to be paid and allowed to his Majestie it may be by them assertined and expresly set downe in there said Graunte to these said Barbadoes Adventures, before they shalbe at further Cost, Charge or troble to setle it which they desire to know as soon as may be for that heare are many hundreds of noble famillyes and well experienced planters that are willing and ready to remove spedily theither to begin a setlement as aforesaid and to beare the brunt thereof, if they shall receave such incorragement as is expected as aforesaid from so noble and worthy undertakers as we do understand are concerned as principalls in said Charter which priviledges and incorragements they are the rather boald to expect Adventures not onely for there vigorous and ready appearing to promote the further discovery and hopeful setlement thereof at such a time as this, when soe great a cloude of obscurity was cast upon it but alsoe from the aptnes of the people heare and persons heare ingaged to further such a work as well for there experienced planters as for the number of there Negros and other servants fitt for such labor as wilbe there required, and doe alsoe find the less cause to doubt of the desired trust to be reposed in them, in regard many of there number consists of persons of good quallity fitt to manage the Government of soe considerable a corporation, whoe with there freinds and associates doe desire to expect to have the sole power of electing all delligates, Governors and officers, and making Lawes, and governing amongst themselves according to the tenor and Priviledges of the said Graunte or charter from his Majestie, which if granted soe, as to incorrage such a free and noble setlement as they beleive and hope is aymed at; will much promote the good and speedy setlement of many other very considerable corporations within the Territory and Dominions of the aforesaid Province.

That alsoe desire that a Proclamation may be procured from the Kinge directed to all Governors in these his Majestie's plantations, requiring them not to hinder any free and uningaiged persons from going theither to setle upon any frivilus pretences whatsoever: but rather to further the good and speedy settlement thereof that possible may be in order whereunto; and that those noble persons to whom the Charter is graunted may the better know whome to appoynt and nominate as Prime Adventurers and undertakers of the before mentioned Corporation, the said Adventurers doe intend by the next to send a list of such persons names as have already subscribed and of the committe by them choasen to manage affaires heare for this yeare and untill some shalbe sent theither to performe the same upon the place unless the said undertakers in England shall please to leave in blancke the place for the said Committe; to put in such persons names as they shall judge most fitt and find willing to goe speedily theither to begin the said settlement there. [*Col. Ent. Book*, No. 20, pages 10, 11.]

My Lord—We humbly advize you will be pleased to appoynt some persons with your Instructions to treate with them on there proposealls, and wee conceave to bringe them to accept of by Lawes onely in steede of Generall Laws, which they desire to have power to make it being fitt the whole Country should make the Generall Lawes and that the Governors they meane to choose should bee only such as in the Citty of Exon, vizt: Mayors, Aldermen, Sherifes, Constables, and the like this wee conceave may sattisfie them, otherwayes they wilbe disturbed in Government which may cause

your humble servants

Tho: Modyford[1]
P. Colleton.[2]

[*Ibid*, page 11.]   *N. C. Records*, I, pages 39, 40.

---

[1] Lately Governor of Barbadoes, 1664, and Governor of Jamaica.

[2] Eldest son of Sir John Colleton, whom he succeeded 1666. Called by Lord Willoughby, "a chip of the old block." Born 1635. Member of the Council Barbadoes 1666, President and Deputy Governor 1672. M. P. Died 24th March, 1694. Succeeeded by his only son, Sir John.

A Declaration and Proposealls to all y^t will Plant in Carolina August 21, 1663.

His Matie haveing by his Charter 24th March 1663 out of his pious & good Intention for ye Propogacon of ye Christian faith amongst ye Barbarous & Ignorant Indians ye Inlargem^t of his Empire & Dominion & inriching of his Subjects; granted unto us Edward earl of Clarending &c. Wee doe hereby declare & propose to all his Maties Subjects. 1. If ye Collony will setle on Charles River as seems desired to do so on Larboard Side &c. 8 Articles. [*Col. En. Book*, No. 20, pages 1, 3.] Printed *Rivers S. C.*, pages 335, 337.

Letter to Col. Tho: Modyford and Peter Colleton Esqr.

Cockepit this 30th August 1663.

Sirs, Wee finde by a letter from Mr Richard Eivans[1] Mr John Vassall and others as alsoe by another from you Coll: Modyford that severall people of Barbados have inclynations to setle and plant in some parte of the province of Carrolina, whome we desire by all wayse and meanes to incorrage, and that it may appeare soe, have inclosed sent you a declaration and proposalls under the hands of all those concerned that are in towne and those that are not have consented to it: which paper we desire you to communicate to all people that are disposed that way and to give what coppyes you please to such as shall desire them and to send others to the Barmothos New England and where elce you think fitt useing your Interest for the propogation of this plantation and assureing the people that what we propose shalbe performed: in which we resolve to be puntuall and circumspect, we are informed that some ill willers to the settlement upon Charles river neare Cape Faire, have contrived the disorder that hapned to those that lately went theither before the ships went from New England and that they went not into the branch of the river in that Hilton was in, but by mistake went into another besides they tooke not the proper time of the yeare, for worke; soe that wee hope that the miscarriage will not discorrage your

---

[1] Member of Barbadoes Assembly 1667, &c., and an eminent planter, owning 300 acres there, 1673.

people; we conceave it wilbe advantageous to the Kinge, his people, and more particularly to your Ilanders to goe on with the setlement where the ayre as we are informed wondrous healthy and temperate, the land proper to bare such commodyties as are not yet produced in the other plantations and such as the nation spend in greate quantities as wine, oyle, currants, reasons, silks &c. by means whereof the money of the nation that goes out for these things wilbe Keept, in the Kinges Dominions and the planting part of the people imploy there time in planting those comodyties that will not injure nor overthrow the other plantations which may very well happen, if there be a very great increase of sugar workes and more Tobacco, Ginger, Cotton, and indicoe made then the world will vent these reasons we conceave will convince the most concerned in your Islands to promote this worke, the proposealls sent are but heads; we conceaving that such as shall undertake, will expect a more formall and large assurance from us according to their owne Methhood; which we shall willingly give when they desire the same, some people heare[1] propose that we should make choyce of a Governor without there presenting; if your people desire the like it shall be done, more freedome then this we may not give; but if any have anyother way to propose that is not loss to us then this, we may consent to it.   Wee have written to my Lord Willoby to countenance at least not to discountenance your proceedings herein, the business is the Kings and nations service more then our owne, the promotion whereof by you is desired & not all doubted by your.

[*Col. Ent. Book*, No. 20, page 8.]

A LETTER TO MY LORD WILLOBY[2] FROM THE DUKE OF
ALBEMARLE.

Cockpit the 31 of August 1663.
My Lord,
    I presume you are not a stranger to his Majestie's Graunte

---

[1] The Vassalls, Sanford, and the Cape Fear adventurers. They settled at Charles River 1664. Modyford's and Colleton's friends wished Port Royal.

[2] Francis, Lord Willoughby, of Parham, Governor of Barbadoes and the Caribees 1663–1666. Lost with H. M. Ship Hope and all on board in a hurricane, July, 1666, on his expedition to St. Kitts.

of the Province of Corrolina to my Lord Chancellor myselfe and others, which we have undertaken to serve him and his people, and not our private Interest there are some persons of your Island of Barbadoes that have by there letters to me set forth there desires of beginning of or contributeing to a setlement in those parts which I conceave will prove rather advantagious than otherwayes to those under your Government for that setlement will devirt many people that designe to plant from planting there commodyties which your plantation abounds in (of which greater quantities being made will sinke the maker) and put them upon such as your lands will not I conceave produce, and as the Kinge hath not yet within his Terrytories in quantity, although his people consume much of them to the exhausting the wealth of the Kingdome, the commodyties I meane are wine, oyle, reasons, currents, rice, silke &c; which commodyties will be of good use and advantagious to your parts, as well as Corne meale flower beefe and poorke; which that Country as I am well informed from persons that have planted in some parts thereof will in short time abound in: for which reasons and being well assured that you in all your actions ayme at the publicke good, I desire that your Lord: will not hinder but incorrage this setlement by which I am sure you will not only doe his Majestie good service but much oblige.   Your Lordship's Humble servant.

My Lord Chancellor is gon to Cornebry who would I believe have joyned with me in this desire if he had been in Towne; I have written my couzen Modyford and Couzen Peter Colleton to promote Carrolina Plantation.   I pray countenance them in it.

[*Col. Ent. Book*, No. 20, page 9.]

———

Coppy of a Commission to Sir William Berkeley[1] to constitute and commissionate a Governor for Albemarle River.   1663. Printed *N. C. Records*, Vol. I, page 48. 50.

———

Instructions for Sir William Berkeley Governor and Captain Generall of Virginia in relation to the setling and planting some parte of the Province of Carolina.   Printed *Ibid*, page 50, 52.

---

[1] Governor of Virginia, commissioned 1641 by King Charles I. Recommissioned by King Charles II 1650 and 1660, till his death, 1677.

THE LORDS PROPRIETORS TO SIR WM. BERKELEY.

Cockepitt this 8ᵗʰ day of Septʳ 1663.

Sir,

Since you left us we have indeavoured to procure, and at lenkth have obtayned his Majestie's Charter for the province of Carolina. A coppy * * we do herewith send you since the sealeing whereof there started a title under a pattent graunted in the 5ᵗʰ yeare of Kinge Charles the 1ˢᵗ to Sir Robert Heath under which there hath been a Clayme by the Duke of Norfolkes Agents and another by Sir Ric: Greenefields heires: but all there that shall plant notwithstanding that pattent are by an Act of Kinge and Councill secured against that pattent: and that pattent by King and Councill made Null &c. * * [*Col. Ent. Book*, No. 20, page 6.] *N. C. Rec.*, I, page 52, 55. *Rivers S. C.*, p. 330.

———

LETTER FROM DUKE OF ALBEMARLE? TO SIR THO: MODY-
FORD SEPT: 9ᵗʰ 1663 ABOUT BARBADOES PROPOSALS &C.
[Enclosing?]

An answer to certine demands and proposealls made by sev-erall gentlemen and persons of good quallity in the Island of Barbados to the Lord Propryetors of the Province of Carrolina: We say That we are well pleased to find soe many publick spirits in the Barbadoes as there seems to be concerned in the Intended discovery of fitt places to plant betweene Cape Faire and the northine lattitude of 31 degrees, and cannot but commend there soe doeing although we ourselves had, before we did know any-thing of that there Intentions; given order for a vessell to be sent from Virginia to discover from Cape Hatteras to Cape Flor-yda all the parts and places fit for the reception of such of his Majestie's subjects as shall desire to plant in those parts.[1] As to your desires, we replye.

That a trew Coppy of our Charter hath beene sent to Barba-dos by Mr. Tho: Colleton[2] who wilbe ready to produce and give

———

[1] In above letter to Sir William Berkeley "we desire you to procure * * some small vessel that draws little water to make that" (Lati-tude 34°) "discovery * * and whilst they are abroad they may look into Charles River &c."

[2] Second son of Sir John Colleton, an eminent merchant and planter of Barbadoes. Created May 28, 1681, Landgrave of Carolina.

Coppyes of the same, and if an exemplyfycation thereof under the broade seale shall notwithstanding be desired by you, we shall upon notice thereof be ready to send the same.

To the 2^d demand we answer that we have sent to Coll: Tho: Modyford and Peter Colleton a declaration and proposealls under severall of our hands of which all doe approve, and doe herewith send a Dupplycate in which is set forth the Meth-hood which we resolve to proceed in for the choyce of Governors, the way of Government, setlement and graunting of land in those parts; from the substance whereof wee shall not receade: which way of Government and of chooseing the Governor and Councell we hold to be better for the people in Generall then the Corporation way that you demand, in which the members choasen to manage the Government doe continue for there lives, and are not to be removed but by there owne fellowes or the Major parte of them, whoe maybe apter to wincke at the misdemeanors of there fellow Governors then the people that are to be governed by them will: in whose power it wilbe, we meane the peoples, at the end of every 3 yeares, to leave out such as have misbehaved themselves: in there election of those that are to be presented to the Lords Propryetors for a new choyse of a Governor and Councill notwithstanding our declaration; if it shalbe desired that more than 6 be of the Councill then may the undertakers propose duble the number they would have, and wee shall choose the Moyty of them.

To the 3^d demand wee consent that the Governor and Counsell shalbe amply and fully impowred from us to graunte such proportions of land to all that shall come to plant in quantity and according to the Meth-hood and under that acknowledgement & noe more, as in our declarations and proposealls is set forth for which they may contract and compound with the Indians; if they see fitt: and if they shall desire a confirmation from us, we shal be ready to give it: in as ample manner as they or there Councill at Law shall contrive, and likewayse we shall empower the Governor and Councill choasen as aforesaid to make choyce of all Officers as well Military and Civill, the Secrytary and Surveyor, onely excepted and arme them with all powers as farr as our Charter will extend, for the well governing of the Collony or place.

We shall likewayse endeavowr to procure his Majesties Letters to the Governors of the Barbados and Carribbia Islands, Virginia, New England and Barmothos requiring them not to hinder any free and uningaiged persons from going to Carrolina to setle upon any frivolos pretences whatsoever but rather to further the good and speedy settlement thereof: we have given power and direction to Coll: Tho: Modyford and Mr. Peter Colleton to treate and agree with you concerneing the premises, not receading from the substance of our Declaration whose agreement we shall ratifie so rest your loveing friends.   [*Col. En. Book*, No. 20, page 12.]   *N. C. Rec.*, Vol. I, pages 55, 57.

———

A TRUE RELATION OF A VOYAGE upon discovery of part of the Coast of Florida, from the Lat. of 31 Deg. to 33 Deg. 45 m. North Lat. in the ship *Adventure, William Hilton* Commander, and Commissioner with captain *Anthony Long* and *Peter Fabian* set forth by several Gentlemen and Merchants of the Island of *Barbadoes;* sailed from *Spikes* Bay *Aug.* 10, 1663:

After Sixteen days of fair weather, and prosperous winds, *Wednesday* the 26 instant, four of the clock in the Afternoon, God be thanked, we espied Land on the Coast of *Florida*, in the lat. of 32 deg: 30 m. being four Leagues or thereabouts to the Northwards of *St. Ellens*, having run five hundred and fifty Leagues; and to the Westward of the Meridian of Barbadoes, three hundred and thirty and one leagues.[1]   This Evening & Night following we lay off and on: *Thursday* the 27th instant in the morning, we stood in with the Land, and coasted the Shoar to the Southward Ankering at Nights, and sending our Boat out a Mornings, till we came into the lat. of 31 deg. but found no good harbour that way.   On *Sunday* the 30th instant, we tacked and stood Northward: and on *Wednesday* the second of *September*, we came to an Anchor in five fathoms at the mouth of a very large opening of three Leagues wide, or thereabouts, in the lat. of 32 deg: 30 min: and sent our Boat to sound the Channel.

———

[1] Hilton's second voyage to Carolina.   He made the land off St. Helena.   The " St. Ellens " he mentions is Port Royal.

On *Thursday* the third we entered the Harbour,[1] and found that it was the River *Jordan*, and was but four Leagues or thereabouts N. E. from *Port Royal*, which by the Spaniards is called *St. Ellens:* within Land, both Rivers meet in one. We spent some time to sound the Channels both without and within, and to search the Rivers in several branches, and to view the Land. On *Saturday* the fifth of *September*, two Indians came on Board us, and said they were of St. Ellens; being very bold and familiar; speaking many Spanish words, as *Cappitan, Commarado*, and *Adeus*. They know the use of Guns and are as little startled at the fireing of a Piece of Ordnance, as he that hath been used to them many years: they told us the nearest *Spaniards* were at *St. Augustins*, and several of them had been there, which as they said was but ten days journey, and that the *Spaniards* used to come to them at Saint *Ellens* sometimes in Conoas within Land, at other times in Small Vessels by Sea, which the Indians describe to have but two Masts. They invited us to come to *St. Ellens* with our Ship, which they told us we might do within Land. *Monday* the 14 *September*, our Long-Boat went with twelve hands within Land to St. *Ellens*. On *Wednesday* the 16th, came five Indians on board us; one of them pointing to another, said, he was the Grandy Captain of *Edistow:* whereupon we took especial notice of him, and entertained him accordingly, giving him several Beads & other trade that pleased him well: He invited us to bring up our Ship into a branch on the N. E. side, and told us of one Captain Francisco, and four more English that were in his custody on shoar; whereupon we showed him store of all Trade, as Beads, Hoes, Hatchets and Bills &c. and said, he should have all those things if he would bring the English on board us; w[ch] he promised should be done the next day. Hereupon we wrote a few lines to the said *English*, fearing it to be a *Spanish* delusion to entrap us. In the dark of the same Evening came a Canoa with nine or ten Indians in her with their Bowes and Arrowes, and were close on board before we did discern them: We haled them, but they made us no answer,

---

[1] St. Helena sound. The Jordan is the Combahee. Early Spanish navigators tell of three harbors. Six leagues north of St. Helens is Oristanum. Four leagues north of it Ostanum [S. & N. Audista?], and eight from it Cayagna [Cayawa?]. *Oldm. Carroll 2*. Ribault went from Port Royal to Audista 1562.

which increased our jealousie.   So we commanded them on
board, and disarmed them, detaining two of them prisoners, and
sending away the rest to fetch the *English;* which if they brought,
they should have theirs again.   At length they delivered us a
Note written with a coal, which seemed the more to continue
our jealousie, because in all this time we had no news of our long
boat from St. Ellens, which we feared was surprized by the *Indians* and *Spaniards.*   But to satisfie us that there were *English*
on shoar, they sent us one man on board about twelve of the
clock in the Night who related to us the truth of the matter, and
told us they were cast away some four or five leagues to the
Northward[1] of the place we then rode, on the 24th of *July* past,
being· thirteen persons that came on shoar, whereof three of
them were kill'd by the Indians.   On *Thursday* the 17th of *September* the Long-boat returned from *St. Ellens,* which presently
we sent on shoar to fetch the other English, the Indians deliver-
ing us three more; and coming aboard themselves, we delivered
them their two men.   Then we demanded of the Chief Commander where the rest of our *English* were: he answered Five
were carried to *St. Ellens,* three were killed by the *Stonohs,* and
the other man we should have within two dayes.   We replyed
to him again, That we would keep him and two more of his chief
men,[2] till we had our *English* that were yet living; and promised
them their liberty, with Satisfaction for bringing us the *English.*
Now to return to the businesse of our Design; the entertainment
we had at S. *Ellens* put us in great fear of the Indians treachery;
for we observed their continual gathering together, and at last
began with stern-look'd countenances to speak roughly to us,
and came to search our mens Bandileers and pockets; yet invit-
ing us to stay that night with them: but we made a sudden re-
treat to our Boat, which caused the Indian King to be in a great
rage, speaking loud and angry to his men; the drift of which
discourse we understood not.   That which we noted there, was
a fair house builded in the shape of a Dove-house, round, two
hundred foot at least, compleatly covered with *Palmeta*-leaves,
the wal-plate being twelve foot high, or thereabouts, & within

---

[1] They were cast away at North Edisto, or between that and Stono.

[2] Shadoo, Alush, and another who escaped.   Hilton took them to
Barbadoes, but they returned and received Sanford on his arrival, 1666·

lodging rooms and forms; two pillars at the entrance of a high Seat above all the rest; Also another house like a Sentinel-house, floored ten foot high with planks, fastened with Spikes and Nayls, standing upon Substantial Posts, with several other small houses round about. Also we saw many planks, to the quantity of three thousand foot or thereabouts, with other Timber squared, and a Cross before the great house. Likewise we saw the Ruines of an old Fort, compassing more than half an acre of land within the Trenches, which we supposed to be *Charls's* Fort, built, and so called by the *French* in 1562 &c.[1] On *Monday September* 21, one English youth was brought from St. *Ellens* aboard us by an Indian, who informed us that there were four more of their company at St. *Ellens*, but he could not tell whether the Indians would let them come to us: For saith he, Our Men told me, that they had lately seen a Frier and two *Spanyards* more at *St. Ellens*, who told them they would send Soldiers suddenly to fetch them away. This day we sayled up the River with our Ship to go through to *St. Ellens*. On *Tuesday* the 22 instant three *Indians* came on board; one of them we sent with a Letter to the *English* Prisoners there. On *Wednesday* the 23[d], we sent our Boat and Men to sound the Channel, and finde out the most likely way to *St. Ellens* with our Ship by *Combeheh*. In the mean time came many Canoas about us with Corn, Pompions, and Venison, Deer-Skins, and a sort of sweet-wood. One of our men looking into an Indian basket, found a piece of *Spanish* Rusk: it being new, we demanded of the Indian where he had it; who said, of the *Spaniards*. In the interim, while we were talking, came a Canoa with four Indians from *St. Ellens*, on standing up, and holding a paper in a cleft stick; they told us they had brought it from the *Spanish* Captain at *St. Ellens*. We demanded how many *Spaniards* were come thither; who said Seven, and one *English-man:* We received their Letter writ in *Spanish*, but none of us could read it: We detained two of the chiefest *Indians* one of them being the Kings Son of *St. Ellens*,[2] and that kept one of the *English* prisoners; the other

---

[1] Charles Fort, built by Ribault in June, 1662, "situated on the South eastern point of Parris Island, open to the ocean, upon a small creek" [Pilot's creek] "where there are still traces of its intrenchments." *Rivers S. C.*, pages 25, 27.

[2] Wommony. He also was taken to Barbadoes, but returned.

two we sent away with a Letter to the *Spaniard*, wherein we
gave him to understand, that we understood not his letter; and
told the *Indians* when they brought the *English*, they should
have their men again, with satisfaction for their pains.   On
Thursday, 24 instant, we sayling further up the River to go
through, at last came to a place of fresh water, and Anchored
there, sending our Boat ashoar with a Guard to get water.   Towards night came the first Indian that we sent to *St. Ellens* with
a letter to the *English*, who brought us another letter from the
Spaniards, and an Answer of ours from the *English*, writ in the
Spaniards letter.   The *Spaniard* sent us a quarter of Venison,
and a quarter of Pork, with a Complement, That he was sorry
he had no more for us at that time.   We returned him thanks,
and sent him a Jug of Brandy; and withal, that we were sorry
we understood not his letter.   This night about twelve of the
Clock we had a most violent gust of winde, but of no long continuance.   On *Friday* 25 *September* we weighed, and returned
down the River six leagues or thereabouts, because we perceived
the Indians had gathered themselves in a Body from all parts
thereabouts, and moved as the Ship did: and being informed by
an Indian that the Spaniards would be there the next day; we
took in Fire-wood, and continued there that night, at which time
one of our Indian Prisoners made his escape by leaping over-
board in the dark.   On *Saturday* the 26, we weighed, and stood
down to the Harbour's mouth, and stayed there till *Monday* the
28.   In all which time came no one to us, though we stayed in
expectation of their coming continually; therefore put out to
Sea, concluding their intentions not to be good.   Being out of
the River *Jordan*, we directed our course S. W. four leagues or
thereabouts for *Port Royal*, to sound the Chanel without from
the poynts of the Harbour outwards; for we had sounded the
Harbour within from the points inward when our Boat was at
St. Ellens: And now being athwart the Harbour's mouth, we
sent our Boat with the Mate[1] and others, who found the N. E.
and E. N. E. side of the opening of *Port Royal* to be Sholes
and Breakers to the middle of the opening; and three leagues
or thereabouts into the Sea, from the side aforesaid, is unsafe to
meddle with: but the S. W. and W. side we found all bold steer-

[1] Probably Pyam Blowers. He and John Hancock were apparently
mates.

ing in N. N. W. two or three miles from the S. W. shoar, sayling directly with the S. W. head-land of the entrance of *Port
Royal:* the said head-land is bluft, and seems steep, as though
the trees hung over the water: But you must note, that if you
keep so far from the S. W. side, that you stand in the N. N. W.
with the bluft head aforesaid, you shall go over the Outskirt of
the E. N. E. sholing, and shall have but three or four fathom for
the space of one league, and then you shall have six and seven
fathoms all the way in: But if you borrow more on the S. W.
side, till you have brought the S. W. head of the Entry to bear
N. N. E. you shall have a fair large Chanel of six, seven, and
eight fathoms all the way in, and then five, six, seven and eight
fathoms within the Harbour, keeping the Chanel, and standing over
to the Northward: we supposed that it flows here as at the River
Jordan, because they are but four leagues asunder, and flows S.
E. and N. W. seven foot and half, and sometimes eight foot perpendicular: the Mouth of *Port Royal* lyes in 32 deg. 20 min.
lat. Now as concerning the entrance of the River *Jordan,* lat.
32 deg. 30 min: or thereabouts, you shall see a range of Breakers right against the opening, two or three leagues off the S. W.
Point; which you must leave to the Northward, and steer in with
the said S. W. Point, giving a range of Breakers that runs from
the said Point a small birth, and you shall have two, three, and
four fathoms at low water; and when you come one mile from
the Point aforesaid, steer over directly to the N. E. Point, and
you shall have six or seven fathom all the way. Within the N.
W. Point is good Anchoring: you shall have five fathoms fair
aboard the shoar: and you shall have five, six, seven and eight
fathoms, sayling all along upon the River, ten leagues, and a
large turning Chanel: It flows . here S. E. and N. W. seven foot
and a half, and eight foot at common Tydes. The River
Grandy, or as the Indians call it *Edistow,* lyes six leagues or
thereabouts from the River *Jordan,* and seems to be a very fair
opening:[1] but because the chief Indian of that Place was on board
us, and the Countrey all in Arms, we not knowing how the winde
might crosse us, it was not thought fitt to stay there: But some
of those *English* that had lived there, being Prisoners, say that

---

[1] Grandy is North Edisto, but this opening, latitude 32° 40', the last
they passed, may have been Charleston harbor, then called by the Spaniards St. George's Bay.

it is a very fair and goodly River, branching into several branches, and deep, and is fresh water at low Tide within two leagues of the Mouth; it seeming to us as we passed by, a good entrance large and wide, lat. 32 deg. 40 min. or thereabouts.   Now our understanding of the land of *Port Royal*, River *Jordan*, River *Grandie*, or *Edistow* is as followeth: the Lands are laden with large tall Oaks, Walnut and Bayes, except facing on the Sea, it is most Pines tall and good: The Land generally, except where the Pines grow, is a good Soyl, covered with black Mold, in some places a foot, in some places half a foot, and in other places lesse, with Clay underneath mixed with Sand; and we think may produce any thing as well as most part of the Indies that we have seen.   The *Indians* plant in the worst Land because they cannot cut down the Timber in the best, and yet have plenty of Corn, Pompions, Water-Mellons, Musk-mellons: although the Land be over grown with weeds through their lasinesse, yet they have two or three crops of Corn a year, as the Indians themselves inform us.   The Countrey abounds with Grapes, large Figs, and Peaches; the Woods with Deer, Conies, Turkeys, Quails, Curlues, Plovers, Teile, Herons; and as the Indians say, in Winter with Swans, Geese, Cranes, Duck and Mallard, and innumerable of other water-Fowls, whose names we know not, which lie in the Rivers, Marshes, and on the Sands: Oysters in abundance, with great store of Muscles: A sort of fair Crabs, and a round Shel-fish called *Horse-feet;* The Rivers stored plentifully with Fish that we saw play and leap.   There are great Marshes, but most as far as we saw little worth, except for a Root that grows in them the *Indians* make good Bread of.   The Land we suppose is healthful; for the *English* that were cast away on that Coast in *July* last, were there most part of that time of year that is sickly in *Virginia;* and notwithstanding hard usage, and lying on the ground naked, yet had their perfects healths all the time.   The Natives are very healthful; we saw many very Aged amongst them.   The Ayr is clear and sweet, the Countrey very pleasant and delightful: And we could wish, that all they that want a happy settlement, of our *English* Nation, were well transported thither, &c.

From *Tuesday* the 29th of *September*, to *Friday* the second of *October*, we ranged along the shoar from lat. 32 deg. 20 min: to the lat. 33 deg: 11 min. but could descern no Entrance for our

Ship, after we had passed to the Northwards of 32 deg: 40 min: On *Saturday* the third instant, a violent storm came up, the winde between the North and the East; which Easterly windes and fowl weather continued till *Monday* the 12th. By reason of which Storms and fowl weather, we were forced to get off to Sea to secure ourselves and ship, and were forsed by reason of a strong Current, almost to Cape *Hatterasse* in lat. 35 deg. 30 min: On *Monday* the 12th aforesaid we came to an Anchor in seven fathom at *Cape Fair*-Road, &c.   *   *   *

Whereas there was a Writing left in a Post at the Point of *Cape Fair* River, by those *New England* men that left Cattel with the *Indians* there, the Contents whereof tended not only to the disparagement of the Land about the said River, but also to the great discouragement of all those that should hereafter come into those parts to settle: In Answer to that scandalous wrighting we whose names are underwritten do affirm, That we have seen facing on both sides of the River, and branches of *Cape Fair* aforesaid, as good Land, and as well Timbered, as any we have seen in any part of the world, sufficient to accomodate thousands of our English Nation, lying commodiously by the said River.

On *Friday* the 4th of *December*, the winde being fair, we put out to Sea, bound for Barbadoes; and on the 6th day of *January* 166¾, we came to Anchor in Carlisle-Bay; and after several known apparent dangers both by Sea and Land, have now brought us all in safety to our long-wish'd-for and much desired Port, to render an Accompt of our Discovery, the verity of which we aver.

ANTHONY LONG,
WILLIAM HILTON,
PETER FABIAN.

A COPY OF THE SPANYARD'S FIRST LETTER.[1]

I am come to this Town of Infidel Indians, to seek some English, which my Governour & Captain-General, *Don Alonzo de Arangows, de Colis,* Cavallier, and Knight of the Order of St. James, for his Majesty, had notice that there was a Ship lost in that Port in which you are, that the men might not run any

---

[1] This is the earliest extant correspondence in Carolina.

hazard of their lives, as those with me here have. *Don Adel-eyers*, with the Governor of the Garison of *St. Augustine*, are gone to ransome and free the Subjects of the King your Master, Charles the Second: wherefore I advise you, that if these Indians (although Infidels and Barbarians) have not killed any of the Christians, and do require as a gift or courtesie for those four men, four Spades and four Axes, some Knives, and some Beads, and the four Indians which you have there, you deliver them, and that for their sakes that shall sayl on this Coast: you may send a Boat, who when she comes athwart the Port of *St. Ellens* may hoist an Ancient twice or thrice, and I will do the same. The shortnesse of the dispatch I desire, for I want provision for my Soldiers, and the way is large. Your Servant desires you would give me a Speedy Answer; and what may be done in your service I shall do very willingly. And if you have none that can interpret the Spanish Tongue, you may write in your own, for here are your Countrey-men that can understand it: but if you can, let it be in Spanish. *From the Capt.*

ALANSO ARGUILES.

From St. Ellens the 22 of Septemb. 1663.

———

THE COPIES OF OUR LETTERS SENT TO THE ENGLISH AND SPANIARDS AT ST. ELLENS, WITH THE ANSWER OF MR. WILLIAM DAVIS, AND THE SPANIARDS ALSO, HERE IN-CLOSED.

Loving Friends and Country-men. Wee are come up the River with our Ship, and are resolved to come through by Com-biheh to St. Ellens, and to get you away by fair means, or other-ways. If that will not do, we have five of your company already: and the Captain of Edistow, and one more are Prisoners with us, whom we intend to keep till we have rescued all the English Prisoners out of the hands of the Indians. Send us word by this Bearer what you know concerning the Spaniards, for the youth Morgan tells us that the Spanyards are come with Sol-diers to fetch you away. Fail not to inform us how things are. Nothing else at present, but remain

your friend and Servant

WILL. HILTON.

From on Board the Adventure, Septemb. 21, 1663.

AN ANSWER TO THE SPANYARDS LETTER NOT UNDERSTOOD.

Honoured Sir; Whereas wee received a Letter from you, the Contents whereof we understand not, because none of us could read Spanish: Our businesse is to demand and receive the English Prisoners from the hands of the Indians, and then they shall have their Indians which we have detained on Board, with satisfaction for their pains. We understand not at present that we have any businesse with you. Not else at present, but remain

your Friend and Servant in what I may

WILL. HILTON.

From on Board the Adventure Septemp. 23, 1663.
To his honoured Friend the Spanish Captain at St. Ellens.

AN ANSWER TO MR. WILLIAM DAVIS HIS LINES WRITTEN
TO US IN THE SPANYARD'S LETTER, VIZ:

Mr. William Davis, Wee received your Lines in the Spanish Letter, but hear nothing of your coming to us. Let your Keepers send you, and that without delay; far you may assure them, That we will be gone, and carry the Indians away with us except they send the English suddenly on Board, and then shall have their Indians upon our receipt of the English. Not else at present, but thank the Spanish Captain for the Pork and Venison he sent us. Remain your loving Friend

WILL. HILTON.

From on Board the Adventure, September 24, 1663.
To Mr. William Davis at St. Ellens.

Sir—wee have received your second Letter, and give you no Answer, for the Reason mentioned in our former Letter to you. Please to inform the Indians, that if they bring not the English Prisoners on Board us without further delay, we are resolved to carry their Indians we have on Board away: But if they will bring the English, they shall have theirs, with satisfaction. Also we thank you for your Venison and Pork.   Not else at present, but remain—Sir,

your Friend and Servant in what I may

WILL. HILTON.

From on Board the Adventure, Septemb. 24, 1663.

To his Honoured Friend, the Spanish Captain at St. Ellens.

————

A COPY OF THE SPANYARD'S SECOND LETTER.

My Governour and Capt. General, as soon as he had News that a Ship, by Nation English, was lost in that Port in which you now are, sent me with Soldiers of the Garison of St. Augustine in Florida, as they have at other times done, to free them from death; for which cause I came to this Port of St. Ellens, where I found all these Indians in a fright, fearing that you would do them some mischief: So having found four men of those that were lost, I thought good to advise you, that you might carry them in your Company, giving some gifts to those Indians which they desire; which is, four Spades, four Axes, some Knives, and some Beads.   This they desire not as payment, but only as an acknowledgment of a kindness for having saved their lives; which they have always done as Naturals who have given their obedience to the King our Master.   And they do also desire you to let go those four Indians which are there: you may send a Boat when you discover the Points of St. Ellens; may hoist an Ancient two or three times and I will do the same.   I desire your Answer may be sodain; for I am scarce of Provisions, and the way is somewhat long: and if you have no body who understands Spanish, you may write in English for here are your Countrey-men who will interpret it.   By the Captain

ALANSO ARGUILES.

From St. Ellens Septemb: 23, 1663.   [*Forces Tracts*, Vol. IV, page 133.]   *Ch. Year Book, 1884, 227, 249.*

PROPOSALS MADE TO ALL SUCH PERSONS as shall undertake to become the first Setlers on Rivers, Harbours, or Creeks, whose Mouth or Entrance is Southwards or Westwards of Cape Romana in the Province of Carolina, and execute the same at their own hazard and charge of Transportation, Ammunition, and Provisions, as is hereafter expressed, &c.

I. Imprimis. It is agreed & consented to by us Thomas Modyford, and Peter Colleton, Esquires, who are impowered by the Lords Proprietors to treat in their behalf; That in consideration of the good service which Captain Anthony Long, Captain William Hilton, and Mr. Peter Fabian have done in making so clear a Discovery on that Coast, They shall each &c. one thousand acres &c.

II. Item to Master Pyam Blowers & Master John Hancock 500 acres apiece &c.

III. To all the Seamen & Adventurers in the said Ship 100 acres &c. IV. To every person &c. (18 articles). *Ibid*, page 255.

———

ARTICLES OF AGREEMENT had and made betweene Edward Earle of Clarendon Lord High Chancellor of England George Duke of Albemarle Master of his Maties Horse and Captaine Gen^ll of all his Forces William Lord Crauen John Lord Berkeley Anthony Lord Ashley Chancellor of his Maties Exchequo^r Sr George Cartrett Kn^t and Barr° Vice Chamberline of his Mat^s Household Sr John Colleton Kn^t & Barr: and Sr Wm Berkeley Kn^t the Lords Proprieto^rs of the Province of Carolina of the one part and Maio^r Wm Yeamans of Barbados for and on the behalfe of S^r Jn° Yeamans Barr° his father Collonell Edmund Reade Symon Lambert Niccolas Edwards Robert Gibbs Samuel Tidcombe Henry Milles Tho: Lake Tho: Maycoke John Somerhayes Bartholomew Rees John Gibbs, Basill Gibbs, John Dickenson Thomas Gibbs, Benjamin Rees, Miles Scottow Nathaniell Meavericke, Bartholomew Rees Junio^r John Arthur, Samuell Smith, Thomas Partrige John Walice, John Brent, John Godfrey George Thompson Robt Williams Lawrence Halsted, Wm Burges, John Tothill, James Thorpe, Robt Tothill, Wm Forster Thomas Merricke, John Merricke, George Phillips Edward Jacobs, Robt Hacket, Benjamine Waddon Robt Johnston Thomas Dickes. Tho: Clutter-

4

booke John Forster Will Sharpe John Ham, John Start Mathew
Grey, John Perie, Richard Baily Edward Thorneburgh Thomas
Liston Anthony Long, Thomas Norvill Giles Hall James Norvill
William Woodehouse Jacob Scantlebury Samuell Lambart John
Forster Wm Byrdall Richard Barrett Edward Yeamans, John
Killicott Isaac Lowell, Thomas Clarke, John Wood John Bellomy
John Greenesmith, Robt Brevitir Thomas Dowden, Niccolas
Browne John Wilson, Robt Sinckler, Thomas Perkins James
Thorpe Robt Richarde, Benjamine Hadlut Christopher Goupher
James Walter James Hayden Senr Wm Birdall, Mordecai Bouden
Junio^r George Nore Humphrey Waterman[1] & himselfe Adven-
turo^{rs} to and Setlers of some part of ye Province aforesaid And
of all others y^t shall Adventure setle and plant in the said Prov-
ince of the other part as followeth

Whereas the said Maio^r William Yeamans is Imployed to
the said Lords Propriato^{rs} by the persons above menconed & by
them declared under there hands to be their Agent and Representative and that they have giuen him full power to treate propose and conclude wth ye said Lords about all matters relateing
to that which they have alleady done as aloe to what shalbe
necesary and convenient tobe done obligeing themselves & their

---

[1] Most men of position and wealth in Barbadoes. Colonel Reade was
of the Council, Colonel Edward Thornburgh afterwards agent of Barbadoes in England, Colonel W. Sharpe an eminent planter with 6co
acres, member Assembly 1674–1676, and a judge, John Merricke, member Assembly and eminent planter. The following came to Carolina or
held lands there: Colonel Lambert (of the Council and Speaker Barbadoes), Robert Gibbes (afterwards Chief Justice and Governor of South
Carolina), Captain John Gibbes (member Barbadoes Assembly and eminent planter 1667–1686), Thomas Gibbes and John Brent (members
Assembly Clarendon 1665), Henry Mills, Thomas Lake (member Assembly Barbadoes 1662–1674), Bartholomew Rees (eminent planter Barba-
does 1679), John Godfrey (afterwards President Council South Carolina),
John Dickenson, George Thompson (member Council South Carolina),
Robert Williams, John Tothill (had land called "Tothill" at Goose
Creek), Robert Johnston (had land Ashly River), Thomas Clutterbuck,
John Foster (eminent planter Barbadoes and of the Council South Car-
olina), John Perrie (later of the Council Antigua), Thomas Norvill
(Thomas Noel? Secretary Barbadoes), Giles Hall (eminent planter
Barbadoes, 400 acres 1673), J. Scantlebury, John Bellomy (held lands
Goose Creek, died there 169–), Thomas Dowden, Ben Hadlut, &c.

Posterityes to accept of stand to and abide by whatsoever the s^d
Maio^r William Yeamans shall conclude of and Agree upon in
relacon to ye Setlement of Carolina or any parte thereof. Now
in pursuance of the powers &^c giuen to ye said Maio^r Wm Yeamans by ye partyes above menconed These present Artickles doe
witnes And it is Covenanted Graunted & agreed by and betweene the said partyes as followeth

Impris. The said Lords for their parte their heires executo^{rs}
and Administrato^{rs} doe covenant and promise to performe fulfill
& keepe all the Concessions and particulers that are to bee by
them performed and keept menconed in the Concessions and
agreem^{ts} hereunto annext contayneing ye man^r of Gouerment
wth severall Imunityes and privileges graunted to all such persons as shall goe or send to plant or as are already planted in
the respective Countyes or Collonyes in the s^d Province of Carolina.

Item. The Lords doe further Covenant and promiss that they
will Cause to be shipt before ye first day of February next Twelue
peeces of Ordinance witn Carrages, Laddles, Spunges and Shott
convenient and necessary & Twenty barrells of powder, one
hundred Fierlocks and one hundred Matchlockes wth Leade &
Bullets fitting as also two hundred pare of Bandalyers for ye
Armeing and Prouiding of a Foart tobe erected and built neare
Port Royall or neare some other harbour River or Creeke whose
mouth or Entrance is Southward or Westward of Cape Romania
in the Province aforesaid by the Respectiue Adventurers before
menconed or by any others vnder their Authority.

Item. The Lords do further Covenant that every one of the
Adventurers of the Island of Barbados and their Associates of
England, New England, the Leward Islands and Barmothos
that hath subscribed and paid or shall subscribe and pay within
forty days after notice of this in the Barbados and the other
places unto the Treasurer or Treasurers appointed or to be
appointed by the Comittee choosen or to be Choosen by the Adventurers that are or shall be to receaue the same for the defraying the charge of carrying peple that cannot pay for ye transportation of themselves to port Royall or some Harbour Riuer or
Creeke whose mouth or Entrance is to the Southward or Westward of Cape Romania and for ye makeing of some Fortification

therefor and towards a Settlem^t of those and other people in
that place and for other necessary charges concerneing the Setlement aforesaid And shall send such proporcons of men Armed
and prouided as there owne Comitte shall agree upon in the first
shipp or shippes that shalbe sett forth to begin a Settlement there
shall haue Graunted to them and their heires forever for every
Thowsand pounds of Suger soe subscribed and paid five hundred
acres of land and soe in proportion for a greater or Lessor some
subscribed and paid as aforesaid to be taken vp wth in five yeares
after the date hereof and setled as other Lands are to be setled
vizt with an able man armed with a good firelocke boare Twelve
Bullets to the pound Tenn pounds of powder and Twenty pounds
of Bullets with six Monthes provizion with in one yeare after ye
takeing vp of ye said Land which land shalbe taken vp to the
south or westward of Cape Romania and by Lotts as is proposed
and prescribed in the Generall Concessions and agreements concerning the setlement of the Respectiue Countyes in the said
Province And shall pay one halfe penny ster : for every acre English measure yearely in manor as in the Concessions hereunto
annexed.

Item.   The Lords doe further Covenant and promiss That
whoever shall goe or send in the first Fleete wth Collonell John
Yeamans, he fayling with ye first Gouern^r or Deputy Gouerno^r
shall haue for his owne head one hundred and fifty acres of land
to him & his heires for ever English measure.   And for every
able man Servt he or shee shall carry or send Armed and prouided as afores^d One hundred and fifty acres of like measure.
And to every such Saruant after the expiracon of his or their
time Seaventy five acres of land to be taken vp by Lotte as
afores^d in the place before menconed.   And to every other Saru^t
that shall there goe after the first fleete such quantityes as in the
Generall Declaracon is exprest, Upon which hundred and fifty
acres of land hee shalbe obliged to keepe one able man and noe
more and in fayler thereof to forfeite the same as in the Generall
Concessions and Agreem^t is exprest for which Land there shalbe
reserued yearelie to the Lords their heires and assignes One halfe
penny ℔ acre English measure to be paid in manner as for other
lands in the Concessions menconed.

In Consideracon Whereof

The said Maio[r] Will Yeamans doth Covenant as well on ye behalf of his father S[r] Jn° Yeamans Bar° and of Coll: Edmund Reade and of all the Adventurers Settlers & planters before exprest and of all others that shall adventure setle and plant as of himselfe that they shall for their p'te pforme fullfill and keepe all ye particulers that are tobe by them performed mencioned in the Concessions & Agreement hereunto annexed And that there shalbe prouided before ye last day of September next two shipps of one hundred & twenty tonns each of them at least with Ordinance convenient in each shipp and wth powder shott and prouizions necessary for the transportacon of such persons as cannot pay for the passage of themselues to y° Southward of Cape Romania there to setle and plant and to erect a foart and on it to plant the Artillery sent by ye Lords afores[d] for ye retreate and preservacon of the first Setlers & of those y[t] shall follow. In witness of truth the said Maior W[m] Yeamans hath herevnto set his hand and seale this Seaventh day of January In the sixteeth yeare of his Ma[tes] raigne Anno'. Dno 1664. [*Shaf. Pap.*, sec. IX, Bdle. 48, No. 3.]

The Concessions and Agreement

of the Lords Propryators of the Province of Carolina to and with the Adventurers of the Island of Barbados and their Associates of England, New England, the Caribbia Islands and Barmothos to the Province of Carolina and all that shall plant there In order to the setling and planting of the Countye of Clarendine The County of Albemarle and the County   which latter is to bee to the Southward or Westward of Cape Romania all within the Province aforesaid.

1. Impris. Wee doe consent and agree That the Governor of each County hath power by the advice of Councill to depute one in his place and Authority in case of death or removeall to continue untill our further order vnless wee haue Commissionated one before.

2. Item. That hee hath likewayes power to make choyce of and to take to him six Councello[rs] at least or Twelve at moast or any eaven Number betweene Six and Twelve wth whose advice

and consent or wth at least three of the Six or fower of a greater Number all being sumoned he is to governe according to the Lymitacons and Instructions following during our pleasure.

3. Item. That the Cheife Registers or Secrytarys which wee haue choosen or shall chuse wee fayling that hee shall Chuse shall Keepe exact enteryes in faire bookes of all publicke affares of ye said Countyes and to avoyde deceipts and Law Suites shall record and enter all Graunts of Land from the Lords to the Planter and all Conveyances of Land howse or howses from man to man As also all Leases for Land house or howses made or to bee made by the Landlord to any tennant for more than one year which Conveyance or Lease shalbe first acknowledged by the Granto^r or Leasso^r or proued by the Oath of two witnesses to ye Conveyance or Lease before the Governor or some Cheife Judge of a Court for the time being whoe shall under his hand vpon the backside of ye said deede or Lease attest the acknowledgement or proofe as afores^d which shalbe a warrant for ye Registers to record the same which Conveyance or Lease soe recorded shalbe good & effectual in Law notwithstanding any other Conveyance deed or Lease for the said Land howse or howses or for any part thereof although dated before the Conveyance Deede or Lease recorded as aforesaid.   And the said registers shall doe all other thing or things that wee by our Instructions shall direct and ye Governo^r Councell & Assembly shall ordaine for ye good & wellfare of ye said Countyes.

4. Item. That the Surveyo^r Gen^{ll} that wee haue Choosen or shall chuse wee fayleing that the Gouernor shall Chuse shall haue power by himselfe or Deputy to survey ley out & bound all such lands as shalbe graunted from the Lords to ye Planters (& all other Lands wthin the said Countyes &^c which may concerne particculer men as he shalbe desired to doe) And a particculer thereof Certifie to ye Registers to be recorded as aforesaid Prouided That if the said Registers and Surveyors or either of them shall soe misbehaue themselues as that the Gouerno^r & Councill or Deputy Governo^r and Councill or the mai^r pa'te of them shall finde it reasonable to suspend their actings in their respective Imploym^{ts} it shalbe Lawfull for them soe to doe vntill further order from vs.

5. Item. That all choice of Officers made by the Governor shalbe for noe longer time then during our pleasure.

6. Item.   That the Governors Councello^rs Assemblymen Sec-
rytaryes Surveyors and all other Officers of trust shall sware or
subscribe (in a booke to be provided for that purpose) that they
will bare trew alleagance to the Kinge of England his heires and
successors and that they wilbe faithfull to the Interest of the
Lords Propryato^rs of the said Province and their heires executors and assignes and endeavor the peace and wellfaire of the
said Province and that they will trewly and faithfully discharge
their respective trusts in their respective Offices and doe equall
Justice to all men according to their best skill & Judgem^t without
Corruption fauor or affection and the names of all that haue
sworne or subscribed to be entred in a Booke and whosoever
shall subscribe and not sware and shall vyolate his promiss in
that subscription shalbe lyable to the same punishm^t that the
persons are or may be that haue sworne and broken their Oathes.

7. Item.   That all persons that are or shal become subjects to
the Kinge of England & sware or subscribe Allegiance to ye
Kinge & faithfulness to ye Lords as aboue shalbe admitted to
plant & become freemen of ye prouince & enioye ye freedomes
& Imunityes hereaft^r exprest Untill some stop or Contradiccon
be made by vs the Lords or elce by ye Gou'no^r Councill & Assembly wch shalbe in force Untill ye Lords see cause to ye Contrary puided such stop shall not anywayse p'iudice ye right or
Continewance of any person y^t hath beene rec^d before such stop
or order come from ye Lords or Gen^ll Assem^bly.

8. Item.   That noe person or persons quallifyed as aforesaid
w^thin ye province or all or any of ye Countyes before exprest at
any time shalbe anywayes molested punished disquieted or called
in question for any differances in oppinion or practice in matters
of religious concernem^te whoe doe not actually disturbe Civill
peace of ye s^d pruince or Countyes but y^t all and every such
person & persons may from time to time & at all times freely
and fully haue and enjoye his and their Judgem^ts and Contiences
in matt^rs of religion throughout all ye s^d pvince they behaueing
themselues peaceably & quietly & not vseing this Liberty to
Lycentiousness nor to ye Civill Injury or outward disturbance of
others any Law Statute or Clause Conteyned or to be conteyned
vsage or Custome of this realme of England to ye contrary
hereof in anywise notw^thstanding.

9. Item.   That noe p^rtence may be taken by vs our heires or

assignes for or by reason of o[r] right of patronage & pow[r] of advowson graunted vnto vs by his Ma[ties] Lett[rs] Pattents afores[d] to infringe thereby ye Gen[ll] clause of Liberty of Contience afore-menioned Wee doe hereby graunt vnto ye Gen[ll] Assemblyes of ye seu[ll] Countyes power by act to constitute & appoint such and soe many Ministers or preachers as they shall thinke fitt & to establish their maintenance Giuing Liberty besides to any pson or psons to Keepe & mainteyne w[t] preach[rs] or Minist[rs] they please.

10. Item.   That ye Inhabitants being freemen or Cheefe Agents to others of ye Countyes afores[d] doe as soone as this our Comission shall arriue by virtue of a Writ in our Names by ye Governo[r] to be for ye p[re]sent (vntill our seale comes) sealed and signed make choyce of twelve Deputyes or representatives from amongst themselues whoe being choosen are to Joyne w[th] him ye s[d] Gouero[r] & Councell for ye makeing of such Lawes Ordinances & Constitucions as shalbe necessary for ye p[r]sent good & wellfare of ye severall Countyes afores[d] but as soone as Parishes Divisions tribes or districcons of ye said Countyes are made that then ye Inhabitants or F.reehold[rs] of ye sev[ll] & respective parishes Tribes Divisions or Districcons of ye Countyes afores[d] (by our Writts under our Seale w[ch] wee Ingage shalbe in due time issued) Annually meete on ye first day of January & Chuse freehold[rs] for each respective divizion tribe or parish to be ye Deputyes or representatives of ye same which body of Representatiues or ye Maio[r] part of them shall wth ye Gov'no[r] & Councell afores[d] be ye Gen[ll] Assembly of ye County for w[ch] they shalbe choosen ye Gov'no[r] or his Deputy being p'sent vnless they shall willfully refuse in w[ch] case they may appoint themselues a P[r]sident during ye absence of ye Gov'nor or his Deputy Gov'no[r].

———

Which Assemblyes are to have Power.

1. Item to appoint their owne times of meeting & to adiorne their Sessions from time to time to such times & places as they shall thinke convenient as alsoe to ascertaine ye number of their Quorum Prouided y[t] such numbers be not less then ye third pte of the whole in whome or more shalbe ye full power of ye Generall Assembly.

2. Item to enact and make all such lawes Acts and Constitu-

tions as shalbe necessary for the well Goverment of ye County for wch they shalbe Choosen and them to repeale Provided y^t ye same be consonant to reason & as neare as may be conveniently agreable to ye Lawes and Customes of his Maties. Kingdom of England Prouided also y^t they be not against ye Interest of vs ye Lords Propryators our heires or assignes nor any of these our p'sent Concessions especially y^t they be not against ye Article for Liberty of Contience above menconed which Lawes &^c soe made shall receaue publicacon from ye Gov'nor & Councill (but as ye Lawes of vs and our Gen^{ll} Assembly) and be in force for ye space of one yeare & a halfe & noe more unless contradicted by ye Lords propryato^{rs} within time they are to be p'sented to vs o^r heires &^c for our Ratification & being confirmed by vs they shalbe continewall force till expired by their owne Limitacon or by Act of Repeale in like man^r as afores^d to be passed and confirmed.

3. Item by Act as afores^d to constitute all Courts for their respective Countyes togeath^r wth ye Lymitts powers & Jurisdiccons of ye s^d Courts as also ye severall offices & number of Officers belonging to each of ye s^d respective Courts Togeather wth there severall and respective Salleryes fees & perquisites Theire appellacons & dignities with ye penaltyes y^t shalbe due to them for breach of their severall & respective dutyes and Trusts.

4. Item by Act as afores^d to ley equall taxes and assessments equally to rayse monyes or goods upon all ye Lands (excepting ye Lands of vs the Lords Propryato^{rs} before setling) or persons wthin the severall precincts Hundreds Parishes Manors or w^tsoever other divizons shall hereaft^r be made and established in the s^d Countyes as oft as necessity shall require and in such maner as to them shall seeme most equall & easye for ye Inhabitants in order to ye bett^r supporting of ye publicke Charge of the said Gouerment and for ye mutuall safety defence & security of ye said Countyes.

5. Item. By Act as afores^d to erect within ye s^d Countyes such and soe many Barronyes and Mano^{rs} wth their necessary Courts Jurisdiccons freedomes and priuiledges as to them shall seeme convenient as alsoo to devide ye s^d Countyes into Hundreds Parishes Leits or such other diuissions or districcons as they shall thinke fitt and ye said diuissions to distinguish by what names wee shall order or direct & in default thereof by

such names as they please.   As alsoe within any part of ye said
Countyes to create and appoint such & soe many ports harbours
Creekes & other places for ye convenient ladeing & vnlading of
goods and Merchandize out of shipps boates & other Vessells as
they shall see expedient wth such Jurisdiccons priuiledges and
francheses to such ports &^c belonging as they shall judge most
conduceing to ye Generall good of ye said plantacon or Countyes.

6. Item by their enacting to be confirmed as afores^d to erect
rayse & build within ye s^d Countyes or any part thereof such
and soe many forts fortresses Castles Cittyes Corporacons Bur-
roughs townes Villages & other places of strenkt & defence &
them or any of them to Incorporate wth such Charters & priviledges as to them shall seem good & our Charter will permit &
ye same or any of them to fortifie & furnish wth such proportions
of ordinance, powder shott, Armer and all other weapons Amu-
nicon & Habillaments of warr both offensive and defensive as
shalbe thought necessary & convenient for ye safety & wellfare
of ye s^d Countyes but they may not at any time demolish dis-
mantle or disfurnish ye same w^thout ye consent of ye Governor
and ye Maior pte of ye Councell of y^t County where such forts
fortresses &^c shalbe erected and built.

7. Item by Act as afores^d to constitute trayne bands & Companyes with the number of Souldiers for ye safety strenth and
defence of ye s^d Countyes & province & of ye forts Castles Cittyes &^c to suppress all Meutinyes and Rebellions To make warr
offensive and defensiue wth all Indians strangers & forraigners as
they shall see cause And to persue an Enymy by Sea as well as
by lande if neede be out of ye Lymitts & Jurisdiccons of ye s^d
County with ye perticculer consent of ye Gouernor & vnder ye
conduct of our Leu^t Gen^ll or Comander in Cheife or whome he
shall appoint.

8. Item by Act as afores^d to give vnto all strangers as to them
shall seeme meete a Naturalizion & all such freedomes and priuiledges wth ye s^d Countyes as to his Ma^ts Subjects doe of right
belong they swearing or subscribing as afores^d wch s^d strangers
soe Natturallized or priuiledged shall alsoe have ye same Imunityes from Customes as is granted by ye Kinge to vs & by vs to
ye s^d Countyes & shall not be lyable to any other Customes then
ye rest of his M^ts Subjects in ye s^d Countyes are but be in all

respects accompted in ye Province and Countyes afores^d as ye Kinges Naturall Subjects.

9. Item by Act as afores^d to prescribed ye quantityes of Land which shalbe from time to time alloted to eavery head free or Saru^t male or female And to make & ordaine Rules for ye Casting of Lotts & leying out of ye same Prouided y^t   not their said prescriptions exceed ye severall proporcons which are hereby graunted by vs to all persons arriueing in ye s^d Countyes or adventuring theither.

10. Item the Gen^{ll} Assembly by Act as afores^d shall make provision for ye Maintenance and support of ye Gouernor and for ye defraying of all necessary charges of ye Goverm^t. As alsoe y^t ye Constables of ye respective Countyes shall collect ye halfe pen

    p. acre payable to ye Lords in their Countyes & pay ye same to ye receauor y^t ye Lords shall appoint to receaue ye same vnless ye s^d Gen^{ll} Assembly shall prescribe some oth^r way whereby ye Lords may have their rente duely collected wthout charge or troble to them.

11. Lastly to enact constitute & ordaine all such other Lawes Acts & Constitucons as shall or may be necessary for ye good prosperity & Setlem^t of ye s^d Countyes excepting w^t by these p'sents are exceppted & conforming to ye Limitacons herein exprest.

The Governors are with Theire Councell Before Exprest

1. Item to see y^t all Courts established by ye Lawes of ye Gen^{ll} Assembly & all ministers & officers civill or Millitary doe and execute their severall dutyes and offices respectively according to ye Lawes in force & to punish them from swerueing from ye Lawes or acting contrary to their trust as ye nature of their offence shall require.

2. Item. According to ye Constitucons of ye Gen^{ll} Assembly to Nominate & Commissionate ye severall Judges Members & Officers of Courts wheither Magistraticall or Ministeriall & all oth^r Civill Officers as Justices Coroners & thir Comissions & powers & authorityes to repeale at pleasure Prouided y^t they appoint none but such as are freehold^{rs} in ye Countyes afores^d vnless ye Generall Assembly consent.

3. Item.   According to ye Constitucons of ye Gen^{ll} Assembly
to appoint Courts & Officers in cases Cryminall & to impower
them to inflict penaltyes vpon offenders against any of ye Lawes
in force in ye said Countyes as ye said Lawes shall ordaine
wheither by fine Imprisonm^t Banishm^t Corporall punishm^t or to
ye takeing away of Member or of life itself if there bee cause
for it.

4. Item to place officers & soldiers for ye safety strenkth &
defence of ye forts Castles Cittyes &^c according to ye number
appointed by ye Gen^{ll} Assembly to Nominate place and Comis-
sionate all millitary officers vnder ye Dignity of ye Leu^t Gen^{ll}
who is Commissionated by vs over ye seu^{ll} trayned bands &
Companyes constituted by ye Gen^{ll} Assembly as Collonels Cap^{ts}
&^c & theire Comissions to revoake at pleasure ye Leu^t Gen^{ll} wth
ye advise of his Councell vnless some p'sent dang^r will not pmitt
him to advize to muster and trayne all ye Sold^{rs} within ye s^d
County or Countyes to prosecute warr pursue an Enymy Supress
rebellions & mewtines as well by sea as land And to exercise ye
whole Millitia as fully as by our Letters pattents from ye Kinge
wee cann impower him to doe Prouided y^t they appoint noe Millitary Officers but w^t are freeholders in ye s^d Countyes Unless ye
Gen^{ll} Assembly shall consent.

5. Item where they see cause af^r Condemnacon to repreiue
vntill ye case may be p'sented wth a coppy of ye whole tryall
Proceedings & proofes to ye Lords whoe will accordingly eather
pardon or comand execution of ye sentence on ye offender whoe
is in ye meanetime to be keept in safe custody till ye pleasure of
ye Lords be knowne.

6. Item in case of death or other remoueall of any of ye representatiues within ye yeare to Issue Sumons by Writt to ye
respectiue deuision or deuisions for which he or they were chosen
Comanding ye freehold^{rs} to chuse others in their steade.

7. Item to make warrants & to seale Graunts of Lands according to theis our Concessions & ye p'scriptions by ye advice
of ye Gen^{ll} Assembly in such forme as shalbe at large set downe
in our Instructions to ye Governo^r in his Comission and which
are hereafter expressed.

For the Better Security of the Proprietyes of all the Inhabitants.

1. Item. They are not to Impose nor suffer to be imposed any tax Custome Subsidy Tallage Assesment or any other duty w'soever vpon any culler or p'tence vpon ye s[d] County or Countyes & ye Inhabitants thereof other then what shalbe Imposed by ye authority & consent of ye Generall Assembly and then only in maner as aforesaid.

2. Item. They are to take Care y[t] Land quetly held planted & possessed seaven yeares after its being first duely surveyed by ye Surveyo[r] Gen[ll] or his ord[r] shall not be subiect to any reveiw resurvey or alteracon of bounds on w[t] p'tence soever by any of vs or any office[rs] or Minist[rs] und[r] vs.

3. Item. They are to take care y[t] noe man if his Catle stray range or graze on any ground wth ye s[d] Countyes not actually appropryated or sett out to particueler persons shalbe lyable to pay any trespass for ye same to vs o[r] heires &[e] Prouided y[t] Custome of Comons be not thereby pretended to nor any pson hind[rd] from takeing vp & appropriateing any lands soe grazed vpon & y[t] noe person purposely doe suffer his Cattell to graze on such lands.

4. Item it is our will and desire ye Inhabitants of ye said Countyes and Adventurers theith[r] shall enioye all ye same Imunityes from Customes for exportinge certine goods from these Realmes of England &[e] theither as ye Kinge hath beene graciously pleased to graunt to vs as also for ye Incorragem[t] of ye Manufacto[rs] of Wine silke oyle olliues fruite Almonds &[e] menconed in ye pattent haue priuiledge for bringing them Custome free into any of his Ma[ts] dominions for ye same time & vpon ye same tearmes as we o'selves may by o[r] patent.

And that the Planting of the Countyes Aforesaid may bee the More Speedily Promoted

1. That the Governors are to take notice That wee doe hereby graunt vnto all persons whoe have already adventured to Carolina or shall transport themselves or Sarv[ts] before ye first day of January w[ch] shalbe in ye yeare of our Lord one thousand six hund[rd] sixty five, theis following proporcons of Land viz[t]. If to

ye County of Clarendon one hundred acres English measure to every freedman & as much to his wife if hee haue one And to every freewoeman y[t] already is or shall arrive into ye s[d] County w[th] a Sarv[t] or Sarv[ts] to plant w[th]in ye time afores[d] one hundred acres Like measure. To a mast[r] or Mistris for every ableman Sarv[t] he or shee hath brought or sent or shall bringe or send as afores[d] being each of them Armed w[th] a good firelocke or Match locke boare Twelve bullets to the pound Ten pounds of powd[r] & Twenty pounds of bullets wth Match proportionable & victualled for six monthes fifty acres of like measure for every weaker sarv[t] he or shee hath brought or sent or shall bring or send as afores[d] as woemen children or slaves aboue ye age of fowerteene yeares And fifty acres like measure for every Christian Sarv[t] y[t] is brought or sent w[th]in ye s[d] time to his or her proper vse and behoofe when their time of servitude is expired.

2. Item to every freeman and freewoman y[t] shall arrive in ye said County Armed & pvided as afores[d] w[th]in ye second yeare from ye firste daie of January one thousand six hund[rd] sixty five to ye first of January one thousand six hund[rd] sixty six w[th] an intencon to plant seaventy five acres of land and seaventy acres for every able man sarv[t] y[t] he or they shall carry or send armed & pvided as aforesaid.

3. Item for every weaker Sarvant or slave adged as afores[d] y[t] shalbe carryed or sent theith[r] w[th]in ye second yeare as afores[d] forty acres of land—To every Christian Sarv[t] y[t] shall arrive ye second yeare forty acres of land of like measure af[r] ye expiration of his servitude.

4. Item to every freeman or freewoeman armed and provided as afores[d] y[t] shall goe & arrive w[th] an intention to plant within ye third yeare from January One Thousand six hund[rd] sixty six to January One thousand six hundred sixty seaven fifty acres of land like measure & for every able man sarv[t] y[t] he or they shall carry or send armed & pvided as afores[d] ye like quantity of land and for every weaker sarv[t] or slave aged as afores[d] y[t] he or they shall carry or send within ye third yeare Twenty five acres of Land & to every Christian Sarvant soe carryed or sent in ye third yeare Twenty five acres of land of like measure aft[r] ye expiracon of his or their time of sarvice.

5. Item. Wee doe hereby grant vnto all psons whoe haue already adventured to Carolina or shall transport themselves or

sarv^{ts} before ye first daie of January wch shalbe in ye yeare of our Lord One thousand six hundrd sixty five theis following proporcons of Lande vizt. If to ye County of Albemarle Eighty acres English measure to every freeman & as much to his wife if he haue one And to every freewoman y^t already is or shall arrive into ye s^d County wth a Sarv^t or Sarv^{ts} to plant wthin ye time afores^d Eighty acres like measure. To a Mast^r or Mistris for every able man Sarv^t hee or shee hath brought or sent or shall bring or send as afores^d being each of them armed wth a good fierlocke or Matchlocke boare twelve bullets to ye pound Tenn pounds of powder & Twenty pounds of bullets wth Match proporconable & victualled for six monthes Eighty acres of like measure & for every weaker sarv^t he or shee hath brought or sent or shall bring or send as afores^d as woemen children & slaves above ye age of fouerteene yeares Forty acres like measure And for every Christian Sarv^t y^t is brought or sent wthin ye s^d time to his or her proper vse & behoofe when their time of sarvitude is expired forty acres of like measure.

6. Item to every freeman and freewoman y^t shall arrive in ye s^d County armed and provided as afores^d wthin ye second yeare from ye first day of January One thousand six hundred sixtie five to ye first day of January one thousand six hundred sixtie six wth an intencon to plant Sixtie acres & Sixty acres for every able man sarv^t y^t he or they shall carry or send Armed & prouided as aforesaid.

7. Item for every weaker sarv^t or slave adged as afores^d y^t shallbe carryed or sent theither wthin ye second yeare as afores^d Thirty acres like measure. To every Christian Sarv^t y^t shall arrive ye second yeare Thirty acres of Land of like measure aft^r ye expiracon of his or theire time of service.

8. Item to every freeman and freewoman armed & provided as afores^d y^t shall goe & arive wth an Intencon to plant wthin ye Third yeare from January one thousand six hundred sixty six to January one thousand six hundred sixty seaven forty acres of land like measure and for every able man sarv^t y^t he or they shall carry or send within ye s^d time armed & prouided as aforesaid ye like quantity of land. And for every weaker saru^t or slave aged as afores^d y^t hee or they shall carry or send within ye third yeare Twenty acres of Land like measure And to every Christian Saru^t soe carryed or sent wthin ye Third yeare Twenty

acres of land of like measure af^r ye expiracon of his or there
time of service.

9. Item wee doe hereby graunt unto all p'sons whoe have
already adventured to Carolina or shall transport themselves or
Saru^{ts} before ye first day of January which shalbe in ye yeare of
our Lord one thousand six hundrd sixty five these followinge
proporcons vizt.   To every freeman y^t shall goe wth ye first
Gou'no^r from ye port where hee Imbarked (or shall meete him
at ye Randeyvous he appoint) and from thence goe wth him to
ye Southward or westward of Cape Romania wthin ye province
afores^d for ye settling of a plantacon there which we name to be
ye County of   Armed wth a good Muskett boare Twelve
bullets to ye pound wth Tenn pounds of powd^r & Twenty pounds
of Bullets wth Bandalears & match Convenient & wth six monthes
provision for his owne person arriueing there One hundred and
fifty acres of land English measure.   And for every able man
Saru^t y^t hee shall carry wth him armed & pvided as aforesaid &
arriuing there ye like quantity of one hundred and fifty acres &
whoever shall send sarv^{ts} at y^t time shall have for every able man
sarv^t hee or shee soe sends Armed and prouided as afores^d &
ariving there ye like quantity of one hund^d and fifty acres.   And
for every weaker Sarv^t or slave male or female exceeding ye age
of fowerteene yeares which any one shall send or carry ariving
there Seaventy five acres of land and to every Christian Servt
exceeding ye age afores^d af^r ye expiracon of their time of service
Seaventy five acres of land for there owne vse

10. Item.   To every Mast^r or Mistris y^t shall goe before ye
first day of January which shalbe in ye yeare of our Lord one
thousand six hundrd sixty five one hundrd & twenty acres of Land
& for every able man sarv^t y^t hee or shee shall carry or send
armed & pvided as afores^d and ariving wthin ye time afores^d ye
like quantity of one hundrd & Twenty acres of land & for every
weaker sarv^t or slave male or female exceeding ye age of fowerteene yeares ariving there sixty acres of land & to every Christian Sarv^t to there owne vse & behoofe Sixty acres of like
measure.

11. Item to every freeman and freewoman y^t shall ariue in ye
s^d County armed and prouided as afores^d wthin ye second yeare
from ye first of January one thousand six hundred sixty five to
ye first of January one thousand six hundrd sixty six wth an In-

tencon to plant Ninty acres of Land English measure and for every able man sarv^t y^t hee or shee shall carry or send Armed and prouided as afores^d Ninty acres of Like measure.

12. Item. And for every weaker sarv^t or slave adged as afores^d y^t shalbe soe carryed or sent theith^r wthin ye second year as afores^d forty five acres of land of like measure & to every Christian Sarv^t y^t shall arriue ye second yeare forty five acres of land of like meassure after ye expiracon of his or there time of service for there owne vse and behoofe all wch Lands soe graunted in ye 9, 10, 11 & 12 artickles preceeding & ye 13th following are ment & intended to be taken vp & giuen in ye County of and not elce where.

13. Item to every freeman and freewoman armed & puided as afores^d y^t shall goe & ariue wth intencon to plant wthin ye Third yeare from January One thousand six hundrd sixty six to January One thousand six hundre^d sixty seaven armed and puided as afores^d Sixty acres of land like measure & for every able man Sarv^t y^t he or they shall carry or send wthin ye s^d time Armed & prouided as afores^d ye like quantity of sixty acres of land. And for every weaker Sarv^t or Slave aged as afores^d y^t he or they shall carry or send wthin ye third yeare Thirty acres of land. And to every Christian Sarv^t soe carryed or sent in ye thirde yeare Thirty acres of land of like measure after ye expiracon of his or there time of service. All wch Land and all other y^t shalbe possessed in s^d Countyes are to be held on ye same tearmes and condicons as is before menconed & as hereafter in ye following paragraphes is more at Large exprest Provided That all ye before menconed Land and all other w'soever y^t shall be taken vp & soe setled in ye said province shall afterwards from time to time for ye space of Thirteene yeares from ye date hereof be held upon ye condicon afores^d of continewing one able man sarv^t or two such weaker serv^{ts} as afores^d on every hundred acres a Master or Mistris shall possess besides w^t was graunted for his or her owne person In failer of wch upon Notificacon to ye p^rsent Occupant or his assignes there shalbe three yeares giuen to such for there compleating ye s^d number of persons or for there sayle or other disposure of such part of there Lande as are not soe peopled within wch time of three yeares if any pson holding any Lands shall faile by himselfe his Agents executo^{rs} or assignes or some oth^r way to prouide such Number of persons Unless the

Gen[ll] Assembly shall w[th]out respect to poverty Judge y[t] it was impossible for ye party soe fayleing to keepe or procure his or her number of Sarv[ts] to be prouided as afores[d] In such case wee ye Lords to have power of disposeing of soe much of such Land as shall not be planted w[th] its dew number of persons as afores[d] to some other y[t] will plant ye same Prouided alwayes y[t] any pson who hath a stocke of Catle Sheepe or such like on his hands shall for every greater soart of Cattel w[ch] hee att ye time of such forfeiture as horses kine &[e] retaine two acres, & for every lesso[r] sort as sheepe hoggs &[e] one acre Prouided alsoe y[t] noe persons arriveing into ye s[d] Countyes wth purpose to setle (they being subjects or Natturallized as afores[d]) be denyed a grant of such proporcons of land as at ye time of there arriueall are due to themselues or saru[ts] by Concession from vs as afores[d] but have full Lycense to take vp and setle ye same in such order & man[r] as is granted & p'scribed all lands notw[th]standing (ye pow[r] in ye Assembly afores[d]) shalbe taken vp by warrant from ye Gov'nor and confirmed by ye Gou'nor & Councell vnder a Seale to be prouided for y[t] purpose in such Ord[r] & meth-hood as shalbe set downe in this declaracon and more att large in ye Instruccons to the Gouernor and Councell.

AND THAT THE LANDS MAY BEE THE MORE REGULERLY LAYD OUT AND ALL PERSONS THE BETTER ASCERTAYNED OF THEIR TITLES AND POSSESSIONS.

1. Item in the boundary of ye County of Clarendon the Governor and Councell (and Assembly if any bee) are to make Choyce of (and confine themselves and planters to) one side of ye mayne riuer neare Cape faire on w[ch] some of ye adventurers are already settled or Intend to setle & ye Islands in or neare ye s[d] River next ye side they setle on Unless they have already setled some Island neare ye other side w[ch] if they haue they may continew thereon.

2. Item. The Governo[r] of ye County of   wth ye advice of his Councell is to bound ye said County as hee shall fitt not exceeding forty myles square or Sixteene hundred square myles.

3. Item. They are to take care and direct that all lands bee devided by Gen[ll] lotts none lesse then two thousand two hundred acres nor more then two & twenty thousand acres in each lott

exceeping Cittyes townes &ᶜ and ye neare Lotts of towneshipes and yᵗ ye same be vndecimally deuided, one Eleaventh part by lott to vs our heires and assignes ye Remaynoʳ to psons as they come to plant ye same in such proporcons as is allowed.

4. Item. That ye Governor of each County or whome he shall depute in case of death or absence if some one be not before Comissionated by vs as aforesᵈ doe give to every person to whome land is due a warrant signed & sealed by himselfe & ye Maior pte of his Councell & directed to ye Surveyoʳ Genˡˡ or his Deputy Comanding him to ley out Lymitt & bound   acres of land (as his due proporcon is) for such a person in such allotmᵗ according to wᶜʰ warrant ye Register haueing first recorded ye same and attested the record vpon ye warrant ye Surveyoʳ Genˡˡ or his deputy shall proceed and certifie to ye Cheife Secrytary or Register ye name of ye person for whome he hath layde out lands, by virtue of wᵗ authority, ye date of ye authority or warrant ye number of acres ye bounds & on wᵗ poynt of ye Compass ye severall Lymitts thereof lye wᶜʰ Certificate ye Register is likewayse to enter in a booke to be prepared for yᵗ purpose wᵗʰ an alphabetticall table referring to ye booke That soe ye Certificate may be ye easyer found & then to file ye Certificates & ye same to keepe safely. The Certificate being entered a Warrant comprehending all ye ptticulers of land menconed in ye Certificate aforesᵈ is to be signed & sealed by him & his Councell or ye Maior pte of them as aforesᵈ (they haueing seene ye entery) & directed to ye Register or Cheefe Secrytary for his p'paring a Graunt of Land to ye party for whome it is layd out wᶜʰ Graunt shalbe in ye forme following vizᵗ:

The Lords Propriᵃtors of ye Province of Carolina doe hereby graunt unto A B of ye County of Clarendon (or in wᵗ County ye same shalbe) in ye province aforesᵈ a plantacon in ye sᵈ County conteyning   acres English measure Bounding as in ye said Certificates To hold to him (or her) his (or her) heires and assignes for ever Yielding & paying yearly to ye sᵈ Lords Propriators their heires or assignes every twenty fifth day of March according to ye English Accᵒ one halfe penny of lawfull English money for every of ye sᵈ acres To be holden of ye Maner of   in free and Comon Soccage ye first paymᵗ of wʰ rent to beginn ye twenty fifth day of March which shalbe in ye yeare of our Lord One thousand six hundʳᵈ & seaventy According to

ye English Accompt Giuen und^r ye Seale of ye County of Clarendon ye   day of   in ye year of our Lord

To which Instrewm^t ye Governor or his Deputy hath hereby
full Authority to put ye Seale of ye s^d County & to subscribe
his name As alsoe ye Councell or ye Maior pte of them are to
subscribe there names & then ye Instreum^t or Graunt is to be
by ye Register Recorded in a booke of Records for y^t purpose
All wch being done according to these Instruccons wee hereby
declare y^t ye same shalbe effectual in law for ye Inioym^t of ye
s^d plantacon & all ye benefitts & profitts of & in ye same Except
ye halfe part of Mynes of Gold & Silvo^r paying ye rent as afores^d
Provided y^t if any plantacon soe graunted shall by ye space of
three yeares be neglected to be planted wth a sufficient Number
of Sarv^{ts} as is before menconed y^t then it shalbe lawfull for vs
otherwayes to dispose thereof in whole or in part This graunt
notwthstanding.

5. Item wee doe alsoe grant convenient proporcons of land
for highwayes & for streets not exceeding one hundred foot in
bredth in Cittyes townes Villages & for Churches forts wharfs
keys harbours & for publicke howses and to each parish for ye
vse of there Ministers one hundred acres in such places as ye
Gen^{ll} Assembly shall apoint.

6. Item ye Gov^{rs} are to take notice y^t all such Lands leyed out
for ye vses and purposes in ye next preceeding Arcle shalbe free
& exempt from all rents taxes & other Charges or duties w^{t}so-
ever payable to vs our heires or assignes.

7. Item.   That in leying out Lands for Cittyes Townes Villages Burroughes or other Hamlets ye s^d Lands be vndecimally
diuided one Eleaventh part to be by lott layed out for vs & ye
rest deuided to such as shalbe willing to build thereon they paying aft^r ye rate of an halfepenny per acre yearely to us As for
there other Lands as afores^d wch said Lands in Cittyes townes &^{c}
is to be assured to each possessor by ye same way & Instrew-
ment as is before menconed.

8. Item.   That all Rules relateing to building of each streete
or quantity of ground to be allotted to each howse wthin ye said
respective Cittyes Burroughes and townes bee wholy left by act
as afores^d to ye wisdome & direccon of ye Gen^{ll} Assembly.

9. Item.   That ye Inhabitants of ye said County have free
passage throughe or by any Seas bounds Creeks Rivers Rive-

lets &ᶜ in ye sᵈ Pvince of Carolina through or by wᶜʰ they must necessarily pass to come from ye mayne Ocean to ye Countyes aforesᵈ or any part of ye Province aforesaid.

10. Lastly it shalbe Lawfull for ye Representatives of the freeholders to make any address to ye Lords touching ye Governor and Councill or any of them or concerning any Greivances whatsoever or for anything they desire without the consent of ye Governor and Councell or any of them.

[L S }   WILL YEAMANS.[1]

Sealed and delivered in the p'sence of vs

Jo. PERYN
THO. WALKER.

[*Shaf. Pap.*, Bdle. 48, No. 3.]

RESOLUTION OF THE LORDS PROPRIETORS.

January 7ᵗʰ 1664–5.

It is this day agreed by the Lords Propryators of Carolina that although the County of Clarendon neare Cape Faire, and all the tract of ground as far as to the Southward of the river St. Mathias and west as far as the South Seas, be for the present, under the Government of Sir John Yeamans, yet notwithstanding it is ment and intended, that that parte of it which is about to be setled to the Southward and westward of Cape Romania be a distinct Government from the County of Clarendon, and that there be a distinckt deputy Governor for the present and that it be called the County of Craven and as soone as it shalbe conveniently setled by the said Sir John Yeamans or any other that there be a distinckt Governor comissionated to governe there. [*Col. Ent. Book*, No. 20, page 22.]   *N. C. Rec.*, I, page 93.

1664–5, Jan: 7,   Mem: To speak to one of the Secretaries to procure the King's warrant to the Commissioners of Ordnance

---

[1] Eldest son of Sir John Yeamans, whom he succeeded as second Baronet 1674. Member of Assembly Barbadoes 1666, 1667, 1674, &c., and one of the most eminent planters, with 300 acres in St. Peter's Parish 1673. He died 167–. His wife, Lady Willoughby Yeamans, and son, Sir John, survived him. (*Pw'r Att'y 1678, Sec. Off.*)

for issuing 12 iron guns, which his Majesty has granted to the
Lord Chancellor, Lord General and others for Carolina. [*Col.
Pap.*, Vol. 19, page 6.] *Am. & W. I.*, §906.

———

ORDER OF THE LORDS PROPRIETORS OF CAROLINA TO SIR JNO. COLLETON.

To ship 12 pieces of ordnance given by the King,[1] for Barbadoes; and to cause carriages, bullets, shot, ladles, sponges,
matches &c. to be provided for said ordnance, with 20 barrels of
powder and 200 muskets, with lead bullets, shot, match and
bandaliers. [*Col. Ent. Book*, No. 20, page 20.] *Am. & W.
I.*, §907.

———

LORDS PROPRIETORS OF CAROLINA TO MR. DRUMMOND.[2]

Cockpitt, Jan. 7, 1664–5.

Their last was by Mr. Peeter Carteret[3] &c. [re County of Albemarle.]   Printed *N. C. Rec.*, I, page 93.

———

LORDS PROPRIETORS TO Sr JOHN YEAMANS.

Sir John Yeamans—Sir, Haveing receaved a very good car-
rector of your abillityes and Inteagryty and of your loyalty to
the Kinge from Sir John Colleton,[4] with an assurance that you
will viggorously attempt the setling of a Collony or plantation
to the southward of Cape Romania which will conduce much to
the Interest and honour of the Kinge and advantage of his people, and more especially that of the first setlers, wee have in the
first place prevaled with his Majestie to conferr the honor of a

———

[1] See page 31.   These guns were lost in Charles River entrance.

[2] William Drummond, of Virginia, Governor of Albemarle, appointed
by Sir William Berkeley 1663 (page 15).   Replaced by Samuel Stevens
1667.

[3] Secretary of Albemarle, appointed September 8, 1663; continued till
167—.

[4] Lord Willoughby to Joseph Williamson July 9, 1667: 'Never was
man so out in his judgm't of men in Barbadoes as your friend S'r John
Colleton who you know named one S'r John Yeamans to exceed all men
for interest in this island.'   *N. C. Rec.*, I, pages 158, 176.

Knight Barronet upon you and your heires, to whome wee have given assurance that you will deserve the same.

In the next place we have by our Commissions which goes by your Sonn, made you our Lieutenant Generall and Governor of that parte of our Province of Carolina, which we conceave may most conduce to the setlement aforesaid and in as much as cann yet be under our Government for many reasons which we have not time to shew, we have in our agreement with your Sonn indeavoured to comprehend all Interests especially that of New England from whence the greatest stocke of people will in probabillity come, our more southerne plantations being already much drayned, wherefore we advize you to contrive all the good wayes you cann imagen to get those people to joyn with you in which there wilbe a common Utility especially by keepinge those in the Kinges dominions that either cannot or will not submitt to the Government of the Church of England.

As for the Six thousand acres of Land by you desired from us we doe here oblige ourselves to graunt the same to you or your assignes to be by you or them taken to the southward or westward of Cape Romania, by lott as other lands are to be taken up, in which we desire you to avoyde the comeing to neare the home Lotts which if you shall doe for any greate proportion, it will thin the people and weaken that part to the indangering of the whole, and alsoe as you take it up or cause it to be taken up and bounded within 3 yeares after the date hereof, you paying one halfe penny per acre English measure yearely the first payment to begin the 25ᵗʰ day of March which shalbe in the yeare of our Lord 1670, according to the English account.

Wee doe likewayse ingage ourselves to graunt to your frind Captain William Merricke[1] or assignes fifteene hundred acres of Land English Measure, in the places upon the tearmes, wee have ingaged to graunt to you, wishing you good success and prosperity in your intended voyage and undertakings we rest

Your very loving frinds.

Cockpitt this 11ᵗʰ January 1664.

[*Col. Ent. Book*, No. 20, page 21.]   *N. C. Rec.*, I, 93, 94.

---

[1] An eminent planter in Barbadoes, with 300 acres there 1673.

THE LORDS PROPRIETORS OF CAROLINA COMMISSION to Sir John Yeamans[1] appointing him Governor of their County of Clarendon, near Cape Fair, and of all that tract Southerly as far as the river St. Mathias and west as far as the South Seas with power to appoint a Council &c.   Jan: 11, 1664,   *N. C. Rec. I,* pages 97, 98.

————

LORDS PROPRIETORS OF CAROLINA COMMISSION to Sir John Yeamans Governor of the County of Clarendon &c. and his Council, To convey lands &c.   Jan: 11, 1664.   *N. C. Rec. I,* pages 95, 97.

———————————————

[1] Eldest son of Robert Yeamans, Alderman of Bristol (executed 1648 for his loyalty).   He went to Barbadoes, became a considerable planter, and 1661–65 of the Council.   Henry and William Willoughby and himself were made Governors of Barbadoes in absence of Lord Willoughby, who calls him "of good conduct and stout."   In 1665 he was made a Baronet and Governor of Clarendon and in October sailed for Cape Fear, but suffering shipwreck returned.   He withdrew from Council 1667, on appointment of William, Lord Willoughby, Governor, who complains of the seditious Barwicke, Lambert, and Sir John Yeamans are the head.   Their correspondents in England are Sir Peter Colleton, "a chip of the old block S'r Paul Pindar &c."   In 1669 he was commissioned to receive St. Kitts from the French, and in December sailed with the Carolina Colony to Bermuda and returned to Barbadoes.   In 1671 he was created landgrave, settled an estate in Carolina, and went there in June.   'But within 2 or 3 days of his arrival he retired to his country house disgusted that the people did not incline to salute him Governor' and murmured 'that S'r John intended to make this a Cape Fear settlement.'   However at Parliament, July 8th, he was chosen Speaker, and December 14, 1671, claimed the Governorship but was refused.   He was commissioned Governor August 21st and again December 26, 1671, and proclaimed at Charles Town April 26, 1672.   Halsted says he 'was disaffected as too selfish.'   He sought the aggrandisement of himself, the planters and trade with Barbadoes, and 1672 Lord Ashly 'is disgusted by his conduct.'   But he passed important acts, organized the colony against Westoes and Spaniards and laid out New Charlestown.   Henct says: 'in 1674 being reduced to a feeble & sickly condition by the warm climate & his indefatigable labors for the success of the settlem't, returned to Barbadoes where he died.'   (Before December, when his successor, Sir William Yeamans, Baronet, was in the Assembly.)

LORDS PROPRIETORS TO [THE BARBADOES ADVENTURERS].

Cockpitt this 11th January 1664-5.

Gentlemen,

We have receaved your letter of the 29th of August and 8th of October by Major William Yeamans who hath made knowne your desires touching your settlement and planting in our Province of Carolina, as alsoe his power from you to treate and conclude with us concerneing the same in which we assure you he hath beene very carefull of your advantage and interest and by his injenuity hath prevayled with us to consent to more, then severall people would have accepted from us, of which we doe noe wayse repent considering your forwardness to setle neare Cape Faire before you had an assurance of any conditions from us, and your resolution to make another setlement to the Southward or westward of Cape Romania which we much desire out of respect to the Nations and your Interest which will thereby receave severall advantages which we hope wil be a motive to press you viggorously forward to that worke, we have done our parte in order there unto, as will appear by our Concessions or Agreement which your Agent Major William Yeamans on your behalfes, to whome and to our Ingagement under our hands and seale, we refer you, Pleas to be confident that there is nothing that may be fitt for us to graunt more, or to obtayne for you from his Majestie but that we shall doe the one and endeavour to procure the other, as soone as we understand that you have begunn the Southermost setlement: wishing you good success & prosperity in your undertakings, we rest

Your very loveing freinds.

[*Col. En. Book 20*, page 20.]   *N. C. Rec.*, I, page 98.

[SUGAR RECEIPTS.[1]]

BARBADOES.   By virtue of an Election of the adventurers for the Province of Carolina did elect me to be one of the Treasurers for the Receipts of all such subscriptions and also for the Re-

---

[1] See page 32.   Captain Thompson, Barbadoes adventurer 1663, their Treasurer 1665.   Came to Carolina 167$\frac{9}{0}$; member of the Council there 1675.   Benjamin Hadlut, &c., see page 30.

ceipts of what Sugars in pursuance of the Generall Concessions under the Great Seale of said Province I doe acknowledge to have received of Coll. Simon Lambert the sume of foure thousand pounds of Muscovado Sugar as witness my hand this 25th Aprill 1665.

Test   GEORGE THOMPSON.

(Indorsed.) BARBADOES. I Sir John Yeamans, Barronett Lieut Generall and Governor of the Province of Carolina doe acknowledge the above mentioned & expressed receipt to be good and effectual to clayme have and enjoy for every thousand pounds of Sugar Five hundred acres of land according to the Generall Concessions under the Great Seale of the said Province Given under my hand this 7th of October 1665.

JOHN YEAMANS.

Test: Ja: Browne.

Entered this October 25th, 1671. This is a true copy of the original Examined the 30th of October 1671.

Jos. DALTON Secretary.

S. C. Council Journal, page 78.

[Similar to Jacob Scantlebury 1000 lbs. Gyles Hall Esq: do. Mr Robert Williams do: Thomas Dowden, Mr Thomas Noevill, Capt: John Godfrey, Mr Benjamin Tadbutt, Lieut Thomas Clutterbuck. (*C. J.*, page 73, 82) Thomas Lake (*Dalcho*, page 15.)]

BARBADOES. By virtue of an Election of the adventures for Carolina wherein Capt. George Thompson was elected one of the Treasurers of all such Subscriptions And also the Receipt of what Sugar in pursuance of the Generall Concessions under the Great Seale of the said Province I as I am appointed to keepe the accounts of the aforesaid George Thompson, as he is elected Treasurer aforesaid, doe acknowledge to have received of the said George Thompson the sum of one thousand pounds of Muscoᵛ. Sugar as witness my hand this 25th Aprill 1665

RANDˢ BRANDT.

[Indorsed with similar certificate by Sir John Yeamans 2 Oct: 1665.] Entered 29 May 1671.

THOS. WOODWARD'S[1] LETTER to Sir Jno Colleton. Albemarle June 2 1665 understands by Mr. Drummond & Mr. Carterett that the Lords Proprietors have appointed him Surveyor of Albemarle &c. [S. P., 48, No. 4.] N. C. Rec., I, page 99, 101.

———

THE SECOND CHARTER granted by King Charles the second to the Proprietors of Carolina 30 June 1665. S. C. Stat., I, pages 31, 40. N. C. Rec., I, pages 102, 114.[2]

———

ACCO: OFF FFEES IN PASSING YE CHARTER & DUPLICATE OF CAROLINA VIZT:

	£	s	d
ffor ye Kings war^{nt} & Secretary takeing noe fee	1	02	06
ffor m^r Attorney gen^{ell} & his Clarks ffees for drawing & Engrossing ye Bill . . .	17	17	06
ffor ye Kings signeing ye Bill & ye Secretary takeing noe fee	1	02	06
ffor ye ffees of ye Signett & privy Seale 8 £ each	16	00	00
ffor fees to ye m^r of ye Pattent office & for Vellam Ruleing, painting & Ingroseing ye Pattent for ye Broad Seale & to ye Clarks .	25	05	00
ffor Ld Chancello^{rs} pursebearer & his Clarke .	1	09	00
ffor Ld Chancello^{rs} Servant, ...	2	00	00
ffor fees of ye Hannap^r Office	24	00	00
ffor fees of ye duplicate of ye pattent office & for ye vellom & engroseing it & to ye Clarks	15	00	00
ffor fees at ye Hannaper office . . .	2	15	00
	106	11	06

———

[1] Appointed Surveyor-General and of the Council of Albemarle September 8, 1663; continued so July 12, 1666 (N. C., I, page 141). 1665, July 12. The King to the Wardens of the Mint: The office of Assay Master is vacant by the death of John Woodward and the absence of Thomas Woodward, his father, who if alive is at some plantation on York River in Virginia (A. & W. I., ₴ 1019). Thomas Woodward was put out 1649, went to Virginia not to return till the King came in again (₴ 187).

[2] Note of the names of the eight Lords Proprietors of Carolina and the bounds of their two patents, &c., June, 1665. [Col. Ent. Book, 20.]

FFEES P^d IN PASSING YE LAST PATTENT FFOR
CAROLINA (July 1665)

ffor ye Kings war^nt & Signeing ye Bill the Secretary takeing noe fee	4	oo	oo
ffor m^r Attorney gen^rll & his Clerks fees for drawing & Ingroseing ye bill &c. . -	11	05	oo
ffor fees p^d at ye Signett office & ye Privie Seall	17	o6	o8
ffor ye Ld Chancello^rs Pursebearer & Clarks .	1	04	oo
ffor ye Master of ye Pattent office for vellam, ruleing &c. Ingroseing ye Pattent and to ye Clerks	16	15	o6
ffor fees at ye Hannap: office at Twitnam . .	20	07	o8
ffor expenses there in attending ye Great Seale	o	03	o6
	71	02	04

[*Shaf. Pap.*, Sec. IX, Bdle. 48, No. 5.]

————

A D^r AND C^r ACCOUNT WITH THE LORDS PROPRIETORS OF CAROLINA 1663 June to april 1666. Each of the Eight Lords Proprietors having as per C^r side subscribed 75l. making 6ool. The Amount on D^r side is 6ool. 8s. 3d: and includes payments for this Book 4s. 3d. a monthly salary of 4l. to Mons: Laperey [engineer & Surveyor for Carolina] 1od. for parchment and wax for engrossing & sealing Sir Wm Berkley's commission [see page 15] 1os: to Sir Rich: Browne's clerk for the King's Order for abrogating Sir Robt Heath's patent [see page 8] 1o6l: 11s: 6d. for charges of the Carolina Patent 24s: for a dinner to M. Samford and Vassall[1] about a treaty with them concerning Carolina 4ol. for engraving a great seal [see page 9] 284l. 12s: 3d. for

————

[1] Robert Sanford and Henry Vassall. 1664, November 14. Lords Proprietors of Carolina to Robert Samford, commission as Secretary and chief registrar for their county of Clarendon in the Province aforesaid, the duties of which office are set forth; with such salary, fees, and perquisates as by them and their General Assembly of the said county shall be appointed. November 24. Lords Proprietors to John Vassall, appointing him Surveyor-General of their county of Clarendon by himself or deputy, the duties set forth, with such salary, fees, &c. [*Col. En. Book*, 20, page 17.] *N. C. Rec.*, I.

arms and ammuntion towards the settlement of Port Royal[1] 5s: for the docket of two patents to send Governor Drummond, 71l. 2s: 4d. M[r] Westlake's fees for the last patent. [Col: Ent: Book, No. 20, end.] *Am. & W. I., 1661, 68,* § 1192.

THE PORT ROYALL DISCOVERY.

Being the Relation of a voyage on the Coast of the Province of Carolina formerly called Florida in the Continent of the Northerne America from Charles River neere Cape Feare in the County of Clarendon and the Lat: of 34: deg: to Port Royall in the North Lat: of 32: d. begun 14th June 1666.

Performed by Robert Sandford Esq[r] Secretary and Cheife Register for the Right Hon[ble] the Lords Proprietors of their County of Clarendon in the Province aforesaid.

Fungor Officijs Anno Domni 1666.

To the Right Hono[ble] Edward Earle of Clarendon Lord High Chancellor of England, George Duke of Albemarle Cap[t] Gener[ll] of all his Ma[ties] forces in the Kingdome of England Scotland & Ireland and Mast[r] of the Horse, W[m] Lord Craven, John Lord Berkley, Anthony Lord Ashley Chancellor of the Excheq[r], S[r] George Cartrett Vice Chamberlaine of his Ma[ties] Household S[r] W[m] Berkley Kn[t] & S[r] John Colleton Kn[t] & Baron[tt] The rtue and absolute Lords Proprietors of all the Province of Carolina.

Right Hon[ble]

It is not p[re]sumption but Duty that p[r]sents this Narrative (howsoever rude and imperfect) to soe Iullustrious, I had rather say a Constellation then a Corporation the matter related was performed under yo[r] Auspice in yo[r] Country & by yo[r] servant. It measures to yo[u] my Lords (as his foot did Hercules) the greatnes of yo[r] Soveraignes Guift And to the World ye great-

---

[1] December 28. 'A particular of Ordnance, Arms, Powder &c. in order to the planting & Settling Port Royal.' The Proprietors in 1664 sent to Barbadoes the ship John and Thomas, with arms and ammunition to be sold to all who desired to undertake, on liberal offers, a settlement at Port Royal. *Rivers,* pages 80, 315.

ness of yo[r] trust and favour w[th] him. It shewes yo[u] in Prospec-
tive how lasting a Renowne yo[u] may adde to yo[r] already most
glorious Names. How boundles a Grandeur to yo[r] longest Posterity. None indeede but God and the King cann move yo[r]
hearts to doe these great things for yo[r]selves & Nation. Yett
that such a Notion be effected may and shall bee the prayers of
Right Hon[ble]

withall submission readiness & fidelity
Yo[r] Lordpp[es] Servant

ROB: SANDFORD.[1]

The Right Hono[ble] the Lords Proprietors of ye Province of
Carolina in prosecution of his sacred Ma[ties] pious Intentions of
planting and Civillizing those his do[ions] and people of the North-
erne America, w[ch] Neighbour Southward on Virginia (by
some called Florida) found out and discovered by S[r] Sebastian
Cabott in the yeare 1497 att the Charges of H: 7: King of England &c. Constituted S[r] John Yeamans Baronett their L[t]
Generall with ample Powers for placeing a Colony in some of the
Rivers to the Southward and Westward of Cape S[t] Romania.
Who departing from the Island Barbados in Octob. 1665 in a
Fly boate of about 150 Tonns, accompanyed by a smale Friggatt
of his owne and a Sloope purchased by a Comon purse for the
service of the Colonyes. After they had beene separated by a
great storme att Sea (wherein the Friggatt lost all her Masts and
himselfe had like to have foundred and were all brought together
againe in the beginning of November to an Anchor before the
Mouth of Charles River neere Cape Feare in ye County of Clarendon, part of the same province newly begunn to be peopled,
and within the L[t] Gen[lls] Commission) They were all blowne

Sir John Yea-mans made L[t] Gen[ll].

---

[1] Perhaps Lieutenant-Colonel Robert Sandford, who, 1662, petitions
the King for redress, having been banished from Surinam and returning to Barbadoes where he had employment, was imprisoned by Lord
Willoughby and sent to England. In 1664 he was there concerned in
the Cape Fear settlement, and November 14th was appointed Secretary
and Register of Clarendon, whither he went and was in the Assembly
1665, and in January, 1666, commissioned by Sir John Yeamans and
sailed on this discovery. Next year the settlement broke up and Sandford went to Virginia, whence, in 1671, he proposed to remove to Carolina.

from their Anchors by a suddaine violent Gust.   The Fly boat
S[r] John was in narrowly escapeing the dangerous shoales of the
Cape, But this proved but a short differrence of their fate, ffor
returning with a favourable winde to a second viewe of the entrance into Charles River, but (destituted of all pilates) save
their own eyes (w[ch] the flattering Gale that conducted them did
alsoe delude, by covering the rough visage of their objected
dangers with a thick veile of smooth waters) they stranded their
vessell on the Middle ground of the harbours mouth to the Westward of the Channell where the Ebbe presently left her, and the
wind with its owne multeplyed forces and the auxiliaryes of the
tide of flood beat her to peeces.

Hee is wracked in ye entrance of Charles River.

The persons were all saved by the Neighbourhood of the shore
but the greatest part of their provision of Victualls clothes &c.
and of the Magazine of Armes powder and other Military furniture shipped by the Lords Proprietors for the defence of the designed Settlement perished in the waters   The L[t] Gen[ll] purposed
att first imediately to repaire his Friggatt (w[ch] together with the
Sloope gate safely into the River when the Fly boate was driven
off) and to sende her backe to Barbados for recruits whilest himselfe in person attended the Issue of that discovery w[ch] I and
some other Gentlemen offerred to make Southwards in the
Sloope.   But when the great and growing Necessityes of the
English Colony in Charles River (heightened by this disaster)
begann clamourously to crave the use of the Sloope in a Voyage
to Virginia for their speedy relief, S[r] John altered that his first
resolution and permitting the Sloope to goe to Virginia retorned
himselfe to Barbados in his Friggatt.   Yett that the designe of
the Southerne settlement might not wholy fall Hee conditioned
with the freighters of the Sloope that in case shee miscarryed in her
Virginia Voyage they should hire Capt. Edward Stanyons Vessell (then in their harbour but bound for Barbados) to performe
the Discovery.   And left a Commission with mee for the effecting it upon the retorn of the Sloope or Stanion, w[ch] should first
happen.

He returns to Barbadoes.

A Commission is left wth Sandford to search Southerne coast.

The Sloope in her comeing homeward from Virginia loaden
with Victuall being ready by reason of her extreme rottennes in
her timbers to sinke was driven on shoare by a storme in the
night on Cape lookeout (the next head land to the North and
Eastward of Cape Feare and about 20 Le: distant) her men all

saved except two, and with many difficultyes brought by their boate through the great sound into Albemarle River neere the Island Roanoake (w[th]in this same Province of Carolina) to the English plantation there.

A Strange chance.

Cap[t] Stanyon in retorning from Barbados weakely maned and without any second to himselfe driven to and agen on the Seas for many weekes by contrary winds and conquered with Care, Vexation and watching lost his reason.   And after many wild Extravagancyes leapt over board in a frenzye leaveing his small Company and Vessell to the much more quiett and constant though but little more knowing and prudent conduct of a Child, who yett assisted by a miraculous providence after many wanderings brought her safe to Charles River in Clarendon her desired Port and Haven.

Sandford begins his voyage.

I had now a Vessell to performe my Southerne Expedition but disfurnished of a Master and none here skilled in Navigation to be persuaded to the Voyage least therefore a worke soe necessary to promote the settlement of this Province should be poorely left without an attempt My selfe undertooke the Office, though noe better capacitated for it then a little reading in the Mathematicks had rendred mee with the helpe of a fewe observations made whilst a passenger in some late Sea Voyages to divert their tedium.

On the 14th June 1666 I entered on my Charge neere six months after the date of my Commission (soe long had theise various accidents detained mee) and on the 16th I left Charles River sayling Westward with a faire gale att East alongst that goodly & bold bay w[ch] on her two Capes Feare and Romania as on two hornes procures all dangers of Flatts and shoales from her owne more gentle bosome.   To make her yett more

Berkly Bay.

signall I named her Berkly Bay from the Right Hon[ble] John Lord Berkly and S[r] W[m] Berkly two of her Noble Lords Proprietors.

I was accompanyed by Cap[t] George Cary Lt: Samuell Harvy Lt: Joseph Woory Ens: Henry Brayne Ens: Richard Abrahall & M[r] Tho: Giles[1] and severall other inhabitants of the County of

---

[1] Cary, Harvy, and Thomas Giles or Gibbes, of Barbadoes, were members of Assembly Clarendon 1665. Woory may have been of Jamaica, where Ralph Woory was Solicitor-General.

Clarendon to ye number of 17 besides my selfe and the shipps Company (wch alas were but two men and a boy) wth mee I tooke a smale shalloope of some three tonns belonging to ye Lords Proprietors and appointed by the Lt: Gen^{ll} for that service in wch I placed Ens: Henry Brayne[1] of some Experience in Sea matters and two other men soe reserveing Eighteene of all sorts in the biggest Vessell whose burden alsoe exceeded scarce fiveteene Tonns.

The 19th in the night it being very cloudy & darke and hee att our helme unawares bringing our Vessell a stayes we lost Company of our Shalloope the 22th about 7 a clock in the morning wee made the land and a fair River to Leward of us (haveing beene driven out to Sea by a Southwest winde from the 18th to the 21st when a strong Easterly gale brought us in with the shoare againe) Wee bore up to this River and a great way kept our depth of six and five fathom water w^{th}out any signe of breakers att length it shoaled, and Wee could plainely discerne a breach in the Easterne board the River when wee first made it bore N. W. by W. of us and by this time we had brought it to N. W. by N. being therefore come into two fath: water and judging our selves on the banke of the visible Easterne shoalings Wee steered more Westerly and presently deepened our Water to three fathom and soe upwards. But the wind being att East and the Water ebbing, If wee had gonne more Westerly Wee could not have luffd in Wherefore I resolved (Noe breach appeareing all before mee) to runn in directly with the River which nowe bore N: N: W: and in standing in that Course one heeve of the lead Wee had but 11 foot water, but the next was two fathom, wch depth and betweene that and two fathom and a halfe continued a great while, and as wee approached the Westerne point of the Entrance it deepened soe that close aboard ye

---

[1] 'Of some experience in Sea matters' and with 'the portugall language,' member of Assembly Clarendon 1665, and after this 'Discovery' a 'great encourager of the Carolina design;' was in 1669 given command of the Proprietors' frigate Carolina. In 1670 he had the best stock in the colony, and asks 5,000 acres 'for the moneys &c. I was out at Cape Faire & for my first discovery with Col: Sanford.' He commanded the Carolina till 1671, when Lord Ashley was 'not satisfied with Brain in any of the voyadges he hath made.' He returned to Carolina 1672, and seems to have died there. His inventory recorded C. 33, 168—?

6

point Wee found five and six fathom water and soe upwards to
nine fathom all the way in it was halfe Ebbe att least when Wee
entred, and I am very much persuaded that if Wee had gonne
soe farr Westerly as till ye River had borne North or N: N: E:
wee had found a much deeper Channell, for though it blew a
very fresh gale att East (wch here is alongst shore and somewhat
upon the Westerne Coast) yett wee could not discerne any appeareance of Flatts att all to the Westward.

Being come about foure or five miles within the River I anchored and a Canoa with two Indians came presently aboard mee
and told mee that was the Country of Edistoh and that the cheife
towne or seate of the Casique was w^{th}in on the Westerne shoare
somewhat lower downe towards the Sea by which relation I
guessed this to be the same River[1] that some English in a former
discovery mentioned by the name of Grandy (if it be not rather
the french Gironde) and only sawe of att Sea but entered not;
that it might noe longer remaine under an uncertaine distinction
I called it from the name of my Lt: Harvy Haven.   It lyes about

Harvy
Haven.

32^{d} 3^{m} & the markes to knowe it by as you come from Sea are
theise, The North East side is a bluffeland, rounding from the
River and stretching East into the Sea, hence a ledge of breakers runn out South before the Harbour's mouth, on which wee
borrowed when Wee made such shoale water in our Entrance.
The Southwest side makes a sharpe lowe flat point bare of trees,
a pretty way from the Entrance West and then shews a ham-
mocke or two of thicke shrubby trees.   From this point the
Coast tends S: W: and then W: S: W: just within the Entrance
is a shewe of a faire Creeke on the Starboard side and another
on the West or Larbord side almost oposite from the uper side
of the East side Creeke a Marsh Island runns out West and
Southerly almost cross the River.   Edged to the Seaward with
a banke of Oyster shells, discernable a good way to Sea as you
come from the Northward and particularly meett with two lowe
trees wch in ye offing and before the Oyster banke is discovered
seeme as Vesseble riding w^{th}in the River.   It flowes here East
and West neere eight foote perpendicular att spring tides the
Woods on each side entring to us seemed to consist most of live

---

[1] North Edisto, latitude 32° 30′.   The Indian town was on Edisto Island, probably near cross roads, by Eding's 'Spanish mount' place.

Oake, the land levell of an habitable height generally with steepe redd bankes here and there appeareing over the Marshes, on which in many places Wee could see the fields of Maiz greenly florishing. The next day being the 23rd June I went with my boate into a Creeke[1] on the East shoare opposite to where the vessell rode a very faire and deepe Creeke or River goeing North and Easterly to appearance a long way being gonne about a mile up I landed and according to my instructions in presence of my Company tooke a formall possession by turffe & twigg of that whole Country from the Lat. of 36 deg: North to 29 d: South and West to the South Seas by the name of the Province of Carolina For Our Soveraigne Lord Charles the Second King of England & his heirs and Successors and to the use of the Right Hon[ble] Edward Earle of Clarendon: Geor: Duke of Albermarle, William Lord Craven, John Lord Berkley, Anthony Lord Ashley, Sr George Cartrett Sr Wm Berkley and Sr John Colleton their heires and assigns according to the Letters Pattents of Our Soveraigne Lord the King. I ranged a little on either side this Creeke passed through severall feilds of Maiz or Indian Corn And following the guidance of a small path was brought to some of the Indians Habitations I found all the land that I passed over whether I went back or alongst the side of the Creeke a rich fatt soyle black mould on the topp and under mixt with a soft redd marle (w[ch] and a stiffe Clay) I after found the most generall foundation of all the land. Noe Swamps, noe Sandy land. On the Outside of the woods some single scattring Pine trees but of the sort which is called spruce. The rest and the Generallity of the timber being Oake, Maple, Ash, Wallnutt, Popler Bayes & the trees tall and straight but not very large growing closer tagether than I have seene in any other part of this Province (the reason I guesse of their being so slender) they are for the most part a well seized building timber and some fewe Wee sawe of Oake and maple that would beare three or foure foot over a very great burthen upon the ground And much of it of such growth as wee knowe to be an excellent feeding for Cattle and so thick and high that it made our travelling very tedious.

The next day I went some miles up the maine River and find-

---

[1] Bohicket Creek. Landed about Rockville, near Bohicket Indian village.

ing a Creeke[1] alsoe on the East side wch opened some groves of Pine trees to our Viewe I putt in there purposely to see that sort of Land and found this if any the Swamps of this Country for this Creeke carryed us into Low broken Marshes and Islands of these pine trees lying almost levell with the water. Wee landed on some of them found them firme and dry (though severall dayes and but the very night before wee had store of raine) and w^{th}out any signes of haveing ever beene overflowed. Yett they are seemingly soe seated as that greate store of raine and frequent must necessarily stand in them, the pines are all spruce the soyle a fatt blacke mould with a scarce discernable mixture of Sand founded alsoe either on marle or Clay as the other lands and bearing a very great burthen and though on the outside Wee sawe only pine trees yett being entered the Wood wee found alsoe Oake and severall other timber trees of a very large seize. Att a venture wee called these kind of lands pine swampe. But I esteeme them a very proffitable tillable ground and some of my Company did after this see an Indian planted feild of this sort which they told me bore as tall Maiz as any. We rowed along way up the Creeke and besides these swamps sawe and ranged through very spacious tracts of rich Oake land and yett Wee were not part the Oyster bankes and frequent heepes of shells nor the salt water. Att my returne downe the River I sent some ashoare to range on the West side who did instantly affirme that the lands there were of an equall excellency with the best of those Wee had other where veiwed and that they believed itt an impossible injunction to be putt to march to the end of the tracts, being therefore well satisfyed with the successe of our discovery hitherto I wayed and stood downe the River intending a short stay att the landing place neerest to the cheife Seate of Edistowe which the Indian had intreated of mee that they might wth the lesser trouble come aboard mee to trade. When Wee were here a Capt of the Nation named Shadoo (one of them wch Hilton had carryed to Barbados) was very earnest with some of our Company to goe with him and lye a night att their Towne wch hee told us was but a smale distance thence I being equally desirous to knowe the forme manner and populousnesse of the place as alsoe what state the Casique held (fame in all theire things

---

[1] Leadenwah Creek.

preferring this place to all the rest of the Coast, and foure of my Company (vizt.) Lt: Harvey, Lt: Woory, Mr Thomas Giles and m^r Henry Woodward forwardly offring themselves to the service haveing alsoe some Indians aboard mee who constantly resided there night & day I permitted them to goe with this Shadoo they retorned to mee the next morning wth great Comendacons of their Entertainment but especially of the goodness of the land they marcht through and the delightfull situation of the Towne. Telling mee withall that the Cassique himselfe appeared not (pretending some indisposition, but that his state was supplyed by a Female[1] who received them with gladnes and Courtesy placeing my Lt: Harvey on the seat by her their relation gave myselfe a Curiosity (they alsoe assureing mee that it was not above foure Miles off) to goe and see that Towne and takeing with mee Capt George Cary and a file of men I marched thither ward followed by a long traine of Indians of whome some or other always presented himselfe to carry mee on his shoulders over any the branches of Creekes or plashy corners of Marshes in our Way. This walke though it tend to the Southward of the West and consequently leads neere alongst the Sea Coast Yett it opened to our Veiwe soe excellent a Country both for Wood land and Meadowes as gave singular satisfaction to all my Company. Wee crossed one Meadowe of not lesse then a thousand Acres all firme good land and as rich a Soyle as any clothed wth a ffine grasse not passing knee deepe but very thick sett & fully adorned with yeallow flowers. A pasture not inferiour to any I have seene in England the wood land were all of the same sort both for timber and mould with the best of those wee had ranged otherwhere and wthout alteration or abatement from their goodnes all the way of our March. Being entered the Towne wee were conducted into a large house of a Circular forme (their generall house of State) right against the entrance way a high seate of sufficient breadth for half a dozen persons on which sate the Cassique himselfe (vouchsafeing mee that favour) wth his wife on his right hand

---

[1] In 1682 and subsequently lands were ceded by the Cassiques of Wimbee, Stono, Combahee, Kussah, Edisto, Ashepoo, Witchaw, and by the Queen and Captains of St. Helena. *Rivers*, 124.

(shee who had received those whome I had sent the evening before) hee was an old man of a large stature and bone. Round the house from each side the throne quite to the Entrance were lower benches filled with the whole rabble of men Women and children in the center of this house is kept a constant fire mounted on a great heape of Ashes and surrounded with little lowe foormes Capt: Cary and my selfe were placed on the higher seate on each side the Cassique and presented with skinns accompanied with their Ceremonyes of Welcome and freind-shipp (by stroaking our shoulders with their palmes and sucking in theire breath the whilst) The Towne is scituate on the side or rather in the skirts of a faire forrest in wch at severall distances are diverse feilds of Maiz with many little houses straglingly amongst them for the habitations of the particular families. On the East side and part of the South It hath a large prospect over meadowes very spatious and delightfull, before the Doore of their Statehouse is a spacious walke rowed wth trees on both sides tall & full branched, not much unlike to Elms wch serves for the Exercise and recreation of the men who by Couples runn after a marble bowle troled out alternately by themselves with six foote staves in their hands wch they tosse after the bowle in their race and according to the laying of their staves wine or loose the beeds they contend for an Exercise approveable enough in the winter but some what too violent (mee thought) for that season and noone time of the day from this walke is another lesse aside from the round house for the children to sport in. After a fewe houres stay I retorned to my Vessell wth a greate troope of Indians att my heeles. The old Cassique himselfe in the number, who lay aboard mee that night without the society of any of his people, some scores of wch lay in boothes of their own imediate ereccon on the beach.

While I lay here I had perfectly understood that the River went through to another more Westerly and was passable for our Vessell and alsoe that it was not much more then a tides worke through this increased my desire of passing this way Especially being persuaded that this next River was Jordan (Hilton intima-teing as much in his Journall and mapp) Wherefore on the 27th of June with the helpe of the tide of flood (the winde being contrary) I turned upp the River so haveing oportunity to try

the whole Channell wch I found generally five[1] and between that
and six fathume deepe and bold home to each shoare till wee
were come about 10 miles from the harbours mouth when the
River was contracted between the Marshes. Yett here (Except
in one or two places where some flatts narrowed the passage)
Wee seldome found less then five fathum water. The River
being narrowe and variously winding noe Gale would att any
time serve us long soe that Wee were forced for the most
part to towe through and that often against the wind which
proved very tedious nor could wee passe but by day, wch with
lying two tides a ground to stopp some Leakes made it Sunday
morning the first of July before Wee came into the next Westerly River, and by it into the Sea againe though by the Travers
I took of our Course I found it performable with light boates in
one tide of flood and an Ebbe. The passage is generally betweene drowned marshes a greate breadth betweene the River
and wood Especially on the Island side, on the East or maine
side of the Marsh is much narrower, and in many places the
River runns close under the banke of wood land wch wee had the
oportunity to veiw and found it to continue its excellency without
change or diminution, The Indians alsoe that inhabitt the inner
parts of it assureing us that it was all alike, The next Westerly
River is a pretty faire river not less broad then Harvey Haven.
But its Channell more crooked narrowe & shallowe. The West
side of itt (as wee found afterwards) is but a necke of land haveing a Creeke or two wch seeme to goe through into the west River
It is for ye Generallity drowned Marshes alsoe yett in same places
the banke is high Crowned here and there with smale ground of
wood, consisting of dry plantable Land, surrounded a good space
with a firme Meadowe or pasture Land and presenting most de-
lectable Seates for summer recesses, I did a little wounder to see
the Sea and noe apparent open passage first to the Westward as
I expected (still imaginning this to be the River Jordan) and
when I was come out of it into the Sea and sawe none of these
marks wch Hilton had prefixed to Jordan I was in a great puzzle
to know where wee were gott. Nothing of the Coast makeing like those drafts which Hilton had given of it. But

[1] Or nine, MS. illegible. They went through Dawho River to S.
Edisto and through S. Edisto Inlet to the sea. Hilton was in St. Helena
and Combahee.

the winde first dying into a calme and then againe blowing contrary wth some Menaces of an Evening storme I putt
into the River againe and being anchored went a shoare on the
East point of the Entrance where I found Shadoo (The Capt: of
Edistow that had beene with Hilton att Barbados) And severall
other Indians come from the Towne by Land to see for our
comeing forth) of whome I asked whether this was the River w^ch
Hilton was in, they told me noe but itt was the next River.   This
assured mee that Jordan was yett further and that Hilton had
noe knowledge of this River and soe could not lay it downe I
demanded the name of this River   They told mee Edistowe still
& pointed all to be Edistowe quite home to the side of Jordan,
by which I was instructed that the Indians assigne not their
names to the Rivers but to the Countryes and people.   Amongst
theise Indians was one who used to come with the Southern Indians to trade with us att Charles Towne in Clarendon and is
knowne by the name of Cassique,[1] hee belongeth to the Country
of Kiwaha and was very earnest with mee to goe wth my Vessell
thither assuring mee a broad deepe entrance and promising a
large welcome and plentiful entertainm^t: and trade, I told him
I must first goe to Port Royall and that in my retorne I would
see his Country, but for his better security hee would needs
accompany mee to Port Royall and soe bee my pilate (as hee
made mee understand) for their River.   And presently hee sent
away his Companion to give notice to the cheife Cassique of the
place of my intention that hee might prepare for my comeing
and himselfe went on board with mee.   That Evening blewe a
storme of winde att S. W. (the frequent Somer stormes on this
Coast) soe violent that (though in the River) I durst not trust to
my ordinary roade, but kept my sheet anchor under foot.

    With the riseing of the morne I weighed and stood out to Sea
haveing an easie gale att N. E: and a Tide of Ebbe, my Course
out lay S. E: between two bankes of shoales lesse then halfe a
mile distant I choase rather to keepe in the Sounding of the
Easterne than of the W: Flatts, both because the winde was
Easterly and soe I could beare up from them when I would and
alsoe because haveing both in goeing out and comeing in the

---

[1] The first appearance of the 'Cassique of Kiawah' in history.   His
persuasions were yet to fix the first colony at Ashley River.

day before borrowed on the Westerne shoalings, I should by
this Easterly Course take knowledge of the whole Channell, I
was scarce shott a mile without the Eastermost point of the Entrance but the winde wholy left me, and the Ebbe (wch the flatts
on either side makeing soe faire a land, I expected should sett
directly out to Sea) did runn with soe strong a Current over the
Easterne Sands that att the second heave of my lead I was cast
from two fathum into six foot water and I drewe five into a rowl-
ing sea on the very edge of a breach I had no way but imediately to lett fall one anchor, soe to stay the Vessell from precip-
itating on her ruine whilst I might carry forth another anchor to
warpe her into deepe water. The first was presently downe,
but to gett out the second wch way to confirme our safety proved
hughesly difficult. Wee lay in soe tumbling a Sea that our
boate could not bee brought to our bowe without danger of
staveing, I had but two men with mee entred to Sea labour, and
the most spirrited and active part of my Company were Gentlemen but little used to any labour. One of the Seamen must
necessarily stay within board to deliver the Anchor and Cable
that was to be carryed out, however the danger made every one
give his best helpe and with much adoe the boate is brought to
the bowe and the Anchor putt into her, but all our strength
could not stemme that tide of Ebbe wch had hurried us into the
perill and must therefore be encountred in the way to bring us
out but a starne wee fall against the whole force of our Oares.
A second attempt is made with doubled strength but one breakes
his thoales another his Oare and nowe cumbred with our owne
uslesse number in a boate of scarce equall seize Wee became
rather weaker then att first yett wee have no other way left but
this to prevent our wreake (heaven not yeilding us one breath
of aide) therefore to worke wee goe againe and refix our boate,
but in theise past fruitless parformances soe much time had beene
spent as had given the Ebbing tide a further advantage against
us to the almost perfecting our destruction, for by this time the
Vessell by her repeated stroakes as it were to rescue herselfe from
those inhospitable sands, gave us warning that her condition was
well neere desperate, yett out goes our boate againe and god
mercifully improved our strength to the getting forth an Anchor,
though not much farther then our Vessell's length) yett soe farre
as brought us into two fathom water the banke on wch Wee had

grounded proveing steepe to, by reason of wch Wee the more easily wrought ourselves out of those unkinde embraces and to the praise of the Almighty Deliverer were snatcht from either an instant descending into the open Gorge of the unsated Ocean, or the more slowe and painfull progresse to our ends in a naked Exposure amongst Nations whose piety it is to be barbarous & Gallantry to be inhumane.   This ill entertainment made us brand the place with the name of Port Perill, It lyes in the Lat. of 32^d: 25^m: or thereabouts.   And may be knowne when you are in the very Entrance by its Easterne point wch is a lowe point of Sand bare of trees or other growth save a fewe stragling shrubs, hence the River goe in N. N. W. and N. W. by N. a smale Creeke running in East just within the point.   The Coast hence to the Eastward tends neerest E. by N. wth Sandy bayes and appeares even and bluffe wth trees when you are in the Off-ing the Westerne part of the Entrance lyes within as in a deepe bay and beare from the East point N. N. by W. or W. N. W. about two miles.   It is a bare sandy bay with a fewe shrubs next the River & thinne scatring Pine trees.   more Southerly the Coast thence Westward tends S. S. W. and all betweene this and Jordan shewes with severall hummacks like broken land or Islands when yo^u are off before itt and especially next to Port Perill appears a wide opening as of a River but it is nothing but bare sandy bayes or oyster bankes with lowe Marshes behinde

Yeamans Harbour.   them Jordan or as we now call it Yeamans harbour[1] from the name of our Lt: Generall opens about two Leagues to the West-ward of this between two bluffe lands from the Westermost of wch the North East end of an Island (wch from Capt Cary wee named Cary Island) runns out E. S. E. and makes all the Coast between it and port Perill lye in the forme of a deepe bay.   All between Yeamans Harbour and Port Perill are shoales and foule ground wch from the West point of Port Perill runne out S. E. before the mouth of Yeamans Harbour to almost an even range wth the outermost face of Cary Island, From the East point of Port Perill a Rowe of breakers range themselves parrallell wth the Westerne shoales and were the same wch had like to have proved soe fatall to us at our comeing out thence Neere a League

---

[1] Wassaw Sound (Morgan River).   The 'wide opening' is St. Helena Sound.   Cary Island is the Hunting Islands.

within Port Perill are three distinct groves of trees elevated on pretty high bankes with lowe Marshes in each intervall they lye neere E: and West and when you are so farre South and Westerly as that the lowe sandy point off the Entrance wholy disappeares Theise shewe themselves as though the mouth of the River were betweene two bluffe lands wth a round woody Island in the middle of itt, In steering in if you come from the South and Westward, keepe East in three fathum water till you bring this seeming Island to touch the Easterne bluffe head and then stand in N. W. by N. and N: W. wth the head Land rather takeing the Soundings of the Easterne flatt then of the W: if the wind will permitt and yo^u will have two fathum water little more or lesse all the way in att lowe water, As you come neere in you will discerne the Easterne lowe sandy point between you and that bluffe land and the sandy bayes along the Easterne Coast steering in wth that Sandy point and yo^u will deepen and have five fathum Water close aboard it.

After we were gott cleare of the Sands The Ebbe being donne and the Gale springing up Wee made Sayle and stood out to Sea but wee were not gott farre ere the winde shifted to South East, and the flood sett soe strong into the narrowe baye that wee could neither board it out nor gaine to the Westward, of the Shoales wch lye before Yeamans Harbour soe to runne in there, wherefore I came to an Anchor in three fathum water till the Ebbe att least might helpe us to worke out against the winde whilst wee rode here Wee espyed to our great rejoyceng the Shalloope whome wee left the 19th of June in the night, Shee was come forth of Yeamans Harbour and stood to and againe before the Southwest Coast betweene it and Cary Island to shewe herselfe not being able to come out to us for the same reason that kept us imbayed, We alsoe fired a gunn and putt out our Colours to lett her Knowe that wee sawe her but could not gett to her for the flatts that interposed.

To goe into Yeamans harbour Hilton's direction is (and itt The goeing into Yeam seemed true to mee as I lay before itt though I went not in) to Harbour. goe in on the West side of the shoalings wch are opposite to the mouth thereof and wch are contiguous wth the flatts of Port Perill giveing a ledge of breakers that lye before the South W^t: Cape of the Entrance to smale birth and soe to steere with the North East land of the Entrance, and the least depth hee sayes is two fathum att lowe water and soe upwards to six or seaven fathum when yo[u] come neere under the said Easterne Land. But I have understood since from Ens: Brayne that between that ledge of breakers w[ch] lye before ye South West Cape and the end of Cary Island is a Channell w[ch] hee affirmes has about three fathum water where shoalest w[ch] also when you are past that ledge of breakers sett over to the North East land of the Harbours mouth. The Ebbe now beginning to make wee weighed and plyed off to Sea with some difficulty boarding it out of the dangerous and foule bay wherein till about three leagues from shoare the deepest water wee could finde was scarce three fathum & in our turning Wee generally into a fathum & a halfe on each side and this though it was high water a place to be attempted with Care when the winde is off as nowe it is, by night wee were gott cleere of all danger into six and seaven fathum water I stood off and on all night & in the morning found

Cary Island. my selfe off the Sea board side of Cary Island in the middle be- tweene two openings this Island fills up almost the whole space betweene Yeamans harbour & Port Royall to seaward it makes an even smooth land pretty bluffe with trees & tends South West and North East about three leagues in length, It shewes two smale openings neere equi-distant from either end and from Each other, From the Westermost opening all Westward the Coast is bold five fathum water within halfe a league of the shoare more Easterly It is not soe deepe.

The morning was Calme and soe continued till about two a Clocke afternoone when a fresh gale sprang up att North East

Woory Bay. w[ch] in a short time opened to us Woory Bay[1] and the mouth of Port Royall. Woory Bay of Lt: Woory is made by the South Westerly end of Cary Island and the Southermost Cape or headland w[th]out Port Royall Called from the first discoverer Hil- ton head w[ch] is the farthest land in sight as you come from the Northeast along by the end of Cary Island whence it beares neerest S. W. and is bluffe w[th] trees large and tall w[ch] as you ap-

Port Royall. proach them seeme to looke their topps in the sea. Port Royall mouth seems opens in the bottome of this bay neerest to the Westerne side thereof the opening is wide little lesse then two leagues the Westermost land of it running out almost South to

---

[1] Port Royal entrance, between Chaplin's Island and Hilton Head.

Hilton head and laying in like a halfe bent bowe makeing the west side of Woory bay ffrom the East side of Port Royall the land tends away East Northerly into Giles streights[1] (the passage on the backside of Cary Island named soe from Mr Thomas Giles) and formes the bottum of Woory Bay. Before this part of the Coast and the end of Cary Island in all the Easterly part of the bay Its shoales and very uneven ground unsafe to meddle with towards the Easternmost angle of it oposite to the entrance into Giles streights lyes a Sand Hill pretty high with some smaller about it visible a good distance off in comeing from the Westward as yo^u part from Cary Island steere away S. W. with Hilton Head and yo^u will come thwart the Channell of Port Royall which yo^u will finde by the deepeing of yor water from five to seaven fathum and upward. It lyes neerer towards the West land and runns in N. N. W. towards the Easterne land of the Entrance (by us called Abrahall point) haveing seldome soe little as seaven fathum water all the way in the shoales in the East part of the bay lye poynting out a good way to Sea therefore it wilbe safe for shipps of burthen to keepe out till they have brought Hilton Head to beare about N. N. E. from them. When I had opened Woory bay sayling S. W. along by the end of Cary Island I had brought the Sand Hills within a Steerne of mee I luffed into the bay to try the Soundings of that Eastermost part of itt & after a little while came on the shoalings and found them soe uneven that it was ordinary to differ two fathum in the heave of a lead. Being therefore satisfyed wth ye dangerousnes of this part of the bay I bore up againe & stood away wth Hilton Head crosse some of the shoales till I came to seaven eight & to above ten fathum water Then I steered away with the body of the West land betweene Hilton head and the Entrance of Port Royall and shoaled my water by degrees to six fathum (wch depth continued a good while & att length to five and foure fathum & to three within lesse then a mile of the wood side Then I brought my tacks aboard and stood North Easterly to gett into the Channell againe and after some time deepened my water to five six & seaven fathum I then steered away wth the East land of the River within Abrahall point still deepning my water till att length the Ebbe being strong and wee makeing fresh way

Giles streights.

from Ens: Abrahall.

---

[1] Trenchard's Inlet. Abrahall Point is Bay Point.

against it wth a large winde I could not for a good space strike
ground with my leads.   About midnight the third of July I came
to an Anchor wthin the River[1] in seaven fathum water, the least
depth I could then finde) a little above the Entrance into Brayne
sound or the passage wch goes through to Yeamans Harbour soe
called from Ens: Brayne who twice sailed itt.   I would advise all
who enter Port Royall to goe in upon the Soundings on the west
side of the Channell till they come a good way within Hilton
head that side being the evenest ground and freest from all danger, They may keepe in six and seven fathum all the way in and
then as they steere more easterly towards Abrahall point they will
finde itt much deeper.   It flowes here E. S. E.   The next morning I removed opposite to the principall Indian Towne and there
anchored before itt, where I had not ridd long ere the Cassique
himselfe came aboard mee wth a Canoa full of Indians presenting
mee with skinns and bidding mee welcome after their manner, I
went a shoare with him to see their Towne wch stood in sight of
our Vessell, Found as to the forme of building in every respect
like that of Eddistowe with a plaine place before the great round
house for their bowling recreation att th'end of wch stood a faire
woodden Crosse of the Spaniards ereccon.   But I could not observe that the Indians performed any adoracon before itt, All round
the Towne for a great space are severall feilds of Maiz of a very
large growth The soyle nothing inferiour to the best wee had
seene att Eddistowe apparently more loose and light and the
trees in the woods much larger and rangd att a greater distance
all the ground under them burthened exceedingly and amongst
it a great variety of choice pasturage I sawe here besides the
great number of peaches wch the more Northerly places doe alsoe
abound in some store of figge trees very large and faire both
fruite and plants and diverse grape vines wch though growing
without Culture in the very throng of weedes and bushes were
yett filled with bunches of grapes to admiracon.   It was noe
smale rejoyceing to my Company (who began to feare that after
Edistowe they should see nothing equally to content them) to
finde here not only a River so much superiour to all others on the
Coast Northward, but alsoe a Country wch their fancyes though

---

[1] In Broad River above the entrance of Port Royal River (Brayne
Sound). The Indian town was on Paris Island.

preengaged could scarce forbeare to preferre even that w[ch] but a little before they had concluded peerelesse. The Towne is scited on an Island made by a branch[1] w[ch] cometh out of Brayne Sound and falleth into Port Royall about a mile above where wee landed a scituacon not extraordinary here rather the whole Country is nothing else but severall Islands made by the various intervenings of rivers and Creekes, yett are they firme good Lands (Excepting what is Marsh) nor of soe smale a seize but to continue many of them thowsands of acres of rich habitable wood land whose very bankes are washed by River or Creeke, w[ch] besides the fertillity adde such a Comodiousnesse for portage as fewe Countryes are equally happy in.

After a fewe houres stay to veiwe the land about the Towne I retorned to my Vessell and there found Ens: Brayne wth his Shalloope come that morning through Brayne Sound from Yeamans Harbour att the mouth of w[ch] wee had seene him two days before, Hee told mee that the same morning that I made Harvey Haven, hee came in with the shoare more to the Estw[d]:[2] and sayled along it till towards Evening when hee entred Yeamans Harbour supposing it Port Royall, and not findeing mee there nor any knowledge of mee, and guessing that I might be more Southerly hee came through to Port Royall and acquainted himselfe with Wommony the Cassiques sonne (who had alsoe beene att Barbados) whome hee easily prevailed wth to beare him Company from place to place into severall Creekes and branches betweene this and Yeamans harbour, soe becomeing both his Guide and proteccon that hee had by this meanes a large leasure and oportunity of veiwing all that part of the Country w[ch] hee did soe loudly applaud for land and rivers that my Companies Comendacons of Eddistowe could scarce out noise him,—Sufficiently satisfyed wth this relation (confirmed by those wth him) I resolved to loose noe time in a second search of that parte but to goe a tides worke up the maine River & see the body of the Country, and att my retorne to enter a faire Creeke on the West shoare opposite to where the Vessell rode, and soe to veiwe that side

---

[1] Pilot's Creek, called by Ribault 'Chenonceau.' They landed on the western side of Paris Island, opposite Scull Creek.

[2] About Stono? Wommony had gone with Hilton.

wch Ens: Brayne had not medled with being the more desirous
alsoe to trye this Creeke because the Indians reported that it
lead to a great Southerne River[1] wch peirceth farre into the Continent and I suppose may be the frenchmens River May or the
Spaniards St Matthias, With the Flood therefore and a favourable fresh Gale of winde I sayled up the River in the Shalloope
neere thirty miles, passed where it divides it selfe into two principall branches the Westermost of wch I went upp and conceive-
ing myselfe nowe high enough I landed here[2] I found the Ground
presently wthin to rise into a pretty hill, and as I ranged further
I crossed severall fine falls and riseings of land and one brooke
of sweete water wch rann wth a mourmoring course betweene two
hills a rarity towards the Sea Coast (to wch our former searches
had bene confind in wch wee had not seene any fresh water but in
wells wch inconveniency was not to be borne with were it not to
be healved by the easie sinking of wells every where.   The land
here was such as made us all conclude not only a possibility that
Eddistowe might bee, but a certainty that it was exceeded by
the Country of Port Royall—Being fully tired wth our March
through a ranke growth of vines, bushes and grass wch every
where fettered our leggs and preclaimed the richnes of the soyle I
retired to my boate and with the Ebbe towards our Vessell Wee
passed diverse faire Creekes on each side the River but entred none
haveing not much time to spare and being satisfyed by the sorts
of wood wee sawe and the bankes That the land was all of like
goodness to what wee had already veiwed only (in one place the
land seemeing lower then usuall and wth a great mixture of pine
or rather spruce) I went in there And after I was somewhat wthin
the woods found it very plashy and water standing everywhere
in holes about ankell deepe or deeper caused as I thinke by the
late raine wch had fallen somewhat plentifully for there appeared
noe signe of constant swampishnes (as in the Cipresse swamps
more Northerly) nor anything that might discourage the manure-
ing it.   The morning was pretty faire spent ere I came downe to

---

[1] Savannah or May River, called by the coast Indians Westoboo.

[2] Probably above Whale Branch, opposite Barnwell's Island. Possibly Coosawhatchie, at Graham's Neck.   Returning landed on Port
Royal Island?

the Vessell againe wherefore I made haste and changed my Com- Sandford
pany and then crossed the River into that Westerne Creeke[1] I Sound.
spoke of wch after three or four miles opened into a great sound
full of Islands of different sizes Southwards.   It went into the
Sea by two or three out letts in our sight westward Wee still
opened newe branches some bigger some lesse, like those wee
had already passed and found to crumble the Continent into Islands, I spent the remainder of this day and the best part of the
next in this sound went a shoare on Severall Islands found them
as good firme land as any wee had seene, exceedingly timbred
principally wth live Oake and large Cedar and bay trees then any
I had seene before on all the Coast   In one of them we entred a
pleasant Grove of spruce, shadeing a very cleare pasture of fine
grasse in wch wee rouzed a brave heard of Deere and thence
called it the Discoverer's Parke.   This Island continnes some
hundred of acres and both wood and Marsh, proper for planting
grazeing and for feeding swine and all the Islands of this Sound
that were in our veiwe (some fewe smale Ones Excepted that
were onely Marsh) are in all appeareance alike good, proportionable to their biggnes wth high bankes richly crowned with
timber of the largest size, Soe that of what wee sawe in this
Sound onely might bee found habitations for thowsands of people
wth convenienencyes for their stock, of all kindes in such a way
of accommodacon as is not comon, And if the Sound goe
through to such a great River as the Indians talke off (wch seems
very probable) It will putt an addconall value upon the Settlem^{te}
that shalbe made in it, It abounds besides with Oyster bankes
and such heapes of shells as wch noe time cann consume, but this
benefitt it hath but in comon wth all the Rivers betweene this and
Harvey Haven wch are stored wth this necessary materiall for lime
for many ages, & lying soe conveniently that whatever neere
river or Creeke yo^{u} cann thinke fitt to sett a house there yo^{u}
may place yor lime kill alsoe and possibly in the banke just by
or very neere finde clay for yor bricke tile & the great and frequent sculls of fish wee mett with gives us expectacon of advantage & employm^{t}: that way alsoe In sume wee could see of
nothing here to bee wished for but good store of English Inhabitants and that wee all heartily prayed for, I gave my name the

---

[1] Scull Creek, Calibogue Sound 'Park' is Bull's Island?

7

Honour of calling this Sound by it, and doe believe that if this place bee setled by us, It may hence receive alonger duracon then from any accesse wth in the reach of a rationall hope.

Within night I retorned to the Vessell and the next day being the 7th of July I tooke in some fresh water purposing that night to leave Port Royall and retorne homeward, haveing in the discovery already made, exceeded all our owne & therefor confident to answere all other Expectacons, besides each mans proper occasions hastened him and the Consideration of the Charge of the Vessell hired att five and twenty pounds sterling per month made us earnest not to detaine her a minute of time unnecessarily Wee alsoe designed ourselves some daies to see the Country of Kywaha one of whose Inhabitants remained still with us for that onely purpose, But a little before night the Cassique of Port Royall came aboard and brought with him a propper yo^{u}ng fellowe whome hee made mee understand to bee his Sister's sonne, Hee demanded ofmee when I would retorne thither, & shewing mee the moone asked whether within three times of her compleating her orbe, I told him noe, but in tenn monthes I would, hee seemed troubled att the length of time and as it were begged mee to come in five, But I continued my first given number, att length hee gave mee this young fellowe told mee hee should goe and retorne with mee and that I must clothe him & then hee asked mee when I would sayle I told him presently that night but hee very much importuned mee to stay until the next day that hee might prepare mee some venison and made signes as hee parted that if in the morning hee should not see mee hee should Crye and soe hee left mee and the Indian with mee I was somewhat pleased wth the adventure, haveing before I came on the Discovery wished that if I liked the Country I might prevaile with the Indians to lett one of their Nacon goe with mee, I leaveing an Englishman in their roome for the mutuall learning their language, And to that purpose one of my Company m^{r} Henry Woodward[1] a Chirurgeon had before I sett out assured mee his resolucon to stay with the Indians if I should thinke convenient wherefore I resolved to stay till the morning to see if the Indians would re-

---

[1] He thus became the first Carolina settler (see post). He was perhaps of the family of Thomas Woodward.

maine constant in this Intencon according to wch I purposed to treate further with them on the morrowe therefore I went a shoare to their Towne tooke Woodward and the Indian with me and in presence of all the Inhabitants of the place and of the fellows relacons asked if they approved of his goeing along with mee, they all with one voyce consented after some pause I called the Cassique & another old man (His second in Authority) and their wives And in sight and heareing of the whole Towne, delivered Woodward into their charge, telling them that when I retorned I would require him att their hands, They received him with such high Testimonyes of Joy and thankfullnes as hughely confirmed to mee their great desire of our friendshipp & society, The Cassique placed Woodward by him uppon the Throne and after lead him forth and shewed him a large feild of Maiz wch hee told him should bee his, then hee brought him the Sister of the Indian that I had with mee telling him that shee should tend him & dresse his victualls and be careful of him that soe her Brother might be the better used amongst us—I stayed a while being wounderous civilly treated after their manner and giveing Woodward formall possession of the whole Country to hold as Tennant att Will of the right Hono^{ble} the Lords Proprietors, I retorned aboard & imediately weighed and fell downe.

An Indian that came wth mee from Eddistowe wth Intencon to goe noe further then Port Royall seing this kindnes & mutuall obligation betweene us & the people of this place that his Nacon or tribe might bee wthin the League voluntarily offerred himselfe to stay with mee alsoe and would not bee denyed, And thinking that soe hee should be the more acceptable hee caused himselfe to be shoaren on the Crowne after ye manner of the Port Royall Indians, a fashion wch I guesse they have taken from the Spanish Fryers, Thereby to ingratiate themselves wth that Nation and indeed all along I observed a kinde of Emulacon amongst the three principall Indians of this Country (vizt) Those of Keywaha Eddistowe and Port Royall concerning us and our Freindshipp, Each contending to assure it to themselves and jealous of the other though all be allyed and this Notwthstanding that they knewe wee were in actuall warre with the Natives att Clarendon and had killed and sent away many of them, ffor they frequently discoursed with us concerning the warre, told us that the Natives were noughts they land Sandy and barren, their Country sickly, but if wee would come amongst them Wee should finde the Contrary to all their Evills, and never any occasion of discharge-ing our Gunns but in merryment and for pastime.

Kywaha.   The 10th of July in the morning I was fayre before ye River that leadeth into the country of Kywaha, but the Indian of the place, who undertooke to bee my Guide, and stayed all this while with mee for that onely purpose would not knowe it to be the same, but confidently and constantly affirmed to mee that it was more Easterly, and att length when I was almost neere enough to goe in with greate assurance and Joy, hee shewed mee a head land not farre off which he affirmed the Entrance to bee. This confidence of his made mee stand away, but by that time I had sayled some two Leagues hee sawe his Error when it was too late, for nowe the winde was soe that I could not fetch the River againe and if it had beene fayre I was sure not to enter it before night, And I did not like the complexcon of the Heavens soe well as to trye that night upon the Coast.

River Ashley.   The River[1] lyes in a bay betweene Harvey Haven and Cape St. Romana wherein wee found 7 or 8 fathum water very neere the shoare, and not the least appeareance of shoales or dangers in any part of itt, It shewes wth a very faire large opening cleare of any fflatts or barreing in ye Entrance onely before the East-erne point, wee sawe a breach but not farre out, I persuade myselfe that it leads into an Excellent Country, both from the Comendacon the Indian give itt, and from what I sawe in my ranging on the Easterne part of Harvy Haven the next Neigh-bouring land to this wherefore in hopes that it may prove worthy the Dignity I called it the River Ashley, from the right Hon[ble] Anthony Lord Ashley, And to take away every little remaine of forraigne title to this Province I blotted out the name of S[t] Ro-

Cape Cartrett.   mane putt before the next Easterly Cape and writt Cape Cartrett in the roome to evidence the more reall right of S[r] George Cart-rett as hee is a Lord Proprietor of Carolina.

The 12th of July about noone I entred Charles River and be-fore darke night landed att Charles Towne in the County of Cla-rendon to the great rejoicing of our ffreinds Who yett received not our p'sons more gratefully then they did the Sound Comen-dacons which they heard from every one of us without one dis-

_____

[1] Charleston harbour.   The Cassique was taken to Cape Fear.

sonant note of that never enough to be valued Country wch wee had seene and searcht in which may be found ample Seats for many thowsands of our Nation in a Sociable and comfortable Vicinity secured from any possible generall & from all probable particle Massacres with such other accommodacons to boote as scarce any place cann parralell in a clime pfectly temperate to make the habitacon pleasant and where such a fertile Soyle cannot faile to yeild soe great a variety of Produccons as will not onely give an absolute selfe subsistance to the place without all manner of necessary forraigne dependance, but alsoe reach a trade to the Kingdome of England as great as that shee has with all her Neighbours, and render Our Soveraigne Lord the King within his owne Dominions and the Land possessed by his Naturall English subjects universall Monarch of the Traffique and Comodity of the whole World.

ROBT: SANDFORD.

For a further Confirmacon hereof take this Testimoniall given of this Country by the Principall Gentlemen with mee in this Discovery who have attested under their hands as much as I have sayd and yett noe more then what thowsands had they beene there would alsoe have affirmed—

Clarendon in Carolina—

Wee whose names are hereunto subscribed haveing accompanied Lt: Colo^{ll} Robert Sandford in a Voyage of Discovery on the Coast & Rivers of this Province to the Southward and Westward of Cape St: Romane as farre as the River Port Royall, And being all of us persons well experienced in the nature and quallity of the severall Soyles in theise Regions, and some of us by means of our Travells throughly acquainted with most part of America Northerne and Southerne Continent and Islands Doe hereby declare and Testefie to the whole world That the Country wch wee did search and see from the River Grandy nowe Harvey Haven to Port Royall inclusive, doth for richnes and fertillity of soyle for Excellency of Rivers, havens, Creekes, and sounds for aboundance of good Timber of diverse sorts and many other requisites both to land and Sea, building and for sundry rare accomodacons both for Navigation and Plantacon Exceed all places that Wee Knowe in possescon of our Nacon in the West Indies, And Wee doe assure Our selves that a

Colony of English here planted with a moderate support in their Infant tendencey would in a very short time improve themselves to a perfect Comon Wealth Injoying a Selfe sufficiency of all the principall Necessaryes to life and abounding with a great variety of Superfluity for the Invitacon of fforaigne Comerce and trade, and wch for its Scite and produccons would be of more advantage to our Native Country the Kingdome of England and to the Grandeur of Our Soveraigne Lord the King his Crowne and dignity then any (wee may say all) his other Dominions in America.   And Wee doe further a vouch that this Country may bee more Securely setted and cheaply defended from any the attempts of its native Inhabitants then any of those other places which Our Countymen have refined from the Drosse of Indian Barbarisme In Witnes whereof Wee have hereunto sett our hands this 14th of July 1666.

Henry Brayne   George Cary
Richd Abrahall   Sam^ll Harvey
Thomas Giles   Joseph Woory.

[*Shaf. Pap.*, Sec. IX, Bdle. 48, No. 7.]

HEN. VASSALL[1] TO LDS. PROP^rs OF CAROLINA 15 AUG. 1666.

Right Honble

It is now a considerable time since I had ye the hon^r to treate wth a Committee of yor Hon^rs chosen from among yor selves, conserning ye setling of a Colony at Cape ffeare, & although there was no absolute accord & fineall agreem^t yet severall Concessions were then offered by ye sd Comittee, & by me dispatched to ye

---

[1] Henry Vassall, of London. He died on this adventure, 1667, *s. p.* His father, Samuel Vassall (page 7), merchant and alderman of London (born 1586, married Frances Cartwright), was (with his brother, William Vassall) Massachusetts patentee 1628. 'A steady asserter of the liberties of England' and first to resist the tonnage tax, he was imprisoned and amerced by the Star Chamber, but got £10,445 compensation, and was M. P. for London 1641. Took the Covenant 1643, was Commissioner for peace with Scottand 1646. Aided Cromwell in the conquest of Jamaica and received great estates there.   Died 1667.

Barbados to ye Adventurers there who did intrust me, who imediately retorned answer y^t they would accept them & accordingly gave me powre to conclude wth yor Hon^{rs}: But in ye Interim
comes one M^r, now S^r Jno, Yeomens, & by his sonne offers other
& contrary Artickles to w^t ye Adventurers did desire, & made
such spetious pretences y^t yor Hon^{rs} made an absolute agreem^t
wth him; & refused to confirme those Concessions formerly offered
me, though I then foresaw & also tould your Hon^{rs} there was
no likelihood he should pforme his Covenant, notwithstanding
he had entred into a penall bond of £1000 to accomplish it. Now
may it please yor Hon^{rs} it is so fallen out as I foretould y^t no materiall part of ye sd Covenant is pformed, but on ye Contrary ye
Adventurers & present Planters highly disatisfied y^t they should
not have those Concessions, at least, which were tendred & uppon wch they went, confirmed unto them; they thought those Concessions[1] hard enough, but those other Intolerable. Wherefore w^t
I humbly request is y^t I may have ye Hon^r of one speedy Con-
ference more wth as many of yor Ld^s as may be, y^t I may put a
fineall end to my Negotiation, & I cannot but hope for a good
one since I am resolved to propound nothing but w^t shall be as
well for yor Hon^s Interest as y^t of ye Colony, ye reason why, I
humbly desire this meeting may be so speedy is because many
in England, New England, Barbados yea & those y^t are actually
uppon ye place do wait for the Isue of this my last addresse wch if
good I do promise wth Gods leave, & yor Hon^{rs} favour to set
fourth a good ship wth men & provitions imediately for Cape
ffeare, & allso manefest to yor Hon^{rs} ye likelyhood of severall
other ships to follow in ye spring, but it is high time y^t those y^t
go this yeare shold be makeing ready: if ye successe of this my
last Addresse shold be insuccessfull (wch God forbid) all those
y^t have intrusted me, though they may have begun a plantation
& some are actually uppon ye place, have advised me y^t they
will draw of & quite give over ye designe, & then it will be seen
whether they be ye Major p^t yea or no: But I feare not but, if I
have but time & opertunity I shall manefest ye necessity of
graunting those things I shall humbly offer in order to ye establishing a Colony y^t may thrive and prosper under yor Hon^{rs}

---

[1] August 21, 1663, page 13.   'Those other,' page 29, dated January,
166$\frac{4}{5}$.

Governm^t, wch y^t it may do under yor Hon^{rs} & yor Successors from Generation to Generation is the prayer of

R^t Honble

Yo^r Hon^{rs} faithfull & most obedient servant

HEN: VASSALL

sole agent for ye Adventurers & planters of Cape ffeare.

Augst 15th 1666.

[*S. P.*, Sec. IX, Bdle. 48, No. 6.]

Right Honourable,

The Gent chosen for an Assembly for the County of Clarendon in Carolina upon a views and consideration had of your Honours charters and Concessions to the said county did supplicate for a Redress cheafely in three things, as to grevious to be required of them,

1 The halfe penny p. acre for all Lands.

2 The undecemall way of division of there lands.

3 The Injuntion on penaltye of forfiture of Keeping one man on every hundred Acres.   They added these Reasons viz:

1 To the first that in all their land where or howsoever taken up theire are of these three sortes viz.   Pine Swamp and Marsh which made up much the greater part of theire proportions and are yet so wholy unprofitable that to pay a halfe penny per acre for them is more then there vallew wherefore they did signifie there Redresse, that those lands, what proportion soever they beare to the good Oake Land Should bee accounted to them as soe many Acres but not as to paye the said rent by those acres; they were rather willing to paye a greater rent for what acres of Oake land they should possess soe as they might bee excused the paying rent for the rest and did propose it as an Expedient to paye one penny per acre Annually for all the Oake land in there respective tracts as the Rent due for the whole: and that your Honours Survay in Bounding out there lands should certifie in perticuler the quantity of Oake lands according to which the Rent should bee Resarved in the deeds of conformation for lands they enforced this with a Complaint that it was sufficiently grevious to them after soe chargeable and hazardous an adventure to which they were onely incouridged by the consideration

of such Quantityes of lands to bee constrained to accept of land soe wholy unusefull, and which did soe much incomode every mans settlement and therefore they hoped your Honour would not add this burthen to their sadd disappointment.

2 To the second, that they arived here the most of them beefore the Conssessions ware framed and had there land assigned to them by certaine meats and bounds on which they have planted and bilt, that therefore to have those lands now cast into such a way of Lotts as the Conssessions contrive, and undesimall part reformed for your Honour will certainly alter all those bounds and remove every mans possession which cannot but bee Ruine to most, nor doe they see how this waye of allotments can be practised in the Future, at least soe as to bee any benefit to your Honour for the good land lying soe widely dispersed what is already taken up though but halfe the proportion due to each person, runns to an extent of at least three score miles soe that what is to take up will lye soe Remote from all conveniencyes that it cannot advantage your Honour to have an eleventh part at that distance, and indeed that Kinde of divition appointed by the Concessions is not at all practicable neare, beecause the good lands doe noe where lye soe contiguous nor soe in any place as equally to Accomodate the whole generall lot, And a very great mischife it would bee to any whose lott shall fall where there is not a foote plantable, they did expresse a great desire that somewhat might be offered to your Honour in vallue of this undecimall part but finding nothing heare really worth your acceptance they durst rather bee silent then propose any ignoble compensation.

3 To the third, having already declared soe fully the nature of the lands in this country they thought it unnessesary to multiply reasons against the keeping a man on every hundred acres it being evident from what is sd that in very many places a hundred acres would not maintaine one man.

This Addresse and Representation beeing made to the Lt Gen^ll and his councell and there concurance in all humble maner desired in petition to your Honour for a release from these reall pressures They certainly Knowing all this to be truely soe as it is remonstrated ware the redier to joine in prayers soe Rationall and soe nessasary, and therefore with one harte and voyce we the governer Councell and assembly or representation for the

county of Clarendon in Carolina beseach your Honours to take
the premises into your serious consideration and to relieve us
according to the true merrite of our cause.

May it please your Lordship

    This humble address as it is above written was perpated[1]
with the allowance and consent of the Honorable Sir John Yeamans Baronet L[t] Gen[ll] under your Lordshipp of this Province
at such time as he was heare with us and presided in our Councells; who at first gave us all the appearance of his purpose to
joyne with us in the subscription thereof. But when it was en-
grossed and presented to him to bee signed he made this answer
that his further thoughts had discoursed unto him an absurditie in
owneing under his hands so perticular a knowledge of the soile in
this County into which he was but newly come, and that, therefore
he did conceive it might give a better reputation to our cause if
he did exempt himself from the Gen[ll] Addresse.   he added that
his intimating to your Lordshipp in his private letter the full satisfaction he had received within himself of the greviousnes and un-
practicablenes of these three injunctions espetially would strong-
lier inforce our arguments to your Lordships and more advantage
the Acceptance of our prayers then his appearing jointly with us
and soe he left us with sufficient Incoredg[mt] to proceed with our
petition by ourselves and with our hopes enlarged that though
hee labored not openly with us hee would yet labor more effectually for us.   Thus therefore and upon these grounds wee doe
presume Right Honorable to press into your presents and being
now heare doe in all humility offer these furthur to your noble
consideration.

    1 That when all the fame of this province was left in that black
Cloud of Reproaches which a party of the first new england Adventurers had wraped the whole country in and noe mans eare
or mouth or hand was open to heare or speake or act in her defence wee then from noe other incitm[t] but the Glory of that
venture which is made for publick advantage did by a vollentary
and full countrybution dispell those mists of scandall and revive
a lusture bright enough to direct and provoke to a seizure by

---

    [1] Proposed? December, 1665? Yeamans left for Barbadoes January,
166$\frac{5}{6}$.

meanes of which expense your Lordshipps have the possession
of a parte which may bee improved to aseminary for the whole
province if the discoridgement from without the place prove not
more fatall then those within it; neither can wee think this seir-
vis really performed for your Lordshipps inferior to that which is
but promised nor is it a frindly argument that because wee have
settled in a worse part of the country wee must have the worse
conditions, since therefore those whome wee credited as your
Lordshipps plenipotentiaryes in Barbados were pleased soe well
to consider of the success of those our contrybutions as in your
Lordshipps name to promise us five hundred acres of land and
soe proportionally for every 1000 of sugar wee hade expended
on that second discovery[1] without which (wee can make it plainly appear) though all else was ready the designe had yet fallen,
since also tis most certaine that if Port Royall bee ever presented
with powerfull invitations to a culture it will bee from the consequence of these our super numerary disburses wee hope it will
not be offensive to your Lordshipp that we deprecate a punishment upon our misfortunes and beg to have that conformed to us
notwithstanding our ill suckses which was granted as the prize
of our vigerous crowding in to your Lordships servis, through all
the obstickles that Mallice or conterary pollicies could object.

2 That those nombers of the Carolina adventurers who made
the seperation and intercepted that treaty which wee had com-
enced with your Lordship, presenting different proposalls and
accepting other conditions ware such as had the whole bent of
there affections towards port Royall and never purposed further
to second there diverted adventures on this county of Clarendon
which then might conduce to the establishing them an interest
in the county of Craven who being now by the said callamity
which fell on Sir Jno Yeamens disappointed in there expectations
there are nessesarily discouridged proceeding heare: and evidence the same not onely by a silent discontinuance, but alsoe by
a clamerous drawing off, those againe on the other side who
ware determinate for this county being stop'd in there carreare
by these unexpected concessions have remayned at a staye ever
since, with too much appearance of never reinclyning there mo-

---

[1] Hilton, pages 18, 32. 'Those who intercepted,' Yeamans, &c.,
page 29.

tion this way. Thus is there an approaching loss to all concerned to the King and nation, loss of dominion and trade to
your Lordshipps loss of the name and Honour of enlarging both
these, to the adventurers loss of money and hopes increased in
us that are here by the loss of our whole substance; and all this
unavodiably unles your Honours reeintegrating that treaty which
your Honours once desended to with us and in us with the adventurers of ould and new England and by granting us these
priviledges which you were once not very far from granting us
(which very probably you will) the Actmenity of such who can
trample on all other difficultyes when supported by that which
they opinion Fredome, the Ruine which with open mouth at-
tends us while being desarted by all, wee are utterly disabled
either to proceed or to retire enforceth us to this cruestnes, yet
ware wee the onely partyes in this cause wee should approach
with much lesse bouldnes, but now wee sue in your Lordshipps
behalves also, yet your Possession of this Province may not bee
utterly lost, and with it all the hopes of our subjecting it to an
English Gouvermt wee are

Yo^r Lordshipp's most humble servants[1]

John Nevinson	Geo Cary	John Vassall
Richard Whittney	Robert Gibbs	Hump. Davenport
John Knight	Tho Clifton	John Brent
Henry Brayne	Will Grig	R. Sandford
Thomas Gibbes	Sam Harvie?	

[S. P., Sec. IX, Bdle. 48, No. 81.]

---

[1] Written in 1666, before Sandford went in June. The signatures are
autograph. Cary, Brayne, Harvie, and Thomas Gibes (if the same as
Thomas Giles) were Sandford's companions. Captain Thomas Gibbes
(second son of Robert Gibbes, C. J. Barbadoes), born at Pandwicke,
Kent, April 24, 1642, was (with his brothers, Basil and Robert and John
Brent) of the Barbadoes adventurers 1663, and an early settler in Carolina. Held lands there and in Barbadoes 1686, and died in Carolina 'an
old bachelor.' Colonel Robert Gibbes, his brother, founder of the Carolina family, born at Pandwicke January 9, 1644, was treasurer in Carolina 1683, High Sheriff and Judge 1682–85, 1692–98, Chief Justice 1708,
in Council 1699, 1710, and Governor 1711. He died 24th June, 1715.
Christopher Nevison, his brother, young Mr. Brant, and four others arrive at Nevis from Todos August, 1666. For Will. Grig and Sam. Harvie, A. & W. I., ₰ 390, has 'Willigrip' and 'Sam: Elam?' N. C., 149,
'Sam: Hames?'

1666.   NOTES is hereby given to all * * that there is a New Plantation begun 2 yeers since on the main land between Virginia & the Cape of Florida at a place called Cape Feare &c. [*Shaf. Papers*, 48, No. 83.]   *N. C. Rec.*, I, page 153, 154.

———

1666.   A BRIEF DESCRIPTION of Carolina on the coasts of Florida & more particularly of a new plantation begun by the English at Cape Feare on that river now by them called Charles River the 29th of May 1664 &c printed for Robert Horne &c London 1666.   *Carroll Col.*, II, page 9.

———

NANCYMOND IN VIRGINY OCTOBER 6th 1667.

Hon[ble] Sir

I presume you have heard of the unhappy loss of our plantation on Charles River[1] the reason of which I could never so well have understood had I not com hither to hear how that all that came from us made it their business soe to exclame against the Country as they had rendered it unfitt for a Christian habitation, which hindered the Coming of people and suplye to us soe as the Rude Rable of our inhabitants ware dayly ready to mutany against use for keeping them there soe long insoe much that after they had found a way to come hither by Land all the Argumts and Authority I could use wold no longer prevail which inforced me to stopp the first shipp that came till I could send for more shipping to carry us all away together especially such weak persons as weare not able to goe by land.[2]   The charge & trou-

———

[1] Samuel Mavericke to Sec. Lord Arlington, Boston, October 16, 1667: The plantations at Cape Feare are deserted, the inhabitants have since come hither, some to Virginia.   Att Bermudoes there hath been such a drought as the fruites of the earth are all destroyed & in Virginia on the 23rd August there was such a dreadfull huricana as blew up all by the rootes y[t] was in the ground overturned many houses &c.   *N. C.*, I, 161.

[2] 'In 1667 he applied for relief to be sent to him & followers,' *Savage*, 367, 'the people at Cape Fear being under distressing circumstances a general contribution by order of court was made thro' the colony for their relief.'   *Hutchinson's Massachusetts*, 238.

ble whereof and the loss of my Estate there having soe ruined me as I am not well able to settle myself here or in any other place to live comfortabley but had it pleased God to bring my Cousin Vassall safe hither wee had binn yet in a flurishing condition. I sent one Whiticar last november on purpose at my own charge to give the Lords an accompt of our condition but he was taken by the way soe I have not had aword from any of you since I received my commisions by Mr Sanford and indeed we ware as a poor Company of deserted people little regarded by any others and noe way able to suply our selves with Clothing and necessaries nor any nomber considerable to defend our selves from the Indians all which was occasioned by the hard terms of the Consessions which made our frinds that set us out from Barbados to forsake us soe that they wold nither suply us with nessaseries nor send shipping to fettch us away yet had we had but: 200:ll send us in clothing we had made a comfortable shift for another yeare and I offered to stay there if but twenty men wold stay with me till we had heard from the Lordships for we had Corn enough for two yeares for a ffarr greater nomber and tho' the Indians had killed our Cattle yet we might have defended our selves but I could not find 6 men that would be true to me to stay soe was constrained to leave it to my great loss and Ruin and I feare you will not have a much better acompt of the plantation at Ronoake unless a better Course be taken to incorage there stay for they are not without great cause of complants this with my very humble servis presented is all at present from

Your honors humble servant

(Endorsed)   JOHN VASSALL.[1]

To the Honorable Sir John Colliton Knight and Baronett at Nerehale these present.

In Essex.   [*Shaf. Papers*, 48, No. 8.]

---

[1] Colonel John Vassall, born 1625, came to Massachusetts, 1635, with his father (William Vassall, of London, who removed to Barbadoes 1646, and died there 1655), was lieutenant 1652, and then captain. Sold his estate in Scituate 1661, went to Jamaica, and then engaged in settlement of Cape Fear. Surveyor-General there 1664, and in Assembly 1665. On its loss, 1667, went to Virginia.

ARTICLES OF AGREEMENT made concluded & agreed on Betweene George Duke of Albemarle Captain Genneral of his majesties Forces Edward Earle of Clarendon William Earle of Craven John Lord Berkeley Anthony Lord Ashley Chancellor of the Exchecquer Lord George Carteret Knight and Baronet Vice Chamberlaine of his majesties Houshould Sir Peter Colleton Baronet and Sir William Berkley Knight the Proprieter of the Province of Carolina In order to the speedy setlement of the said Province.[1]

1. Imp   It is agreed that each Proprietor doe at or before the twenty fifth day of May next Pay to Mr John Portman Gouldsmith the sum of Five hundred pounds sterling.

(2) That this money by the consent and direction of the major part of the persons above mentioned testefied by wrighting under their hands be laid out in shipping, Armes, Amunition, Tooles, and Provissions for the Setlement of Port Royall within the Province of Carolina aforesaid.

(3) That the Proprietors or Persons above mentioned or major parte of them doe appoint an husband who shall by and with the Consent and direction of the said Proprietors, or the major part of them contract for Shipps Armes, Amunition, Tooles, provissions, or what other thing shall be thought necessary and after such things are contracted for any three of the Proprietors by a noat under their hands order Mr John Portman to pay soe much of the money deposited as will pay for them And this noat soe signed shall be a sufficient warrant to Mr Portman for his paying the money.

(4) That this husband be oblidged to render unto any one of the Proprietors an account of his proceedings whenever thereunto required.

---

[1] 166⅞, March 24. 'Mem: of the persons concerned in Carolina' to the King. The Dutch no planters & should the English & their slaves be removed Surinam must sink. These planters are willing to quit Surinam & in regard many of them are desirous to remove to Port Royal in Carolina. Offer if his Majesty will send a ship of war to demand these people & protect their ships, they will at their own charge send two ships to transport those willing to Port Royal with victuals &c. (endorsed) Rec'd & read 24 mch 169⅞. Suspended till we hear from Holland. *A. & W. I.*, ₰ 41.

(5) For the Better carrying on the worke of Planting and setling the said Province it is hereby absolutly and fully concluded
and condiscended to by all the Proprietors above named that
had of them shall and will from time to time For the space of
Fower years next ensueing bring and pay in unto such person
or persons as shall be from time to time appointed by the said
Proprietors or the major part of them to receive the same such
sum and sums of money as shall be by the said Proprietors or
the major part of them thought fitt and ordered to be brought
in and paid soe as the same doe not exceed the Rate or Proportion of two hundred pounds per anum for each Proprietors Share
And that in case any one or more of the Proprietors for the time
being shall refuse or neglect to pay in either his or their respective sum of Five hundred pounds above mentioned or his or
their money soe ordered to be paid being required thereunto by
the Rest of the said Proprietors or the major part of them who
shall have first brought in their said Respective money that then
such Proprietor or Proprietors soe refuseing or neglecting to pay
his or their said Respective sums of Five hundred pounds or his
or their moneys soe Ordered to be brought in or any part thereof
by the space of three months next after such Request shall upon
payment to him or them of all such moneys as he or they hath
or have for his or their Share or Shares formerly Expended
about the Province of Carolina aforesaid together with interest
for the same according to the Rate of tenn pounds per cent per
annum For the time he or they hath or have binn out of such
money shall relinquish and convey to the Rest of the said Proprietors who shall have then brought and paid in their moneys
as aforesaid and their heires all the share and shares of such Proprietor or Proprietors soe refuseing or neglecting together with
all his or their Interest or advantage whatsoever which he or
they may or cann claime by vertue of his majesties Letters Pattents Lately granted to the said Proprietors or of any matter or
thing therein contayned In wittness whereof we have hereunto
put our hands and seales the 26th day of Aprill in the yeare of
our Lord 669 and in the 21 yeare of Car 2^d by the Grace of God
of Eng: Scotland France and Ireland King defender of the Faith
&c. H. Cornbury, Craven, Jo Berkeley, Ashley, G. Carteret P.
Colleton.   Signed and sealed and delivered by the Lord Viss-
count Cornbury the Earle of Craven the Lord Berkeley the

Lord Ashley Sir George Carteret and Sir Peter Colleton in the presence of

SAM: JOHNSON

(Endorsed, by Locke)   WILL: PINNOCKE.

Articles between the Proprietors 26. April 69.

[*S. P.*, Bdle. 48, No. 9.]

1669. JUNE 15. WHITEHALL. Warrant to the Commissioners of Ordnance To deliver to Joseph West, for the defence of the plantation called Carolina in the West Indies, four iron demi-culverin and eight sacres, with ship carriages, ladles, sponges and linstocks & 12 rounds of shot for each. *Am. & W. I.*, §75.

SHAFTESBURY PAPERS:—FIRST SET OF THE CONSTITUTIONS FOR THE GOVERNMENT OF CAROLINA; BY JOHN LOCKE.

1. Our Soveraigne Ld. the King haveing out of his royal grace & bounty granted unto us ye province of Carolina, with all ye roialtys proprietys, jurisdictions, & priviledges of a county pallatine, as large & ample as ye county pallatine of Durham, with other great priviledges for ye better settlement of ye governmt. of ye sd. place, and establishing the interest of ye lds. proprietors with equality and without confusion, & y^t ye governmt. of this province may be made most agreable unto ye monarchy under wch. we live, & of wch. this province is a part, & y^t we may avoid erecting a numerous democracy. We ye true & absolute lds. & proprietors of ye province aforesd. have agreed to this following forme of governmnt., to be perpetualy established amongst us unto wch. we doe obleige our selves our heirs & successors in ye most bindeing ways y^t can be devised.

2. Out of the eight proprietors there shall be chosen by themselves a palatin, who shall continue during life, whose son shall not be capable of immediately succeeding him after his death; but ye eldest in age of ye other proprietors shall succeed to pre-

---

2. The eldest of the lords proprietors shall ~~always~~ be palatin, & upon ye decease of ye palatin ye eldest of ye seven surviveing proprietors shall always succeed him.

vent the makeing ye office in this litte governmt. hereditary, &
to avoid the mischief of factions in elections.

3. There shall be seven other chief offices erected, viz. ye
cheife justices, chancellrs., constables, high-stewards, treasurers,
chamberlaines, admiralls, wh. places shall be injoyed by none
but ye lords proprietors, to be assigned at first by lot & upon
the vacacancie of any other of ye seven great officers by death
or otherwise ye eldest proprietor to have his choise of ye sd.
place.

4. Each province shall be divided into countyes, each county
shall consist of eight segnioryes, eight barronyes, & four precincts, each precinct shall consist of six collonyes.

5. Each collony, signiory, & barrony shall consist of 12,000
acres ye eight siginioryes being ye share of ye eight proprietrs.
and ye eight barronyes of ye nobility, both wch. shares being
each of them a fifth part of ye whole, are to be perpetually annexed ye one to ye proprietors ye other to ye hereditary nobillity, leaving ye collonyes being 3 fifths amongst ye people y' so
in ye setting out & planting ye lands the ballance of governmt.
may be preserved.

6. At any time before ye yeare 1701 any of the lds. proprietors
shall have power to relinquish, alienate, & dispose to any other
person his proprietorship and all ye signeoryes powers and interest thereunto belonging wholly & intirely together & not otherwise. But after ye yeare 1700 those who are then lds. proprietrs.
shall not have power to alienate (7) or make over their proprie-
torships with ye signiories or privileges thereunto belonging or
any part thereof to any p'son whatsoever otherwise yn. as in article 18, but it shall descend unto their heires male, & for want
of heires male it shall descend on that landsgrav or casique of
Carolina who is descended of ye next heire female of ye said
proprietor, & for want of such heires it shall desend on the next
heir general., & for want of such heirs the remaining seven

(7) make over or let.

p'prietors shall upon ye vacancy choose a landgrav to succeed ye deceased proprietor, who being chosen by the majority of ye seaven surviving proprietors he and his heires successively shall be proprietors as fully to all intents & purposes as any of ye rest.

7. And y^t ye number of eight proprietors may be constantly kept if upon ye vacancy of any proprietorship ye surviving seaven

~~or casique~~

proprietors. shall not choose a landgrade ∧ to be a proprietr. be-

bienniall

fore ye second ∧ ~~session of~~ parliament after ye vacancy, then ye

next bienniall

∧ parliamt. ~~at ye next session~~ but one after such vacancy shall

~~or casique~~

have power to choose any landgrave ∧ to be propriets., but who-soevr. after ye yeare 1700 either by inheritance or choise shall succeed any proprietr. in his p'prietorship & signiorys there-unto belonging shall be obliged to take ye name & armes of that proprietr. wm. he succeeds, wch. from thenceforth shall be ye name & armes of his family & their posterity.

or casique | inheritance or choice come to be a

8. Whatso~~evr. landgrave~~ ∧ shall ∧ (11) be ~~chosen in to a~~ proprie-torship shall ~~take ye~~ signioryes annexed to ye sd. proprietorship, but shall relinquish all ye barronyes belonging to his landgrave-

or cassiqueship

ship ∧ to be (12) disposed of *by the proprietors as in ye following Articles.*

9. To every county there shall be three as ye hereditary no-bility of this pallatinate, who shall be called ye one a landgrave & ye other two cassiques, & shall have the place in the Parlia-ment there, ye landgrave shall have four barronyes, and ye two

ly

cassiques each of them two a peice hereditary ∧ & unalterably an'exed to & settled upon the said dignity.

---

(11). Whatsoever landgrave ~~or cassique shall~~ any way come to be a propr whosoever by inheritance ~~or choice (11)~~ *shall any way come to be a proprietor.*

(12) Disposed of as in Artic. 12.

8. Whatsoever landgrave or cassique shall any way come to be a propr. shall take ye signiorys annexd. to ye sd. proprietor-ship, but his former dignity with the barronys annexd. shall de-volve into the hands of ye lds. proprs.

10. The first landgrave & cassiques of every county shall be nominated not by ye joint election of the proprietors altogether, but the eight proprietrs. shall each of them seperately nominate and choose one landgrave & two cassiques (7) for ye eight first countys to be planted, & when the said eight countyes shall be planted ye proprietrs. shall in ye same manner nominate & choose eight more landgraves & sixteene cassiques for ye eight next countyes to be planted, and so proceed in the same maner till the whole province of Carolina be set out & planted accord-

ing to ~~ye proprietrs.~~ ^{proportions} in these fundamentall constitutions.

11. Any landgrave or cassique at any time before ye yeare 1701 shall have power to alienate, sell, or make ovr. to any other person his dignity wth. ye barronyes thereunto belonging all entirely together, but after ye yeare 1700 noe landgrave or cassique shall have power to alienate, sell, make ovr. or let the hereditary baronys of his dignity, or any part thereof, otherwise y^n as in article 18, but they shall all entirely wth. ye dignity thereunto, belonging, desend unto his heires male, & for want of such heires, male, all entirely & undivided to ye next heir generall, & for want of such heires shall devolve into ye hands of ye proprietors.

12. That ye due numbr. of landgraves and cassiques may be alwayes kept up if upon ye devolution of any landgraveship or cassiqueship ye (16) ~~proprietors~~ shall not settle the devolvd. dignity wth. ye barronyes thereunto an'exd. before the (17) ~~second session of Parliament~~ *after such devolution ye Parliamt. at the* ~~bienniall~~

~~next session but one~~ after such devolution shall have power to make any one landgrave or cassique in ye roome of him, who dying without heires his dignity and baronyes devolved.

13. No one p'son shall have more than one dignity wth ye signioryes or barronyes thereunto belonging, but whensoevr. it shall happen y^t any one who is already p'prietr. landgrave, or cassique, shall have any of those dignityes decend to him by

---

(7) To be the eight landgraves & the 16 cassiques for the

(16) The Palatins Court shall not

(17) Second bienniall Parlmt. after such devolution the next Bienniall Parlmt. but one.

inheritancy it shall be at his choice to keep, wch. of ye 2 dignityes (with ye lands annexed) he shall like best, but shall leave
the other wth. ye lands an'ex'd to be enjoyed by him who not
being his heir apparent & certaine successr. to his p'st dignity is
      of bloud
next (17) afterwds.

14. Whosoevr. by right of inheritance shall come to be landgrave or cassique shall take ye name & armes of his predesessor
in that dignity to be from thence forth ye name & armes of his
famely & their posterity.

15. Since ye dignity of proprietor, landgrave, or cassique
cannot be devided & ye signioryes or barronyes thereunto annexed must for evr. all entirely decend wth. & accompany that
dignity when evr. for want of heires male it shall decend upon
ye isue female ye eldest daughter & her heirs shall be preferd.,
and in ye inheritance of those dignitys & in ye signiorys or barronyes annexed there shall be noe coheires.

16. After ye yeare 1700 whatsoevr. landgrave or cassique shall
without leave from ye Palatins Court be out of Carolina during
two successive bienniall Parliamts shall at ye end of ye second
bienniall Parliamt. after such his absence be sum'oned by Proclamation, & if he come not into Carolina before ye next bienniall
Parliamt. after such sum'ons, then* ~~it shall be lawfull~~ for ye
Grand Councill at a price set by ye sd. Councill & approved by
ye Parliamt. to sell ye bar'onyes with ye dignityes thereunto belonging of ye sd. absent landgrave or cassique altogether to any
one to wm. ye sd. Councill shall thinke fit, but ye price so paid
for ye sd. dignity or baronys shall be deposited in ye Treasury
                            heirs or
for ye sole use & behoofe of ye former owner or his ∧ assignes.
                       respective
17. In every signiory, barrony, & mannory ye ∧ Ld. shall have

---

(17) unless where a landgrave or cassique comes to be proprietor & then his former dignity & barronyes shall devolve as
in Art. 8.

* then the Grand Council shall have power thence forward to
receive all the rents & profits ariseing out of his baronys, untill
his returne or death, & to dispose of the said profits as they
shall think fit.

~~tenants in controversy one amongst another shall have noe appeale~~. power in his owne name to hold court there for trying of all

(2) ~~from wch. his~~

causes both civill & crimminal ∧ ~~but where~~ it shall concerne any other p'son being noe inhabitant, vassall, or leet-man of ye sd.

or mannor

barrony, signiory, he upon paying downe of forty shillings unto ye proprietrs. use shall have an appeal from thence unto ye County Court, ~~& if ye Ld. be cast ye said Ld. shall pay unto ye apealant ye sd. forty shillings wth. other charges~~. ‡

~~18~~. 19. The Lords of signioryes & barronys shall have power onely of granting estates not exceeding 3 lives or one & thirty yeares in two-thirds of ye sd. signiorys or barronys, & ye re-remaining third shall be all wayes demesne.

19. Eevery mannor shall consist of not les than 3,000 acres, & not above 12,000 acres in one entire peice, but any 3,000 acrs. or more in one peice, & the possession of one man shall not be a manor unles. it be constituted a manr. by ye grant of the ~~Lords Proprietrs~~. Palatin's Court.

20. Every lord of a manor. w'thin. his manr. shall have all the powers, jurisdictions, & privileges wch. a landgrave or cassique hath in his barronys.

21. ⊠ Any Lord of a manor. may alienate, sell, or dispose to

his mannor

any other person and his heires for evr. ∧ all entirely together wth. all ye privileges and leetmen thereunto belonging, so far forth as any other collony lands, but noe grant of any part there-of, either in fee or for any longr. terme yⁿ 3 lives or 21 years, shall be good against ye next heire; nether shall a manor for want of issue male be devided amongst coheires; but ye man'or, if there be but one, shall all entirely decend to ye eldest daughtr.

her

& ∧ heires, if there be more man'ors then one in the possession of ye deceased, the eldest sister shall have her choice, ye second

---

‡ ~~18~~ (2) But when it shall concerne any ~~other~~ person being noe inhabitant, vassall, or leet-man of ye sd. barony signiory, or mannor, he upon paying downe of 40s. to ye Lds. proprietors use shall have an appeale from ~~them to ye County Court~~, the Signiory or Barony Court to the County Court, & from the Manor Court to the Precinct Court.

next, & so on, beginning agn. at ye eldest till all ye man'ors be taken up yt. so ye priveleges wch. belong to manrs. being indevisible, ye lands of ye man'or to wch. they are an'exed may be kept entire, & the man'or not loose those priveleges wch., upon parcelling out to severall owners, must necessarily cease.

22. In every signiory, barrony, & man'or, all ye ~~tenants or~~

respective

leetmen shall be under the jurisdiction of ye ∧ Lord of ye sd. signiory, barony, or man'or w'thout a'peal from him, ~~unles as~~ ~~in ye Article 26~~, nor shall any leetman or leetwoman have liberty to goe of from the land of his particular lord, & live anywhere else without licences obtain'd from his said lord under hand & seale.

23. All ye children of leetmen shall be leetmen, & so to all generations.

24. No man shall be capable of having a court leet, or leetmen, but a proprietor, landgrave, or cassique, or lord of a man-

hath not voluntarily enterd himself

nor; nor shall any man be a leetman who~~se contract to be~~ a leetma~~n is not entre~~d in the registry of the County Court.

25. Whoevr. is lord of leetmen shall upon ye mariage of a leetman or leetwoman of his give them 10 acres of land for their lives, they paying to him therefore ~~⅑ of all ye yearely increase~~ ~~& growth of ye sd. acres~~.*

26. In case ye lord of any signiory, barrony, or manor, shall have made a contract or agreemt. wth. his tenants, wch. agreemt.

of ye county court

by consent is registred in ye ~~next precinc~~t registery ∧ then in such case ye sd. tenant may ap'eal unto or bring his complaint originally in ye county court for ye performance of such agreements & not otherwise.†

supreme

27. There shall be eight ∧ courts or ~~councills for ye dispatc~~h

ing

~~of all affaires~~, ye first called ye Palatin's Court, ~~to~~ consist ∧ of ye

---

*not more than ⅓ of all the yearely produce & growth of ye sd. 10 acres.

† 26. Noe landgrave or cassique shall be tried for any criminall

in the chief justice

cause but ∧ ~~one of the Suprem~~e Courts, & that by a jury of his peers.

Palatine and ye other, seaven proprietors. The other seaven courts of ye other seaven great officers shall consist each of them of a proprietr. & six councellers added to him, under each

of these latter seaven ^courts shall be a colledge of twelve assistants, ~~out~~

the twelve assistants ^out of ye severall colledges shall be chosen two out of the landgraves by ye landgraves chamber ~~during ye Sessions of Parliamt.~~ ‡ two out of ye cassiques by ye cassiques camb. ~~during the Session of Parliamt~~, two out of ye landgraves cassiques or eldest sons of the proprietrs. by ye Palatines Court, four more of ye twelve shall be chosen ~~by~~ by the com'ons chamber ~~during ye Session of Parliamt~~ out of such as have beene or are members of Parliamt. sherriffs, or justices of the County Court, the other two shall be chosen by the Palatines Court out of the aforesd. members of Parliamt. or sherriffs or justices of the County Court, or ye eldest sons of landgraves or cassiques or yonger sons of proprietors.

28. Out of these colledges shall be chosen six councellers to be joyn'd wth. each proprietor in his court of wch. six one shall be of those who were chosen into any of the colledges by the Palatines Court out of the landgraves, cassiques, or eldest sons of proprietors, one ^of those who were chosen ~~out of those who were chosen into any of~~

~~the colledges~~ by the landgraves chambr. & one ^out of ~~of~~ those who were chosen ~~into any one of ye colledges~~ by ye cassiques Chambr. two out of those who were chosen ~~into any one of ye colledges~~ by the Com'ons Chamber, & one out of those who were chosen by the Palatines Court ~~into any of the colledges~~ out of the proprietors yonger sons, or eldest sons, of landgraves or cassiques, or com'ons quallified as aforesd.

29. When it shall happen that any counciller dyes, & thereby there is a vacancy ye grand councell shall have power to remove any counciller that is willing to be removed out of any other of the proprietors courts to fill up this vacancy, p'vided they take a man of ye same degree & choice, ye other was ^of whose vacant place ^is to be filld; but if no counceller consent to be removed or

‡ q during ye Session of Parlmt.

upon such remove ye last remaining vacant place in any of ye Proprietors Courts shall be filld up by ye choice of ye Grand Councill, who shall have power to remove out of any of the colledges any assistant who is of ye same degree & choice yᵗ coun-

siller was ₍of₎ into whose vacant place he is to succeed; ye grand councill also shall have power to remove any assistant yᵗ is willing out of one colledge into another provided he be of ye same degree & choice, but ye last remaining vacant place in any colledge shall be filld up by ye same choice & out of the same degree of p'sons ye assistants was of who is dead or removed. No place shall be vacant in any proprietrs. court above six months; no place shall be vacant in any colledge longer yⁿ ye next Session of Parliamt.

30. No man being a membr. of ye grand councill, or of any of ye seaven colledges, shall be turn'd out but for misdemeaners, of wch. the grand councill shall be judge, & ye vacancy of ye p'son so put out shall be filled, not by the election of ye grand councill, but by those who first chose him, & out of ye same degree he was ₍of₎ who is expelld. (1)

31. All elections in ye Parliamt., in ye severall chambers of the Parliamt., & in ye grand councill shall be passed by baloting.

32. The Palatins Court shall consist of ye Palatin & seaven proprietors, wherein nothing shall be acted without ye presence and consent of the Palatin or his deputy & three others of the proprietors or their deputyes ₍This Court₎ shall have power to call Parliaments to pardon all offences, to make elections of all officers in the proprietrs. dispose,‡ & also ~~they~~ shall have power by their order to ye Tre'ar. to dispose of all publick Treasure, excepting mony granted by ye Parliament & by them directed to some ₍particular₎

---

(1) But it is not hereby to be understood that ye grand council hath any power to turne out any one of ye Lds. proprietors or their deputys. The Lords proprs. haveing in themselves an

~~nor~~

inharent original right ~~are not under ye jurisdiction of ye grand council.~~

‡ to nominate & appoint port towns

publick use, and also~~they~~ shall have ~~an~~ negative upon all acts, orders, votes, & judgmts. of the grand councell & ye Parliamt. (1) & shall have all ye powers granted to ye proprietors. by y^r patent,* except in such things as are limited by these fundamentall constitutions ~~& forme of governm~~t.

*from our Soveraigne Ld. ye K.

33. The Palatin himself when he in p'son shall be either in ye army or in any of the proprietor's courts shall then have the power of generall or of y^t proprietor, in whose court he is then present, & ye proprietor in whose court ye Palatin yⁿ p'sides shall during his p'sence there, be but as one of ye councill.

Chancellors.

34. The ~~Councellors~~ Court, consisting of one of ye proprietors & his six councillers, who shall be called vice chancellors, shall have ye custody of ye seal of ye Palatinate, under wh. all charters of lands, or otherwise com'issions & grants of ye Palatins court shall passe, etc.* To this court also belongs all state matters, dispatches, & treatyes, wth ye neighbour Indians, or any other so far forth as is permitted by our charter from or. Soveraigne Lord ye King. To y^{is} ~~office~~ also belongs all ~~innovations~~ of ye law of liberty of conscience, & all disturbances of ye publique peace upon pretence of religion, as also the licence of printing.

Court Invasions

~~35~~. The twelve assistants belonging to this court shall be calld. recorders.

35. The Chancellor or his deputy shall be allwayes Speaker in Parliamt. & President of ye Grand Council, & in his & his deputyes absence one of his Vice-Chancellors.

The Chief Justices Court, consisting of one of ye p'prietors & his six councillers, who shall be calld. Justices of ye Bench, shall judg all a'pealls both in cases civill & criminal, except all such cases as shall be under ye jurisdiction & cognizance of any other of ye proprietors courts wch. shall by try'd. in those courts

---

(1) Except only as in articles _{7 & 12} & allso _{shall have} a negative upon all acts and orders of the Constables Court & Admirals Court relating to warre.

*And it shall not be lawfull to put the seale of ye Palatinate to any writing wch. is not signed by the Palatine or his deputy & 3 other proprietors, or their deputies.

respectively.   The government & regulations of ye registryes of writings and contracts shall belong to ye jurisdiction of this court.

_{masters}

The twelve assistants of this court shall be calld. ~~marshals.~~

36. The High Constables Court, consisting of one of the proprietors & his six councellrs. who shall be calld. marshals, shall order & determine of all millitary affaires by land & all land forces, armes, ammunition, artilary, garrisons, & fortes, &c., & whatevr. belongs unto warr, his twelve assistants shall be calld. Lieutnts. Generlls. in time of actual warr.   The High Constable, whilst he is in ye Aarmy shall be General of ye Army & ye six councellers, or such of them as ye Palatins Court shall for y^t time & service appoint, shall be the im'ediate great officers under him, & ye lieutnts. genells. next to them.

37. The Admirals Court, consisting of one of ye proprietors. & his six councellers, calld. consuls, shall have ye care and in-

_{oles}

spection over all ports, ~~martes~~, & navigable rivers so farr as the tyde flows, & also all ye publique ship'ing of Carolina & stores

_{maritime}

thereunto belonging, and all ~~naratiive~~ affaires.   This court also shall have ye power of the Court of Admiralty, & also to heare and trye by law-merchent all cases in matters of trade between ye merchants of Carolina amongst themselves arising without ye limits of Carolina, as also all controversyes in merchandising y^t shall happen betwene denizons of Carolina & foraigners.

The 12 assistants belonging to this court shall be cald. proconsuls. (42.)

38. The Treasurers Court, consisting of ~~one~~ proprietor & his six councillers, calld. under-treasurers, shall take care of all mat-

_{that}

ters ~~of~~ concerns ye publique revenue and treasury.

The twelve assistants shall be calld. auditors.

39. The High Stewards Court, consisting of a proprietor and

(42.) In time of actuall war the High Admirall whilst he is at sea shall command in chief, & his six councellers, or such of them as the Palatins Court shall for y^t time & service appoint, shall be the immediate great officers under him & the proconsuls next to them.

his six councillors, who shall be calld. comptrollrs., shall have ye care of all foraigne and domestick trade, manufactures, publick buildings and worke-houses, highwayes, passages by water above the flood of ye tide, draines, sewers & bankes against inunda-
                              & all things in order to trade & travell
tions, bridges, posts, carriers, (6) faires, markets, ∧ & all things in order to travell & com'erse, and anything that may co'rupt, deprave or infect ye com'on aire or water, & all other things
                    trade.
wherein ye publick ∧ com'erse or health is concernd, & also ye setting out & surveying of lands, & also ye seting out and ap-
              places
pointing ∧ for townes to be built on in ye precincts, & ye p'scrib-ing & determining ye figure & bignes of ye sd. townes according to such models as ye sd. court shall order, contrary or diffring from wch. models it shall not be lawful for any one to build in any town.

40. This court shall have power also to make any publick building or any new highway or enlarge any old highway upon any man's land whatsoevr., as also to makes cutts, chan'ells, bankes, locks, & bridges, for makeing rivers navigable, for draining of fens or any other publick uses, the damage the owner
                              which
of such lands (on or through where ∧ any such publick thing shall be made) shall receive thereby, shall be (34) valued ∧ by a jury of twelve men of ye precinct in wch. any such thing is done, and satisfaction shall be made accordingly by a tax, either on ye county or that particular precinct as the grand councill shall thinke fitt to order in that particular case (33).

---

(6) corruptions of or infections of the common aire & water, and all things in order to publique commerce, trade & health & trade.

(33.) And if it be a signiory or barony on or through wch. any such publique thing shall be made, then the damage the owner of ye sd. signiory or barony shall receive therby shall be valued by the High Stewards Court, & satisfaction shall be made accordingly by a tax on ye county.

(34) be valued & satisfaction made by such ways as the High Stewards Court shall appoint the Grand Councill shall appoint.

The 12 assistants belonging to this court shall be calld. sur-veyers.

41. The Chamberlaines Court, consisting of a proprietor & his six councillers, calld. vice-chamberlaines, shall have ye power to convocate, ye Grand Councill shall have ye care of all ceremonys, presedency, heraldry, reception of publick messen-gers & pedigrees, the registryes of all births, buryalls, & mari-ages, legittimation, & all cases concerning matrimony, or arise-ing from it, & shall also have power to regulate all fash'ons, habitts, badges, games, and sportes.

The 12 assistants belonging to this court shall be calld. Pro-vosts.

42. All causes belonging to or under ye jurisdiction of any of ye Proprietors Courts shall in ym. respectively be tryed, & ulti-mately determind without any farther appeal.

43. The Proprietors Courts shall have a power to mitigate all fines & suspend all executions, either before or after sentence, in any of the other ~~respective~~ inferior courts respectively.

44. In all debates, hearings, or tryalls in any of ye Proprie-tors Courts ye 12 assistants belong ^ing to ye said court respectively, shall have liberty to be p'sent, but shall not interpose, unless their opinion be required, nor have any vote at all; but their ^business shall be by direction of the respective courts to prepare such business as shall be com'itted to ym.; as also to beare such offices & dis-patch such affairs, either where ye court is kept, or else where, as ye court shall think fitt.

45. In all ye Proprietors ~~Courts~~ any three shall make a quo-rum.

46. The Grand Councill shall consist of ye Palatine & seven proprietrs., & ye 42 councillrs. of the severall Proprietors Courts,

---

45. In all the Proprietors Courts the proprietor & any three of his councellors shall make a quorum; Provided always, that for ye better dispatch of businesse it shall be in the power of ye Palatins Court to direct what sort of causes shall be heard and determind by a quorum of any three.

who shall have power to determine any controversyes that may arise between any of ye Proprietors Courts about their respective jurisdictions* to make peace & war, legues, treatyes, &c., with any of the neighbour Indians. To issue out their generall orders to the Constables & Admiralls Court, for the raising, disposing, or disbanding the forces by land or by sea, to prepare all matters to be proposed in Parliamt.; nor (1) shall any tax or law, or other matter whatsoever, be proposed, debated, or voted in Par. liamt. but what hath first past ye Grand Councill, & in forme of

a bill to be passed is by then present ₍ₑd₎ to the Parliamt., nor shall any bill soe prepared,† t~~o be enacted, whether it or~~ ~~law or otherwise, or passed into an Act of Parliamt., or~~ be at all obligatory, unles it be three severall dayes read openly in ye Parliamt., & then afterwards by majority of votes enacted during ye same session, wherein it was thrice read & also confirm'd by the Palatin, & three of ye proprietors as is above sd.

47. The Grand Councill shall allwayes be judges of all causes & appeals yt concernes the Palatine, or any of ye p'prietors or any counciller of any Proprietors Court in any case wch. otherwise should have bin tryd in ye court in wch. the sd. councillor is judge himself.

48. The Grand Councill by their warrants to ye Treasurers Court shall dispose of all ye mony given by ye Parliamt. & by ym. directed to any particular publick use.

49. The quoru' of ye Grand Councill shall be thirteen, whereof a proprietor or his deputy shall be alwayes one.

50. The palatin or any of the proprietors shall have power under hand and seale to be registred in ye Grand Councill to

---

*or betweene the membrs. of one ~~of~~ & the same court about their mannr. & methods of proceeding.

(1) any matter whatsoever be proposd in Parliamnt. but what hath first passed the Grand Councill, wᶜʰ after having been read three severall days in the Parliamt. shall be passed or rejected.

† & presented by the Grand Councill to the Parlt., to be enacted whether it be an anticipated law or otherwise, be voted or past into an Act of Parlt.

make a deputy who shall have ye same power to all intents &
who
purposes y^t he himself ~~y~~ deputes him, except in confirming Acts
70
of Parliamt. as in Article ∧ all such deputacon. shall sease &
determine of themselves at ye end of 4 yeares, & at any time
shall be revokeable at ye pleasure of ye deputator.

51. No deputy of any proprietor shall have any power whilst
ye deputator is in any part of Carolina, except ye proprietor
whose deputy he is be a miner.

53. The eldest of the proprietors who shall be p'sonally in
(1.)
Carolina shall of course be ye palatins deputy, ∧ & if no propri-
(1.)

This to be {
in {

etor be in Carolina ∧ he ~~shall choose his deputy out of the heirs~~
~~apparent of any of ye proprietors, if any such be there,~~ & if
there be no heir apparent of any of ye proprietors above 21 years
old in Carolina, then he shall choose for deputy any one of ye
landgraves of ye Grand Councill, and till he have by deputation
under hand & seale chosen anyone of the fore men'coned heires
ap'arent or landgrave to be his deputy, ye eldest man of ye
Landgraves, & for want of landgraves ye eldest man of ye cassiques who shall be p'sonally in Carolina shall of course be his
deputy.
Each
54. ~~The~~ proprietors deputy shall be allwayes one of their owne
six councellors respectively. (3)

---

52. During the minority of any proprietor his guardian shall
have power to constitute & appoint his deputy.

~~(1) The eldest heire apparent of any propr above 21 years~~
~~old shall of course be his deputy, unlesse there being more heires~~
~~apparent than are above 21 yeares old, he shall under hand &~~
~~seal make any other of them his deputy~~

in his absence out of Carolina
(3) And in case ~~there be~~ any of the proprietors hath not ∧ a
deputy in Carolina commissioned under his hand & seale, ye
eldest nobleman of his court shall of course be his deputy
~~in his absence out of Carolina.~~

55. In every county there shall be a court consisting of a sherrif & four justices of ye county, being inhabitants & having each of ym. at least five hundred acres of freehold within ye said county, to be chosen & com'issionated from time to time by ye Palatines Court, who shall trye and judge all ap'eals from any of the Precinct Courts.

56. For any p'sonall causes exceeding ye value of 200*l*., or in tytle of lands, or in any criminall cause, either party upon paying 20*l*. to ye proprietors use shall have liberty of appeal from ye county court unto ye respective Proprietors Court.

57. In every Precinct ~~Court~~ there shall be a court consisting of a steward & four justices of ye presinct, being inhabitants & haveing 300 acres of freehold within ye sd. presinct, who shall judge all criminall causes except for treason, murther, & any other

& all criminal causes of ye nobility,

qu.

offences punished with death ⌄ & all civill causes whatsoever and in all p'sonall actions not exceeding fifty pounds without appeal, but where ye cause shall exceed y^t value or concerne a title of land and in all criminall causes there, either party upon paying five pounds to the proprietors use shall have liberty of appeal unto ye County Court.

58. Noe cause shall be twice tryed in any one court upon any reason or pretence whatsoevr.

59. For treason, murther, & all other offences punishable wth. death, there shall be a Com'ission twice a year, at least, granted

grand

unto one or more members of the ⌄ council or colledges who shall come as itennerant judges to ye severall countyes & wth. ye sheriff & four justices shall hold assizes to judg all such causes. But upon paying of 50*l*. to ye proprietors use, there shall be liberty of appeall to ye respective Proprietors Court.

---

55. In every county there shall be a court consisting of a sherif & four justices of ye county court for every precinct one. The sherif shall be an inhabitant of the county, & have at least 500 acres of the freehold within the sd. county, & the justices shall be ~~each of them~~ inhabitants, & have each of them 500 acres apeice, in the precinct for wch. they serve respectively. These

chosen

5 shall be ⌄ commissioned from time to time by ye Palatine Court, ~~& shall trie & judge all appeales from any of the Precinct Courts.~~

60. The grand juryes at the severall assizes shall ~~have~~ upon their oathes & under their hands & seals deliver into the iternant judges a presentmt. of such greevances, misdemeanors, exigences, or defects, wch. they shall thinke necessary for ye publick good of ye contry wch. p'sentmt shall by ye itennerant judges at ye end of their circuit be deliver'd into ye grand councill at their next sitting, and whatsoever therein concernes ye execution of lawes already made ye severall Proprietors Courts in ye matters belonging to each of them respectively, shall take cognizance
of ∧ & ∧ such order about it as shall be effectuall for ye due exe-
   it give
cution of ye lawes; but whatever concernes ye makeing of any new lawes shall be referd. to ye severall respective courts to wch. yᵗ matter belongs, & by them prepared & brought to ye Grand Councill.

61. For termes there shall be quarterly such a certaine numbr. of dayes not exceeding 21, at any one time as ye severll. respec-tive courts shall appoint' of ye time for ye beginning ~~of~~ ye terme in ye Precinct Court, shall be ye first Munday in Jany., April, July, & October, & in the County Court ye first Munday of February, May, August, November, and in ye Proprieters Courts, the first Munday of March, June, September, & December.

62. ~~For jurys~~ in ye Presinct Court no man shall be jury a man under fifty acres of freehold. In ye County Court, or at the assizes, no man shall be a jury man under two hundred acres
quer of freehold. Noe man shall be a grand jury man under three hundred acres of freehold, & in ye Proprietors Courts, no man shall be a jury man under five hundred acres of freehold.

                      it   not
63. Every jury shall consist of 12 men, ∧ & ∧ shall ∧ be neces-sary they should all agree, but ye verdict shall be according to ye consent of the majorietie.

64. It shall be a base & vile thing to plead for mony or reward nor shall any one, except he be a neer kinsman not farther off yⁿ cousen german to ye party concern'd, be admitted to plead another man's cause till before ye judg in open court he hath taken an
                  not
q oath yᵗ he doth ∧ plead for mony. or reward, nor hath, nor will receive, nor directly nor indirectly bargain'd with the party

9

whose cause he is going to plead for any mony or other reward
for pleading his cause.

65. There shall be a Parliamt. consisting of ye proprietors or
their deputyes ye landgraves & cassiques & one freeholder out
of every presinct to be chosen by ye freeholders of ye sd. presinct
respectively.   They shall sit alltogether in one roome, & have
every member one vote.

66. No man shall be chosen a member of Parliamt. who hath
lesse then five hundred acres of freehold within ye presinct for
wch. he is chosen, nor shall any have a vote in choosing ye sd.
member, y^t hath lesse y^n fifty acres ~~within~~ of freehold within the
said presinct.

67. A new Parliamt. shall be assembled ye first Munday of the
month of November every 2d yeare, & shall meet & sit in the
towne they last sate in wth. out any sum'ons unless by ye palla-
tines $_{\wedge}$ ^{court} ~~or his deputy, together wth. any 3 of ye proprietors or
their deputyes~~ they be sum'oned to meet at any other place, &
if there shall be any occasion of a Parliamt. in these intervals, it
shall be in ye power of of ye ^{Palatin's Court} ~~palatine wth. $_{\wedge}$ any three of the
proprietors~~ to assemble them on forty dayes' notice at such time
~~Court~~ & place as ^{ye sd. court} ~~they~~ shall think fitt; & the Pallatines $_{\wedge}$ ^{Court} ~~or his deputy
wth. ye advice & consent of any three of ye proprietors or their
deputyes~~ shall have power to desolve ye sd. Parliamt. when they
shall thinke fitt.

68. At ye opening of every Parliamt. ye first thing that shall
be done shall be ye reading of these fundamentall constitutions
wch. ye pallatine & proprietors & ye rest of the members then
present shall subscribe.   Nor shall any person whatsoevr. sitt or
vote in ye Parliamt. till he hath y^t sessions subscribed these fundamental constitutions in a booke kept for y^t purpose by ye
clerke of ye Parliamt.

69. ~~And~~ in order to ye due election of members for this Bienniall Parliamt., it shall be lawfull for ye freeholders of ye respective presincts to meet ye first Tuesday in Sept. every two yeares
in ye same towne or place, y^t they last mett in to choose Parliament men and there choose those members, y^t are to sitt ye next
November following, unles ye steward of ye presinct shall by

sufficient notice thirty dayes before appoint some other place for their meeting in order to ye election.

70. No Act or order of Parliamt. shall be of any force unles it be ratified in open Parliamt. during ye same session by ye pallatine, or his deputy, and three more of the proprietors or their deputyes, and then not to continue longer in force, but untill ye end of ye next bieniall Parliamt. unles in ye meane time it be ratified under ye hand, & seale of ye pallatine himselfe, & three more of ye proprietors themselves, & by their order published at the next Bieniall Parliamt.

71. Any proprietor or his deputy may enter his protestacon. against any Act of ye Parliamt. before ye Pallatine or his deputyes consent be given as aforesaid, if he shall conceive ye sd. Act to be contrary to this establishmt. or any of these fundamentall constitutions of ye governmnt. & in such case after a full and free debate ye severall estates shall retire into four severall chambers, ye Pallatine & proprietors into one, the landgraves into another, ~~&~~ ye cassiques into another, & those chosen by ye

presincts unto a forth, & if ye major part of any _∧ four ~~of these~~ ^{of these}
estates shall vote y^t ye law is not agreeable to this establishment,

&   fundamentall constitution of ye Governmt. y^n it shall passe ^{these}
no further, but be as if it had never beene proposd. ✕

72. To avoyd multiplicity of lawes, wch. by degrees allwayes change, ye right foundacons, of ye original government, all acts of Parliamt. whatsoevr., in what forme soever past or enacted, shall, at ye end of sixty yeares after their enacting, respectively sease & determin of ym. selves, & without any repeal become null & voyd as if no such acts or lawes had ever been made.

73. Since multiplicity of com'ents as well as of lawes have great inco'veniences, & serve only to obscure and perplex, all maner of com'ents & expositions on any part of these fundamentall constitutions, or on any part of ye com'on or statute law of Carolina are absolutely prohibited.

✕ The quorum of ye Parlt. shalbe one halfe of those who are membrs. & capable of sitting in ye house y^t present session of Parlt., the quorum of each of ye chambers of Parlt. shalbe one halfe of ye members of that chamber.

74. There shall be a registry in every presinct wherein shall

mortgages

be enroll'd all deeds, leases, judgments, ∧ or other conveyances wch. may concerne any of ye land within ye said presinct, & all such conveyances not so enter'd or registred shall not be of force against any person not privy to ye sd. contract or conveyance.

75. No man shall be register of any presinct who hath not at least three hundred acres of freehold within ye sd. presinct.

76. The freeholders of every presinct shall nominate three men, out of wch. three the chiefe justice court shall choose & com'ission one to be register of ye sd. presinct, whilest he shall well behave himself.

signiory, barrony, &

77. There shall be a regestry in every ∧ collony, wherein shall be recorded all ye births, marriages & deaths that shall happen within ye sd. collony.

78. No man shall be register of a colony y^t hath not above fifty acres of freehold within ye sd. collony.

that is borne in Carolina

79. The time of every ones age ∧ shall be recorded from the day that his birth is entred in ye registry, and not before.

80. No mariage shall be lawfull, whatever contract or cere- monys they have used, till both the partyes mutually owne it before

where they were married

~~of the place where the woman dwells~~

ye ~~collony~~ register ~~&~~ ∧ he enter itt wth. ye names of ye father &

~~of~~ each

mother of ~~such~~ ∧ party.

81. No man shall administer to ye goods, or have right to them, or enter upon ye estate of any p'son deceased till his death

respective   be registerd in the ∧~~collony~~ registry.

respective   82. Hee y^t doth not enter in ye ∧ ~~collony~~ registry ye death or

or is borne

~~ponalty~~ birth of any person y^t dyes ∧ in his house or ground shall pay to ye Ld. Register one shilling p. weeke for each such ne- glect, reckoning from ye time of each death or birth respect- tively to ye time of registring it.

83. In like maner ye births, mariages, & deaths of ye lords proprietors, landgraves, and cassiques shall be registred in the Chamberlains Court.

84. There shall be in every collony one constable, to be chosen an'ually by ye freeholders of ye collony, his estate to be above

one hundred acres of freehold within ye sd. collony, & such

County

subordanate officers appointed for his assistance as ye ~~Presinct~~

sd. county

Court shall find requisit, & shall be establishd by ye ~~Presinct~~ ^
Court, ye election of the subordinate annual officr. shall be also
in ye freeholdrs of ye collony.

85. All townes encorporate shall be governed by a major,
twelve aldermen, and twenty-four of ye com'on council, ye sd.
com'on councll to be chosen by ye p'sent householders of ye sd.
towne, & ye aldermen to be chosen out of ye com'on council,
& ye major out of ye aldermen by ye Pallatins ~~& ye Proprietos~~.
court.

86. No man shall be permitted to be a free man of Carolina,
or to have any estate or habitation within it y' doth not acknowledge a God, & y' God is publickly and solemnly to be worshiped.

87. But since ye natives of y' place who will be concernd in
or. plantations are utterly strangers to Christianity, whose idoll-
atry, ignorance, or mistake gives us noe right to expell or use
ym. ill, & those who remove from other parts to plant there, will
unavoydably be of diffrent opinions concerning matters of
religion, ye liberty whereof they will expect to have allowed ym.,
& it will not be reasonable for us on this account to keep ym.
out y' civil peace may be maintaind amidst ye diversity of opinions,
& our agreement & compact with all men may be duly & faithfully
observed, ye violation whereof upon what p'tence soever, cannot
be without great offence to Almighty God, & great scandal to
the true religion y' we p'fesse, & also y' heathens, Jues, and other
disenters from the purity of Christian religion may not be scared
and kept at a distance from it, but by having an oppertunity of
acquainting themselves with ye truth & reasonablenes of its
doctrines, & ye peacablenes & inoffencivenes of its professors,

perswasion

may by good usage and ^ ~~preservacion~~, & all those convincing
methods of gentlenes & meeknes sutable to ye rules & designe
of the Ghospel, be wone over to imbrace and unfeynedly receive
ye truth. Therefore any seaven or more persons agreeing in
any religion shall constitute a church or profession to wch. they
shall give some name to distinguish it from others.

88. The termes of admittance & com'union with any church or profession shall be written in a booke, & therein be subscribed by all ye members of ye sd. church or profession.

89. The time of every ones subscription & admittance shall be dated in ye sd. booke or record.

90. In ye termes of com'union of every church or p'fession these following shall be three, without wch. noe agreement or assembly of men upon pretence of religion shall be acco'ted a church or profession within these rules.

   1. That there is a God.

   2. That God is publickly to be worshiped.

   3. ~~Thirdly.~~

That it is lawfull and ye duty of every man being thereunto calld by those y^t governe to bear witnes of truth, & that every church or profession shall in theire termes of com'union sett downe ye externall way whereby they witnes a truth as in ye presence of God, whether it be by laying hands on or kissing ye ~~Ghospel~~ ^{Bible} as in ye Protestant and Papist churches, or by holding up ye hand or any other sensible way.

91. No person above 17 yeares of age shall have any benefitt or protection of ye law or be capable of any place of profitt or honor. who is not a member of some church or profession, having his name recorded in some one & but one religion record at once.

92. The religious record of every church or pfession. shall be kept by the publick register of ye presinct where they reside.

93. No man of any other church or profession shall disturb or molest any religious assembly.

94. Noe p'son whatsoevr. shall speak anything in their religious assembly irreverently or sedistiously of ye Governmt. or governors or states mattrs.

95. Any p'son. subscribing ye termes of comunion of any church or profession in ye record of the sd. church before ye presinct register, and any ⁵ ~~one~~ members of the church or profession shall be thereby made a member of ye sd. church or p'fession.

96. Any p'son striking out his owne name out of any _^ ^{religious} record,

or his name being strook out by any officer thereunto authorized
<u>each</u>   <u>respectively</u>
by ~~any~~ church or p'fession ∧ shall cease to be a member of y^t
church or profession.

97. Noe p'son shall use any reproachfull revileing or abusive
language against ye religion of any church or profession y^t being
the certaine way of disturbing ye publick peace, & of hindring
ye coversion of any to ye truth by ingageing ym. in quarrills &
animosities to ye hatred of the professors & y^t profession wch.
otherwise they might be brought to assent to.

98. Since charrity obliges us to wish well to the souls of all
men, and religion ~~ough~~ ought to alter nothing in any mans civil
estate or right, It shall be lawfull for slaves as all others to enter
themselves & be of what church any of them shall thinke best,
& thereof be as fully members as any freemen.   But yet noe slave
shall hereby be exempted from that civill dominion his mastr.
hath ovr. him, but be in all other things in ye same state & condicon. he was in before.

99. Assemblyes upon what p'tence. soevr. of religion, not observing & performing ye above sd. rules, shall not be esteemd.
as churchs, but unlawfull meetings, & be punished as other
riotts.

100. No person whatsoevr. shall disturbe, molest, or p'secute
another for his speculative opinions in religion, or his way of
worshipp.
                                        <u>power &</u>
101. Every freeman of Carolina shall have absolute ∧ authority
ovr. his negro slaves of what opinion or religion soevr.

102. No p'son. whatsoever shall hold or claime any land in
Carolina by purchase or gift, or otherwise, from ye natives,
or any other p'son whatsoevr., but meerely from and under ye
Lds. proprietors upon paine of forfeiture of all his estate, move-
able or unmoveable, and perpetuall banishment.
                    <u>possesse</u>
103. Whoevr. shall ~~posse~~ any freehold in Carolina, upon what
title or grant soever, shall at ye farthist from and after ye yeare
1689 pay yearely unto ye proprietors, for each acre of land,
English measure, as much fine silver as is at this p'sent in one
English pen'y, or ye value thereof, to be as a cheif rent & ack-

nowledgment to ye proprietors & their heires and successors for ever, & it shall be lawfull for ye p'prietors by their officers at any time to take a new survey of any mans land, not to out him of any part of his possession, but y^t by such a survey the just number of acres he possesseth may be knowne, and ye rent thereupon due may be paid by him.

104. All wracks, mines, minerals, quarries, of ge'ms and prec-
pearle fishing,
ious stones, with whale fishing, ∧ and one half of all ambergreece by whomsoevr. found shall wholy belong to ye proprietors.

105. All revenues & p'fitts arising out of any thing but their distinct particular lands & possessions, shall be devided into ten parts, whereof ye Palatin shall have three, & each proprietor one, but if ye Pallatin shall governe by a deputy his deputy shall have one of those $\frac{3}{10}$, and the Palatin ye other $\frac{2}{10}$.

106 All inhabitants & freemen of Carolina above 17 yeares of age & under sixty shall be bound to bear armes & serve as soldiers whenevr. ye Grand Council shall find it necessary.

108. A true coppy of these fundamental constitutions shall be kept in a great book by ye regiser of every presinct to be subscribed before ye sd. register. Nor shall any person, of what condition or degree soever, above 17 yeares old, have any estate or possession in Carolina, or protection or benefit of ye law there, who hath not subscribed these fundamental constitutions in this forme.

I A. B. do promise to beare faith & true alleagence to or. Soveraigne Lord King Charles ye Second, and will be true & faith-
Palatin &
full to ye ∧ Lords Proprietors of Carolina, & with my utmost power will defend ym. and maintaine the Governmt, according to this establishment in these fundamtall. constitutions.

109. ~~And~~ whatsoever alien shall in this forme before any presinct register subscribe these fundamentall constitutions shall be thereby naturalizd.

110. In the same manner shall every p'son at his admittance into any office subscribe these fundamentall constitutions.
in number 111
111. These fundamentall constitutions & every part thereof

shall be & remaine as ye sacred unalterable forme and rule of Governmt. of Carolina for ever.   Witnes or. hands & seales this 21st die July in ye yeare of or. Lord 1669.[1]

[*Shaf. Pap.*, Sec. VIII, No. 3.] 33 *Report Dep. Keeper Public Records*, Appx. 3, p. 258.

GOVERNOR SAYLES' COMMISSION.[2]

July 26. 1669.

Geo. Duke of Albemarle, Cap^n Gen^ll of all his Maties forces, Edward, Earle of Clarendon, W^m, Earle of Craven, John, Ld Berkley, Anthony Ld Ashley, Chancell^r of ye Excheque^r, Sir Geo. Carteret, Barron^t: Vice Chamberlaine of his Maties House-hould, Sir Peter Colleton, Barronett, & Sr Wil. Berkeley, Kn^t.

To our trusty & Welbeloved Will. Sayle, Esq. Govern^r of all that Territory or parte of o^r Province of Carolina that lyes to ye Southward & Westward of Cape Carteret, & to our trusty & Well Beloved o^r Councll^rs & Assistants to our said Governo^r, Greeting—

---

[1] The original 'First set' of Fundamental Constitutions—conceived by Shaftesbury and drawn by Locke, 75 leaves, bound in vellum, entirely in Locke's hand.   In the year 1669 the Lords 'did encourage severall people to come in their Vessells to inhabitt this part of their province & with the said people did alsoe send (see *Sayle's Commission*) Funda-m^ll Lawes, Constitucons under the hands & Seales of six of their Lordshipps bearing date 21st July '69, as the unalterable forme & rule of Governm^t for ever.'   But in 1687 ' disputes having arisen in Carolina to the effect that certain constitutions dated 21 July 1669 are the only con-stitut^ns that can be in force,' declared them to be 'but a copy of an imperfect Originall;' though 'ye records in the secretarys office &c shew that nothinge betweene the L^ds Prop^rs & the people hath been transacted soe sacredly & with soe much solemn caution.'   *Rivers*, 418, 88, 116.

[2] 1662.   Petition of Captain Thomas Trafford to the King.   That Will Sayle, a severe separatist, surreptitiously possessed himself of the Government of the Bermudas and exercised cruel tyrannies over the inhabitants for which he was by the then Committee of Foreign Plantations adjudged fit for banishment.   But by the exorbitant power of Desbrow and Jones, two persons proscribed by Parliament who were sent thither, Sayle was settled in the government.   Prays to be sent over to take it. (Captain Florentia Seymour was appointed to succeed Sayle as governor, Sept., 1662.)   *A. & W. I., ₴ 372.*

10

Bee it knowne unto all men that Wee ye L^{ds} & absolute Pro-
prieto^{rs} of ye Province afores^{d}, for divers good causes & consideracons, but more especially out of ye trust & confidence reposed
in yo^{u} o^{r}. s^{d} Governo^{r} & Councello^{rs}, for ye faithfull managem^{t} of
ye power & authority by us to yo^{u} given to ye best availe & im-
provem^{t} of o^{r} Interest & Dominion in ye Territory afores^{d}, have
given granted & by theise presents doe give & grant dureing
o^{r} pleasure unto yo^{u}, o^{r} s^{d} Goveno^{r} by & wth ye consent of o^{r}
Councell, or any sixe of ye tenn, Whereof three at least are to
be of those appointed by us as o^{r} Deputys, full & absolute power
& authority for us & in o^{r} names, to lett, sell, convey & assure
such Lands in o^{r} s^{d} County, to such person & persons & for such
Estate & Estates, & wth such Provizos, Condicons & Limitacons
as we by o^{r} Instruccons & Concessions, hereunto annexed, have
directed & as yo^{u} shall be directed by such other Instrucons &
rules as from time to time yo^{u} shall receive from us & not otherwise, hereby rattifying & confirming whatever y^{u} shall doe pursuant to ye s^{d} Instruccons & Concessions & to such Instruccons,
Rules and Direccons as afores^{d}, as alsoe to make, doe performe
and execute all & singuler act & acts, thing & things, powers &
authoritys whatsoever, wch Wee o^{r}selves may, cann might or
could doe in, for, conserning or relateing to ye Goverment, both
Civill and Millitary, of ye s^{d} Terretory, by vertue of ye Lett^{rs}
Pattents of his most Excellent Matie, Charles ye Second, King of
England, Scotland & Ireland, Defend^{r} of ye faith, bearing date
at Westminster, ye 20th day of June, in ye 17th yeare of his
raigne, to be exercised nevertheless according to such Instruccons, & wth such Limittations, Restriccons, Condicons & Provisoes as are hereunto annexed, & in these presents are hereafter
contained.   Hereby ratifying & confirming & allowing all &
every such act & acts, thing & things, wch o^{r} s^{d} Govern^{r} & o^{r} s^{d}
Councello^{rs} in o^{r} names shall doe in ye premises, pursuant to ye
authority hereby comitted, & wch is not contrary to o^{r} Instruccons, and o^{r} fundamentall constitucons & forme of Goverm^{t} here-
wth sent under o^{r} hands & seales.   Provided alsoe, y^{t} ye Execu-
tive parte of all ye s^{d} Powers herein given shall be made & exercised by yo^{u}, o^{r} s^{d} Governo^{r} by & wth ye advice & consent of
ye maio^{r} parte of our Councell.   And if it shall happen that o^{r}
s^{d} Governo^{r} shall depart or be absent at any time from our Terretory afores^{d}, unless other provision be by us made, That then

it shall & may be lawfull for o[r] s[d] Governo[r] by ye advice & approbation of ye maio[r] parte of his Councell, under his hand & seale, to nominate & appoint a Deputy, Giveing & Granting unto ye person soe appointed, as full, large & ample powers as wee, by theise presents unto o[r] s[d] Governo[r] have given, anything in this present Comission in anywise to ye Contrary notw[th]standing.   And if in case o[r] s[d] Governo[r] should happen to dye or departe w[th]out nominateing any person to be his Deputy, Wee doe then give & Grant unto o[r] s[d] Councell full power & authority to appointe some person to be Governo[r] till o[r] pleasure be further knowne therein, & signifyed to ye contrary.   And ye person soe appointed shall have ye same power to all intents & purposes as was by this present Comission granted unto o[r] Governo[r] soe dead or departed.   Given under o[r] hands & ye Great Seale of o[r] Province, this 26th day of July 1669.   [*Col. Ent. Book*, 20, pages 41, 42]   *Rivers S. C.*, page 340.[1]

COPPY OF INSTRUCCONS ANNEXED TO YE COMISSION FOR YE GOVERN[r] & COUNCELL.

27 July, 1669.

In regard ye number of people w[ch] will at first be sett downe at Port Royall, will be soe small, together wth want of Landgraves & Cassiques, that it will not be possible to putt o[r] Grand

----

[1] This commission was sent in blank and Sayle's name put in at Bermuda by Sir Jno. Yeamans. Colonel William Sayle, of Bermuda, being in England, 1646, procured a patent for planting the Bahamas, fitted a ship, sailed to Bermuda and thence, 1648 (with Rev. Patrick Copeland aud seventy more of his covenant), to the Bahamas, were there wrecked, and after sore privations Sayle with eight more sailed in a shallop to Virginia, and returning removed his friends to Bermuda again (p. 3).   There he became governor but was superseded by Captain Seymour in 1662.   The Carolina touching at Bermuda, February, 1670, Yeamans named Sayle as governor in his stead, 'a man of no great sufficiency yet the best I could get'—experienced 'in several places' but old and weak, 'a zealot, an independent these 24 years.'   His son Nathaniel attended him to Carolina.   There, weak with ague and age, he forsook Port Royal, allowed disorder and waste, shewed poor spirit against the Spaniards and did 'several things ill.'   December, 1670, Brayne left him sick and wished him safe in his own house at Bermuda again.   At noon, March 4, 167$\frac{0}{1}$, he died 'at least 80 years old' and West was chosen governor.

Modell of Goverm[t] in practice at first, and that notw[th]standing wee may come as nigh ye afores[d] Modell as is practicable.

1. As soone as yo[u] arrive at Port Royall yo[u] are to summon all ye freemen that are in ye Collony, And require them to elect five persons who being joyned to ye five deputed by ye respective Propriet[rs], are to be ye Counsell wth whose advice & consent, or at least sixe of them, all being summoned, yo[u] are to governe according to the Limitacon & Instruccons following, observing what cann at present be putt in practice of our fundamentall Constitutions & forme of Goverm[t].

2. Yo[u] are to cause all ye persons soe chosen to sweare Allegeance to o[r] Soveraigne L[d] the King, & subscribe fidellity & submission to ye Proprietors & ye forme of Goverm[t] by them established. But in case any man for Religeon's sake be not free to sweare, then shall he subscribe ye same in a Booke for that use Provided, w[ch] shall be deemed ye same wth swearing.

3. Yo[u] & yo[r] Councell are to choose some fitting place whereon to build a Fort under ye protection of w[ch] is to be yo[r] first Towne, placeing yo[r] houses soe as ye Gunns of y[r] Fortes may command all yo[r] Streets. 4. Within this Forte is to be kept all yo[r] Stores of all sorts.

5. If yo[u] place yo[r] first Towne on an Island, that whole Island shall be divided into Collonyes, & reserved for ye use of ye people, & suffer no Signiory or Barrony to be taken up in it. But if yo[u] plant yo[r] towne on ye maine, then shall ye sixe next adjoining Squares of twelve thousand acres be all Collonyes, soe that the people may at first plant together in convenient numbers.

6. Yo[u] are not to suffer anyone to take up lands w[th]in two miles and a halfe of any Indian Towne, if it be of ye same side of a River, we hopeing in time to draw ye Indians into o[r] Goverm[t]. And would have ye quantity of a Barrony left about every Cassiques house or Towne.

7. Yo[u] are by & w[th] ye consent of yo[r] Councell, to establish such Courts, and so many as yo[u] shall for ye present thinke fitt for ye administracon of Justice till our Grand Modell of Goverm[t] cann come to be putt in execution.

8. Yo[u] are to sumon ye freehoulders of ye Collony & require y[m] in our names to elect twenty persons, w[ch] together wth o[r] Deputys for ye present are to be y[r] Parliament, by & wth whose consent

or ye maio[r] parte of them, yo[u] are to make such laws as yo[u] shall from time to time finde necessary w[ch] laws being rattifyed by yo[u] & any three of o[r] five Deputys, shall be in force as in that case provided in the 12th & other Articles of o[r] fundamentall Constitucons & forme of Goverm[t].

9. Yo[u] are to take notice that we doe grant unto all free persons above the age of sixteene yeares y[t] doe come to Port Royall to plant before the 25th day of March, 150 Acres of land for themselves & 150 Acres more for every able man Serv[t] they bring wth them or cause to be transported into the s[d] Collony. And 100 Acres for every Woman Serv[t] and Man Serv[t] under 16 yeares of age. And one hundred Acres to any Serv[t] when out of their time to his or her owne proper use.

10. To every free person that shall there arrive to plant & inhabitt before ye 25th day of March 1671, one hundred Acres. And 100 acres more for each man Serv[t] they bring wth them or cause to be transported into ye s[d] Collony, And 70 Acres for each Woman Serv[t] or Man Serv[t] under sixteene yeares of age. And to every serv[t] that shall arrive before ye time last menconed, seaventy acres to his or her proper use for them & their heirs forever.

11. To every free person that shall there arrive before ye 25th day of March 1672, wth an intent to plant seaventy acres, and 70 Acres more for each man Serv[t] they carry wth them And 60 acres for each woman Serv[t] or man Serv[t] under 16 yeares of age. And to every Serv[t] that shall arrive before ye time last menconed, seaventy acres to his or her proper use for them & their heires for ever when there time of servitude is expired.

12. Yo[u] are to cause ye Land to be laid out in Squares containeing each 12,000 Acres, every of w[ch] Squares that shall be taken up by a Propriet[r] is to be a Signiory. And each Square that shall be taken up by a Landgrave or Cassique is to be a Barrony, and each of those squares w[ch] shall be taken up or planted on by any of the people shall be a Collony, And reserved wholly for ye use of ye people as they come to setle, keeping the proporcon of twenty-fower Collonyes to eight Signiorys & eight Barronyes.

13. Yo[u] are to order ye people to plant in Townes, And one Towne at least in each Collony soe ordering & laying out the Townes as yo[u] & yo[r] Councell shall thinke most convenient &

profitable for ye people y^t are to inhabitt them.   Yo^u are not to
suffer ye Inhabitants of any of ye Collonyes to have a greater
proporcon of front of their Land to ye River then a fifth parte
of his depth.

14. Any person haveing brought Serv^{ts}, to plant shall make
ye same appeare to y^{r}selfe & Councell who shall thereupon issue
out a War^t to ye Surveyo^r Genner^{ll} to lay him out a parcell of
Land according to ye proporcons menconed in theise o^r Instruccons.   And ye Surveyo^r haveing done ye same, And ye War^t
wth ye Surveyo^r Gen^{rlls} returne thereon being recorded.   And ye
person to whom this Land is granted, haveing sworne or subscribed Allegiance to o^r Soveraigne L^d ye King, And fidellity &
submission to ye L^{ds} Propriet^{rs}. And ye fundamentall Constitucons & forme of Goverment yo^u are und^r ye Seale (for that use
provided,) to pass this following Grant:

Geo: Duke of Albemarle, Captn Gen^{ll} of all his Maties Forces,
Edward, Earle of Clarendon, William, Earle of Craven, John L^d
Berkley, Anthony Ld Ashley, Chancell^r of ye Exchequer, Sr Geo.
Carterett, Baron^t Vice-Chamberlaine of his Maties Household, S^r
Peter Colleton, Bar^t & Sir William Berkeley, Kn^t, The true and
absolute Lords and Proprieto^{rs} of ye Province of Carolina, Doe
hereby Grant unto A B, of the County of   in ye Province
of   a plantacon in ye Towne of   in ye county
afores^d containeing   Acres English measure, bounded
to have and to hould to himselfe, his heires & assignes forever,
yeilding or paying to ye s^d George, Duke of Albemarle, Edward, Earle of Clarendon, William, Earle of Craven, John L^d
Berkley, Anthony Ld Ashley, Sr Geo. Carterett, Sr Peter Colleton & Sr William Berkley L^{ds} Prop^{rs} as afores^d their heires & assignes, every 29th day of Septr wch shall be aft^r the 29th day of
Septr 1689, one penny of lawfull English mony or ye vallew thereof, for every of ye s^d Acres to be houlden in free & common Soccage Given under ye Great Seale of   ye day of
in ye yeare of o^r Lord   This Grant yo^u & three more of your
Councell are to signe, and cause to be recorded in the Register
Office, ye wch shall then be deemed a full & firme Conveyance of
ye Land therein menconed, unto ye person unto whom it is
granted & his heires & assignes forever, he paying ye rent &c.

15. We haveing sent a stocke of Victualls, Cloathes & Tooles
for ye supply of those people, who through Poverty have not

beene able to supply themselves sufficiently for such an enterprize, to prevent abuses in ye distribucon whereby one may come
to want, & another have too much, yo[u] & ye maio[r] part of o[r]
Deputys by direccon in wrighting, are to order o[r] Storekeeper
how much of each sort shall be delivered weekly to ye respective persons, wherein yo[u] are to have speciall regard to those
that are not able to furnish themselves.

Yo[u] & ye Maio[r] parte of o[r] Deputys, are by o[r] Order in wrighting to direct o[r] Storekeeper how much of ye Indian trade sent
shall be delivered to any of ye Indian Cassiques to purchase their
friendshipp & allyance, Wherein wee desier yo[u] to be as good
husbands as may be, that there may be left a considerable store
to answer all Emergencyes, And never lett ye Indians know what
quantity yo[u] have, it haveing been observed to be prejudiciall to
those that have suffered them to see all their Store.   July 27th
1669. [*Col. Ent. Book*, 20, pages 43, 46.] *Rivers S. C.*, page
347.

COPPY OF M[r] WEST'S[1] COMMISSION AS COMAND[r] IN CHEEFE.

27 July, 1669.

George Duke of Albemarle, Capt[n] Genn[ll] of all His Ma[ties] For-
ces, Edward, Earle of Clarendon, William, Earle of Craven, John
L[d] Berkeley, Anthony L[d] Ashley, Chancell[r] of the Exchequer, Sir
Geo. Carteret Bar[t], Vice Chamberlaine of his Ma[ties] Household,
S[r] Peter Colleton, Bart., & S[r] William Berkeley Kn[t], the true &
absolute L[ds] & Propriet[rs] of Carolina.

To our trusty & welbeloved Joseph West, Greeting—We doe
hereby constitute & appoint yo[u] during o[r] pleasure, Governo[r] &
Commander in Cheife of o[r] fleet & ye persons embarqued in it,
bound for Carolina, or that shall embarque in our s[d] fleet before
its arriveall in Barbados; over w[ch] yo[u] are to place officers & cause
them to be duely exercised in Armes, and to doe all & every
other thing or things w[ch] unto y[r] Charge of a Coman[r] in Cheife belongeth.   And wee by virtue of his Mai[ties] Letters Pattents, bearing date at Westminster, ye 20th of June, in ye 17th yeare of his

---

[1] Captain West, 'a moderate, just, pious & valiant person,' Cassique,
Landgrave, and three times Governor of Carolina, 'to whom we chiefly
owe the settlem[t],' and for near twenty years the chief man there. See
Rivers, 92, 140.

Raigne, have power to Grant, Comanding all inferio[r] Officers of o[r] s[d] fleet & forces yo[u] to obey as their Comand[r] in Cheife, according to this o[r] Comission, & ye powers thereby given unto yo[u]. And yo[u], yo[r]selfe, alsoe are to observe & follow such order & directions as from time to time you shall receive from us. And in all things to governe y[r]selfe as unto ye duty & place of a Govern[r] & Comand[r] in Cheife doth belong, w[ch] place yo[u] are to execute till another Govern[r] for y[t] parte of o[r] Province y[t] lyes to ye Southward or Westward of Cape Carterett shall appeare w[th] Comission under o[r] hands & Great Seale of o[r] Province, to whom you are then to submitt, & this Comission to become voyd to all intents & purposes. Given under o[r] hands & ye Greate Seale of o[r] Province this 27th July 1669. [*Col. Ent. Book* 20, page 39,] *Rivers*, page 342.

COPPY OF INSTRUCCONS FOR MR. JOSEPH WEST.

M[r] West, Yo[u] are wth all possible speed to saile wth ye fleete under yo[r] comand for Kinsaile, in Ireland, Where yo[u] are to endeavor to gett twenty or twenty-five Serv[ts], for our proper account & as soone as yo[u] have gotten them on board yo[u] are to saile directly to Berbados & yo[u] are not to suffer any person whatsoever to putt one Serv[t] on Board o[r] Shipps, till o[r] number be compleated.

Yo[u] are to take ye best order yo[u] cann wth yo[r] Shipps to avoid loosing one another att Sea & appoint what shall be done by each Vessell in case they loose yo[r] Company.

If any Passenger that is ye Master of a Family should dye att sea & leave no Executo[r], or should leave ye Shipp, his Servants are to be reserved to ye use of ye Propriet[rs], it being they that pay theire passage, & by consequence have most right to them; w[ch] Serv[ts] you are to imploy in prepareing loading of timber & other materials for o[r] Shipps.

When yo[u] are at Kinsaile yo[u] are to apply y[r]selfe to M[r] Southwell[1] & M[r] Thomas Gookin for ye procureing of yo[r] Ser[ts], &

----

[1] Mr. Robert Southwell, father of Sir Robert, a merchant there, and probably Mayor or 'Sovereign.'

also use ye assistance of Capt. O'Soolivan.[1]   And haveing staid   dayes at Kingsaile, and not haveing compleated yor number, & findeing noe likelyhood to doe it, though yo^u should stay a day or two longer, yo^u are to saile wth ye first opertunity to Berbados.   Yo^u are to suffer noe freeman y^t hath noe Serv^{ts} on board to goe out of ye Shipp, unlesse he give very good security for his returne.

Yo^u are not to suffer any man whether Seaman or Passenger, to take his Serv^{ts} on shoare at Barbados, unlesse he give bond in double of vallew for their returne on board againe.   Yo^u are to give Orders to ye Comanders of our Shipps to obey this rule, who are hereby required to obey the said Orders.   [*Col. Ent. Book*, 20, page 38.]   *Rivers*, page 342.

COPPY OF INSTRUCCONS FOR Mr WEST ABOUT O^r PLANTACON.

Mr West, God sending yo^u safe to Barbados, yo^u are there to furnish y^{r}selfe wth Cotton seed, Indigo Seed, Ginger Roots, wch roots yo^u are to carry planted in a tubb of earth, y^t they may not dye before yor arrivall att Port Royall; alsoe yo^u may in another tubb carry some Canes planted for a tryall—alsoe of ye severall sorts of vines of that Island & some Ollive setts; all wch will be procured yo^u by Mr Thomas Colleton, if yo^u applye yo^{r}selfe to him.

When yo^u arrive at Port Royall yo^u are in some convenient

---

[1] Petition of Captains John Staplehill and Florence O'Sullivan to the King.   That Petitioners each raised a company of foot in Barbadoes at their own cost by commission from Lord Francis Willoughby for the expedition to St. Christopher's, and being on board the Bachelor and Coventry, seized two great French ships at Todos Santos, near Gaudaloupe, but by a fatal hurricane were forced ashore with their prizes. After defending themselves eleven days against M. De Lyon, Governor of Gaudaloupe, they were forced from want of ammunition to yield; were prisoners eleven months at Gaudaloupe, then sent to France and forced to give engagements to pay 260 livres.   Have attended five months, and destitute of friends and money; pray for a timely supply to preserve them from perishing and enable them to pay their debts and be further serviceable to his Majesty.   (Endorsed.)   Read in Council April 20.   Brought in May 1, 1668.   July 1 (ordered) Governor of Barbadoes to pay them £20 to gratify them for their service.   Petition of same, July 10, praying present payment.   *A. & W. I.*, 1740, 1789.

place on one side of ye Towne & where it may be least Inconvenient to ye people, to take up as much land for our uses as our
proporcon will come to at 150 Acres p^r head of 30 Serv^{ts}, & in
yor land lett there be some marsh, and not much, ye rest to be
of as many varietys of soyle as may be. amongst wch be sure
there be some Sandy land.   Our reason for this is that being
unacquainted wth ye nature of ye soyle, we shall have conveniency of trying wch sort of soile agrees best wth ye severall things
plant^d in them.   On this Land yo^u are to cause to be erected
convenient houseing for yo^{r}selfe & yor Servants, makeing them
warme & tyte, wch is a great meanes of preventing sickness.
Theise houses you are soe to place that upon ye devision of o^r
Land each man may have a share of y^m.   As soon as yor houses
are built, yo^u are to sett yor people to falling and clearing yor
land to make it fitt to plant against ye Seasons come, not forgetting to putt yor Ginger & Canes into ye Ground as soone as yo^u
arrive, for feare they dye—both of wch love a rich soyle & light
mould, in wch sort plant them Yo^r seeds yo^u are to keep till March
& y^n plant some of y^m in Sandy land, some in light black mould
y^t lyes high, & some in land that lyes low; doe ye same againe
in Aprill, ye same in May & June, by wch meanes yo^u will come
to finde wch soyle agrees best wth every specie planted, & what
is ye properest time to plant in.   Yo^u are to doe ye same as to
ye soyle wth yor vine & Ollive Plants, & this will be done wth a
man or two; ye rest of yor people are to be employed about
planting Indian Corne, Beanes, Pease, Turnipps, Carretts &
Potatoes for Provisions.   The proper season to plant Corne &
Beanes & Pease yo^u will be informed by ye Natives; ye others
will thrive at any time, & y^u are never to thinke of makeing any
Comodity yor buisiness further than for experience sake & to
have yor stock of it for planting encrease till yo^u have sufficiently
provided for ye belly by planting store of provissions wch must
in all your contrivances be looked upon by yo^u as ye foundation
of yor Plantacon.   Iff yo^u have time yo^u may fence in a small
peece of ground for ye reception of ye Cattle we shall cause to
be brought from Virginia, and to putt them in all night.

   Yo^u are alwayes to have one or more to looke after yor Catle,
who must bring them home at night, & putt them in yor enclosed Ground, otherwise they will grow wild & be lost.

   Yo^r Grape vines plant in a Sandy mould & drye, & as soone as they will afford other Slipps plant them alsoe y^t yo^u may increase yor stock of plants.

As soon as yor Ginger is ripe yo^u are to digg itt, & plant as much ground wth it as that will fill, that yo^u may increase yor stock.   The manner any planter of Barbados will shew you.   And if yo^u finde that Ginger thrives well, that is to be ye first Comodity you are to fall upon, When you have sufficiently provided for victuall.

Yo^r Cotton & Indigo[1] is to be planted where it may be sheltered from ye North West Winde, for they are both apt to blast. Iff any of yor Shipps touch at Bermudas, order them to bring from thence ollive Plants & Stones, But noat that sticks cutt & planted like Osiers come to perfection, & beare sooner by seaverall yeares then plants from ye Stone.

Yo^u are from time to time to give us acc^o of yor proceedings herein, how much land yo^u have fallen, what yo^u have planted, & how every specie thrives, alsoe what Catle yo^u have rec^d from Virginia, how many Calves yo^u have every yeare, And what quantity of Hoggs, Sheep &c, and what yo^u want.

Yo^u may take from Barbados halfe a doz. young Sows & a Boare, wch will be furnished yo^u by Mr Thomas Colleton, iff you shall not have enough left to doe it of ye thirty pounds p^d yo^u to carry to Ireland.

When you come to Port Royall yo^u are to take what care you cann to helpe y^t of our Shipps that returnes to Barbados to a loading of timber &c.

Yo^u are in all things to consult, advize & communicate wth Mr John Rivers, Agent for ye Lord Ashley.   And wth Mr Agent for Sr Peter Colleton, That they may be able to give a particuler account of all transactions there.   [*Col. Ent. Book* 20, page 34, 35.]   *Rivers S. C.* 344.

———

Copy of Instructions to Mr. Joseph West, Storekeeper.

Mr. Joseph West, you are to cause to bee erected within o^r Fort at Port Royall 2 houses wch are not to bee thached, in one of

---

[1] Locke wrote for Lord Ashley a treatise on culture of vines and olives and silk. Cotton, indigo, and tobacco were tried and did well, *S. P.*, 44, 56. 'Indico like to be a comodity 1671' & 1673, tobacco was so.

wch you are to putt o^r Stores of Warr, in the other, the Victualls, Cloathes, Tooles &c.

The key of that in wch our Stores of Warr, you are to deliver unto Mr John Rivers, who is to have the charge hereof, you are to make an Inventory of all you deliver him & take his rec^t thereon.

You are to deliver such quantitys of the Indian trade for presents to the Indian Kings, as o^r Govern^r & any three of o^r Deputys, if so many bee alive in Carolina shall direct you, the residue you are to lye out in Victuall & other necessarys for the use of the Colony, takeing rec^t from every man for what you furnish him. You are weekly to deliver to such persons as o^r Governour & any three of o^r deputys, if so many bee alive in Carolina shall direct you, the following proportion of victuals & no more, vis: to every three men 9 lb. of beef & 14 q^{ts} of pease, or if they will not have pease then 14 lb. of flower, or 14 lb. of oatmeale, or tenn pounds & three quarters of bread, or some of the one & some of the other, as your stores of the respective spetie shall hould out, not exceeding this proportion to any man. You are to deliver the cloathes tooles & fishing trade wee have provided, to such men as the Govern^{or} & any 3 of o^r Deputys, if so many bee alive in Carolina shall direct you, still keeping enough for the use of o^r owne plantation.

You are not to deliver to any man a double proportion of any thing nor no more than is necessary for him. If you finde that there is a want of cloathes or Rugs, you are then wth your Indian trade to buy skins to suply that defect.

You are to keep exact acc^{ts} of what you deliver to every man, takeing his rec^t for the same & once in 3 mo^s to accompt wth every man & take his obligation under hand & seale, to pay unto Geo. D. of A. W. Earle of Cr., John Ld B., A. Ld A., Sr Geo. C. & Sr P. C., what shall bee then due unto them wth 10 p^r C^t interest for the time it shall remain unpaid, wch obligations are to bee made beefore the register, who is to record the same.

In regard there is no mony in Carolina, you are in ye accompting to recon upon such Comodityes as the Country doth produce, & vallue the goods at the rate they cost us in England, recconning the Comodityes at the rates following, viz: Ginger scalded at 2^d the lb.; scraped Ginger at 3^d p^r lb:, Indigo at 3^s p^r lb.; Silke, at 10 s. the lb.; Cotton, at 3½^d p^r lb.; Wine, at 2 s:

the G[ll]; Oye Olive, at 3 s the G[ll]; Wax at 9[d] the lb.; pype staves at a halfe penny p[r] stave; and in any of these comodityes are you to receive o[r] debts at the rates specified above. You are as nigh as you can to observe what is loaden on o[r] ships from Port Royall for any other port, & also what shall bee brought in any of o[r] ships into Carolina, how many passengers, what goods, & for whose acc[o] of w[ch] you are from time to time to give us notice, & also how the Com[drs] of o[r] Ships doe beehave themselves. If it should happen that so many of o[r] Deputyes should dye or depart out of Carolina, that there should not bee three there, then are you to observe the orders for the delivery of the Indian trade, provizions, &[e] that shall bee from time to time given you by o[r] Governo[r], & so many of o[r] Deputys as are alive & in Carolina. [*Col. Ent. Book* 20, page 31, 32.] *Rivers*, page 350.

INSTRUCTIONS FOR M[r] HENRY BRAINE.

M[r] Henry Braine, You are under the Comand of M[r] Joseph West, (whom wee have apointed Com[dr] in Chief of o[r] fleet till their arrivall at Barbados) to saile to Kinsale in Ireland, & from thence to Barbados as hee shall direct and order you, & when you are at Barbados, you are to observe the orders of o[r] Governour for your proceedings to Port Royall, And to returne from Port Royall to Barbados or to Virginia as you shall bee directed by S[r] John Yeamans, M[r] Thomas Colleton & Majo[r] Kingsland,[1] & there take in passengers & other fraught for Port Royall: if you goe to Virginia you are to apply yo[r]selfe to M[r] William Burgh, in Chocatuck Creek, in James River, in whose hands you shall finde instructions what you are to doe; if you come to Barbados, you are to deliver what goods you shall bring from Port Royall for the Proprietors acc[o] to M[r] John Hallet,[2] & take his &

---

[1] Nathaniel K., a large planter in Surinam and Barbadoes, member assembly Christ church 1666–76, with 340 a. '79. In 1671 Halsted recommends him for Governor of Carolina.

[2] Commissioner Jamaica emigration 1664, and an eminent merchant and planter in Barbadoes, with 300 acres 1673. Treasurer of the Tobago fund and a justice. 1674 Major of guards receives the new governor. 1675 Comptroller. Saltodudos is Salt Tortugas.

M[r] Thomas Colletons advice for your proceedings from thence, either to Saltordudos & Virginia, or to Virginia directly, or back to Port Royall.

When you are at Port Royall, you are to Consult wth M[r] West, & o[r] Governo[r] there, to what port you shall goe from thence, & are to saile to that port that any two of you there shall agree on, all being present at the consultation, if alive.

You are from time to time to send us an acc[o] of your proceedings, what fraught your ship hath made, & what you have delivered into the hands of o[r] Factors or any of o[r] Agents. [*Col. Ent. Book*, 20, page 33.] *Rivers*, page 345.

Coppy of Instruccons to M[r] John Rivers.[1]

M[r] John Rivers, yo[r] are to take charge of o[r] Storehouse att Port Royall containeing o[r] Materialls of Warr, and are from time to time to deliver out such quantity of Guns, Powder Shott & other Stores, as ye Govern[r] and Councill shall direct yo[u] by their order in wrighting and not otherwise, except it be some powder & birding Shott for ye use of o[r] Plantacon. Yo[u] are to keepe account of what Gunns, Powder & fowling Shott, yo[u] doe by order of ye Governo[r] & Councell deliver to any one, and take ye persons rec[t] for ye same for whom you deliver it, The w[ch] Receipt to avoid multiplicity of acc[ts]; yo[u] are to deliver to M[r] West, who is to charge ye s[d] Party wth it in his Books & account wth him for ye same. [*Col. Ent. Book*, 20, page 37.] *Rivers*, page 345.

M[r] O'Sullivan's Com'n as Surv[r] Gen:

George Duke of Albemarle, Capt: Generall of all his Majesties forces Pallatine, Edward Earle of Clarendon William Earle of Craven John Lord Berkley, Anthony Lord Ashley Chancellers of the Excheq[r] S[r] George Carteret vice Chamberlain of His Majesties Household and S[r] Peter Colleton Barronet, the True and Absolute Lords and Propriators of All the Province of Carolina in America,

---

[1] Kinsman of Lord Ashley. Sent to Carolina as his agent. Was taken by the Spaniards at St. Katherines, May, 1670, and imprisoned at St. Augustine until freed by the intercession of the Spanish Ambassador. He returned to England.

To our trusty and well beloved Florence O'Sullivan[1] of Saint
Margarett Westminster Gent: Greeting:

Wee being well assured of your wisdom, prudence and integrity have thought fitt and doe by these presents, nominate constitute and appoint you Our Surveyor Generall of the Province
aforesaid during our pleasure as by yourself or such as you shall
depute appointe & commissionate to lay out bounds and survey
with chayne and other Instruments, all alliotments and parcells
of land generall or particular, publick or private whether relating to us particularly or to other persons by grant from us according to such warrants and directions as you shall from time
to time receive from us our Governor and Councill of our province aforesaid or the major part of them as Also true Certificates
to make of the scituations bounds quantities and lines of all
lands soe laid out, mentioning the persons for whome and the
order you received for soe doeing the coppy of which certificates
you shall in faire writing register and record in your office in its
true figure, with the name of the righte owners of such Ground
is laid out by virtue of the respective warrant from our Governor
and Councill within our province of Carolina aforesaid Soe that
upon any difference or controversy in Tytles of land as to its
first settlement and inhabiting And as to the finding out the first
right owners it may be more easily discussed And these and all
other act or acts, thing or things which doe may or shall belong
or in any wayes appertayne to the office of our Surveyor Generall within within the said Province, you are faithfully to doe and
performe according to such orders and instructions as you shall
receive from us the Lords Proprietors or our Governor or Gov-

---

[1] An Irish soldier of fortune. Served in West Indies 1666. Taken
prisoner to France and when released joined this expedition and was
appointed deputy and surveyor-general. 'A very dissentious, troublesome man,' 'shamed of nothing,' his plausibility could not cover his
incompetence and ill practices. He was dismissed as deputy, had to
share his surveyorship with Culpeper and then lost it. He was chosen
to parliament 1672. Wa; an officer of militia 1672-76, and May, 1674,
had charge of a signal gun on the island which still bears his name. He
was arrested in the Culpeper disturbances, but was Commissioner of
Public Accounts 1682-3. The proprietors granted him 2,340 acres in
Christ Church which he devised to his daughter Katherine, who sold to
John Barksdale. In 1692 Daniel Carty left £5 'to Katherine Sullivan,
dau^r & orphan of fflorence O'Sullivan, dec'd.'

ernors and Councill or the major part of them to the best of your judgment and skill And for your doeing the same or any of them you shall receive such salaries fees and perquisites as by us and our Governor and Council of the said Province or the major part of them shall be appointed And all such privileges & liberties as to the Office or place of Surveyor Generall doth belong or appertayne according to the Generall Costume, or most approved usage of other plantations of his Majesties subjects. Given under our hands and the Great Seale of our Province of Carolina in the one and twentieth year of our Sovereign Lord Charles the Second by the Grace of God of England France and Ireland King, Defender of the Faith &c Anno Dom: one thousand six hundred and sixty and nine.

Albemarle   Craven   Jo. Berkley
Ashley   P. Colleton.

This is a true copy of the original.

Exam^d this 28th October 1671 ℔.   Jos. Dalton Secr.

[*S. C. Coun. Jour.*, page 54.] [1]

Rivers Accompts.

		£.	s.	d.
July { 16. received of Mr Thomas South	. .	10	00	0
24. received of him againe	. . .	05	00	0

Laide out.

		£.	s.	d.
For 2 Shirts and a p^r of Drawers	. . .	01	02	0
For 1 paire of Shooes	. . . . .	00	16	0
For 1 Hatt and band	. . . . .	00	06	6
For Water hire to Wapen .	. . . .	00	06	6
For Water hire to Bugbies hole 4 times	. .	00	18	0
Paid to Mr Miller for a boy	. . . .	00	19	0
Paide to Mr Wote for bringing to me a bricklaier and a Blackmore	. . . . . .	00	11	0
For my lodging for 3 weekes	. . . .	00	01	6
For 3 paire of worsted stockins .	. . .	00	15	0

---

[1] For 'coppy of ye Deputacon, July, 1669,' *See Rivers, 341.* The deputies first appointed were Jos. West, for Duke of Albemarle; Wm. Scrivener, for Lord Berkley; Stephen Bull, for Lord Ashley; William Bowman, for Lord Craven and F. O'Sullivan, for Sir P. Colleton?

For 2 paire of yarne stockins 00 07 0
For 2 paire of Sheets 00 17 0
For 6 Towels 00 04 0
For 12 Nacpkins 00 09 0
For 3 Pillobes 00 03 0
For a Boat to Gravesin 00 07 0
                                            ———————
                                            08   8 6

Wanting 1 Bed 2 Blancots.
1. Rug 1 Pillo.   Laid out in all £. 15. 01ˢ. 3ᵈ.

(Endorsed, by Lord Shaftsbury.)
Rivers accompts—Carrolina—July 1669.

[S. P., Bdle. 48, No. 10.]

———

FROM ABOARD THE CAROLINA NOW RIDING IN THE DOWNES.
                        August the 10ᵗʰ 1669.
May it please your Lordship,

This (after begging your Honors pardon) is to give your Lordshipp a perfect Accompte that wee are with our shipps now ridinge att an Anker in the Downes And may itt please your Honor I hope to your Lordshipps sattisfaction I have taken all the care I cann although very troublesome to fitt out and make ready with what expedition I possible could all the shipps now onely by the permission of the Almighty expecting a good winde and being well fitted with and by the leave of God I doe intende to waye and sett to sayle expecting under God a good and prosperous voyadge for Ireland into the port of Kingsale and upon our arivall from thence your Honor shall receive a more fuller Accompt then I att present can give your Lordshipp I have here enclosed sent your Honor a particular Accompt of what passendgers are aboard first Masters and then servants and then those persons that are single and have noe servants which with your Lordshipps pardoun is all att present from
                        Your Lordshipps most humble and
                              obediente servant.
                                    JOSEPH WEST.
[Endorsed]
    For the Right Honᵇˡᵉ the Lord Ashley att his House neere
    Excetter House in the Strand London.
            [S. P., Bundle 48, number 11.]
    11

A LIST OF ALL SUCH MASTERS,[1] free passengers and servants which are now a board the Carolina now ridinge in the Downes. August the 10th 1669.

Masters	Servants	Numbers of Names
Capt: Sullivan	Ralph Marshall	
	James Montgomery	
	Rich: Allexander	
	Stephen Wheelwright	8.
	Tho: Kinge	
	Eliz: Dimmocke	
	Eliz: Mathews.	
Step: Bull		
	Robert Done	
	Burnaby Bull[2]	
	Tho: Ingram	
	Jonathan Barker	7.
	John Larmouth	
	Dudley Widzier.	
Ed: Hollis &		
Jos: Dalton	George Prideox	
	Thomas Younge	
	Henry Price	
	Will: Chambers	
	John Dawson	11.
	Will: Roades	
	Alfra Harleston	
	Jane Lawson	
	Susanna Kinder.	
Tho: Smith		
Paule Smith	Aice Rixe	
	Jo: Hudlesworth	
	Jo: Burroughs	
	Hugh Wigleston	9.
	Eliz: Smith	
	Andrew Boorne	
	Francis Noone.	

---

[1] Master here means *Pater Familias*. Servants included kin, dependents, employees and servants. Thus B. Bull was probably brother to Stephen. Marshall, Donne, &c., were 'gentlemen' freeholders and men of education. John Burley was son of a rich father, &c.

[2] Captain Burnaby Bull, a successful planter, living, 1690-93, on Ashley River. 1701 had grant 500 acres there. Bond of Burnaby and Stephen Bull, Esquires, sued 1703. He died 1716, and by will, March 20th, empowered William Elliott and Shem Butler to sell lands. *Book P.*, page 92.

Hambleton[1]

	Tho: Gourden	
	Will: Lumsden	
	Jo: Frizen	
	Step: Flinte	
	Edw: Young	10.
	Jo: Thomson	
	Samuell Morris	
	Tho: Southell	
	Agnis Payne	
	Jo: Reed.	

Jo: Rivers

	Tho: Poole	
	Rob: Williams	5.
	Henry Burgen	
	Math: Smallwood.	

Nich: Carthwright

	Tho: Gubbs	
	Jo: Loyde	
	Martin Bedson	6.
	Step: Price	
	Will: Jenkins.	

Morris
Mathews

	Abra: Phillips	
	Reighnold Barefoot	5.
	Mathew Hewitt	
	Eliz: Currle.	

Will: Bowman

	Abraham Smith	3.
	Millicent Howe.	

Doctor Will
Scrivener

	Margarett Tuder	2

Will Owens

	John Humfreys	
	Christopher Swade	4
	John Borley	

Tho: Midleton
Eliz: uxor ejus

	Rich: Wright	4
	Tho: Wormes	

---

[1] 1671? Petition of Major Edward Hamilton to the King. His many faithful services and sufferings for the Crown have ruined his estate. Prays for the Government of Nevis, likely to become void by the great age of the present Governor, Colonel James Russell, a native of Ireland, where Petitioner was born and resideth. *A. & W. I.*, 393.

Samuell West

Andrew Searle   3
Will: West.

Joseph Bailey

John Carmichaell   2

Passengers that have noe servants.

Mr Tho: Rideall
Mr Will Haughton
Mr Will Kennis
Mr Tho: Humfreys
Eliz: Humfreys
Marie Clerke
Sampson Darkenwell
Nathanyell Darkenwell
Mrs Sarah Erpe
Eliz: Erpe
Martha Powell
Mrs Mary Erpe
Thomas Motteshed

Totall Number now aboard is   92.[1]

[Endorsed]
A perticular of all the passenger aboard the Carrolina.

[*S. P.*, Bdle. 48, No. 11.]

---

[1] Neither West nor the Proprietors' fifteen servants are named.   Major Hamilton was not aboard.   His steward, J. Reed, Mr. Thomas Humfreys, his wife and child, and Mr. William Bowman left the ship in Ireland.   The following reached Carolina: Captain O'Sullivan, Mr. Cartwright, Mr. S. Bull, Mr. Dalton, Messrs. P. and Thomas Smith (afterwards Landgrave and Governor), Mr. Mathews, Dr. Scrivener, Mr. Owen, Mr. S. West, Mr. Kennis, Mrs. Sarah Erpe (lot 37 C. T., 1681), Mrs. Mary and Elizabeth Erpe, Mr. Marshall, Mr. Donne, Mr. B. Bull, Mr. T. Ingram, Jonathan Barker, S. Wheelwright (commissioned Surveyor 1673), W. Chambers (lot C. T., 1681), Affra Harleston (the benefactress of the Church), Jane Lawson (1694, Dr. Robert Adams leaves Jean Lawson £8; 1701, Jane Lawson, of Berkly county, sells 54 acres Ashley River), Susan Kinder (lot C. T., 1672), Mathew Smallwood (bound over 1674; Palawanee Island granted him, *A. A.*, 2, 599, 1728 Mathew Smallwood, deceased, administratⁿ to Mary Smallwood), John Burley, W. West (witness will E. Roberts, 1671), and Major Hamilton's servants, *S. P.*, 38, and probably T. King (Thomas King, joyner, deceased, 1706, Mary K., widow), J. Humphreys, C. Swade, Elizabeth Curle, Millicent Howe, Serle, Price, Jenkins, Carmichael, and all Captain O'Sullivan's servants and others.   A few servants joined at Kinsale;

ffrom ye Downes this 7th of
Augt 1669.

Right Hono^{ble}

I have (herein inclosed) sent yor Lordship an Inventory of all the apurtinances belonging to ye Carolina ffrigott, and also a list of all the seamens names that doe belong unto herselfe, the Port Royall, and the Albemarle wth their distinct salleries.

My L^d (our shipp having been stayed here by the comon inconveniences incident to shipps outward bound) our provision is far spent (considering our uoiage) for Although six are put to foure mens allowance we have not aboue ten or twelue dayes beare left; therefore I beseech yor Loship to consider our want when wee come to Ireland, where we are to take in a great number of passingers. God hath been pleased this morne to send us a faire wind, and our shipps are just now come to saile; I hope the Lord will make our uoigage and designes prosperous.

Yo^r Lordships most Hum^{ble}

HENRY BRAYNE.

Addressed:

To the R^t Hono^{ble} Anthony Lord Ashley at Exet^r house in the strand   London.

———

AN INVENTORIE of all the Apertinances and men that doth belong to the shipp Carolina ffriggatt now Rideing in the Downes saufe att an Anchor this 17th day of August in the yeare of our Lord one thousand sx hundred sixty & nine.

Imp^rmis.

Masts yards wthstanding & Runing Riging all full wth one spare Topmast & ⅔ of A maine yard wth two good pumps sixtene great guns 6 of them of 4 pound shott 8 of 3 pound shott & ye other two of one pounder & two Takells to each

———

Sir John Yeamans, Mr. Barrow and his wife, Mr. H. Hughes, Mr. Thomas Norris, Mr. John Jones, Mr. H. Simons, J. Collins, H. Cartwright, James Marshall, George Beadon, A. Churne, William Carr, Samuel Lucas, C. Edwards, and others at Barbadoes. Dr. H. Woodward at Nevis; Governor Sayle and his son at Bermuda; Captain Bailey, Mr. Rivers, J. Collins, M. Bedson, Margaret Tuder, and W. Carr were taken at Wallie. Mr. Barrow and wife and probably Mr. Middleton and wife, Mr. Hollis, Mr. Rideall, Mr. Houghton, S. and N. Darkenwell, T. Motteshed, and others were on the Port Royal.

gun & two guns more that was keept in the steed of sume perticulers that was wanting of the ships Inuentory ye weight about 1500ˡⁱ p pᵈ.

Gunners Stores.

two hundred & thirty Round shott 20 doubble head shott
tenn Barˡˡˢ of Corne Powder
fourtene Ladles spunges & Wadhooks
Twelve heads & Ramers of each
Eighty pounds of Sheet Leade
Two hundred weigh of Musquett shott
ten swords & seauen hangars
ten collars of Bandelears & one bundle of pistoll ditto
Six Pistolls & ten half Pikes
one Rehme of Paper Royall
Three ordinary Lanthorns & two muscouy dᵒ one dark Lanthorne & twenty powder hornes
three pounds of Brass Wire & one pound of starch
thirty-six tackle hookes: Thirty-six Tackle Cloths.
Thirty six thimbles: six formers for Cartridges
one wood budgbarrell one Tin budge ditto
Six Ladle stands, & two Tand hides
Two Iron melting Ladles one ᵐ of small nailes of sorts
Twenty eight pounds of Cork for Tomkins [Tompions] seauen sheep skins Eleven Cartridge Cases one small hand vice & ten pound of tallow.

Sailes:

one new maine Saile of Hollands Douck
one new foresail of ditto
one new foretopsaile & mainetopsaile of french canu.
one new miz. [?] and one maine staysaile
one new spritsaile two new small sailes
one oold maine and fore topsailes ditto
one old studing saile three old small sailes

Anchors.

	c.	q.	li.
one sheete Anchor weight	08	0	00
one Best Bower ditto wᵗ	06	0	00
one small ditto Anchor	05	0	00
one Kedg Anchor wᵗ	01	0	00

Cables.

| one new Cable nine inches for sheete Anchor . | 20 | 0 | 00 |

one Best Bower Cable halfe worne w^t about .   14   o   oo
one new Horser of six Inches for small Bower   07   3   16
one new 3 Inch warpe for kedg Anchor   .   02   2   14

Cordige.
 one Quoile of three Inch Roope w^t   .   .   02   o   14
 one ditto of one Inch Rope .   .   .   .   oo   3   oo
 half a Quoile of two Inch Rope   .   .   .   oo   2   16
 one Quoile of Ratling w^t   .   .   .   .   oo   i   06
 one new main & fore stay w^t .   .   .   .   o3   i   16
 one sett of maine & fore shrowds .   .   .   07   2   14

Leads lynes &c.
 two dipsea leads & foure hand Leads
 two dipsea lynes & two hand lynes
 one duz. & half of Logg lynes & two white Hambroug ditto
 light sayle needles & one palme
 one paire of Canhookes one fidd Kamber
 six mardling spikes twelve Inch Blocks
 six Inch & half Blocks
 twelve Hookes & thimbles six dead eyes
 twelve scrapers
 one new Longboate wth windless wth six handspikes
 Eight oares one new Grapnell and Chaine belonging to her
  one top chaine for maine top

Cooks Store.   c.   q.   li.
 two Copper kettles weight .   .   .   .   oo   2   15
 three lardg Mustard Bowles.   two duz of quarter Canns
 two duz of Bread Basketts & foure Ballast Basketts
 two wooden Ladles & two skimming Dishes
 three duz of wooden spoones & ten tapps & Cannells
 four duz. of trenchers & six broomes
 two duz. & halfe of butter dishes
 two sauce pans two paire of large Bellows
 two iron bound pailes—two wooden tinder boxes
 one tin tinder box foure water pumps
 one small Beame & Scales to weigh Bread
 & weights from foure pound to half a quarter
 one sett of oyle measures
 one scrubing Brush & two small ones
 two water scoops foure larg trayes
 one paire of tonges one fire shouell one Gridiron

one frying pan six buckets
one funell to fill water
three doz of wooden platters
one doz. & halfe of pease boules
Casks.
sixtene tun of Beare & water Cask. Iron bound
Saile Cloth.
fifty yards of Titlery (?) Canuas
thirty ditto of french ditto
foure Meridian compasses
foure halfe houre glasses
foure halfe minit ditto one Watch Glass
Carpenters Stores.
three new Augers
one cross cut saw ould
ten pound of thrums
one pich Ladle one Iron Loggerhead to heat pitch
Eight hinges nine Ring boults
foure port hinges three puttack plates
Six iron bound dead eyes two eye bolts three chaine plates
    two double Hookes three Reaming Bolts two Iron Wedges
    fiue port Hookes one boome Iron for ye boate
Two iron Clamps foure bolts three Iron hoops
Two port hinges one Iron Saucer for Capstan
two pump hookes foure pump bolts.
one Iron Driuer one hoock for shipp side.
one boome Claspe six bower pump boxes.
eleuen upper boxes three chaine boxes.
one foote & halfe square of pump leather.
seuen paire of hinges & oaches.
three paire of Cross Gametts & one paire small hinges.
one halfe Bagg of sheathing nailes about 40^{ll} w^{t}.
one halfe ditto of twenty peny ditto.
two thousand five hundred of ten peny nailes.
two thousand of six penny ditto.
fouer^{m} of pump nailes of sorts.
foure^{m} of Lead ditto of ditto.
foure^{m} of foure peny nailes.
two thousand of scupper nailes.
three hundred of fourty peny ditto.

three hundred of thirty peny ditto.
foure hundred of twenty foure peny ditto.
Coopers Stores.
one Bung borer one tap borer.
five hundred of Riuets for Iron Hoops.
three punches two Socketts.
two Iron setts or drifts.
three could chizells one Buckhorne.
one pump shaue one dubble head hamer.
one Tarjars.

———

A LIST OF ALL THE SEAMEN that doth now belong to the shipp Carolinas their pay begining from the third day of Augt 1669.

	li.	s.	d.
Henry Brayne entred upon pay the 25th of July 1669 at the rate of five pounds p^r month and then reced twenty pounds sterling by a noat charged to Mr Portmain wch was Reced is .	05	00	00
Aug^t—John Comings mate entred upon pay at the rate of three pounds sterling p^r month . .	03	00	00
Richard Dyas Gunner entred upon pay at the rate of thirty five shill^s p^r month is . . .	01	15	00
Richard Cole Carpenter entred upon pay at the rate of three pounds five shillings p^r month .	03	05	00
Peter Salter Trumpeter entred himselfe at the rate of thirty five shillings p^r month . . .	01	15	00
Arthur Roper Botswines mate entred himselfe at the rate of thirty shillings p^r month . .	01	10	00
John More entred himself at the rate of thirty shill p^r month	01	10	00
Thomas Joy entred himselfe at the rate of thirty shill p^r month	01	10	00
William Orr entred himselfe upon pay at the rate of thirty shillings p^r month	01	10	00
Thomas Sumers entred himself at the rate of thirty shillings p^r month	01	10	00
Georg Gray entred on pay at the rate of thirty shill p^r month	01	10	00

Henry Jones young man entred on pay at ye rate
   of twenty shill p^r month   .   .   .   .   OI IO OO
James Shepard entred upon pay at the rate of thirty
   shillings p^r month .   .   .   .   .   .   OI IO OO
John Williamson entred upon pay at the rate of
   thirty shill p^r month   .   .   .   .   .   OI IO OO
James Roberson entred into pay at the rate of
   thirty shillings p^r month   .   .   .   .   OI IO OO
John Rippett entred upon pay at the rate of thirty
   shillings p^r month .   .   .   .   .   .   OI IO OO
Allixander John Stowne entred into pay at ye rate
   of thirty shills p^r month   .   .   .   .   OI IO OO
Henry ffarro entred himselfe at the rate of thirty
   shills: p^r month   .   .   .   .   .   .   OI IO OO
Hailes Porter Carpinters mate entred upon pay at
   the rate of thirty shillings p^r month.

I und^r written doth Acknowledge that I have Reced and taken
into possession all the perticulars of this saide Inventory the w^{ch}
I shall give a just an accompt. of to ye best of my power when
I am there to required by the Lords Proprieto^{rs} of Carolina or
their order wittness my hand this 17th of Aug^t *1669.*

HENRY BRAYNE.

———

A LIST OF ALL THE MENS NAMES that doth now belong to
   the Port Royall now Rideing saufe att Anchor in the downes
   this 17th of Augt 1669.

June—John Russell master entred upon pay ye
   twenty fourth of June 1669 at the rate of fiue
   pounds sterling p^r month is   .   .   .   .   05 OO OO
   and he have reced three pounds ster in part.
Augt ye 3^d—William Allan Carpinter entred upon
   pay at the rate of three pounds p^r month   .   03 OO OO
Peter Stanford Boatswaine entred upon pay at the
   rate of thirty shills p^r month .   .   .   .   OI IO OO
Tobias Cox entred upon pay at the rate of thirty
   shills: p^r month   .   .   .   .   .   .   OI IO OO
Lewes Corson entred himself at the rate of thirty
   shills p^r month   .   .   .   .   .   .   OI IO OO

Georg ffarro entred upon pay at the rate of thirty
    shills p^r month   01   10   00
Robert Chappell mate entred himselfe to goe the
    uoidge at the rate of three pounds sterling p^r
    month Augt 9th 1669   03   00   00

A LIST OF ALL THE MENS NAMES y^t doth now belong to the
    Albemarle sloop now Rideing saufe at Anchor in the downes
    this 17th day of Augt 1669.

Edward Baxter master entred upon pay to goe in
    the sloop at the rate of three pounds ster^l p^r
    month till she arrive at Carolina and then he is
    to come entred mate in ye ship Carolina at the
    rate of fiuety shills p^r month   03   00   00
Augt 3—Georg Buggy entred upon pay at the rate
    of thirty shillings p^r month   01   10   00
John Rogers entred upon pay at the rate of thirty
    shills. p^r month   01   10   00
Georg Young entred himselfe at the rate of twenty
    five shills p^r month   01   05   00
Henry Buck entred upon pay at the rate of fiftene
    shills p^r month   00   15   00

    This List I acknowledge to be just p^r under

HENRY BRAYNE.

[S. P., Bdle. 48, No. 12.]^1

THE ACCOMPT OF THE COSTS OF THE SHIP CAROLINA AND
HER SETTING TO SEA VIZ.

Paid Mr Thomas Knight for said Shipp &c.   .   430   00   00
P^d Capt Potter for sheathing and caulking her   106   00   00

---

    ^{1} Frigate, a long, light built, square stern vessel. The Carolina was
probably about 200 tons, cost £430, repairs, &c. £500, crew 18 men. Port
Royal probably under 100 tons, cost £125, crew 7. Albemarle about 30
tons, cost £50, crew 5. For their fate, see post. Brayne, Coming, Dyas,
Cole, Joy, Sumers, Williamson and perhaps others of the crews settled
in Carolina 1670. The last four probably left descendants there. Deyos
had lands 1674. Cole (from whom Coles island?) was of parliament 1672,
died about 1697? William Joy lived in Christ church parish 1692.
Thos. Sumers in Chestertown 1698, 1706. Williamson died about 1701.

P^{d} ditto for Timber & planks for her	008	00	00
P^{d} for a new long boat for her	014	00	00
P^{d} for a new Cable for her	031	05	00
P^{d} for 51^{cwt} 3 ^{qrs} of Cordige for her at 30^{s}	077	11	00
P^{d} for 6^{c} 1^{qr} 9^{lb} of new Cordage at 27 p. is	008	12	00
P^{d} for 30. Hamborough Lines at 18^{d} p. Line	002	05	00
P^{d} for 3^{c} 3^{qr} of spunn yearne at 20. p. is.	003	14	00
P^{d} for 4 deep sea lines at 8^{s} per line	001	12	00
P^{d} for 28^{lb} of fine Marlin	001	01	00
P^{d} for 15 hand lines at 3^{s} per line	002	05	00
P^{d} for a new suit of Sailes	58	00	00
P^{d} for mending the ould sailes with materials	14	00	00
P^{d} for main yard and 2 top Gallant masts	00	08	00
P^{d} for a Capstell boat oares and handspiks	06	09	09
P^{d} the carver for worke done aboute the ship	02	00	00
P^{d} to seamen for worke done on board	10	03	00
P^{d} Carpenters for worke done on board	19	16	00
P^{d} the smith for worke done for said Ship	27	00	00
P^{d} for a sheet Anchor with 8. at 24^{s} p. is	09	12	00
P^{d} for Anchor Stocks	01	10	00
P^{d} for Blocks	07	10	00
P^{d} for Deale boards and Battens	13	00	00
P^{d} for severall necessarys as Dishes, Cans, &c,	07	00	00
P^{d} for 4 barrells of Tarr	04	00	00
P^{d} for a barrell of Pitch	01	08	00
P^{d} for 2^{c} 2^{qrs} of Rozin	01	10	00
P^{d} for 3. cant Sparrs	00	19	00
P^{d} for a Jack and Ensigne 2 Pendants & vanes	05	13	00
P^{d} for 2 Iron bound Broces	01	06	00
P^{d} for clensing and fixeing the armes	01	10	00
P^{d} for entring the Shipp & a victualling bill	00	07	06
P^{d} for 7600 of Wood for Deunidge	06	01	06
P^{d} for 2 Copper Kettles and other necessaries	05	10	08
P^{d} for a Poop Lanthorne	01	06	00
P^{d} for Compasses and Glasses	01	19	00
P^{d} the Painter	06	00	00
P^{d} the Plummer	03	00	00
P^{d} for Carpenters stores	12	00	00
P^{d} Coopers stores	02	03	00
P^{d} more for Iron worke	12	00	00

P^d for a sheet anchor stock	oo	15	oo
P^d for 6 doz of trunnells	oo	o6	oo
P^d for 24 foot of Elme board	oo	o6	oo
P^d for brimstone and other necessaryes . .	oo	o3	o6
	930	17	11

AN ACCOUNT OF THE COSTS OF THE SHIP PORT ROYALL AND HER SETTING TO SEA.

Paid for the Port Royall Friggat . . .	125	oo	oo
P^d for a new boat for her	o4	oı	o6
P^d for 12 small anchors	o2	oo	oo
P^d for a nue cable for her 6. 2. 7. at 27. 6. .	o8	16	oo
P^d for 7^c 2^{qrs} 18^{lb} of new Cordage at 30^s p. is	11	o8	o6
P^d for 3^c 2^{qrs} 11^{lbs} more of new Cordige at .	o4	16	oo
P^d for nue sailes for her	o9	10	oo
P^d for timber, Rosin and other necessaries .	o8	10	oo
P^d for carpenters worke done aboard s^d Ship .	10	14	oo
P^d for a nue Pump and boxes	oı	o8	oo
P^d for entring the Shipp	oo	o6	o8
P^d for a nue Jack and Ensigne . . .	oı	15	oo
P^d for clensing and fixing her Armes . .	oı	o2	oo
P^d for Oares and hand spikes	oı	oo	oo
P^d for blocks for the Ship	o4	oo	oo
P^d for dishes, Canns &c	o3	oo	oo
P^d for a Ketle for said Ship	oı	18	oo
	199	o5	o8

AN ACCOUNT OF THE COSTS OF THE ALBEMARLE SHALLOP AND HER FURNITURE AND SETTING TO SEA.

Paid for the Albemarle Shallopp . . .	50	oo	oo
Paid for nue sailes for her	10	oo	oo
Paid for timber, rozin and other necessaries .	o5	oo	oo
P^d for Carpenters worke done on board the sloop	o9	o4	oo
P^d for a nue Ensigne for her	oo	15	oo
P^d for entring the sloop and victualling bill .	oo	o6	o4
P^d for hand spikes for her	oo	o9	oo
P^d for blocks for her	o2	12	oo
P^d for a nue yaule	o2	o3	oo

P^d for joyners worke done for the Shallop .	oo	o8	oo
P^d for 2 Compasses and 2 Lanthornes . .	oo	12	oo
P^d for hand lead and line	oo	o3	o6
P^d Clearing at Gravesend	oo	o9	oo
	82	o1	1o

An Accompt of the Costs of the Provizzions bought for the Expedition to Carolina.

Paid for 154^c 2^{qrs} 17^{lbs} bisk^t at 11^s 6^d p. is .	88	17	oo
P^d for 112^{qrs} 6 bushells of pease . . .	157	1o	oo
P^d for 59½ bushells of flower at 6^s 8^d p. bus^l .	19	16	oo
P^d for 58 bush^{ls} of Oatmeale at 4^s 6^d per bush^l .	12	19	o6
P^d for 162^c 2^{qrs} of beefe at 22^s per ^{c} . .	178	15	oo
P^d for 43 bushells of white salte p. bush^l .	o3	18	1o
P^d for 54 bushells of bay salte at 2^s 4^d p. bush^l .	o6	o5	oo
P^d for 1o firkins of butter at 12^s per firkin .	o8	1o	oo
P^d for 2^{cwt} of Cheese at 1£ 3^s 6^d is . . .	o2	o7	oo
P^d for 48 Gallons of Oyle at 2^s 8^d is . .	o6	o8	oo
P^d for 400 stock fish	o7	16	oo
P^d for 100 Couple of Haberdine fish at 14^d p Cp^{le}	o5	17	oo
P^d for 13 tonn ½ of beere at 1£ 19^s p. tonn is	26	o6	oo
P^d for 2 tonn & a barrell of beere for the Port Roy^l	o4	o2	oo
P^d for 16 doz: of Candles at 4^s 4^d per doz: .	o3	o9	o4
P^d for Garden seeds	o1	15	oo
P^d John Bishop for butter and cheese . .	oo	15	oo
P^d for 30 Gallons of Brandy	o5	o5	oo
	540	11	o8

An Account of the Costs of Cloathes bought for the present expedition to Carolina.

Paid for 100 Bedds, Ruggs & Pillows at 8^s 6^d .	42	1o	oo
Paid for one leather bed	o1	1o	oo
Paid for 30 Hammocks at 22^d	o2	14	oo
Paid for 100 Cloath suits at 16^s . . .	8o	oo	oo
Paid for 20 doz: Shierts at 32^s p. doz: . .	32	oo	oo
Paid for 1o doz: of drawers at 22^s p. doz. .	11	oo	oo
Paid for 1o doz. of redd capps at 14^s p. doz. .	o4	oo	oo

Paid for 20 doz. of shoes at 27ˢ p. doz. . .	27	00	00
Paid for a flagg for the Fort at Carolina . .	01	15	00
Paid for 10 doz. of Stockings	07	00	00
Paid for needles and thred	02	15	00
	212	04	00

An Account of the Armes, Powder and munition of Warr
         for the expedition to Carolina.

Pᵈ for 200 French fyerlocks muskets at 17ˢ .	170	00	00
Pᵈ for 13 fouling peeces at 24ˢʳ . . .	15	12	00
Paid for 58 swords	06	05	00
Paid for 200 pike heads	03	06	00
Paid for 200 Collers Bandeleers . . .	13	06	00
Paid for 30 barrells of powder at 3£ 12ˢ p. barrˡˡ	108	00	00
Paid for 10ˡᵇˢ 2qʳˢ of Muskett shott . . .	05	05	00
Paid for 30 barrells of small shott . . .	26	00	00
Paid for 6 paires of shott moulds . . .	01	09	00
Paid for 1000 of Flints	00	16	00
Paid for 6 Chests to pack these goods in .	01	10	00
Paid for 100 of Match	01	10	00
Paid for sheet lead, paper Royall, tand hydes powder hornes, 14 sheep skins, and severall other things belonging to the Guns . .	12	05	00
Paid for 12 suits of Armour[1]	09	16	00
Paid for a fother of lead to make shott . .	13	05	00
Paid for 200 deale boards	08	10	00
Paid for a drum	01	00	00
	397	15	00

Accompt of the Costs of the Tooles and Iron ware
      bought for the present expedition to Carolina.

Paid for 15 of Iron and 50 of Steele . .	12	12	00
Paid for a whole sett of smiths' tooles . .	08	18	00
Paid for a sett of stock makers tooles . .	01	12	00
Paid for 6 sett of Carpenters and Joyners tooles	09	10	00
Paid for 2 sett of Coopers tooles . . .	02	13	00

[1] Probably breast and back plates and morions. *Fother*, 'a load, a quantity.' *Johnson Dic.*

Paid for 10 Carpenters adzes . . .	01	00	00
Paid for 10 broad axes at 3ˢ per axe . .	01	10	00
Paid for 2 doz. of hammers at 14ˢ p. doz. .	01	08	00
Paid for 20 cross cut saws at 5ˢ 6ᵈ . . .	05	10	00
Paid for 10 Whipsaws	02	15	00
Paid for 2 tennant saws & one Carpenʳˢ joynter	00	09	06
Paid for 10 steele hand saws	01	00	00
Paid for 4 setts of Iron Wedges . . .	02	02	00
Paid for 3 doz. of ordinary Augers . .	01	01	00
Paid for 6 syeths and sneiths ffitted . .	01	06	00
Paid for 20 m of 20ᵈ nailes at 8ˢ 4ᵈ p. . .	08	06	00
Paid for 40 m of 10ᵈ nailes at 5ˢ . . .	10	00	00
Paid for 60 m of 8ᵈ nailes at 4ˢ 2ᵈ . . .	12	10	00
Paid for 40 m of 6ᵈ nailes at 3ˢ . . .	06	00	00
Paid for 100 m of 4ᵈ nailes	08	06	08
Paid for 80 m of 3ᵈ nailes	05	06	08
Paid for 3 doz. of strong eyed hows at 16ˢ ·	02	08	00
Paid for 10 doz. of Grubbing axes at 17ˢ .	08	10	00
Paid for 20 pickaxes 1. 1. 9. at 30ˢ. . .	01	19	11
Paid for 10 doz. of broad hoes . . .	08	10	00
Paid for 7 doz. of Narrow hoes at 12ˢ . .	04	04	00
Paid for doz. best narrow hoes at 14ᵈ p. hoe	05	16	08
Paid for 10 doz. of felling axes at 17ˢ . .	08	10	00
Paid for 6 doz. of Stockbills at 12ˢ . .	03	12	00
Paid for doz. of Spades and Shovels . .	03	12	00
Paid for 18 Stock locks & 1 doz. of hooks & hinges	02	12	03
Paid for 17 barrells & 4 Fatts[1] to pack them in	01	17	03
Paid for 9 English iron Potts at 2ᶜ 2qʳˢ 21ˡᵇˢ at 26ˢ .	03	10	06
Paid for one flemish iron Pott at 2ᵈ p ℔ . .	00	09	03
Paid for 2 brasse Ketles at 49½ˡᵇˢ at 16ᵈ p. ℔ .	03	06	00
Paid for 6 frying panns at 43ˡᵇˢ ½ at 5ᵈ . .	00	08	01
Paid for 10 of pothooks at 10ᵈ . . .	00	08	04
Paid for a brasse tind pott & stue pann . .	01	10	00
Paid for 3 steel mills	06	00	00
Paid for 2 of hand skrues	03	16	00
Paid for 12 iron crows at 28ˢ ℔ C . . .	04	01	06
Paid for 4 chaind hooks, 2 fisgys & 2 harping Irons	00	16	00

---

[1] Vats, for moist goods.   Sizzards are scissors?

Paid for 1000 bricks and 6 Grind stones . .	01	10	00
Paid for 2p^r of Cartwheeles and 12 wheelebar-row wheeles	05	16	00
Paid for ½ a Chatherne of Coales . . .	00	10	00
Paid for a p^r of Stilliards	00	10	00
	188	09	07

An Account of the Cost of Caske for this present Expedition to Carolina.

Paid for 8 tunn ½ of hhds for beefe at 22^s per tunn	09	07	00
Paid for 8 tunns of Great Butts for bread and pease at 17^s	07	00	00
Paid for 20 tunns of hhd at 17^s 6^d p. tunn .	17	10	00
Paid for 21 barrells for Oatmeale & flower .	03	03	00
Paid for 2 tunn of hhd to pack Cloathes at 17^s 6^d	01	15	00
Paid for 14 tunn of Water Caske at 23^s . .	06	02	00
Paid for 6 bucketts and 3 tunnells . . .	01	05	00
Paid for trimming 4 tunns of Caske and other things	02	00	00
Paid for 420 Iron hoops w^t 14^c 3^{qrs} 8^{lbs} at 25^s .	18	10	07
Paid for hooping 20 tunn of Caske . . .	01	15	00
Paid for 7 tunn ½ of beare Caske at 23^s p. tunn	08	12	06
	87	00	01

An Account of the Costs of Fishing Trade sent to Carolina.

Paid for 3 seanes one of 60^{yds} and 2 of 40 .	11	10	00
Paid for 5 casting netts at 16^s per nett . .	04	00	00
Paid for 17 doz. of fishing lines of all sorts .	05	12	00
Paid for 63 doz. of fishing hooks of all sorts .	02	10	00
Paid for 107^{lb} of twine at 11^d per ℔ . .	04	18	00
	28	10	00

An Account of Indian Trade sent to Carolina.

Paid for 240^{lbs} of glasse beads . . .	14	00	00
Paid for 300 hatchets	12	10	00

12

Paid for 100 hoes	04	11	08
Paid for 100 hollowing adses	07	10	00
Paid for 4 grose of knives at 20ˢ p. grosse .	04	00	00
Paid for 3 doz. of white hafts at 3ˢ 6ᵈ p. doz. .	00	10	00
Paid for 2 grosse of sizzard at 2ˢ 6ᵈ p. doz. .	02	12	00
Paid for 10 striped suits at 10ˢ 6ᵈ p. suite .	05	05	00
	50	18	08

An Account of Charges of shipping goods and other disbursements.

Pᵈ for the king's warrant for 12 Gunns &c. .	06	00	00
Pᵈ a fee for Mʳ Jones the Lawyer . . .	02	00	00
Pᵈ Mʳ Braine several disbursemᵗˢ about the ship	04	05	00
Pᵈ for the Custome of the goods with serchers fees &c.	08	15	00
Pᵈ lighteridge, porteridge and Waighters .	07	15	00
Pᵈ for packing & repacking the beefe . .	05	02	06
Pᵈ clearing the ships at the Custome House .	03	17	00
Pᵈ for wrighting & engroseing the laws . .	04	00	00
Paid shipping the seamen	07	06	00
Pᵈ clearing the ships at Gravesend . .	02	05	00
Pᵈ the Master of the Port Royal for some disbursᵐᵗˢ	00	05	06
Pᵈ for a free Cockett for the 12 gunns[1] . .	00	05	06
Pid pyloting down the Carolina . . .	05	05	00
Paid clearing 15 servants at Gravesend . .	01	02	06
	58	04	00

Pᵈ for a Chirurgeons Chest & Instruments .	30	00	00

Pᵈ Henry Braine Master of the Carolina in advance of wages	30	00	00
Pᵈ the seamen of the severall shipps at Gravesend	31	16	00
Paid more to the seamen	14	19	00
	76	15	00

[1] The guns given by the King for Carolina, page 93.

ACCOUNT CURRANT OF THE DISBURSEMENTS FOR THE
EXPEDITION TO CAROLINA IS:

To money paid by the Duke of Albemarle .	500	oo	oo
To money paid by the Earle of Craven . .	500	oo	oo
To money paid by my Lord Berkeley.			
To money paid by my Lord Ashley . .	500	oo	oo
To money paid by Sir George Carteret . .	500	oo	oo
To money paid by Sir Peter Colleton . .	500	oo	oo
To the Duke of Albemarle	50	oo	oo
To the Earle of Craven	50	oo	oo
To Sir Peter Colleton	45	oo	oo
To the Lord Ashley.			
To the Lord Berkeley.			
To Sir George Carteret.			

℔ CONTRA C[r].

Paid the costs of the ship Carolina as in fol: 2 .	930	17	11
Paid the costs of the ship Port Royal folio 3 .	199	05	08
Paid the costs of the Albemarle fol: 4 . .	082	01	10
Paid the costs of Provizzions as in fol: 5 . .	˙540	11	08
Paid the costs of cloathes as in fol: 6 . .	212	04	00
Paid the costs of stores of Warr as in fol: 7 .	397	15	00
Paid the costs of tools & Iron ware fol: 9 .	188	09	07
Paid the costs of Caske as in fol: 10 . .	87	00	01
Paid the cost of Fishing trade fol: 10 . .	28	10	00
P[d] the acc[t] of Costs of Indian Trade fol: 11 .	50	18	08
P[d] the costs of charges and shipping goods &c.			
fol: 12	58	04	00
Paid a Chirurgeons Chest and Instruments .	30	08	00
Paid wages paid the severall seamen . .	76	15	00
money paid M[r] West at Kinsaile . .	30	00	00
	2913	01	05
Lent Capt: O'Sulivant	10	00	00
Paid M[r] West for his paines	20	00	00
	2943	01	05

Paid for the Cargo with Charges sent to Virginia & consigned M[r] W[m] Burgh for account
of the Duke of Albemarle &c.[1]   .   .   .   270   17   06
    26£ 5[s] 6[d] in M[r] West's hands being parte
of the 61£ he received of M[r] Portman by
order of my Lord Ashley and hath not given
account of   26   05   06
                                  3240   04   05
Abated on the severall bills which ought to be
deducted   39   07   11

Expended in all   3200   16   06

[*S. P.*, Bdle. 48, No. 13.]

Right Honorable

    I have received your Lordshipp's of the 16th of July last
joyned with Sir George Cartrott to procure some servts in these
parts to serve your Lordshipps and particularly at Port Royall
in the Province of Carolina, and showing the conditions to bee
allowed them at the end of their service which I did fully enlarge
and explaine to all the persons that I thought fitt to take notice
thereof and consulted with all such as I thought intelligent in
these affairs to advise mee how to rayse such servants but hitherto I could not obtayne any for the thing at present seems new
and foreigne to them, and withall they had been terrified with
the ill practice of them to the Caribda Islands where they were
sold as slaves that as yet they will hardly give credence to any
other usage; and withal they are loathe to leave the smoke of
their owne cabin if they can but beg near it; but indeed the chief
obstacle that I observe at present is the many buildings repayr-
ing and contrivances that are in all the towns in this Country
since the settlmt of the 49 interests which has made work for
those who will serve and again it is harvest time when they may
earn or steal a sheaf but that is near over.

    The last night arrived your Lordshipps Shipp Carolina friggott
Joseph West commander and M[r] Florence Solovane by whom I

---

[1] Received after Burgh's death by Bennett and Godwin, who invested
it in provisions and cattle for Carolina, see *S. P.*, Nos. 21, 28, 48.

received your lordshipps letter of the 27 July. The daie before came in the Albemarle the Port Royall not being yet arrived. I have upon receipt of your Lordshipps second letter used all indeavers and have proferred unto those present a very intelligent person in those affaires newly landed out of England and is very well informed and satisfyed in the designe and they have sent him into the Country where hee is confident he shall prevail with some and now that your shipps are here where they may have great entertainment and passage they will be much the easier persuaded and I doubt not but some wilbe got before the shipps part; and I know most of the people of this Country will give some credit to mee in the worth and advantage of this designe, because they know I never had anything to doe with the West India trade, but have ransomed many of them that have beene snatched up and privately conveyed on board the shippe bound that way.

My Lord I humbly beseech you to believe that whensoever it lyes in my power I shall most affectionately and faithfully serve your Lordshipps and all those most Honorable partners concerned and am rejoyced to see and observe such Honorable undertaking, and wish with all my heart all prosperity and success unto them and thus with my most humble service unto your Lordshipps my most Honored my Lord Duke of Albemarle and the rest of those Honorable Lords and persons concerned in these affaires I humbly take leave and remaine My Lord

Your Lordshipps most faithfull & humble Servant

ROBERT SOUTHWELL.

Kinsale 31ˢᵗ August 1669.

[Endorsed] To the Right Honorable the Lord Ashley one of His Majesty's most Honorable Privy Councill of England these presents   London.

[S. P., Bdle. 48, No. 14.]

———

KINGE SAYLE September the 10ᵗʰ 1669.

May it please yoʳ Loᵖᵖ

This is to give yoʳ honoʳ An Account that wee wᵗʰ our 3 Shipps have binn heere 12 dayes the winde beinge now come vpp fayer I doe intende God willinge to set to sayle & quitt this

Harbor, for (if itt may please yor Lo^{pp}) I cleerly find yor hono^{rs} Expectacons will nott be any wayes Answered heere in gettinge of s^rvants & wee have Lost A brave winde by cominge heere for wee by the Assistance of the Sovraigne[1] heere & other gents have vsed all Indeavo^{rs} butt all to noe other ende or purpose then Losse of tyme & Expence of Moneys, for I am nott assured of A mann that will goe from hence May itt please yor Lo^{pp} heere is some gents that are nott in the waye Mr. Boweman & others butt I hope that they will bee aboard before wee sayle, there is one Mr. Reade A deputy or Steward to Majo^r Hambleton that is Cleerely runn a way butt nott wthout some Advantagge to yor Hono^r for hee hath Left 9 Servan^{ts} aboard butt there is one Humfreys that yor Lo^{pp} putt vpon the designe that is runn A way wth his wife & childe And hath like a rascally knave reported very high & scandalous words against the Proprieto^{rs} Although hee had noe reason for itt beinge well vsed & provided for May itt please yor Hono^r I have rec'ed 30£ by Sr George Cartwrights order & have layed itt out in provisions & Necessarys for our voyadge & soe soone as I come to Barbadoes yor Hono^r shall receive A p'ticular Account of the disbursem^{ts} from

Yo^r Hono^{rs} Moste humble & obedient S^rvant

JOSEPH WEST.

Endorsed—[by John Locke.]

Jos: West to Ld Ashley 10 Sep^t '69.

Addressed: These for the Right Ho^{ble} the Lorde Ashley att

his House neere Exeter House in the Strand

Post paid 4^d.   London.

———

KINGE SAYLE September the 17 1669.

May it please yor

Hono^r.   This is to give yor Lo^{pp} An Account that vpon my dep'tinge this Harbor wch I gave yor Hono^r an Account of in my last l're the winde Imeadyatly veared about against vs & hath hitherto deteyned mee heere butt wth the first oportunity of winde I will God willinge quitt this place hopinge for a good & prospe-rous voyadge to the Barbadoes May itt please yor Lo^{pp} I have

———

[1] Mr. Southwell.   In those days the head of the Corporation of Towns in Ireland was called Sovereign.

rec'ed A l're from Mr Blany[1] with 2 Bills Inclosed from Sr Roberte Southwell[2] for 30£ charged vpon Mr Southwell his father in King Sayle wch I have nott as yett passed, neither doe I intende to passe them Except necessity Enforces mee by A Longe stay heere for want of a winde I beinge already suplyed wth 30£ by Sr George Carterites Order wch in my last l're to yor Lo^{pp} I menconed (wch wth first begginge yor Hono^{rs} pdon is all att p^{r}sente from   Yo^r Hono^r Moste humble Obedient S^{r}vant

JOSEPH WEST.

Endorsed—[by Locke].

Jos: West to L: Ashley—17 Sepr 1669.

Addressed—Thes for the Right Honble the Lorde Ashley att his House neere Exeter House in the Strande   London.

[S. P., Bdle. 48, No. 16.]

AT A MEETING OF THE PROPRIATORS OF CAROLINA HELD AT THE COCKPITT THE 21st OF OCTOBER 1669.

Present.   The Duke of Albemarle   The Earl of Craven
        The Lord Berkeley   The Lord Ashley
        Sir George Carterett   Sir Peter Colleton.

The Duke of Albemarle was elected the first Pallatin of Carolina.   The Earle of Craven the first High Constable.

The Lord Berkeley the first Chanceller.

The Lord Ashley the first Chief Justice.

Sir George Carteret the first Admirall.

Sir Peter Colleton the first High Steward.

[Col. Ent. Book, No. 20, page 46.]   N. C. Rec., I, page 179.

October the 29th 1669

AN ACCOUNT OF WHAT MONEYS HAVE BEENE PAID BY MEE ON THE ACCOUNT OF CAROLINA:

	£.	s.	d.
June the 14th. To John Rivers by your Lordships order	02	00	00

---

[1] Robert Blaney, Lord Ashley's secretary.

[2] Secretary Council for Plantations 1673–75, Clerk of the Privy Council to King Charles II, envoy to various courts, and principal Secretary of State in Ireland 1690. Died 1702.

July the 6.	To m^r Florence O. Sullivan	.		10	00	00
" " 18.	more to John Rivers	.	.	10	00	00
" " 25.	more to him	.	.	05	00	00
" " 27.	To Mr West	.	.	05	00	00
" " 29.	More to John Rivers	.	.	02	00	00
Aug the 11.	To M^r miller	.	.	01	00	00
	Totall	.	.	35	00	00

Memorand^m on an account formerly delivered to your Lordshipps

			500£	Venter.[1]
19£.	To John Rivers.	and	050 "	Hudsons Bay.
10	To Sullivan.			
05	Mr West.		550	
1	To Miller.		35	
35			585	

(Endorsed)

Disbursements on the accomp^t of Carolina.

[*S. P.*, Bdle. 48, No. 17.]

BARBADOES November the 8th 1669

May itt please yor Hono^r

   These are to Informe yor Lo^{pp} of our beinge att Barbadoes where wee shall stay vntill the 23^d Instant; & then hopinge to quitt this Islande for our desired Port; the People here seemingly show a great Inclinacon for Porte Royall Sr John Yeomans beinge resolved to goe downe doth give good Encouradgm^t & wee hope to make our Complem^t vp 200 p'souns; The Albemarle sloope wch wee lost 3 dayes after wee quitted Ireland Arrived safe heere 3 dayes after vs & ye 2^d instant in the morninge itt blew hard & the sloops cables broake & shee a shoare vpon ye Rocks & is lost: Sr John Yeomans & Esqr Colleton[2] are about

---

   [1] Lord Ashley's venture in Carolina.

   [2] Thomas Colleton. The ships left the Downs after August 17. The sloop, Carolina, and Port Royal made Kinsale 29, 30, and 31; left there September 11? put back and sailed again after 17th; arrived at Barbadoes late in October. The Albemarle was wrecked November 2, and the Colleton's sloop, '3 Brothers,' hired in her place.

buyinge of or hieringe of another sloope & alsoe another vessell that will cary downe 60 or 70 people wee have had very bad weather att Barbadoes & ware in much dainger wth our shipp for one of our cables broake; And the Port Royall hath lost a cable & Anker: Our dependance & Principle hopes are beinge yor Hono^r wth the Rest of the Right Ho^bles havinge binn pleased soe hono^bly to sett vs forthe wch is the life of our designe & yor Hon-o^rs ffame, nott to lett vs fade in our Infancy butt bee pleased to send vs A supply in the Springe wch from yor Hono^r wilbee received wth great Joye and much fortifye vs against ruin for al-though I have vsed all diligent Care Imadginable yett our stores are Eaten very deepe into And wee shall not have att our Land-inge above 3 Months Provisions: Since wee Arived heere to save provisions Esqr Colleton hath taken 20^tie servants into Sr Peeters Plantacon & Major Kingsland hath taken some they beinge now allmoste all ashoare May it please yor Hono^r those S^rv^ts wch did belonge to Major Hambleton I have & doe order them as for yor Hono^rs vse: by reason they are left w^thout a Master for their steward quitted the shipp & overrun them in Ireland & I doe intende to keepe them vntill I receive from yor Hono^r farther Orders. I doe hope before wee quitt Barbadoes to make yor number of servants vpp wth them May itt please yor Hono^r I have here inclosed sent yor Lo^pp A Coppy of the Proposalls wch are Published heere for the Peoples encouradgm^t & knowledge wch is all the Informacon att p^rsent that cann bee given by

    yor Hono^rs Moste Humble & Obediente S^rvante

                             JOSEPH WEST.

[*Endorsed*]—Carolina and Barbadoes.

[*Addressed*]—These for the Right Ho^ble the Lorde Ashley Cooper
          at Little Exeter House in the Strande London.

      [*S. P.*, Bdle. 48, No. 18.]

HENRY BRAYNES NOATE OF PERTCULARS TO BEE SENT FOR
      THE CAROLINA. 11 Nov. 69.[1]

one cable of 9 enches the same length of our sheet cable
one quile of 3 ench roope
one ditto of 2½ ditto

---

[1] So endorsed in Colleton's hand; the date by Locke.

one ditto of 2 inch
two ditto of 1 inch
2 doz of hambrough lynes
2 doz staives of marling
2 doz ditto of housing
1. quile of rutling
1. grapnell for long boat about 50^{lb} w^t
one fore topsaile having butone from m^r Shaw sailemaker
one boult of french canvas
one p^{ce} of vitterie ditto
one Anchor about 3^e weight for m^r Russell

I desire your Honour to lett m^r Hooker and m^r Shaw furnish me with these perticulars for what we had from them proves
verie well and if you will send more of each perticular it will
serve alsoe for the port Royall which she will in a short time
want

Your Honors servant to com^d

HENRY BRAYNE.

The 11th of 9^{ber} 1669.

[*S. P.*, Bdle. 48, No. 19.]

NICHOLAS BLAKE[1] TO (JOS. WILLIAMSON).

Barbadoes Nov; 12 1669.

About three months past was the most violent hurricane known
by any alive; at Nevis the sea came 150 yards up into the land
*   *   *   Arrival of three vessels to carry 'tis said Sir John
Yeamans to Surinam to transplant the English for Port Royal;
he will have few people hence, and if they be not vigorously
recruited they will endure much hardship; they must be exempted from all taxes, for new settlements are like young scions and
must have time to root and grow and in seven years will bring
fruit.   *   *   *

[*Col. Papers*, Vol. 24, No. 94.]   *Am. & W. I.*, §126.

Wm FREEMAN[2] TO COL: GEO: GAMVEL, LONDON.

Nevis, Dec: 19, 1669.   Sir John Yeamans one of the Com-

---

[1] Of Bilboa p'n, Christ Church, Barbadoes, 1668–79.
[2] Lieutenant-Colonel, member Council, and Commissioner for St. Kitts.

missioners appointed to receive his Majestys interest in St Christopher's passed here about 10 days ago with three vessels full of people for settling Port Royal on the main near Cape Fear; * *

[*Col. Papers*, Vol. 24, No. 96.]   *Am. & W. I.*, §131.

AT A MEETING of the Proprietors of Carolina at Sir George Carteretts Lodgings at Whitehall the 20th of January 1669

Present   The Earle of Craven   The Lord Berkeley
          The Lord Ashley   Sir George Carteret
          Sir Peter Colleton   Sir Tho: Clarges for Christopher Duke of Albemarle.

George Duke of Albemarle the first pallatin of Carolina being dead The Lord Berkeley being the eldest in years of the surviving proprietors succeeded him and was admitted the second pallatin of Carolina.

The Earle of Craven continued his place of Constable.

The Lord Ashley continued his place of Chief Justice

Sir George Carteret continued his place of Admirall

Sir Peter Colleton quitted his place of high Steward and made election of that of Chancellor.

The Duke of Albemarle sent his Commission to his Deputy in Albemarle County by the tytle of Treasurer.

The Lord Berkeley comissionated Samuell Stephens[1] to be his Deputy and Governor of Albemarle.

The Earle of Craven deputed John Jenkins The Lord Ashley Mr. John Willughby

Sir George Carteret Mr Peter Carteret Sir Peter Colleton Mr Godfry

The Duke of Albemarle sent a blank to the Governor.

[*Col. En. Book*, No. 20, page 47.]   *N. C. Rec.*, I, page 180.

---

[1] Governor of Albemarle October, 1667, *N. C.*, 162, 181. On his death, 1674, the Assembly chose Peter Carteret, see page 50, but he went to England, 1676, 'leaving the adm'n in ill order & worse hands.' Colonel Jenkins, who succeeded, was dispossessed; he led the rioters with Culpeper and Willoughby, but on Harvey's death, 1680, was chosen Governor. Captain Willoughby, 'imperious among his equals courteous to his inferiors,' was a judge and deputy 167—80. *N. C.*, 258, 326. John Godfrey *post*.

Jo: Dorel and Hugh Wentworth to Lord Ashley
17. Feb: 69-70.

Somers Island. Feb. 17. 69-70.

Right Hono^ble

Your shippe Carolina being forced from her intended Port
into one of our harbours¹ it begott an acquaintance betwixt me
and a servant of yours one Captain O. Sullivan which is gone
your Surveyor Generall, He haveing acquainted me with your
designe of settling Carolina and desire of promoting new Plantations caused me to presume upon your Honours favour and to
trouble you with the perusall of these lines, which may acquaint
your Honour that our Island of Barmudoes being over peopled
and the natives thereof much straitned for want of land being
now yearly able to spare a Hundred inhabitants for the settlement of new Plantations and many people haveing gone from
this Island to settle Santalucca, Trinidadoe, Antego and Jamaica
have most part of them dyed, but about three or fower years
since some of our people have gone for the Bahama Islands and
costing amongst them for spanish wracke and Ambregrise which
sometimes they found, at last they settled on an Island which at
first they named Sayles Island² but when more of our people went to
settle they named it Newprovidence, for the Generallity of our people that went they were soe poore that they were not able to transport themselves, But myselfe and one Mr Hugh Wentworth an
Inhabitant here did get two shipps and have transported most
part of the Inhabitants upon the Accompt of creditt giveing of
them time for their payment till they can rayse it of the Plantation by their Labour. There is about 3. hundred Inhabitants
upon it my selfe haveing settled a plantation there with eight peo-

---

¹ The three ships left Barbadoes about November 2, 1669, reached
Nevis December 9; were soon after scattered by storms. The Port
Royal beating back and forth in the Bahama channel, was wrecked near
Abaco; the sloop was driven northward and put into Nansemond, Va.,
in January; the Carolina 'with difficulty attained' Bermuda (before February 8). We know of the horrors of this voyage only that 'the stern
of the ship broke in,' and Mrs. Comings' prayer that 'God will preserve
me as he hath in many great Dangers when I saw his wonders in ye
Deepe & was by him Delivered.'
² Where Governor Sayle was 1647, see page 4. Settled 1666 by Captain John Wentworth and the Bermuda settlers.

ple on it 8 negroes and five English. The Island lyeth in the latitude of 25 degres and a halfe and is very healthfull and pleasant accommodated with Gallant Harbouring for shipping some part of the Island good land and some part of it wast land, The people there have now noe want of provisions, and our Natives here most inclinable to settle there, by reason the Island is soe healthfull. It produceth as good Cotten as ever grew in America and gallant Tobacco, They have made but little as yet There greatest want at present is small Armes and ammunition, a godly minister and a good smith. If the Spaniard become your enemy at Carolina he will come through the Gulf with his shipps and harbour them at New Providence and stay there for a south east wind which for the most part bloweth there and in three days time will be in the River of Port Royall on the back of your people, and it is the nearest place for Neighbourhood of any Plantation in America and should your Lordshipp engage us here to accommodate your people with live Cattle or other necessaries from hence with our shipping that Island would be a refuge to us for if the winds hold westwardly or Northwardly that we could not recover Port Royall then we could stand southwardly and gaine that Island for a recruite and need not stay long there for a winde to carry us to Port Royall.

My humble request and suite to your honours is that you would patronise our poor Inhabitants of New providence by gaineinge a Patent for New Providence and the rest of the Bahama Islands that the poor people may have protection there and be governed according to his Majestys' Laws and enjoy such priviledges for their incouragement of a better settlement as other Colonies and Plantations hath and that your Honour will be pleased to have a Remembrance therein for them, we have been the first beginners and incouragers of the settlement of New Providence and shall be ready to serve your Honour or your Commands and subscribe ourselves

Your Honour's most humble servants

JOHN DORRELL senior

HUGH WENTWORTH[1]

17. Feb: 69-70.

[S. P., Bdle. 48, No. 55.]

---

[1] Merchants of Bermuda, promoters of the Bahama settlement, and helpful in that of Carolina. Wentworth was appointed, April 24, 1671, Governor of the Bahamas; died at Barbadoes 1671. *A. & W. I.*, 509, 510, 694.

The Fundamental Constitutions of Carolina ("Second Set")[1] 120 articles &c March 1. 1670. [*Col. Papers*, Vol. 25, No. 13.] Printed *S. C. Stat.*, Vol. I, pp. 43, 56. *N. C. Rec.*, I, pp. 187.

--- ---

JOHN LORD BERKELEY of Stratton Pallatin of Carolina To all whom these presents shall come greeting.   Know ye that out of your Confidence and Trust I put in   I doe heareby constitute and appoint you the said Anthony Lord Ashley to be my Deputy as Pallatin of Carolina, for mee and in my name to doe and execute all those thing and things, Powers and Jurisdic-tions which I by vertue of the Fundamentall Constitutions and forme of Government of the Province of Carolina as Pallatin might doe; and I will that this my Deputation continue in force untill my returne into England, or that I revoke the same by granting a Deputation to some other of the Proprietors of the said Province Wittness my hand and Seal this 9th day of March 1670.

JOHN BERKELEY.[2]

(Endorsed) Carolina—Lord Berkeley deputation

Lord Ashley 29 Mar. 70.   [*S. P.*, Bdle. 48, No. 20.]

--- ---

NICHOLAS BLAKE TO JOSEPH WILLIAMSON.

Barbadoes March 23, 1669–70.

*   *   Believes it is no news in England that the two sons Lord Willoughby left behind him are dead;[3] these parts have

---

[1] The first set is dated 21st July, 1669, page 93. This second set, that published in Locke's works, was also 'to remain the sacred & unaltera-ble form & rule of governmt of Carolina forever;' but a third was dated 12th January, 1682, a fourth set 17th August, 1682, and a fifth 11th April, 1698. 'Feb. 167$\frac{9}{3}$ the Gov'r did propose to the council in the name of the Ld Prop'rs a book of new Fund'l Const'ns dated march 1669 & after-wards in 1677 the same were again by the sd Col. West proposed in Par-liam't as before in Council but were received in neither.' *Rivers*, 420, 461. *A. A.*, I, 16.

[2] Going as Lord Lieutenant to Ireland.

[3] Antigua 1670. Governor Bynum to Lord Willoughby 'sent your excellency the sad news of the death of the Lieut. General' (Henry Willoughby) 'and of the manner of the death of James Willoughby in this Island.' *A. & W. I.*, 508.

been nothing smiling or fortunate to that noble gentleman * *
Wishes they were as strong as the French in men-of-war; one
of the Commissioners, Sir John Yeamans, went for Port Royal
but is returned re infacta, having taken but 150 men, which
should be at least 10 times as many for the first settlement, unless they make account to be cut off within the year by Spaniards or Indians.   *   *   *   [*Col. Papers*, Vol. 25, No. 17.]
A. M. & W. I., § 163.

FROM THO GODWIN THE 26ᵗʰ APRIL 1670 FROM VIRGINIA.[1]

Honored Sir

These by Capt Covell with the goods according to invoice
and bill of ladeing are. received about the time of that shipps
arrival Mʳ Burgh died leaving his wiffe executrix, who sent for
the goods and about that time they came down from the shipp
to here she also died leaving all that concerned her and her husbands business in trust with us The goods you sent are not yett
opened nor will not bee till we hear further from Port Royall
being in dayly expectation of some shipp from there and upon
the arrivall whereof we shall Comply with your orders in buying
hoggs, cattle and what else is desired by those that shall come
for it In which we shall pursue your instructions and endeavour
the best we can for your advantage as well in sale of goods as in
buying with it what you would have to be bought for the service
of that designe as also in the despatch of such shipps or vessels
as is or shall be employed upon that account Sir John Yeomans
we heard was att Barmudas and from thence returned home to
Barbados after he had sent away Capt Saile Governor to Port
Royall A sloope which came out with them from Barbados was
here in January John Baulk Master being forced hither by bad
weather with about thirty people some of which were putt off
here to procure food for the rest which having done she sailed
away from here about the beginning of February.

---

[1] So endorsed.   The Three Brothers.   She reappears at St. Katherina.
Richard Bennett, 'one of Ld Arlington's family,' member Council, Virginia, and Major-General first military district; died 167—.

We have had no more at present but to subscribe our selves
Your Honors servants

RI. BENNETT
THO GODWIN.

Nansamund River in Virginia April 28th 1670.

(Endorsed) For the Honorable Sir Peter Colleton Knt at St. Jameses these   London

By the shipp Coventry Capt Gosoling

[*S. P.*, Bdle 48, No. 21.]

LORD ASHLEY, &c., TO SIR J. YEAMANS—MAY 1670?

To Sir John Yeamans Bar^t These.

Sir Your letters of the 28th of November[1] we have received, by which we perceive the effectual paines you have taken in our Port Royall designe for which we give you many thanks, We find you are mistaken in our Concessions that wee have not made provision of Land for negroes for by saying that we grant 150 acres of land for every able man servant in that we mean negroes as well as Christians And the same in other proportions which you may cause to be laid out to those who carry negroes as to the former adventurers to Carolina that paid in their 1000^{lbs} of Sugar towards the discovery And subscribed, we should now give you order for the performing our first Concessions to them, and as soon as we have that lyst, shall doe it, but in the mean time that wee [?] who are the most forward to adventure, may not be discouraged you may cause to be layed out to the first 50 of them that send servants to plant their portions of land, according to their sugar paid in ast to the reverting of the   appertayning to the Landgraves and Casiques to us upon   of the it was only that the balance of our Government might be the better upheld And is no greater restraint upon them then we have put upon ourselves about our proprietorshipps however at our next meeting we shall thinke of some way that may take off that scruple and yett uphold our balance: by Captain Prince we shall send 30 Barrels of flour for a future supply of victuall

---

[1] Before the ships left Barbadoes? Concessions, page 31, 32. The MS. is imperfect; supply 'lands,' 'want,' and 'heirs,' page 96.

and send letters of credit to New Yorke to be made use of in
case of extremity.   Wee rest your affectionate friends

ASHLEY

G. CARTERET

P. COLLETON.

This is a true Copy of the Original, Examined this   January
167½

pr Jos: Dalton Sec[r]   [*Coun. Jour. MS.*, page 76.]

MR. CARTERET'S RELATION.

Barmuda Febu[r] 26th Sayling from thence we came vp with
ye Land betweene Cape Romana & Port royall & in 17 days ye
weather being faire & ye winde not friendly ye Longe boate
went Ashoare ye better to informe as to ye certainty of ye place
where we supposed we were, vpon its approach to ye Land few
were ye natiues who vpon ye Strand made fires & came towards vs
whooping in theire own tone & manner making signes also where
we should best Land, & when we came a shoare they stroaked
vs on ye shoulders with their hands saying Bony Conraro Angles.   knowing us to be English by our Collours (as wee supposed) we then gave them Brass rings & tobacco at which they
seemed well pleased, & into ye boate after halfe an howre spent
with ye Indians we betooke our selues, they liked our Company
soe well that they would haue come a board with us.   we found
a pretty handsome channell about 3 fathoms & a halfe from ye
place we Landed to ye Shippe, through which the next day we
brought ye shipp to Anchor feareing a contrary winde & to gett
in for some fresh watter.   A day or two after ye Gouerno[r] whom
we tooke in at Barmuda with seuerall others went a shoare to
veiw ye Land here.[1]   Some 3 Leagues distant from the shipp,
carrying along with us one of ye Eldest Indians who accosted
us ye other day, & as we drew to ye shore A good number of

---

[1] Reached Bermuda by February 8, and stayed over several sermons of
Rev. S. Bond.   Left 26th, got to land 15th or 16th March, anchored in
Seewee (Bulls Bay) at north end of Oni:see:cau, now Bull's Island, 16th
or 17th.   *C. J.*, June 28, 1672, *Rivers*, 94, fix arrival March 17, but this
may be the day they reached land, anchored, or Governor Sayle landed.
The Indian town was on the main, perhaps near Oak Grove.   Lawson,
in 1701, saw a deserted Indian residence at Seewee Bay.

13

Indians appeared clad with deare skins haueing with them their bows & Arrows, but our Indian calling out Appada they withdrew & lodged theire bows & returning ran up to ye middle in mire & watter to carry us a shoare where when we came they gaue us ye stroaking Complim^t of ye country and brought deare skins some raw some drest to trade with us for which we gaue them kniues beads & tobacco and glad they were of ye Market. by & by came theire women clad in their Mosse roabs bringing their potts to boyle a kinde of thickening which they pound & make food of, & as they order it being dryed makes a pretty sort of bread, they brought also plenty of Hickery nutts, a wall nut in shape, & taste onely differing in ye thickness of the shell & smallness of ye kernell.   the Gouerno^r & seu'all others walking a little distance from ye water side came to ye Hutt Pallace of his Ma^{ty} of ye place, who meeteing vs tooke ye Gouerno^r on his shoulders & carryed him into ye house in token of his chearfull Entertainement.   here we had nutts & root cakes such as their women useily make as before & watter to drink for they use no other lickquor as I can Learne in this Countrey, while we were here his Ma^{tyes} three daughters entred the Pallace all in new roabs of new mosse which they are neuer beholding to ye Taylor to trim up, with plenty of beads of diuers Collours about their necks: I could not imagine that ye sauages would so well deport themselues who coming in according to their age & all to sallute the strangers, stroaking of them.   these Indians understanding our business to St Hellena told us that ye Westoes a rangeing sort of people[1] reputed to be the Man eaters had ruinated y^t place killed seu'all of those Indians destroyed & burnt their Habitations & that they had come as far as Kayawah doeing the like there, ye Casseeka of which place was within one sleep of us (which is 24 howrs for they reckon after that rate) with most of his people whome in two days after came aboard of us.[2]

Leaueing that place which is called Sowee, carrying ye Cas-

---

[1] 'That live back in an entire body' (in a palisaded town on west bank of Westo:boo River) 'have guns, attack these & carry away their corne & children & eat them,' or sell their captives in trade with the northward colonies. See *post*.

[2] About March 20, this ubiquitous 'very ingenious Indian' left at sea with Sandford in 1666, reappears to decide the fate of Port Royal.

seeka of Kayawah wth us a uery Ingenious Indian & a great Linguist in this Maine, ye winde being very Lofty soe that we could
not deale with ye shoare   we droue to the southward of Port
royall, where we made a faire opening & findeing by obseruation
& otherwayes ye Contrary we stood fiue minutes to ye northward & soe gott ye shipp into Portroyall riuer (the opening
there appeared not to us as Collⁿ Sanford did relate) ag^t which
shoales ley of a bout fiue Leagues to sea.[1]   W N W Hilton head
boare from us when we steared in, & in stearing in w. n w: &
n w b w: we had 2½ fathoms at low water with breakers on both
sides, but when you are within you haue 5. 6. 7. 8 & 9. fathoms
water & a cleare Riuer.   I cannot say much of the channell
being but a Land man. but this ye Gouerno^r Capt Brayne and
myself took ye Longe boate to goe upon discouery & stood
of to sea about 5: or 6: miles close aboard the northwardmost
Breakers, we had no lesse than 5: fathoms at low water ye tyde
being spent & the winde proueing calme we were forst to make
in for ye shoare with ye tyde of floud Leaueing this to Cap.
Brayne who will giue you a more pfect Acc^t then I can.   A small
kinde of whale white about ye head & Joule is very plenty in
this Riuer in two howres time I beheld about 10: or 11: of ye
kinde, & some p^rtend & undertake to say to be of ye Sparma
kinde that were worth ye Experim^t to finde out ye truth of it,
we were two dayes at Anchor ere we could speake with an Indian.
when we did they confirmed what heard at Sowee. we weighed
from Port royall riuer & ran in between St Hellena & Combohe
where we lay at Anchor all ye time we staide neare ye Place
where ye distressed Indian soiourned, who were glad & crying
Hiddy doddy Comorado Angles Westoe Skorrye (which is as
much as to say) English uery good friends Westoes are nought,

---

[1] Page 73. Got to Port Royal about March 21, stayed two days, and
then to St. Helena (the town was perhaps on north end of that island
near site of St. Helenaville), lying there held the first South Carolina
election for five commoners of the Council, Jos. Dalton, R. Donne, Ra.
Marshall, Paul Smyth and S. West; sent the shallop (which West and
Brayne had bought in Bermuda) to Kiawah and waited her return.
These breakers of ' Martin's Industry,' the exposed situation of Port
Royal ' in the very chaps of the Spaniard,' and the persuasions of the
Caseeka turned them to Kiawah. They arrived early in April. Wilson,
1680, and St. Augustine report, *S. C. Col.*, 4, page 11, also say the ships
arrived at Ashley River in April, 1670.

they hoped by our Arriuall to be protected from ye Westoes, often making signes they would ingage them with their bowes & arrows, & wee should with our guns they often brought vs veneson & some deare skins wch wee bought of them for beads. many of us went ashore at St Hellena & brought back word that ye Land was good Land supplyed with many Peach trees, & a Competence of timber a few figg trees & some Cedar here & theire & that there was a mile & a halfe of Cleare Land fitt & ready to Plante. Oysters in great plenty all ye Islands being rounded wth bankes of ye kinde, in shape longer & scarcely see any one round, yet good fish though not altogether of soe pleasant taste as yor wall fleet oysters. here is also wilde turke which ye Indian brought but is not soe pleasant to eate of as ye tame, but uery fleshy & farr bigger. ye sloupe wch wee haue with us bought at Barmuda was dispatcht to Kayawah to veiwe that Land soe much Comended by the Casseeka   brings back a report y^t y^t Lande was more fit to Plant in then St Hellena which begott a question whether to remove from St Hellena theither, or stay some were of opinion it were more prudent forthwith to Plant prouisions where they were then betake themselues to a second voyage though small it would not proue a better change ye Enterance into that harbour being as difficult as ye other. the Gouerno^r adhearing for Kayawah & most of us being of a temper to follow thoug wee knew noe reason for it Imitating ye rule of ye Inconsiderate multitude cryed out for Kayawah yet some dissented from it yet being sure to take a new voyage but difident of a better convenience those that Inclyned for Port royall were looked upon straingely soe thus wee came to Kayawah. the Land here & at St Hell^a is much at one ye surface of the earth is a light blackish mould under that is whiter & about 3: or 4: feet is a clay some read wth blew vaines & some blew wth read vaines soe is all ye Land I haue seen.

Endorsed by Locke. Mr Carterets[1] relation of their Planting
                      at Ashley River   *70.*

[*S. P.*, Bdle. 48, No. 23.]

---

[1] Nicholas Carteret settled his plantation and servants and went on the ship to Virginia and back, then to Barbadoes September 23, and witnesses Yeomans' will there 1671; commended by Sayle; held lands at Ickerby 1672, 74.

Mr. Mathews' Relation.

The sloupe which we had at Barbadoes,[1] & parted wth at sea did Arriue at Keyawah on Munday ye 23rd of May: 1670. An acc^t of whose voyage from St Katherina & Passages there I thought fit to send yor Hon^r as I had it from Mr Maurice Mathews who was in her.

On Saturday May ye 15th we came to an Anchor in St Katherina A place about ye Latt: of 31^d: where wee intended to wood & watter the Indians very freely came aboard whom we Entertained, from this day to ye 18: they traded with us for beads & old Clothes, & gaue our people bread of Indian Corne, Peas, Leakes, Onyons, deare skins, Hens, Earthen pots &c. vpon ye 16 day Came Aboard An Indian Semi Spaniard with a p^rsent of bread &c. to our Master, & promised him Porke for truck. seu'all of our people had been just at theire houses & told us of braue plantations with a: 100: working Indians & that they want nothing in the world, our Master upon ye: 17: instant about 8 in ye morning with his mate & Mr Riuers three seamen & one man servant which had been theire Just before went a shoare with truck to buy porke for ye sloupes use, theire were two men servants more which went a shoare ag^t ye sloupe to Cut wood &c & one woman with a girle to wash some Linnien at ye wattering place, our Master promised to be aboard next tyde, but he came not, we hollowed to them right ashoare about 4 of ye clocke but they made no answere this raised a doubtfull feare in us, that night we kept a strickt watch & next day about: 10: of ye clocke we heard A drume, & p^rsently saw 4 Spaniards Armed with muskets & swords, with ye drume came downe one of these & standing behind a tree holding forth A white cloath hailed us & bid us yield & submit to ye soueraignty of S^to Domingo & told us it were better soe for o^r Capt was in chaines. I holding up a white shirt told him if we should haue our people wee would depart in peace but he cryed No, No, & giuieing ye word to some in ye wood, Indians & Spaniards wee receiued a volley of musket shott & A cloud of Arrows which ye Indians shott upright, & soe they continued for an howre & a half, then they Left of, & comanded three

---

[1] 'Three Brothers' left Nansemond in February. St. Katherines, Ga., called Wallie, a Spanish mission. Captain Baulk, his mate, Mr. Rivers, W. Carr, Marg't Tuder? Marten Bedson? and others were taken.

of us ashoare, we told them we would send on with Letters to
them, & sent them A boy a shoare who swimed with a note to
ye Master & another to ye fryer ye note to the fryer treated of
free passage with all our people, ye boy they receiued courteously, cloathing him at ye watter side with deare skins &c.   A little
after they bid us not use any armes, & they would ye Like. And
bid us expect an answer to oʳ Letter.   we were glad of this &
agreed, but about half an houre after they comanded shippe & all
ashoare.   we told them we had neither winde nor boat to obey
them (not a breath of winde stirring) & gaue them faire words
intending with ye first Winde to gett without shott, but they fired,
& shott att us feircely.   then a small breeze arising of ye Lande
& we with much adoe haueing weighed oʳ small bower & cut oʳ
best, hoisted sayle and away & came to an anchor out of theire
reach, but before this I being at ye Helme, John Haukes (on of
ye sea-men) shott at them which made all keep behind trees.
wee haueing out three muskets had not a bullet till at Last we
found seu'all upon ye deck which reshooting did a little help us,
as we stood to our sailes, but they fired still but by gods mercy
hit no body, but our sailes were much damaged.   ye next day
about noone we hoistsd & away, turneing it out they stll keeping
watch on the shoare.   Saturday May ye 19ᵗʰ we sailed about ye
shoare wᵗʰ ye winde at South, this night we came to Anchor in
two fathoms & a halfe watter ye next morning we weighed Anchor & steered alongst shoare about. 10. of ye Clock we made
A. cannew coming of ye shoare towards us, which proued to be
of 4 Indians they with signes of friendship came aboard.   We
Entertained them courteously, they told us the place right Ashoare
from thence Odistash & as we understood them told us there were
English at Keyawah, they further told us of a Capᵗen Sheedou,
& made signe that he would speak with us upon this we detained
ye Cheifest of them & sent one a shoare to that pʳsone they spoke
of, with a Letter to desire him to come A board without much
Company ye three Indians that went with our Messenger a shoare
promised to returne after sun set.   A bout twilight they returned
with our messenger & Capᵗ Sheedou, & one Capt. Alush (who
were at Barbadoes)[1] & many more, this Sheedou told us that

---

[1] Indian captains of Edisto, with Hilton, pages 20, 64. 'Carry,' its
first South Carolina use in that sense?

ye English with two Shipps had been at Port royall & were now at Keyawah he further promised us on ye morrow to carry us thither, About 9 of ye clock came another Cannow but we sent them after a little stay away being all too numerous—ye next morning we came to saile for Keyawah where we found ye Barmudian sloupe going out A fishing who pilated us into Keyawah river.

Endorsed by Locke.   Mr Mathews relacon of St Katherina Ashley River 70

[*S. P.*, Bdle. 48, No. 22.]

GOVERNOR SAYLE TO LORD ASHLEY.

Much Honord and noble Lord.

I hope yor Lordsp hath recd an accot (Long before this tyme) of Gods prouidences and dealeings with yor Seruant and Colony here in Carolina from my selfe Mr. West &c.   Though we are (att p'sent) vnder some straight for want of provision (incident to the best of new Plantations) yet, we doubt not (through the goodness of God) of recruits from sundry places to wch we haue sent.   But there is one thing wch lyes very heauy vpon us.   The want of a Godly and orthodox Minist' wch I and many others of vs haue euer liued vnder, as the greatest of o' Mercyes.   May it please yor Lordsp in my Late Country of Barmudas there are diuers Ministrs of whom there is one Mr Sampson Bond,[1] heretofore of Long standing in Exeter Colledge in Oxford, and ordayned by the late Byshop of Exeter, the old Dor Joseph Hall: And by a Commission from the Earle of Manchester and Company for the sumer Islands, sent there in the yeere 1662, for the term of three yeeres, vnder whose powerfull and soul-edefying Ministry I haue liued about eight yeeres last past: There was

------

[1] Not in Foster's Oxford.   He remained at the Bermudas many years after Governor Sayle's death.   Opinions differ, 'Falmouth, 1651 to stir up others to the pious work of propogation of the Gospel in N. England &c one man in o' west partes put in to be a treasurer wch is not well beloved wth us, but rather feare he will deceive you of itt, his name is Mr Sampson Bond, a notorious Insynuating Hypocrite as by most of us conceived, &c.'   R. Lobb to E. Winslow, *N. E. His. Reg.*, 1883, p. 392.

nothing in all this world soe grieuous to my spirit, as the thought
of parting with his Godly society and faythfull ministry: But I
did a little comfort myselfe that it might please ye Lord by some
good meanes or other to enclyne his heart to come after vs, who
hath little respect from some who are now in Authority in Barmudas, wch is a great discouragm^t to him; wch Is taken notice oft
in other places, and he is inuited to Boston in New England and
to New Yorke by the Gouerno^r there, with tenders of Large
incouragement, If he will come to ye one or other place: I haue
Likewise writt most earnestly to him desiring that he would
come and sitt downe with vs, Assuring him it is not only my
vrgent Request but withall the most hearty request of ye Colony
in Generall, who were exceedingly affected with him and his
Ministry all the tyme they were in Barmudas, And we shall all
haue Assured Cause to Bless God for him, so long as we shall
liue, might he be gained to be ou^r settled minis^r.   Sr John Yeoman was soe much affected with him, that he promised me he
would procure a Comission from the King to make him ou^r min-
ist^r and to the vttmost endeauo^r to procure him a Considerable
Sallary for his incouragem^t.   But I can heare of nothing done
by him herein, wch hath imboldened me (in the name of all ye
rest) most humbly to beseech yor Lord^{sp} to put on bowells of
great Goodness and Compassion towards yor Colony here, in
procuring (wch yor Lord^{sp} may easily and speedly doe) a Comission and Competent Sallary for him for about fiue or seuen yeeres
(till the Lord shall enable vs to mayntayne him ou^rselues) to be
paid to him or his Assignes in London, Barbadoes, or elsewhere:
I doe most faythfully assure yor Lord^{sp} that this Mr Bond is so
well known, well reported off, and so beloued in most the Cara-
bee Islands that were it known abroad that he were yor Minist^r
here, It is the iudgm^{mt} of sundry prudent persons, It would (in
a little tyme) gaine many hundreds of Considerable persons to
this place: Oh that it might not be deemed too much boldness in
me to beseech yor Lord^{sp} with ye desired Comission to hono^r
him with yor Lett^r wch If it be sent to yor Comissio^r att Barbadoes, It will soon be dispatcht to him: I shall not (att p^rsent)
give yor Lord^{sp} any further trouble takeing my leaue with my
fixed purposes to the vttmost during life to further this yor
Lord^{sps} (hytherto) Blessed designe euer praying for an encrease
of those yor Manifest fauo^rs of all kinds and degrees of eminent

Gifts and graces from God, and likewise for an encrease of yor most deserued Hono^r and noble dignityes from his sacred Maiesty.

Resteth yor Lords^{ps} in all humility and ffaythefullness to Hono^r obey &c.

WILLIAM SAYLE.[1]

ffrom Albemarle point in Ashley Riuer June 25th 1670.

Endorsed by Locke. Wm Sayle 17 July, 70.

To my Lord Ashley   Ashley River.

Addressed: For the Right Honorable Anthony Lord Ashley Att little Exetur House in the Strand   London.

[S. P., Bdle. 48, No. 24.]

JOSEPH WEST TO LORD ASHLEY.

May it please yor Lo^p

In my last to yor Lo^p dated ye 28th of May, I gave yor Lo^p an Account by the way of Virginia of our proceedings in Carolina, and how wee came to quitt Port Royall, and to begin our settlement at Kyawaw:[2] May it please yor Lo^p since the departure of the ship for Virginia, wee sent the shallop back againe to St Katherina with 2 letters, one for the Governour of St Augustines,

---

[1] With seal. Duplicate of this letter but with a different seal, date Oct. 24, 1670, S. P., No. 41.

[2] Now Old Town Plantation. The town was on a low bluff, the first land on the north side of a winding creek, a flat point of dark pine forest projecting into the wide marshes of Ashley river; a fair prospect on an April morning and (but for sparcer pines) much the same a few years ago, as then; now changed by axe and plough. Across a narrow neck behind the town a palisade and ditch (still traceable) enclosed some nine acres; beyond near the spring and oak grove was the Indian village. From Kiawah Sayle sent 'the Bermuda sloop up the river to discover it,' the ship to Virginia, with the Barbadoes proclam'n and West's letter 28th May, enclosing these 'Relacons' and the 'Three Brothers,' under N. Sayle, with letters to the Gov'r Don Pedro Melinza? to Wallie (where they lost Capt. Bailey and Jno. Collins) and then June 27 to Bermuda with this letter.

the other for ye ffryer at St Katherina to demand the men y^t were detained there by the Spaniards. (Yo^r Lo^{ps} Kinsman Mr Rivers being one of them:) and when y^r shallop came thither, 2: or 3 of our people went a shore contrary to orders, without Hostage, and the ffryer reced them seemingly wth much kindness, and told them upon his ffaith they should not be wronged, whereupon there was 4 of our men went to his House, where he treated them very Civilly, and told them y^t our men were at St Augustines, not as prisoners, but had theire Liberty about the towne and were Entertained at an English man's house; but when our men were taking theire leave of the ffryer, Hee, betweene a Complement and Constraint detained 2 of them, upon pretence that hee could not lett them goe till hee had an Answer from St Augustines, whereupon after 3 days stay, our men in the shallop being informed by the Indians that there were 3 ships at St Augustines wch would come to surprize the shallop were forced weigh Anchor for their security & come for Kyawaw leaving those 2 men more behind at the ffryers house.   Now yor Lo^p may please to knowe that wee are forced to send the Barbadoes shallop to Bermuda for a supply of provision for feare the ship should miscarry at Virginia for wee have but 7 weekes provision left and y^t onely pease at a pint a day a man the Country affording us nothing, wch makes it goe very hard with us and wee cannot Employ our servants as wee would because wee have no victualls for them: Our Corne, potatoes, and other things doe thrive very well of late praised be god. but wee cannot have any dependance on it this yeare, but if wee have kindly supplys now wee doe not question but to prouide for ourselues ye next yeare. and y^t it will prove a very good settlement and answer yor Lo^{ps} Expectacon wch is ye desire of

Yo^r Lo^{ps} most humble and faithful serv^t

JOSEPH WEST.

Albemarle poynt at Kyawaw June ye 27th *1670.*

Endorsed by Locke.

Joseph West—27 June 70 To my Ld Ashley. Ashly River.

Addressed—For the Right Honob^{le} Anthony Lord Ashley at little Exeter House in the Strand   London.

[*S. P.*, Bdle. 48, No. 25.]

The Council to the Proprietors.

Right Hono^rable

My service presented vnto yor Hono^rs—May it please yor Hono^rs since the writing of our former letter by way of Virginia, wee have sent vnto the Spaniards to demand the Captaine of the shallop and the rest of the men detained by them, and wee gaue strict orders to those whom wee sent to make the demand as afores^d not to trust themselues with the Spaniards, but some of them as soone as they did arriue at Sta Catherina being deluded by the ffryers faire pretences, contrary to our orders, went ashoare to him, and soe wee haue lost two men more, namely Mr Joseph Bailey, and John Collins.[1] Wee sent a letter vnto the Gouerno^r of Sta Augustine, and another to the ffryer of Sta Catherina, but noe Answer can be got from them: Therefore wee desire yor Hono^rs orders and directions how we shall further demeane ourselues in this matter. Two of our Councill[2] haueing acted in the s^d Embassie quite contrary to our Instructions, we haue at present suspended from the Councill table. Wee haue not aboue one months' prouision in the Collony, for as we are forced to send the shallop to the Sumer Islands for prouision to keep our people from perishing and we are forced to charge Bills upon yor Hono^rs Agents at the Barbadoes to pay Sugar for such prouisions as wee take up at the Sumer Islands: Our necessityes are soe great that wee must either doe this or else dessert the settlement, wch were a great pitty, ffor indeed, my Lords, I am confident there was neuer a more hopefull designe set on foote. I haue been in seuerall places, yet neuer was in a sweater clymate then this is. Wee haue discouered abundance of good land as a man would desire to looke on, wee doe Judge and I doe belieue there is good land enough for millions of people to liue & worke on, There is nothing that wee plant but it thriues very well. Wee sowed some flax and it thriues very well, the land as I doe conceiue will beare Sugar canes & I doe beleiue good

---

[1] 'A person of good worth and a good linguist;' imprisoned at St. Augustine. West kept his four servants and the Council reserved his lands, but he unlike Collins 'Marshal of Kiwah,' seems not to have returned to Carolina. Captain Jno. Collins, of C. T., died 170⁸⁄₉ leaving to his wife Elizabeth and sons Jonah, John and Alexander, Carnadey, Washishoe, and Tibwen plan'ns and Bull's island.

[2] Scrivener and Donne who alone do not sign?

wine, Tobacco, silk, all sorts of English graine & manufactry may be plentifully produced here.   In tenn or twelue yeares doubtlesse yo[r] Hono[rs] may haue returne from hence suitable to your great expences.   Therefore I beseech yo[r] Hono[rs] that we may Imploy yo[r] Hono[rs] shipps to fetch more people that this honor[ble] designe might not fall for want of an Industrious man- agement, w[ch] a little more expences will preserue.   Myself & Councill doe use our vtmost endeavours for the advancement of yo[r] Hono[rs] Interest in this Country, & for that purpose I haue wrote to the people of the Sumer Islands & to New England to gaine what people wee may to promote the designe, and we shall further make vse of all opportunityes and advantages whereby we may propogate this worthy designe, and expresse our selves

Yo[r] Hono[rs] most faithfull humble servant

William Sayle

Flor: O: Sullivan	Stephen Bull
Joseph West	Paul Smyth
Ralph Marshall	Samuel West

Jos: Dalton—Secret[ry].

Endorsed by Locke.   William Sayle & Councill.

To Proprietors—*70*   Ashley River.

Addressed: To his Grace George Duke of Albemarle Cap[t] Genn[ll] of all his Ma[ts] fforces &c.: and the right hono[ble] the rest of the Lords propriet[rs] of the province of Carolina in America.

at   Whitehall   humbly p[r]sent.

[*S. P.*, Bdle. 48, No. 42.]

MR. OWENS' PARLIAMENT.

Albemarle point ye 4[th] July 1670

Mr Maurice Math[s]	Mr. Hen: Hughes
Mr. John Jones	Mr. Tho: Smith
Henry Symons	D[r] Henry Woodward
Hugh Carteret	James Marshall
Anthony Charne	Will: Kennie
George Beadon	*Jonathan Barker
*Thomas Ingram	Thomas Norris

Will: Owen

We ye free houlders haue by virtue of ye Goun[rs] order and sumons in pursuance of Au'tie to him giuen by Lords proprietors Institutions and Instruccons for Gou'nm[t] elected and chosen ye seu'all persons aboue named in ord[r] to ye establishm[t] of Laws for the p[r]sent and better Gou'm[t] of ye people within this province who being added to ye fiue persons alreadie in ye Councill Compleate ye number of 20 as is by ye said Institutions Warr'ted and directed.

Endorsed:

Mr. Owen's Parliamt[s] returne July 4[th] 1670[1]

[*S. P.*, Bdle. 48, No. 26.]

———

CAPTAIN BRAYNE'S ADVICE.

Sir

You maye please to be enformed that coming to account with Captain Thomas Godwin and mister Richard Bennett for the Goods shipt and moneys disbursed by them for your shipp the Carolina in furnishing her out with a supply for your plantation at Keyawah or port Royall, I found that Major Generall Bennett had layd out fower score pounds fifteene shillings six pence sterling more than what came to his hands from Sir William Berkeley and Captain Godwin for the Reimburseing whereof. I have drawn bills of Exc: on you payable at sight to mister Arthur Bailey and M[r] Thomas James or either of them.

Not at all doubting but that you will please to honour those bills with your acceptance I humbly take leave and Rest

Your Honors Humble servant to com[d]

HENRY BRAYNE.

Nansamund River in Virginia the 30th of July 1670.

---

[1] This 4th of July parliament, the first in Carolina, was neither legally called nor recognized. Thos. Smith was afterwards 'much esteemed for his wisdom and sobriety,' sheriff of Berkley, Member of Council and Cassique 1691, and in 1693 landgrave and governor. He was m'd 2d 'by Rev. Wm. Dunlop, March 22, 168$\frac{2}{3}$, to Sabina de Vignon dowager Van Wernhaut,' widow of John D'Arsens, whose Carolina barony he acquired 1689; he died 1694. H. Symons came from Nevis? was in the Council 1691, and died 1695 ? leaving considerable estates to his wife Frances. Barker and Ingram were said not to be qualified.

More 10ˢ for a Boare delivered aboard after the accompt was past, and 10ˢ for a bond upon the clearing the shipp is 20ˢ.

HENRY BRAYNE.

Endorsed :

Captain Brayne leter advise 30° Jul. 70.

[*S. P.*, Bdle. 48, No. 27.]

PROVISIONS AT ASHLEY RIVER.

140 men at River Ashly[1] they had in River 7 weeks provisons from the 25ᵗʰ June which is to the midle of August.

At Barbados is 30 barrels of 200 bushells of flower and 20 barrels of about 4500 lb beef which is provisions for 140 men 90 days more which is to the middle of november   The Carolina had from Virginia the produce of a cargo of 270ˡᵇ what that is I cannot tell but cannot be lesse than 6 months if we are not cheated which is to the middle of may.   Besides all this they have crops which if it produce according to Virginia will be at least 1000 bushells of Indian corne besides Roots and beanes which crop I judge was ripe by the middle of August

[*In Sir P. Colleton's hand.*]

Endorsed by John Locke.   Provisions at Ashley river 70

[*S. P.*, Bdle. 48, No. 28.]

COUNCIL TO THE PROPRIETORS.

May it please yoʳ Honoʳˢ

In observance of our dutyes we shall not omitt any opportunity of giueing yoʳ Honoʳˢ a faithfull Accᵗ of all our proceedings in this place, pursuant therevnto wee here doe offer to yoʳ Honoʳˢ that for some time since the dispatch of the Carolina from this place to Virginia & the sloop to Bermuda to bring Provisions and other supplyes that yoʳ Honoʳˢ care had intended for vs, wee haue been put to purchase our maintenance from the Indians, & yᵗ in such small parcells, as we could hardly get another supply before the former was gone, in which time of our soe

---

[1] West hoped for 200, Blake mentions 150, less the Port Royal's 35 leaves, say 120, and a few from Bermuda, &c.

great Exigencyes the spaniard not being ignorant of it sent out a party of their Indians ag^t us as we received intelligence from the Indians y^t are our friends, who lay for some time in a place called Stonoe neare our Rivers mouth, vntill the Carolina ffriggot arriued here wch was the 22th of Augt last in wch time we receu'd seuerall Allarums though they neuer yet came soe far as to Action, more then when Mr. Henry Braine came upon the Coast, and went ashoare in his long boat thinking to meet with our owne Indians being so neare the Riuers mouth, they fired upon him and his company with small shott, notwithstanding y^t the s^d Indians had shewed them a white flagg:[1]

But before y^t time we had put our selues in a reasonable good posture of receiueing them though they had come much in odds, hauing mounted our great Guns, & fortifyed ourselues as well as time & the abilityes of our people would giue leaue, & moued good courage in our people, besides the assistance of some Indians y$^:$ were our friends.

After the shipps arrived we sent out a p'ty of our Indians with two of our own people to discouer their Camp but when they expected to come upon them, the Spanish Indians were retreated back againe as our Indians informe us at the noise of our great Gunns, but whether there were any Spaniards among them we cannot yet receiue certaine intelligence, other then one who according to our Indians description we iudge to be a ffryer, neither can we as yet know the number of Indians that lay ag^t us they exceeding the number of an Indians acc^t.

The Carolina's safe arrivall has very much incouraged our people, the more for y^t she has brought us provisions of Indian Corne, pease, & meale for eight months, soe as we make noe question but (by God's assistance) throughly to defend & maintaine yor Hono^{rs} Interests & our Rights in this place till we receiue a further Aid which we very much stand need of, y^t soe plantations may be managéd & yor Hon^{rs} finde what we indeavour to p'suade that this country will not deceiue yor Hono^{rs} & others Expectacons, for wch purpose we haue dispatched the Car-

---

[1] The Carolina reached Virginia June 6, left Aug. 8, got to Morris island where they landed, Aug. 22, and came in 23d. Sailed for Barbadoes Sept. 15, but was delayed till 23d.

olina to Barbadoes where we vnderstand are a considerable number of people ready to be shipped for this place, y^t she may make a returne before winter wch will conduce much to the safety of this place & the ease of our people, y^t haue been too much ouerprest with watching already, & what we must stand to vpon euery occasion, & yet blessed be God we haue not lost aboue foure of our people[1] who dyed vpon distempers usual in other parts, soe far may be yor Hono^{rs} be further convinced of the healthfulnesse of the place.

The stores of all sorts doe very much want a supply especially cloathing, being all disposed of allready & many of the people vnsatisfyed, & the winter is like to proue pretty sharp; The powder was all damnified especially when the sterne of the ship broke in, soe as there is a great necessity of Ten barrells of powder more.

Wee haue rec'd some cowes & Hoggs from Virginia, but at an imoderate rate, considering the smalnesse of their growth 30^s for a hog, a better then wch may be bought in England for 10^s. If yor Hono^{rs} had a small stocke in Bermuda from thence may be transported to this place a very good breed of large cowes, Hoggs, & sheep, at farr easier rates.

The Bohama Islands lyeing neare this coast from the latt 34. to 37. being lately setled,[2] & as yet in noe patents soe far as we can vnderstand may be worthy yor Hono^{rs} care to take notice of, for from thence wee can be supplyed with salt, & shipps goeing home without freight (if any such should be) may take in a loadeing of Brazellettoe wood.

We are in great want of an able minister by whose meanes corrupted youth might be very much reclaimed, and the people instructed in the true religion, and that the Sabbaoth and service of Almighty God be not neglected.

The Israelites prosperity decayed when their prophets were wanting, for where the Arke of God is, there is peace & tran-

---

[1] 'Only one of those that came out of England.'

[2] Lat. 24, 27. By Bermudians, 1666. Granted 1 Nov: 1670, to Albemarle, Craven, Berkley, Ashley, Carteret & Colleton.

quility, that the want thereof may neuer be knowne to yor Hono^{rs} or this place are the prayers of

yor Hono^{rs} most faithfull humble Servants[1]

William Sayle	Flor: O. Sullivan
Ste: Bull	Joseph West
Will: Scrivener	Ralph Marshall
Paul: Smythe	Samuel West.

Jos: Dalton—Secr^y.

Albemarle Point Sepr. 9th 1670.

Endorsed: Council at Ashley Riv: to L^{ds} Proprietors 9° Sept. 70.

Addressed: To The right hono^{ble} Anthony Ld Ashley chancello^r of his Mat^s Co^{rt} of Excheq^r and the rest of the Lords Proprieto^{rs} of Carolina   at   Whitehall *London*   humbly p^rsent.

[*S. P.*, Bdle. 48, No. 31.]

———

May it please your Lordshipp

Att the request of Mr Joseph Dalton we doe hereby certifye to your Lordshipp that the said Joseph Dalton was elected to be one of the Councill by the people according to the Lords Proprietors directions, and we in confidence of his abilities and Integrity have constituted and appointed him to be our Secretary and Register for this Collony; Wee finde him sufficiently quallifyed for, and capable of the said imployment wherein he has demeaned himself with great care and great dilligence, but for a Continuance or any Grant thereof we have directed him to your Lordshipps pleasure for an order, to

Your Lordshipps most faithfull and humble servants

William Sayle

Step. Bull	Joseph West
Will Scrivenor	Flor O'Sullivan
Ralph Marshall	Samuell West

---

[1] These Sept. letters went in the Carolina to Barbadoes. Duplicates of *S. P.*, 30, 34, &c., are entered in 'Carolina letter book of the Earl of Shaftesbury.' *A. W. I.*, 252, has *S. P.*, 28, 'note in handwriting of Jno. Locke' instead of 'Sir P. Colleton' as above.

Endorsed by Locke.

Council at Ashley river recommendation of J. Dalton to be Secretary and Register 9° Sept. 70

[*S. P.*, Bdle. 48, no. 29.]

———

JOSEPH DALTON[1] TO LORD ASHLEY.

May it please your Lordshipp

To wast a small time in the perusall of a few rude lines it takes boldnesse to wait upon your Lordshipp more out of an affectionate duty than a curious nicety designeing no other but that your Lordshipp may have a through understanding of all things in this place that may conduce to your Lordshipps Interest and the good of this happy (I hope) settlement.

Your Lordshipp has had a full account of the harbours, scituations and hopefullnesse of this place, which indeed deserves noe other than an excellent commendation.

The Collony is indeed safely setled and with a very propritious aspect there only remaines the preservation of it which consists cheifly in two things, carefull supplyes and a wise politicke Government which two diamonds I have borrowed for this structure from the ruines of other settlements of this nature of the English especially who have been very unsuccesfull of late, which in my weake opinion might be very easily prevented and by a free disbursement of a penny in the morning may have a pound at night. By carefull supplyes I meane a speedy peopling of this place to the effecting of which the best way is for your Lordshipp to have a ship of a considerable burthen to be wholly imployed for three or four yeares in transporting of people and their goods to this place gratis they finding themselves provisions which though it may seem to draw something out of your Lordshipps Treasure yet it will but be as good put into the ground for a better harvest and a perfect store of all necessaries

---

[1] A learned & able man, chosen to Council 1670, & made Sect'y & Register & most useful in those & other offices; Oct. 7, 1673, he went thro' the wilds to treat with the Esaw Indians, returning safe Feb. 1674; in May he asked to go home, but in Dec. was in the Council & gives his lands 'next Ickerby' for newcomers. He was Sect'y till 1677, and died 167–. 'May 20, 1682, Mr. Wm. Reach having purchased Mr. Dalton's plantation of his heirs, &c.' *H. S. Col.*, I, 205.

belonging to a new settlement till they have a produce of their owne, the want of which have been sometimes fatall always injurious, hunger starved infancy seldome produces strong maturity consumptions may be reasonably prevented but chargeably recovered; This place craves your Lordshipps care for stores of all sorts cheifly servants Apparell: As for the Government aforementioned it lyes in your Lordshipps breast to effect neither doe I reflect upon the present Government the gravity whereof I do reverence, yet I will take boldnesse to represent to your Lordshipp very briefly the charge that lyes upon Government in this place.

We are here settled in the very chaps of the Spaniard whose clandestine actions both domesticke and forraigne are not unknown to your Lordshipp nor can be blotted out of the memoryes of the West India planters soe tender skinned are his managements that they start bloud with a prick at a thousend miles distance and therefore must be avenged if they can, either secretly, or by publicke hostility; this we have in some measure experienced though to no great losse other than the inforced omision of planting, to secure ourselves; which we doe not doubt yet to performe as well as we have hitherto done haveing severall advantages of him, for first the Indians that are under him dare not trust for his long continued tyranny among them has taught them how to desire liberty; and well he knowes that they will be the cheife Instruments to cut him off if ever an enemy comes against him in probability able to encounter him, secondly we have a perfect road to him through our owne Indians but if he comes to us he may possibly make an approach per terrorem but he is soe surrounded with false friends that upon a small skirmish he will finde it a difficult matter to cleare himself.

One principall grudge he has against us I humbly conceive may be partly from a jealousy of the King of Spaine requie (?)[1] which passes the Westward of us to Mexicoe which lyes not much above 300 leagues very neare west from this place, according to the estemate of M[r] Hen: Woodward our Interpreter, who has had a good oppotunity dureing his confinement at S[t] Augustine to discover the truth thereof, the which he gives good reason to believe The people here are in very good plight,

---

[1] Uncertain in MS. the plate fleet seems meant.

especially since provisions came from Virginia, only they have
had a sad repulse of their desires in propogating their plantations
with provisions and such produce as might inable them to discharge their dutyes to the Lord Proprietor by these alarmes
being more like souldiers in a garrison than planters to whose
conditions your Lordship if but throughly senceble, would use
no small clemency in a favourable mitigation of freight for their
goods being in some measure a recompence for their losses.

We heard of the losse of the ship port Royall upon the
Bohama Iselands but the truth thereof is not yet manifested:
there is an absolute necessity for a speedy dispatch of ships to
this place, and that one Ship of force still be here, whilst the
rest are abroad; Your Lordshipp may by a penny know how a
shilling is coined, my desire was only to give a hint (or be as a
sparke for a nobler flame without any strangely affected idiom or
dialect, if I have done well I have my reward, if otherwise my
Lord be pleased to pardon my lavishnesse, pardon a penn stupi-
fied with zeale for the prosperity of Carolina: I should now subscribe my dixi. but that I beg leave to speake a word or two to
this certificate to your Lordshipp directed from our Government
and Councill.

Since it has pleased our Government and Councill for reasons
best known to themselves to conferre upon me the office of their
secretary and Register for this Collony, wherein I have expressed great dilligence and care in reduceing all proceedings to an
orderly method which I hope I have effected to a losse of much
time (which I might have well expended otherwise) and that
without one farthing of advantage to myself, I humbly desire
that I may not be denied some part of that favour your Lordshipp has intended for the first adventurers, being one of the
first that set forward this designe, and that as I have strugled
through the worst I may have your Lordshipps favourable Grant
(bene gerente) to have a small share of the better that soe your
Lordshipps service may not have any countenance of discouragement in it; but therein as it now stands or upon any misdemean-
our I am very willing to submit to your Lordshipps pleasure.

We have very little paper in the whole Collony being most of
it lost and damnified in the voyage which proves a great impediment to this office though I made the best shifts I could with a
small quantity of my own which I had saved.

Noe provision being made for this office, there is not one booke wherein to record anything, I hope the want thereof for the future will be remedied by your Lordshipp especially a booke to Register Grants in which ought to be of a considerable bulke in folio.

I shall trouble your Lordshipps patience noe more at this time, being ready to observe all your Lordshipps commands to, or concerning me, a duty that I shall alwayes adore as I am

Your Lordships most faithfull humble servant

Jos: DALTON

Albemarle Point Sept 9th 1670

It will be a very great invitation for people to come hither for to cause to be published in England and other his Majesties plantations a freedome of trade & that without custome for seaven yeares, without which they will hardly beleive

Addressed: To, The right honoble Anthony Lord Ashley Chancellor of his Majesties Court of Exchequer at Whitehall London humbly present

Endorsed by Locke.

Jos: Dalton to Lord Ashley 9th Sept: 70.

[*S. P.*, Bble. 48, No. 30.]

GOVERNOR SAYLE TO LORD ASHLEY.

Right honoble

I humbly begg yor Lords'ps patience in the p'vsall of these lines wch is a relation of the Country wch yor Honor hath the happiness to bee a proprietorA more healthfull frutfull and pleasant place the world doth not afford abounding wth good land and many pleasant Riuers; I beseech of yr honor to be mindfull in sending vs supplies and more people which is our greatest want yt thereby wee may bee strengthened agt our enemies, for the Spanyard watcheth onely for an opportuny to destroy vs, we further desire yt yor honors wold send vs a pinke[1] of about Eighty Tunn, for one vessell is not sufficient to attend vs, In our generall letter to yor honors a more pticular Account is sett downe att large, vnto wch I reffer your Lords'p. for a more satisfactory information; As

------

[1] A narrow sterned merchant vessel.

to the trust imposed vpon me as yor Gouerno^r I shall indeavor to Discharge to the vttmost of my Abillity, whilst that I am:

Yo^r hono^{rs} ffaithfull serv^t to Comand

WILLIAM SAYLE.

Albemarle Point Sepr ye 10th 1670.

Endorsed by Locke.   W. Sayle to Ld Ashley 10 Sept. 70.

Addressed: These ffor the Right hono^{ble} the Lord Ashley
London.   [*S. P.*, Bdle. 48, No. 32.]

H. WOODWARD TO SIR JOHN YEAMANS.

Albymarle Pointe in Chyawhaw Sept. 10. 1670.[1]

R^t Honble S^r

I could not soe well haue pleaded my exscuse, & tardinesse in not giuen y^r Hon^r a particular relation by ye way of Virginia, & Barmudoes of our proceedings, & transactions; since yor Hon^{rs} departure for ye Barbadoes & our settinge forward for ye Maine: It being my fortune to bee gone uppon ye discouery of Chufytachyqj[2] y^t fruitfull Provence where ye Emperour resides; in y^t same juncture of time, when ye said Vessells set sayle from our Port of Chyauhaw: whereuppon at my returne from Chufytachyqj I understood y^t Mr. Jones had satisfyd yor Hono^r in those particulars, as for my aforesaid journai I haue discouered a Country soe delitious, pleasant & fruitfull, y^t were it cultivated doutless it would proue a second Paradize. It lys West & by Northe nearest from us 14 days trauell after ye Indian manner of march-

---

[1] This letter was enclosed in Sir Jno. Yeaman's to Ld Dudley, Nov: 15, 1670. *Post. A. W. I.*, 337.

[2] Cusitawaichee? 14 or 10 days W. by N. fruitful, red clay, white and black stone, to the W. over rising land are bells. 'Tatikequyas country bounds on the Spaniards, pearls & mines there.' Perhaps about Silver bluff or higher between the Oconee & Salwege. The Act 1691, mentions the Cussetas (the most powerful nation of the Muscogee) in that region, thence they extended over N. Georgia waters of Coosa, Etowah, Oustenaulla & Tennessee (where they got the pearls); later they retired further south & 1695 Archdale calls them 'subjects of the King of Spain.' Map in *Year Book* 1883, 376, has 'Cafitaciqui' on head of Santee (placed at head of Saluda). DeSoto's town is put at Santee, at Silver bluff, at fork of Salwege & other places. Santee is north, Silver bluff seems too low & the fork of Salwege was new to Woodward, 1674.

inge. I there contracted a leauge wth ye Emp^r & all those Petty Cassekas betwixt us & them, soe y^t some few weeks after my re-turne, ye Carolina being longe in her dispatch from Virginia our Prouision failed us & had not myne wth Mr Jones[1] diligence wth some few others releved ye Gen^{ll} wants by what Provisions wee procured of the Natives it had gone very hard wth us, in which scarsecytie of Provision wee receeved an Allarum from ye South-ward by ye Indians of St Helens y^t Spanish vessells & 30 Peery-augoes of Spaniards & Indians intendinge to worke us what mischeife they could. (And as I conceive they haueing intelligence of our Expectations of a supply in ye Carolina) awaited at Sea to trepane our Shipp: y^t soe depriueing us of our Supply & block-ing us up: our necessitys increasing wee consequently must have surrendered: for wch intent the Perryaugoes lay 10 leagues dis-tance from us at ye mouth of Stonowe Riuer, & there shipps of at Sea. Yet it pleased God y^t our ship arrived safe to us wth a most convenient Supply. Ye Enimy not being remoued, & yet being sensible thereof, theire Indians being terrifyd at ye Scaleing of some of our Great Guns. And ye Spaniard as wee suppose being frustrated of his expectation of starving us, cowardly re-treated to St Augustines never attempting anythinge against us soe y^t at prst wee have noe other news but y^t he hath threatened to destroy ye Indians of St Helens, of Cumbohee & of Edistowe y^t are our friends.

Thus as to ye estate of our Gen^{ll} affaires. As to our family necessity. I suppose Mr. Jones hath made yor hon^r ffully ac-quainted as to my particularre wants. I am most beholden to yor hono^{rs} Agent here than any thinge from ye Publicke, All though I must confesse they have made hon^{ble} recomendations of mee in there Gen^{ll} letters I shall endeavour by ye next to send y^o Hon^r some of our American raritys, our troubles at pres^t not permittinge mee ye vacancy as to travel ye Country, It being most of my businesse to awaite in towne & to give an account of what relations ye Natives bringe us either from ye Southward or ye Northward soe y^t least I might seeme too prolixe I rest my respective seruices presented to yor Hon^r not forgetting my re-

---

[1] *A. W. I.*, 337, reads 'with (Owen) Jones diligence.' Probably Mr. John Jones, Sir J. Yeaman's agent, member Owen's parliam't 1670, & 'Euan Jones,' of Charlestown, 1673.

spects to Mrs Mavel Carter & ye rest of y^r Hon^{rs} family & relations.

I rest y^r Hon^{rs} most obliged Servant

HENRY WOODWARD.[1]

Endorsed by Locke. H. Woodward to S^r Jo: Yeomans 10 Sept 70

Addressed: To ye right Honorable Sr John Yeomans Kn^t Baron^t
   Barbadoes   [*S. P.*, Bdle. 48, No. 33.]

———

F. O'SULLIVAN TO LORD ASHLEY.

Right Honoble

 I writt a particular account of all things to your lords by the
Carolina by the way of Virginie I am doubtfull whether or noe
they are come to your hands for fear of which I have now made
bold to trouble your Honor with these lynes that you may understand in what condition we are in: The Country proves good
beyond expectation and abounds in all things as good Oake, Ash,
Deare Turkies, partridges rabbitts turtle and fish the land produceth anything that is putt in it for wee have tried itt with Corne
Cotton and tobacco and other provisions, which proves very well
the lateness of the season considered, the country is stored with
severall pleasant fruits as peaches strawberrys and other sorts we
are settled at Kaaway near 20 leagues to the Northward of Port
Royall it not prouvinge according to report we build our towne
upon a point of land called Albemarle point seated upon the River

---

[1] With Sanford 1666, left with the Pt. Royal Indians, & treated well
till taken by the Spaniards. Searle surprising St. Augustine took him
away; while surgeon of a privateer he was wrecked at Nevis & joined
the ships for Carolina, there he was useful as interpreter & 'discoverer.'
In June he journeyed to Cusitachique & returning got supplies of the
Indians. In July, 1671, went by land to Virginia, & 1674 made discovery to the Westoes, & 1677 the Lords commend these discoveries
'by his industry & hazard,' grant him 2000 acres & com'ns as Deputy
& Indian agent. He was in the Westo wars 1680–81, & incurred the
Lords displeasure but was pardoned, & April 4, 1683, com'd to make
discoveries & search for mines inland. In 1685, while in the Yemasses
he was arrested by L'd Cardrosse, March 21, 168$\frac{5}{6}$, wrote 'his father-in-
law, Col. Godfrey,' Presd't, of this. He probably died soon after. His
estate was at head of Abapoola creek. He left 2 sons. Col. John Woodward d. 1726, & Rich'd Woodward, Esq., d. 1725.

that leads in from the sea called by us Ashley river where we are afortifieing ourselves I have made several descoveries into the Country and find it very good and many pleasant Rivers I cannot give a better Caracter of it than it deserves. We humbly thank your Honor for your care in ordering us provisions, att Virginia the shipp returned to us in good time for all our provision was gone soe that we were forced to live upon the Indians who are very kind to us we hope your Honor will continue your care over us till we are in a condition to help ourselves. Our ship is now on her departure for Barbados from whence we expect more people and fresh supplys We expect from your Honor a ship from England with more people. You would doe well to grant free passage to passengers for some small time for many would be willing to come that are not able to pay their passage. pray send us a minister qualified according to the church of England and an able Counsellor to end controversies amongst us and putt us in the right way of the management of your Colony we hope now the worst is past if you please to stand by us. You please to send instructions that the land may be laid out to the people as it lyes that the bad and good may go together by that meanes the people will not inhabit att a distance and it will prove more beneficial to your Honor In my last I informed your Honor that the sloop we took with us from Barbados loosing us at sea fell into one of the Spanish bays called Sancta Katherina where the master & mate Mr Rivers, with several others goeing ashore was taken by the spaniards and sent prisoners to St Augustens where they still remain and would have intersepted the sloop but she escaped we sent letters one to the Fryer where they were taken the other to the Governor of St Augustens to demand them but they denied us and got two more of our men they offered them no injuries butt intended to wood and water and soe depart. Pray your Honor to take some care for the reliefe our men.

I question not butt that you are senseable Sir John Yeoman left us att Barmudoes where we took one Col Sayle for our Governor I procured there 20^{ll} creditt in provisions which assisted the people very much I made bold to charge it upon your Honor to be paid to Capt Jos. Dorrall there or his order I am sorry to give your lordshipp an account of the loss of the Port Royall upon the Bahama Ilands all being lost but the master and two or three more soe beggin your Honor's excuse I humbly desire your answer which will be very acceptable to

Your faithfull servant

FLOR: O SULLIVAN

Albemarle Point Sept: the 10 1670

I humbly desire your honor to speak to my lord Craven that he would be pleased to make choice of one Mr Ralph Marshall for his deputy a person fitt for the imploymt he is one of the council and desires to be employed by my lord his Deputy Mr Bowman left us in Ireland.

I humbly desire your Lordship to Order the Governor and Counsell what I shall have for my sallery for they refer itt wholly to your honor for according to their proposal I am not able to live, the country is troublesome to survey ten pounds is little enough for a thousand which is all I desire.

Capt Braine denied to carry me pipe staves to Barbados unless he might have half for his own part, which is a great grievance to us and much disheartens the people I beseech your honor rectifie those abuses:

Endorsed by John Locke.   O'Sullivant to Lord Ashley 10 Sept: 70.   [*S. P.*, Bdle. 48, No. 34.]

———

THE COUNCIL TO THE LORDS PPOPRIETORS.

Albemarle Point Sept; 11th 1670.

May it please your Honors,

Wee cannot omitt to lay before you the difficulties which Dr Woodward from the first discovery of these parts and of the settlement here, with the great use he stands us in at present: for at the first haveing remained some considerable time amongst the natives of these parts being treated with the greatest love and courtesye that their rude natures were acquainted withal, untill the Spaniard haveing notice of his aboade at St Helena carryed him thence to St Augustine where necessarily he must have remained prisoner if Serle[1] surprizing the Towne had not

---

[1] Capt. Robert Searle, the buccaneer 'March 18, 1670, arrived also at Pt. Morant the Cagway, Capt. Searle with 70 stout men, who hearing Sir Thomas was much incensed against him for that action of St. Augustine, went to Macary Bay and there rides out of command.' *A. W. I.*, 161, 172, 261.

transported him to the Leward Islands, where shipping Chyrur-
geon of a privateere whereby to procure something to defray
his charges home, being desirous to give your Lordshipps an
account of these parts, unfortunately the 17th of August 1669
was cast away in a Hurricane at Meavis,[1] whereby being disabled
to perform his voyage; Wee happening to touch at Meavis
where he was awaiting in order to his transportation for England
voluntarily deserted that designe, purposely to manifest his ready
inclynation to promote your Lordshipp's service in this expedition
and by his constant travelling and inquiry amongst the natives
who being greatly affected towards him, is able to give your
Lordshipp's a more exact Account of the discovery of several
places and rivers then ever we heard before, he hath lately beene
fourteene days journey westward up into the Maine, as farr as
the fruitfull Country of Chufytachyque[2] the Emperour, unto whom
by the Casseca of Kaiawah he made knowne the settlement of the
English in these parts, with their desires of a true league and
friendshipp; wherewith being very well satisfyed, he highly approved of a peace with the English nation and accordingly sent
persons with the D[r] in his returne to assure us of his good affections
and ready assistance upon all occasions to them of this Colony,
whom according to promise at the expiration of 40 dayes[3] wee in
Person expect and cannot otherwise thinke but that in time his
friendship may be very considerable to the English in this settlement. The Doctor hath lately been exceeding useful to us in
the time of the scarcity of provision, in dealeing with the Indian for
our supplyes who by his meanes have furnished us beyond our
expectations, he would willingly have embarqued this time for
England cheifly to wait upon your Lordshipps in person, and in
the best measure he could to have provided some servants and
other necessaryes for his speedy returne and comfortable settlement amongst us in these parts, who accordingly had come but
that wee cannot well dispence with his absence from the Collony

---

[1] At Nevis, the ships touched there Dec. 9, page 158.

[2] He went end May, and returned July. DeSoto's town was on a
great river. Woodward mentions no river or town; perhaps he met the
Emperor at an out village or camp about or north of Silver bluff. The
Caseeka, pages 68, 80, 167, appears no more.

[3] The Spanish report delayed him. From his people Bull and Owen
expect him in 10 or 4 days.

being of very great advantage by his familiar acquaintance amongst the natives, and his knowledge in their language, we therefore recommend him to your Lordshipp's consideration and as he is useful to us upon all Accounts here soe we humbly desire your Lordshipps would have thought on him suitable to his de-merits, thus we humbly take leave, and remaine

Your Lordshipps most faithfull humble servants

William Sayle

Will; Scrivener	Joseph West
Flo; Sullivan	Ralph Marshall
	Joseph Dalton. Secretary.

Endorsed:

To the Right Honorable Anthony Lord Ashley Chancellor of his Majestie's Court of Exchequer and the rest of the Lords Proprietors of Carolina at Whitehall London   humbly present.

Council at Ashley River to the Lords Proprietors 12° Sept: 70.

[*S. P.*, Bdle. 48, No. 36.]

STEPHEN BULL[1] TO LORD ASHLEY.

Albemarle Poynt September the 12th 1670.

Moste hono[rd] Lord

Accordingto my duty I have heere sent yo[r] Hono[r] an Ac-comp[t] of our settleing and condicon wth a small Informacon of the gen'all Judgm[t] & opinion of this place & a relacon of some p'ticulers And in my last L're to yo[r] Hono[r] I sent A full relacon of our voy-adge from Bermuda of the Lands Islands Rivers tymber ffish &

---

[1] Came to Carolina as L'd Ashley's deputy, opposed leaving Pt. Royal, but at Kiawah was, after West, the most useful man in all duties of the settlem't, the Council & with the Indians. L'd Ashley praises his be-havior in the governm't as agreeable to them and his own high charac-ter. In 1672 Mathews succeeded him as deputy, but in April he was chosen to parliam't & the Council. In June was commis'd Capt. of the Forts. In 1673 surveyor, & May, 1674, L'd Cornbury's deputy. Feb., 1675, he laid off the new fortifications. Sat in Council 1675 to 1682, & 1683 was ass't judge; 168$\frac{3}{4}$ Surveyor Gen'l & in Council 1684, 87 & 1691, 99. Col. Bull was Com'r taxes 1703, & then retired from public life to his large estates. His will is 170$\frac{8}{9}$; he died soon after and was buried at his seat, Ashley Hall. His family is one of the most distinguished in Caro-lina.

other noble perquisits which we discov'ed att Porte Royall & this Place, wth such reasons as could obtaine from Governo^r for desertinge Porte Royall wch in my judgem^t & seu'all other gentle^n was very much In[viting] for A setlem^t & Admirable good land.[1]

May itt please yor Hono^r notw^{th} standinge wee have quitted Porte Royall yett in this place heere is very good lande & in probability wth yor Hono^{rs} Incouradgm^t in sendinge shipps to us wth people & some supplyes duringe our Infancy vnder god there is noe question to bee made but that this is likely to bee one of the best setlem^{ts} in the Indies wee have founde in all places that wee [have been] in since wee quitted England that the people gen'ally harbor a good opinion for this place & in sev'all places there are divers p'souns that would come to vs if they could gett Passadges & if yor Hono^{rs} would bee pleased to grant Passadges ffree for a yeare or two from barbadoes & the Leward Islands to some p'souns that are not able to transporte themselves wee should then in a shorte tyme bee well peopled & yor Hono^{rs} Teritorys much enlardged May it please yor Hono^{rs} this Cuntrey is fitt for almost any Produce there is nothinge that wee sett soe or plant butt thrives beyond our Expectacons wee came soe late heere that wee could nott Plante any Corne butt little more then to make an experim^t & itt hath retorned to a greate helpe seede Corne for this next yeare I brought hither seu'all trees as orrenge Lemon Lyme Pomcitterne Pomegrainett ffiggtrees & Plantons & they like the ground & thrive & fflourishe very bravely & I question nott butt they will come to Maturity wee conceive this to be as healthfull A place as ever was setled wee have lost butt fower p'souns since wee satt downe heere, & those was sickly p'souns & in A declininge condicon of health before wee landed there is some p'souns that have had the feaver and Ague butt we observe little Mortality in the distemper neither is the distemper neere soe high as is vsuall in other Places wee have lately taken up in A cemicircle about the Towne tenn acres A head for our present Plantacons & wee have chosen in this River Above & below the Towne our greate Lotts—there is lande sufficient heere for some thousands of People where they may make very brave & happy setlem^{ts}.

---

[1] That letter is lost. The MS. is torn. He proved his faith by large settlem'ts there afterwards.

May it please yoʳ Honoʳ when the shipp Carolina dep'ted hence about the 26 of May last for Virginia she left us as wee conceived about 10 or 11 weekes Provision of Pease & A small quantity of wheate & Oatemeale very inconsiderable att a quart ℔ diem for a mann & wᵗʰin 15 or 16 dayes after the shipps dep'ture wee over haled our stores of Provisions & wee found that there could nott bee made vp above 2 moneths Provision att a Pinte of Pease ℔ diem A mann & halfe of them diminished butt *ne' scitas non h' et leg' m* beinge our case wee cheered vp ourselves & wee found very great Assistance from the Indians who shewed them selves very kinde & sould vs Provisions att very reasonable rates & takeinge notice of our necessitys did almost daylie bringe one thinge or another otherwise wee must vndoubtedly have binn putt to ex-treame hardshipps & they doe seeme to bee very well pleased att our Settlinge heere expectinge protecon vnder vs wᶜʰ wee have promised them agᵗ another sorte of Indians that live back-wards in an intier body & warr agᵗ all Indians they are called Westoes & doe strike a great feare in these Indians havinge gunns & powder & shott & doe come vpon these Indians heere in the tyme of their cropp & destroye all by killinge Caryinge awaye their Corne & Children & eat them & our neibouringe Indians doe promise Ayd vpon all Exigencies wᶜʰ they have manifested. Dcʳ Woodward hath traveled vp to the greate Emperoʳ of this p'te of the Indies whoe liveth about 10 dayes Journey vp in the Maine the Emperor received very kindly makinge him welcome after his Manner & made A firme League of ffreindshipp & hath sent downe skinns to our governoʳ & sent worde that about 10 dayes hence hee wilbee wᵗʰ vs himselfe. About the 18ᵗʰ of August last wee received newes that the Spaniard wᵗʰ all the In-dians about Sᵗᵉ Augustine & the Spanishe Keyes was come to a River about 6 miles from vs & vpon the recepcon of the Larum havinge continuall notice for 7 or 8 dayes before of their cominge wee had putt our selves in reasonable good Posture to defend ourselves agᵗ an Enemy the Indians informeth vs that there was about 200 Spaniards & 300 Indians & one as wee conceived to bee A ffryer & thanke god for itt our Menn nottwᵗʰstandinge hard workinge in ffortification shortnesse of Provision & stricte dutyes in watchinge yett they were possesst wᵗʰ good courradge & were very ready & desirous to fight the Enemy & all the In-dians about vs came in wᵗʰ their full strength to our Ayde & att the same Interim the Carolina ffriggott came in allmost to the mouth of the River seeinge seu'all Indians ashoare supposed them to be our owne Indians & Capt Brayne wth some of his menn went Ashoare & 3 or 4 of the Indians made towards them & Capt Brayne havinge one of our owne Indians wth him whoe cryed out that they were Enemyes & Capt Brayne returned towardes his boate & then 20 or 30^{tie} that were in Ambushcade came out & fired 7 or 8 Musquets vpon Capt Brayne butt hee rec'ed noe hurte & wth in 2 dayes they wthdrew their Camp & Marched hoame. Our Indians Informeth vs that the Spanishe Indians seeinge the scalinge of our great gunns & seeinge the shipp that they were possesst wth such feare that the Spaniard could nott bringe them vp nor gett them to staye our Indians alsoe Informeth vs that they had 3 shipps & 12 Perriaugers[1] wch relacon wee doe much credditt for there was noe variance in all Indians daylie reportes in their Campe amongst other things there was a vizard lost wch vizard represented an Indian & wee conceived that that vizard was to keepe some Englishman that they had wth them vndiscovered   May itt please yor Hono^r our gou'no^r is ill of the feave^r & Ague & beinge Aged & falen into A relapse I doe much feare his recovery there is seu'all thinges wch he hath Either Acted or Indeavored to Acte wch have nott binn altogeather Agreable to the Concessions butt it is rather Imputed A selfe will then any thinge of designe or his owne Intereste & hee beinge in this weake condicon I p'sume to beg yor Hono^{rs} p'don & att p'sente wave incertinge p'ticulers.

May itt please yor Hono^r Capt Suliv^t is a p'soun that doth acte very strangely & heere is nott any p'soun in the Collony butt complaines of his vnjust practices beinge A very dissencious troublesome Mann in all p'ticulers hee is bound both to the good behavi^r & Peace Exactinge strangely for ffees & hath made all the seamen att the retorne to give him a Paper oblidginge them to pay after the rate of 10^{li} for a 1000 Acres & 5^s for A Certificate wch is almost treble the rates of other setlem^{ts} wee doe looke vpon him not altogeather soe able or capable of that Imploy as hee hath confidence to report himselfe wee finde in our smale towne lotts very strange & grosse Errors wch would

---

[1]At Stono & landed on Folly & Morris islands. *Sp*. Piragua, canoes or boats for inland navigation.

much shame most People butt hee is of another nature shamed of nothinge vsinge private watches to overreach People, & is A very troublesome p'soun & is daylie complained of for ill Actings May itt please yor Hono^r Mr. Rivers beinge vnfortunately taken wth the Spaniard & his Imploye voyd if yor Hono^r please to thinke my service convenient I should bee very glad to serve in the same capacity wch if yor Hono^{rs} pleaseth shalbee very obediently observed in all orders & direccons by

Yo^r Hon^{rs} Moste obedient S^{r}v^t & Deputy

STEPHEN BULL.

Endorsed by Locke.   S. Bull to Ld Ashley 12 Sept. 70.

Addressed: These ffor the Right Honble the Lorde Ashley Cooper Att Exeter House wth my duty   p^{r}sent.

[*S. P.*, Bdle. 48, No. 35.]

WILLIAM OWEN[1] TO LORD ASHLEY.

May it please yor Lord'pp.

It was not for want of Dutie y^t I did not waite yor Lord^{pp} when I resolved here but ye shorte time I had to provide myself and yor Lord^{ps} recesse from the Cittie deny'd me that hono^r I know yor Lord'p is again and again Inform'd of ye p^{r}sent Condicon of the settlem^t yet however I hould myself most obliged to p^{r}sent somthing to yor Lord^{pp} p'ticularlie.

Although we are somthing to ye northward of Porte Royall yet considering ye Condicon we were att our arriuall, & the Inlett there being not as it was rendered we haue made choise for ye better, hauing pitcht on a pointe defended by ye maine riuer with a brooke on ye one side, and inaccessible Marshe one ye other wch att high tides is euer ouerflowne: ioying itself to ye

---

[1] Was known to L'd Ashley and kin to his steward, Mr. Blaney, well educated & clever, but of a restless & captious spirit. He opposed Sayle at Bermuda, but coaxed him to leave Pt. Royal & call a parliam't. He opposed West, was ever 'stirring up the people' and in many suits. In 1671 Sir P. Colleton made him deputy, & his ability was useful in the Council. He had a house in Charlestown & a plant'n on Ashley river above; went 'discoveries' among the Indians & 1673 to treat with the Esaws. He was Secretary in 1677 & Deputy from 1671 to 1682, & died soon after.

mainland in a small neck not exceeding fiftie yards which now is pallizadoed, and with a verye small charg might be made Impregnable: for neither by water on ye one side nor by land on ye other cann ye enemie make any considerable attack but y[t] a handfull of men may defend with securietie, if this neck of land would be seuered from the Continent.

My Lord I think I shall not much err when I say y[t] a good Inlet, a healthie Countrie, securietie, and seasonable supplies performs a settlm[t].

the Inlett here is faire and kind onlye att half ebb breakers appear one both sides the going in, w[ch] to those that are acquainted proue good marks, when to strangers they may be a terrour, here yo[r] Lord[pp] shipp the Carolina had 3 fathoms better att her comeing in and as to matters of health, I think it may be reckon[d] with ye cheifest for if att this time when the Countrey is close, pertaking of all ye damps, vapours, and exhalacons, y[t] weedes, foule creekes, and swamps cann dilate it is kindlie and wholesome, yo[r] Lord[pp] may well conclude it better when its opened and cleansed; there dyed but one person of all them that cam out of Engl[d] and he of a Lingring and a Consumption distemper. My Lord the greate pointe in this designe is securietie for as we are neere a jealous and a potent neighbour soe he will neuer want engines to disquiet us and although it may be said that he cares not for ye Land, yet will not be pleased that any stranger should be neere him to see or know his strength or actings; and as vessells are bound hither strangers to ye coast and countrey must frequentlie be distrest as the winds are various on the parts where he inhabits soe he will euer entertain them to their disadvantage, he hath alreadie begun as M[r] Colleton's sloop hath found whereof yo[r] Lordp[p] hath had an account though I know not in what maner, ye Spaniard is of himselfe but inconsiderable 200 leagues to ye southward of us and we cannot reasonablie ap[r]hend anything of disturbance from himself especiallie when soe firme a peace is establisht att home, yet ye fryers will neuer cease to promote their tragick ends by ye Indian whom they instruct onlye to admire the Spanish nacon and pay them adoracon equall to a dietie, possessing them with an oppinion that ye Spanish people is of an Angelicall production, and that they are Ye onlie masters of ye world and that all other people are their slaues and vassalls and those people that are not subject to

15

them are to be destroied, and who euer refuse it, or correspond
with them are accursd with these assertions with ye Advantage
of the Indian language wch they gradually speake, they Incline
the Indians to doe anything, but since Searle playd that pranck
att St Augustines som of ye most Intelligible Indians on this side
the Cape doubted of ye veritie of ye frier's Doctrine and now
our settleing here putts ye priests our neighbours upon new
pointes there are onlye foure betweene us and St Augustines our
next neighbour is he of Wallie wch ye Spaniard calls St Katarina
who hath about 300 Indians att his devoir with him joyne ye rest
of ye Brotherhood and cann muster upp from 700 hundred Indians besides those of ye main whom they vpon any vrgent occasions shall call to their assistance, they by these Indians make
warr with any other people y^t disoblige them and yet seeme not
to be concerned in ye matter.   St Augustines of itself is but an
Impotent Garrison haueing not aboue 200 souldiers and is ye onlie
certaine strength ye Spaniard hath to Leuell de Cruz onlye in
Appalachia they haue 3 files of men whom they place there for
Intelligence of w^t shall happen of Importance on ye Coast, ye
Spaniard cannot affect our settleing here neither cann he tell w^{ch}
way to Impede it, but as ye fryers our neighbours are a little
startled att it soe they Imploye all ye meanes they cann to terrifie
us for where they are att present seated I meane those 4 vpon ye
Spanish Keyes if ye settlem^t here thriues, must approach neere
to y^{em}, the greate reuerence wch they exact from ye Indian will
in a verie shorte time decline, for by their converseing wth our
Indians who are more and better satisfied of ye Grandeur of ye
English wch they doe assure them of (seu'all of ours haueing
bein att Barbadoes and Latelie att Virginia wch places they much
talke of and admire) telling all their acquaintance y^t we haue
greate freinds and stronger then ye Spaniards wch makes them
not a little proude of our frendshippe this the fryer is sensible of
strictly corresponding with ye Indian att St Hellina by whose
meanes he gets Intelligence of our affairs, and is of y^t restlesse
temper y^t he promotes all ye mischeife he is able to defeate this
designe he hath latelie sent to St Hellina to tamper with ye Indians for frend^{pp} and alarm^d us with 10 periagoes of Indians of his
country and among whom were seu'all Spaniards ye Indians here
made us signe y^t they had 2 fryers amongst them and that they
intended to distroye us our Indians tould us y^t they had a shipp

at sea wch would come into ye riuer and that the Indians would come and attack us by land, thus they kept us in arms for 10 dayes they hauing advanc^d as farr as our riuers mouth where for 6 dayes they Incamped and hindered our correspondence with our freinds of Edistah, Asha-po and Combohe, yet ye more north-erne Indians as those of Wando, Ituan, seweh and sehey, came to our assistence and I am persuaded y^t in 10 dayes time we might haue muster'd neere 1000 bowemen they seemed verie zealous in our behalfe their Cassekas making verie ample speeches to incite their bands of bowemen to ingage for us crying out the Spaniard to be nought and y^t ye English comraro were Hiddie dod . . . a word of great kindnes amongst them I have seene one of their Capitanos speake to his people halfe an hour together, with ye greatest passion y^t could be inveigheing ag^t ye Spaniard & applauding ye English for the Hoes Axes beades and kniues wch they had brought them and shewing us with his bowe & arrowes and an ould sword we gaue him w^{tt} massacre he would doe. we onlye made vse of them as scouts wch they would performe with care, and as we did not depend vpon their courage soe ye fryers were sorrie to heare doubtlesse y^t we had soe much gained ye Indians, while we were thus in arms makeing all ye preparacon we could to receiue them and if they did not Intend suddenlie to attempt us we made account to force them home ye Carolina appeared vpon ye Coaste from Virginia whose boate goeing ashoare att ye mouth of ye riuer and thinking they had bein our owne Indians might haue bein injured but aye Indian wch the ship caried to Virginia gave notice y^t they were Spanish Indians and nought yet being resolued to trye w^h they meant Capt Bryan and ye Indian made towards one of them who seemed Intent to approach, our Indian goes before and tells him he should lay aside w^t weapons he had seemed to doe soe but as our Indian drew neere him he discouered his bowe and Quiuer hang'd along his back and soe made from him ye strang Indian springs after him and Capt Braine hastening to his rescue, caused ye other Indian to run away vpon this appeared to ye Number of 40 att som distance off houlding forth a white thing like a handkerchefe but suspecting their deuice returned to their boate who in their return had 7 or 8 guns fired att them by those Indians or Span-iards who appeared att distance and since we haue not heard from them but our Indians tell us they are gone this is the third affront ye Spaniard offered us by Indians since they heard of us here, to Question ye Spaniard on this account he will deny and disowne all things of this kind of hostile affaires and putt all vpon ye Indian whom he cannot restraine as he will alleage or y^t it is ye actings of som p'ticular Banditos when as in treuth it is owne Contriman, there are seu'all for Certaine att St Aug'ins who haue Comissions of reprizalls for ye damage Capt Searle hath don here, the Spaniard att Sta Katharina was not afeard to owne it, as for ye strength ye Spaniard cann make by his Indians and his Garrison of St Augustins we neede not feare, for I dare assure yor Lord'pp y^t fortie good actiue persons may driue all ye Spanish Indians and people vpon ye Keyes betweene us and that towne to ye verye walls of it, and we neede not be concerned (vnlesse ye Hauana supplie them with men) w^t they are able to doe, while we are here on this designe these prancks and policies of ye Spaniards will deter others from comeing here, who iudge of things meerely by reporte wch is euer greater y^{en} ye matter itself, if we had but 500 persons here, ye fryers on ye Keyes adjacent would remoue with all ye speede they could for as they are mischievous soe they are verie timerous and cautious of their own Indians who hearing of our groweing strength would deter the Spaniard.

My Lord I wish we did well knowe how to demeane ourselves for as their is a mixture of Spaniards and Indians and a strict League att home wch we would not giue the least incouragm^t to infringe and Consious of our owne strength if ye Spaniard were in good earnest soe we seeme to appeare onlye defensive, wch if we seeme to continue we shall hazard our reputacons among our owne Indians who we must now depend vpon for they Looke vpon it somthing strange if we doe not goe to Wallie and shoote as they call it, that they may come along, we excuse it all we cann to please them, as for them att home we haue them in a pound, for to ye Southward they will not goe fearing the Yamases Spanish Comeraro as ye Indian termes it.[1] ye Westoes are behind them a mortall enemie of theires whom they say are ye man eaters of them they are more afraid than ye little children

---

[1] Then settled near St. Augustine, revolting 1680, 85 they pushed thro' the Westos (then warring with the Savannas & English) and settled near Pt. Royal.

are of ye Bull beggers in England.[1] to ye Northward they will not goe for their they cry y^t it is Hiddeskeh, y^t is to say sickly, soe y^t they reckon themselves safe when they haue vs amongst them, from them there cann be noe danger ap^rhended, they haue exprest vs vnexpected kindness for when ye ship went to and dureing her stay att Virginia provision was att the scarcest with us yet they daylie supplied vs y^t we were better stored att her return than when she went haueing 25 days provision in store beside 3 tunn of corne more wch they promised to procuer when we pleased to com for it att Seweh.

The Emperour[2] of Tatchequiha a verie fruitfull countrey som 8 days iourney to ye Northwest of vs we expect here within 4 days som of his people being alreadie com with whom he would haue bein had not he heard in his way y^t ye Spaniard had defeated vs his frend^pp with us is very considerable against ye Westoes if euer they intend to Molest us he hath often defeated them and is euer their Master the Indian Doctor[3] tells us y^t where he liues is exceedinge rich and fertill generally of a red mould and hillie with most pleasant vallies and springes haueing plentie of white and black Marble and abundantly stored with Mulberries of wch fruite they make cakes wch I have tasted to ye westward of this countrey there appeares a Tract of high and rising Land ouer wch the Indians of that countrey make signes that there are bells and as we conceive as they demonstrate som of ye fryers they make signes of shipping y^t way too wch if soe it must needes be ye Spaniard, they pointe also Northward and tell us y^t there be people who ride vpon greate deere as they terme it putting things across in their mouths wch we thinke to be ye people att ye falls of Virginia and from thenceward they say they haue there Horses these people are generally of greater Limb and bulk then those with us and farr ruder then them vpon ye sea coaste.

My Lord this designe well prosecuted will render itself as well

---

[1] 'Something terrible, something to fright children with.' *Johns.* Strange supernatural beasts; this superstition exists in America, as the 'Bugger ponds' of S. W. Georgia attest.

[2] Called also Cotachico, of the Cusitaws, see May 23, 1674. 'Hath 1000 bowmen in his towns.' He came to Kiawah 1672, with 100 men to renew this amity.

[3] One of Tachequias' 'medicine men,' called in the Muskoge 'Hitch: lalage' 'cunning men, seers.' *Adair,* 80.

profitable as honorable and doubtlesse when this Countrey is firmelie settled verie considerable things may be effected a small number of people not exceeding 500 men would render vs secuer and 500 more would p'fect the settlem^t soe y^t we neede not ap^{r}hend ye least of dread from Spaine or Indian and yor Lord^{pps} care for supplies of necessaries for a shorte time I hope will make us in som measure capable to stand vpon our owne Leggs the countrey being fertill and of a wonderfull growth, and hope in a little time be able to invite others to their Advantage.

My Lord I haue troubled you with a long indigested indian relacon wch I hope you will pardon the distance being greate and oportunitie scarce & ye dutie I owe to yor Lord^{pp} soe greate, and that I may be ye better enabled to serve yor Lord^{pp} wch of all other thinges I should be ye most glad   I am to pray yor Lord^{pp} by yor order to dispence with me for som time for ye fraught o$_1$ such goods I shall exporte hence and wch goods and serv^{ts} I shall haue procured to be sent to me upon my owne account, haueing not brought with me but two servants from Engl^d being vnwilling to carry any from Barbadoes consideringe ye scarcetie of provision wch would betide us, yor Lord^{pp} would advantage my settlem^t exceedingly in this particular.

I pray God blesse yor Lord^{pp}; I humbly take my leave and remaine—my verie good Lord

yor verie dutifull and obliged serv^t

WILL'M OWEN.

Ashley River 7^{ber} ye 15° America 1670 Lat. 31 45m:

Endorsed by Locke.   Wm. Owen to Ld Ashley 15° Sep^t 70.

Addressed: These To ye R^t hon^{ble} Anthony Lord Ashley one of ye Coms^{rs} of his Matie Treas^y Chancell^{or} of his Ma^{tis} Excheq^r and one of his Ma^{tis} most hon^{ble} privie Councill.

[*S. P.*, Bdle. 48, No. 37.]

JOSEPH WEST TO LORD ASHLEY.

May it please yor Lo^p

In my last to yor Lo^p by the way of Bermuda of the 27th of June, I gaue yor Lo^p an Acco^t of the proceedings of our men

that went to Sta Katherina in the shallop to look for yor Lo^{ps}
Kinsman Mr Riuers, and the rest of the men there detained by
ye Spaniards, of whome as yet wee haue heard nothing: But
doubtlesse the Spaniard hath an Intent to keepe them, and to
cutt us off if possibly hee can; Wee haue oftentimes bene al-
larrum'd by them for they came within 12 miles of our settlement, where they lay when ye ship came in from Virginia w^{ch}
was the 23^d of August, and had like to haue taken theire Boate;
but about 2 dayes after the ship came in they returned back to
St. Helens, the greater part of them being Indians: but the
Arriuall of the shipp and the noyse of our great Guns did strike
such a Terrour upon the Indians, that the Spaniards could not
perswade them to come upon us (as wee are informed by the
Indians y^t are our friends, who haue bene very ready to assist us
against the Spaniards and seem'd to haue more courage. May
it please yor Lo^p ye ship hath brought us from Virginia a considerable proporcon of provision, and some live Cattell, an Acc^t
whereof I haue sent to Sr Peter Colleton, I haue kept some of
the Cattell for ye vse of yor Lo^p plantacon, wee haue not as yet
taken up any Land but what adjoynes to the Towne, and y^t at
ten Acres ℔ head, because wee will not seperate before there are
more people come. Mr Brayne doth informe us of many people
in readiness to come from Berbadoes as soone as the ship shall
arriue there, therefore wee haue dispatch'd the ship away that
shee may be here againe before winter, for wee belieue the Spaniards will slip noe opportunity to doe us an Injury, although hee
is soe farr from us, wch wee belieue to be at the least 90 Leagues
to St Augustines. Wee haue already and (in a small time) shall
haue soe well fortifide ourselues, y^t wee shall not neede to feare
all the strength the Spaniards can make against us. Our people (God be praised) doe continue very well in health, and the
country seemes to be very healthfull and delightsome. Our
Corne and other things planted at our first comeing doe thriue
very well, onely our Garden Seeds wch were not good, and I belieue the Ground will beare anything that is put in it, and y^t it
is as hopefull a Designe as euer was put on foot: As for our
Gouerno^r hee is very aged, and hath much lost himselfe in his
Governm^t: and would haue cal'd a Parliam^t amongst us allthough
wee could not make 20 ffreemen in the Collony, besides the

Councell,[1] and had made an order for it, had not wee y[t] were yo[r] Deputies and some few of the Councell vigorously withstood it, I doubt hee will not be soe advantageous to a new Collony as wee did expect.   I hope yo[r] Lo[p] wilbe pleased to send mee new Instruccons for ye disposeall of the propriet[rs] stores, for these I haue (the Govern[r] tells me) are not sufficient, because they are onely signed by yo[r] Lo[p] and S[r] Peter Colleton: I haue sent to S[r] Peter an Acc[t] of what things will be necessary for a present supply of stores, w[ch] are now growne very short in many things, and doe hope y[t] yo[r] Lo[p] will be pleased to send to us in the spring.   In ye Interim I shall use my vtmost Endeavours to manage yo[r] Lo[ps] affaires here untill I receiue further orders from yo[r] Lo[p].   I haue taken into yo[r] seruice 4 Servants belonging to Cap[t] Balye, and shall keep them & Major Hambletons till I re-ceiue further orders.   Thus (in discharge of my Duty) I haue giuen yo[r] Lo[p] this trouble, and shall assure yo[r] Hon[r] I will lay out my selfe to ye vtmost to manifest myselfe as really I am, my Lord

Yo[r] Lo[ps] most humble & faithfull serv[t]

JOSEPH WEST.

Albemarle poynt at Kyawah Septemb: *1670.*

Addressed: For the Right Hono[ble] the Lord Ashley Chancello[r] of the Exchequer at Little Exeter House in ye Strand—London.

Endorsed by Locke.   Jos: West to Lord Ashley.   Sept. 70.

[*S. P.*, Bdle. 48, No. 38.]

———

MEMORIAL TO THE SPANISH AMBASSADOR.

His grace the Duke of Albemarle the Earle of Craven the Earle of Clarendon the Lord John Berkeley Lord Leiutenant of Ireland the Lord Ashley Chancellor of the Excke[r] Sir George Cartaret Vice Chambelain of his Majesty household Sir Peter Colleton Baronet and Sir William Berkeley Knt being concerned

---

[1] Gov. Sayle, West, Bull, Scrivener, O'Sullivan, deputies; Dalton, Donne, Marshall, P. Smith, S. West, Council'rs.   Beadon, H. Carteret, Churne, Hughes, Jones, Kennis, Mathews, Jas. Marshall, Norris, Owen, T. Smith, Symons, Woodward and Barker, Ingram, Michael Moran & Rich. Cross-ley claimed to be.

in a plantation bordering on the south of Virginia did the last year send some English people in a sloop to that their plantation who by foule weather haveing been put out of their course did about the 15th of May '70 come to anchor off St. Katharina in Florida where by the kinde usage of the Inhabitants coming abord them and a present of bread and other things sent to the Master of the Vessel and a free & friendly intercourse between them for several days wherein many of the English had gone ashore and returned without question or difficulty Mr John Rivers a kinsman and agent of the Lord Ashley with the Master of the sloup and his mate and six or seven men one woman and a girle were at last encouraged to goe on shore where they were by order of a Fryer the chief man of that place seized on   & detained prisoners The Fryer refusing to restore them upon demand but instead thereof commanded the sloop to yield and endeavoured by shot from the shoare to force them to it.   The sloop thereupon set sayle for the s'd plantation.   From whence it was shortly after sent back with two letters one to the Fryer and the other to the governor of St. Augustines to demand the delivery of the English that had been left prisoners by them. The Fryer at their arrival gave them fair words and his faith that those that would come on shore should not be injured by him who notwithstanding after three days delay not only refused to set those he had formerly seized on at liberty but kept two more of those who coming to demand their companions had upon his parol ventured them selves into his power.

The Lords and others above mentioned concerned in this affair desire that his Excellency the Lord Ambassador would be pleased to give his effectuall orders to the governor of St. Augustines and the s'd Frier that all the persons belonging to them who have been seized and detained at St. Katherinna may be set at liberty and restored to them.   These people nor any of their company having not donne any acts of hostility or given any provocation to the s'd inhabitants of St. Katherinna or any of the King of Spains subjects whereby the Fryer may have any just pretext to make them his prisoners And the said Lords &c having sent those persons with a designe only to plant and carry on the fore mentioned plantation without disturbing any others whatsoever are very willing to continue an amicable correspondence with the subjects of the King of Spain nor shall they allow any piracy nor permit any of their people to invade others with force or use any acts of hostility. [N. B.—*All the preceding is in Locke's hand and also on margin.*]

' Delivered to the Spanish Ambassador 9 Sept 72.'

The Lords and others above mentioned concerned in this affaire and particularly the Earl of Shaftesbury who hath lately heard from his kinsman M[r] John Rivers that he is prisoner at St. Augustines does desire his Excellency the Lord Ambassador would be pleased to procure an Effectual order from the Council of Spain to the Governor of St. Augustines or who ever else has in Custody any of the affore said English men or women that the said persons who have been seized at St. Katharinna and divers times detained may be set at Liberty and restored to them, those people or any of their Comp having not done any acts of hostility or given any provocation to the said inhabitants of St. Katharinna or any of the King of Spains subjects whereby the Fryer or any other person might have just pretence to make them prisoners. And the said Lords etc having sent those persons with a designe only to carry on the before mentioned plantation without disturbing any others what soever are very willing to continue an amicable correspondence with the subjects of his most Catholick majesty nor shall they allow any Piracy nor permitt any of their people to invade others with force or use any acts of hostility. The said Lords etc doe alsoe desire that a duplicate of such effectuall Orders (as shall by the Counsell be sent to America) may be sent hither to them that they may convey it to the Governor of St. Augustines soe to secure the delivery of the said M[r] John Rivers and the rest of the prisoners if the other Duplicate sent imediately from Spain should miscarry.

[*The following in Locke's hand.*]

As many of the names of the said prisoners as are known to the said Lords as followeth: M[r] John Rivers, Cap Bayley, John Collins, William Car, Margaret, & Martin. The rest of their names they know not.

Endorsed : Memorial about the prisoners at St. Katherina delivered to the Spanish Ambassador. 1 Oct. 70.

Ashley River.

[*S. P.*, Bdle. 48, No. 40.]

LORD ASHLEY TO J. DORREL AND HUGH WENTWORTH
29 OCTOBER 70.

London Exeter House 29th Oct: 70.

Your letter from Bermudos of the 17th Feb: 69, I received and returne you my thanks for the willingnesse you therein expresse of puting yourselves and the rest of the Inhabitants of New Providence into my hands. In compliance with your desire I have gott of his Majestie a grant of the Bahama Islands to the Duke of Albemarle, the Earle of Craven the Lord Jno. Berkley, Sir George Carteret, Sir Peter Colleton and my selfe. Six of the Proprietors of Carolina, who having heard that you M[r] Hugh Wentworth are by the consent of the people chosen Governor there we doe approve of it, and we shall as soon as our Patent is pass'd the great Seale send you Commission[1] to be our Governor and such farther instructions as may be for the welfare of the People there, we resolving to establish the same Government in New Providence which we have settled at Carolina as far as that place will allow, and doe give to the Inhabitants that have been transported thither by you, and are planted there with you, the same termes we doe to those who went first over into Carolina and are now planted there on Ashley River which I believe are the best have been ever given any where, and for yourselves you shall find by the next dispatch after the Patent is passd, that I shall take care of your concernment to your satisfaction. That you may not repent either the charge you have been at there or the puting your affairs into my hands. In the meane time the Proprietors desire you would send me word by the first oppertunity what number of men and women are at present on New Providence what quantity of Ground they have taken up and how much good land yet remaynes vacant with the nature fertility and product of the soile, scituation and conveniency of the Ports and other advantages and disadvantages of that place. Besides this you are alsoe desired to send what information you can of the rest of the Bahama Islands, their number, bignesse, healthinesse, Ports and soile, particularly which amongst them is the best, besides that you are already settled on, and fittest for Plantation with the scituation and circuite of

---

[1] See page 160. It was his brother Jno. Wentworth. His commission 24 April, 1671, page 161.

it and alsoe in what latitude the most Northerne of the Bahama Islands lyes.

As to your particular request for small Armes &c. we shall take care as soon as an intercourse can be settled between our Plantations by ships which we shall imploy there of our owne. That you as well as other parts of our Plantations shall be supplyed with all necessarys at reasonable rates. I had brought me some time since by Mr Day a Linnindraper in Cornhill London, a bill of Exchange charged upon me by Flor. O. Sullivan to be paid to Captain Jno. Dorrels order the sum is £20. and the date Somer Island 8 Feb; 69. There comeing noe letter of advise of it either from him or you and the letters I have received from both of later dates taking noe notice of any such money, I have not pay'd it nor was ever O. Sullivan entrusted by me or any of the Proprietors as our Agent, but had only the place of Surveyor for the measuring out the Plantations at Carolina a Mr West being our Agent commissioned by us in that affaire, but if it be soe that O. Sullivan has taken up soe much money of you Mr Dorrell we will take a course that he shall doe you right therein.   I am
                    Your very affectionate friend
                                                ASHLEY.
     London Exeter House October 29. 70.

Who ever of the two receives this letter is desired to communicate to the other.

You will see by the constitution of our Government that in the division and allotment of the land one 5th is to be in the possession of the Proprietors one 5th settled on the Nobility and 3. 5^{ths} possessed by the people. You are therefore to take care that two 5^{ths} of the good land in New Providence be set apart for the Proprietors and the Nobility that shall be made by them, you are like to have soe particular a concernment in this that I cannot doubt but you will be very careful of it.

[S. P., Bdle. 48, No. 55, p. 5.]

LORD ASHLEY TO JOSEPH WEST. 1° NOV. 70.[1]

Your letter of 27 June last I received and hope that your settlement in Carolina in soe commodiouse a place as you have

------

[1] West's letter, p. 173.   The Amber rumour was false, specimens only occur in Carolina.   Ashley river, p. 80.

chosen will have a success answerable to soe promising a beginning to which your care and prudence will very much contribute,
and, I doubt not but you will answer your expectation we all
have of your management of this affaire a greate part whereof I
looke to lie upon you, and I in particular doe very much rely
upon you in it.   Since the receit of your letters we are informed
that the Portroyal which we conceived had foundered in the
storme which parted her from you, was run on shoare on some of
the Bahama Islands, Pray let there be care taken to get to you as
many of the men as were saved which will be a good addition to
your number and strength, and soe order the management of
your provision, that neither they nor any others may want, but
yet that as much as may be your people may be maintained by
the product of the country, which if you take a right course in
planting provisions enough, I am informed that for the future
they may bee.   As for Mr Rivers and the rest kept by the Spaniards at St Katherina the Spanish Ambassadour has given me
assurance these shall be redelivered, wee are told here that there
has been a great quantitye of Ambregrise, upwards of 200 weight,
taken up by some of our people of Ashley River, whereof we
receiving noe accompt either from you or Governor Sayle we
imagine it might be by the sloop at her goeing out to Bermudos,
I desire you to make diligent enquiries into this matter, expecting that whilst we are not only giving the fairest conditions, and
makeing the equalest laws for the people there, but also are at
charges to transport and maintain them in a fruitful country,
where we designe and labour they should be happy, they will not
any of them, make soe ungrateful a returne as to goe about to de-
fraud us of our just rights, since halfe thereof by the constitutions of
our Government would belong to us even from strangers, for whom
we had done noe more than barely admitted them into our country, we shall endeavour to establish our Government on strict
rules of equity and Justice, and as we shall take care that noe
body there shall be oppressed in his just rights and lyberties, soe
we expect that noe body should offer to injure us by such fraud
which we will not suffer him to use to his neighbour.   I looke to
hear from you concerning this, and by every oppertunity of sending concerning the state and progresse of our affairs there, and
that you may not hereafter mistake the name of the place you
are in, you are to take notice that the River was by Captain

Sandford long since named Ashley River, and is still to be called soe, and the Towne you are now planted on we have named and you are to call Charles Towne.   Your present Palatine is the Lord Jno: Berkley Lord Lieutenant of Ireland who succeeds in the roome of the deceased Duke of Albemarle

I am Your asssured friend

ASHLEY.

[S. P., Bdle. 48, No. 55, page 3.]

1670 Nov: 3. RELEASE FROM ANTHONY LORD ASHLEY of his eighth part of the proprietary of Carolina to Thomas Stringer of Sᵗ Clement Danes, co: Middlesex, upon trust for the benefit of the son & heir of the said Lord Ashley & his heirs male forever with power to said Lord Ashley to revoke and make void the same.   *signed by* Lord Ashley, with seal.

Endorsed: "The Release of Carolina to Mʳ Stringer."[1]

[S. P., Sec. ix, No. 43.]

"BARBADOS PROCLAMATION."[2]

Barbadoes November the 4ᵗʰ 1670 for Carolina.

Whereas certaine Intelligence is now come from Ashley river in the province of Carrolina by the Carrolina friggott Capt. Henry Braine commander now residing in the bay of Carlisle that all those people which departed hence aboute 12 months paste in the said friggott for the settling of that province are in very good health and safely arrived at the said Ashley river and settled in a very rich aud fertile soyle situated in 32 degrees 45 minutes north latitude   The river being so convenient for shipps of 3 to 400 tunns that on skidds they may load and unload theire goodes from the shipp on the branch of the river which beyond all mens expectations doth produce all manner plants which this Island doth afforde they having had experience thereof by plant-ing of sugar cannes cotton ginger tobacco potatoes yames corne and other of this country provision which doth flourish and

---

[1] MS. unprinted; he was L'd Ashley's secretary.

[2] So endorsed by Locke, signed by Sayle at Kiawah, sent May 28 on the ship to Virginia, she returned Aug. 23, sailed for Barbadoes Sep. 23 & arrived Oct. 31.   *S. P.*, 48.   For Hilton, see pages 18, 32, 53.

increase to all the peoples satisfaction that are there settled they having noe want of provision but sufficient without the help of the country provision for a long season which from Virginie Burmudas and this island hath been supplyed on the Lord pro- prietors there Accounts and that from this day forward they will have noe need of supplyes for the future the stocks that which is now in the ground that will next spring be planted sufficiently will maintaine them and to spare. The Indians that boarder on them being soe friendly for a inconsiderable vallue they supplye them with deer fish and fowle in a great abundance as likewise in assisting them to cleare and plant their land Now for the better Expedition in settling of the said province and encourage- ment of all manner of people that have a desire to tranceport themselves sarvants negroes or utensils the Lords proprietors of the province of Carrolina hath provided the Carrolina friggott aforesaid for the tranceportation of the said people who will be ready to depart this Island in 30 dayes after the date hereof.

Wherefore this is to give notice to all such persons as formerly under write one thousand pounds of Muscouadoe sugar or more towards defraying the charge of setting forth Capt Hillton on the discovery of the said province of Carrolina and ware to have a vallerable quantity of land allotted them in consideration of their disbursement in the said province after the setting thereof the Lords proprietors are now pleased to confirme the saide quantity of land. To all such persons as have underwrite as aforesaid according to the termes then promised and now to have the said lands runn forth to every such person that before the 25 day of March next Insueing the date hereof shall make demand thereof from the Agents of the said proprietors where they are now settled and shall sende people to take possession thereof.

As Likewise these are to give notice to all persons who have nott underwrite as aforesaid that are minded to transport them- selves sarvants or goodes for the said province of Carrolina for this present Expedition on the aforesaid friggott shall have the benefitt of the insueing Articles confirmed unto them at their arrivall in Ashley River by the Governors and the Agents of the Lords Proprietors and for their accomadations aboard the saide shippes all such persons as are not able to pay theire passage or furnish themselves with provisions for the said voyage shall have convenient and good accomadation of victuals drink etc. giving their obligations to pay unto the Agents of the Lords propriators within two yeares after their arrivall at the said Ashley River the sume of five hundred pounds Marchantable tobacco cotton or ginger or any of the said spetie they shall first produce. And all such persons as are able to putt in there production and other necessaries shall pay butt one hundred pounds of Muscouadoe sugar in Bardadoes or two hundred pounds of cotton ginger or tobacco within two yeares time as aforesaid and all such persons that are willing to tranceport themselves on these termes they may repaire to the house of Mr Jno Strode Marchant at St. Michaels towne[1] where they shall finde Capt. Henry Braine to have their agreemts confirmed. Major Natha Kingsland att windward Mr Tho Colleton at the cleift Sir Jno Yeemans at Leward these may also advertize all such persons that are minded to tranceport themselves as above said to putt their names timely in the secretary's Office according to the custome of this place to prevent the shippe staing for their tickets. *Annexed.*

The grants of the Lords propriators of the Carrolina to those that settle therein:

To every freeman that shall arrive there to plant and inhabit before the 25 March 1672 one hundred akers of land to him and his heires for ever and one hundred akers more to every man sarvant he brings with him or causeth to be tranceported into the said Colony and 70 akers for every woman sarvant or man sarvant under 16 yeares of age and 70 akers to every sarvant that shall arrive before the time last mentioned to his or her proper use when their time of sarvitude are expired to them and their heires for-ever.

The propriators doe keep a storehouse in the country out of which those which are not able to furnish themselves with victuals cloaths and tooles shall be supplied at easie rates upon trust untill they are able to pay.

All persons that are able to make up 8 in one family or will joyne together to that number shall have liberty to settle upon there lands granted as above said by the Lords propriator in .such place as they shall thinke most convenient and benefitiale to themselves All which and every other priviledge and immunity

---

[1] Had 50 acres & 40 negroes 1679. Settled a plan'n in Carolina 167$\frac{0}{1}$, and afterwards his son there.

granted to the inhabitants of this Collony will be performed upon their arrivall and for the truth and assurances of the same I have hereunto sett my hand this 21 May 1670 Wm Seale Governor.

All goodes and Marchant dize that shall be tranceported out of England to ye s^d Colony for ye use of ye Inhabitants therein by a grante from ye King pay noe custome nor duty for seaven yeares in England likewise by the said grant noe comodityes of the growth of Carrolina shall pay any dewes or dutyes in England or the domions till seaven tunns of any one particular spetie be tranceported in one vessel for England and then nott to begin till seaven yeares be expired after the tranceportation and landing of the seaven tunns of any one particular spetie and then only for that spetie the truth of the coppy above this is certyfied by mee.

[*S. P.*, Bdle. 48, No. 44.]

To Sir John Heyden—7. Nov: 70.[1]

Sir,

The courtesie wherewith you entertained our people at theire passage to Carolina and the forwardnesse wherewith you have assisted our new settlement there, make me believe that you will easyly be perswaded to continue this kindnesse you have soe frankely begun though I should forbear to tell you that you have thereby oblieged severall persons of some consideration in England whom when you shall have occasion to make use of them you will not find unmindfull of this favour. As for myself I assure you I have soe particular a sense of this kindnesse done me with soe obliging circumstances that I shall be very glad of any opertunity you will give me to repay you my thanks otherwise then by bare acknowledgements I cane send you in a Letter and whenever I may be serviceable to any concernment of yours you may be confident it will be as safe as my interest here cane make it.

I begg this farther favour of you in a businesse of some moment to us we being informed that some of our People that went last to plant in Carolina have taken up above 200 weight of Ambergreece a part whereof doth of right belong to us the Proprietors. I desire you would search into the truth of this matter

---

[1] Deputy Gov'r Bermuda, came there May 15, 1669.

16

and if any Part of it be in the Island you would seise on it for our use.

I am, your very affec^ate friend and servant

7. Nov. 70.   ASHLEY.

[*S. P.*, Bdle. 48, No. 55, p. 9.]

HENRY BRAYNE TO LORD ASHLEY.

My Lord,

My last was from Virginia and now liekwise I have sent within boath letters[1] I have given your Lordship to understand the truth of the most of my proceedings and our Instructions and what hoopes we have of our settlement if it be but well managed for the Corst and Country will answer any men's expectation boath as to navegation and plantation and the greatest of our wants is good men of reason fitt for a Commonwelth for though the Governer is anchient and crazie yet if there was but a wise Counsell that was Planters and knowing how to setle such a Country which by such men's contrivances if it bee good for them selves by the same rule I and others being governed by them and working alick it must needs be good for me and the rest of settlers and a great incouragement to lay out our moneys but as we are constraint to follow the rules of those that are soe ignorant that we now have acting all things to their owne ruining we must of necessity ruining our selves or at least wise a great loss to our time and what we doe lay on to premoat the Country but I hoope by the goeing downe of sume persons in my ship that be recommended to the Governor which if he take them into his Councell things wilbe better carried heareafter with much more less charge to your Lordships, and to our better ease profitt and sattisfaction then heatherto it hath bine for I assure your Lordship there is but 4 or 5. men of the Councell that have any reason which is Capt: West, Mr Bull, Mr Scrivener and one Mr Dun and Mr Dalton those good honest men but knowes nothing of planting which if we had but so many more that did know what did belonge to it the most of our agrevances would soone be remedied as to the rest of your Councell they knowes nothing unless it be to scould or abuse any person that did seack their good and welfare but espetially Capt: O. Swilowvun our

---

[1]12 June, lost & 30 July, *Ante*, p. 177.

Surveyor Generall who doth by his absurd language abuse the Governor, Councell and Contry and by his rash and base dealings he hath caused everie one in the Country allmost to be his Enimie and espetially he hath given the people a verie great Jelousie of him as to his act of surveying for I assure your Lordship all lands that he hath pretended to lay and run out is verie irregular not knowing how to give us any sattisfaction in things of plaine cases in soe much that we are everie day almost togeather by the ears and espetially with him pretending knowledg but acts nothing to make it out for at the verie day I came away hardly any person was sattesfied as to there small lotts I know not when they wilbe layd out unless your Lordship will take sume speedie Care that we may have a better surveyor which if your Lordships think good heare are verie able, sober, wise men that would be willing to undertake it if your Lordships would impower Sir John Yeamans, Mr Colliton, and Major Kingsland to gett us one which I am confiden are verie fitt and better deserves it which would give us all verie good sattisfaction or at leastwise that we might have libberty to survay at present till a better doth present my Lord I have heatherto bine as greate an incourager as any one ordinary man upon the designe and I may say I have the best stock of any three men in the Collony except your Lordshipes Interest haveing put on 6 head of Cattle that my people have milk enough twice a day I have there alsoe 7 hoggs more I had but in spite or rashness was killed lickwise I have put on 3 sheep. 6 geese 8 turkies 12 foules with provitions enough for my people which is one lusty negro man[1] 3. cristian servants and a oversear I brought out of Virginia and 10 head of Cattle I have ordered to be brought on this next sumer by my owne vessell from Virginia but the greatest of my agreavances is that I have not as yett a convenient pece of land that is worth the making a settlement on and as yett verie little Incouragement from your Lordshipes for when I was at Sir Peter Colleton's house his Honor was pleased to promise that he would gett me a patten for 5000 Acres of land for the monys, sugers servant and else that I was out at Cape Faire and for my first discoverie with Coll. Sandford the which

---

[1] The first negro mentioned in Carolina; Yeamans may have sent some from Barbadoes. See page 164.

if your Lordshipe would be plesed to grant me the said quantity
of land for my futer Incouragement I should for ever pray and
that I may have liberty to take it up in any part of the provunce
the which if your Lordship doth grant I wil be bound that I will
not settle it tell our place that we have made a beginning now
be thoroughly and saufly settled and then I will if please
God put on 30. hands of my owne and 50. or 60. more I will
gett to settle by me on there owne lands adjasent which if your
Lordship would be pleased to give me liberty to take out 3 or
fower small gunes out of the ship if I see occation beinge of noe
service heare aboard I would not question but to settle as
saufe and secure as any place in the world was ever settled and
I doe beleave it would be much for the promoting of your Lordships Interest if your Lordshipes think it convenient I desire the
Duke of Yourk's Commission or else one from your Lordshipes[1]
which if your Lordshipes doth impower me I hoope your Lordship will find that I shall not any waies goe beyond your Commands and by it I may doe your Lordships good service heareafter   this I doe not desire of an ambition of Honour but as I
conceave it may be rite usefull my Lord I am heartily soerie
that M[r] Rivers my good friend and the rest are detayned by the
Spaniard and as I have the portugall language I have a very
great ambition that I could procure there libberties which if
your Lordship layes your Commands upon me the next sumer
I would try what I could doe in it: M[r] Colliton and M[r] Stroud
the marchant doth take abundance of paines and they have taken
up one hundred pounds sterling fur the furnishing of our ship
with necessaries and provitions for our semen and passingers that
goes downe with us   M[r] Stroud is a great incourager of our
designe haveing provided almost 20 servant betwext himselfe and
one Justice Harvie my Lord we doe dearly want an other vessell
that may saile at a small charge which if your Lordships send
one this bearer my mate[2] is verie fitt and able to take charge of
him knowinge him to be a verie able man and accoynted well
with our Virginia, Newingland and the Leward Islands   If your
Lordship hath a mind to continue me in the ship I desire your
Lordship to give me a little better power that I may not be

[1] As a ship of war or privateer against the Spaniards.
[2] Jno. Coming, going home in Cap. Gilbert.

thretned by such as our Governors and Councell to turne me out of the ship or by any other mens envies for their owne private Interest I have little else to trubble your Lordship at present with praying for your Lordshipes and your Honor^able Ladies good Helth I am

Your Lordships exact serv^t to command

HENRY BRAYNE.

Barbadoes this 9th of Novr 1670.

Endorsed : To the Right Honorable the Lord Ashley.

Present London.

[*S. P.*, Bdle. 48, No. 45.]

———

SIR JOHN YEAMANS TO LORDS PROPRIETORS.

May it please your Lordshipps

I have formerly given your Lordshipps an Accompt of your Affaires relateing to Port Royall, to the time of the departure from hence of your Fleete thitherwards[1] And that through the greate desire I had to serve your Lordshipps principally in a matter tending soe much to the Increase of the Honor and Benefitt of the English Dominion I had embarqued myselfe thereon And alsoe in consequence thereof how by the hand of God through the violence of stormes and contrary winds your Fleete became dispersed and that Shipp wherein I myselfe was with much difficulty had attained the Harbour of Burmoodoes, where the refitting and waiting a faire oportunity had relapsed soe much time that I found myselfe through necessity engaged to reterne from that Island hither to be in a readines for the executing His Majestie's Commissions before that time directed to myselfe and some others Com^rs for the Negotiateing with French Com^rs the Affaire of St Christophers.[2] And that therefore before my departure thence I had according to the best of my understanding directed your publique concernements and by your blanke Commission

---

[1] Lost letter Nov. 28, 1669. See page 164.

[2] Com'n March 22, 1669, to Sir Jno. Yeamans, Col. Philip Bell, &c., to demand part of St. Christophers, &c., under treaty of Breda. *A. W. I.*, 33, 36, 39, 65.

substituted Colonel Wm Sayle a Burmodian the Governor Who although a man of noe great sufficiency yett the ablest I could then meete with and by whome I had greate reason to hope many of that Island would be the sooner invited to your settlement.

Now I have further to acquaint your Lordshipps that your Shipp the Carolina arrived here from thence some fewe days past by whome I have Intelligence of the welfare of the people there of the continued health they have enjoyed from the time of their arrivall.

The wholesomnesse of the Aire, the fruitfulness of the Earth even to Admiracon that the scituation is pleasant beyond ex-pression That the Natives are friendly and faithfull giveing them ready assistance in all things they can desire of them and with whome they have contracted a perpetuall Peace and Friendshipp by Articles ratified betwixt them and their supreeme Cossique.[1] But I am also further informed that whilst these matters were ac-complishing the Spaniard seated at St Augustine appeared in a warrlike Posture in their shipps before their Harbour but de-parted without attempting anything And that they endeavoured to stirr up the Indians to prevent your settlement threatning dis-truction to those Indians that continue friendshipp to the Eng-lish.   But your people doe not apprehend any danger from those designes only they doubt that the poorenes of Spiritt shewne by Governor Sayle in this occasion and the fears he hath betrayed in this smale commotion hee hath lost them soome esteeme with the Indians and may draw on them great Inconveniencyes in the future.   To prevent which if God permitt I intend to sayle thither myselfe towards the latter end of the Somer comeing If I can have conveniency for my transportation, where I will wholly lay myselfe out to Doe your Lordshipps and that Collony all the service I am able otherwise must bee forced to waite some other somer passage And for the present I shall endeavour the speedy dispatch and returne of your Shipp thither with what passengers I cann encourage to that Designe.   The welfare of that Colony now principally depending upon the increase of their strength and Numbers.

My Lords I hold it my Duty further to give your Lordshipps

---

[1] The Emperor of Cusitachique.

notice that sundry Gents in theise parts desirous to be concerned in your Province haveing perused the Concessions in your Charter for the Government are become absolutely dissatisfied and discouraged and from proceeding thereon upon consideracon of the 6th Article thereof and others consequent, wherein you determine that the lands appertaining to all Landgraves Cassiques with the Dignityes shall go to the Heire male, and for want of such issue escheate to the Proprietors Now they say that all such lands soe assigned by your Lordshipps being altogether without improvements And from whence noe produce cann be reapt without vast disbursements Nor advantages hoped for till the second Generacon. It wilbe an undertakeing not warranted by discretion to hazard soe greate an Estate upon such an uncertaine Lymitation and therefore will by noe meanes be induced to lay out their mony in that settlement, unless it may redound to them and their heires for ever. But as to the bare title of Honor they are contented if your Lordshipps will have it soe that in default of Heires Male it may be in your Lordshipps Giuft againe Farther they say they are not satisfyed how inferior Persons that hold under theise Landsgraves or Cassiques shalbe dealt with in case of such an Escheate as aforesaid And whether they shalbe putt to compound with your Lordshipps in such case for their Inheritances. Farther there are some that take exception for that your Lordshipps have not in your Concessions aforesaid acquitted the produce of the Country from Customes and Impositions answerable to his Majestie's Grant to your Lordshipps which they conceive your Lordshipps have omitted for your Advantage.

In all which Particulars if your Lordshipps shall think fitt to explaine yourselves by some Instrument as publique as that of your Concessions from whence those doubts are drawne It will abundantly satisfye many here who are men of Purse and parts to promote your Lordshipps Designes in this Settlement and in the meantime If your Lordshipps shalbe pleased to send mee a Pattent for a Landgrave with directions for laying out the Barronyes thereto belonging by a Tenure free and unfettered soe that the Estate I intend to buy there may in its resurrections become the benefitt of my Posterity It wilbe a meanes the sooner to free those Persons from the doubt and Jelosies I have mentioned and to encorage them to goe on chearefully in the greate worke

your Lordshipps have designed.   And to that end alsoe fully to engage the utmost endeavours of My Lords
Your Lordshipps most obedient & humble servant
JOHN YEAMANS.

Barbadoes Nov. 15. 1670.
Endorsed : Sir John Yeamans to Lords Proprietors 15. Nov: 70.
[*S. P.*, Bdle. 48, No. 46.]

FROM SIR JNO YEOMANS NOVEMBER 15° 70.[1]

May it please your Lordship,

I have this day written to the Proprietors of the Province of Carolina acquainting them with the Occurrences of that Place hitherto, and of some matters which I conceived needful for them to effect towards the benefit thereof in the Future to which I most humbly referr your Lordship.

My Intentions to goe in person thither this summer comeing, and my great ambition to serve your Ldsp gives me the confidence at present to that end to tender my humble service to your Lordship and to beg that your Lordsp will be pleased to lay your Commands upon me, In your ship the Carolina which lately arrived here from thence my Agents sent me 12 Cedar Planks which I have directed to be loaden on Capt. Gilbert presenting them to your Lordsp as the first fruits of that glorious Province which promising in abundance all those good things the heart of man can wish for, doth at present infinitely abound in this excellent sort of Timber.   I have here inclosed your Lordshipp a Letter sent me from one Mr Henry Woodward The Person left at Port Royall by Coll: Robert Sandford upon the first discovery made which I desire may be imparted to the rest of the Lords Proprietors   And as I am informed the said Woodward has made a very large discovery in the Colony but is much unwilling to declare it to the Government there being desirous to be sent for to make it out to your Lordsps which if granted will Redound much to the Prejudice of the Setlement   He being the only Person by whose meanes wee hold a faire and peacable Correspondence with the Natives of the Place But I question not but

---

[1] To L'd Ashley.   See *S. P.*, 53.   (*A. W. I.*, 337 has 'to L'd Dudley,' but it is evidently to a Proprietor.)   Enclosing Woodward's letter, page 186.   His 'large discovery' is the pearls & silver of Cusitachique.

at my Arrivall there to have a full and perfect discovery from him of all his Proceedings, and soe send it for your Lordships further Satisfaction the Consideration of which is left to your Lordshipps and the rest of the Lords Proprietors by

My Lord Your Lords^{pps} most humble servant

JOHN YEOMANS.

Barbadoes the 15° Novemb^r 70.

[*S. P.*, Bdle. 48, No. 55, p. 72.]

SIR JOHN YEAMANS TO SIR P. COLLETON.

Sir

Yours of the 28th August last I recd with a copie of the 30th May last the originall whereof never came to my hands the miscarriage of which doth not a little trouble me.   about six weekes since here arrived one Mr Berrow [1] who was in the Port Royall friggott bound for Carolina and a person very industrious in the taking an exact accompt of the transacceons of their unhappy voyage which hee brought me with severall papers and Plotts of the Bahamy Islands which I gave to my friend your Brother Mr Thomas Colletton for perusall, and to send you coppyes thereof, which he hath not as yet retorned me.   Soe that to the particulers of them I must refere you to him.   Some few dayes since here arrived the Carolina friggott from Carolina by which we have a large and ample accompt of the peoples arriveall and good health there, only their deficiency in Strength and number of People as you will perceive by my generall letter to all the Lords Proprietors for what supplyes those parts cann afford.   I have by my dayly care and Industry withdrawne severall persons from their resolutions of other settlements as Colonel Sharpe [2] from New Yorke who intended a large settlement there but has suspended the same untill a moderation be made to the severall Excepcons specified in my generall letter here inclosed to the

---

[1] Christopher Barrow, was put on the Pt. Royal at Nevis, by Sir John to pilot her to Port Royal, by his advice they took a southerly course. After the wreck near Abaco, he and his wife went to New York, thence to Barbadoes.   He was of Bristol, and visited Carolina 1678.

[2] Col. Wm. Sharpe, an eminent planter of Barbadoes with 600 acres, 'an ingenious man and of good interest,' member of Council 1666, &c. of Assembly and Speaker 1674-76 and a judge.

Lords, with one to Lord Ashley[1] which pray deliver I presume the Carolina friggott may be ready about three weekes hence to depart for said province wherein by my perswasion is bound Capt Godfry and M[r] Thomas Gray who was my chiefe Agent of all my Affaires here,[2] with a very considerable strength of servants and many others unknowne to you soe needles here to name here is lately passed an Act in this Island to prevent depopulation in which there are great penaltyes imposed upon such persons that shall endeavour and perswade any to goe hence for other Colonyes which will be a greate hinderance of Supplyes from hence I have onely at present to desire your concurrance and urgency with the Lords for a speedy Answere to my generall letter wishing you health and prosperity I assure you

I am   Your very faithfull servant

JOHN YEAMANS.

Barbadoes the 15th of November 1670.

Endorsed: These for my Honored Friende S[r] Peter Colliton Barronett   present.   [*S. P.*, Bdle. 48, No. 47.]

MEMORANDA—*in the handwriting of John Locke.*

Wm. Owen Sept. 15-70.   (Page 196.)

Charlestowne—Defended with a creek on the one side and a salt marsh overflowne at high tides on the other the neck that joynes it to the main land not exceeding 50. yards palisaded and easily defensible.

Inlet.   Difficult to strangers but 3 fathom water.

Healthy.   But one that came from England dead and that of a lingring distemper.

---

[1] Page 220.   *A. & W. I.*, 337, misprinted, 'Lord Dudley,' see 186.

[2] He reached Carolina in 1670-1, settled plantations there, was chosen to parliam't and the council, and being brave, active and efficient, bore part in every action.   He subdued the Kussoes, seated James town and made discoveries up Ashley and Cooper rivers for which he received Lord Ashley's thanks.   In 1672 he was made Duke Albemarle's deputy and major against the Westoes and 1673 was sent against the Stonos. But in June, Gray, Culpeper, Robinson and others, headed civil disturbances, fled the Province, were attainted by the parliam't, and their estates forfeited, and Grays vessel seeking to remove his family and goods, was seized.   He probably retired to Barbadoes.

Navigation. Ships in their voyage to Carolina there being various windes on the coast will be apt to fall in upon the Spanish plantacons who are 200 leagues to the Southward.

Spaniards. 4 Preists between us and St Augustines 1° at Wallie or St Katherina with about 300 Indians who with the other 3 can muster about 700 Indians besides those of the maine whome sometimes they call to their assistance. These without owneing it they set on upon those they have a minde.

St Augustines'. An important gareson with about 200 souldiers and at Apalachia[1] they have 3. files of men for intelligence came with 10 periagos and incamped at the rivers mouth 6. days. We need not feare the Spaniards unlesse supplied from the Havana.

Indians. Of Edisto Ashapo and Combohe to the South our friends. Of Wando Ituan Sewee and Sehey to the north came to our assistance and were zealous and resolute in it 1000 bowmen In our want supplied us.

Q. Spaniards. What we shall doe to the Spaniards if we invade them we brake the peace, if we sit still we loose our reputation with the Indians our freinds.

Westoes. Inland man eaters.

Country. To the northward more sickly, about Ashley River fertile and of a wonderful growth.

Tatchequea. A very fruitfull Country 8. days jorney by the North west the Emperor our friend and enemy to the Westocs and to hard for them.

The land of his country very fertile, hilly, full of white and black marble, mould red, people biger and ruder than our Indians.

Q. Settlem't. 500 people will secure the settlement 1000 perfect it. desires supplys of necessarys till that time, and for himself a dispensation of frieght in exportation and importation for some time.

S. Bull. *12. Sep. 70.* (*Page 192*).

Ashley River. Good land plenty everything thrives beyond expectation. Oranges, Lemons, Limes, Pomcitrons, Pomegranats, Fig trees, Plantanes 10 Acres p^r head taken up about

---

[1] Owen writes or misspells 'impotent,' page 198. Apalachicola. The words in italic here are on margin in original.

the towne and the greater lots upon the river above and below. Healthy, some people have had agues and fevers but neither mortal nor violent.

Passage free for a yeare or two from Barbadoes Leeward Islands to such as cannot transport themselves.

More people, shipps and supplys to be sent.

To serve my Lord himselfe in Mr Rivers's roome.

Indians. Supplied y^r want of provisions without inhanceing the price upon our necessity, ready to assist us. Afraid of the Westocs who are an inland people, invade them about their harvest, men eaters, have guns. Friendship with the Emperor of T   who sent a present of skins to the governor.

Governor. Sick of a feaver and in danger some things ill done by him rather through self will then designe or interest.

O. Sylivant. Dissentious troublesome, bound to the peace and good behaviour, Exactor of unreasonable Fees noe able surveyor. Knaveish.

H. Brayne 9° Nov: 70.   (Page 214.)

Council of reasonable men and good planters.

Q That Sir Jo: Yeamans, Mr Colleton and Major Kingland may be impowered to get an other Surveyor in O. Sylivants room, or survey themselves. 5000 akers of land for his incouragemen^t promised by Sir P. Colleton and to take it up any where, His present stock at Ashley River being more then any bodys and ready to bring on more. Three or 4 small guns out of the ship to secure his plantation. A commission from the Duke of Yorke or the proprietors Command to attaque the Spaniards for the recovery of Mr Rivers. Another vessel and Comins to command it, a man skild in those parts. More power soe as not to be subject to the Governor and Councel.

Country. Good.

Mr. Colleton. Laid out for supply of the shipp £100.

Mr. Strode. A great incourager of the plantacon is sending 20 servants thither in partnership with justice Harvey.

Governor. Ancient and crazie.

Council. Men of reason in it West, Bull, Scrivener, Dun, and Dalton but ignorant of planting. The rest unfit espetialy O. Sylivant an ill man and no surveyor.

J. West. Sept. 70. (Page 204.)

Q. New Instructions for disposall of the stores because those he hath signed by your Lordship and Sir P. Colleton alone are not allowed by the Governor as sufficient.

Servants. Hath taken into your service 4 servants belonging to Captain Bayly.

Country. Healthy, delightful, bears anything.

Cattle. Some of the Virginia Cattle taken up for your Lordship's private plantation.

Governor. Aged and unfit would have cald a parl^{mt}.

Ship. Dispatched in haste to Barbadoes to fetch people and returne before winter.

Charles towne In a little while will be soe fortified as not to feare any attaque.

Wm. Sayle. (Page 185.)

Q. Supplys and more people. A Pinke about 80 tun.
Country. Pleasant, Healthy, Fruitfull.

Sir Jo: Yeamans: 15° Nov. 70. (Page 220.)

Desires your Lordships Commands in particular resolveing to go to Carolina next summer. Presents the Cedar Plants. Commends the Country. Woodward necessary to the plantation as interpreter. Sir Jo: hopes to get out of him what he hath to say to the Proprietors without leting him come home.

Jo: Dalton 9° Sept: 70. (Page 182.)

Desires a ship to transport people for 2. or 3. years, thes want servants and clothes. The Spaniards dare not trust the Indians under him because of their tyrany. 300 leagues to Mexico from Ashley River. Desires mitigation of freight for the planters goods they haveing been hindered from planting by alarms and fortifiing. Desires a ship of force to be always there, and to be continued Secretary. Want paper and a booke to register grants.

Endorsed: Extract of Lord Ashleys Letters 70.

[*S. P.*, Bdle. 48, No. 39.]

CAPT. BRAYNE TO THE PROPRIETORS.

Barbadoes Nov. 20th 1670.

My Lords,

My last unto your Lordships was from Virginia dated the
12th of June last wherein I rendered a full accompt of all our
procedings from Burmuda to port Royall; from thence to Ashley River; before called Keywahah; where we are now settled
and so to Virginia; where I did arive the 6th of June and finding
M[r] Burgh deed I applied my selfe to Major Generall Bennett
and Captain Godwin the persons that had your Lordships goods
in possession; and when they understood my business they was
verie forward to putt all things in prosecution for my dispatch
and acquainting Sir William Bercley of our Countryes afaires he
was verie ready to assist us and ordered one hundred pound
sterling for the better supplying of our wants, the efects of which
and your cargo sent with eighty odd pounds more I tooke aboard
as by the inclosed accompt or invoice you may see; haveing
dispatch I fell down with my Shipp, the wind taking me short I
was forced to come to Anchor with two vessells more in my company, being the 4th of August and the 6 and 7th day wee rid out
a Hurry Cane being verie ill provided for such purposes but God
be thanked I saved my shipp; but one of my company was staved
to peces breaking loose and runing in the night against another
shipp did force her ashore, and lickwise that wind hath done a
great deale of damadge to the Planters Cropes and Houses that
Tobacco wilbe extraordinary scarce, The storme being over I
gott up my top masts and yards the wind scinkhing favoring I gott
up my anchors and sett saile the 8 day of August and the 22[d] of
that Instant I arived at our River's mouth and came to anchor
to stop the tide of ebb: and seeing some Indians on shore I tooke
my boat M[r] Carteret and one of the two Indians of our Country
which I had to Virginia with me and 2. or 3. servants with a gun
or two and went towards them and coming neere we spied a
Flagg of truce about quarter of a mile from two or three of
those Indians that the boddy of them had sent downe to the
water side to invite us on shore, but our Indian was verie sure
thay was none of our Country Indians which made me begin to
mistrust that they ware eyther spanish Indians or those that we
call westows and rowing alongst shore about ½ mile from them
we went on shore and sent our Indian toward them and coming

prettie neare our indian had spied a bow made fast alongst his back whereupon he made signe to the other Indian that he might heave hime away which he did cast the bow upon the sand and then they came toward one another and the rest behind at ther place of rundizvous about half a mile from them; and when they mett the straing Indian sprung to our Indian and indevered to take hoult of hime but being a brave, bould spritly fellow hee sprang from hime and made twoards us; we seeing that; thought it the best of pollicie to make twoard the Enimie to make them stand fore we had gott our Indian before us; and getting into the boat we rowed off and I think there was about 9 or 10 musquits fired after us but neaver a shott did reach Tidde of flud being made we weighed anchor and the next day being the 23 we arived at the towne now called Albemarle poynt where we found them all in armes. Our Governor and the rest did judg us to be one of the Spanish ships that the Indians of our Country in my absence acquaint them that thay saw at sea, but whether they did see any spanish ships I know not for thay might be as well Inglish men come through the Goulfe from Jamacca; or it may be thay saw non at all however the sight of us after knowledg did take away most of their fears and doubts; and after I acquainted the Governer and Captain West of what had past betwixt my selfe and the Spanish indians;[1] thay ordered me to put my Cattle and hogg and lumber on shore keeping my provitions aboard and bringe my shipp in a posture for a defence which the 25th day she was all cleared and seeing noe licklyhood of opposition I desired the Governer to send out a party to goe against those Indians which did oppose us (if he though good) he did call his councell but being in opposition one to the other there was nothing don though all my seamen was all ready and willing to goe; the Governer did well in it for not sending for ought I know but this I am certing where Indians finds thay are lett alone in their roagerie; it doth the more increase their bouldness and annimat them on to more mischift; which on the contrary had we a routted them as all the whole country was willing, I question weather ever any Spaniards or Indians would ever attempt to come soe neare us; my Lords I have bine somthing tedious but the reason is because

---

[1] See pages 179, 194, 199, 203, the alarm was Aug: 18.

your Lordshipps should have the full truth and understanding
of our opposers that you may the better judg. and contrive for
our heraeafter saufty and quiet; the men are not as yett come
back from the Spaniards though there was a sloop sent for them
the time that I was on my voyadge to Virginia for I suppose by
our Gov^{rs} & Councills ill contriving as I did understand by M^r
Bull and Mr Owine two ingenious persons that insteed of bringing of Mr Rivers and the rest that was seized thay left Captain
Bayly in the Fryers hands and went away he being a person of
verie good worth and a good linguister, which persons my
bowells doth yearn to have them oft if I had power to act;
hoopin your Lordships will consider something in it after I had
waited 6 dayes with my shipp in readyness I consulted with the
Governer and Captain West as to my farther proceding eyther
to take in timber for Barbadoes or what else thay could think on
better for the Countreyes good and their owne saufty whereupon
they answered mee that all the time I was absent thay was faine to
put the people to a pint of pease a day by which sharp allowance
was the cause that there was little worke don and noe timber ready
or fitt to be shipped off and the distraction that thay ware in about
those spaniards; thay thought it better to fortifie themselves as
strong as thay could and to send me away emediately to Barbadoes that I might come time enough to gett in before the foule
weather did come in; upon this conclusion I putt my provisions
ashore fitted my ship and soe soone as I received my dispatch I
fell downe to the River's mouth Sept: 15th and the 17th I gott all
my water aboard and the wind blowing verie hard easterly I could
not gett out, and the 20th day I spied the shollup^1 that whe heired
in Barbadoes when wee went downe to port Royall; and she
turning 24 hourer to gett into the River I sent my Boat to assist
them; and when she arived I understood that she was deep loden
with Corne; but passingers not above two in regard the noyse
of the spaniard, seasinge those men beinge reported by some
that went in the sloop which is one reason that thay are afraid to
venter another thing as I did understand thay did not licke the
Governer which I did read in some letters that was sent from
Burmuda to some of our gentlemen that came out of Ingland

---

^{1} The 'Three Brothers' was next sent to the Bahamas and went on to
Barbadoes arriving there in December.

the Governor having noe more service to command mee I tooke
my leave of him Captain West and went abourd and the 23 day
of Sept: the wind came up at north I weighed anchor and sett
saile for Barbadoes, wheare I arived the 31 day of October;
beinge becalmed and with contrary winds 12 or 14 dayes in my
passaidg; yet however I hoope I am come time enough finding
heare abondance of people that is makinge ready to goe downe
with me; and the more willinge because our Contry is though
(by those that lives there) verie healthie and everie one in generall doth give a good report of it and all verie well sattesfied
and contented; assuering themselves that in one 2. or 3. years
thay shall live verie happy and comfortable; and a good part of
our seamen have a great fancie to settle having some stock
allready upon it; and are now goeing to your Lordshipps for
their wages to fitt themselves out; longer I would a kept them
off from their pay but could not fearing that I should a don
more harme by restrayninge them then I should a don good; by
keeping them from their monys which is justly due; hoopinge
your Lordshipes will make them good payment according to the
tennar of my noats charged to your Lordshipes; Captain God-
frie[1] is goeinge downe with me a verie ingenious person and 5.
hands upon his perticular accòmpt; Mr Gray Sir John Yeamans
his oversear with 10. able men; the most part Carpinters and
Sayars; Mr Stroud the marchant and Justice Harvy is sending

---

[1] 'A very able man and good planter,' a Carolina adventurer 1663–5
and 167$^9_1$ 'he and Lt Gray going thither things will be better,' he was
made Ld Craven's deputy, improved the laws and agriculture, settled
towns and plant'ns, subdued the Kussoes and 1672 commanded against
the Westoes and drove the Spaniards from St. Helena. In the scarcity
he brought food from abroad, he led against the Westoes and in every
civil enterprise and warlike action of the Colony. Sat in the Council
1673–4 and April 1675 acted as Governor in West's absence; was in
Council 1676–8 &c., and 1682–3 in Morton's; June 3, 1684, Duke Albemarle's deputy and May, July 1685 Presid't of the Council and in Colleton's 1686–7. He had estates on Ashley river, 'Mandee' & 'Tuera'
plant'ons on Dalho branch of Wapachecoone creek and elsewhere He
died 1691 leaving his widow Mary, dau'r Mrs. Woodward & son Capt.
Jno Godfrey (who left will 1705, widow Elizabeth, 3 sons John, Richard
& Benjamin & dau's Jane m'd Jas Stanyarne esq: Mary m'd Wm. Cattel
esq: Eliza m'd Chas Hill, chief justice & Sarah m'd Benj. Whitaker, ch:
justice).

17

downe his sonn with 10. or more hands with hime; Sir John Yeamans hath provided a great many that will in a short time be ready; my selfe and friends shall gett about 10. hands and sev- erall others that it is our opinions wee shalbe forced to gett another vessell hoopinge I shalbe ready to saile about a mounth after this date, supposing that I shall tuch at the Leward Islands; espetially at Antegua abundance there beinge ready to desert it being a meare grave and will never advance the King's interest the Contrys nor theirs that lives in it wishing that my power was a little stronger then it is I would doe your Lordshipes nor my selfe noe harme and doe a great deale of good to a great many soules that would willingly come off and transport them- selves farther from them terrible Hurry Caines that doth everie yeare distroye their Houses and crops; and lickwise it being so onhealthy with many other evills that I sertingly know in soe much that I pitty their conditions thay at Antegua (I suppose) is now sensible of our making ready to come to them having sent down the proposals 5. or 6. days agoe which if more people doth present heare then we can take in then I suppose we shall gett another vessell and tuch there if not it is nothing out of our way to sale (as our designe is soe lickly to be prosperous) we doe dearely want an other vessell that may sayle with an easie Charg and that may be profitable; eyther a pink of 70. or eighty toon or a good Ketch[1] of about 50. or 60. toon, which I am confident might be had verie reasonable and might be fitted out with an easie charg; which if your Lord- shipes would be pleased to send such a shipp or Ketch you would find a great many good convenences boath for your owne In- terest the Countries and else; first that the port Royall was cast away upon the Bahama Islands; by the masters owne willfullnesse when he might a saved her as the report goes, soe that we have none but this shipp that I am upon to depend on and she have bine a long time of the ground; within few months more her sheathing will goe to decay and must of necessity eyther be fitted abroad at a verie great charg or else must come home; and that cannot be unless there is another in her roome; which if there

---

[1] Pink, a narrow built vessel, with two masts, a ketch broader and strongly built, with fore stay sail, jib and two masts far aft, both with square lower and top sails and fore and aft sails.

ware one and now as I shall (as I suppose) carrie downe 150. or 200 people more besides what else will come at the spring from other places the Country by that time, wilbe (if plese God to prosper our indevers) in a verie good and saufe esquepadge and saufly settled, soe that I shall now loade with timber for Barbadoes and by God's assistance may theare arive by Aprell next and then is the prime time for a freight; which I question not but that she would be loaden with sugar as deep as she could swim; and in a probable way might arive in the Thames; about the latter end of July next which freight would pay my seamen's wages and then it would be a verie good time to fitt her out for our country; that we might arive before the foule weather comes in; and by good reports of our Country and the incuradgement that I should give there to people I wod not question but to have 2. or 3. hundred people out of London; but this cannot be don with any convenience unless we have another small vessell to supply my place or steed onless your Lordships can otherwise contrive for your more convenence; however my mate[1] having an inclynation to goe home and he being a verie honest trustie and able man and if such a vessell should present and fearing there might not a pilott or fitter man present I though it good with permition to recommend him to your Lordships knowing him to be a very faithfull trusty and able man and verie fitt for such a purpose having allready an Interest in our Country, and verie well knowing about our coast & rivers Newingland, Virginia and all the Leward Islands; and as to any other passiges of Country governer people or else of your Lordships concerns I shall leave this bearer my mate Mr. John Com-

---

[1] John Coming, of the hardy race of Devon sea rovers, 'a very honest, trusty and able man,' experienced in the western isles and coasts, went mate of the 'Carolina,' 1669, settled a plant'n at Ashley river and went with the ship to Virginia and Barbadoes, thence home in Cap. Gilbert. Returned May, 1671, in the 'Blessing,' reached Ashley river Aug: 13, charted the entrance ('Coming's point' attests it) and went to New York and back. Ld Ashley commends his diligence and success. He married Affra Harleston and Feb., 1672, they give half his land for new Charlestown. He succeeded Halsted and 1674, 78, commanded the Prop'rs Ship 'Edisto.' He was then a successful planter ('Comingstee' & 'Blessing' plant'ns, Cooper river preserve his own and his ships names). May 13, 1691, he was made Duke Albemarle's deputy and sat in the Council till his death 1 Nov: 1695, at 'Comingtee.'

ing who can give your Lordships as much sattisfaction as your Ld[ps] servant to command.

HENRY BRAYNE.

Endorsed by Locke.   H. Brayne to the Lords Proprietors, 20 Nov. 70.

[*S. P.*, Bdle 48, No. 48.]

————

CAPT. BRAYNE TO SIR P. COLLETON.

Barbados, Nov: 20th 1670.

Hono[ble] Sir

My last unto your Honour was from Virginia wherein I certified your Honour and our Lords of the most of our proceedinges and there also I received a letter from your hands wherein you advised me to take in Cattle, Hoggs provisions and else for our Collony and with all to follow your former instructions which I have heatherto don as neere as possible I could; only in my first Instruction there is one thing that your Honour comanded me (which is not as yet don;) haveing noe great need at present which was that I should deliver what goods I brought from port Royall or elce unto M[r] Hallett and to take his and M[r] Thomas Colliton's advice for my proceding which it was not by your Brother thought convenient supposing that M[r] Stroud would be a more convenient man for that purpose than the other for severall reasons as I did informe your Honor in my first letter from barbados in which I did desire your Honor's advice in it but as yett I have heard nothing from you to contradict my first order nyther shall I breek it untell your Honour comands me but this I can asure your Honour that M[r] Stroud is a great settler and promoter of our designe haveing gott allmost 20 people to send downe betweene himself and Justice Harvy and very Just he is in all his dealings but as he is a marchant I suppose your Honour will have not much better dealings from him then from an other Honest man of his Calling: M[r] Thomas Colliton and M[r] Stroud have taken up some moneyes about 100£ Sterling for the furnishing our ship with necessaries and provisions for the carring on our designe and abundance of paines thay do take in it hooping it wilbe verie succesfull which I do not questian its well doeing; if it please the Lord to give me a quick pasaidge or at least wise that I can but gett in well which I doe not much doubt

unless contrarie wind and foule weather doe take me coming upon
the coast being so late in the yeare; but as I have heatherto delt
with it I shall doe the utmost of my indeavors to answer my
greatest desires &c.   Deare Sir I have not received any letter
from under your Honour's hands never since I came from Ingland only that at virginia and the coppie of an other that your
Honour sent off a long date which I received from squire Colliton wherein I understand your Honour's great care in the sup-
pliing our wants but I am heartily sorry in that you did not send
me the suite of sailes sheat cable cordidg and Else I writt for
and it is as great a wonder to me as your Honour should admyar
how I should alredy want having bine now almost 18 mounths
of the ground and soe ill furnished as I was when I came out and
allwaies furnished vesells with what thay did perpetually want;
and as you say I was well furnished I shall leave it to your Honour to judg whether it twas or noe as your Honour may see by the
accounts of the shipes stores wee sent home the which in the trew
Coppie of the origenall accomp᠈ or Inventerie of all that the
shipe was found with when I was riding at Grave End Aug᠈ the
3. 1669. the which originall I did send to my Lord Ashley with
the accomp᠈ of Everie seaman that did then belong to the ship
and their names and what thay was shipt for a mounth.   M᠈
Cartrett[1] doth verie well know it for he sent home the same and
at the same time; whether it came to your Honours vew I know
not; but I am verie sure I was not neglectfull in it.   I give your
Honour many thanks in that you have expressed your love
towards me as to the continuing me in the ship; upon the Condition I behave my selfe well and follow orders with this Check
or else; that your Honour sent to me to give your Honour an
accomp᠈ of the shipes stores and the men and that I would give
neither; and with all to give M᠈ Colliton an accoump᠈ heare at
Barbados with this at the end which if you refuse to doe or give
I should think myselfe mad to continue you in the shipe nor will
I pay any seaman wages tell you have an accomp᠈ what thay
was shippt for and what is due to them.   As to those words and
thoughts I must cleare with Honesty whether for my good or
harme.   I did send an accomp᠈ of both as I said before; and
never did desire to give it sence that I can remember; for I

---

[1] Nicholas Carteret, for sails, &c., see pages 157, 137, 142.

asure your Honour it is not my way of dealing and as your
Honour doth scruple my giveing your Brother an accomp[t] I
have faithfully dun it who can finde (as I think) noe falt in
them; the same for your Honour's sattesfaction I have now sent
home and in every perticular I have given an accomp[t] of the
spending of it to the vallue of 5[s] and what is wanting of the
Inventory I have still in possession with other necessaries I have
had since for the ships Accomp[t] which accomp[t] shall allwaies be
ready to render when your Honour heareafter comands it that is
to say what Charg the ship is at how it tis spent and what she
doth heareafter gett which at present her gaines is but little only
2400[lbs] of Sug[r] I was to have for the passaidg of a young man
and 13 ho'h of tobacco that I brought from virginia to barbados
the which I received part in Courdidg at virginia for the ship
and sume part in pease for the ships use which I have still and
the rest I turned into M[r] Strouds hands which is verie sure for
us when I came from virginia to our Collony I thought to a taken
in afreight of Timber for Barbados supposing by the produce of
that I should not aput you to any more charg heareafter supposing the ship should rather be a gainer than alooser but finding
our people of the Collony in such a distracted condition and
being tide up by my Instruction to follow the orders of our Governer and Cap[t] West they thought it good and the savest way
to send me hear for more people which was the truth I did not
now load neyther was there any timber made ready for me; but
now (I hoope) by the going downe of Cap[t] Godfrey M[r] Gray
and some other ingenious planters things wilbe better carried then now thay are, questioning not in the least if plese
God all things falls out according to Expectation (but that)
I shall loade her as deepe as ever she can swim or as full as she
can hould; In my letter to the lords I have writ of my coming
home at the spring if your Honour and thay thinks good with
my reasons to it; but if you think it not convenient then I shall
desire your Honour to send me the vallue of 50£ sterling: in
commodities that is fitt for nue yourk as sarge shues stockings
hats blew lining Cotton bayes and such lick commodityes it wilbe
verie convenient to pay Carpinters work when I fitt the ship and
as much usefull to pay my seamen for necessaries thay will want
and it may save your monyes which if you sends the disposall
of which I shall give your Honour a just accomp[t] for if I comes

not home then I think it wilbe most convenient at my returne
hether to make an other trip doune with passingers to our cun-
try there to load timber and heather a gaine and from hence to
nue York there fitt my shipe (which wilbe noe great charg)
making use of Mr Philip Carteret[1] with what Rume Sug^r masassar and else I shall have we may verie well load her with Cattle and some provitions and what passingers I may gett there
and away for our Country which as to this and the madgagment
and contrivences of all things of this nature I hoope your Honour
will give power unto Mr Thos: Colliton and Mr Stroude Sir John
Yamons Major Kingsland with my selfe or any of them as your
Honour thinks most convenient and as the Governer Capt West
and myselfe had the contrivance I desire if your Honour think
fitt to impower only Capt West and my selfe in it or som other
third person as Capt Godfrey or Mr Gray for I assure your
Honour our Governer is not (as I conceave) fitt for severall
reasons as I certinly know in any such case nor indead in any
Else as to his place being a person verie anchant or Aged and
verie feble haveing gon threw a great deale of sickness of late
Inclyning much to the lettergie dropsie and other deseases that
what small reason he had is almost taken from hime in soe much
that (without any thing of prejudice to the ould Gentleman I
spake it) he is hardly Compus mentes and with all my hart could
I wish him saufe to his oune house againe at Burmudas for I am
really persuaded that if it is noe better with him the next somer
then this was to him it is much doubted not only by me but by
Capt West and severall others that he cannot live for I left him
sick when I came away whether he is recovered I know not more
I could say of him but it goes against my nature the which I
shall leave it to other men which I suppose have writt something
of him but this your Honour may take my word and I will
paune my life of it that he is one of the onfittest men in the
world for his place and by him being Governer doth keepe our
settlement verie much back and verie chargable it wilbe to
your Lordshipes as to the settlement by his Illcontrivances
then if there had bin a wiser man all things being don heath-

---

[1]Afterwards Sir Philip, Governor of New Jersey, of which Sir George,
his father, was a proprietor.   He predeceased his father.

erto verie erigular for want of men of Judment for though
the governer is crazie yett if we had a wise Councell or three
or fouer men of reason that was planters that knew what did
belong to settle such a Country then by their Judgment thay
would ask nothing but what should be for theirs and the countryes heareafte good and your Lordships Interest which by the
same rule as thay would contrive for the good of themselves I
being a planter and a settler haveing the greatest Interest of any
one particular man in the Country following as I must the same
methwod I should doe well but on the contrary if we are guided
by those that knoweth nothing that doth belong to a settlement
or at least to planting as I am constrainst to doe as they doth if
thay undoe themselves for want of Judgment I must lyckwise be
undone per force but I hoope our agreavance wilbe somthin
made better by the goeing doune of those persons that I now
carry who are and wilbe recommended to the governer for some
of his councells Sir those accomp^t that I have sent to your selfe
and Lords which I am verie confident are verie Just I desire thay
may be excepted and past that when I heare from your Honour
I may ball. my bookes and as to my owne perticular accomp^t
having not charged you with one shilling more than in my Just
rite as you may see I desire that the ball. of it may be paid unto
Mr Peter Jones your Secretarie [1] if liveing and his recp^t shalbe
your discharg for soe much that you pay and at the recevall of
it I have ordered him to lay it out in necessaries for our Country
for the better carring on of my busines but if he doe not live
with youe then I pray your Honour to cause it to be layd out
and sent according to my instructons I desire if your Honour
and the Lords think good to procure me a commision from the
Duke of York or at least wise one from the lords and lickwise to
Intrest me in all manner of concernes as to the shipe or shipes
masters or men that I might if accation ware to call them to an
accomp^t and upon accation necessarie to shift them I meane such
that doth or may belong to your Honors and as to any accomp^ts
that may heareafter come of this ships concernes that belonges to
my duty pray kiend Sir have nothing of ajelosie of me but asure

---

[1] Of St. Clement Danes, London, Lords Proprietor's treasurer, May,
1674. He was dead Dec. 4, 1674.

your selfe that I am and wilbe your trusty and faithfull ser^t to
my power praying for your Honor's, prosperity I am

Your Honour's ser^t comd.

HENRY BRAYNE.

Sir, I have tested my Company having noe more then my
selfe fivetene men and one boy which is as little as possible, I
can saile her with saufty and your Honour may be confident that
I shall putt the Lords to noe more charg then is just necessarie
now haveing more comand in my business then I had when I
came out of Ingland.

Idem H. B.

I have sent 8. barr^els of powder home in Mr Gilbert as by his
recp^t heare in closed which was damnifive in the storme the
which I desire it may be chainged and sent over by the first of
which I will keep 3. barr^els the other 5. I will deliver to Captaine
West.

I desire your Honour that if there be any accation to put 3. or
4. of our shipes goons on shore at our Country that your Honour would give me the liberty upon good considerations for our
owne security thay being needless in the ships and might be usefull heareafter to myselfe and others settlars.   Idem.

Endorsed by Locke.   H. Brayne to Pet. Colleton 20. Nov. 70.

[*S. P.*, Bdle. 48, No. 49.]

———

H. BRAYNE TO LORDS PROPRIETOR.   20 NOV. 70.

Barbados Nov^ber 20th 1670.

May it please your Lordshipes

Capt Gilbert[1] the Bearer heareof as I doe understand by
hime hath a great inclination to our Country which if your Lordshipes did give hime any incouragment I doe really beleave he can
gett abundance of his sect or friends to settle; he having a verie
good shipe for that purpose and I have heard him often say that

---

[1] James Gilbert, a quaker? left Barbadoes (with Capt. Coming, the
'damnified powder,' and these letters) Nov. 24, returned Feb., 1671.

he would come and see us if he could have incuragement as to afreigh that might be worth his time.

Your Lordshipes Most Humble Ser^t

HENRY BRAYNE.

Addressed: To the Right Honorable the Lord Ashley and the rest of the Lords proprietors of Carolina present.

Endorsed: paid Capt Gilbert 2^s 3^d, *and by Locke:* H. Brayne to Lords Proprietor.   20 Nov. 70.

[S. P., Bdle. 48, No. 50.]

N. CARTERET TO SIR G. CARTERET.

Barbadoes November 22nd 1670.

On munday the 22nd of August in the morne we came in between the Breakers and turning it to windward in hopes to gett into the River we were forct the tide of ebbe being made to drop anchor and stay for the tide of flood.   Cap' Brayne one seaman and the passenger[1] we brought from Virginia my selfe and one of the Indians we carryed with us in the Shipp went ashore in the skif to gett grass or the like for the Cattle.   As we came neare to the Land we perceived some Indians on the strand with a flagge of truce which as we neared proved to be a white Hankerchif which made us question amongst ourselves how the Indian might come by it and when we were close aboard the shoare we made our Indian call to them (but they not answering) he told us they were Westoes, and if they ketcht us they would eat us, at lenght we espied a great number of them which lay in Ambush behinde the banke which caused us to row of againe, but I being desirous to know the result of what might be, desired Cap' Brayne to goe ashoare at a place more distant which was done, and when we were gott on the strand we held up a cravatt spread a broad for a flagge of truce and made signes for one to come towards us. then one of them moveing forward we sent one to meet him who as he approached the Indian threw down his cloths and spread his armes abroad to signify he was unarmed and that the Indian might doe the like the Indian seemed to throw down something from him but as he approached

---

[1] Perhaps T. Biggs.   Landed Morris Island.   See page 195.

nearer our freind perceived his bow and Arrows which were tied to his back above his head which caused him to returne to us becaus he was told by our Indian they were Westoes our Indian then seeing the other throw down his Armes was desirous to goe and endeavour to bring one of them to speak with us and goeing did tell them (at a convenient distance) that wee were English and that we were very good freinds then they beckoned him to come nearer but he not suffering them to come no nearer then 30: yards to him they sprang upon him and he ran back towards us but seeing them with in some 8 or ten yards of our Indian I ran to rescue him which gave a stop to theire pursuit then we retreating to our boat I looked back and saw severall more of them who fired five musketts at us before we went into our boate and two after we had but one Muskett with us which I fired at them These Indians were very good marksmen for theire bullots gras'd just opposit against us and had they given theire Peeces their full charge they had undoubtedly shott some of us. When we came into the Reiver we found our freinds ready to receive us in an unwelcom manner but when sure of us they received us joyfully theire hearts are good, and will dy rather then yeild. The Indians were Spanish Indians with many Spaniards among them sent from St. Augustine but they went as they came. after Your Hon[r] hath perused this I need not writte the want of more people. It seems when we were gone to Virginia the Governour and Counsell sent the sloop that came from Barbadoes with the Gouvernours son to command her and severall gentlemen and freemen to treat about the delivery of the persons that were lost out of the sloop at St Katherina (of which I writt to your Hon[r] from Virginia) 30 leagues to the southward of Keyawah. Cap[t] Bayly and another which was the Marshall of Keyawah went a shore with Letters one to the Fryer and others to be sent to the Governour of St Augustine but they were both detained, the reason as I was informed was for want of Credentiall and fortifying Letters and therefore were detained as Pirates soe that the gentleman and the Marshall as far as is understood both lost. I doubt not but your Hon[r] and the rest of our Lords will have a particular of this buisness from them that were there which makes me desist from writeing any more of it.

Endorsed by Locke: N Carteret to Sir G Carteret 22 Nov. 70.

[*S. P.*, Bdle 48, No. 51.]

THOS. COLLETON TO SIR P. COLLETON.

Deare Bro^r

The shipps staying till now I have the oppotunity to give you an accomp^t that I have prevayled with Mr. Howell and Guy[1] to give mee 6^{mos} after sight for payment of the Bills of £282 for Negroes for the Windward plant: so that now there is 2. bills viz: one for £230. stock payable to Mr Jno. Colvill Henry Johnson and John Little and Comp: the other for £52. sterling payable to Sir Andrew Ricard Mr. Henry Johnson and Mr Tho: Heatly[2] which please to honore with acceptance and good payment at the time I do not doubt but to send you befor said time much more Effects from said Plantation Captain Brayne hath shewed mee his accompts and sends them home by this conveyance his Virginia accompts are very extravigant and cheats I thinke; I meane those hee had from them that furnished the ship their for never was such rates given wherefore you ought to take care to have better factors for the future and things better ordered at Carolina then now they are for it was a shame that the ship should come away without a stick for you; in her and one hundred men upon the place besides seamen and all for feare of two or three Spaniards and a few Indians I finde the people theire to minde soely there owne interest and not the proprietors for they thinke the proprietors are bound to maintaine them now they are their without their assistance to the proprietors in any thing I finde they are in divizions amongst themselves through the pride and insoelence of some and ignorance of others which I hoope this supply will reconsile you may please to take notice that the ship brought from Virginia 8 or 9 head of Cattle more then yours and others things whetheir you give that fraight or noe I know not, though there was noe thing upon your accompt aboard this time yet your vessell was pretie full of Lumber and wood on the seamens and some others accompt (I must confess it was not well stowed) which I tooke no notice of not being willing to disoblige the seamen or any other till this

---

[1] Rich. Howell (or Fowell?) Esq: and Col. Rich. Guy eminent planters of Barbadoes, each with 200 acres 1673. Col. Guy was member Assembly St. Michaels 1674–5. They had 605 acres, 405 negroes there, 1679.

[2] Sir A Ricard, a merch't and landowner in Jamaica, residing in London 1670. Johnson & Heatley were merch'ts in London & members of the new Royal African Co.

voyage was over which I hoope will give the maine stroake to
the business and for the future if Captain West the Governor
and Braine will follow my orders things shall be carryed better
for the future if Captain West the Governor and Braine will follow my orders things shall be carryed better for the doeing it the
more conveniently please to send mee a full power or joyne mee
with some body else to call any to accompt: to turne out or to
put in order your shipping (but in cases of necessity) and to send
a positive order to the Governor and Captain West to follow my
orders and directions as to the loading and dispaching her from
thence and as to the quality and sizes of Timber and if need bee
for a quick dispach to hyer or presse sawyers Carpenters or
others and to pay them for their labor out of your Stores at an
easye rate by which means your vessell will do a great deale
more and neare beare her charge if not all and give you and
everyone else more sattisfaction I looke upon the present Governor as very unfit for the place and if the Bermudians doe not
come to him this next yeare that then he ought to be changed
for a more active prudent man but if hee had but a good counsell hee would doe well enoufe yett however you may please to
lodge a blank Commission with me and impower me and some
others upon a Case of necessity to send or put on another
Governor for you are so remote and soe long befor you can
hear from thence that all may bee lost before you can remedie
it of this please to consider well and if you doe anything in it dispach it to mee first.

Capt. Braine hath discharged severall of his seamen here and
charg'd noats on the Prop[rs] for their wages and shipt new ones
in theire roome at easye rates and hath reduced his comp[a] from
20 to 16 under which number he cannot saile the ship hee sayeth
nor will not this winter time indeed there is some reason for it
that Coast being bad at this time of the yeare and two or three
of his men lastyeth[1] in the Country as Planters some of those
that goeth home goes in order to bring their familyes and to
settle there in which you ought to incourage them those seamen
that is shipt hear will bee paid here wherefore please to give me
power and instructions at large what I shall doe in this and all
other affaires belonging to the designe if you sent a cargoe of 40

---

[1] Restyeth or stayeth? Cole, Williamson and Sumers?

or 50£ in such commodyties as is fit to aparrle seamen I believe it would bring your seamen's wages out reasonable. Capt. Braine desires mee to write in his favour to you to paye him the money that is due to him by his wages and disbursements. I believe that new yorke will bee a better place for Cattle and Horses then Virginia for that wee may buy Cattle their at about 50ˢ per head and Horses much more reasonable then in Virginia and boath them and Cattle much larger and our Comodyties there yealds a greater price and the runn but little farther and provizions cheeper then in Virginia soe that I am clearly of opinion that New Yorke or new Jarsye will bee much fitter for our stocking Carolina then Virginia I have had layeing ready at the Brige some time 6 barrells of Molasses between 2 and three tonns of Rum 1. hhds of [illegible] & 2 hhds of bottons wᵗʰ 2 Barrells of lime juce which might amount to 40000 lb tobacco but cannot meete a Conveyance to James River or New Yorke Though severall shipps have departed for Virginia; I had got some aboard but the Master put it ashore againe and would not deliver it on James River at Nancemum soe that haveing an oppertunitye to ship off I must let it rest till our sloop[1] comes in from Carolina which I dayly expect and then if I can get a good fraight back againe I shall send her the and send effects that may goe along with her to New Yorke which shall produce its vallew in stock and returne thither againe and soe with her loading of timber hear which I thinke the best way to imploy our sloope and I think it will alsoe bee the best way to imploy the Carolina Frigott and now and then to tooch at Virginia to trye what people will goe from thence soe a small stock may ley their upon occation. Please with the Proprietors to consider well of these affairs and give mee as I have before desired full power and Instructions in all things that I may confidently goe aboute and [torn away] your affairs for since you have begun soe well their is now noe goeing back without looseing reputation and Interest if I can order my affairs hear after the Crop I intend with your consent to make a trip and see things a little better settled and carryd on Wee doe not doubt now of 80 people from Barbadoes besides what I may expect from the Leward Islands I tell you

---

[1] Named after themselves, '3 Brothers;' she arrived before Dec: 26. 'Bottons,' perhaps *bottoms* from sugar boilings.

with the least   Indeed the Proprietors are much obliged to Mr.
Jno. Strode[1] for if they had appointed him their Agent hear he
could not have done more nor have promoted the designe more
to advantage then he hath done hee hath ingaged severall of
his relations and is comin partner himself by this dispach where
I goe his halfes that the people wee persuade may see that wee
doe act as well as perswade them by which means wee shall
ingage this and the next turne I believe above one hundred and
50 people for all their dependance is on us and hee will shipp
upon the Carolina or upon the Jno. and Thomas a ship of our
owne that wee dayly expect (which hee is persuading me to
send) which wee hope to get full fraighted as well as the Carolina for in our ingagem[ts] and profession that way wee have
gotten more peoples Harttes then you can immaggen   The seamen and all applyes themselves to him as if one of the Proprietors or their cheefe agent in my absence and I doe believe that
hee is soe for they aply themselves to him for advize eate with
him and make use of his house as if belong'd to the Proprietors
wherefor I intend you and some of the Prop[rs] to thanke him for
his kindnesse and to give him a grant of some considerable par-
sell of land which will oblige others to serve you and continue
his zeale and affection to the place who thinke is the greatest
actor yet, but myselfe and will next yeare carry a trade thetheir
who hath boath purse and industry to follow it, It was the desire
of Capt. West and Mr. Braine &c, the last time the Carolina
parted from hence to intreat you to concerne him in the place of
Captain Hallet who is as neare a stranger to us all and much
more morose and out of the way and his conveniencye more
remote for Timber then his and J. Strodes Understanding in this
way more and I believe his interest in New England will bring
a great many from thence soe Capt. Braine hath intreated me
now to make the same Motion which I doe and second it with
my owne that hee may be imployed to dispose of your Effects

---

[1] 169$\frac{6}{7}$ 'Jno. Strode of Barbadoes m'cht to Hugh Strode of same island
m'cht plant'n 500 acres in Goose creek on Wando river in Carolina formerly purchased by Is. Mazyck,' and 1697 he makes his 'son Hugh
Strode of Carolina m'cht attorney to settle with Cap. Jas. Moore in
managm't of my plant'n affairs.' His lands passed to Jno. Strode
(another son?) who dying 170–; his widow, Susanna, m'd Hon. Jas.
Kinloch.

hear Else if you judge it will never goe currantly on and I as I have before doe assure you I have noe concerne of my owne in it and that hee never was the man that ever spoke to mee about this affair soe begging you to send your answer per first to these Concernes.   The Carolinas bare comming in of running rigging sayles and provizions she not being able to goe to sea without two sayles and sufficient provizions for one hundred people and for the seamen for three months and new running rigging.   I have bin constrayned to take up one hundred pounds upon bills of Exchange at 5℔ per Cᵗ, very difficulty because of the greate mens mony they ware drawne upon but Sir Peter might have had what hee would by this means I shall bee able to buy all things at the best rate and bringe the Monye out a greate deale cheeper then formerly which will bee alwayse your best waye for the future hear if you give me power some times I can have for the other when I have noe occasion wee buy all provision now for reddy Monye and almost all things for the merchant is loath to trust with else the Lords Proprietors hath occasion for hear their best way will bee to send Mony over for their occations in peeces of ⅜ Bills are drawne upon my Lord Ashley, Sʳ George Carteret and yourselfe which please to see paid honorably or else I shall have noe more on sd accᵒ a just accompt with receipts after the shipps Departure shall come to you and it shall be always my endeavour to doe all things to the best advantage for the Lords Proprietors our vessell wee intend to send is not yet come in and our partnership is but for two years I have but an eight part which is for encouragement.

The bills were made payable to Mʳ Tho. Counnell[1] and Compᵃ owners of the ship   The nett Merchant vallue recᵈ heare of Mʳ Beunnell[1] and Mʳ Thos Pelham what wee buy for ready monye heare wee vallue sugar at but 10 or 11 per Cᵗ what wee pay away at 12ˢ 6ᵈ.   Please to consider that the difference of takeing up of sugar for Bills of Exchange is 30 p. Cᵗ then to buy for ready Monye for I shall produce as much goods provizions &c for 10ˢ 8ᵈ as I shall doe upon accᵒ for 12ˢ 8ᵈ when reduced into sugar then to remitt the some for London at 14ˢ 8ᵈ p. Cᵗ the price currant heare for sugar for ready Monye will bee at least 30 p. Cᵗ more then to take up monye at 5 per cent. and lay the

---

[1] The same person?   Tho. Pelham lost a plant'n at St. Kitt's, 1672.

same out for your occations.   But henceforward if I receive full power to load the ship at Carolina as affor mentioned I doubt not but I shall save the Proprietors this charge and pay the men's wages of the produce of her loading the shipp wants sayles and all things wherefor please to send stores over for her I have written you a former which goes by Gilbert.

I am Your most affectionate Brother and humble servant

THO. COLLETON.

Endorsed by Locke.   Mr. Tho. Colleton to Sir P. Colleton 23° Nov. 70.

[*S. P.*, Bdle 48, No. 52.]

PROPOSALS AND WANTS—(*In Locke's Hand*[1]).

Woodward.   He desires to come to England wanting necessaries and servants but cannot be spared being interpreter and familiarly acquainted with the Indians he in their want haveing procured supplys from the Indians.   *Council.*

Desires to come home to informe the proprietors of what he has discovered and will tell noebody else.   *Mr. T. Colleton.*

Unfit for Woodward to come home though he desire it and hath something to discover to the Lords Proprietors because their only interpreter and mediator with the Indians.

Sir J. Yeamans.

He is most beholding to Sir John Yeamans his agent though the proprietors have made honorable recommendation of him, he is forced now to stay at home to interpret the Indians intelligence.   *Woodward.*

Colony Wants.   Want more men clothes powder it having been damnified.   A Minister.   *Council.*

Another vessel of 50 or 70 tun   Iron hoops for 8 tun of punchine.   *Brayne.*

Servants Clothes.   A ship to transport people gratis.   A ship of force to be always in the river Paper A large folio to register grants. *Dalton.* Men.   *Sir J. Yeamens.*

---

[1] The words here in italics, left and right of the text, are in the original, in the left and right margins. For letters see Council 179, 191, Woodward 187, Dalton 182, West 203, Sayle 185, Proclam'n 210, Yeamans 220, Brayne 214, Colleton, 240, Mathews' is lost.

18

Noe wants but of Company Cattle and good liquor and an understanding planting Council.   *Mathews.*

3 Dozen of shoes 3 doz shirts 3 doz Irish stockings for servants.   *West.*

Coopers and Carpenters but one Carpenter there 8 Barrels of dammified powder sent home by Capt Gilbert which he desires may be returned 3 for him and 5 for West.   *Brayne.*

People and a Pink of 80 tun.   *Sayle.*

Clothes espetially shoes and stockings and shirts coarse Kersys, Bays and blew linnin better to be sent then cloths ready made which doe little or noe service. A Gunsmith, powder. *West.*

Cattle. Cheaper supplyed from Bermudos those from Virginia being extraordinary deare.   *Council.*

Horses and Cattle larger and cheaper at New York then Virginia.   *Mr. T. Colleton.*

Virginia Cattle and provisions excessive deare and their cattle small, larger and cheaper to be had from Bermudos. A Virginia hog of 30ˢ not worth 7ˢ in England.   *West.*

Ship Carolina. To be loaded back to Barbadoes with timber and to be there in April and thence load home with sugar and then sheath the ship in England which will be cheaper then abroad.   Undertakes to get 300 people from London.   Desires supplyes for the Carolina and more powder and sayle cable etc as formerly desired.   *Brayne.*

Desires power to him alone or with others to order the sea affaires, and to order the Governor and West to hire or presse carpenters and others to load the ship as he shall direct.   To provide better factors in Virginia.   The things brought thence being excessive deare 40 or 50ˡᵇ Cargo in seamens cloths convenient to be sent to pay the seamen.   The best way to employ the Carolina is from Barbados to New York with sugar Rum and Molessus when Barbadoes commoditys are dearer and provisions cheaper.   From New York to Carolina with Cattle from Carolina to Barbados with timber.   For the wants of the Carolina he hath taken up 100ˡᵇ at 5. ℔ ct.   And for what shall be laid out in Barbadoes for the future if he had commission to take up mony he could sometimes take it up at the par but it is cheaper to take up mony at 5 per cent then to deale otherways which will cost 30 per Cᵗ and therefore it is the Proprietors best way to send mony for their occasions.   *Mr. T. Colleton.*

If he may not come home next spring he desires 50^{lb} to be returned him to New York in serge shoes stockings hats blew linen Cotton bays & to pay seamens wages and Carpenters.

Brayne.

PROPOSALS.

F. Constitutions. Desires the escheat of Baronys for want of heires males to be altered as hindering undertakers.

Mr. T. Colleton. Sir Jo. Yeamans.

Ship Carolina. If he come not home next spring he will make another trip to Barbadoes and thence carry Rum Molessus and sugar to New York and there fit the ship cheaper, and thence carry Cattle provisions and passengers to Carolina The management of this to be put into Mr Colleton Mr Strode Sir Jo. Yeamans Major Kingsland Capt Godfrey Mr Gray. Mr West and his owne hands.   *Brayne.*

Ship Port Royal. The greatest part of the passengers of the Port Royal stayed on the Bahamas. Russell the master now coming for England. Q Whether the ship were not cast away through his neglect and whether he have not disposed of some of the ships things.   *West.*

Governor and Council. If the Bermudians come not in the next yeare a more active governor would be better Proposes Leiutenant T. Gray and Capt. Godfrey to be taken into the Council The governor and planters too slugish To lodg a blank commission in his and others hands for another governor in case of necessity the proprietors being soe remote. *Mr. T. Colleton.*

Escheat of the Nobility's land for want of heires male hinders undertakers who will not be at the charge of planting in such uncertainty Q Upon escheat what shall become of the undertenants? Feare of customs hinders planters. *Sir Jo. Yeamans.*

INFORMACON.

Lots. Noe ground taken up but 10 acres per head about the towne.   *West.*

10 Acres per head taken up about the towne to be deducted out of the maine lot.   *Mathews.*

Governor and Governm't. Aged unfit.   *West.*

A weak man.   *Mr. T. Colleton.*

A very weak man a servant in the Council and P. Smith an arrant knave and ignorant preacher Laws made post factum

Pecuniary fines and corporal punishments designed on freemen without their consent Commends West Bull and the Dr.

Mathews.

The people there depend lazily on the Proprietors supplys are divided amongst themselves.   *Mr. T. Colleton.*

Want a council of knowing planters men of reason are West Bull Scrivener Dun Dalton but ignorant in planting. *Brayne.*

Saile a man of noe great sufficiency His feares upon the late alarme may draw a great inconveniency.   *Sir Jo Yeamans.*

Sayle unfit crazy lethargic almost senseless now sick. *Brayne.*

INFORMACON.

O Sulivan. Disliked.   *Mr. T. Colleton.*

Unfit ignorant in surveying of noe understanding.   Ill natured buggerer of children sent another mans pipe staves to Barbados a very ill man.   *Mathews.*

Of ill language and life unskilled in surveying everybody dis-satisfied with him and your letters sent out by him Desires that Sir Jo Yeamans Mr Colleton and Major Kingsland may be impowered to get a Surveyor from Barbados or that they may survey themselves.   *Brayne.*

Brayne. Has at Carolina of his owne 6 Cattle 7 Hogs 3 Sheep 6 geese 8 turkeys 12 fowls 1 negro 3 servants 1 overseer desires 5000 acres of land provided him by Sir P. Colleton for his venture at Cape Feare and discovery with Sanford which he will plant with 30 hands and get to him 50 neighbours but not till Charlestowne is planted and desires 3 or 4 small guns out of the ship to fortefie his plantation Desires a commission from D. York or Proprietors and next summer if commanded would try to recover the prisoners at St. Augustins.   Desires more power and not to be subject to the council but absolute power in the affaires of the Ship Desires his accounts to be passed and the bills paid to Mr P. Jones if he be in Sir P. Colletons service.

Brayne.

Bahama. The history of the voiage of the Port Royall and severall plots of the Bahamas taken by Mr Berrow and copys sent to Sir Peter Colleton.   *Sir Jo. Yeamans.*

Provisions and Stores. Sloop brought from Bermudas between 3 and 400 bushels of corne and some other necessaries the produce of 12000 of sugar charged on Mr Colleton in Barbadoes the people have engaged to pay the sloops hire for this trip to Bermudas and for the 10 per C^t will alow as much as the proprietors pay in Barbados.   *West*.

4 cows and a bull of the Virginia Cattle kept for owne Plantation the rest the Governor and deputy have disposed of but are not willing to defray the freight and other charges. The Planters refuse to give bond to the Proprietors for what they have received but consent the Register shall record it he cannot keep any thing for the use of the private plantacons.

INFORMATION.

Chufytachyque. A very pleasant delitious fruitfull. *Council*.

Country 14 days journey from Charlestowne West and by North. Woodward hath made a league with the Emperor thereof and the Petty Cassiques in the way. The country a 2nd Paradise.   *Woodward*.

The Emperor hath 1000 bowmen in his towne Woodward says tis a 2nd Paradise.   *Mr. T. Colleton*.

Indians. Assisting with provisions intelligence and armes.
                                                          Council.

Stout and when the Spaniards came ready to fight. *West*.

Honest, Just Two Cassiques sonnes clothed and civily treated by him in Barbadoes. The Indians supply provisions and help to plant.   *Mr. T. Colleton*.

Faithfull freindly and in league perpetuall. *Sir. Jo. Yeamans*.

Spaniards. 12 Periagos in a river 12 miles to the south and one ship off at sea most of those Indians 2 days after the arrival of the Carolina they returned to Port Royall terrified with our great guns noe news of them since.   *West*.

Many Spaniards amongst the Indians from St. Augustines. Bayly and another detained at St. Katherina for want of Credentials as pirates.   *Carteret*.

Spaniards. Alarmed by the Spanish Indians but not attaqued they lay at Ashley river Mouth and the Frier suspected to be amongst them they exceeded an Indian account. *Council*.

At the mouth of the river they were like to surprize Brayne made 9 or 10 musquet shot at his boat.   *Braine*.

Often alarmed by the Spaniards two days after the Carolina came in the Spaniards returned to St. Helena the Indians with them being frighted by noise our guns.   *West*.

At the mouth of the river make 5 shot at Brayne upon the Carolina going up the river they got away.   *Mathews*.

12 Periagos of Spanish Indians lay 4 or 5 days in the river Stonow to the Southward of us and two days after the Carolina came in they returned to Port Royal frighted with our ships guns.   *West*.

30 Periagos lay at the mouth of Stonow ten leagues from Ashley river with Spanish Indians of St Helens and 3 vessels off at sea to block us up.   The Indians frighted by our great guns retreated and the Spaniards to St Augustines threatening to destroy the Indians of St Helens Combohee and Edisto that are our friends.   *Woodward*.

Towne.   Fortified and guns mounted.   *Council*.

Well fortified beyond feare of the Spaniards   Almost soe well fortified as not to feare the Spaniards.   *West*.

Provisions and Stores.   Now for eight months.   *Council*.

Before Braynes returne from Virginia the allowance a pint of pease a day.   *Brayne*.

The Shalop also loaden with corne came in 20ᵗʰ Sept.
                                                      Brayne.

Have been hindered from planting by fortifying themselves and alarmes.   *Dalton*.

18 months provisions at Charlestowne for more people then are there.   *Mr. T. Colleton*.

Sent to Barbados for 3 hogshead of Rum and Molessus and 2 or 3 cwt of sugar and some Bonavise.   *West*.

Provisions in their want procured from the Indians by Woodward and Jones.   *Woodward*.

Country.   Good Healthy but 4 dead and those of distempers usuall in other places though the men have been pressed with watching.   *Council*.

Healthy pleasant corne and other things planted thrive well soyle will beare anything gardens seeds did not thrive sent to Barbadoes for Indian corne, Ginger ginger to plant.   *West*.

Cotton olives sugar canes grow there very well.   Plenty of fish and foule abundance of oysters with good perle.   Turtle hares rabbits otters badgers a fine country.   *Mr. T. Colleton*.

Mould generally without fault.   Large cedars towards Port Royal.   Rivers deep and safe.   Air beyond admiracon healthfull.   *Mathews*.

Good for planting and navigacon.   *Brayne.*

Healthy earth fruit full to admiration situation pleasant beyond expression abounds with cedar and all good things.

Sir Jo Yeamans.

Healthy pleasant fruitfull abounding in good land and many pleasant rivers.   *Sayle.*

Ashley river bears vessels of 3 or 400 tun to unlade on skids from the ship on the bank.   *Mr. T. Colleton.*

Ship Carolina.   Arrived at Ashley river from Virginia 22 Aug and 15 Sept went for Barbados.   Went to Barbados without timber the smallness of the allowance haveing hindered the men from working soe that noe timber fit busy to in fortifying themselves upon this alarme and hasty to dispatch me away for Barbadoes that I might returne with more people before winter He went by the Governor and Wests order.   *Brayne.*

Out of repair and in want of almost every-thing.

Mr. T. Colleton.

Timber was ready but not shipped for hast of sending away to Barbados for more people.   *West.*

Brought from Virginia 8 or 9 cattle more then belong to the Proprietors and to Barbados timber and lumber on the seamens and others account none on the Proprietors Some seamen discharged at Barbados and paid by Mr Colleton and new ones taken in at easier rates The ships company reduced from 20 to 16.   2 or 3 of the seamen stay in Carolina as planters the seamen taken in in Barbados will be paid there for which he desires instructions and all other concernments of Carolina.

Mr. T. Colleton.

Mr Colleton furnished the shipt to the value of 100^lb He to have 2400^lb of sugar for transporting a man and 13 ho'h of tobacco from Virginia to Barbados whereof part send and part hand over into Mr Strodes hands The ship will more then beare her owne charges.   Ships company now is himself 15 men and a boy.   *Brayne.*

Planters goeing.   Most of the seamen comeing to England with a designe to returne to Carolina and plant there from Barbados are going Capt Godfrey with Mr Gray Sir Jo Yeamans overseer with 10 and in all from Barbados and Antigo 150 or 200 soe that if multitude of passengers make it necessary Brayne intends to hire another ship 2 came with him from Virginia and 2 in the sloop The noise of the Spaniards seising our men at St. Helena a little dis-couraged others from comeing.   *Brayne.*

Many going from Barbadoes and several of considerable estates many removing from Antigo weary of the Hericanes. Sir Jo Yeamans buying a vessel at New York to transport cattle and stock from thence to Carolina 80 or 100 now goeing in the Carolina out of Barbadoes and severall understanding planters sent to the Leeward Islands to prepare them from whence he thinks many will goe.   *Mr. T. Colleton.*

Stopped severall from planting elsewhere Capt Godfrey and Mr Gray goeing now in the Carolina.   *Sir Jo Yeamans.*

M^r Jo: Strode a very zealous promoter of this plantation persuades his relaçons to goe thither and goes partner himself deserves thanks and a grant of some lands Strodes interest in New England lik to procure people from thence and is a fitter man than Hallet to be the Proprietors agent He and Strode designe to send a ship of their owne to Carolina next yeare, and beleive 150 will be persuaded to goe with the Carolina next turne from Barbadoes.   *Mr. T. Colleton.*

He sends as many people as he can get the welfare of the plantation depending on the increase of people will goe himself the latter end of the next summer.   *Sir Jo Yeamans.*

The land shall be made good to the former subscribers of 1000^{lb} or more of Muscavados sugar towards Hiltons discovery if they demand it before 15th day of March next All others not subscribers as abovesaid if they lay in provision of their owne shall pay for their passage either 100^{lb} of Muscavadoe sugar in Barbados or 200^{lb} of Cotton Ginger Tobacco or other the first product of the country within 2 yeares to the proprietors. All passengers that doe not lay in provision shall pay 500^{lb} of the lik product.   *Proclamacon.*

PROPOSALS.

Sir Jo Yeamans.   Desires a patent for landgrave without limitation.   *Sir Jo Yeamans.*

Jo Strode.   Desires Strode may be agent in Halets place being an honest man a great promoter of this designe haveing got between him and Justice Harvey almost 20 people. *Brayne.*

Comings.   Recommended to the Master of the vessel to be bought he being trusty knowing skilled in the coasts of New

England Virginia Carolina and the Leeward Islands and haveing an interest in Carolina. *Brayne.*

Capt. Gilbert. Recommended as lik to increase the plantation if encouraged. *Brayne.*

Brayne. Desires more power Promises a draught of the coost. *Brayne.*

Dalton. Recommended to be Secretary and Register. *Council.*

Desires to be continued Register and Secretary. *Dalton.*

West. Desires new instructions for disposeing of the stores these that I have being Lord Ashley and Sir P Colleton hands only the Governor says are insignificant. *West.*

Carteret. Commended as ingenious and fit for employment. *Sayle.*

Endorsed: Extract from letter from Carolina Nov 70.

[*S. P.*, Bdle. 48, No. 53.]

———

ARTICLES BETWEEN FOSTER AND GRAY.

Barbadoes December 23ᵈ Anno 1670. An act:[1] of sundry particulars provided for the shipping aboard the Carolina frigatt, Henry Briant Commander and is for setling in the Province of Carolina and provided by Mr. Thomas Gray 1670 Impʳ account of the names of persons indented with and the time they serve in the said place. Thomas Witty, a sawyer, is to serve two years. Thomas Patterson, a carpenter, is to serve 2 years. Richard Poore, a sawyer, is to serve eighteen months. John Cole, a planter is to serve 2 yrs. 6 months. Moses Flower is to serve two years. John ton is to serve two years. Samuel Buzard, Tayler, is to serve two years. Joan Burnet, a woman

---

[1] Schedule to partnership articles Mr. Jno. Foster and Capt. Tho. Gray for three years &c. if either dye estate to be equally divided, houses &c. equalized and by lot &c. Foster to ship yearly to Gray 6 servants and goods to value 5,000lbs. muscovado sugar for improv'mt of sd. estate &c. penalty £1,000. *signed* John Foster *wit:* Jno. Yeamans, Nich. Carteret, John Sherleh? *Cou. Jour.* 'Division of goods' Jan. 13, 167½ to Mr. Foster ser'vts Thos. Witty, Wm. Davise, Jno. Ratlife, Jas. Powell, goods &c. to capt. Gray ser'vts Rich. Poore, Rich. Barginer, Edw. Howell, Joane Burnett &c. *Rivers*, 383.

servant serves 3 years. John Ratcliffe to serve two years.
Account of Sundry other goods &c.

Examined 8 July 1671   Jos. Dalton Sec^r.

[*Coun. Jour.*, 71–73.]

ORDER ON SUGAR RECEIPTS.   (*Page* 30, 53).

Barbadoes December 24th 1670. (Maj^r Robert Johnston).

Col: Sayle: Att the request of Maj^r Robert Johnston, I do
hereby certify you, that he hath formerly been one of the Adventurers for the settlement of the Province of Carolina and there-
forre upon the acct of one Thousand pounds of sugar which he
hath disburst towards the advancement of the Publique interest
ought (according to the Proclamation) to have five hundred
acres of Land assigned to him for such his adventure, which I
desire may be granted, and the bearer hereof Capt. Henry Brayne
(unto whom he hath given power) will take care to see it effected,
which is all at present but that I am your lov: friend

JOHN YEAMANS.

This is a true copy of the Originall.   Examined this XVth
December 1671.   Pr Jos. Dalton Sec^r. *Ibid*, page 77.

ORDER ON SUGAR RECEIPTS.   (*Page* 164).

Whereas the Proprietors of Carolina did about Eight months
past send an Order to Sr John Yeamans Barronett for the ordering of the laying out the Lands which was granted to Adventurers and underwriters and who have paid for the discovery made of
the Province of Carolina by Hilton at the rate of five hundred acres
of land for every thousand pounds of Sugar soe paid And to those
that shall settle the said Land before the 25th March next by sending one or more people to possess it and doe keepe possession
thereof.   Now these are to certify the Governor and Councill of
Albemarle Poynt in Ashly River, in the said Province of Carolina that Bartholomew Reese of Barbadoes hath adventured and
paid one thousand pounds of Sugar on said account wherefore
wee doe desire accordingly five hundred acres of land may be
layed out for him, he taking care to possess it as above said Also
one thousand pounds of sugar more that was paid upon the above

said account, that the Receipt is wanting that was in the custody of Henry Brayne which after made appeare to you by the said Brayne then to grant unto the abovesaid Reese five hundred acres of land more.

your friends and servants

JOHN YEAMANS
THO. COLLETON.

Barbadoes the 24th December 1670.

Entered this Dec: 15th   This is a true copy the Originall Examined 15th December 1671.   Jos; Dalton Sec^r   [Similar to Mr Benj: Hadlitt or Fadbutt]¹   *Ibid*, page 79.

T. COLLETON TO GOVERNOR AND COUNCIL.

Barbados the 26th X^{ber} 1670.

Gentlemen

Yours by my sloop three brothers came lately to my hands with the desires of speeding people to you, in order to which, the Carolina will God willing sayle to-morrow with about sixty or seaventy passingers, and hath orders to touch at the Leward Islands to see what more she can get; she being provided with provisions &c: for one hundred and twenty passingers besides her Crew, and also Mr Jno: Strode and my self doe send a vessell of our owne the John and Thomas, Tho: Jenner Commander with about forty persons to settle with you, upon our own accomp^{ts} to whome we hope you will be kind, not only in your adviseing them, and assisting them in their sitting downe, but

---

¹ Barbados.   By virtue of an Election of the Adventurers for the Province of Carolina did elect me to be one of the Treasurers for the Receipts of all Subscriptions and also of the receipt of what sugars in pursuance of the Generall Concessions under the Great Seale of the Province I doe acknowledge to have received of Lieut. Thomas Clutterbuck the sum or quantity of 604 pounds of muscovado sugar three hundred ninety and six pounds of Ditto sugar more being paid to Mr. William Rossewell ℔ order of Mr. John Rorkeby Treasurer as ℔ receipt, as witness my hand this 25th aprill, 1665.   ℔ GEORGE THOMPSON.

Test   Rand^t Brandt.

Underwritten, I Sir John Yeamans Barronett Lieut. Generall &c. page 54, entered Dec. 15th, 1671. (Tho. Modyford, Jno. Hallet, Jno. Rokesby &c. were com'd by Sir Tho. Modyford Gov. of Barbadoes may 10, 1664, to treat with any free inhabitants of Barbadoes desiring to go to Jamaica.)

also in helping to dispatch our ship loaded with timber hither againe, by which meanes you will not onely incourage us to continue our trade with you in shipping, and to settle a factory among you, but alsoe bring a great many people to you, and a trade alsoe, when now the vessells from you comeing empty doth disincourage the same; what I have desired for our own ship, I doe intreat for the Carolina, and doe assure you, if she doe not come back loaded upon the Lords proprietors Accomp^ts this time, she will hardly come back to you againe, for here, the seamens wages most of them are to be paid, and how to produce mony without effects, I know not, and this is the only way to fill you with people, and to bring you a trade when empty vessells I doe assure you will never doe it, it hath cost 200£ sterling to set the Carolina to sea this time, and next time twill cost a great deal more of which please to consider   I am

Yours &c

THOS. COLLETON.

Directed: To the Governours and Councell of Albemarle poynt in Ashly River In Carolina per Mr Tho: Jinner L: D: C: [Q. D. G?][1]

Vera Copia Ex^r this xix^th March 167⁰ Jos: Dalton Reg^rs.

Endorsed by Locke : T Colleton to Governor and Councell at Ashley river 26th Dec. 70.

[*S. P.*, Bdle. 48, No. 54.]

MEMORANDA—All in Locke's hand. [2]

Woodward hath been 14 d journey westward to Chufytuchyque's Empire a fruitfull country, league made with him, By Woodward's means provisions procured from the Indians in plenty He desires to come home wants necessarys and servants but cannot be spared being familiarly acquainted with the Indians and skld in their language.   Council Ashley River 12 Sept 70 (p. 190)

In their want of provisions supplyd by the Indians but spareingly, Alarmed by the Spanish Indians lying at the

---

[1] Que Dei Gratia? See p. 281. The ships sailed Dec. 27?

[2] Extracts 18 letters from Carolina 7 pages in Locke's hand enclosed in letter Lds Prop'rs to Earl Shaftesbury, 20 Nov., 1674, *post.*

rivers mouth but not assalted, guns mounted and the towne fortified Indians ready to assist. The fryor suspected to be amongst them who exceeded an Indian account. Provisions now for eight months need further aid. Country good Carolina gon to Barbados to bring more people. Lost but 4 of the English who died of distempers usuall in other parts notwithstanding they have been overpressed with watching. Great want in the stores especially in clothes and powder that which was intended them being all damnified. The cattle from Virginia at extraordinary rates which would be cheaper supplyd from Bermudas Bahama Islands from 34 to 37 d. N L. convenient for Salt and Braziletto wood. want a minister Council Ash: Riv: 9° Sept 70. (p. 178.)

9 or 10 Musquet shot made at Brayne at the mouth of Ashley river by supposed Spanish Indians. Before Brains returne from Virginia the allowance a pinte of pease a day and soe noe timber cut to be sent to Barbadoes 20° Sept Your Shalop came to Ashley river from Barbadoes laden with corne and 2 passengers the noise of the Spaniard seizing our men and dislike of the governor hindering others Many people prepareing to goe to Carolina from Barbados looking on the country as good and healthy and the conditions good.

The seamen most comeing to England with a designe to returne to Carolina and plant there Capt Godfrey with 5 goeing, Mr Gray S^r Jo Yeamans overseer with 10 ready to sayle from Barbados in a month many ready to goe to Car: from Antigo (desires more power) when he intends to call and if overladen with passengers to take another vessel Another vessel of about 50 or 70 tun necessary The Carolina must either come here to be sheatd and fitted or it must be done abroad at a greater charge. he thinks he shall 150 or 200 people with him proposes to load back to Barbados from Car: and to be there in April and from thence to load home with sugar. undertakes to get over 300 people from London recommends Comming his mate as a man fit to be master of the other vessel he being trusty knowing and sk'ld in the coasts of N. England Virginia Carolina and Islands and having an interest in Carolina H Brayne Barbados 20° Nov 70 (p. 229).

Recommends Capt Gilbert as a person who if encouraged was like to increase this plantation H Brayne Barbados 20 Nov 70 (p. 237).

Council at Ashley river recommend J Dalton to be Secretary and Register.

Proposes to have a ship to transport people gratis a supply of servants and clothes hindered from planting by fortification Indians their friends 300 leagues from Ashley river to Mexico West people in a good plight A ship of force to be always at Ashley river. desires to be continued register and secretary want of paper and a large folio for registering grants. Jos Dalton 9° Sept 70 Ashley riv: (p. 182).

Noe news of the English detained at St. Katharina often alarmed by the Spaniards 2 day after the coming in of the Carolina the Spanish Indians returned to St Helena frighted at the noise of our guns our Indians stout and ready to assist us noe ground taken up but 10 acres per head about the towne 90 leagues to St Augustines fortified well Country healthy and pleasant soyle beares anything corne and other things planted thrive well. The governor aged and unfit desires new instructions for desposall of the stores. Jos: West to Ld Ashley. Sept: 70 (p. 202).

Desires supplys for the Carolina and iron hoops for 8 tun of punchine and more powder promises a draught of the coast H Brayne to Sir P Colleton 23 Nov 70 (p. 245).

Many going to Car: from Barbados and severall of considerable estates many removing from Antigo weary of the Herycane. Sir Jo: Yeamans buying a vessell at New York to transport cattle and stock from thence to Car: 18 months provisions for more people then are there: Canes ginger Cotton olives grow very well there plenty of fish and foule abundance of oysters with good perle turtle hares rabits otters badgers. honest just people. Two Cosseques sonnes clothed and civilly treated in Barbados by T C. The Carolina out of repair and in want of almost everything. Like to carry back with her 80 or 100 people and severall understanding planters. Desire the cause of escheat of Baronys for want of heires male to be altered a fine Country the Emperor of the Caphatachaques hath 1000 bowmen in his towne. Woodward Sayth tis a 2ⁿᵈ paradise and will not discover what he hath found there but desires to come home to the proprietors O'Sullivan disliked the Governor a weak man proposes Capt Godfrey and Lieutenant Tho Gray to be taken in to the Council. Governor and planters there somewhat slugish. If the Bermudians come not in this next year a more active governor would be better Sent to the Leeward Islands to prepare them for Car: and expects many passengers from there: Thomas Colleton 19° Nov 70 (missing).

History of the voyage of the Port Royall and severall plots of the Bahamas taken by Mr Berrow and sent to Sir P C. Stoped severall in Barbados for planting else where.   Capt Godfrey and Mr Tho Gray Sir Jo: Yeamans agent goeing in the Carol: to Ashley river Want of men at Car: Sir Jo: Yeamans 15° Nov: 70 (p. 221).

The mould in generall without fault. brave large cedars towards port Royall the rivers deep and safe the air beyond admiration healthful noe want but of company and cattle Spanish Indians at the mouth of the river make 5 shots at Brayne upon goeing of the Carolina up the river they goe away 10 acres a head about the towne to be deducted from the maine lot want cattle company and good liquor Governor very weak man a servant in the Council and P Smith a knave and arrant preacher O'Syllivan unfit and ignorant in Surveying of noe understanding illnatured buggerer of children.   Sent another man's pipe staves to Barbados a very ill man laws post factum. pecuniary fines and corporal punishment on free men designed without their consent commends West Bull the D^r they want an understanding planting council.   Matthews to M^r T Colleton. [1]

23° Aug when our provisions were spent the Spaniards with 12 Peryagoes came into a river to the Southward of us called Stonowe where they lay 4 or 5 days the greatest part of them Indians and 2 days after the ship came in they returned to Port Royal frighted with our ship and guns.   Our Indians ready to assist and give us intelligence. The ship sent away without loading of timber which was ready to expedite transporting of people from Barbados well fortified soe as not to feare all the Spaniards can doe   All healthy every thing hopefull and thrives besides the gardens seeds desire 3 doz of shoes 3 dozen of shirts 3 doz of Irish stockings for servants sent to Barbadoes for 3 hheads of rum and molessus 2 or 3 C^{wt} of sugar some Bonavise[2] Indian corne to plant and ginger roots and vines want coopers and carpenters but one carpenter there Jos. West 15 Sept 70 (missing).

[1] This letter of Mau: Mathews is missing, date about Sept. 15, '70.

[2] BONAVIST (*Lablab vulgaris*). A species of tropical pulse—kidney bean. *Murray's English Dictionary*.

Virginia commoditys very excessive deare and therefore to
take care to have better factors there complains that the Carolina
came away without timber the people at Ashley river depend
lazily on the Proprietors supplys divided amongst themselves
Ship brought from Virginia 8 or 9 cattle more then the Proprietors and to Barbados timber and lumber on the seamens and
other account none on the Proprietors.   Desires power to him
alone or with others absolutely to order the sea and merchant
affairs and to order the governor and West there to presse or
hire Carpenters to load the Ship as he shall direct a blanck commission which lodged in his or others hands for another governor
in case of necessity some seamen dischargd at Barbadoes and
pd by M^r T Colleton and new ones taken in at easier rates and
the ships company reduced from 20 to 16.   2 or 3 of the Seaman
stay in Carolina as Planters.

To seamen taken in at Barbados will be paid therefore[1] which
M^r T Colleton desires instructions and all other concernements
of Car: A cargo of 40 or 50^{li} in seamens clothes convenient to
be sent.   Horses and cattle cheaper and larger at New Yorke
then Virginia.   Barbados commoditys dearer their provisions
cheaper best way to employ the Carolina from Barbados to New
York with sugar rum and Molesus from New Yorke to Carol: with
cattle from Car to Barbados with timber 80 people going from
Barbados besides others from the Leeward Islands M^r Jo: Stroude
a great promoter of this plantation persuades his relations to go
thither and goes partner himself he beleive by the next turne
they shall persuade 150 people to goe from Bar sending Jo: and
Tho: a ship of theire owne with the Car: thanks to be returned
to Strode for his kindness and a grant of some lands to him,
next yeare will trade thither Strodes interest in New England
like to procure people thence and a fitter man [than] Hallet to
be the proprietors agent.   100^{li} taken up a 5 per C^t for defraying the charge of the Carolina   It is better to take up mony to
by commodity which some times may be done at the par if he
have commission then to buy upon trust which will be 30 per
C^t The best way to send mony for their occasions.   T Colleton
23° Nov 70 (p. 245).

The country good for navigation and planting want a council

---

[1] P. 241. 'Those &c shipt hear will be paid here wherefore.'

of knowing planters men of reason are West Bull Scrivener Dun Dalton but ignorant in planting O'Syllivan a man of ill language and life and unskilld in Surveying everybody dissatesfied with him and their lots set out by him desires that Sir J Yeamans Mr Colleton and Major Kingsland may be impowered to get one from Barbados or Survey themselves He has there 6 cattle 7 Hogs 3 Sheepe 6 geese 8 Turkeys 12 foules 1 negro 3 Servants 1 overseer desires 5000 acres of land promised him by Sir P Col. for his ventur at Cape Feare and discovery with Sanford which he will plant with 30 hands 50 neighbours but not till Charlestowne is planted and desires 3 or 4 small guns out of the ship to fortifie his plantation desires a commision from D of Yorke or Proprietors and next summer if commanded would trie to regaine the prisoners at St Augustines Mr. Stroud a great incourager. he and Justice Harvey send almost 20 servants. Mr Colleton furnished the ship and shipes company to the value of 100^li Another small vessel wanting to which Coming as skillfull in those seas is recommended desires more power and not to be subject to the council H Brayne to Ld Ashley 9° Nov 70. (p. 214.)

Sayle a man of noe great sufficiency Healthyness of the air Earth fruitfull to admiration situation pleasant beyond expression Natives friendly faithfull and in league perpetuall 3 Ships appeare before the harbour Sayles feares on this occasion may draw on inconveniency from the Indians Goe himselfe the latter end of next summer Sends now as many passengers as he can get the welfare of the plantation depending upon the increase of peoples Thinks escheats of nobilitys land a prejudice to undertakers who will not be at the charge of planting on such uncertainties Q Upon escheat what shall become of the under tenant? Customs not taken of another hinderance of planting desires a patent for a Land grave without limitacon Sir Jo: Yeamans 15 Nov 70. (p. 217.)

Desires Strode may be agent in Hallets place he being an honest man and a great promoter of this designe having got between him and Justice Harvey almost 20 people Mr Colleton taken up 100^li for furnishing the ship wishes for sayles cabols etc as formerly 2400^lb of sugar for transporting a man and 13 hsh of tobaco from Virginia to Barbados whereof part pd pt Mrs Strodes hands. Noe timber brought to Barbados because none ready

19

through dispatch to fetch people by the Governors and Wests
orders The ship more than beare her charges in voyages If he
may not come home next spring he desires 50ˡⁱ to be returned
to him in serge shoes stockings hats bleu linen Cotton bays etc
to New York to pay seamen and Carpenters   If he comes not
home he would make another trip to Barbados and so returne
with passengers then carry back woodtimber to Barbadoes and
from thence Rum sugar Molessus¹ to New Yorke and then fit
his ship cheap and thence carry cattle and provisions and passengers the managemt of this he desires to be put into Mʳ Colletons Stroude Sir Jo: Yeamans Majʳ Kingsland West Capt Godfrey Mʳ Gray and his owne hands the Governor unfit crazy lethargic almost senselesse Sick now.   Want of a wise planting
council desires his accounts to be passed and his bill pd to Mʳ P
Jones desires a commission from D Yorke or Proprietors and
absolute power in the affaires of the ship His ships company
himself 15 men 1 boy 8 Barrells of damnified powder sent him
[home ?] by Capt Gilbert which he desires may be returned 3 for
him and 5 for West.   desires 3 or 4 guns out of the ship to
guard his plantation   H Brayne to Sir P Colleton 20 Nov 70
(p. 232).

Intends to goe to Carolina next summer desires L Ashley commands Country abounds with Cedar and all good things Unfit
for Woodward to come home though he desires it and have
something to discover to the Ldˢ Proprietors because he is the
only enterpreter and mediator with the indians   Sir Jo: Yeamans
to Ld Ashley 15 Nov 70 (p. 220).

Chufytuchyque a fruitful province delitious pleasant a 2ⁿᵈ paradise 14ᵈ journey West and by North from Ashley river has
made a league with the emperor and petty cassiques betwixt us
want of provisions supplyd by the Indians in the absence of the
Carolina at Virginia by his and Mʳ Jones his Industry in his
want 30 Peryagoes lay at the mouth of Stonow riv: 10 leagues
from us with Spanish Indians of St Helens and 3 Spanish vessells off at sea to block us up the Indians frighted with our great
guns and the Spaniards retreated to St Augustines without attempting anything but have threatened to destroy the Indians

---

¹ See page 235, where 'malassas' is copied 'masassar.' Mr. Carteret
there named is not Sir Philip, son of Sir George, but his kinsman, Capt.
Philip Carteret, Gov'r of New Jersey 1664-81.

of St Helens Cumbohee and Edisto that are our friends   He is most beholding to Sir Jo: Agent though the proprietors have made honorable recommendation of him   He is forced to stay at home and intrepret the Indians Intelligence.   Hen: Woodward to Sir Jo: Yeamans 10° Sept 70 (p. 186).

Sloop arriv'd from Bermudas with between 3 or 400 bushells of corne and some other necessaries the produce of 12000 of sugar charged on Mr Colleton in Barbados the people have engaged to pay the sloop hire for this trip to Bermudas and for the 10 per Ct will allow as much as Proprietors pay in Barbados   The greatest part of the passengers of the Port Royal staid at the Bahamas Russell the master comeing for England   Q Whether the ship were not cast away through his neglect and he have not disposed of some of the ships things   J West to Sir P Colleton 22 Sept 70 (missing).

Healthy fruitfull pleasant abounding in good land and many pleasant rivers greatest want of people and a pink of about 80 tun. Wm Sayle to Ld Ashley 10 Sept 70. (p. 185.)

Country produces sugar canes ginger Cotton tobaco potatoes yames corne and all other plants of barbados   The river bears vessels of 3 or 400 tuns to unload on skidds from the ship on the banks noe need of supplys for the future   The Indians supply provisions and help to plant.   The land made good to the former subscribers of 1000lb or more of Muscavadoe sugar towards Hiltons discovery If they demand it before 15° March next.   All passengers not subscribers abovesaid 100lb of Muscavados sugar in Barbados or 200lb of cotton ginger or tobaco or other products to the Ld Proprietors within 2 yeares but those that cannot lay in provisions for their passage shall pay 500lb for their passage and provisions   Barbados   proclamation 4° Nov 70 (p. 210).

Carolina arrivd from Virginia 23° Aug 12 Periagos then 12 miles of in the river to the south greatest part Indians and one ship off at sea Indians very ready to bring intelligence Spanish Indians like to surprise Brayne at the rivers mouth fired muskets at him.   2 days after they returned to Port Royal noe news of them since terrified by the ship and great guns almost soe well fortified as not to feare the Spaniard force   Timber ready for the ship but not loaded for hast to fetch people from Barbados before winter people healthy though provisions thats 8 months provisions brought corne and all they planted thrived but garden

seeds and the ground will beare anything   Taken up 10 acres
per head about the towne Governor old and unfit 4 cowes and a
bull of the Vir: cattle kept for Sir Peters owne plantation   The
rest the governor and the deputy have disposed but are not well
to defray the freight and other charges   The planters refuse to
give bond to the proprietors for what they have rec'd but
consent the Register shall record it he cannot keep anything for
the use of the private plantacons desires new instructions for disposeing the stores those being only under yours and Ld Ashleys
and therefore as the governor says insignificant Hard usage in
Virginia for cattle and provisions 30ˢ pd for a hog in England
not worth 7ˢ Cows small cattle large and cheaper to be had from
Bermudas Want of clothes especially shoes shirts and stockings
coarse kerseys bays and bleu linen to be sent better than clothes
ready made which doe little or noe service a gunsmith and powder 4 servants belonging to Capt Bayley taken into Sir P's service noe news of Mʳ Rivers.   J West to Sir P Colleton 15 Sept
70 (missing).

Spanish Indians at the mouth of the river fired 7 muskets at
Braines company many Spaniards amongst them from St Augustines.   St. Katherina 30 leagues to the southward of Ashley
river where Capt Bayley and another detained as Pyrates for
want of Credentials.   N Carteret to Sir G Carteret 22 Nov 70
(p. 238).

Desires more people another vessell and commends Mʳ Carteret.   Wm Sayle to Sir P Colleton 15° Sept 70 (missing).

Endorsed: Extracts from letters from Carolina in Sept &
Nov 70.

[S. P., Bdle. 48, No. 95.]

SIR PETER COLLETON TO JOHN LOCKE.

Mʳ Ogilby[1] who is printing a relation of the West India hath
been often with me to gett a map of Carolina wherefore I humbly
desire you to gett of my Lord those mapps of Cape feare and
Albemarle that he hath and I will draw them into one with that
of port Royall and waite upon my Lord for the nomination of
the rivers &c.   And if you would doe us the favour to draw a

---

[1] John Ogilby, cosmographer to the King, his maps *A. W. I.* 714, 1433.

discourse to bee added to this map in the nature of a description such as might invite people without seeming to come from us it would very much conduce to the speed of settlement and be a a very great obligation to your most faithful friend and servant

P. COLLETON.

Thursday [1671 ?]

Addressed : To my Honoured frend Mr John Lock. present.

WRITERS OF CAROLINA.[1]

Authors		Writers	
Herera ⎫		Peter Martyr	
Oviedo ⎬ Spaniards		Fabian	
Acosta ⎭		Clement Adams	
Thumany ⎫		Baptista Ramusius	
Laudoneer ⎭		Franciscus Lopes de	
Jo: de Laet.		Gamara	

Galeacius Butrigarius ye Pope's nuncio in Spain all these prove or allow the English right from 25 deg: N. L. to ye Northward of Newfoundland.

Travellers: Sebastian Cabot employ^d by Hen: 7th 1496. 4 years after Columbus and 1 year before America discover^d from 25d. N. Lat: the north p^ts

Queen Elizabeth—   Robt Thomson and Hugh Eliot 1565
Roger Bodenham 1569 John Chilton 1570. Sr John Hawkins 1570
Nicholas Philips   Hen. Hawks Sr Francis Drake
Jo: Oxenham   Sr Francis Drakes circumnavigation 1577
Sr Thomas Cavendish 1586 Sr Walter Raughly Virginia 1584
Sr Ralph Lane ⎫   Sr Robt. Dudley ⎫
Jo: White   ⎬ 1585 Sr Geo Summer   ⎪
S^r Jo: Chidly   S^r Jo: Hawkins ⎪
Sr Ric Grenville 1587 Sr Fra: Drake   ⎬ 1595
Tho. Heriot   ⎫   S^r Jo: Baskerville ⎪
Wm Nichelson ⎬ 1591 Sr Nic: Clifford ⎭
Christ: Newport ⎭   Sr Anthony Shirly 1596
Hen: May 1593.

G. Ld Clifford Earle of Cumberland 1586, 89, 92, 94, 97, 98.
Sr Sam Argal expelled the French out of Canada ann: 1611.
Sr David ⎫ Kirke expelled the French out of Quebec Todosac
Sr Lewis ⎭ Mons Royall on the River Canada.

---

[1] So endorsed by Jno Locke and the mem: following are written by him on the two inside pages of above letter.

Sr Walter Raughly's hist: of Virginia

Collection of ye Commodyties of Virginia

Albemarle from 35½ to 36½ Ashley Ashley River Berkeley Cartaret Cape Roman. Clarendon Cape Feare. Colleton Craven north side of port Royal. Edisto 32d 30m S C. Port peril 32.d. 25m. Kiwaha 32d. 40m. Situation Discovery Soyle & shore Subterranea Fossilia Aire & Temperature Water Rivers Lakes Fish Plants & Fruits Insects Birds Beasts Inhabitants number Bodys Abilitys of mind Temper and inclinations Morality and customs Religion Economy.

[*S. P.*, Bdle. 48, No. 82.]

MAP OF CAROLINA '71—(*So endorsed by Locke*)

Map of Carolina with part of Virginia &c the Gulf of Mexico, Bahama Islands &c shewing the capes and rivers from Albemarle river to the Cape of Florida &c partly in pencil.

[*S. P.*, Bdle. 48, No. 80] *A & W I.* § 715.[1]

JO: WEST TO LORD ASHLEY 2° MAR 7¹/₀.

May it please your Lordship,

In my last to your Lordship of the 15th of September by way of Barbadoes,[2] I gave your Lordship some Acc^t of the Spaniard, since which time wee have lived very peaceable and quiett, without alleigances [allarumes] and have heard noe more of them: I hope ere now your Lordship hath taken Order for those poore mens Release who were soe unhandsomely detained at St Katherina. May it please your Lordship the shallop wee sent to Bermuda for a suply of provisions arrived here safe the acc^t whereof I have sent to Sir Peter Colloton: We thought good to send her from hence to the Bahama Islands, to see if they could gett a Freight of people there, but shee could not find ennough to defray her charge soe shee went from thence to Berbados. May it please your Lordship here arrived from Barbados the 8th

----

[1] Like map with additions in *Charleston Year Bk* 1886, p. 249.

[2] By the Carolina. The ships left Barbadoes Dec. 27? The John & Thomas arrived Feb. 8, and Carolina 16 or 17. Letter, page 202.

of February last (to our great encouragem^t) a ship belonging to Mr Tho: Colloton and Mr John Strode with about 40 passengers, the list of whose names and to whom they belong I have sent to Sir Peter Colloton: 8 dayes after here arrived the Carolina Frigate, with about 70 passengers with whome came Capt Godfrey and 6 servants on your Lordships acc^t viz 2 men and woeman and 3 small children, which wilbe a great charge to the plantation, wee haveing nothing as yet but what is brought. I have cleared this yeare above 30 Acres of ground and built convenient houses for ourselves and servantes and palizadoed it^1 soe that wee are able to defend ourselves against 1000 Indians, it being all compleated before the arrivall of the ships: Capt Godfrey is come here to manage Sir Peter Collotons Interest in partnership with your Lordship, the man I believe is very able and a good planter, I shall advise with him in all things that may advance your Lordships Interest. Wee intend this yeare to plant most of our ground with provisions it being the life of a new settlement onely something of every Comodity for Experiences the better to know what the land will produce, the last yeare all things blasted in October before they could come to perfection, but wee do not question this yeare but all things will come to their full growth before the cold weather comes, which is something sharpe especially in a morning: The planters that came now from Barbados doe say that they doe not question but the ground will produce as good ginger, Cotton &c as they have in Barbados. My Lord, in my last to Sir Peter Colloton I advised him (if your Lordship and Sir George Carterett thought fitt) to part the partnership as soone as you could and to appoynt your Agents to Act for you severally, for I find when soe many are of one family, yet one depends upon the other, and soe oftentimes businesse is neglected of great concernment, there may be severall other reasons for it, which I shall at present leave to your Lordships wisedome to consider, and humbly beg your Lordships pardon for my boldness. My Lord, the stock wee have from Virginia doe thrive very well, especially Hoggs, the cattle

---

^{1} A star shaped fort is shown on plat of Lds. Prop'rs plantation, the first land on south side of Old Town creek, long called (from Gov. West) 'Old Governor's point,' now 'Hillsborough.'

being of a small Kind, and will be of very little profitt only for Breede. I believe wee may have Cattell from new Yorke and Bermuda at easier Rates than from Virginia and one Cow shalbe worth two. Your Lordship may please to understand that our Governor doth lye at this time in a very weake condition, by reason of sickness and past all hope of recovery, I hope your Lordship will please to take some speedy course to send us an honest able Gent to be our Governor and one that desires to feare God above all wordly Interest; for if wee endeavour to propagate and cherish the service of God amongst us and to root out evill and wickedness wee may expect a blessing on our undertakeings, otherwayes not, I heare that Sir John Yeomans is comeing amongst us againe, if soe my Lord, tis to be feared that a hopefull settlem⁺ will soone be eclipsed. One thing more I have to mind your Lordship of that you would please to encourage some able godly minister to come to us, for hee may be a meanes of doeing God good service here, in stirring and awakening poore people that are dead in their trespasses and sinnes. I have now (my Lord) one humble request to make if your Lordship thinke it fitt to graunt mee, that is, when the right hon^ble Proprietors please to send hither the great seale of their province I may be thought wortthy to be trusted with it, for I suppose it may prove some benefitt to mee hereafter. Which is all at present, only my poore prayers to the Allmighty to preserve your Lordship in Honour and health in this life; and happiness in the world to come I rest, My Lord

Your Lordships most humble and faithfull serv⁺

JOSEPH WEST.

Albemarle Poynt in Ashley River March 2nd 16$\frac{70}{71}$.

I have not recd any letter from your Lordship since our departure from Ireland.

Addressed: For the right Honble Anthony Lord Ashley Chancll^r
of his Ma^ts Exchequer at little Excester house in
the Strand   These   London.

Endorsed by Locke. Jo: West to Lord Ashley 2° Mar 7$\frac{0}{1}$.

[1 p. with seal, *S. P.*, Bdle. 48, No. 56.]

JOSEPH WEST TO SIR G. CARTERET.

Right Honourable,

In my last to your Honour of the 15th of September I gave your Honour an Acc' how the spanyards approached neere our settlement with an Intent doubtless to cutt us oft, since which time wee have lived very quietly from being Allarmed by him, who doubtless will not let slip any Oppotunity that may disturbe us: The Indians and wee doe agree very well; and to our great comfort here is lately arrived the Carolina Frigate, and another ship belonging to Mr Tho: Colleton, and Mr Strode Marchant of Berbados, with about 100 passingers in all, we have at present setled as neere the Towne as wee can, that wee may be the more ready to repaire there upon all Occasions.   I have for the present taken up 300 Akers neere the Towne upon the Acco' of your Honour's Partnership with my Lord Ashley and Sir Peter Colleton for present planting: I have this yeare cleared about 30 Akers of land, and built convenient houses for ourselves and servantes and pallizadoed it round soe that wee are able to defend ourselves against 1000 Indians: here is come in the Carolina one Capt Godfrey to act in behalfe of Sir Peter Colleton which I believe is a very honest man and a good Planter, I shall advise with him in all things that may advance your Honour's Interest; Wee intend to plant what provisions wee can this yeare, it being the life of a new settlement in the first place to provide for the Belly and to make some Experiment of what the land will best produce; I believe that English graine will agree very well with this soyle, I sowed some English Wheat in November and it doth thrive very well.   The Winter here doth prove something sharp and cold but noe hard frost onely in a Morning before the Sunne hath any power.   May it please your Honour our Governor is very aged and lyeth now in a very weake condition past all hope of Recovery, my humble Request to your Honour is, that you with the rest of the Lords Proprieters would please to appoynt an honest able Gent to be our Governer, and one that hath a desire above all things to feare God, for if wee doe not endeavour to propagate and cherish the service of God, and to Roote out evill and wickedness wee must not expect a blessing upon our undertakings, I heare that Sir John Yeomans is comeing amongst us againe, if soe, I doubt it will something dazle a hopefull Flourishing settlement.   May it please your Honour wee are now in a great forwardness towards the settling of a new Collony, and I hope the Lords Proprietors will not be slack in sending us timely supplyes from England, where they may buy all things at the best hand, I have inclosed the Copie of an Invoyce of goods I have received from M[r] Tho. Colleton in Berbados upon the Acc[t] of your Honours Partnership, where your Honour may see what rates you pay for some Commodities; I have also received 6 servantes from Berbados 4 of them are a woeman with 3 small children not able to help themselves.   May it please your Honour now I come to give you my Judgm[t] concerning your Partnership, which I suppose will be for all your advantages to part before wee goe upon the great Lott; for being such a great Family together one depends upon the other, and oftentimes business of great concernment is neglected, for I find in these Countrys it is very Inconvenient to keepe great Familyes together, without they be divided into severall Gangs and an Overseer in every Gang to lead them; There are severall others Reasons to be given but I shall leave it to your Honours wisedome to consider of it.   Your Honour may please to take notice that the stock wee had from Virginia doe thrive very well especially Hogs increase very fast, the Cattell are of a small kind, and will turne to little profitt onely for Breed; I believe wee may have Cattell from new Yorke at as easie rates, and of a larger breed, I hope in few yeares the Country will answer all your Honours expectations; I have endeavoured to get some Cedr for your Honour but cannot yet meete with any worth sending.   I hope your Honour will please to see that my sallary be paid to my Wife for my service here to the Lords Proprietors and that your Honour will order mee the moneys your sonne James[1] owes mee, that I may be supplyed with such things as I want being unprovided now of all things necessary.   One thing more I humbly Request of your Honour and the rest of the Lords proprietors if you shall please to think it fitt, viz, to be trusted with the seale of your Province when you send it hither for it may be some benefitt to mee heareafter,

---

[1] Capt. James Carteret, created Landgrave of Carolina, May, 1671. He was in New Jersey, 1671; chosen by malcontents their 'President,' left there for Carolina, but returning to New York, 1673, m'd a dau. of Thos. Delavall, the Mayor, and went to England, 1679.

soe beging your Honours pardon for my boldness with my poore prayers to the Allmighty for your Honours health and length of dayes, and happiness in the world to come, Which is the hearty desire of Sir

Your Honors most humble faithfull serv^t

JOSEPH WEST.

Albemarle Poynt in Ashly River March 2nd 16$\frac{70}{71}$

I have not read any letter from your Honour since we arrived in Carolina.

Endorsed : For the Right Honble Sir George Carteret Vice Chamberlaine of his Maj^{ts} Household at his Lodge-ings in Whitehall   These   London.

West's Letter to Mr Vice Chamberlaine, March 2nd 7$\frac{1}{0}$.

[1 p. with seal, S. P., Bdle. 48, No. 57.]

JOSEPH WEST TO SIR P. COLLETON.

Honord S^r

In my last by your shallop by way of ye Bahama Islands[1] where they could not answer your our expectations, for ye people would not come off before they were provided with Provisions. Since wch time wee have lived very peaceably & Quiet from Alarms by ye Spaniard, who wee suppose will noe more come near vs, S^r to our great encouragem^t ye 8th of Feb. heare arrived fro' Barbados ye John and Thomas, Capt Jenner commander, wch your brother and m^r Strode sent upon theire own Acc^t with

---

[1] Of Sept. 22, by the Three Brothers, see p. 259, the Carolina brought 64 people including Capt. Godfrey and servants 2 men, 1 woman, 3 children, Cpt. Gray and serv'ts Sam Boswood, Joan Burnet, Jno. Cole, Jno. ——ton, Moses Flower, Enoch Howell, Tho. Pattison, Rich. Poore, Jno. Ratcliffe, Rich Bardiner? Wm. Davis? Jas. Powell? Tho. Witty, Capt. Geo. Thompson, Mr. Jno. Culpeper, Mr. Jno. Robinson, Mr. Jos. Dowden, Tho. Finden, Tho. Holton and serv'ts, Geo. Canty, Phil. Comerton, Jas. Donohoe, Jno. Faulconer, Original Jackson, Jno. Norton, Jas. Needham, Edw. Roberts, Oliver Spencer, Tho. Thomson, —— Teague, Henry Wood, Jas. Jones? Jos. Pendarvis? Tho. Screman? Tho. Turpin? Jno. Pinke? also serv'ts, B. Fitzpatrick, Jno. Griffin, &c. (Mr. Jno. Foster, Cpt. Gyles Hall, Mr. Christo. Portman, Mr. Jno. Pinkard? probably sent serv'ts but came later themselves). The John and Thomas had 42 men, women and children, including Mr. Jno. Maverick and serv'ts, Phil. Jones, Rich. Rowser, Christo. Field? &c.

about 40 people to settle here, 8 days after arrived ye Carolina
with about 70 People, ye particular acc^t of theire names and to
whom they belong is inclosed, most of y^m being unprovided with
Provisions wee haveing none in Store, for there was a Destribu-
tion of all y^t came from Virginia & Bermuda by order of ye Gov-
ern^r & Deputys, as I gave you an acc^t in my List wch would
have served us very well untill wee had some produce of ye
country, but now it will goe something hard with vs if ye supply
should not come timely wch your brother sent by ye way of Bermuda. I have cleared this year about 30 acres of ground and
built convenient houseing for our selves & servants wch was all
compleated & Palisadoed in before ye Arrival of ye shippes, we
have been something weak handed and our men have been sickly
and weak, but god be praysed wee have not had one Dyed out
of our Family sinc^e wee came into ye countrey; wch I Look^e
vpon as a great mercy from God, I hope most part of ye old
Standers will plant enough this year to produce Provisions for
ye next. Capt Godfrey is come hither from your brother to act
for you in part of Partnership, whom I do think is a very honest
man & a good Planter; I shall advise with him in all things; wee
are resolved to plant most of our ground with Provisions wch is ye
Life of a new Settlem^t only to make this year full experiment of
what ye country will produce best, wee having had but little
Knowledge as yet. Ye winter here is something cold and sharpe,
but noe great frost only morneings, neither have I seen any
snow here; wee had a great blast here ye Latter end of October
wch did kill all things, ye cotton was codded very well but it came
to nothing, Ginger wee had none to make tryall of, For all ye
Rootes and other things I had of your brother were all Lost in
ye Port Royal. Ye stocke wee had from Virginia doe thrive
well, especially ye Hoggs increase much, ye cattell are of a very
small kind, I believe you may have a better Stocke from New
York or Bermuda and come at as easy a Rate as These. The
Inhabitants here have assisted Capt Jenner towards Ladeing his
ship with Pine (Trees) timber, Hee hath made a Quick dispatch
from hence, I have ready fallen as much timber as will Load ye
Carolina, and hope to dispatch her for Berbados within 15 Days
it will be a great hindranc^e to our Planting now falling out just
in ye season. S^r our Governor is very Aged and weake, and I
believe past recovery of this fitt. I hope ye hono^{ble} Proprieto^{rs}

will appoint an honest able man to be our Govern^r and one y^t desires to fear god above all worldly interest, for if wee doe not endeavour to Propagate & cherish ye (word of) servic^e of God amongs^t vs and to roote out evill and wickednesse wee must never expect a blessing on our undertakeings, I hear y^t Sr Jno Yeomans is comeing amongst vs againe, if soe I doubt it will something cloud a hopefull Settlem^t. I hope S^r you will please to order my Sallery to be duely payd to my wife y^t shee may furnish me with such necessarys as I want, for I am very bare of all things now ye shallop m^r Brayne and I bought in Bermuda is very usefull to ye countrey, I hope ye Proprietors will please to consider us something for her service, I have one thing S^r humbly to request of ye Proprietors, y^t when they send ye Seal of their Province here I may be trusted with it, for I think it may be a Plac^e of some benefitt hereafter; Soe with my hearty desire and prayers to ye Almighty for your health and happiness in this world and in ye world to come

I rest Your Hono^{rs} most humble and faithful servant

JOSEPH WEST.

Albermarl^e Point March 2nd 16$\frac{70}{71}$.

S^r I have not received any letter from you or any of ye Proprietors since our departure from Ireland: Pray S^r will you be pleased to send a good fouling peec^e of 7 foote Long well fortifyed and Double Locked.

Addressed: For ye Hono^{ble} Sr Peter Colleton Barron^{nt} neer
　　　　　Clarendon House in St James's Streete
　　　　　These　　London.

Endorsed by Locke: J. West to S^r p. Colleton 2 Mar. 7$\frac{0}{1}$.

Also by Colleton: Pray do not send this away as I have no
　　　　　copy.

[1 p. with seal, *S. P.*, Bdle. 48, No. 58.]

STEPHEN BULL TO LORD ASHLEY.

Albemarle Point 2nd die Marcij 1670.

May it please yor Hono^r

About 13 [23] days since here arrived a Shippe from Barbados the John & Thomas wth about 42 Passengers sent hither by Tho. Colleton ――― ffarmer[1] & John Stroud Esq^{rs} wth one Mr Maverick[2] a gentl that is intrusted to settle an Estate for them & wthin 8 or 9 days After the Carolina ffriggott safely Arived here wth about 70 or 80 persons in number to setle wth Capt Godfrey Capt Thomson Mr Gray Mr Culpeper and severall other gentl & may it please yor Hono^r wthin 5 days after their arrivall for our better Strength & Comfort we have showed all the respect that could bee & Setled them amongst us & the better to compleat their coming in wee have parted wth & thrown up severall Lands wch wee had taken up & made Every ffamily a very good seat for their p^{r}sent Sitting down and Planting & wee are Sett Downe as close togeather as Conveniency will admit and the greatest distance that any p'son or ffamily is Seated is wthin lesse than 2 Miles Either up or down the River, from the Town, and those gentl' are satisfied to Every one of their p'ticuler desires, & promise to give an Accompt in Barbadoes & other p'tes of their Contented Setlem^{ts} wch will bee a Means to Invite seu'all others to follow.

May itt please yor Hono^r the Indians doe still Continue their accustomed kindenesses to us & I doe not believe that they will very hardly make any warr vpon vs but show kindnesses vnto vs & Looke vpon themselves over awed by our gunns, the Last yeare in our Extreme wants of Provisions I was Imployed by the Collony to Get some Corn from the Indians to supply our wants & I went about 30 Miles from the Town & Lay out seu'all nights & found great kindnesses amongst them & very well rec'ed & treated according to their Customs & Manner & as I went amongst them from one place to another they declared very great kindness and showed great Joy that wee are Setled amongst

---

[1] Sam. Farmer, Esq. Joined in attempt to deliver Bristol to Pr. Rupert and fled to Barbadoes; on its subjection by Parliam't was dismissed the assembly. In 1663–5 was Speaker and sent home by Ld. Willoughby and imprisoned as 'a great magna charter man and petition of rights maker, the first that started up that kind of language here;' was released and in Barbadoes assembly 1667. He was an eminent planter with 500 acres and member of Council 1670–76, &c.

[2] A Barbadoes planter, settled this Carolina estate north of the Lds. Prop'rs and planted it 1671–73, &c.; was chosen to Parliam't 1672. In 1698 Jno. Mavericke on bond Da. Davis adm'r Wm. Davis, dec'd.

them and promise assistance against the Spaniard or any Indian Nacon that shall oppose us.

May please yo[r] Hono[r] wee have had very Cold weather this winter Especially when the wind is att North or North west the wind is very sharpe when itt frezes I have seen Ice about an inch thick of one nights freezing butt not Snow the wind is very Sharpe in my Apprehens'on Colder than in England butt very Clear days & little or No Rayne all winter, our Cattell & hoggs are in ffarr better case all the winter heere than in virginia heere is as good duch grasse in the sumer & fegg in the winter that Cattoll wilbee broad fed & kept att very easy rates as in any p'te of the world as I do humbly conceive & very good feedings for hoggs of Acorns Hiccory Nutts Berrys & roots that they thrive & feede at very easy rates & once in two or three dayes blowing a horn & throwing A handful of Corn the hoggs will all repaier hoame or when wee please, Our Gou'no[r] is very weake & nott likely to live yett I doe nott p'ceive that any of this Countrey Distemper hath Seized him butt Aged his Spirits are cleerly fflatted & complaines of noe sicknesse. May it please yo[r] Hono[r] I should be much hono[rd] if y[r] Lordshipe would bee pleased to signify in a letter which is the Humble Desire of

Y[r] Hono[rs] Most humble & obedient deputy and S[rv]

STEPHEN BULL.

Addressed: These   For The Right Ho[ble] Lord Ashley Att
    Exeter House in the Strand.
Endorsed by Locke. S. Bull to L[d] Ashley 2 Mar: 7⁰/₁.
    [1 p. with seal, *S. P.*, Bdle. 48, No. 59.]

THE COUNCIL TO THE PROPRIETORS.

May it please your Honours

This hasty Messenger comes sorrowing without any Company onely to acquaint your Honours with the decease of our Grave and honourable Governor Coll: William Sayle elected at Barmuda[1] as hath been formerly signified, who dyed of a Con-

---

[1] P. 119. Col. Wm. Sayle, Governor of that part of the Province of Carolina, s'd & w'd from Cape Carteret otherwise called Cape Romanoe, codecil to his will made in Bermuda in February last gives, &c., my Mansion House and town lot in Albemarle Point, in the Province of Carolina, to my Eldest son Nathaniel Sayle, &c., all my other lands, &c., in s'd Province to my two sonns Nath: Sayle and James Sayle their heirs, &c., dated 30th Sept., 1670, wit: Paul Smith. Jos. Dalton, Secrett: Proved April 10, 1671, by Nath: Sayle, *Rivers*, 384.

sumption this day about noone, very much lamented by our people, whose life was as deer to them as the hopes of their prosperity.   Now it hath pleased God to remove our governor from
us, what remaines, but as a languishing body, we humbly desire
that some worthy hono^{ble} person may be dispatched to take this
great charge in hand, whose wisedome, and sanctity may cherish
that infant Reformation untill it has obtained soe much strength
as to walk alone, curbing the vicious, countenancing the ver-
tuous, with qualifications suteable for Actions as well military as
civill: if this be onely God's favour to a people, then the want
thereof must needs be judged the contrary, which we doe wish,
and hope may not happen to this place, though many others
seemingly in a better condition then we are suffered thereby;
Therefor doe we humbly offerr this to your Honours considerations, not by way of advice, but as the overfloweing of our desires for the prosperity of Carolina, which we hope is noe lesse
taken care of by your Honours then aimed at by us.   And till
such time as we shall receive the effects of your Honours care
herein, we shall endeavour to conserve your Honours Interests
and the peoples priviledges in this place to the utmost of our
skill, and powers.   And for that purpose according to your
Honours direction and the approbation of our said governor in
his life time, we have elected Capt. Joseph West to be governor,
till we heare your Honours pleasure herein.[1]   It has been bruited
in this place that your Honours have designed to commissionate
Sir John Yeomans againe as governor of this province, though
we have good reason and hopes to believe the contrary, yet it
doth breed a very great dissatisfaction in the people, for he who
without any regret would look upon our bleeding condition at
Barmuda, and though often requested thereunto would not contribute the least assistance to stanch the wound, when he was
safe, which for anything he knew was mortall: and hath heretofore tainted the like, cannot reasonably expect that we should
repose any trust of our preservation in him now, should he seem
to be in danger.   Wee shall trouble your Honours noe more
at present; Capt. Thos: Jenner Commander of the John and
Thomas being ready to sayle from hence to Barbados, but shall
leave the inlargem^{t} hereof and other affaires to be dispatched by

---

[1] See Sayle's Commission, page 119; *Rivers*, page 88.

Capt. Braine who will saile from hence very suddenly.   In the meane time we desire leave to subscribe ourselves

Your Honours most faithfull humble servants

Stephen Bull,	Will: Scrivener,
Flor. O'Sullivan,	Paul Smyth,[1]
Ra: Marshall,	Samuell West,
Ro. Donne.	

Albemarle point In the province of Carolina, March 4th, 167$\frac{0}{1}$.

Jos. DALTON: Secr.

Addressed : To The right hono^ble Anthony Lord Ashly Chan-cell^r of his Ma^ts Co: of Excheq^r and the rest of the Lords propriet^rs of the province of Carolina At White-hall London.

Per Capt Tho. Jenner L. D. G.,[2] humbly your serv^t

Endorsed by Locke : Councel at Ashley river to Lords Proprie-tors, 4. Mar. 7$\frac{0}{1}$.

[1 p. with seal.   *S. P.*, Bdle 48, No. 60.]

To the Right Honble Sir Peter Collington, Knight.

The humble Declaration of John Russell late M^r of the Porte Royall concerninge his Condicon

Shewinge to your Honour After wee sett sayle and departed from England wee sayled to Kingsale in Ireland where Capt

---

[1] Came to Carolina with his brother? Tho. Smith and 7 servants, and tho' called 'a knave and ignorant preacher' was chosen to the Council March, 1670, and held influence with Gov. Sayle, he sat till Aug., 1671, and soon after died or left the Colony.   Mr. Ralph Marshall came at the same time; was chosen to the Council at St. Helena and recommended for L'd Craven's deputy as 'a person fit for the employment,' was elected Councellor, April, 1672, and sat till Yeoman's death, when he became Duke Albemarle's deputy, and Dec. 4, 1674, Councellor again, serving with ability for several years.   His plant'n was at Orange grove, on Ash-ley river, and he was living there 1683, 1690.   April 18, 1694, Governor Smith issued a war't to Mr. Ralph Marshall on behalf of his 2 daughters, Katherine and Elizabeth Marshall, for 2 lots in Charlestown.

[2] Q. D. G. ? Capt. Jenner sailed for Barbadoes Mar. 5 (the Carolina followed Mar. 21).   He had lands at Jamestown, May, 1672.

20

West shipt a mate on board us, from thence we sayled to the Barbadoes where the Right hon[ble] Sir John Yeomans was pleased to embarque himselfe on board of us (hee being appoynted as Governor for the settlement leavinge Barbadoes meeting with bade weather wee were forced to putt in att Nevis where Sir John was pleased to send on board me one Christopher Barrowe[1] with Instructions to pilott the shipp to Port Royall, when, the wind comeinge about faire wee sett sayle from Nevis haveinge not above a fortnights Water for 44 People)[2] and had good weather untill such tyme as wee came nere the Land where wee found a great alteration in soe much that wee were forced to part from our Fleet, and haveinge beene six Weeks beating from place to place by reason of continuance of foule weather we were beaten of the land 3 severall tymes and were driven to such great want of water that wee were all ready to perish, our allowance beinge butt a Pinte and sometymes halfe a pinte a Day, and afterwards many of us were forced to drinck theyre owne Urine, and salt water, Beinge in this dismall dispayreinge condition and haveinge by the advice of Christopher Berrow beaten or driven much to the southward expectinge fayre weather, through his persuasion wee endeavoured to touch at the Bahama Islands and neare to the Island of Munjake neare Abeco being in the Latitude of 26. 14 minutes, wee were most unfortunately cast away beinge a place where neyther our Pilott or myself ever were before and both altogether unacquainted with, and the Rocks lying 3 or 4 Leagues off the Shoare, soe that wee could not possibly putt in or runn a Shore. Butt by Gods great mercy, by the help of our Boate wee putt all our People safe upon the Island, where through the neglect and Delayes of our inhumane Carpenter whoo hath been the occasion of our long and tedious stay many of our People lost theyre Lives there, I was forced to putt the Carpenter upon an other Island and to

---

[1] Page 221. Dame Willoughby Yeamans, of St. Peter's parish, Barbadoes, widow and adm'x of Sir Wm. Yeamans, dec'd, and guardian of her son, Sir Jno. Yeamans Bart, an infant, Sept. 1678, appointed 'my well beloved friend Christo. Berrow, of the Cittie of Bristol, mariner, my atty to collect debts in Carolina,' &c.

[2] Pages 158, 160, n. 191. Crew 8 and passengers 36, some p. 137 n. Some servants of those, p. 134, 135, and from Barbadoes; most staid at the Bahamas. His carpenter was Wm. Allen.

make a Boate myselfe, by reason that hee would not worke, with which Boate wee landed ourselves upon an Island called Ellutherea inhabited, a place likewise unknown to us, where by the Inhabitants Directions I hyred a Shallop and sayled from thence to the Island called new Providence, where wee gott transportation for most of us to the Burmoodoes the rest wee left at Providence except Barrow and his wife who went to a place called New Yorke, from Barmoodoes, I have since safely arrived att London and have made bold to give you the trouble of this Accomp¹ humbly peticoninge your Honour to take itt and mine and the rest of our conditions into your Honours charitable consideration haveinge lost all desireinge your Honour to allowe us for the tyme that our sayd shipp raigned.

Your honours most humble serv¹

March the 4th 1670.   JOHN RUSSELL.

Wee were cast away 12th January, 1669.

Endorsed by Locke : Russells relation of the Port Royal 4 mar. 70.

[*S. P.*, Bdle. 48, No. 61.]

———

JOHN STOW[1] TO SIR P. COLLETON.

March the 11. 1670.

Whorthy Sir

I thought good being nowe come from the barbados and haveing order frome your brother Thomas Colleton, and bringing frome him about 7 tun of provisions for to send to Col. Sayle to Carolina and likewise three tunne more here which is bought. I have hired a shipp to goe there and there will be some quantity of pasengers and I doe not question but that here is a gret many young men here but that they will be good corssters there and if that any of you shipes should put in here they may have a pilot, And soe I doe desire that you whould be pleesed to write me word where I shall direct my letters for there will be a commerce betwixt me and them at Carrolina and therefore Sir take noe exception because I direct my letter upon the charge and soe I rest yours to command to my Power.

Sir I have charged bills of exchange on your brother in Bar-

---

[1] Capt. John Stow at Bermuda, he was member Assembly there 1673. The ship was the Blessing, Capt. Jas. Farmer. See page 281.

badoes for fiftie seven pounds sterling the which is for the fraght of goods sent hither from Barbados and provisions brought here for Carolina and have consigned them to Capt West and in his absence to Col Sayle not else I am

Sir your friend and servant

John Stow.

Addressed :   These for my Honnered Friends Sir Petter Colleton upon the Exchange.

Indorsed by Locke :   Jo Stow to Sir P Colloton 11 Mar 70.
[1 p. with seal.   *S. P.*, Bdle. 48, No. 62.]

———

Gov. Sir John Hayden to Lords Proprietors.

Bermuda, Mar. 17, 16$\frac{70}{71}$.

May it please your Grace and Right Honble Proprietors

In obedience to your commands signified in a letter from white Hall bearing Date Nov: 7th 1670.   I have not omitted any oppotunity to promote his sacred Maties and your Lordshipps Interest in Carolina since the receipt of which letter here is arrived from thence, one of Collonel Sayles sonnes,[1] who brings us the good news of the health of the People and of some good progress in that your plantation.   since when I have made it my business to procure a shipp from hence which is now effected and intends (God willing) to sett forward by the latter end of this month; with such provisions this small Island cann afford. And indeed I find that People very well affected to that under-taking.   And now I shall have an opportunity to serve your Lordshipp in the conveyance of the pacquet to the River Ashley hoping by this means to begett a correspondence with a succes-sive Intelligence of their affaires.   I have inquired after the Ambergreece mentioned in your Lordshipps letter,[2] and cannot

---

[1] Capt. Nathaniel Sayle in sloop 3 Brothers left Carolina June 26 and returned from Bermuda Sept. 20.   Proved his father's will April, 1671; came to Bermuda and back to Carolina Dec., 1671, and had lands and negroes there 167$\frac{3}{4}$.   He died before Jan., 167$\frac{5}{6}$, when Jas. Sayle claims this estate for 'heirs of Nath. Sayle.'

[2] Pages 213, 207; a grey concrete found floating on many seas and coasts or taken from sperm whales; used as a costly perfume.   Capt. Farmer, of Bermuda, was a member of assembly there 1673.

heare of any, But shall give instructions to Capt James Farmour master of the shipp, blessing going hence to examine more effectually uppon the Place, and shall render your Lordshipp an Accomp^t according to the success, which I wish may prove well, as a good omen to this your Royall enterprize in promoting whereof none shall be more willing then

Your Graces most humble servant

J. HEYDON.

Addressed: To the Right Honble the Duke of Albemarle his Grace and the Right Honble Proprietors of Carolina: att Whitehall.

Endorsed by Locke. Ashley River Sir John Heydon L^{ds} P^s 17 mar. 7$\frac{0}{1}$.

[1 p. with seal. S. P., Bdle. 48, No. 63.]

JOS: DALTON TO LORDS PROPRIETORS.

May it please yor Hono^r:

Yo^r Hon^r will find here inclosed three letters or transcripts marked A: B: C: severally,[1] A: giving yor Hono^r an acco^t of the Gen^{ll} affairs of this place; B: the Remonstrance of the Council, for ye rest of the first Adventurors, as well as for themselves; and C: a Relation of the Demeano^r of Mr William Scrivenor Dep^{ty} to our very good Lord, Lord Berkely, and Mr William Owen one of the ffirst ffreeholders

I am yor Hon^{rs} most faithfull humble serv^t

JOS: DALTON.

Albemarle Point In the province of Carolina March 21st 167$\frac{0}{1}$.

Address: To the right Hono^{ble} Anthony Lord Ashly Chancello^r of his Ma^{ts} Co^{rt} of Excheq^r and the rest of the Lords proprieto^{rs} of the province of Carolina at Whitehall London

℗ Capt Henry Brayne Q. D. G. p^{r}sent.

Endorsed by Locke: J. Dalton to L^{ds} Proprietors Mar 21st $\frac{70}{1}$.

[S. P., Bdle. 48, No. 64.

---

[1] These papers are evidently by Mr. Dalton.

A.

May it please yor Hono^{rs}

Since o^{rs} of the 9th September, hath safely arrived two ships from Barbados, namely the John & Thomas with about 42 people, men, women, & children, and the Carolina with about 64: who are not a little wellcome to vs, in regard that the great burthen which hath soe long been vpon vs, and the people, to the sinking of some, may in some measure be eased: yet this Bee has its sting, many of whom have brought little or noe provision with them: Our letters by them inform vs, that a good opinion doth Generally pass in all parts concerning this place, (y^t not undeservedly) and probably, may be much advanced by ye good report that those who are lately arrived here have given to their friends and acquaintanc^e some of whom being persons of good repute and fame and known^e to be experienced planters: In our last of the 5th instant, we did briefly signify to yor Hono^{rs} the death of Coll William Sayle our late Governo^r, and the election of Capt Joseph West; reserving the reasons of such our choice till this, it being an Act seemingly to vary from yor Hono^{rs} directions, & what might be the opinion of some others, yet (it may be) yor Hono^{rs} will approve of it, if you will be pleased to consider: That our late Governo^r dying in a time, when we stood in as great need of a head, as ever we did since we came to this Collony for the managen^t of affairs now beginning to increase and y^t most neerly concerned the secure settlem^t of this country, we thought it altogether inconvenient to choose a stranger, who would be longer in learning than the thing in doeing, and to avoid all innovations: and finding none of the old Inhabitants to be soe well skilled in the affaires of this Collony, and having had good experience of his great care and able assistance in the skilful managem^t thereof, being a person wholely imploying himself for yor Hono^{rs} Interest, and the carefull incouragm^t and orderly Governing of the people: hath incouraged us with the consent of all the people, and the approbacon of our late Governo^r in his life time, to choose and proclaime the said Capt Joseph West Governo^r & Commander in Chief, to all intents as largely as our late Governo^r was commissionated by yor Hono^{rs}, vntill yor Hono^{rs} pleasure, and further care be signified therein:

for that now two seates in the Council are vacant, (viz) the right hono^{ble} the Lord Craven's Dep^{ty} and Sr George Carterets.[1]

The provisions that yor Hono^{rs} have been pleased to cause to be transported to Barbados, for our supply, were by yor Hono^{rs} Agents there shipped aboard Capt. John Stoe of Barmuda, but we have not yet rec'd any, nor the letters therewith: yet we have some reason to believe they may be safe, and that ye said Stoe waits at Barmuda to bring people from thence in the Spring, whom every day we doe expect: Some of the people who did arrive here last in the ship Carolina, have made their claimes[2] of severall quantities of land, pursuant to yor Hono^{rs} Concessions formerly, of 500 acres of land for every 1000^{lb} of sugar, that any person should vnderwrite towards the defraying of the charge, of setting forth of Capt Hilton, on the discovery of this province, and Mr Colleton yor Hono^{rs} Agent in Barbados his publicacon, that the same should be performed, to all y^t should send people to take posession thereof, and make their demands before the 25th of March next, but having received noe instructions from yor Hono^{rs} concerning the same, and being fully satisfied of the truth thereof, upon their earnest requests, and y^t noe discouragem^t might thereupon be given, we passed an order, that what lands should be made appeare to be granted by yor Hono^{rs}, upon what consideration soever should be assured, and laid out to them, as in Mr Colleton's said publication is specified, and we have incouraged to expect yor Hono^{rs} further returne hereto; which we humbly desire.

We have with much adoe, our people being weake by reason of scarcity of provisions, pallasadoed about 9: Acres of land, being a point, whereon we first set downe for our better security, and mounted seaven great Gunns, all the other carriages haveing been lost with the ship Port Royall. And when the people have done planting, we shall proceed to finish all, being very forward in our p^rparation: We have here inclosed sent yor

[1] Bowman left in Ireland & West now Palatine's deputy. Page 132.

[2] Entered in Secretary's Office by Capt. Geo. Thompson May 29, 1671, Mr. J. Scantlebury, Gyles Hall, Esq., Mr. Ro. Williams, Capt. Jno. Godfrey, Mr. Tho. Noevil 19 July; Col. S. Lambert, 25 Oct., Lt. Thos. Clutterbuck, Mr. Tho. Lake, Maj. Ro. Johnston, Mr. B. Hadlit, B. Rees, (these 4 are orders dated Barbadoes, Dec. 24, 1670) Dec. 15, 1671, Tho. Dowden, 13 Oct., 1672. *Pages 18, 30, 54, 211.*

Hono[rs] a copy of M[r] Colleton's letter to vs, by w[ch] yo[r] Hono[rs]·
will perceive, that we are forced to encourage, and invite people,
not only by our tongues, and pennes but also by our axes, which
hitherto we have very willingly effected, for yo[r] Hono[rs] Interest,
and the advantage of others, (not of ourselves) though in the
time of planting, we having assisted in the loading of the John
and Thomas with timber, which is now gon, and the Carolina,
now ready to sayle.

We must further acquaint yo[r] Hono[rs] that the land not lyeing
as yo[r] Hono[rs] were formerly informed in England, we cannot
possibly observe all yo[r] Hono[rs] directions therein, for all the land
being Interwoveen, with great Creeks, and Marshes, and sometimes a neck of land running between two Rivers, half a mile, a
mile, between River and River, and such small depths, as will
not answere a depth, sufficient to the breadth of any great quantity of land, as yo[r] Hono[rs] have directed to be laid by the water-
side, and most of the land will not admit of the joining of one
line upon another, or the exact fifth part of a depth, by reason
of the aboundance of creeks and marshes, and irregular points
of land as afores'd, but as neere as we can, we shall observe yo[r]
Hono[rs] said Instructions, though the reasons afores'd, hath inforced vs somewhat to vary from them.

When we arrived here, we thought it most conducing to our
safety, to build a town, where we are now setled, it being a
point with a very convenient landing, and safely fortified, being
almost surrounded with a large Marsh, and Creek, and after the
first joint planting, upon our arrival, w[ch] necessity had soe put
upon us; That the people might have sufficient land to plant,
and keep a small stock, and that we might keep as neer together
as we could, for the better security of this place, we were forced
to grant them towne lotts cont: eleaven poles or thereabouts ℈
head, and Tenn acres ℈ head to plant as afores'd; which tenn
acre lotts were, and are laid out to them, & about the Towns
from the South, westwards to ye North, by w[ch] we humbly conceive,
we shall p[r]vent any sudden surpriseall; this modell we were
forced to exercise at first for our better defence, and speedy concourse to the Towns, not knowing what use we might make
thereof, before more people did arrive. And now more people
are come, we find that if they be not suffered to choose their own
conveniencyes, it may prove a great retarding of a speedy peo-

pling this Country; for non omnibus arbusta juvant; some delighting to be near the sea, and others from it, the denyall of wch we find to have been fatall to the late Settlem^t of Sta Lucia &c: which to p^{r}vent in this, and as we have endeavoured to make a perfect settlem^t with the best security we can; We hope yor Hono^r will allow of what we have hitherto done, not having any oppertunity of speedy resolution of our dispondings. We doe assure yor Hono^{rs} that we have, and shall come as neere to yor Hono^{rs} Instructions, as we may, having a tender regard to a reall settlem^t which we humbly conceive yor Hono^{rs} doe desire, for which we humbly desire yor Hon^{rs} approbacon by the next. .

Having given yor Hono^{rs} an acco^t of the irregularity of our land, we must be forced to acquaint yor Hono^{rs} with the irregularity of our Surveyo^r Gen^{ll}, who though he has rec'ed warr^t upon warr^t, & our speciall charge for the same, hath not yet compleated any man's land in the Collony, nor caused soe to be done, and that he might be encouraged to doe this, before more people should arrive here, we did promise him 2^d per acre; as much againe as any Artist in Surveying would do the like, which he altogether has neglected; soe that we were forced to imploy two Gentl in the Collony to marke out every man's land gratis, before any more people should come, to p^{r}vent any difference that might arise between the old and new comers; which we doe impute to his inability, the rather that we are soe informed by some artists that have lately arrived here, who have taken notice of his workings; however we have once more put him to compleat the bounds of lands, pursuant to his former warr^{ts}, which if he does not effectually follow, we doe intend to Imploy one Mr John Culpeper[1] a very able Artist to finish the same, (to p^{r}vent all incon-

---

[1] From Barbadoes, Surveyor in Carolina 1671, mapped Charlestown and its vicinity and Aug. 28 was made Sur. General's deputy, and Dec: 30 Surveyor General; served with skill and diligence, and 1672 was chosen to parliam't, in 1673 'a civil disturbance broke out, Mr. Culpeper headed the malcontents,' and 'being in danger of hanging for endeavoring to set the poor to plunder the rich,' fled to Albemarle. There he was Collector of Customs, and in 1679 with his faction riotously resisted and expelled Capt. Biggs, who claimed the office. He was 'a person never in his element, but while fishing in troubled waters, was forced to fly from Ashly river for his turbulent and factious carriage there. He both here and in New England plotted and encouraged rebellion, this being the second disturbance he hath made here besides what he hath

veniences that may arise from the arriveall of more people, the land not being bounded) who will vndertake to doe it, returne a plat, & keep a record of the figure thereof, according to yor Hono^rs directions therein, for ten shillings a day vnder five hundred acres, and above five hundred acres one penny ℔ acre, untill we receive yor Hono^rs further directions concerning the same, and yor Hono^rs declaracon of M^r fflor: o'Sullivan our Surveyo^r Gen^ll or other Surveyo^rs ffees, or what Surveyo^rs shall be Imployed here, that people may not be discouraged, or kept ideling too long, for want of laying out of their land.

We desire that yor Hon^rs will be pleased to send by the first oppertunity, two bales of parchment, one hundred weight of well tempered wax, and the seale, which yor Hono^rs provided for the passing of Grants, that the people may have the grants of their lands, (which they very much desire) as yor Hono^rs have directed; And a parchm^t booke to record the said Grants in, six other good paper books differenceing in their bulk, to be used in the Register's Office, and at the Councill. We have formerly given yor Hono^rs an account of the great necesity, there is of a supply of yor Hono^rs stores of all sorts, of tooles, cloathing and provisions, the want whereof hath not a little pinched the first Adventurers, haveing had noe recruit since their first arrivall hither nor have they been able to raise comodities sufficient to produce any, neither will they be in a capacity soe to doe, till they have made sure of a good stock of provisions in the country, to answere all emergencyes: the want whereof, how p^rudiciall it is to all labour, and good improvem^t, we have sufficiently experienced; whereof we hope yor Hono^rs will not be backward to help vs at a dead-lift, by a timely supply of the stores, And that yor Hono^rs will be pleased to cause some Cattell, & hoggs to be brought to us from New Yorke, where we understand is a very good breed, with some horses fit for plowing, which the people doe intend to fall vpon, as soon as ever they can get materialls, by means whereof the people will be sooner able to discharge themselves from yor Hono^rs storebooks, and raise some adwantages to themselves, and the Country be brought into a

---

done at Ashly River, New England and Virginia.' In 1680 Mr. Culpeper ('late of St. Margaret's Westminster') was tried at Westminster Hall for High Treason in raising a Rebellion in Carolina, but acquitted. *N. C.* 255, 331.

flourishing condition of plenty of all things in a very short time to the great satisfaction of yor Hono^{rs} and of

Yo^r Hono^{rs} most faithfull humble Serv^{ts}

Stephen Bull	Samuell West[1]
Paul Smyth	Robt Donne
	Ra. Marshall.

Jos. Dalton Regr^s.

Albemarle Point In the province of Carolina   March xxith 167$\frac{0}{1}$.

Endorsed by Locke.   Councell at Ashley river to L^{ds} Proprietor 21° Mar. $\frac{70}{71}$.

A.   [*S. P.*, Bdle. 48, No. 64.]

B.

Albemarle poynte March ye 16th 1670.

The humble Remonstrance of the Councell, for, & on the behalfe of themselves, and the severall ffreeholders, being the ffirst Adventurers to the Province of Carolina, in America.

May it please yor Hono^{rs}

Wee cannott Imagine, butt that yor Hono^{rs} are very senceable of the grievous pangs, & many sorrowes, that all new Setten^s (wee meane the people concerned therein) doe sufferr, before that happy Issue (Hope) cann bee brought forth, beinge only in the concepcon vpon arrivall: whereof wee have had a full, nay a double Share.   Now after soe Painfull travells, wee doe heere p'sent, an Infant Setlem^t to y^r Hono^{rs} (though in a meane dress) yett if cherrished by yor Hono^{rs} favo^{rs}, may proove not less serviceable, then yor Hono^{rs} have designed; butt, such is our misery, that unlesse yor Hono^{rs} bountye doe Countermande, the after

---

[1] Came in the Carolina 1669, with 2 servants, was elected to Council at St. Helena, and sat until the new election July, 1671. In April, 1672, he was chosen to Parliam't, and Aug., 1673, to the Council again, and served to 1677, &c. His plant'n was on Ashley river, below Accabee. Samuel West, of St. Andrew's, died 1731—probably his son; had wife Sarah and children Mary, m'd, 172$\frac{1}{2}$, Henry Toomer, Isabel, m'd, 172$\frac{2}{3}$, Tho. Elliott, Sarah, Samuel (of Charlestown neck, 1730–58), Charles (d. 1768, in Georgia, and has descend'ts there), and Willoughby, d. 1758.

birth is likely to proove more fatall to us, than all our former troubles; wch have binn none of the Least. Yo^r Hono^rs have formerly rec'ed, (wee hope), some Account from vs, of our tedious, unpleasant voyadge, what great damage wee have sustained thereby, the difficulty of our arrivall in this place, wth the unusuall hardshipps, & hazzards wch wee did patiently undergoe, Incouraging ourselves wth this, that the fruition of our desired Lande, which ℔ mare, ℔ terras, wee have soe longe pursued, would p^rsently cause us to forgett all our former discouradgm^s when after all this, & much more, fitter to be lamented then rehearsed, vpon our joyfull greetings of this happy shoare, (happy to all others, however itt prooves to vs), wee did confidently apply ourselves, to yor Hono^rs Stores for such necessaries, as was expedient for us in this place, not doubting, butt what was freely delivered to us out of yor Hono^rs Stores, pursuant to those large incouradgm^ts wch brought vs hither, butt should in some smalle tyme, humbly return to yor Hono^rs, Crura Thyme: This fair promising ffruite was blasted in the bloome, ffor beinge att once assaulted, wth want of Lodging, Scarcity of provisions, & a Lapsed Springe, Endeavoring every thing that would seeme to promiss reliefe, being more willing to say, this we have done, than, this we might have done, we did bestirr ourselves in Planting of Corne, Pease, pumpieons, &c wch though somewhat unseasonably comitted to the Earth, yett itt pleased God, to give us the comforte of a promisinge Cropp, butt, before wee could come to taste of our hard Labours, our provisions failed vs, and the Spaniard well knowing our Condicon, besett vs: wch caused the losse of all our planted provisions, and the overpressing ourselves & people wth continuall watchings, to the Losse of some; having noe other thing to support vs, but a pint of pease, a mann a day, some of wch were damnified, & that almost at an end; onely a very smale assistance wch wee rec'ed from the Indians; and although ruine did threaten vs on all sides, by the Spaniard, or Starving, or both: Yett thinking itt beneath vs to Submitt to the Tyranie of either; how hardly soever itt might fall vpon vs, wee were resolved to incounter the one. And stand vpon the defence of yor Hono^rs Interests, to the utmost of our powers against the other; both of wch itt hath pleased God to Subdue unto us, & send releif of some farther provisions, Att the very pointe of our Extremity; Yett noe assistance of people did arrive, alledging that they would see, what would become of vs for one Yeare, before they would transport themselves, or any thing of their Concernes hither; thus have wee binn as forlorne, & gazing to all the world hitherto only like souldiers in a garison, to defend yo[r] Hono[rs] rights; Our whole tyme beinge thus imployed, in publick works, for our further security, wee have been wholely debarred from makinge any other provisions for ourselves, then wholly to depende vpon yo[r] Hono[rs] Stores for Supplies of provisions, & other necessarys, Att Excessive rates, Especially the hire of M[r] Colleton's Sloope to Bermuda, w[ch] our great Exigencies hath inforced vs upon; whereby we have deeply involved ourselves, in yo[r] Hono[rs] Store Books, That wee shall Nott, by anything wee cann doe, bee able to dischardge ourselves in haste. All p'sons here after Ariving, may very well promise to themselves, A Speedye advantage. Butt the Contrary hath happened to us, for soe long tyme as wee have binn heere, wee have binn in our retrogradacon from itt, soe that wee may seeme to bee the first ruined, not the first setled of Carolina; w[ch] wee might believe, if wee did not think, that your yo[r] Hono[rs] Clemency w[ch] hath formerly Incouraged us, whilst upon the Adventure; will nott bee abated, (now the hazard is overcome), wee, therefore, doe humbly offer these Addresses to yo[r] Hono[rs] Considerations, to Mittigate, what yo[r] Hono[rs] wilbee pleased to thinke, lyeth too severely vpon us, as we are charged in the Store Books: And to lett fall what influence else, yo[r] Hono[rs] may think sufficient, or oppertune, (bee it by the qualificaions of the freight, of our goods, & concernes, for some tyme yet to come or otherwise) to sweeten the hardshipps of our late Adventures & to recover the Shattered, & almost worne out fortunes, of

      Yo[r] Hono[rs] Most ffaithfull Humble Serv[ts]

Stephen Bull,	Flor: O'Sullivan,
Paul Smythe,	Ro: Donne,[1]
Ra: Marshall,	Samuel West.

Alber. Poynt in the province of Carolina, March the xxi[th] 167⁰⁄₁.

---

[1] Came from England, 1669; was chosen to the Council, March, 1670; suspended for his action at Wallie, but reinstated, and sat till Aug., 1671; was Captain in the Kussoe War, but afterwards cashiered. He was elected to Parliam't, April 20, 1672, and commanded the company at Oyster Point (where his plant'n was) in July, and in the Westo troubles.

Endorsed by Locke: Council at Ashley river Remonstrance 16
Mar: $\frac{70}{71}$.

B.   [*S. P.*, Bdle. 48, No. 64.]

———

C.

May itt please yo[r] Hono[rs]

Itt is nott a little trouble to vs, that wee should have occasion, to p[r]sente before yo[r] Hono[rs], those vnsavory accout[s] in this
Collony, w[ch] wee have indeavored, soe much to suppress; occasioned by troublesome spirritts: A mallady that all regularity in
Gov'nem[t] are more or less subject to, whose fate is to bee knowne
in the world only as if they were designed to bee vnknowne; w[ch]
rather then they will nott avoyd, will att all tymes, & vpon all
seeminge occasions, to the annoyance of all men, appeare in
their Na'rall deformity, w[ch] is soe much rejected: thus from tyme
to tyme since our Arrivall in this place, have wee found the like
intrusions, w[ch] hithertoe wee have smothered, butt of late, those
sparks meeting wth more fuell, have binn indeavored to bee
blown vpp into a flame, by M[r] William Owen chiefly & M[r]
Will'm Scrivener,[1] Dep[ty] to our very good Lord, the L[d] Bertly,
w[ch] wee are as vnwilling to take notice of, or remember, as to
give yo[r] Hono[rs] the trouble, were itt Nott to purge the aire from
such infeccons.   Thus, vnwillingly willing shall wee briefly represent to yo[r] Hono[rs], the true & various transaccons of the s'd
will'm Owen, & will'm Scrivener tending to the incitinge of

June, 1675, he was in the Council, and in Dec., 1676, a deputy. Dec.
29, 1680, 'Robert Donne of Charlestown upon Wandow river in Carolina
& Jane his wife formerly Jane Rivam ? convey to Tho. Berrick a plant'n
15 acres on E. side of Wandow river Bounded S. & W. on Edw. Mayo
& N. on Jno Williamson' &c. and 168– Arthur Middleton, Esq., conveys
him half lot 42 in Charlestown (now the Library), in Jan., 1683, he proved
Jno. Cottingham's will and died soon after, for Aug. 18, 1683, 'Jane
Cliffe widow, relict & adm'x of will of Robert Donne late of this province,
dec'd,' conveys to her dau. Eliz. Neale, house and half of 'lot 42 in
new Charlestowne,' &c.

[1] Came from England, 1669, as L'd Berkley's deputy, 'a man of reason
and parts,' 'one of the most understanding of our statesmen here,' in
March, 167$\frac{0}{1}$, suspended from the Board for joining Owen in exciting the
people.   He died about June? 1671.   (Dec. 9, 'Susan Kinder's lot
next lot of Mr Wm Scrivener in his life time.')

Mutinies amonge the People, little respecting the safety of themselves, or others.

Att Bermuda when Sr J^o Yeomans was pleased, soe ffarr to
humor an ignoble Spirritt, as wholly to wthdraw his care from
the manadgm^t of the designe, wch hee was Intrusted wthall, leaving
us to the Sufficiency of our owne bottoms, either to stand or
fall; the s'd will'm Scrivener, & will'm Owen esp'ially, would
have p'swaded the people to a Publicke difference or Suit, ag^t
the s'd Sr J^o Jeomans, nott regarding the discouradgm^t & ill
opinion, that therevpon might arise, of those people whom wee
did, & doe much Expect assistance, for this Collony: wch wee
did as well as wee could Salve; And the s'd Sr J^o Yeomans having p'swaded Collonell william Sayle to accept of the Com'issons, wch hee had there brought blanke, as Gov'no^r of this place:
& caused the Name of the s'd Coll Sayle in the s'd Com'issons
to bee incerted; The s'd Coll Sayle being a p'son of good report, & well Experienced in New Settlem^{ts}, And rather then this
designe should fall, wee did consent thereto, & accepted him,
as Gov'no^r; the s'd Willm Owen being dissatisfied, that his
contrivance was nott observed, has ever Sinc^e binn labouring
vnder a violent Ague of distraction: When wee Safely arrived
att Port Royall that the s'd Late Gov'no^r Pursuant to yor Hono^{rs}
directions Sum'oned all the ffreemen, & there to Ellect & choose
five men to bee of the Councill, as yor Hono^{rs} have directed;
The ffreemen proceeding to Ellection, having by that tyme
throughly discov'ed the s'd will'm Owen, wholely rejected him:
& chose Mr Paule Smith, Mr Rob'te Donne, Mr Ralphe Marshall, Mr Samuell West, & Mr Joseph Dalton, to bee their rep-
resentitives, wch accordingly was recorded; butt the s'd will'm
Owen finding his desiers (alwaies itching to bee in Authority)
frustrated, could nott butt Censure the legality of the Election,
wherevpon the s'd ffreeholdo^{rs} or the major p'te of them, mett a
second tyme, & confirmed their former Election, by subscribeing
of their sev'all names: This instead of a reformacon in the s'd
will'm Owen, (wch wee could well have wished) prooved one
sparke more to his fire, as hereafter will appeare.

About the 4th of July last, the s'd late Gov'no^r & Councell,
having binn informed how much the Sabboth Day was Pro-
phanely violated, & of div's other grand abuses, practised by
the people, to the greate dishonor of God Almighty, & the des-

truction of good Neighbourhood; the s'd Gov'no[r] & Councell did
seriously consider, by w[ch] way or means, the same might bee
redrest, & finding, that the Number of ffreehould[rs] in the Collony
nott neere sufficient to Electe a Parliam[t]; the s'd late Gov'no[r],
by & wth the advice, & consent of vs his Councell, did make
such orders, as wee did think convenient to suppress the same,
vpon w[ch] the s'd Gov'no[r] did Sum'ons all the People to heare the
said Orders,[1] all the s'd ffreemen consenting therevnto the s'd
Gov'no[r] & Councell caused the s'd orders to bee published;
wherevpon the s'd william Owen, willing to doe anything, though
ever soe ill in itt selfe, rather then not to apeare, to bee a man
of acc'on, indeavored to possesse the people, that w[th]out a Parliam[t] noe such orders ought, or could passe; the rather, being
seconded by the said M[r] will'm Scrivener, and while the s'd
Gov'no[r] & Councell were discursing That, & other matters, the
s'd will'm Owen p'swaded the people, to Elect a Parliam[t] among
themselves, w[ch] they did) & reterned to the s'd Gov'no[r]; The
Originall, being the writing of the said will'm Owen, wee have
sent heere inclosed to yo[r] Hono[rs], two of w[ch] Parliam[t] men were
then in dispute, whether they were Serv[ts] or ffreemen;[2] And in
the whole Collony there were butt two men (vizt) Mich: Moran
a Laboring Irish mann; & Rich: Crossley one whom his M[r]
Sett ffree, for his Idlenesse, butt how the s'd will'm Owen Did
proceed in the Elec'on, wee doe nott yett vnderstand, All the
rest of the ffreemen being moved, by the s'd will'm Owen, in
another Spheere then their owne, After that the s'd will'm Owen
had taken their Names, w[th]out any farthere notice takinge of the
s'd will'm Owen, or their Elec'on into dignity, (as the s'd Owen
p'swaded them itt would bee) lefte the s'd Owen, & his Paper,
& followed their other Labours, w[ch] indeed neerely concerned
them & vs to.   And the s'd Owen having noe inclinac'on to bee
alone, went home for Company; Thus may yo[r] Hono[rs] discov'
one p'te more, of the s'd Owen disposicon, because the Altitude
of his body, will nott Show himselfe taller than any other man,

---

[1] These ordinances for keeping the Sabbath and preserving stock are
the first we have note of, p. 296.

[2] Pages 176, 204.   Ingram & Barker.   This shews that Hollis, Middleton, Rideall, Houghton, S. & N. Darkenwell & Motteshed never arrived.   Baily, Rivers & Collins were taken at Wallie and Brayne, Coming, N. Carteret, N. Sayle & Dyas were away.

by the Head & Shoulders, hee will climbe vpon the pinacle of any Desperatt Attempt, to bee seene above others, bee the hazard ever soe dangerous: This is nott all, for after the Arivell of the two shipps, namely the John & Thomas, & the Carolina, wth more people, wee the p^rsent Gov'no^r & Councell finding the aforemenco'ed disorders likely to bee renewed, about the 11th instant, caused a republicacon of y^r s'd Orders, formerly made by the late Gov'no^r & Councell, & revised by the p^rsente Gov'-no^r, that all p'sonns might bee Excluded, from any plea of Igno-rance concerning the same, wch All the Antient ffreehoulders for-merly had, & wth the New ffree men then did assent vnto, & well aproove on; butt the s'd will' Owen finding himselfe swalloed vp in a gen'all consent; invents a New Stratagem, & Singles out the Cheife of the people, Especially the New Comers, & Possess them, that hee had discov'ed, that the great seale of the Province nott beinge in the Collony, whatever land they had or should take up, & their Improvem^ts therein, would nott bee assuered to them, butt might bee taken away att pleasure, vnlesse a parliam^t bee forth^wth chosen to p^rvent the same; this takes wth the people (most men being Naturally inclined, sooner to receive the beleife of a seeming injury, then a reall truth) That they should venter soe far for land, the tytle whereof was vncertaine, & therevpon the people might well bee incited to an Incredulity of the p'for-mance of yor Hono^rs other Declaracons; Now the s'd Owen hath hit the marke, hee is what hee would bee, the leader of a company of people vpon any tearm^es; he is now the peoples prolocuto^r, & therefore must have roome in the Councell, to show himselfe & the peoples grievances; thus before the s'd Gov'no^r & Councell, & att the ffronte of the people Champion like, hee would vndertake to reveale, what hee long had Stud-died, the true Interpretacon of yor Hono^rs Instrucons, & the peoples rights, & Priviledges involved therein, wth various argu-mentacons; (wch wee shall rather Silently Pitty, then give yor Hono^rs the trouble of reading them): The s'd Gov'no^r having patiently heard, what the s'd Owen had to say, & finding, that the s'd Owen had ill advised the people, directed his Speech to the s'd people, & gave them to vnderstand, that by vertue of Authority, derived from yor Hono^rs Instrucons, Dated the 26th July, 1669: wth the Consent of his Councell, hee did Conceive, he had Sufficient Power to Convey, & assuer to them, All such

21

lands, for such Estates, & wth such provisoes, & limitacons, as yor Hono^rs by yor Instrucons, & consessions, on that behalfe had directed, & would carefully doe the same, vntill hee had received the s'd seale of the Province, from yor Hono^rs; And when the s'd seale shall come, All their Grants should for the better Confirmacon of their tytles Pass vnder the s'd seale: And as for the Election of the Parliam^t, wch the s'd Owen had soe long Studied Rhetoricaly to Demande, the s'd Gov'no^r declared, that That tyme was some what vnseasonable, & that hee did intend to sum'ons the people for the Election of a parliam^t when opp'tunity did serve or necessity of makinge lawes did requier, vpon w^ch, All or most of the s'd ffreemen, being fully satisfied of the truth thereof, (& vpon the s'd Gov'no^rs com'and) were about to w^thdraw themselves; as that all doubts were removed from them; The s'd william Scrivener the countenancer & coadjutator of the said Owen perceiving that the time & paines wch the one had spent in contriving, & both in manadginge something, (if they knew what), was likely to proove noe discourse for them hereafter, & that they were likely to loose the tytle, of men of vnderstanding: for som tyme before being observeed to sitt very silent, on a svdden arose vp, wth somwhat more then an ordinary heat vpon his spiritt, & the better to colour his new kindled anger, as if in hast, desired the people to take Notice, That hee did conceive, their proposalls were very just & reasonable, & those whoe should deviate from them, were disturbors of the Peace & infringers of the Peoples libertys; wch soe farr as wee could p'ceive then, made little or noe impression vpon the people), beinge satisfied wth the Gorv'no^rs said declaracon, and dep'ting soe quietly, Yett forasmuch as the Acc'ons & Speeches of the sd Scrivener & Owen, then and formerly, (a p'te whereof, are heer, butt moderately recounted.)   Tending to the Sleighting, & utter destruction of this p^rsent gov'm^t, setled by y^r Hon^rs, & the inciting of seditions & Mutinyes among the People, and consequently the ruin of this Setlem^t, the same Day we the sd Gov'no^r & Councell made an order, that the sd Scrivener from thenceforth, should be suspended and debarred from all votes, & Priviledges in Councell, to other Councello^rs belonging^e.   And that the sd Scrivener and Owen bee, & be deemed incapable of bearing any Publick office, or Imploymen^t in this Collony, vntill wee receive further Orders, from yor

Hono^{rs} concerning the same: Thus having given yor Hono^{rs} a relacon of what wee have done, wee shall now, give an Account of what wee intend to doe; having hithertoe endeavored as much as in us lyes, to have all our Acc'ons well resented abroad, that soe the merritt of this place, & the manadgm^t thereof (keeping tyme, the harmony might bee approved of, by all Judicious Eares, and having (blessed bee god) binn successfull in our reports of this place, & confirmed by those, that thereupon are now becom eye wittnesses, wee should be very sorry, that anything should be Acted here, that might proove distastefull abroad; being very sencible, that the name of a Parliam^t is strangly resented abroad; that the quality of our Parliam^t men, might not give an occasion of Disputing in other p'ts, & noe great necessity att p'sent of a Parliam^t our tyme being well imployed, if wee cann imploy it well, in Planting & other necessary works that lyeth vpon vs, knowing how treacherous reports are, wee have therefore deferred the sum'oning of a Parliam^t till the shipps begon, att wch tyme the heat of Planting being over, we shall, (now some more people are come), proceed to the prosecucon of yor Hono^{rs} Instrucons, by and wth the Consent of the Parliam^t or the major p'te of them, to make such lawes, as wee shall finde necessary in this Place; in the meane tyme wee humbly desier yor Hono^{rs}, farther to Inlardge yor Instrucons, (vizt) how long this Parliam^t is to continue; as we humbly Conceive itt wilbee moste convenient, for 2 or 3 yeares yett to com, that they bee dissolved vpon pleasure of the Gov'no^r & Councill for the tyme being, & a sum'ons for a new Election, may bee issued out att any tyme; by means whereof many people arriving here, from tyme, to tyme, some of worth, such as a Parliam^t may bee found ere Long, whose wisedome, & experience, may nott onely consent, butt assist, yor Hono^{rs} Gov'no^r, & Councell, for the tyme being, in the making of all such Acts, & Lawes, as may bee to the best avail of yor Hono^{rs} Interests, & the peoples good in this Cuntrey wch are the only desiers, & the thing aymed att, by

Yo^r Hono^{rs} most obedient humble Servants

	Joseph West	Ste. Bull
	Fflor: O'Sullivan	Paul Smythe
Jos. Dalton, Regr^s.	Ro. Donne	Ra. Marshall

Albermarle Poynte in the province of Carolina March the xxist 167$\frac{0}{1}$,

Endorsed by Locke: Goveror & Council at Ashley river to
Lords Proprietors 21° Mar. $\frac{70}{71}$.

C.   [*S. P.*, Bdle. 48, No. 64.]

GOV. WEST TO LORD ASHLEY, &c.

May it please yo[r] Honn[rs]

Since my last to yo[r] Honn[rs] of ye 2[d] Instant it hath pleased
God to call for our Govern[r] who was very aged & nature quite
decayed in him, ye 4th instant in the morning hee finding himselfe very weake & sensible sent for ye Councell and nominated
myselfe to succeed him in the Governm[t] vntill yo[r] Honn[rs] pleasure bee further knowne: the Councell being all very ready to
give their consents.   But being conscious of my owne weakness
I dare not be a suitor for soe great a charge: But desire to continue noe longer than yo[r] Honn[rs] may finde out a Gent[n] y[t] may
be more Encouregem[t] to a new Settlem[t]: and propogate & cher-
rish the service of God and yo[r] Honn[rs] Interest here.   May it
please yo[r] Honn[rs] That to leave the people last come Inexcusa-
ble about the 11th instant I called all ye ffreeholders of the
Collony together to heare ye publicacon of some orders made by
the late Govern[r] & Councell for ye better keeping of the Sabboth day, & for preserving our stock this yeare; But some hot
spirited persons[1] being ambitious of perpetuating theire owne
wicked Inclinacons spurned at all order & good Governm[t]
fearing to be reduced from a sordid beastly life, y[t] they will
rather not live than bee induced to live well; such hath been
(especially) the life of one M[r] William Owen amongst us, hee
haueing some relacon to yo[r] Lo[pps] secretary M[r] Blany who hath
many times since our departure out of England appeared in the
head of the people, & stirring them up to differences, as yo[r]
Honn[rs] may see more at large in a gen[ll] Letter from myselfe &
Councell An Answer whereof I hope yo[r] Honn[r] will please to let
us haue by ye first: In ye meane time I shall endeavour with diligent care to propagate & advance ye publique good & yo[r] Honn[rs]
Interest.   I haue since ye late Govern[rs] decease reduced the
people into two Companeys that they may the better be disci-
plined, wee cannot yet make in the Collony 150 men, y[t] are fit

-----

[1] West's letter page 266.   For Owen's side see page 300.

to beare Armes, & wee are still forced to lye upon our guard, keeping good watch, not trusting the Indians further than security will allowe, ffor I am very sensible (though they carry themselves never soe faire) yet they are very treacherous and will let slip noe opportunity that may destroy us. In my last to yor Honn^{rs} I gave you an Acc^t of some transaccons here and now I shall give yor Honn^{rs} a briefe Acco^t of yor owne Plantacon. I have taken up for present planting about 300 Akers of ground. I have cleared this yeare about 30 Akers and built convenient Houses for ourselves & serv^{ts} and Inclosed the Houses wth Pallisadoes, wch doth containe betweene 6 & 700 foote and have soe placed them y^t one Angle shall cleare another soe y^t wee doe not feare all ye Indians y^t shall attempt us, wch worke was all compleated before the Arriveall of the 2 ships. In the Carolina one Capt Godfrey arriued here from Barbadoes to manage Sr Peter Colletons Interest in yor Partnership, who I beleive to be a very honest man and a good Planter, I am very glad of his Assistance and doe hope wee shall answer yor Hono^{rs} Expectacons. Wee intend to plant most of our ground this yeare with provisions, it being the life of a new settlement to provide in the first place for the belly. Wee haue already sowed Pease and planted some Indian Corne—and although I think it something too soone yet the pease doe thrive very well and some English Wheat wch I sowed about 2 months before Christmas, and I believe y^t English graine will agree very well with this soyle: Wee haue also planted Ginger and severall other things, and doe hope to make a full experim^t this yeare of what comodities the Country will best produce. The winter here doth prove something sharpe and colde, soe y^t I feare this will not prove a Cotton Country,[1] but our new Commers like it very well, and say they believe it will produce any Comodities y^t the Charibbe Islands doe, as Cotton, Ginger, Indigo, &c. and they haue written severall Letters to their friends in Barbadoes to encourage them to come, and I believe wilbe a meanes of drawing many to us in a short time: Our stock doth thrive very well especially Hoggs wch doe increase very fast, being somewhat troubled wth them this yeare by reason wee have not time to fence in our planted grounds. The 4 Cowes I kept for ye use of y^r owne Plantacon,

[1] The Barbadians were right and West mistaken.

one of them hath calved, and another is ready to calve, but they are very small Breed, and wilbe but little Proffit, except onley for stock.   I am Informed that there is at New Yorke a very large Breed of Cattell, and y^t one Cow will give 2 gallons or more at a meal, halfe a dozen such Cowes would be a great helpe to our family; likewise Horses are there very cheap and of a good Breed some for present use wee want very much to drawe downe Timber to ye waters side, and most of ye ground wee plant this yeare may be plowed the next, wch would be a greate helpe to cleare the ground: I have (with what Expedicon I could) dispatched ye Carolina laden wth Pine Timber some of wch wilbe fitt for Masts for small ships, & for poynts for windmills.   The Inhabitants lent me their Assistance to bring it doune to ye waters side; I suppose they have peticon'd yor Honn^{rs} to take off Mr. Colletons sloope hire from this place to Bermuda shee being upon y^t voyage about 3 months[1] at 30^{li} ℔ mensum, wch I haue charged to ye severall Inhabitants, they haueing engaged to pay ye same (if yor Honn^{rs} require it) before I would signe the Bills to produce the provisions in Bermuda, likewise they desire you would please to mitigate ye freight of any other goods yor Honn^{rs} shall send to ye first Adventurers they haueing spent much time in watching & publique Employm^{ts} May it please yor Honn^{rs} Captn Sullivan hath been very negligent in laying out of the peoples lands there being not one mans proporcon yet compleated in the Country, and I doubt hee is not capable of what hee hath undertaken.   I intend to put him upon it to run out every mans lands and if I find his insufficiency to suspend him vntill yor Honn^{rs} pleasure be further knowne and to Imploy another Surveyor who is come from Barbadoes and doth proffer to run out all parcells of land above 500 Akers at a Penny ℔ Acre.   I hope yor Honn^{rs} will please to send the Seale for ye grants and 2: or 3 bayles of parchment and a considerable proporcon of good wax; Likewise ye Pattent yor Honn^{rs} had from his Matie wee haueing not soe much as a Copie of it.   Youre Stores growe very short, I haue now very little of any thing left but a few nayles; I hope yor Honn^{rs} will please to send timely supplyes according to ye Invoyce I sent to Sr Peter Colleton, and to send mee Instruccons for ye disposing of them and what I shall charge

[1] June 26 to Sept. 20, 1670.   The surveyor was John Culpeper.

for freight wch I haue not as yet done for all ye Cattell & provision from Virginia, haueing had noe Order soe to doe. Here is
wanting amongst us a good Doctor, and a chest of good medi-
cines, those few people y^t haue dyed amongst us, I believe most
part for want of good lookeing after, & that wch is fitt for men:
Wee haue not (thankes be to God) had one dyed out of our
ffamily[1] since wee came ashore which I looke upon as a very
great ffavour from God: Our Servants haue bene sickly as well
as others but now they are indifferently healthfull, and I hope
season'd to the Country I hope yor Honn^{rs} are thinking of sending a supply of Serv^{ts} from England, for some of these wilbe out
of their time the next yeare, and wee find that one of our Serv^{ts}
wee brought out of England is worth 2 of ye Barbadians, for
they are soe much addicted to Rum, y^t they will doe little but
whilst the bottle is at their nose: I did in my last to yor Honn^r
and formerly to Sr Peter Colleton advise yor Honn^{rs} to part Partnership before wee went upon ye great Lott, my reason is because
wee cannot order it soe that there be an equal division made
when you come to part without wee make 3 settlements and that
cannot well be done because the Land lyes in such Irregular figures, and ofttimes when 2 or 3 familyes joyned together one
depends upon ye other and soe business of Concernm^t is neglected there are severall other Reasons may be rendered, but yor
Honn^{rs} haue wisdome to consider of it, and I hope you will please
to excuse my boldness; ffor with what truth & affection I haue
served yor Honn^{rs} I desire it should rather be read in my Actions
than my words. I hope yor Honn^{rs} doe please to pay my sallery
to my wife for y^t shee may supply my wants which are at present
very great being unprovided of all necessaryes. I hope alsoe
yor Honn^{rs} wilbe pleased to consider mee something for ye managing yor particular affaires in P'tnership, I being vncertaine of
any thing as yet, and I hope to approve myselfe a true Servt to
yor Honn^{rs} in ye vsing my best Endeavours for the managem^t of
yor affaires here. May it please yor Honn^{rs} the late Goven^r hath
had severall things out of yor Stores amounting to neere 40^{li} I
desire to knowe yor Honn^r pleasure about it, for hee expected
100^{li} ℔ Ann as promised by Sr John Yeomans: The Inclosed is
a List of ye People that came last from Barbadoes in ye Caro-

---

[1] West's 'family,' Hamiltons', Baileys' & Rivers' servants & others.

lina & ye John & Thomas,[1] I haue taken obligacons to yor Honn^{rs} for about 20 people to pay 500^{li} of Tobacco ℔ head 2 yeares hence, or three pounds two shillings & sixpence in pype staves, at a halfepenny ℔ staffe, ye rest Captn Brayne hath taken bills to be paid in Barbadoes at 200^{li} ℔ head, of wch I haue given Mr. Thomas Colleton a particular Acco^t this in discharge of my Duty to yor Honno^{rs} I cease writeing but I shall never cease to be

Yo^r Honn^{rs} most humble & faithfull Servt

JOSEPH WEST.

Albemarle poynt in Ashly River March ye 21th 16$\frac{70}{71}$.

These seamen belonging to the Carolina are Deb^r to yor Hon^{rs} stores here: I shall desire yor Hon^{rs} will bee pleased to stoop ye monys If thay bee not paid   If thay bee I will Indeuor to gett it here.

			li.	s.	d.	
John Cominges D^r	-	-	2	14	6	) these men haue
John Williamson D^r	-	-	5	10	00	} servants & stockes
Richd Dyers D^r	-	-	7	13	07	) here.

Addressed: To ye Right Hono^{ble} Anthony Lord Ashly, Sr George Carterett, and Sr Peter Colleton: at little Exeter house in ye Strand.   London.   These.

Endorsed by Locke.   Jos: West to Ld Ashley & Sr George Carteret & Sr Peter Colleton.   21° Mar. $\frac{70}{71}$.

[2 p. with seal.   *S. P.*, Bdle. 48, No. 65.]

————

WILLIAM OWEN TO ROBERT BLAYNEY.

Ashley River. Florida.

Lat. 32: 40: m: Mar: the 22: $\frac{70}{71}$.

Sir,

As I am obliged from time to time to give you an acc^t of what happens in this parte of the world soe I should desire you att your owne time to dispensce what you please thereof to my Lord for as all the people in the countrey have an esteeme to his Lordshipp as knoweing his prudence and wisdom and that his care of us att this distance will not impaire in the conservation of our Civill rights soe we dayly expect to heare that his Lord-

———

[1] Unluckily missing.   See partial list, page 271.

shipp hath made choise of a person as Governor fitt for such an
Imployment and although it may be said that att this time its
but inconsiderable yet the continued growth of the countrey by
the Concourse of people who shall here suddenlje arive will in
a shorte time raise it to a matter of noe small moment and the
true reporte of the Countrey being comunicated to Barbados by
the persons who thence here lateljc arived for which they there
onlje waite will suddenlje drawe multidudes to this place besides
those from New Engld and other parts who are alreadje fitting
for this Countrey and as many persons come from those severall
places soe its not otherwise to be thought but that they wilbe of
different judgments and as well pleased with the Constitutions
of the Government when managed with a tempered and understanding person for here are alreadje som gents of verje good
parts and doe expect that noe deviation from the Lords Conces-
ions be in noe case countenanced by their Lordshipps, it being
the onlje thing which will when heard abroade be the great Incouragement for all maner of Judgments to resorte here, for that
then things duelje considered the cheife parte of the fabrick of
this designe and settlement depends upon the prudent managm^t
of things abroade in order to it and the good conduct of all
affaires upon the place, without which there be not any of estates
abroade will adventure to this place, as the Governor must be of
able parts soe he should be noe overgrowne zelote, and I am
dubious whether the later hath not don a discourtezie alreadje;
for the Governor that is now deceased whom we tooke in att
Bermuda declared he had bein and independant these 24 yeares
[2d page MS. begins.] whom it seemes was verie well knowne
att Ronoake and Virginia and in som other places and with
whom they were not well pleased, he latelie dyeing partly with
age and partly with a kind of a lethargicall distemper desired
that Mr West the storekeeper for the proprietors should succeed
him in the Governm^t whom it seemes and onlje he had alone
made him Governor att Bermuda and none other of the Lords
Deputies privie nor present as att the election of our new Governor they declared, my Lord Barkleys deputie who indeed is
the most understanding amongst our statesmen here insisted that
West was not so competent for the Imploy his buisines of the
store lyeing upon his hands and that the Governors warrant for
the deliverie of things out of the store to himself from himself

would not sound soe verie well and therefore prayd that the Government might rest in the hands of some certain persons with the deputies in regard there was not any one fitt for the place att present yet this was carryed against him; soe now the former Governor being deceased and buried West is Governor a storekeeper and a deputie and the same day that the other Governor was Interred the new Governor feeling au'tie creeping upon him undertakes to make a speech to the people, the sum of all that he would have said was that he did assure them he would afflict and inflict punishment upon them if they did sweare and prophane, not a word of Incourag^{mt} to industrie and planting &c, some few days after he sends an officer by him called a Martjall[1] (which the directions of the Government knowes not) to require all the freehoulders to be att the storehouse, we are about 200 and od soules here alreadie of whom there be abouts 40. or 50 freeholders[2] who when we cam after som time were called in before the Councell Table where our Governor setting aside elocution said they had made verie good lawes for the beating doune of sinn and sweareing still, caused it to be read, which imported equall fines upon poore people here as the greatest of estates are subject to in England and in default of good pay^{mt} gagging and whipping som tould him the law of England knew noe such thing as gagging and severall other wise particulars which that paper did importe others inquired the nature of sending for them, to that they answere that it was to promulgate those lawes that they had made to which it was replyed that they might as well have posted them if that was all, however they desired that they might have a view of the paper to which it was verie learnedly answered that they were noe children to part with their papers; at which som standing by smiled. [2d page ends, on margin follows:]

Att length he tould us that he did verie suddenly intend to have a booke where every man should subscribe religion the people wondered where the booke hath been all this while it

---

[1] Thos. Thomson from Barbadoes, succeeded Jno. Collins, and held the office 1671, 3.   He owned land and town lots July, 1672.

[2] Those page 204 and Godfrey, Gray, Culpeper, Mavericke, G. Thompson, Dowden, Holton, Finden, Canty, Comerton, Faulconer, Jackson, Norton, Roberts, Spencer, T. Thomson, Wood and perhaps Mr. Robinson, Jas. Jones, Donohoe, Needham, Pendarvis, Teague and Turpin, &c.

being one of the maine things in the instructions to the Governor
the people desired that they might withdraw and consider of
what they had heard and having so don they unanimouslie agreed
to adhere to the Lords concessions sayeing that when lawes were
to be made they were to be fraimd by 20 persons freehould[rs] in
the nature of a parlem[t] and that those being not founded upon
the bazis of the Lords Instructions for the goverm[t] they could
not assume to themselves an inclination to concur with them.
[Here 3d page begins.]

To that the Governor answered that they were but ordered,
att this the people tould him that the King of England did not
by orders impose either precuniarie or corporall punishment
upon any of his subjects and could but wonder that a subject
could doe it to a subject the consequence they did not I perceive
understand, by and by the Governor inquired, what you would
have a parliament the people verie modestlie tould him that they
desired that lawes for governing of them should proceede from
that patterne which the Lords had prescribed for them, it were
safe in them to obey and in him to command, but if he went
otherwise to impose upon them it would prove both disobliging
to the Lords and injurious to the people yet nothing of this doth
he cleerely understand; they tould him also that it was necessarie that a parliament should be to prevent strives and contentions
betweene those that shall come hereafter I meane sudenlie and
those that are now in the Countrey for the foundation of the
settlement being not pursuant to the concessions the question
may be whether a firme title in the case of land besides the great
seale of the province they have not, which the grant should be
sealed with all (but how warrantable doe you judge they have
in som writeings as conveyances sett their owne seales, we tould
them if upon the arivall of another Governor and upon view of
the Concessions if that their actings and our titles were not pursuant as neere could be to the directions for the Government
they expired in themselves and soe brought upon all a dis-
couragm[t] and we by that meanes might be deprived of our
labour he tould us but whether in England it may not be
called presumption that before another Governor should come to
the Government here, he should confirme all that they had don,
and for the assureing of lands they tould us that they would do
it and were takeing care about it but how we cannot tell; soe

that hereby you may cleerely perceive the Judg^{mt} and reason in our affaires, I cannot otherwise beleive but the man is honest but whether of parts and reason sufficiently qualified in judging of Civill rights I cannot tell; but a man for this place must be of parts learneing and policie and of a moderate zeale not strickt episcopalle nor yet licentious nor rigid presbiterian nor yet hypo-criticall but swayeing himselfe in an even Ballance betweene all opinions but especially turneing his face to the Liturgie of the Church of England, this Countrey doubtless will in a few yeares be a place of plentie and Trade and all persons that are come into it to settle are pleased with it, and as they com so they draw more, we are incouraged by the gent which lately arrived from the Barbados who doe informe us that by the later end of the yeare we cannot be lesse then 1000 people [on margin 3d page] but in the mean time we are straitened for provision untill our Cropp is off ye ground wch now we hasten to put in the pro-vision that was sent from Engld to Barbados being thence ordered by ye way of Bermuda and noe absolute contract made for the transporte there of to this place soe that it will com by Com. Long.[1]   we had but one supplye wch was in augst from Virginia and a little from Bermuda about the same time wch consisted only in corne and pease, yet are we carefull and want not hopes that within these 18 months we shallbe able to eate and drink plen-tifully   soe God bless you

I am S^r yor most obliged humble servant

WILLM OWEN.

[Here 4th page begins.]   but I had almost forgot to tell you the issue of our debate which when we had urged all wee mod-estly could that things might be acted onlje by the rule of the Concessions which bore the Lords true pourtrature and livelje representation; my Lord Berkleys deputie stood upp sayeing that he apprehended that what we had offered was but just and reasonable and therefor could not dissent in what we had pro-posed and said that whosoever should deviat from the Lords proprietors dirrections for the Government did injure their pre-rogative and infringe the peoples libertie which he would by noe meanes doe, whereupon the Governor for his protestation caused

---

[1] Come when Christmas comes?   *A. & W. I.*, 473, has 'Tom Long.'

him to be suspended from the Councill, the rest of the Lords deputies concurred with the Governor in his suspension which is an act that cannot be well resented by the Lords neither cann any Governor as the Lords have qualified it here expell any of the Lords deputies from the Councill being upon the matter coequall with himself without a breach of the Lords rights the rest of the deputies concurring herein introduce a Trample upon the Lords priviledg which is an Injurie to the Lords, which they doe not understand or att least will not indeavour to adjust; a small president in pointe of aut'ie within a little time will introduce a greater and time (if not rectified will) corroborate evill as good in a case of this nature, many here admire where my Lord Ashley hath met with his deputie and I am sorrie to heare them discourse of it how that he studied hard in a great strong house att London for a considerable time together, and hath appeared upon severall accounts (to their Knowledge in London) suitable onlje to the Qualitie of that academie &c Informer &c and one Pights Questers.

Deare Sir

I have not omitted any opportunity to send you an account of this Countrey which is both pleasant and fertill and of a new settlement the healthfullest as hath bein heard of. If I had 10000£ per. anum in England yet would I have an Interest here and if Ginger continues a price no doubt not of more then an ordinarie Liveing. I want only 25£ or thereabouts in bills or otherwise for Barbados to be returned in comodities such as are vendible in Bermuda, to buy me young heifers to stock my great lott with one Cooper and a Carpenter and then I should be soone settled and make comodities if I had a stock I could sett upp my Smith[1] which would be of advantage to me whereas now I can imploy him onlie in the feild. [4th page ends, on its margin comes:]

I have heard that the new Governor will write to the proprietors and bespatter me all he cann on purpose that I may not be concerned in anything for he hates anything that takes notice of his way he charged me the other night for inserting the people to mutinie I tould him I did not understand what he meant, one standing by tould him inciteing att which I could but smile which

---

[1] His servants were Jno. Humfreys and Christ: Swade.

inraged him so that I was comitted to the Martialls hand which
I did little value knoweing that there was noe such thing in nature
the next day the Countrey was to meete and there they all declared that there was not the least thought of any such thing
and prayed I should not be debarrd of my libitie so he discharged me for both sayeing he did not comitt me for speaking
for the people but for scratching my head and misdeameaneing
myself in his presence and thus inserting the people to mutinie,
it seems was the other day when we argued to have the concessions pursued, and against fines and punishm^{ts} without the rules
of the proprietors [Here on top margin 4th page.] y^n in a greate
furie he askt me whether I would not take the oath of allegiance
I answered I would take both allegiance and supremacie and
tould him I had taken ye oath of allegiance twice (but here we
have ye latitude to subscribe to a booke) you said he did not
take it in ye ould Governors time, nor sayd I nor did I denye
it, indeed ye ould Govn^{rs} election was not legall [5th page
begins.] R soe when he perceived it would not doe he tould me
that I should have noe priviledge there (a word he doth not
understand) I answered he might doe what he would soe by
this meanes he thought to take away my inclination from appearing in the behalfe of the people, the truth of it is they are now
senscible of their ignorance and the labrinth they would involve
the people in by their simplicitie and would deterr any bodie
from acquainting the Lords proprietors with the state of things
and to that end he hath ordered that noe Trade should be carried
off before he should see them, I beseech you make it your bus-
nes to inquire about us and give noe credit to what they say ex
parte and I pray you if anything comes from them tending in the
least to anything of dishonor, injustice discourteousnes and but
the publick good and welfare of this Countrey ye cleere hon^r of
the Lords and the good of us all by me att any time proposed
that you look not upon it as they rend^r but as it wilbe made
here to appeare and as it is in itself, therefore that I may not
suffer for the present in the oppinion of any bodie soe compose it
that as to my deportm^t here that it be examined by any man of
reason and knowledge and if a new Governer doth come that
my particular be recomended to him and that if in the least he
finds me otherwise then endeavouring the good and amitie and
the incouraging of industrie then I will forfeite my life and

acknowledge myself guiltie I cannot imagin that they wilbe so simply ridiculous as to rend[r] themselves soe poore and meane as to doe it but be it what it will I be adjusted by the Testimonie of all the Countrey that if in the least it tends to any disrepute for anything said or don since I cam to this place that its malicicious and erronious I pray speake to my Lord and procure his L[re] to Sir Jno. Yeamans to see me righted if he comes Governor or to any other person that is to be appointed which I pray hasten for the good of the settlm[t] I thank God I am as forward in my planta-tions as any man in the Country and rather and they that the Councill most of them have not one serv[t] [1] nor any concernes but only once seemed to be zealous in the ould Governors time and for their knowledge in anything besides ignorance God de-liver us all only their Clark and he hath much adoe to under-stand and what they would have him to insert. I pray mind this affaire I had much adoe to convey this the person that brought understands the affaires all as well as cann be. [2]

Addressed: To Robert Blayney Esq[r] att ye r[t] hon[eble] ye Lord
Ashley att exeter house in the strand London.

Endorsed by *Locke:* W[m] Own to M[r] Blany 22 mar. $\frac{70}{71}$
Ashley River These.

[*S. P.,* Bdle. 48, No. 66.]

"AN OLD LETTER."

Honnored S[r]

The mouth of our River w[ch] by the Indians is called Kia-wa but by vs Ashley Riuer is scituate in ye Lat of 32[d] 35[m] an ex-cellent climate & neere to w[ch] Latitude & in ye same parallel are many healthy, fferteele & prosperous Kingdoms Countrys & Prouinces & not at all to fflatter yo[r] Honno[rs] or ye world so farre as I have read heard or believed I question not but this may compare wth any in ye world for either health, pleasure, profit or delight our Riuer large and spacious but a broad Marsh of each

---

[1] Donne and Marshall had none; P. Smith and S. West few. See Brayne's opinion, page 214: their clerk was Jos. Dalton.

[2] "This is a most confusing letter and it is probable the transcriber has not copied all in the right order—which I scarcely think he has." *W. N. S.* (He put margin 2d, top page 4th and marg. 3d pages, after 5th page; the order here adopted resembles that of *A. & W. I.,* 473.)

side yet the Creeks are very thick wch runn vp boldly to ye Land soe that in most of ye Creeks shipps of 3 or 4 hundred tunns may with skidds load or disburthen themselves upon the shore[1] the Rivers and Creeks ffull of diverse sorts of excellent good ffish all ye Sumer the Country soe plaine & Leuyll that it may be compared to a Bowling ally full of dainty brooks & Riuers of running Water wch are gennerally sweet & good & excellent purgers & clearers of vrin. ffull of faire large & Stately timber. Gallant Groues of Pines, 70—80—100 feet long straight as an arrow and very large wth all; Delightfull forrests of Oake, Ash, Walnutt Poplars & almost all others wth some Cedar y^t full of diuers sorts of excellent fruits as strawberrys mulberrys Peaches, Apricocks Bullys Nutts wth a multitude besides. The Woods may rather be called a Garden then an vntild place in respect of ye Variety of Garden herbs wch Grow wild & vnregarded of ye brutish natiues ye Woods & Riuers plentifull of all manner of winged foule. I speake wth in compass I haue seene millions of ducks in a fflock in soe much that they haue darkened ye skye. Inumerable of Turkeys Geese Cranes Herons Curlews wth abundance other smaller birds as Pidgeons[2] Turtle doues, Partridge, Phesant, and many others. It would rauish a man to heare in a morning ye various notes & ye chanting Harmonious sounds wch these dainty Wing'd creatures soe delicately warble forth in ye Aire. And for hunting here is pleasure enough mixt wth something of profitt. The woods are full of Deere, hares Connys & diuers other beasts worth looking after. Good turtelling in time of yeare. Our Cattle (though in more Northwesterly Countrys are Ready to starue all ye Winter here are fitt for ye knife all ye yeare. Hoggs, sheep goates & all other serviceable creatures thriue here very well. Yet we are something in feare of ye Wolues[3] wch are too plenty. And as for ye

---

[1] Page 210. Walnut or hickory? bullaces there were but no apricots. Ash says, 1680, 'the peach tree in incredible numbers grows wild.'

[2] Pigeons are not now seen on the coast and seldom of late even in the mountains. Pheasants were, perhaps, ruffled grouse, but hardly on the coast; Woodward may have seen them inland.

[3] Wolves still appear occasionally in the mountains. Act 169⅚ required of Indians 'one woolfes, tygers or beares or two catt skinns' yearly. Acts 'to encourage destroying beast of prey' 1700, 1703, 1726, 1733 gave 5s: to 20s: for every wolf, Tyger, bear or wild catt, and 1786, 'for a panther or tiger 10s: for a wolf 10, for a wild cat 5s.'

Snakes wch are here we mind them not at all, not one of us thanks be to God binn hurt or touched by them. The place is very healthy not one Master of a ffamily since ye Settlem^t hath died here excepting o^r good Aged Gouerno^r Colonel William Saile who was at least 80 years of age—not one man now in ye Collony there being about 200 y^t is at all distempered wth any sickness. Not anything we plant here but comes vp & thriues very well. All sorts of corne pease & other Graine like to prosper here exceedingly. Wee are in great hopes of Ginger Indigo Tobacco & Cotton[1] to be our maine Comodities, they all come up very well Potatoes like to thriue. Our towne called Albemarle point is scituate on a point wch is almost encompassed w^tn a large Marsh & may easily be strongly fortifyed wth a broad trench, it contains about 80 acres of Land. Our Winter soe mild & temperate y^t it may rather be termed a continuall spring y^n could weather the ffrost neuer causing Ice nor hardening ye Ground only leauing a white hoary dew wch is suddenly dryed vp wth ye least blast of ye sunn. Our Sumer not extreame hott to Ingender in ye Aire contagious Infections. The woods so cleare of copps or vnderwoods that a man may ride his horse[2] a hunting. And generally it may be said of this place as we read of ye Land of Canaan, the habitation of the then elect & chosen people of god it is a Land flowing with milk & honey, it Lyes in the same Latitude wth that & as farr as I have read or understand is endued as plentifully wth ye Benefitts & blessings of Almighty God. I pray God send us more thankfull spirits and gratefull hearts in acknowledgment of this great mercy of God in thus seating us then those stubborne hard hearted stiffnecked and rebellious Jews.

Endorsed : An old Letter. (About March 1671?).

[*S. P.*, Bdle. 48, No. 85.]

---

[1] A true prediction. 80 for 8 acres, page 283. See pages 173, 196.

[2] Had they horses already? Mares were brought from N. York Dec., 1671, and possibly before from Virginia, page 242. They had many, 1673, *C. J., Sep. 3.* Horses were strange to the S'n Indians, page 201. The Cusitaws called those at Virginia 'great deer.' But horse in the Creek tongue is *echolucco*, 'the great deer.'—*Bartram.* See *Adair,* 'horserope,' *hissooba* (Elk), *tarakshe* (to tie).

22

MARCH 24, 1671, WARRANT to Sir Thomas Chicheley, Knt., Master of the Ordnance, To deliver to such as Anthony Lord Ashley shall appoint, four sacres, four minions and four drakes, with ship carriages to each, to be used in the plantation of Carolina in the West Indies (¾ p. *Dom. En. Bk.* 19, p. 53). *A. & W. I.*, § 478.

LORD ASHLEY TO JOSEPH DALTON.

Mr. Dalton,

You are in soe good Esteeme with us all here that you need not doubt from us those Incouragements to which you may have any just pretences.   Wee are all willing to continue you in the office of Secretary in the discharge of which Imployment wee have noe complaynts against you, and I hope you will soe behave your selfe in your trust as to give us reason alwayes to thinke you as wee doe now, the fittest man for that Place you will by this ship receive a Paper Booke[1] as you desired and what other things or persons your friends here shall send you their Transportation & freight free   I take kindly from you the Letter you sent me and am.

Your affectionate friend

ASHLEY.

Exeter House, Aprill 10. 1671.

[*S. P.*, Bdle. 48, No. 55, p. 13.]

LORD ASHLEY TO GOV. SAYLE.

Colonel Sayle,

The River and Place you have chosen to plant on though it be not that wee intended when our ships went out of England yet it is soe much better and soe well fitted to all the ends of our Present Designe that wee very much approve of your remove from Port Royal to Ashley River[2] and think that Charles Towne where you are settled is very convenient for our new settlement both for its strength and that plenty which the Nobility of the soyle round about will afford the Inhabitants From this hopefull

---

[1] In it the extant Council Journals were probably kept as they begin soon after the Blessings arrival.   See p. 330, *Dalcho* 10, 11.

[2] The name perhaps eased L'd Ashley in abandoning Pt. Royal.

begining wee expect much good success which wee promise to
ourselves from your Integrity and experience and carefull management of that Trust wee repose in you, But yet I must com-
playne to you that you have refused an observance of our Instructions because signed onely by Sir Peter Colleton and me
Wee two having the great care of this businesse left to us had
reason to expect that our orders would not be disputed   Nor
cane wee immagine you would vary from them unlesse upon
measures that will be more advantagiouse to the common Interest
of   then those wee sent you.   Wee have been exceedingly
concernd and at great Charges for the supplying you with all
Necessarys and wee must in Justice expect from the People
there, and you in Particular, that you will be very carefull of our
Interest and Expectations (which are very moderate and faire)
should be justly and punctually complyed with   I am forced to
minde you this, in that our ship the Carolina in September last
went away for Barbadoes, not for our advantage but other mens,
who were not hinderd by the hast of that voyage from loading
Timber for themselves.   And the stay of above 20 days upon
the River would me thinke have afforded time to take in some
upon our Account had our concerns been regarded I must recommend to you the Desire wee all have that you would be very
punctuall in observing the instructions you receive from us.
Amongst which there is none of more consequence than the
security and thriving of our Settlement, than that of planting in
Townes, in which if men be not overruled theire Rashnesse and
Folly will expose the Plantation to Ruin.   The difference whereof
is apparent in New England and Virginia In the pressing of this
soe absolutely on the People, wee have noe other designe but
their safety and advantages.   Neither shall they or you in Particular want any incouragement from us whilst every one in his
place will but contribute his Part to the Promotion of the common Good of the Plantation the chiefe thing that wee aime at.

   Mr O. Sullivan charged upon me a Bill of £20. which he pretends he took up for the use of the Passengers and layd out in
Provisions for them in Bermudos.   He had noe authority from
me or any of the Lords Proprietors to doe any such thing M^r
West being commissioned by us as our Agent, I desire to know
whether you gave him any order for soe doeing or whether the
People wee sent stood in any such need when they were in the

Bermudos and whether M[r] Sullivan did with his money buy necessary Provisions which he distributed among the Passengers.[1] In answer to your Desires concerning M[r] Samson Bond wee writt formerly both to him and you to let you know that if he would come to Carolina he should have 500 acres of land £40. per annum and an house but though wee allow him this Salary and Alotment of land to be the Preacher among you yet wee give neither him nor you Authority to compell any one in matters of Religion having in our Fundamental Constitutions[2] granted a freedom in that Pointe which wee resolve to keep inviolable

I am Your very affec[ate] friend

ASHLEY.

Exeter House 10. Aprill, 71.

[S. P., Bdle. 48, No. 55, page 15.]

———

LORD ASHLEY TO STEPHEN BULL.

M[r] Bull,

Your behaviour in our Government I finde is agreable to the good character I have received of you wherein you doe a very acceptable thing to the Lords Proprietors and me in Particular, from you may assure yourselfe of a due acknowledgement and you may be confident that I shall be carefull of you and your Concerns there, whilst you are not wanting to encourage the continuance of my kindnesse in those wayes which have hitherto deserved it   I am very well satisfied with the goodnesse of the climate and Country you are pitched in the Particular accompt whereof which you have given me in your Letter I thank you for, and I desire you to continue your Correspondence with me, and to send me as often as you have oppertunity notice of the whole state of our Plantation and the Neighbourhood.   Wee have now sent you another ship[3] filled with People and designe

---

[1] O'Sullivan, see pages 160, 189, 208. Mr. Bond, page 171.

[2] Sec. 87, &c. In 2d set was inserted (contrary, 'tis said, to Mr. Locke's judgment by one of the Proprietors), Art. 96, establishing ' as the country comes to be sufficiently planted &c the Church of England, which being the only true and orthodox, and the national religion of all the Kings dominions, is so also of Carolina &c.'

[3] The Blessing, sailed May 14? Bull's letter, p. 192. His brother was perhaps John Bull, of London, mercht., of new Royal African Co.

not to stop in our supplyes till you are a thousand strong.   Wee onely expect that the Peoples cariage and regard to our Interest should be answerable to the care wee have of them and intend to continue.   I have acquainted your brother that the things or persons hee will send you shall be freight free

I am Your affec^{ate} friend

ASHLEY.

Exeter House Aprill 10, 1671.

[*S. P.*, Bdle. 48, No. 55, page 27.]

LORD ASHLEY TO WILLIAM OWEN.

Mr Owen,

I returne you my thanks for the Letter you sent me wherein you have given soe discreet and impartiall an Information of the state of our affairs there and the Correspondence wee have or may expect from our Neighbours round about us that I think wee may well take our measures from thence.   To this purpose we intend not to slacken our hands till wee have brought such an addition of People to you as you have therein mentioned to be sufficient for the support and security of that Plantation but whilst wee are at great charge and are very carefull to promote the interest and good of the Plantation and supply the People with those things that their present necessitys require Wee hope they will not fayle to answer our expectations but will be like-wise carefull of our just interest there And soe long you need not doubt of our constant Assistance And that I may from time to time be able to judge what may be most convenient and advav-tagiouse for your Settlement you will doe me and yourselfe a kindnesse (as often as you have oppertunity of sending) to give me notice of the condition of your Affairs and all the concern-ments of your Colony from whose hands, haveing already re-ceived soe rational and useful an Accompt I promise myselfe I shall be impartially informed of all things of moment there. And what ever may be fit to be taken into our consideration, and particularly I desire you to send me word whether the In-dian Cassiques your Neighbours be absolute supreame Lords, in theire owne Territorys, or else be Tributary Princes and pay subjection and homage to any greater King who is theire Em-peror.   You will always finde me ready to favour all your

reasonable Desires.   And you need not doubt but the rest of the
Lords Proprietors will not be sparing of an Incouragement to a
man that shall be carefull of and contribute to the Publique welfare of our People there.   Wee have according to your request
granted you Freight free for what things or Persons your friends
shall now send you out of England and have signified soe much
to them.

I am Your very affec^{ate} friend,

ASHLEY.

Exeter House Aprill 10, 71.

[*S. P.*, Bdle. 48, No. 55, p. 37.]

To Sir Jno: Yeomans.

Sir,

I thanke you for the favour of your letter and Present and
am very pleased to receive the first fruits[1] of our Plantation at
Ashley River from your hands who have been soe forward to
promote our settlement there and doe still oblige us by the continuance of your kindnesse to it Wee have expressed the sense
wee have of your Assistance to that Designe in a Patent for
Landgrave, which wee herewith send you.   And have soe far
considered your Exceptions to the descent and devolution thereof
as to establish that part of our Constitutions[2] according to your
desire soe that it shall not be in any danger of goeing out of the
Family, as long as any one of it remaynes Wee haveing noe
other Aime in the frameing of our Laws but to make every one
as safe and as happy as the state of Humane Affairs is capable
of, and soe to order every ones condition as that altogether may
make us a quiet equall and lasting Government wherein every
mans Right Property and Welfare may be soe fenc'd in and
secured that the preservation of the Government may be every
ones Interest   And in order to the general good of the Plantation
I must recommend to you as very necessary to our Government

---

[1] Cedar planks, page 220.   April 5, 1671, Draft of a patent for Landgrave of Carolina to Sir John Yeamans.   In John Locke's handwriting
with corrections and additions.   *Latin 2 pp.   Endorsed.*   (*S. P.*, 48, No.
78.)   *A. & W. I.*, 484.   Like patents to John Locke and Jas. Carteret.

[2] Sec. 11, Yeaman's letters, pages 164, 219.

the Planting of People in Townes   The Cheife thing that hath
given New England soe much the advantage over Virginia and
advanced that Plantation in so short a time to the height it is
now at I desire therefore that when you goe to Carolina this
summer that you give your direction and Assistance in it and
put them in such a way of settling in Towns as may be most
equall and convenient for the Planters and soe order the home
Lots in every Colony (Wee requiring that all the Inhabitants of
every Colony should set there houses togeather in one Place
which Place wee leave to the choice of the Inhabitants themselves)
that those who are to come after may share in the conveniency of
the Townes and have an equall Proportion of home Lots left
them.   I have moved the rest of the Lords Proprietors in the
behalfe of Mr Woodward who have sent him £100 besides which
I have sent him £20 of my owne, which is not all wee intend to
doe for him; onely wee desire that whilst his stay there is necessary to maintaine the Correspondence betweene our People and
the Indians he would be perswaded to stay there where wee
shall be sure to be minedfull of him.   Of these and the other
concerns of our Plantation wee know you will take care when
you goe thither.   From whence I hope to hear from you, who
by the continuance of your Correspondence with me will obleige,

        Sir Your affec^{ate} friend and servant

                                        ASHLEY.

    Exeter House 10. Aprill 1671.

            [S. P., Bdle. 48, No. 55, p. 73.]

            ———

        LORD ASHLEY TO HENRY WOODWARD.

Mr Woodward,

    I thinke myselfe obliged to take care of you and your con-
cernments and whilst I may doe you any kindnesse you shall
have noe reason to repent the paynes you have taken, and the
ventures you have run in Carolina in order to our settlement
there.   To make you some present acknowledgement for what
you have done for us, I have recommended your services to the
rest of the Lords Proprietors, and wee have out of our Publick

stock ordered you a hundred pounds which you may take up
either part or the whole in servants or goods out of our stores
at Charles Towne such as you like best or else may have any
part of it sent from England, Barbadoes, Virginia or any other
place with which you have Commerce in such commodityes as
you desire In any of which Ports wee will give you creditt accordingly, Besides my share in the £100 sent you out of the common stock of the Lords Proprietors I send you £20. as a particular gratuity from my selfe which you shall have returned to
you from any Port where wee have Trade in such things as you
shall make choice of.   Besides the Correspondence you manage
for us with the Neighbour Indians I heare you have been 14
days journey up in the Country with a great Emperor there with
whom you have made a League and where you have discovered
things · which you thinke not fit to reveale to any but us ourselves.   You have done very discreetly in that silence, And I
wish that the condition of our People there did not yet a while
need your stay amonge them.   For the keeping up the Friendship and commerce (among) with our Neighbours with whose
language and Customes you are soe well (accustomed) acquainted.
That noe body cane be soe helpful to our settlement in that part
as you And our Planters till they have learnt the Natives language and get into a better knowledge of them cannot I feare well
spare you Wee must therefore for sometime yet deny ourselves
the satisfaction of those discoveries you reserve for us till you
come to England and doe desire you would not leave our Plantation till the Indians and our People are growne into soe good
an Acquaintance one with another as not to need an Interpreter
between them.   If those Inland Countrys have given you any
knowledge or conjecture of Mines there I earnestly desire you
not to give the least hint of it to anybody whatsoever For feare
our People being tempted by the hopes of present gaine should
forsake their Plantation and soe run themselves into certaine
Ruine which has followed all those who formerly though in
greater Numbers then wee have there now marched into this
Country in Search of Gold and Silver.   Pray therefore if there
be any such thing keep it secreet to yourselfe alone but if it
should be convenient, as perhaps it may to give me some hint
of it in Letters to me Pray call gold always Antimony and Silver

Iron by which I shall be able to understand you without any danger if your Letters should fall into other hands.

I am Your very affec^{ate} friend

ASHLEY.

Exeter House Aprill 10. 71.

[*S. P.*, Bdle. 48, No. 55, page 77.]

WEST 27 APRILL 71.

Mr West,

I am to informe you that the plantation you manage is noe more upon the private account of Sir G. Carteret, Sir P. Colleton and myself but upon the account of all the Lords Proprietors soe that the cattle that you have taken for that plantation or anything else out of the Stores for that use is not to be satisfied for to the publique stock.

This we have donne to avoid confusion amongst our selves. I am somewhat unsatisfied that the Carolina when she went to Barbadoes had noe timber at all loaden in her upon our account and yet a great deale upon private mens of which at least we should have had our share for f./rait.   But I am not satisfied with Brain in any one of the voyages he hath made[1] and I thinke it necessary to tell you that both myself and the rest of the Lords Proprietors are apprehensive that Sir P. Coll: may have advantage of us by his interest and mingleing of trade with the Barbados.   I expect you make noe words of this but that you keepe yourselfe steddy to the interest of the Lds and suffer not Sir P. Colleton to make either in your affair or any other of the affairs upon the publique stock in that place an advantage beyond the rest of the Lds to their prejudice.   I did expect from you and doe still an account to be kept (and a copy thereof sent us from time to tyme) of our Stores to whome delivered and at what rates, that soe we may be repaid in worke timber or goods, as may best consist with the ease of the planters.   I must confess freely to you I have not been a little unsatisfied about it for a discouragement of that nature strikes at the very being of the plantation.   For if we be not satisfied that we have faire dealeing we shall stop our supplying.   Therefore pray let us have an

---

His ship went to London Aug., 1671? and returned no more.

exact and satisfactory account by every ship. I did not think the Governor would have disputed any instructions he had seen signed with Sir P. Colleton's hand and mine I doe not understand upon what measures he did it and cannot imagine he should deviate from those rules we had set unless it were to order the disposeing of our Stores more to the Lds P^rs advantage, in some things which possibly at this distance we could not foresee. I approve well of your takeing Capt. Baylys 4 servants into our imploym^t. But if Capt: Bayly or any one authorized by him require it we would have them restored we enterteining them only in our service till they can returne to his

I am Your very affec^ate friend

ASHLEY.

Exeter House 27° Apr: 71.

[*In Locke's hand.* S. P., Bdle. 48, No. 55, page 88.]

CAPTAIN HALSTEDS [1] INSTRUCTIONS.

1 May 1671.

1. Capt Halsted, God sending you safe to River Ashley, You are to deliver ye eight lesser Guns [2] with theire Carriages to ye Governor & Councel there, & you are with all convenient speed to procure a loading of timber, pipe staves & other Commoditys to ye Ship Blessing, fit for ye Market of Barbados, of wch you are to get ye best information you can of persons upon ye place, and if need be to make use of ye Lords Proprietors Servants under ye care of Mr West to helpe to fell and load ye same.

2. Dureing ye loading of ye Ship you are to take an acc^t of Mr Joseph West, concerning those following particulars. What they were. How they have been disposed of. How those y^t have been disposed of are to be payd for, & what remaines. 1. The

---

[1] Mathias Halsted, of the 'Blessing,' reached Carolina Aug. 14, 1671, sailed to New York, returning Dec. 13 to Ashly river, there quarreled with the Council and was imprisoned, then sailed to Barbadoes, was there March, 1672, and in Carolina again, whence, June, 1673, he took the Blessing to England. He was there discharged, and Nov., 1674, the L'ds Propr's 'are very much importuned by that idle fellow Halsted, who used us so ill.'

[2] Minions and drakes, see page 310, the sakers at the Bahamas.

Provisions of Victuals put on shoare at theire first landing.   2.
The Provision of cloths.   3. The Stores of War.   4. What
Cask was put on shoare, yᵗ ye rest may be accounted for by Mʳ
Braine.   5. The Fishing Trade.   6. The Indian Trade.   7.
£26. 5ˢ 6ᵈ, ye remainder of £61 pᵈ Mʳ West by Mʳ Portman
upon my Lᵈ Ashley's order, wᶜʰ £26 5ˢ 6ᵈ Mʳ West never accounted for.   8. The Cargo from Virginia.   9. The Provisions
received from Bermudos.   10. The Lords Propʳˢ finde yᵗ Mʳ West
and Mʳ Brayne at theire being at Bermudas, drue upon Mʳ
Colleton two six thousands pounds of Sugars & since yᵗ 12,000
pounds more of sugar hath been drawne upon Mʳ Colleton.
Wee desire to know what this 24,000 pounds of sugar was layd
out in, and how ye effects disposed of.   11. The Beefe & Flower
sent by Mʳ Colleton.

3. At your comeing alsoe to Ashly River, you are to deliver
ye cargo to Mʳ West and take his receite for all ye particulars
thereof.

4. If you have anytime dureing ye Ships loadeing at Ashley
River, ye are to take a view of ye Countrey, especially of ye
River Ashley & thereon to seeke for a healthy highland, convenient to set out a Towne on as high up as a Ship can well be
carried, and of this to bringe up a particular exact Description,
ye same thing you (if you have time,) are to doe in Wando
River, and alsoe Sewa River.

5. You are to informe yʳselfe alsoe dureing ye stay you shall
at any time make in Carolina, concerning ye healthynesse, rich-
nesse & other Propertys of ye soyle, ye usefull Productions of
ye Countrey, & enquire wᵗ masts ye Countrey products, of wᵗ
Diameter ye largest, and whether ye great ones grow near ye
sides of any Rivers by wᶜʰ they may by water be brought to the
ship, & to bring Samples of Casini[1] and theire dying Stuffes, &c.

6. As soone as ye ship is loaden you are to goe with her to
Berbados, & there touch at Augustins & enquire of ye health
of yᵗ Island, & if you find you may safely trade there you are
to sayle to ye bridge Towne, & there dispose of ye Timber,
&c. on board ye best you can for our advantage, selling it if

---

[1] The famous Cassiny, whose admirable and incomparable virtues are
extolled by the French and Spanish writers, *Car. 2*, page 70. Austin's
bay and St. Michael's town, Barbadoes.

possible you can for ready money, if you cannot you are to consult with Mr J^{no} Strode, & take all other ways you can to informe yourselfe w^t persons you may trust.

7. If you have trade at Berbados, you are to consult with Sir J^n° Yeamans & Mr Tho: Colleton of ye best course you can take to get a quicke fraught of Passengers for River Ashley (ye carrying of Passengers being ye maine end of our sending out this Ship,) and you are to lay out ye produce of ye Cargo of Timber, &c, & what you shall get for fraught of Passengers, &c in Rum and Sugar and other goods fit to make a Cargo for ye trade of Virginia.

8. At Berbados you are to enquire and bring us an acc^t w^t those Bills charged upon us by Mr Colleton were for.

9. As soon as you have gotten your loading of Passengers you are to sayle to River Ashley againe, and as soon as ye Ship is there delivered you are to sayle to Virginia and there lay out ye produce of y^r Rum & Sugar in Cattle, wch you are to transport to Ashley River, and these deliver to Mr West, ye remainder of y^r Cargo you are to lay out in Provisions, &c, fit for ye market of Berbados, if there be not any need of them in Carolina.

10. Dureing your stay in Virginia you are to state ye acc^{ts} between us & Mr Godwin & Mr Bennet, concerning wch you must remember.   1st That they gave us noe acc^t at all w^t our Cargo[1] yielded wch came into theire hands, as appears by their letters, & whereof you have an Invoye was sold for there.   2^d Mr Bennet states his acc^t to us in money, whereas ye Scale of Commerce in that Countrey being Tobacco, we have reason by ye prices wee finde sett downe in his acc^t to thinke he recond all those things too dear, w^{ch}, 3^d Wee have more reason to suspect because he hath not as Mr Godwin has set downe in his acc^t ye Persons from whom he bought those things wee had of him. Concerning all these acc^{ts} of Virginia, ye rates of ye things therein mentioned, & ye way how wee may have right done us you are to apply y^{r}selfe to Sr William Berkley & Sr Henry Chichley & Mr Applewaight, and to informe yourselfe by any other ways y^t you can.

11. God sending you safe to River Ashley you are to sayle to

---

[1] See pages 152, 163, 177, 178, 326.   Sir W. Berkeley, Gov. Virginia.

Berbados with another Cargo of Timber, &c, ye produce whereof you are to invest in a Cargo fit for ye Bahamas, and if Passengers doe present, to sayle from thence to Ashley River, and from Ashley River to New Providence, and there to deliver ye Boxes and Letters sent by you, & ye 4 Sakers with theire Carriages, & ye shot belonging to them, and ye 2 Barrells of Powder to ye Governor there, for ye use of ye Island, and make use of his assistance for ye sale of ye rum and Sugar for ye procureing you a loading of Brasiletto wood, and w^t else is to be had there fit for ye Market of England, with w^{ch}, if ye ship be full you are to come directly for London, if shee be not, you are to touch againe at River Ashley, and fill her with ye best Stocks of Cedar you can finde, & from thence to sayle for London.

12. If you shall judge it unsafe to trade at Barbados by reason of any infectiouse disease there, you are then with as much safety as you can to deliver ye Timber to Mr J^{no} Strode, & haveing gotten on board things necessary to load salt, you are to sayle to the Salt Tortugos, and there load your Ship with Salt, & sayle with her to Virginia, & from thence, as above directed.

13. In all ye trips you shall make to any place in ye West Indies, yo^u are still to remember y^t ye cheife imploym^t, wee send our ship for is to carry people to our Plantacon at Ashley River, wch designe you are mainly to intend and to minde ye other businesse of Traffique but as it may be in subserviency to y^t, and in concurrence therewth, may helpe to beare ye charges of our Ship whilst shee is abroade.

14. In all ye places you goe, you are to learne as much as you can any of ye husbandry of Manufactures of ye place, wch may be usefull to our people in Carolina, as particularly in Virginia ye sorts & ordering of mulberry trees, silkworms & all belonging to ye right way of makeing ye best Silk, Tobacco, Indigo, Cotton &c., & this to communicate to our people at Ashley River, & particularly you are to carry from Virginia some of ye best sort of mulberry trees for Silkworms & plant them there.

15. You are to consult with ye Governor & Councel at Ashley River about ye best way of disposeing of our Stores, and our being repayd by ye People for w^t wee trust them with, and to informe them y^t as wee aime at theire thriveing, and to that end have been soe much out of purse, soe wee expect from them

faire and punctuall dealeing in repaying us for what wee let them have, upon wch faire dealing of theires will depend ye continuation of our Supplys.

16. If you shall by any accident at any time before your second voyage to Berbadoes touch at Bermudos, you are there to leave with Mr J^{no} Dorrell sen^r, ye Duplicates of our Dispatches[1] to New Providence, to be sent forwards thither by ye first opertunity.

17. If dureing y^r being abroad you shall finde y^t a Trip to any other place, or in any other order than w^t wee have here directed shall better serve to ye Lords Prop^{rs} designes of carrying people and turne to better account; Wee then leave it to your prudence, still keeping in your eye our mayne designe as in Article ye 13, onely wee would not have you at all goe to Jamaica upon any pretense.

18. You are to take an account of ye ships stores & ye expences thereof, from time to time dureing ye whole voyage.[2]

	CRAVEN,	G. CARTERET,
Whitehall, May 1°, 1671.	ASHLEY,	P. COLLETON.

[*Col. Ent. Book*, 20, p. 68.]   *Rivers S. C.*, p. 359.

———

'CAROLINA INSTRUCTIONS.'

1 May, 1671.

To the Governor and Council of Ashley River,

1. You are within thirty days after receit hereof to summon ye Freeholders of ye Plantation, & require them in our names to elect 20 persons who, togeather with our Deputys as our Rep-

---

[1] L'd Ashley to Hugh Wentworth, Gov'r of Bahama islands, April 12, 1671. He will receive with this the King's Patent for Providence and the rest of the Bahamas, &c., of which he has procured a Commission for him to be Governor, will readily do anything for him 'for the beginning of this and putting of it into my hands' &c. Intends that he and his posterity shall reap the benefit of having led a colony of English there. Nor shall he be unmindful of Mr. Dorrell who has a good share, &c., and has laid out money in transporting people thither. (*S. P.*, No. 55.)   *A. & W. I.*, ≀498. *See page* 161.

[2] This 18th article and the Prop'rs signatures are in Locke's hand.

resentatives,[1] for ye present are to be your Parliam', by and with whose consent, or ye major part of them, you are to make such Laws as you shall finde necessary wch Acts shall be in force as in y^t case is provided in our Fundamentall Constitutions & Temporary Laws.

2. After ye same maner till our Fundamentall Constitut^s can be put in practice·yo^u are to call a Parliam^t ye first Monday in Novemb^r every two years, and as often besides as ye state of our affaires in o^r Plantat^n shall require.

3. You are to require ye Parliam^t to choose five men whom they thinke fittest to be joyned with our five Deputys, who with ye five eldest men of the Nobility are to be your Grand Councell. * * *

7. When ye place for ye Town is chosen &c ye Surveyor shall lay out streets according to ye model herewith sent as near as ye particular scituation of ye place will admit &c. * * *

13. You are alsoe to send us a Description of River Ashley & Wando River, drawne by a Compasse and Scale, and a map of ye Country divided into Squares of 12,000 Acres apiece by lines runeing East & West, North & South.

14. If any people shall, with armes invade you and with Acts of Hostility molest you in your Plantacon, you are to defend yourselves against them and doe for your preservation and future Security what y^u shall finde requisite, but * * *

19. You are to take notice y^t wee have made Mr James Carteret, Sr Jno Yeamans and Mr J^{no} Locke, Landgraves, and you are accordingly to set them out theire Barronys according to our Fundamentall Constitucons and Temporary Lawes whenever they or either of them &c. shall require &c.

20. In ye granting and seting out every mans Lot you are to reserve convenient high ways from ye Colony Towne to ye Plantations y^t shall be beyond it, and from one Colony Towne to another.

CRAVEN,   ASHLEY,

G. CARTERET,   P. COLLETON,

White Hall, 1st May, 1671.

---

[1] The Governor represented Duke Albemarle, Palatine, 5 deputies: Lords Craven, Berkeley & Ashley, Sirs G. Carteret & P. Colleton, the Prop'rs residing in England and 5 Commoners, the people.

20 articles, with mem: in Lockes hand: That ye Model of ye Town mentioned 7,[1] was of streets runing strait, whereof ye largest was 80 foot, ye back street to y[t] 40 foot, ye next, 60 foot, & ye back street 30, w[ch] streets divided the Towne into squares, each of whose sides was 600 foot. [Col. En. Bk 20, pp. 62, 65] *Rivers S. C.,* pp. 366, 369.

"Temporary Laws, Carolina." (*May* 1671?)

It is resolved and agreed by ye L[ds] Propriet[rs] y[t] till by a Sufficient number of Inhabitants ye Governm[t] of Carolina can be administered according to ye Forme established in ye Fundamentall Constitutions.

1. That ye Palatine name a Governor, and each of ye L[ds] Propriet[rs] a Deputy, w[ch] Deputys, with an equall number of others chosen by ye Parliam[t], shall continue to be ye Councellors till ye L[ds] Propriet[rs] shall either order a new choice or ye Countrey be soe peopled as to be capable of ye Governm[t] according to ye fundamentall Constitutions; and when there shall be any Landgraves or Casiques created by ye L[ds] Propriet[rs], soe many of ye eldest in age of them that are resident in Carolina, as shall be equal to ye number of ye L[ds] Propriet[rs] Deputys, shall be alsoe of ye Councell, y[t] soe ye Nobility may have a share in ye Governm[t] and ye whole administration may still come as near ye forme designed as ye Circumstances of ye groweing Plantacon will permitt.

2. The Governor, with ye Lords Prop[rs] Deputys, ye Landgraves and Cassiques y[t] are Councellors, and those chosen by ye Parliam[t], shall be ye Grand Councell, and shall have all ye power and authority of ye Grand Councell and other Courts till they come to be erected.

3. Besides ye Deputys for Councellors, The Chiefe Justice shall choose & constitute ye Provost Marshall. The Chancellor, ye Secretary. The Treasurer, ye Receiver. The High Steward, ye Surveyor. The High Chamberlaine, Register of Births, Burials & Marriages. The Admirall, Marshall of ye Admiralty.

4. The Article in ye Fundamental Constitutions beginning

---

[1] 'A model of a town was sent, which it will be well if the people of Carolina are able to build 100 years hence.' *Oldm. Car.* 2. p. 405.

thus [All ye Revenues & Profitts,] shall not take place till ye Lords Proprietors y^t have layd out money in carying on ye Plantacon be reimbursed with such satisfaction as shall be agreed on amongst them.

5- To suite ye begining of ye Government to y^t proportion of Land upon wch ye ballance of ye Settlem^t principally depends, and y^t by takeing up great Tracts of land sooner than they can be planted; great gaps may not be made in ye Plantation to ye prejudice of ye commerce, and exposeing ye safety of ye whole by stragling and distant Habitations. In ye first takeing up of Land each Proprietor shall have but 3 Signiorys, and each Landgrave and Cassique one Barrony set out for him till by increase of ye Inbabitants part of seventy-two Colonys shall be possessed by ye people, after wch time it shall be free for everyone to take up ye proportion of Land due to his dignity.

6. All Lords of Baronys and Mannors shall be obleiged to have each upon his Barrony 30 persons, and upon his mannor 15 persons respectively within seven years after ye date of his Grant, and whatsoever Lord of a Barrony or Mannor shall not have soe many persons on his Barony or Mannor respectively at ye end of ye s^d seaven years shall be lyable to such fine as ye Parliam^t in Carolina shall think fit, unless ye L^ds Prop^rs shall allow him longer time for ye planting his Barrony or Manor with people to that proportion.

7. All acts y^t shall be made by ye Parliam^t before our Govern' of Carolina be administred according to our Fundamentall Constitutions shall all cease and determine at ye end of ye first Session of Parliam^t y^t shall be called, chosen, and shall sit according to ye Articles concerneing Parliam^ts established in our Fundamentall Constitutions.

CRAVEN,   G. CARTERET,
ASHLEY,   P. COLLETON.

[*Col. Ent. Book,* 20, page 66.]   *Rivers, S. C.,* page 351

SIR H. CHICHLEY.[1]   71.

Sir,

I and the rest of the Lds Proprietors of Carolina are fallen into the hands ot two men of the country of Virginia who have

----

[1] Knt., Lieut.-General of the forces, 1673, and deputy Gov'r of Virginia, 1674. His brother, Sir Thos. Chichley, Knt., page 310.

23

by noe means used us well.   But soe ordered Affairs that where as wee might (upon a just estimate of what they have received from us and wee from them) expect that they should be in Debt to us, instead thereof they have charg'd Bills upon us here.   A more particular Account and State of the whole matter between us and the neighbours Mr Rich. Bennet and Mr Tho. Godwin you will receive from the bearer hereof Captain Halsted whom wee have been at the charge to send to Virginia on purpose to adjust and procure right to be donne us in these Accounts For it is not easy to us nor can wee patiently bear the Affront to have Bills drawne upon us which wee must refuse to pay unless wee will admitt of very unreasonable Accounts and readily pay whatsoever is Demanded.   Wee wish those Gent had considered that our Reputations were not easily to be brought in Question, or would not have made choice of us to impose upon.   However we Doubt not but the Justice of your Country will doe us right and wee shall not be forc'd to looke elsewhere for Redresse in this Matter which wee shall not leave till we have fairly cleared between us.   Sir the ill handling I have received from your Neighbours hath occasioned you this trouble and the Relation I have to your brother makes me confident you will doe me the favour to give our Agent Captain Halsted all the Assistance you can in this business Though wee are well assured by persons here well acquainted with the Affairs of Virginia that the prices in their Accts especially Mr Bennets are very extravagant yet you will doe us a kindness to shew Capt. Halsted the overvalues they have put upon theire Commodyties and what artifice they have used in the reconing to our Prejudice as alsoe what the commodyties wee sent them might reasonably yeild in your Market. This if you please to give yourselfe the trouble to doe, and to instruct him what course he is to take (if they refuse of themselves to come to reasonable Termes) for the expediteing the businesse and procureing a Quick Dispatch you will very much oblige

Sir Your very affecate friend

ASHLEY.

Exeter House May the 12th 71.

[*S. P.*, Bdle 48, No. 55, page 89.]

WM. SAILE 13° MAY. 71.

Sir,

Just as our ship is ready to saile[1] I receive an informacon from Barbadoes that Mr Woodward when he was up in the Emperor of Tatikequias country had then discovered that it bordered upon the Spaniards and that probably there were mines there. I apprehend this may be apt to tempt some of our people covitous of present booty to some attempt that way which you are to take notice we doe absolutely prohibit you and you are to take care not only that you suffer not the people out of greedinesse to molest either the Spaniards on that side or any of our neighbour Indians in their quiet possessions but we alsoe require that you avoid all searches too far that way least the Spaniards by that means discovering how neare you border on them should joyne all theire forces there and elsewhere to cutt you off and therefore that the people may goe noe farther up into the country then what shall be necessary to their planting. This you are to looke well after as you will answer it to his Majestie whose pleasure it is that we should keepe our selves within the rules of the peace. Neither doe we thinke it advantageous for our people to live by rapin and plunder which we doe not nor will not allow Planting and Trade is both our designe and your interest and if you will but therein follow our directions we shall lay a way open to you to gett all the Spaniards riches[2] in that Country with their consent, and without any hazard to yourselves, and therefore I must presse it upon you that you bind the peoples mind wholy to planting and trade, wherein if they will with industry and honestly imploy themselves they will not only answer his Majesty's and our ends of sending them thither but finde themselves with great safety and ease become masters of all that is desirable in those parts. If you finde that any such report is got amongst the people that farther up in the country there are mines of gold and silver I desire you would endeavour

---

[1] The Blessing, she sailed next day? By her went many people and all these papers April 10th to this: Sayle's were claimed by the Council in Carolina Dec. 20.   Information was from Yeamans, p. 220.

[2] Woodward, p. 186, in Yeamans, p. 220, L'd Ashleys policy checked inland discovery, *C. J.*, Oct. 7, 1673, but his prediction proved true.

to suppresse it and put it out of their heads by all means you can.   I am Your very affec^{ate} friend

ASHLEY.

Exeter House, 13° May. 71.

[*In Locke's hand: S. P.*, Bdle 48, No. 55, p. 91.]

THE SHIPP BLESSING.

A List of Bills as they were Signed 25th of May 1671 to be p^{d} by Mr Portman.

£	s	d		£	s	d
050	11	9	John Lewin sailemaker in St Katherines - - - - -	49	80	00
152	02	4	Thomas Martin Baker at ye Blewanck^{r} Limehose - - - -	151	—	00
148	10	4	Rich Whitepane Butcher in Little Eastchip - - - - -	146	00	00
2	17	2	Andrew Gimlow Cooke in Wappin	2	10	00
15	03	1	Hen: Man Boatmaker in Ratcliffe -	14	13	00
52	09	2	Robt Hooker Roapmaker in Shadwell - - - - - -	52	0	00
25	12	0	Wm Smith smith in Shadwell - -	24	10	00
18	18	5	Wm Hitchcock blockmaker in Wappin - - - - - -	17	10	00
1	05	7	Peter Williamson Compass maker in Wappin - - - - -	1	04	00
16	01	0	Robt Tayler brazier in Wappin -	16	00	00
1	01	0	Mary Hadock ffor Oakum in Wappin - - - - - -	1	00	00
3	00	7	John Watts oar maker in Wappin -	3	00	00
3	04	0	Reynold Peters bricklayer in Wappin - - - - - -	3	04	00
10	01	5	Robt Kingston turner in Wappin -	9	80	00
31	09	10	Ann Phillipps Brewer in Wappin -	31	00	00
32	06	8	Robt Kingston & Robt Thomson deale marchants in Wappin -	30	00	00
57	09	8	Ann Coxe Smith in Wapping -	54	00	00
9	13	1	Tho: Partridge plumer at ye Hermitage - - - - -	9	00	00
4	09	0	Hen: Williamson slopseller Mark lane - - - - -	4	00	00

5	14	5	Phillip Lane in Ratcliffe tallow Chandler - - - - -	5	14	00
0	16	0	John Dawson turner in Wappin -	—	16	00
22	15	6	John Kent ffishmonger at ye Her-mitage - - - - -	22	00	00
6	11	10	John Benbridge tarr March^{nt} in Wappin - - - - -	6	00	00
22	03	08	Edwd Tho: Norman Atway Ship Chandler in Tower S^t - -	21	00	00
3	10	0	Wm Carr Painter in Wapping -	3	10	00
46	12	4	John Goodman Cooper in Shadwell	45	00	00
12	01	5	Clarke Apothecary in Wappin	10	00	00
115	04	6	Rich: Potter Shipwright in Wappin	113	00	00
36	10	4	Rainsford Waterhouse Ship chand-ler - - - - - -	36	00	00
908	06	1		882	01	00
5	00	0	Julius ffowles pilate - - -	5	00	00
913	06	1		887	00	00
137	1	7	Julius ffoules	£ 5		
156	10	10	P. J. ffor Sev^{nts} &c	38	3	5
882			P. J. for Sug^r to Mr West	29	04	—
1175	12	5		72	07	5

[S. P., Bdle. 48, No. 74.][1]

---

[1] Sir J. Yeamans arrived in Carolina from Barbadoes about 1 July, 1671. (With or soon after him came Jno. Foster, Esq., Capt. Giles Hall, Messrs. Christ. Portman, Jno. Pinkard, Jno. Yeamans, Tim. Biggs? Amos Jeffords? Wm. Murrel, &c.) He claimed the government as sole Landgrave in the Province; a Parlia'mt was called by West July 8 and elected July 11, and Sir John chosen Speaker, but disputes arising it dissolved July 16. Five councillors were elected, and Sir John retired into the country disgusted and sent Dr. Woodward to Virginia, West Sept. '71. The Blessing sailed about May 14, 1671, touched at Barbadoes? and Bermuda, and reached Carolina Aug. 14th with 96 people— Mr. Edw. Mathews, Henry Pretty and perhaps Mr. Jno. Gardiner, Rich. Cole, Peter Hearn, Jos. Oldys, Tho. Hurt, Tho. Archcraft, other passengers and many servants, perhaps Rich. Nicklin, Wm. Argent, Rich. Batin, Wm. Barry, Jno. Chambers, Jno. Cooke, Tho. Laford, Ro. Lewis, Wm. Loe, Mich. Lovell, Tho. Munkaster, Dennis Mahoon, Phil. Onill, Jno. Rivers, Jas. Willoughby, &c.

1671 AUGUST 21 Lords Proprietors of Carolina commission to Sir John Yeamans, Governor of Carolina South and West of Cape Carteret granting him power to let set assure and convey lands with consent of his Council and as set forth in his instructions Also to execute all powers and authorities in relation to the government and in case of his absence to appoint a deputy. *Similar to a Commission to Gov. Wentworth of the Bahamas* (*A. W. I.*, 509). *The name of* Major Arkhurst Esq. *has been carefully erased and that of* Sir John Yeamans, Bart: *written over it by John Locke who in a mem.* (*at p. 76*) *writes that* on Dec: 26, 1671 Sir J. Yeamans was made Governor by a Commission in the same form under the Great Seal of the Province signed John Berkeley, Ashley, G. Carteret and P. Colleton. [*Col. En. Bk.*, 20, page 72.] *A. & W. I.*, § 606.

THE COUNCIL JOURNALS.

Council Journal[1] *25th August, 1671.* Charles Town in the Province of Carolina. Coll. Joseph West, Governour.

In the session of Parliament vizt. the 25th day of August 1671 at Charles Towne upon Ashley River in this Province of Carolina aforesaid pursuant to the Lords Proprietors directions The said Parliament[2] out of themselves chose five persons namely,

---

[1] 'The Grand Council which is the Senate of Carolina,' L'ds Prop'rs letter, 1682. *Rivers*, 396. This extant Journal is probably in Dalton's hand in the book mentioned, p. 310; the first five pages [Aug. 14.24 ?] are lost, *Dalcho*, 10. An order 18 Aug., 1671, directing Halsted's voyage to New York and account thereof on his return is mentioned Jan. 6, 167½. The members now were Gov. West, Sir G. Carteret's deputy, but acting Palatines deputy, Capt. Godfrey, L'd Craven's, Ste: Bull, L'd Ashley's, Wm. Owen, Sir P. Colleton's, Sir Jno Yeaman's, L'd Berkeley's, and Mr. Foster for Duke Albemarle?

[2] Elected under Instruc'n 1, page 322. Mr. Hughes came from England, 1669, settled a plant'n and servants, was chosen to Owens parliam't 1670, was in Council, 1671, and gave half his lands for new Charlestown, 1672 he was in parliam't and Capt. Godfrey's lieutenant. 1674 his wife was still in England. He died in Carolina, 168–? I[4], p. 169. Capt. Portman came from Barbadoes 1671? Settled a plant'n near 'Orange grove,' was chosen to the Council. April 20, 1672, he was elected to the new parliam't and the Council again. He sailed June, 1673, in the Blessing, but soon returned, was captain 1674 and Oct., 1675, in the Council, serving till 1676. He went to Barbadoes, and Oct., 1679, sails for Carolina in the sloop Endeavor, but probably returned to Barbadoes.

Mr. Thomas Gray, Mr. Maurice Mathews, Lieut Henry Hughes, Mr. Christopher Portman and Mr. Ralph Marshall and the same day returned the names of the said persons and presented them to the Governour and the Lords Proprietors Deputies to be joyned with the said Governour and Deputies as Members of the Grand Council for the people therein to act and doe as the Lords Proprietors have directed. *Sec: Stat: Off: Coun: Jour:* p. 6. *At a meeting of the Governour* and Councill August 28, 1671, sitting & present: The Governor, Sir John Yeamans, Capt. John Godfrey, Mr. Stephen Bull, Mr. Wm. Owen, Mr. Thos. Gray, Mr. John Foster, Mr. Maurice Mathews, Mr. Henry Hughes, Mr. Ralph Marshall. Upon full and mature deliberation had by the Governor and Councill upon the matter of the oath (as a Councellor &c., *Rivers*, 370). The question was raised whether the said oath ought to be taken by all that are of the Councill. Affirmants Mr. Henry Hughes Mr. Maurice Mathews Mr. Christopher Portman Mr. Thos. Gray Mr. Ralph Marshall Mr. Stephen Bull. Negants Sir John Yeamans refusing the question, the question was altered and put to him whether the Lords Proprietors Deputies as they are Councellors ought to take the oath Saith they ought to take it reserving the Lords rights. Soe saith the Governour. For a better encouragement of the Seaman belonging to the Lords Proprietors ship Blessing Capt. Mathias Halsted Commander It is ordered by the Governor & Councill that the said Seamen namely Thomas Weedland, Daniel Ming, Edward Ottaway, Thomas Bonick[1] Adrian Johnson, Richard Plummer, Edward Doe, Wm Boe, David Abercromby and Lawrence Chapman or their attorney or attorneys shall have Liberty to take their severall proportions of land in this Province as largely as is granted by the Lords Proprietors to other persons comeing at the same time, soe as the said Seamen doe come or send servants to inhabitt their said severall shares of land within the time afore limited all or such of the said Seamen soe fayling shall forfeit all and every such parcel of land taken up by virtue hereof, to be disposed of to any other person or persons willing to take up the same.

It is ordered by the Grand Councill that all and every the

---

[1] He only, perhaps, stayed in Carolina. May, 1684, a Charlestown lot was granted Tho. Bornick and Mary, his wife.

Seamen who have formerly taken up any land in this Province by any order warrant or other indulgence from the Governor and Councill and shall neglect to settle the same before the expiration of two years from the date thereof such persons soe fayling shall forfeit their severall shares of land to be disposed of as above directed. Upon hearing the petition of John Norton & Originall Jackson &c., see *Rivers*, p. 370. Capt Florence O'Sullivan Surveyor Generall of this Province and John Culpeper surveyor having this day come before the Governor & Councill did then and there declare an agreem^t &c.[1]

Maurice Mathews[2] to Lord Ashley.

The Riuer Ashley lyes in ye Latitude of 32° deg^rs 40 mints: as I Best guessed by all the Artists y^t haue been here yett; the Soyle is generally fruitfull, to the content of ye Best and Wisest

---

[1] "That s'd Surveyor Gen'l allow s'd Jno. Culpeper ¾ the fees, &c., divided according to the several notes given, &c., by the persons for any land so layd out ¾ to s'd Culpeper for his labour and paines therein and ¼ to the s'd Surveyor Gen'l, &c., s'd Culpeper shall likewise layout and finish all lands, &c., about Charles Towne and within the Compass of the ten acre lots and other small lots of land at present designed for the interment of people nere the Towne for their better safety and security, &c."

[2] An able, brave and active gentleman, who sailed, 1669, with his serv'ts to Barbadoes, thence in the sloop's dreadful six months' voyage to Kiawah. There he was of Owen's Parliam't, 1670, settled lands at Ickabee, made discoveries among the Kussoes, and June, 1671, up Ashley river. He was chosen to the Council, but suspended by Gov. West. Dec. 15 Ld. Ashley, for love of his uncles, made Mr. Mathews his deputy; he was made captain and by the Indians their casseeka. 1673, he went to the Esaws for help against the Westos, was captain in many actions of the time and Ld. Ashley's deputy till made Surveyor-General April 10, 1677, and May 22, 1679, was Ld. Craven's deputy. 1680, Capt. Mathews, 'an ingenious gentleman and agent for Sir P. Colleton's Carolina affairs,' had large plant'ns at Cotebas and Wadboo; was appointed to settle a beaver trade, and, 1682, to set out Craven and Colleton counties, Com'r to the Indians, and with Gov. Morton to buy lands of them. He engaged in the Westo wars, for which the Prop'rs, 1683-5, ordered his dismissal as deputy and Surveyor-Gen'l, and again, 1685, from the Council, but, 1686, for his services in buying lands of the Indians, gave him 1,000 acres. In 1690-91 Col. Mathews, with Capt. Moore, made discoveries in the Apalachian mountains. He died before 1694.

Plant^{r}s we haue; the mould is Black ½ A foot deep, in some places A foot, & more or Lesse according to itts propinquity to ye Water or pine Land, for in most Places ½ A mile or A mile from the Riuer side you will finde A veine of pines, wch is bad Lande, & hath its breadth according to ye vicinity of other riuers; great Creeks, marhes, or Savanoes on the other side, elce ye Intersection or Encroachm^t of other sorts of timb^r, but this Pine land, besides its Turpentine yeilds very good pasturage haueing Little or noe vnderwood, this Land bears very good white, red, black wat^r Spanish, & liue oak; Ash, Hickery, Poplar, Beach, Elme, Laurell, Bay, Sassaphrage, dogwood, Black Wallnutt. Where these 5 Last grow I generally obserue itt is good land, here is Cedars in sertaine places in Abundance, cypress here is (or all of vs are mistaken y^t haue seen of itt) this Cypress is Wonderfull Large and tall, and smooth, of A delicate graine & smells. some y^t did belonge to Captn Jen^{rs} shipp sent hither by Mr. Thomas Colleton, did say itt was not ye true Cypress; butt something elce, & y^t they in New England did sell it very deare for masts being much better for y^t use then Any wood in ye World butt whatsoever itt bee. I haue some reason within me not to belieue them; ore let it bee what it will it will hereafter be A good Comodity to ye prying planter y^t Lookes Abroad & it please god there shall some of itt come for England ye next opportunity, here is some holly, elder & witch hazell, & tenn thousand more plants, herbs, fruits then I know, figgs, & peaches enough plums of diuers sorts or kind of cherries, Berryes of sorts, Abundance, Indeed we haue had this yeare a great drought, butt although all things were put back, ye first raine wee had wch was on ye 16th of may did bring all things which seemed dead soe on y^t we not ouer much minded it, not doubting of A reasonable Crop, Indian Corne thriues very well, English pease there is noe feare will doe very well, butt ye next yeare wee must plant them I suppose about Christmass, ffor ye pease our Workmen spilt in ye Woods Last Septemb, grew well, & did come to very great perfection in february; when I & A great many more did eat of them Guiney Corne growes very well here, butt this being ye first I euer planted ye perfection I will not Auer till ye Winter doth come in, ginger thriues well butt ye perfection &c. Cotton growes freely butt ye perfection &c. Indigo for ye quantity (by the

approbation of our western planters I speake itt) I haue as good
as need bee, butt being butt Little & very little or none in ye
Colony I did nott Cutt it once, butt haue kept itt for Seed; some
whereof I haue already gathered, Potatoes doe very Consid'a-
bly; pumpkins, Water & musk melions thriues Admirably &
with little trouble.   Tobacco does very well   I haue now in Cure
as good as euer was smoakt, ye drought yᵗ I spoke of before,
the Indians say they never knew the like before.   The Indians
all About vs are our freinds; all yᵗ we haue knowledge of by
theyre Appearance and traid with vs are as followeth:

S* Helena ye Southermost;¹ Ishpow, Wimbee, Edista, Stono,
Keyawah, where we now liue, Kussoo to ye westward of vs,
Sampa, wando, Ituan, Gᵗ Pa;² Sewee, Santee, Wanniah, Elasie,
Isaw, Cotachicach, some˙ of these haue 4 or 5 Cassikaes more,
or Less Truly to define the power of these Cassikaes I must say
thus; it is noe more (scarce as much) as we owne to ye Topakin
in England, or A grauer person then our selues; I finde noe
tributaries among them, butt intermariages & pouerty causeth
them to visitt one Another; neuer quarelling who is ye better
man; they are generally poore & Spanish; Affraid of ye very
foot step of a Westoe; A sort of people yᵗ liue vp to the westward [which these say eat people and are great warriors]ᵗ; The
Generall Letters will informe of Treatys & matters of peace we
haue had of Late with them; before Winter comes in I hope if
God giues Leaue there will be A greater discouery made
Amongst them; About 2 or 3 months agoe [Mʳ Thos Gray]³ Mr.

---

¹At Pt. Royal; the Ashepoo, Wimbee, Edisto, Stono, Keyawah,
Wando, Ettiwan, Seewee, Santee, Sampit and Winyah were on those
rivers; the Kussoes on the freshes of Ashley and Edisto rivers; the Esaws
on bounds of N. Carolina east of the Catawbas; Cotachicach are the
Cusitaws. 169⅝, 'the natives of Sante Helena, Causa, Wimbehe, Com-
behe, Edistoe, Stonoe, Kiaway, Itwan, Seewee, Santee, Cussoes have
freely offered that each Indian bowman capable to kill deere bring in
yearly one woolfes skinn &c.' 1707, 'those called Cusabes, viz: Santees
Ittavans, Seawees, Stoanoes, Kiawaws, Kussoes, St Helena &c.' *and
Bohicotts. A. A.*, 2, 108, 309.

²*A. W. I.*, 610, has 'Sᵗ Pa.' Is it 'Sampa' repeated? or Sampit?
Sieur S. map 1680? shews the 'Sompa' W. of Cainhoi on N. side of
Wando river and the 'Wando' on the S. side opposite.

³Given, *A. & W. I.*, ⅝ 610; accidently omitted in our MS?

William Owen and myself made A discouery of this Riuer both by the Land & Watter when ye Carolina frigott Landed her Company here a small Bermuda shallop was sent vp to discouer the riuer; She in 2 or 3 dayes returned & reports y[t] the riuer 20 or 30 miles vpwards spent itt selfe in a marsh; butt I could never bee persuaded to it, nor ye Gent y[t] went vp with me w[ch] caused vs to take ye Trampoor and goe by land towards the head of the riuer, About 30 miles or more vpwards wee came Among the Cussoo Indians[1] our friends; with whome I had been twice before; from whome taking a point of the Compass we steered towards the head of the riuer; y[t] after noone as wee trauiled we found Cypress trees innumerable, very tall and large, they y[t] haue ye best skill here say it is the very best sort itt was not aboue 3 hours before wee came to the riuer, which wee found very narrow & betweene & vpon A continued Rock Like Barbadoes sandstone, there about we saw Ceedar & Cypress in noe small numb'; this done wee came home & ye next day after went vp againe by Watter in A boate and in one tide went vp farther then the aforesaide shallop had been.   Between 20 or 30 mile vp from ye Towne in this Journey wee saw seuerall excellent sauanas containing A vast quantity of Land; in one about 500 Acres wee saw dile & y[t] which wee call in England Withy; ye marshes of each side cease; & the riuer is wholy betweene & vpon A Rock,[2] very good Land, timber abundance, & cheifly white oakes, Cedar much near ye water side, & not a little Cypress, when wee went vp About 60 miles from the riuers mouth wee were stopt by trees y[t] Lay thwart ye Riuer throwne downe by weather or fallen by age, wee did seuerall times carry our boate ouer the trees; but ye Tide spent and night approaching, & our victuals not soe much as wee thought we came back, when you are about 12 Leagues within the riuers mouth ye Tide diuides itself, one branch runing norward; ye other it is which I haue been speaking of; The north riuer is commonly called Wandoe, they that haue been oftenest vp them say it is Excellent good Land, and as well Timberd as this; but truly y[t] as yet is vnknown to them, for they neuer vp this nor y[t] branch Aboue 10 or 15 miles; I haue been vp that riuer Aboue 10 miles from the diui-

---

[1]At head of Ashley river, extending across Stono to Edisto.

[2] Marl. *Dill* (sax. dile), herb, like fennel; *withy*, willows.

sion of both; & 20 or 30 by land I found y^t Land as good as any in this, & as well timbred. I hope before Winter to make a further discouery of it; fish there are in both riuers multitudes, As Bass, mullets, Old Wiffes; &c Places, scad, Thornbacks, drumes, &c. About ye riuers mouth & vp the riuer beyond ye mashes, vpon an Ebbe you shall finde the fish playing in crouds. they seem to be Trout or young salmons; or what euer they are; o^r Gou^r Capt West did assure me y^t the greater sort of them were Sturgeons, this was A weeke after the discouery when I went vp to shew him some land ducks & gees here and in the winter in multitudes. The Winter begins about the middle of 8^{ber}, & ends about ye middle of february, here is a heauy frost wch 2 hours sun Exhales. Ice here was last winter in our water pales but noe thicker then a shilling.

I beseech y^r Lordship pardon ye errors of clarke in this for ye ship being come to saile I haue not time to better it.

Endorsed by Locke.   Mr. Mathews to Ld Ashley 30th Aug^t *71*
Ashley river.

[*S. P.*, Bdle. 48, No. 75.]

GOV: WEST TO LORD ASHLEY.

May it please yor Lo^p

The safe arriuall of the ship Blessing the foureteenth of August last, gaue me the receipt of yor Lo^{ps} l're [page 317], by which I p'ceive the plantacon I now manage, is to be upon the publick Account of the Lords propriet^{rs} I shall use my uttmost endeauo^{rs} to answer the Lords expectacons of me, in all respects; I doe not doubt but to approue my selfe a faithfull serv^t to the Lords Propriet^{rs} and shall by the next send your Lo^p a p'fect account of all the goods and prouisions I have had in my custody, how disposed of, to whome, and at what rates; had I rec'ed any order for it before it had not been to doe now Inclosed is an Account of the thirty-six pounds rec'ed last by yor Lo^{ps} order, the other twenty-fiue pounds was accounted for with the three hundred, and seaventen pounds I rec'ed to pay sev'rall disbursm^{ts}, also herein inclosed is the account of the thirty pounds rec'ed to procure serv^{ts} in Ireland, wth another Account of fifteen pounds rec'ed in Barbadoes.

My Lord I must acknowledge the charge and Trust of yor

Lo^{ps} affaires in this Countrey upon me to be such, y^t I would seeme to degen'ate, should I not remember to yor Lo^p what are the disturbances of this Collony (though modesty may persuade to the contrary) wherein, I doe assure yor Lo^p I shall be very faithfull and just, free from any rancor, or mallice, and to noe other end but that yor Lo^p (knowing what o^r distempers are) may the better p^rpare a remedy.

Wee haue allwayes had some differences in the Collony but when Sr John Yeamans arriued here, I was in good hopes, y^t he with us, appearing to quiet the people, might giue good satis-faction, wherefore I aduised wth him for y^t purpose, he gaue me good assurance to beleeue, he intended it, but w^{th}in two or three dayes he retyred himselfe to his Countrey house,[1] being dis-gusted (as since I p'ceived) that ye people did not incline to salute him Gou'ne^r More people being now arriued the 8th of July last I summoned all the ffreemen, and required them in the Lords propriet^{rs} names to elect twenty persons to be of the parliament according to yor Lo^{ps} directions,[2] wch in three dayes was performed and their names returned; I appoynted them a meeting to putt themselves in an order of proceeding; Sr John being then chosen Speaker, declared that it was necessary for them to w^{th}draw to choose a Clarke, and after some argum^{ts} be-tweene Sr John and my selfe about it I p'mitted them; they stayed two hours from me hauing as I am informed had seu'all disputes whether I was made Gou'no^r according to the Lords propriet^{ts} directions at wch seu'all of the parliam^t being dissatis-fyed they broke up and came to me. Sr John declaring the re-sult of their consultation wch was that they found by the Lords Instructions there must be three Dep^{ties} to confirme all acts of Parliament, two only being liuing besides myselfe[3] it would be in vaine for them to proceed unless I would surrender the power of a Gou'no^r and make the third Deputy, if soe, then they would proceed. I then giuing my resolution to the contrary they tooke the power immediately to disolue themselues from being a parliam^t and Sr John Yeamans and his party went hastily

---

[1] At Wappoo point, palisaded and garrisoned by his negroes.

[2] Page 120, the first legal parliament; the names are lost.

[3] Pages 118, 121. Stephen Bull and F. O'Sullivan? Scrivener was probably already dead. O'Sullivan was suspended later.

away much dissatisfyed, thus was I left wth out either parliam^t or councell it being their oppinions that the Councello^{rs} chosen into Parliam^t did cease to be Councello^{rs} till a new election should bring them in.   The people did all resent this distraction and began to murmur saying Sr John intended to make this a Cape-fare Settlem^t wherefore to passify the people I summoned them in fiue dayes after to elect fiue men to be of the Councell, herein Sr John could not conceale his practise in Barbados to giue eu'y man his free vote, but he must make a p'ty to ou'rule the vote, preaching this doctrine y^t in all elections to choose such as will stand at the greatest distance from the Gou'no^r

Sr John has privately sent Dr Woodward away to Virginia by land [1] wthout any knowledge wch when I heard I was very much concerned at it, for many inconveniences attend it, wee want o^r Interpreter, and if he arriues safe in Virginia, there is a way laid for o^r Serv^{ts} to range in, wee haue lost two allready I wish noe more undertake the voyage, I had sent for him back but he was gone to fare for me.   [See page 89.]

Yo^r Lo^p will find in o^r publick l're,[2] the relacon of a very ill office done by an Irishman upon an Indian betweene Sr Johns and Mr Thomas Grayes & though the Indians seeme to be satis-fyed, yett as the grand Councell is compleated I shall endeauo^r to be thoroughly informed of the truth and man'er how the In-dian's life was taken away, a full account whereof yor Lordship shall receiue by the next.   I wish Sr John Yeamans may be cleare of it the Irish man is upon his Bayle, for feare the Indians

---

[1] Before starting he made his will, dated Jul. 17, 1671.   'To all Chris-tian people I Henry Woodward now resident at Ashly River in the province of Carolina being now minded to journey Northward of the said River and in respect the same may be very hazardous and danger-ous I do make my will and testam't; what lands I have as one of the first settlers &c. to Hon. Sir Jno Yeamans Bart. &c.   Item, whatsoever goods may or shall arrive on my behalf either from the said Proprietors or any of my relations to the above Sir Jno Yeamans and until such time as the certainty of my Death or returne be knowne I do constitute and appoint the aforesd Sir Jno Yeamans Bart my attorney &c.'   *Henry Woodward* O.   Witness: Gyles Hall, Jo. Dowden.   Proved *for power atty. since Woodward was alive?* Dec. 23, 1671, *before* Jos. West, *by* Capt. Gyles Hall and Mr. Joseph Dowden.   *Pro. Ct. Char'n.*

[2] Missing, see page 353.   Brian Fitzpatrick, 'a noted villan, deserted to the Spaniards, who had come to St Helena,' 1672.   *Hewet*, 61.

recant their League: Thus I haue and euer shall discharge my conscience towards God and my duty towards yor Lo^p.   And howsoever yor Lordship may receive diuerse aduertisements from hence, which may giue yor Lo^p occasion to thinke all will not go well wth us; giue me Leaue to incourage yor Lo^p to beleeue, y^t the Collony at this time is in a uery good state and condicon, and I doubt not but to preserue the same, till yor Lo^p shall make better prouision for us, in the meane time I shall use all my endeauo^{rs} to expresse myselfe.

Yo^r Lo^{ps} most faithfull humble Servt

JOSEPH WEST.

Charles Towne upon Ashley Riuer Carolina Sepr 3^{r1} 1671.
Addressed: To the Right hono^{ble} Anthony Lord Ashley, Chancello^r of his Ma^{ts} Excheq^r at Exeter house in the Strand.   London.   p^rsent.

Endorsed by Locke.   Jos: West to Ld Ashley 1 Sep^t 71
Ashley river.

[*S. P.,* Bdle. 48, No. 76.]

CULPEPER'S DRAUGHT OF ASHLEY RIVER.

See Frontispiece and Charleston Yr Book 1883, do: Made July–August? and Sent on the Blessing Sept. 1, 1671, see p. 356.   Endorsed:

A. Sr. Jno. Yeamans Land Conto. Acres 70.   B. Land to be divided betwixt Sr. Jno. Yeamans & Tho. Gray 160.   C. Mr. Tho. Gray & Mr. Jno. ffosters Land 140.   D. Mr. Tho. ffindens Land cont 40.   E. Teague Land 20.   F. Oliver Spencers Land cont 30.   G. Mr. Joseph Dowdens 30.[2]   H. Cap. Giles Halls Land 20.   J: K. Land taken up By Samuell Bosswood Thos. Thomson, Henry Wood[3] & others but as yet nott devided 100.   L: The Right Honble. Anthony Lord Ashly Sr.

---

[1] Sept. 1st? *as endorsed and A. &. W. I*⅖ *612,* when Blessing sailed.

[2] A Barbadoes planter came to Carolina 167⁰⁄₁, had land there 1680.

[3] Sam. Boswood, taylor, servant to Mr. Gray came from Barbadoes 1670, had land in Charlestown 1671 and 1675, 80, at Accabee.   Jas. Boswood 1701, 1729, Christ church parish, may have been his son.   Henry Wood, carp'r, came from Barbadoes 167⁰⁄₁, his family were settled in St. Andrew's parish for many years.   Henry Wood & Mary, his wife, 1720, &c. see *Register.*   " 1741, on 22 march last departed this life Mr. Henry Wood in the 68th year of his age.   He was the 3d child born in this Province," *S. C. Gazette.*   1758, Henry Wood, sen., died April 6.   *Ibid.*

Geor: Carterett & Sr. Peter Colletons Lands 420.   M. Mr. Jno. Maver-
rick & Comp" 285.   N. Cap Robert Dunnes Land 150.   O. Cap Joseph
West (our present governor) Land cont. 200.   P. Cap. George Thompson 170.   Q. Mr. Tho: Ingrams Land Cont. 150.   S. Capn Sullivans &
Comp: 100.   R. Land Reserved by governor & Counsell to be disposed
of at their pleasure I suppos for a minister or governor 100?   T. Mr.
Thos. Smith & Comp: 100.   V. Mr. Will: Owens Land 60.   The
small division betwixt wt^r & towne are two acre & 4 acre lotts belonging to Hugh Carterett George Beadon & others cont. about 20.   A
Little nearer but behind the Towne Cap Sayle hath 16 & by him there
is laid out for a Churchyard 4—cont 2194 Acres.   W. Mr. Jno. Robinson & Mr. Jno. Culpeper cont: Acres 60.   X. Mr. Maurice Mathews,
Cap. Henry Bryen & Mr. Stephen Bull & Mr. Nicho. Carterett 190.   Y:
Mr. Joseph Daltons Land 80.   Z. Mr. Thos Holtons 100.   1: 2: 3.
George Canty phillip Cumerton & James Donahue Cont. ten Acres
apeice 30.

There are divers other Settlements scattering up & downe in this
Draught where I have made markes for * houses but I thought Itt sufficient to gift yr Lordshipps this accompt of what Land is taken up nearest
the towne there is others hair marked which is nott Laid them out by
Reason they marked for the present wth other men for shares the greatest part of the Land where the marke (&) is pine Land which is generally Refused the passengers wch arrived In the Ship Blessing are to be
setled up Stonoe Creeke where Lyes very good land & they Like it well.

[*S. P.*, Bdle. 48, No. 73.]

COUNCIL JOURNAL SEPTEMBER 5th 1671.

At a meeting of the Governour and Councill September the
5th 1671 sitting and present: The Governour Sir John Yeamans
Capt John Godfrey Mr. Stephen Bull Mr. Wm. Owen Mr. Thos.
Gray Mr. John Foster[1] Mr. Maurice Mathews Mr. Henry Hughes
Mr. Ralph Marshall.

The Governor and Councill having considered how to dispose
of the people arrived in the Lords Proprietors Ship Blessing
agreeable to the said Lords Proprietors directions and most convenient for the Security and wellfare of the said People have
ordered & ordeyned (nemine contra dicente) a certayne parcell
of land conteyning five and twenty acres from the marsh joyning

------

[1]An eminent Barbadoes planter and adventurer 1663, 5, settled plant's
in Carolina with Mr. Gray, came there 1671, was Propr's deputy and an
active planter.   He had lands (near Crafts farm) till 1675, but returned
to Barbadoes where, 1673, he had large estates.

to the West side of the land layd out for Mr. Thomas Gray nere this Towne and soe running along Stonoe Creeke,[1] be layd out for the Towne whereof five acres shall be reserved for a church-yard &c. *Rivers, 370.*

At a meeting of the Governor and Councill September 9th 1671 sitting and present: The Governour Sir Jno Yeamans Cap[t] John Godfrey Mr. Stephen Bull Mr. Wm. Owen Mr. Thos Gray Mr. Christo: Portman Mr. Maurice Mathews Mr. Henry Hughes Mr. Ralph Marshall. Upon hearing the matter of the petition of John Norton[2] &c. Upon consider[n] &c of the address made by Rich[d] Rowser and Phillip Jones[3] servants to M[r] Jno Maverick and how industrious and useful the said persons have been in this Collony &c. *Rivers, 371.*

At a meeting &c Sept 23[d] 1671 sitting &c (*same*)[4] *Rivers* 372.

At a meeting of the Governour and Councill September 27th sitting and present (*the same*) The Governour and Councill taking into their serious consideration the languishing condition that this Collony is brought into by reason of the great quantity of corne from time to time taken out of the plantations by the Kussoe and other Southward Indians and for as much as the said Indians will not comply with any faire entreaties to live peaceably and quietly but instead thereof upon every light occasion have and doe threaten the lives of all or any of our people

---

[1] The bluff of Coburg plant'n between Jourdins and Colletons creeks on Wappo creek west of the Devils Elbow towards Pompey's cut. See *Year Book*, 1883, p. x. The town was not built.

[2] Came from Barbadoes on the Carolina 1671, and planted with Jackson till 1673. In 1673 he agrees to pay Col. Godfrey 7,000 lbs. sugar in Barbadoes. 1691 Jno. Norton and Sarah, his wife (dau: of Jon'n Fitch, sen), sell lot 79 to Jon'n Amory, esq. He had lands at Stono, and 1701 a grant 960 acres, Washua and Data islands, in Granville Co: and by will 30 Sep. 1705, gave $\frac{1}{3}$ to his wife Sarah and $\frac{2}{3}$ to his children Wm. Norton, d. s. p. Jno. Norton d. 1740, Geo. Norton of Stono 1710, 36, Jon'n Norton 1740, Dorothy m'd Jno. Cowen, Jane m'd Thos Goreing and Sarah m'd Randolph Evens. *B'k T.* 522, 32. *A. A.* 1712.

[3] They came from Barbadoes 1671, later settled in Christ church parish and left descendants. 1708, Wm. & Sarah Rowser, and 1728 Richard & Susana Rowser lived there. *Christ Ch. Register.*

[4] The bracket words are to save repeating the names, which in MS. are usually in two columns deputies and councellors.

24

whom they will sufore (?) to them and doe dayly persist and
increase in their insolencyes soe as to disturb and invade some
of our plantations in the night time but that the evill of their intentions have hitherto been prevented by diligent watchings.
And for as much as the said Indians have given out that they
intend for and with the Spaniards to cutt off the English people in
this place &c *Rivers*, 372 Ordered & ordeyned by the said Governour &c Councill (nemine contra dicente) that an open Warr
shall be forthwith prosecuted against the said Kussoe Indians and
their co-adjutors & for the better effecting thereof that Commissions be granted to Capt. John Godfrey and Capt. Thomas
Gray to prosecute the same effectually.   And that Mr. Stephen
Bull doe take into his custody two Kussoe Indians now in Towne
and them to keepe with the best security he may till he receive
further orders from this Board.

———

To Sir Jo. Heyden *Sept: 18. 71.*
Sir,

I have sent to you by this Conveyance a small Chest with 3.
Locks directed to Sir Jo: Yeamans marked C A.[1] which I desire
you to send to Ashley River in Carolina by the first oppertunity,
I give you many thankes for all former favours by which you have
very much obliged me to be
Sir   Your very affec^{ate} friend and servant
Ashley.

London Sept: 18. 71.
[*S. P.*, Bdle. 48, No. 55, page 94.]

———

To Sir Jo: Yeamans. *Sept: 18. 71.*
Sir,

I am very glad to hear that you are at Carolina, wee shall
expect good success to our new settlement when it shall be
countenanced and conducted by so judicious and worthy a Person, wee have therefore sent you a Commission for Governor
and doe rely upon you that you will be both industrious and
firme to us in the settling the Government wee have established.
Above all things let me recommend to you the making of a Port

---

[1] With Yeaman's commission as Governor &c., see letter following.

Town upon the River Ashley and to chuse such a place as may healthyest and seated upon the highest Ground, and as far up the River as shipps of burden will goe. The Place they are now planted in is so Moorish that it must needs be unhealthy and bring great Disrepute upon our new settlement where as a Towne in a healthy Place will give more Reputation, Security and Advantage to us then ten times that number of People scattered about the countrey When you have chosen a Place for the Towne.

You must lay out six Colonys about it which make a Precinct and none of the Proprietors signiorys or of the Nobility's Barronys must be intermixt, It is necessary that you lay out the great Port Town into regular Streets for be the buildings never so meane and thin at first yet as the Town increases in Riches and People the voyde spaces will be filled up and the buildings will grow more beautyfull If you designe six score squares of 300 foot each to be divided one from the other by Streets and Alleys it will be a good Proportion of a Towne, and let noe man have above one of those Squares to one house. And to each of these Squares let there be allotted fower score Acres in the same Colony and 400 in some of the other 5. Colonys of·the same Precinct, Those that build first to chuse theire Lotts and Shares first, your great Street cannot be lesse then one hundred or six score broad your lesser Streets none under 60, your Alleys 8. or 10. foote A Pallisado round the Towne with a small Ditch is a sufficient Fortification against the Indians There is a necessity that you leave a Common round the Towne soe that noe Enclosure may come nearer then the 3. part of a mile to the Pallizado. This will add conveniency, Beauty and security to the Place, and will afford roome to enlarge or better fortifye the Town hereafter, you may for the Present (when you have designed and measured both the Towne and the Common and mens shares) give leave to the Inhabitants to make use of this Common to Plant sow Corne or make Gardens for the better clearing of the Place if it be incumbered with wood.

But upon noe Termes to grant to any man a lease longer then 5. or 7. years that soe at the end of 7. years it may all come in to ly as a Common for the Cattle of the Towne Every square of the Towne to have its proportionable Part in the feeding of it, by our Fundamentall Constitutions there is to be one Port Towne upon every navigable River and all People are bound to lade and unlade at some Port Towne and the Proprietors have obliged themselves to grant noe more then one Port Towne upon a River for 31. years.

There is one thing more that I especially recommend to you that you will take care of the Lesser Townshipps in the severall Colonys that the houses be placed both orderly and conveniently togeather so as the nearnesse of the Neighbourhood may be a security to each other, If men are not overruled in this wee find by the experience of both Virginia and Maryland that men will expose themselves to the Inconvenience and Barbarisme of scattered Dwellings in unknown Countreyes.

If any Private (man) Person has taken the land which you finde most convenient for a Towne there is a necessity that they give way and that you provide for them in some other Place, wee must trust you with this and measure all our future Expectations from you by this, that in the settling of this our First Port Towne you seeke onely the Publique Interest and doe it with the most Equality and not let any Private Designe of Ingrossing the Land (that is lykely to be of soonest and greatest Advantage) hinder the speedy building and increase of the Place. Sir, I desire to hear as often as you can from you as being very much resolved to be

Sir   Your very affec^{ate} servant

Ashley.

London. Sept: 18th 71.

[S. P., Bdle. 48, No. 55, page 94.]

Council Journal, Oct., 2, 1671.

At a meeting of the Governor and Councill at Charles Towne this October the 2^d sitting and present.   The Governor Sir Jno Yeamans, Capt: Jno Godfrey, Mr Ste: Bull, Mr Wm Owen, Capt. Tho. Gray, Mr Chris. Portman, Mr M. Mathews & Mr H. Hughes Upon consideration had of the disposing of the Indian prisoners now brought in for their better security and maintenance   It is resolved and ordered by the Grand Councill that every Company which went out upon that expedition shall secure and maintaine the Indians they have taken till they can transport the said Indians, but if the remaining Kussoe Indians doe in the meane-

time come in and make peace and desire the Indians now prisoners then the said Indians shall be sett at Liberty having first
paid such a ransom as shall be thought reasonable by the Grand
Council to be shared equally among the Company of men that
tooke the Indians aforesaid. See *Rivers*, 105.

At a meeting &c October the 4th 1671 sitting &c (*same but
Bull & Mathews*) Upon consideration of the most secure dispos-
ing of the store of Gunpowder &c six barrels shall be lodged in
the Lords Proprietors plantation in the custody of Capt: John
Godfrey, 3 barrells more in Sir John Yeamans house in this
Towne & the remainder to continue in the Lord Proprietors
Storehouse aforesaid. *Rivers*, 373.

At a meeting of the Governor and Councill at Charles Towne
this October 14th sitting &c. The Governour Sir John Yeamans
capt John Godfrey capt Thos Gray Mr. Maurice Mathews, Mr.
Henry Hughes. Upon hearing the matter of the Petition of
Edward Roberts[1] one of the inhabitants of this Collony against
James Needham it is ordered by the Grand Councill that Capt.
Thomas Gray doe keepe in his hands what goods he has be-
longing to the said James Needham till the matter be heard.

At a meeting of the Governor and Councill at Charlestowne
this October 24th sitting &c. The Governor, Sir John Yeamans
Mr. Stephen Bull Capt. John Godfrey Capt. Thos Gray, Mr.
Chris. Portman, Mr. Ralph Marshall, Mr. Maurice Mathews.

Upon consideration had of the better disposing of people that
hereafter shall arrive in this place. It is advised & resolved by
the Grand Councill that Capt. John Godfrey, Capt. Thomas
Gray, Mr. Stephen Bull, Mr. Maurice Mathews and Christopher

---

[1] From Barbadoes. This 14 Oct: 1671, 'Edward Roberts being at this
time p^rsent of a good sound & ꝑfect memory although much weakened
& impaired in body by a disease wch dayly hangeth upon me &c doe
ordeyne &c to John Faulconer all my land &c 200 acres wch I markt &
pitcht upon adjoining Mr. James Needham & facing the river called
Ashly river also all that small patch of land purchased by me & intended
as a Town Lot 12 poles between the Town lot of Henry Wood, carp^r,
& Sam^{ll} Boswood, taylor, both inhabitants of Charles Town. I being
in daily expectation of the arrival of a ship from Barbadoes & of things
to be to me consigned or sent in the said ship &c *Edward Roberts* O.
Witness John Norton, Originall Jackson, William West. Proved ix Dec.
1671 by Norton & Jackson. *B'k* 1693 &c., p. 1.

Portman doe with what convenient speed they may goe and view all the places on this River and Wandow River and take notice and make returne of what places may be most convenient to situate Towns upon that soe the same may be wholy reserved for these and the like uses. *C. J.*, p. 10.

At a meeting of the Grand Councill at Charles Towne this October 26th sitting &c   The Governour, Sir Jno Yeamans, Capt. Godfrey, Mr. Bull, Mr. Owen, Capt. Gray Mr. Marshall Mr. Portman and Mr. Mathews.   Upon serious consideration this day had of the better safe guard & defence of this Collony it is ordered &c that all and every person or persons now in this Collony except such as are members of the Grand Councill or officers attending the same shall appeare in arms ready fitted in their several Companies according to the list now given &c. *Rivers*, 373.

At a meeting of the Grand Councill at Charles Towne this October 28th sitting &c (*same except Owen*).   Capt. John Godfrey Capt. Thos Gray and Mr. Maurice Mathews are appoynted by the Grand Councill to prepare the matter following vizt. the Secretaries Fees, the Marshalls Fees, the rates & scantlings of merchantable pipe staues and to modell the proceedings of the Councill in determining of differences between party and party to be proposed in Parliament.[1]

At a meeting of the Grand Councill at Charles Towne this november sitting &c   The Governor Capt. Godfrey, Mr. Bull, Mr. Owen, Mr. Mathews, Mr. Marshall.   Upon the opening of the matter of the Petition of Anthony Churne[2] against Mr. Wm. Owen &c. *Rivers*, 375.

WANTS.   (*All in Locke's hand.*)

Owen to Sir P C.[a] Ashley river suspected not to be soe big as at first imagined.   Brackish a good way up a high water that it meeting with Stonow the next southern river.   good land about it, and in it Salmon trouts, flounders very big tench Sturgeon, all in great plenty   Store of supposed Ciprus trees on the

[1] Our earliest statutes and code of procedure. [For note[a] see next page]

[2] Came with the fleet from Barbadoes 1669, was a freeholder and of Owens parliam't July, 1670, had lands near Ickerbee and Orange grove 1674, witnessed Hugh Carterets will 1687, and probably died soon after.

banks very tall and strait Wando thought to be the better river. The harvest like to afford the first planters provisions for the greatest part of the year notwithstanding draght

Clothing for half the people.

Winter begining in end of October and Spring in February N W winds cold   But 4 sick in the year of ague and fever and all recovered.

Mr. Mathews to Sir P C.[a]   Land good good pasturage amongst the pines Savanas Cypresse plenty sweet wood and very good for masts Promises of a good crop notwithstanding the drouht Pease spilt in the woods in Sept at perfection in Feb. Indigo grows well and comes to perfection Tobacco thrives and is very good Indians poore and timorous and their Cassiques have little authority.   Ashley river 30 miles up runs narrow between freestone rocks and there abouts Cedar and large Cypresse in abundance.   Many Savanas upon Ashley river within 30 miles of the towne The Land on Wando good Plenty of fish in those rivers Winter begining about the middle of October and ends the middle of Feb: Ice seldom and thin.

Coming to Sir P C.[1]   Two hundred familys ready to remove from New Yorke to Ashley river they will give ⅓ of their cattle for transporting the rest.

A flye boat of 300 tun to transport people and cattle and carry pipe staves to Barbados which will clear herself The Blessing like to be laded back with people and cattle as much as she can carry A ship of 100 hundred tun goeing with them from New York to Carolina: M[r] Foster hath bought a sloop of 30 tun, to load Cattle at Virginia for Ashley river and to plye there.   The Barbadians endeavour to rule all.

A main topsaile of 11½ Clothes and Spleet saile of 11 square clothes to be at Barbadoes in January and a suit of Colours.

A sloop[2] of 150 tun going from Barbadoes to Ashley river with passengers.

---

[a] These letters, written about Aug. 30, 1671, are missing.   Mathews' is like his to Ld. Ashley, page 332.   These, West's, Sep. 1, and other August letters went by the Blessing.

[1] Missing.   From New York about Sept. 30, 1671; the 100 ton ship was the Phœnix, bot. page 48.   The Blessing was about her size.

[2] This, in *A. & W. I.*, page 278, begins Dalton's letter.   Sloop perhaps the Charles.   See Roberts, page 345, Bull, *post*, C. J. Jan. 23, 167½.

Dalton to Sir P C.[1]   Winter cheifly in Jan.   The place healthy and begets a good Stomach.   Lay abroad in the fields on the ground severall winter nights to gether without any inconvenience rayny Season March and July.[2] moderate showers at other times once a weeke A crop of pease and corne from the same ground in a yeare Crop like to be good.   Provisions tools clothes seeds of all sorts and books of husbandry.   Three or 4 paper books more.

O Sullivan to Sir P C.[2]   Complaints of the Governor West and disorder about the Surveyor Generalls place West refuseing to direct warrants to him and Sir Jo: questioning the goodnesse of those titles whose lots are not set out by the Surveyor General.

Another malapart Expostulateing letter about his Surveyorship.

Coming to Lord Ashley.[3]   H Wentworth will accept of the governement if the Lords Proprietors will admit of his proposals.   Sir Jo Yeamans hath bought in Virginia 100 head of cattle to be transported to Carolina Bermudians likely to remove to Ashley river if they could have passage when their tobacco and provisions are out of the ground.

Halstead to Lord Ashley.[4]   Desires to Know what he shall doe with 3 letters he has directed to Col Saile two from my Lord Ashley and one from Sir P C: West a person faithfull and stout but noe good governor.   Col Kingsland or Col Morris[5] recommended to be Governor.   Sir John Yeamans dis-affected as too selfish Intends to discover the rivers of Carolina suspects Ash-

---

[1] Missing letters; date Aug. 20? 1671; sent by the Blessing.

[2] Average 1738-49.   April, Nov: Jan: had least rain 2 & 2½ in: June, July, Aug: most 5 & 7, yearly 47.60.   1876–95, Nov: Dec: Feb: had least 3& 3½ and Sep: Aug: July most 6 & 7½, yearly 56.85.

[3] Missing; from Bermuda about July 30, 1671? page 161.

[4] Missing; from Carolina Aug. 20, 1671? For Sayle's letters from Ld. Ashley, page 310; the other is lost. C. J., Jan. 6, 167½.

[5] Page 129.   Col. Lewis Morris, an eminent planter of Barbadoes with 400 acres, 1673.   Member of the Council 1666, 'a gentleman of the Country, of good interest and conduct and an honest man tho' a Quaker.' In 1668 made Com'r to treat for St. Kitts, 'the wch if he should accept' Ld Willoughby thinks ' Monsieur would be astonished at thee and thou.' Yet he was 'very ready to swagger in black small clothes and a sword.' See *A. W. I.*, 635.

ley river to be only an arme of the sea Woodward sent by Sir Jo. Yeamans to Virginia by land.

A Deputation for himself.

The Spaniards at the Havana intend to disturb the settlement next somer.[1]

A flye boat strong and well fitted for a close fight.

Godfrey to Lord Ashley.[3] He the sole manager of the Proprietors plantation since 1ˢᵗ of March 70 20 acres of provision planted. Provisions ginger Indigo etc planted were destroyed by the drought and the seed lost. But got a very hopefull plantation, the Indians say such droughts are [not] usuall. Gagging one of their enacted punishments great stirs about calling a parliament O Sullivan noe surveyor Desires to be Surveyor Generall, a divine and physician Cattle and horses would turn to great profit Sir Jo Yeamans intends to stay all the winter brought negroes and expects more. The number of Deputy to be kept up and their power not to determin in two years.

Sir J. Yeamans to Lord Ashley.[2] West proud and peevish denyed a Parliament for feare his election or actions should be questioned. Sir P C writ to him that the Proprietors were sending 300 people. Tobaco 7 years Custom free will draw the Virginians. Sir Jo: sent word to Virginia that from Carolina they could carry their good whither they would Many rich men lik to remove from Barbados. Gray an active man hath brought a good stock. He and the Barbadians at Carolina intend to have a ship of their owne.

Q. 1 Surveyor General to be chosen by Governor and Council 2 as also Deputy and all other officers 3 How those shall be emploied that sell their land.

J. West to Lord Ashley. Sir J. Yeamans setting up a Barbados Party and expects 500 people from Barbados before next spring. People expected from New England.

More people from England.

The crop hopefull and like to produce sufficient provisions for

---

[1] *Spaniards.* See *A. W. I.*, 916, 921; *post*, Sep. 8, 72. *Fly boat*, a large broad bowed vessel used in coasting trade.

[2] These letters of Godfrey, Yeamans and West, written early in July? 1671, soon after Yeamans arrived and these 'stirs' happened, page 337, are missing. *A. & W. I.*, page 278, has 'not usuall.'

the first planters Promises to send a draught of the river and towne[1] and some Cedar.

Received from Bermuedos 30 bar of flower and 4000[lb] of Beef etc The account sent to Sir P. C: and flower much damaged by weevels and therefore presently distributed The Barbadians as well as the rest want provisions and rely on the Lords Proprietors. The towne cald Charlestowne.

Mrs. Sayle to Lord Ashley.[2] Desires some consideration for her husbands service, something being promised by Sir J: Yeamans.

WANTS.

Godfrey to Sir P C.[3] Received 8 servants on Sir P's account and 16 on the Proprietors.   Hath planted 25 acres of corne some Potatos and some pease.   The new comers all sick of the bloudy flux occassioned by the green corne.   Indigo Ginger Tobaco Cotton Potatoes Yams and pease grow well.   Intimates that Sir John Yeamans, Owen Gray Mathews and O Syllivan are the contrary party to the Governor West.

Drums Spear heads Cords Snares Braces and Colours.

West to Sir P C.[3] The place very healthy some of the last servants sick of the flux by eating green corne.

A set of Smiths tools, Drums field colours Carpenters Sawyers and a Cooper A stock of cattle from New York, Horses and a plough.

Indigo as good as grows Commends Godfrey for a good planter and honest man Godfrey intends to goe higher up the river and they two not to part this yeare.

Halsted to Proprietors.[4]   Rectifyes some particulars of his former accounts about the servants Scaped the polemoney at Gravesend by his commision All the passengers gave bond for 6[lb] in 3 yeares except Ed: Mathews who refused till arrived at

---

[1] Missing; date July, 1671? Culpeper's draft sent by Blessing, page 355.

[2] Missing; from Bermuda July, 1671, when the Blessing touched there?

[3] Missing letters of Godfrey and West, Aug. 20, 1671, sent by the Blessing, which brought these servants, Aug 14. *Braces* of drums, the *cords* on the sides for tightening the *heads* and *snares.*

[4] Missing; like Comings, page 348, from Bermuda, July 30? 1671. Wentworth, page 161. Mr. Edw. Mathews arrived Aug. 14, settled his servants near Charlestown; was chosen to parliam't April, 1672, and in June had 4 men for war service. His family and fate are unknown.

Carolina 3 servants dead, received by Sir J Heyden kindely. Patent and commision delivered to H Wentworth. Intends to be at Barbados Jan: next. Capt J Darrell[1] and Capt F Tucker in Bermudas very civil. Capt. Darrells proposals for victualling refused to pay port dutys at Bermudos because of his commission.

J. Darrels proposals. Beef 1^{lb} per cwt. Fish 8^s per cwt. Butter 6^d per lib. Candles 7^d per lib. to be delivered in Bermudos. Freight to Carolina 40^s per tun. Live cattle of one years growth at 3^{lb} per head to be delivered at Charles towne.

Halsted to Proprietors.[2] An Indian killed by Fitz patrick about whom Sir J. Yeamans and West had a hot contest he suspects both Sir Jn: and Gray to have a hand in the Indians death. To be paid by the Colony 52^{li} per mensem for his voiage to new Jersey in pipe staves at 3 farthings a piece. Coming ready and active to give directions for this coast Coming a good and carefull seaman. Pipe staves to be set at a low rate to draw customers and trade.

Intends to shift mates for the increase of pilots Seamark a Buoy and constant sounding at the charge of the Colony. A Fishing towne and a Look out to Pilot in ships Sold 80 bushels of peas at prime cost for pipe staves at ½ penny a piece having noe instructions to deliver them to the Governor to get intelligence and to raise a stock.

Order to the governor and councill to assist him in the discovery of the Country and Mr Coming and Culpeper, to attend him.

Paper books paper ink quills. small armes sayns casting nets Ironworks. Clothing.

Will be at Barbados in Feb: The governor and others at New York troubled at the inclinacon of the people to Carolina

---

[1] John Dorrell, pages 160, 207. See Ld. Ashley to J. Wentworth, Dec. 12, 1672, 'a business proposed by him seems very fair,' but April 10, 1674, he 'raised jealousies,' and May 17, 1675, with T. Colleton, inclined Wentworth from the proprietors. *A. W. I.*, 986, 1262, 561. Capt. Francis Tucker, 1663, commanded Pagett's Fort, Bermuda, and held land there and on St. David's Island.

[2] Missing. The Blessing sailed Sept. 1st, 1671? with August letters; touched at Virginia? about 15th? (whence Biggs and Berry, &c., wrote) and on to New York, Sept. 30? whence Halsted and Coming wrote, page 346.

10 per cent. customs and hard winter makes them weary where they are.

His commission from the Duke may be continued which is of great use to him.

Answers to Berry's and Morris' letter and copys of the laws and concessions to be dispursed in New England and Virginia.

A flye boat will give reputacon to the port carry 120 cows and and 50 passengers. Sayle with 18 hands carry 100000 pipe staves which will people the country and stock it and get in the debts in pipe staves without charge the flye boat to be at Barbados the middle of June &t.

In Barter for Cottons Searges &t there is to be had at New Yorke Beef and pork at less then 1^d per lib. Bread 8^s per C^{wt}. Pease 20^d per bushell.

H Wentworth dead at Barbados where Halsted intends to be at the end of Feb from thence to Carolina with passengers and at Barbadoes again in the middle of June thence to Carolina with passengers Rum and Molessus and thence to New Yorke and soe on   A considerable quantity of ginger Indigo and Tobaco fit for the market of England to be expected in 3 years in Carolina.

Expects the Lords orders in Barbados from Feb to the middle of Aprill.

96 passengers delivered at Ashley river[1] From New Yorke they shall now carry 14 cows and mares which is all the Blessing can carry and 30 passengers another ship with them carrys 50 cows and mares and 20 passengers 200 familys ready to remove from New Yorke if they had convenient transportacion. He shall be necessitude to draw bills in Aprill.

Letters to Morris Sanford and Berry to be directed to M^r Jn Jollise in Boston. A copy of the Butchers bill to be sent him.

Governor and Councill to Lords Proprietors.[2] The stores have

---

[1] From England. Other ship the Phoenix? Hugh Wentworth died Aug. 1671? See p. 161. John Joyliffe, commissioner, at Boston, 1685.

[2] Missing; date Sept. 1, 1761, page 338. West and Bull held over, Sir John was Ld. Berkeley's deputy vice Wm. Scrivener, dec'd, Godfrey Ld. Craven's vice Bowman, resigned, and Owen Sir P. Colleton's vice O'Sullivan, removed. Their commissions perhaps came on the Blessing Aug. 14; Foster perhaps acted under a blank deputation of Duke Albemarle.

been well disposed of and care shall be taken for repayment.
The towne surrounded with a creeke the banks bold that ships
ride by it the farthest house from the towne two miles off the
ground about it 3000 acres.   They will search for a convenient
seat for a towne.   Charlestowne seated high and healthy what
sickness hath been among them hath been occassioned by want
of other conveniencys An Indian after divers insolencys slaine
satisfaction made to the Indians about it.   The Blessing sent to
New Jersey for provisions to be paid for at 52^l 13^s per mensem
in pipe staves at 3 farthings.

The present Council

		Mathews
Governor West	Mr Bull	Portman
Sir Jn Yeamans	Owen	Hughes
Mr Godfrey	Gray	Marshal.

They will follow the instructions and thinke the next yeare
they shall have provisions enough with overplus.

Two or three ships to be imploied there to carry goods and
passengers Negros, New York cattle Stores of pease corne and
flower Irish frieze bandel linin and broges nails of all sorts stock-
locks hooks and hinges Drums colours small armes and fine powder Draught of armes for the Judicature[1] A bill of 100^{lib} weight
For Indian trade hats and beads bleu and white some great
ones Carpenters and boats 20 feet in the keele A paire of vitry
Canvas a coyle of inch rope 12 handlines fishing hooks and lines
and a set of gun smiths tools.[2]

WANTS.

Gray and Lord Ashley.[1] Ready to serve my Lord on all occas-
sions intends to discover Cooper river which he think the better
but Edisto river best which is fresh 12 miles up and is 15 feet
deepe at Low water.   Hath a family of 24 Ashley river navigable.

Boats for discovery.

For sloops of 20 tun, 60 miles from the mouth, better land
and better timber up the river the sides and bottom of the river

---

[1] For the Court seals and to blazon above the bench? In 188——a
number of such beads were found in an Indian grave near Old town.
Vitre canvas, see pages 140, 158.

[2] Locke's MS. is four pages, very small and closely written.

rock of sand stone, pleasant hills and valys and large dry Savanas with very good grass. He chose land for himself but was
deny'd it by the governors West accused for commanding Scrivener and Mathews out of the Council and for declareing he
cared not what became of the Government.

A good governor.

The country very good.

Mathews to Lord Ashley.[1]   Soile fruitful, mould black 1 or ½
foot deep, about a mile from the river usually a tract of pines,
the land there not soe good but yet yields good pasturage Good
white red black water Spanish and live Oak Ash Hickery poplar Beech Elme laurel Bay Sassafras. dogwood, Black walnut,
Cedar Cypresse wonderfull large and tall of delicate grain and
smell, better for masts than any wood in the world.   Holly
Elder witch hazel and 10,000 others figs peaches, plums of divers
sorts the draught did noe great injury to their crop   The rest
the same as in his letter to Sir P. C.

Culpeper to Lord Ashley.   Promises a draught of the rivers
thereabouts and description of the land   The draught he hath
sent of Ashley river noe more for want of a boat and men Stono
river runs into Edisto river which hath a better entrance than
Ashley river the land high and fruitfull and the water fresh.

J. West to Lord Ashley.   Promises account of the stores the
next opportunity hath herewith sent an account of 36^{lib} 30^{lib} and
18^{lib} A parliament summoned but break up without doeing anything because there were not 3 Deputys this imputed to Sir J.
Yeamans who at the peoples elections of such as should be of
the Councill told them they should choose such as were at greatest distance with the Governor.   Woodward sent by Sir J. Yeamans by land to Virginia want of an interpreter the meantime
and fear of teaching the servants to run away two being there
already.   He intends to make a strict inquiry into the death of
the Indian suspects, Sir Jn and Gray had a hand in it.

West to Lords Proprietors.   Received the Blessing Cargo
most want was of Clothes All comers depend on the Proprietors

---

[1] This and the next four letters about Aug. 30, 1671, went by the Blessing. Gray's, both Culpeper's and West's to the Prop'rs are missing.
Mathew's, Aug. 30, and West's, Sep. 1, to Ld. Ashley are given pp. 333,
336, and Culpeper's draft, frontispiece.

supply and expect 5 yeares for payment for which concessions
were produced under Sir P. C's. hand the people refused to give
bonds but by order of the Council gave receits in the book
and are to pay 10 per cent but as yet hath received noething
It was Col Sayle and the Councels fault that the Carolina went
away without the timber which was then ready.

Instruction concerning those that die in debt to the Lords
Proprietors as to their lands and goods.

Godfrey and he cannot part till the crop is in which is much
more than they expected.

Halsted disposed of about 100 bushels of peas to the old
Standers who had lesse need of them to the Proprietors disadvantage Promises an account of stores.

The pines being pitch pines and ponderous not good for masts
Boats for discovery

Complains of Woodward being sent away by Sir Jn.

Culpepper to Lords Proprietors. Sent a draught of Ashley
river and promises a perfecter   Noe place that he hath yet seen
on Ashley river fit for a towne   Wando river he thinks hath
which is reported to run up broad a great way.

Berry Morris Sandford ⎱ Intending to remove from Virginia
  to Lords Proprietors.[1] ⎰ to Carolina Proposes. A flye boat
drawing 12 foot water and at least 5 foot between decks.

To carry cattle at ⅓ the owners providing meat and water for
them.   and their persons carried free they provideing their owne
victuals.

Many inclined to remove from Virginia to Carolina.

Maning[2] *to T. Colleton.* Proposes to furnish provisions and
cattle to be delivered a New York with hey for their passage.

A cow under 5 years—40 gall Rum of 3 years—30   A
mare to breed or draw—50   Bread and flower per C'—10
Sheep goats and hogs—10   19 Ews and a ram—80   Yoak of
oxen—70.

Brigs to Halsted. Many ready to remove out of Virginia but

---

[1] The next 3 letters are missing. Berry, Morris, &c., and Timothy
Biggs? wrote from Virginia middle of Sept., 1671, when the Blessing
touched there; Manning from New York later.

[2] Perhaps Capt. Jno. Manning, of New York, who, left Com'r in Chief
there 1673, surrendered to the Dutch.

want transportation some are frightened with a remembrance of Cape Fear.

Endorsed. Extract from letter from Carolina Nov. 71.

[*S. P.*, Bdle. 48, No. 77.]

———

THE COUNCIL JOURNALS.

At a meeting of the Grand Councill at Charles Towne this november. sitting & present: The Governor Sir Jno Yeamans Capt Jno Godfrey Mr Ste Bull Mr Wm Owen Mr Maurice Mathews Capt Thomas Gray Mr Chr. Portman and mr Ralph Marshall. Mr Henry Hughes came this day and made his complaint &c against Thomas Screvman Gent: &c. *Rivers,* 375.

At a meeting of the Grand Councill at Charles Towne this november the ——. sitting &c: The Governor, Godfrey, Bull, Owen, Mathews, Marshall & Portman. Capt: Thomas Gray having this day made his Complaint &c against Sir Jn° Yeamans Barrᵗ &c. *Rivers,* 376, for felling and carrying away several quantityes of timber from off a certayne parcell of land neare this Towne belonging to him the said Capt. Gray, It is therefore ordered by the Grand Councill aforesaid that an injunction be issued out under the Governours hand requiring that neither the said Sir John Yeamans nor Capt. Gray nor any of them shall fall worke upon carry or take away any timber from the said place until the matter or cause of difference between them be heard and determined which they the said Sir Jno Yeamans and Capt: Gray being present then and there did submit to be tryd and concluded by this Councill upon the 25ᵗʰ day of November next peremptorily.

At a meeting of the Grand Councill at Charles Towne this november 25ᵗʰ sitting &c. The Governor, Godfrey, Owen, Marshall & Portman. Capt: Thos Gray & Sir Jno Yeamans Barrᵗ having this day personally appeared before the Grand Council in order to the tryall of the differences between them pursuant to their agreement in a former order of the Grand Councill dated the sixteenth instant & for as much as the Quorum of the Grand Councill are not present It is further agreed on by and between the said Capt. Gray and Sir John Yeamans that the injunction formerly issued out to the said Capt. Gray and Sir Jno Yeamans which is this day determined shall. be continued on them till monday next the twenty seaventh instant of November inclusive and noe longer upon which said day they doe submit the said difference to be tryed and fully concluded and determined between them the said capt. Gray & Sir Jn° Yeamans by the Grand Councill or soe many of them as shall be assembled soe as three of the Lords Proprietors Deputies be present. Upon hearing of the matter &c of Richard Cole, Carpenter, against Joseph Dalton, Gentleman &c. *Rivers*, 377.

At a meeting &c this november the 27th sitting &c The Governor, Godfrey, Bull, Owen, Mathews, Portman & Marshall. Capt. Thomas Gray this day brought his Complaint before the Grand Councill against Sir Jno Yeamans, Baronet, for working upon a certain parcell of land belonging to him the said Capt. Gray bounding upon the land formerly laid out for the said Sir Jno Yeamans his tenn acre lott and carrying away severall parcells of timber from thence to the said Grays great damage pursuant to their agreement before the Grand Councill the 25th instant november—desires the same may now be tryed & determined by the Grand Councill—The Grand Councill having considered of the premises the question is putt whether the said Capt. Gray had the primary possession of the land in Controversy or noe, It is resolved (nemine contra dicente) in the affirmative. And upon further consideration had of the evidences brought in and examined It is adjudged and resolved that the said Sir Jno Yeamans ought to have the moiety of the said land bounding upon the said Sir Jno Yeamans his tenn acre lott as aforesaid and it is ordered by the Grand Councill that the said land in controversy shall be admeasured and equally divided between said Capt. Thomas Gray and said Jno Yeamans which dividing line shall begin on Ashley River at the tree formerly marked by the said Capt: Gray and said Jno Yeamans for that purpose giving also an allowance of land for all or any marsh which shall be in either of the said divisions to the party in whose division it shall happen. *Ibid*, 16.

At meeting of the Grand Councill at Charles Towne this IXth December 1671 sitting &c The Governor, Yeamans, Godfrey, Bull, Owen, Gray, Mathews' Portman & Marshall. Upon consideration this day had of the Complaint made by Susan Kinder against Capt. Florence O'Sullivan It is ordered by the Grand

25

Councill that the Capt. Florence O'Sullivan doe upon monday next admeasure and lay out or cause to be admeasured and layed out for the said Susan Kinder[1] tenn acres of land to be taken out of the North part of the tenn acre lott belonging to mr Owen and mr William Scrivener in his life time. M[r] Stephen Bull M[r] Wm Owen and M[r] Ralph Marshall are appoynted by the Grand Councill to consider of and prepare some matters to be proposed in Parliament (that is to say) Masters tradeing with Servants, Servants with Servants and Servants purloyning their masters goods, Servants coming from England how long to serve, and Servants coming from Barbadoes how long they shall serve from their severall arrivalls   That none may retail any drinke without license   The Speedy payment of the Lords Propriators Debts and of what rates Artificers and labourers shall worke therein.

For as much as for the ascertaining the rates & scantlings of Pipe Staves by the statute in that case made & provided. It is enacted and ordeyned that the Grand Councill from time to time should nominate & appoynt one or more viewers, either of whom shall examine & view all pipe staues wherein any difference shall happen upon payments or exchanges between party & party in this Province of Carolina.   It is therefore ordered and ordeyned by the Grand Councill and the said Grand Councill doe nominate and appoynt George Beadon & John Pinke[2] Coopers to be present viewers of all pipe staues in this Province as aforesaid and that the said George Beadon & John Pinke, Coopers or either of them shall view & upon their view declare what pipe staues shall be said to be merchantable according to the rules and directions of the said Statute whensoever they or either of them shall be thereunto called by any person or per-

---

[1] Came in the Carolina 1669, page 134. Dr. Wm. Scrivener opposed West in March, 167⁰⁄₁; was suspended from Council and died soon after.

[2] Came in the fleet from Barbadoes, 1669; was of Owens parliam't, 1670; viewer of pipe staves, 1671; had lands and lots in Charlestown, 1672, on Ashly river, 1675, &c., and 1684 lots 35 and 36 in New Charlestown (Beadon's alley); 1693–5 appraiser Cartwright's and Pendarvi's estates; 1699, 1702, Geo. Beadon Sen. and Jun. made packers. *A. A.,* 2, 178. He died 17—; his name is still in Carolina. John Pinke viewer of staves, 1671, was a cooper in 1674; from his poverty he was given tools by the public.

sons whatsoever And that they the said George Beadon and John Pinke or either of them for their labour and paines therein shall have and receive such fees or other reward as in and by the said Statute is set forth and allowed. *Ibid*, 17.

Upon consideration of the address this day made by Mr. Joseph Dowden[1] to the Grand Councill liberty is granted by the said Grand Councill for him and his boy named John Griffin for their transportation to Barbadoes in order to the better managing of his affairs in this place. Upon consideration this day had of the petition of Richard Cole, carpenter, against Mr. Joseph Dalton, the said Richard Cole is dismissed and left to proceed in his action according to the rules of the Statute in that case made and provided.

At a meeting of the Grand Councill at Charles Towne this December 14th 1671 sitting &c The Governor Sir John Yeamans Capt Jno Godfrey Mr Stephen Bull, Mr Wm Owen, Capt Thomas Gray Mr Christopher Portman Mr Ralph Marshall & Mr Maurice Mathews.

Sir John Yeamans Landgrave came this day and in the Grand Councill declared that as he the sole Landgrave in this Province according to the fundamental constitutions and according to a letter from the Lords Proprietors to him directed a coppy whereof he does produce he conceives he is vice Pallatine and thereupon requires the Government and care of affairs in this Province.[2]

Upon serious consideration had thereof and of the Fundamental Constitutions and the Temporary Laws agreed on by the Lords Proprietors and here remaining and the true coherence between them It is resolved and advised (nemine contra dicente) that it is not safe or warrantable to remove the Government as it is at present untill a signall nomination from the Pallatine or further orders or Directions be received from the Lords Proprietors. *Ibid*, 18.

---

[1] A Barbadoes planter, settled in Carolina 167⁰⁄₁, had a plant'n south of the Proprietors, on Ashley river, 1673, 75.

[2] Page 107. The Blessing arrived from New York Dec. 13, 1671, with this letter or copy (also perhaps Ld. Ashley's, April 10, and the Landgraves' patent, page 314, tho' these probably came Aug. 14, 1671).

To JOHN COMING—*71, Dec. 15.*[1]

M[r] Comeing,

I have received your letter and am very well satisfied with your behaviour, ability and the service you have done us this voyage and the good Character wee receive of you from other hands.   You have by this good Cariage made your selfe valuable to us and wee are resolved to continue in our imployment a man that hath been so diligent and succesfull in his business and wee doubt not but will continue to be soe.   I take notice in particular of the care you have taken to instruct others in the Navigation of Ashley River and the directions you have spread abroad for the information of those who may have occasion to sayle thither.   This was very well done and like one who minded the business hee was upon.   Wherein whilst you imploy that industry and care you have hetherto done, you shall be sure to receive all the incouragement and kindness you can justly expect from

Your very affec[ate] Friend

ASHLEY.

Exeter House Dec: 15th 71.

[*S. P.*, Bdle. 48, No. 55, p. 98.]

To SIR JOHN YEAMANS *15° December 71.*

Exeter House 15° Dec: 71.

Sir,

I hope er'r this you have received the Commission wee sent you to bee Governor by the way of Bermudos,[2] and that you will in pursuance of our Constitutions and Instructions endeavour to accomodate things there to the advantage and settlement of the Plantation, one maine Pointe whereof is the setting downe togeather in Townes.   Wee have in Favour of the first Planters

[1] These December and early January letters came by Capt. Jeffreys, who left London Jan. 13 ? 167½, and reached Carolina April 19 ?

[2] This com'n, Aug. 21, 1671, sent with letter, Sep. 18, 1671, p. 342, it seems was not received Dec. 13, when he claimed as Landgrave. Another com'n 26 Dec. 1671, was sent by Capt. Jeffreys and on producing this April 19, 1672, he was proclaimed.

altered our minds about the Port Towne on the River Ashley as you will find by our Generall Letter which though through the little care was taken to lay it out into Convenient Streets at theire first comeing it cannot be made soe exactly regular and beauty-full as wee wish, yet wee desire you would use your Endeavour to have the Streets layd out as large orderly and convenient as possibly may be,[1] and when that is done the houses which shall hereafter be built on each side those designed Streets, will grow in beauty with the Trade and Riches of the Towne. To prevent the like inconvenience hereafter I desire you would bee early enough in choosing a place and laying out the Modell of an exact regular Towne on the Next River and thereof to send us the Draught. Charles Towne we intend for the Port Towne on Ash-ley River where wee will oblige all shipps that come into that River to unload all theire goods and to take in all theire loading except Tymber and such other very bulky Commodyties as cannot without great trouble be brought to the Port Towne and thus on all the Navigable Rivers as they come to bee planted on Wee intend to have in the most convenient Situations Port Townes. I looke upon you as my Friend and therefore expect you should beare plaine dealeing from me in private which is this that though Wee had resolved to make you Governor, yett you were making yourselfe by the People a little too Quicke. I begg that you would trust me when I assure you that a man of your Abilitys doth not need nor will find anyother way successfull but that direct one of serving us and endeavouring the Good of the Plantation.

I am glad to hear soe many considerable men come from the Barbadoes for wee find by deare Experience that noe other are able to make a Plantation but such as are in a Condition to stock and furnish themselves, the rest serve onely to fill up Numbers and live upon us and therefore now wee have a competent Number untill wee are better stocked with Provisions I am not very fond of more Company unlesse they be substantiall Men.

The first of your Queres is answered by our haveing appointed M[r] Culpepper a man of your own approbation our Surveyor Generall[2] To the second concerning our Deputys I hope you

_____

[1] This was attempted July 22, 1672, post, *Dalcho*, 18.

[2] Lord John Berkeley, Palatin of Carolina and the rest of the Lords Proprietors of Carolina. To our Trusty and welbeloved John Culpeper

will not expect our Deputies should be named by any but ourselves and to the 3rd if men sell theire lands it is expected by us
the Lords Proprietors that the Governor and Councill should
take care that our Debt if he ows us anything be secured and
that being done they may dispose of themselves and their land
as they thinke fitt.   I desire you would doe me the particular
kindnesse to take with you Mr Mathews my Deputy Mr West and
Captain Halsted if hee be there and with them take up for me a
Colony of 12000 Acres in some convenient, healthy, fruitful,
place upon Ashley River   I am Sir,

Your very humble servant

ASHLEY.

[S. P., Bdle. 48, No. 55, page 100.]

LORD ASHLEY TO MAURICE MATHEWS.

Exeter House 15. Dec. 71.

Mr Mathews,

Besides the kindnesse I have for you upon your Uncle's the
Chalanors account, the industry you have imployed in discovering the Country, and the account you have given mee of it hath
me choose you for my Deputy for which I have herewith sent
you a Commission [1] and I doubt not but you will continue for

---

gent: Greeting, Be it knowne unto all men that we the Lords and absolute Proprietors of Carolina for divers good causes & consideracons,
but more especially out of the trust & confidence reposed in the said
John Culpeper for the faithful and skilful management of the Office of
Surveyor Generall of all that territory or part of our Province of Carolina which lyes to the Southward and Westward of cape Carteret, with
full power and authority to act and doe all those things, which by our
Fundamental Constitutions Temporary laws or Instructions, our Surveyor generall may or ought to doe.   In witness whereof we have hereunto set our hands and seals this 30 Day of Dec: 1671.   *Craven, Ashley,
G. Carteret, P. Carteret.   Col. Ent. Bk.*, 20, p. 77.   *N. C. Rec.*, I, 211.

[1]Anthony Lord Ashley to Maurice Mathews.   Whereas each of the
Lords Proprietors hath power to make a deputy to be his representative
in Parliam^t & in the Grand Council, & to exercise such powers in the
absence of the deputator out of Carolina as by our Fundamental Constitutions more fully appear out of the trust & confidence in your wisdom,
prudence, & integrity; hereby appoint said Maurice Mathews my deputy
in Carolina, &c., Dec. 18, 1671.   *Col. En. B'k*, 20, page 76.   *A. & W.
I.*, § 698.

the Establishment and Enlargment of the Plantation all that vigour and activity which has given me occasion to take notice of you, and which I shall be carefull to incourage as you shall give me reason to doe it. To this purpose I put into your hands oppertunitys of deserving my kindnesse, and desire you would have an eye to my private and publique concerns there, of which you will doe an acceptable thing to give me a constant and faithfull account. In particular I desire you would consult with Sir John Yeamans and that he and you would togeather lay out for me 12000 acres of fruitefull healthy Land in the most convenient place for a pleasant seat upon the River Ashley.[1]

I am Your very affec^ate Friend

ASHLEY.

[*S. P.*, Bdle. 48, No. 55, page 102.]

––––––

To STEPHEN BULL. 71.

Mr Bull,

The acquaintance I have with some of Mr Mathews's neare Relations here in England, hath made me choose him to succeed you as my Deputy. I would not have you interpret this as any unkindnesse or disrespect to you, who though you were a stranger to mee, when I put the trust into your hands, yet I shall continue to you this advantage of haveing been my Deputy, that upon all occasions I shall be ready to doe you any good, and to shew that I have a respect for you, the freight of your goods which came in our shipp Blessing is according to your desire given you free, and I have sent order to Captain Halsted to deliver you up your bonds which hee tooke of you for the frieght of those goods.

I am Your very affec^ate Friend

ASHLEY.

Exeter House Dec: 16° 1671.

[*S. P.*, Bdle. 48, No. 55, page 99.]

––––––––––––––––––––––––––––––

[1] On Ashly river, above 'Middleton Place,' still called 'the Barony.'

LORD ASHLEY TO CAPT. HALSTED.

Exeter House 16° Dec. 71.

Captain Halsted,

I am very glad to finde that I have not been mistaken in the man whom I imployed in our Carolina Affaires and that you have acquitted yourselfe soe well to all our satisfaction Since I in particular relyed upon you This gives me great Encouragement to continue you in our Service, though wee have formerly sent orders and doe now againe for the comeing home (as you will finde more at large in our Publique Letter and the Instructions therewith sent you) yet it is so far from any dislike wee have of you that at your returne wee intend to send you againe and should not now call you home were it not the better to accommodate our affairs to the Advantage of the Plantation and you may assure them there at your comeing away that wee intend to send you and Mr Comeing againe to Carolina in such a shipp as shall bee most convenient for our businesse there.   In the meane time I would have you in all the places where you shall touch to encourage men of Estates to remove into Carolina.   But forbeare to invite the poorer sort yet a while, for wee finde our selves mightily mistaken in endeavouring to gett a great Number of poore People there it being substantiall men and theire Familyes, that must make the Plantation which will stock the country with Negroes, Cattle and other Necessarys, whereas others relye and eate upon us.

I understand Hugh Wentworth is dead at Barbadoes, I am sorry for his death, but am now satisfied that John Wentworth his brother who is now at Providence,[1] was the fitter man to bee Governor, and hee whom wee purposed to make soe, but that the shuffling of names of men whom we did not personally know made us mistake and whilst we were over carefull to be in the Right, made us applye theire names amisse.   This when you see John Wentworth you must assure him of for wee have now rectifyed the mistake and if Hugh were alive we should not comply

---

[1] Pub. letter, page 372. Capt. Jno. Wentworth settled the Bermuda colony 1666, "on an island they first called Sayles island," and then New Providence; was chosen Gov'r by them and commissioned by Gov: Modyford, of Jamaica. Appointed Gov'r by the Lds. Prop'rs Dec. 23, 1671. *A. W. I.*, 710, 712.

with his Termes.   What more you are to treat with him of and
how in this and the rest of our Affairs you are to order your
selfe you will finde particularly in our General Letter and Instructions to which I refer you.   I have writt to Sir John Yeamans
and Mr Mathews to take up a Colony for me on River Ashley
which if I like I will forthwith stocke,   I would have you view
the land taken up for me and give me your opinion of it.   I
would alsoe have you informe yourselfe concerning Mr Mathews
whom I have made my Deputy.   The things that most particularly I desire to know is his honesty, his skill in Planting and his
Ability to manage a Plantation.

When you go to the Bahamas I would have you make as
exact observations of those Islands as you can especially those
two which are Planted and give me by the first oppertunity the
best Information that you can and also to enquire out the Char-
ecters of the most considerable men there that wee may know
whom to imploy and trust

I am   Your very affec^ate Friend

ASHLEY.

I have writt to Sir John Yeamans to take you and Mr Mathews with him and to take me up a Colony on Ashley River   I
would have it a commodiouse pleasant Place in a healthy and
fruiteful soyle wherein I very much depend upon your skill and
assistance.

[S. P., Bdle. 48, No. 55, page 103.]

LORD ASHLEY TO JOSEPH WEST.

Exeter House 16 Dec. 71.

Mr West,

Your letters I have received and am abundantly satisfied in
all that I doubted of before which I had not done had you sooner
given us an account of your management of our Affairs there.
Wherein I find now you have been a very honest man to us, and
have taken that care of our Concerns in the Distribution of our
Stores and secureing our Debts which wee could desire, wee are
all soe well satisfied herein that wee resolve for the future to put
our stores and the whole disposall thereof wholy into your hands
to be governed wholy by your discretion according to those Instructions wee shall send you.   Without any Direction or order

from the Governor and Council there Which was onely necessary whilst the whole Plantation was to be supplyed by us but now that wee think that every man there may by his own Industry be not onely provided with victualls enough but with other Commodyties to pay for Clothes and Tools and other Necessarys out of England Wee intend from time to time soe to furnish our Stores that Industriouse People who will pay ready truck may be supplyd with things they want at reasonable and moderate Rates, but doe not intend that the Lazy or debauchd who will never be good for themselves or the Plantation shall run farther in our Debts to the increase of our charge and disparagement of our Settlement.

You ought not to be dissatisfied to finde another man made Governor it was noe personal dislike or disrespect of you that occasioned it but the nature of our Government which required that a Landgrave should be preferred to any Commoner[1] soe that any body else as well as you must have given place to Sir John Yeamans but as our opinion of your Discretion, Vigilancy and Fidelity is not hereby at all lessened soe I am confident neither will your care and concernment for our publique or private Affairs there slacken in the least   I looke upon you as one who doe in earnest mind the Interest and prosperity of our Settlement Wherein you will be sure to meet with my kindnesse and such Incouragements from mee as will assure you that

I am Your very affec^{ate} Friend

ASHLEY.

[S. P. Bdle. 48, No. 55, p. 105.]

———

To Mr WEST.

We being assured from thence that Charles Towne and the country about it is healthy have altered our minds concerning the remove of our servants farther up the river and would have you now goe on in the plantation where you had begun and imploy them all there chiefly in planting of provisions.

[S. P., Bdle. 48, No. 55, p. 104.]

---

[1] This fiction was kept up till 1712, and each Governor appointed was made Landgrave also.

INSTRUCTIONS TO YE GOVERNOR & COUNCIL OF CAROLINA
at Charles Towne on Ashley River.

16 Dec. 1671.

1. In the Government of our affairs in the Plantacon committed to y^r care, you are to follow such rules as we have given in our Fundamentall Constitutions, Temporary Laws & Instructions formerly sent.

2. You are to take notice that in all our Instructions formerly or hereafter to be sent, that of the latest date (where they at all vary from one another) is always to take place.

3. You are always from henceforth to fill up ye Councill from time to time, with a number of Councellors chosen by ye Parliam^t equall to ye number of our Deputys.

4. You are to prepare such Bills as you shall thinke convenient for ye good of ye Plantacon, & to present them by ye Parliam^t to be passed (if ye Parliam^t thinke fit) into laws. For there is noething to be debated or voted in ye Parl^t, but w^t is proposed to them by ye Councill.

5. You are upon all occasions to afford Cap^n Halsted all ye assistance you can, in ye discoverys we have ordered him to make up ye rivers or in any part of ye Country where you are planted.

Whitehall 16th Dec, '71.   *Signed & sealed*

	CRAVEN	G. CARTERET
In Lockes hand,	ASHLEY	P. COLLETON

[*Col: Ent: Bk.* vol. 20. p. 79.]   *Rivers*, 369.

TEMPORARY LAWS to be added to ye former.

8. Noe Indian upon any occasion or pretense whatsoever is to be made a slave or without his owne consent to be caried out of our Country.

9. If it happen that any of our Deputys shall by death or departure &c cease to be our Deputys &c ye eldest of ye Councellors chosen by ye Parliam^t shall be &c Deputy &c till the said Proprietor &c make another Deputy &c.[1]

Col. En: B'k 20, p. 79.   *Rivers*, 353.

---

[1] Halsted, 351. Tem: laws, 324. C. J., Aug. 13, 1674, Dec. 10, 1675.

THE COUNCIL JOURNALS.

At a meeting &c. this December 20ᵗʰ 1671 sitting &c. the Governor, Sir Jno Yeamans Mʳ Step. Bull Capt. Jno Godfrey, Mʳ Wᵐ Owen, Mʳ Mau: Mathews, Mʳ Chr. Portman, Capt. Tho Gray Mʳ Ra. Marshall.   It is ordered by the Grand Councill that Mr Stephen Bull and Capt. Thoˢ Gray doe assist Mʳ Michael Smith and others lately arrived from New Yorke to find some convenient place to erect a Towne for their present settlement.

At a meeting &c. this December 20ᵗʰ 1671 sitting &c. (*same except Yeamans*) Capt:Mathias Halsted Commander of the Lords Proprietors Ship Blessing having brought three severall letters sealed from some of the said Lords Proprietors directed to Col: Wm. Sayle Governor of Carolina at Charles Towne on Ashley River and for as much as the said Coll. Sayle is deceased and Mr. Nathaniel Sayle heire apparent and executor to the said Coll. Sayle hath made his address to the Grand Councill that the said letters may be delivered to him And for as much as it is considered & advised by the Grand Councill that probably the said letters (being directed to the said Coll. Sayle as Governor of this Province from some of the Lords Proprietors as aforesaid) may afford matters of advice and instructions to this Government & better ordering of affairs It is therefore resolved & ordered that the said Capt. Mathias Halsted shall upon Saturday next being the 23ʳᵈ instant December between the houres of ten and eleaven in the morning deliver the said letters to be read before the Grand Councill But if the letters upon perusall shall be found only to concerne the said Coll. Sale in his private capacity then the said letters shall be delivered to the said Mʳ Nathaniel Sayle as he hath requested.   [See pages 310, 327.]

Upon consideration had of the report this day given into the Grand Councill by Mʳ Stephen Bull and Capt. Thos Gray It is advised and resolved that thirty acres of land shall be laid out most convenient to the water for landing, in a place described by the said Mʳ Bull and Capᵗ Gray on a Creeke Southward from Stonoe Creeke for a Towne for the settlement of those persons who lately arrived from New Yorke in the Ships¹   and

---

¹ The Blessing? arrived Dec. 13, 1671 with 20 people, the Phoenix with 30, Mr. Michael Smith, Mr. Rich. Conant, Mr. Richd. Chapman, Mr. Jno. Boon? Chas. Miller? Jas. Smith? &c.

Phoenix which said Towne shall be called and known by the name of James Towne[1] wherein shall be allowed five poles for every   in each family who shall inhabitt there and the lands without the said Towne shall be laid out for tenn acre lotts to the said Inhabitants   And it is further ordered by the Grand Councill that noe land shall here after be taken up in the said Creeke but tenn acre lotts (that is to say) tenn acres of land for every person in each family who shall settle and inhabitt thereon as aforesaid.   *C. J.*, 19.

At a meeting &c. this December 23rd 1671 sitting &c. (*all nine*) It is ordered by the Grand Councill that Capt. Godfrey and Capt. Gray or one of them doe view and direct the Surveyor Generall or his Deputy in the manner and forme of the tenn acre lotts about James Towne as they ore either of them shall Judge most agreeable with the situation and conveniency of the said Towne.   It is ordered by the Grand Councill that all and every the Surveyors in this Collony who marked any lands pursuant to a former order of the Governor and Councill dated 27th May last doe returne certificates of the situations & marks of such their lands into the Secretaries Office before the expiration of twentyeight days next ensuing that soe their right and interest to the said lands may be preserved according to the intent of the said order.   Upon consideration this day had of the approved usage conceived and established in other parts of his Majestys Dominions for the entry of Shipps upon their arrivall in their severall Ports and to prevent all inconveniences that may attend the omission thereof in this Province.   It is ordered ordeyned and declared by the Grand Councill that all masters of ships now in this Port or hereafter to come in the same shall make an Entry of their severall shipps in the Secretaries Office in this Province[2] specifying the day of their arrivall and from whence they

---

[1] Commonly called Newtown was (I believe) at Buckners, the first high land of James island, on the N. W. side of Newtown creek, a crescent bluff 12 feet above the creek which runs deep against its foot for ¼ mile.   The land slopes gently N. W. to a savanna some 200 yards wide. Both James island and Newtown creek get their names from this town.

[2] Taken from the Barbadoes acts and often re-enacted, see act 9 April, 1687, 'for entrys of ships and giving out of tickets.'   *A. A. 2*, p. 32. Like acts existed in other colonies.

came and doe there give in a true and full lyst of all
and every the passengers they doe bring to settle and
inhabitt here, And doe also then and there enter into Bond
not to carry of any person or persons inhabiting this Province
without Special lycence for the same, And it is further ordered
ordeyned and declared that it shall not be lawful for any master
or masters of Shipps hereafter arriving in this Port to land any
goods or commodities brought in the said Shipps before he or
they have made such entry given in such lyst and entered into
such Bond as aforesaid.

At a meeting of the Grand Council at Charles Towne this 30th
December 1671 sitting &c. The Governor capt Jno Godfrey
Mr Stephen Bull, Mr William Owen, capt. Thomas Gray, M^r
Maurice Mathews, Mr Christopher Portman Mr Ralph Marshall.
For the more formall & expeditious erecting of James Towne
capt. Jno Godfrey capt. Thomas Gray, Mr Stephen Bull and M^r
Joseph Dalton are appoynted by the Grand Councill upon
Wednesday next being the 3rd day of January 167½ to goe and
view the place appoynted to seate the said Towne upon, and
upon their view, consult advise & direct the surveyor Generall
or other sufficient surveyors to lay out and modellize the said
Towne as they shall think most agreeable with the situation and
conveniences of the said place Yett soe as the whole Towne may
be laid out in Squares, each Square to contayne one half acre of
land which shall be deemed a Towne lot for one family allowing
eighty foot by the water side for a wharfe or publick landing
place and such fitt and convenient streets as they shall think
suitable to the said Towne and to appoynt all other things which
they shall judge necessary in the said Towne either for enlarge-
ment of the said Towne Market Places or otherwise And it is
ordered by the Grand Councill that the Surveyor Generall or
whatsoever surveyor or surveyors have used to practice in this
Collony shall then and there give attendance to doe and performe
such directions as aforesaid And it is further ordered by the
Grand Councill that all and every person or persons intending
to settle in James Towne aforesaid shall likewise be then and
there present to draw their severall lotts according to the directions of the persons afore mentioned and that all and every person or persons taking up any of the said lotts shall build one or
more sufficient habitable house or houses upon his lot before the

1st day of Aprill next And if any person or persons shall build one sufficient habitable house upon each lott within the time afore limited, every of which said houses shall be twenty foot long and fifteen foot broad at least And it is also ordered and ordeyned by the Grand Councill that whatsoever person or persons shall neglect to build upon his lott or lotts in the said Towne to the dimensions and within the time limitted such person or persons soe failing shall forfeit his or their severall lott or lotts unbuilt as aforesaid to such person or persons who will presently settle the same according to the directions afore mentioned.

———

1671. MAP OR PLAN in colors shewing course of Ashley, Cooper and Colleton Rivers, also Charles Town, Waping [Wappoo?] and Comings point, with scale 10 miles. *Parchment, S. P.,* 48, No. 73; *A. W. I.,* 666.

———

"CULPEPERS DRAUGHT of the L^{ds} P^{rs} Plantacon, Carolina 1671." *30 by 18 inches shewing the star palisade and bounded N on* 'the Landing place' (*on Old Town creek*) Mr Samuel West *and* Mr Jno Mavericke, *W. on* 'land not taken up' *S. on* Mr Jos. Dowden *and* Jas Jones *and E. on* 'marshes of Ashly river.' *Inscribed.*

Carolina. These plotts Represent the shape & forme, the Larger of 340 acres of Land which by virtue of a warrant under the hande of the hon^{ble} Col. Joseph West governor of the abovesaid province & of his Councell I measured bounded & layed out for Anthony Lord Ashly Sr George Carteret & Sr Peter Colleton three of the Lords proprietors &c the smaller draught being laid out &c by the same authority for the said Sr Peter Colleton & Partners containing 160 acres &c the warrant for 340 acres 10 May 1671 & the other 5 Dec. 1671 said parcels of land situate lying & being in the aforesaid province Butting & Bounding on each other &c or on other mens Lands whose names are mentioned about the said plott performed according to the dates of the Severall warrants & certified By *John Culpeper. S. P.,* 48, No. 79.

———

LORDS PROPRIETORS TO CAPT. HALSTED.

2 January, 1671-2.

Capt. Halsted,

We have received your Dispatches, both from Barbadoes & New York [pp. 350, 352], and are extremely well satisfied with your management of our affairs, and the account you give us thereof.   Having taken new resolutions concerning your stay abroad, you are to govern yourself by these following Instructions.

1. If these Instructions meet you at Barbadoes & a sufficient freight of passengers or goods for Carolina present there, you are with all speed to loade and saile for Ashley River.

2. When you have unloaden at Ashley River, you are to take in ye Carriages sent by Capt Jeffreys,[1] belong^g to the Guns appointed for Providence, & with them and other things directed to Providence you are to saile thither.

3. If no sufficient freight present at Barbadoes for Carolina you are then to saile from Barbadoes directly to Providence.

4. God sending you safe to Providence, you are there to deliver up to Capt. John Wentworth the Commis^n herewith sent you, &c.

8. Having dispatched all things in Providence according to our Instructions you are to take in what Brasiletto wood or other Commodities present fit for ye market of London upon freight or otherwise & from thence sail to Ashly River, & there complete y^r loadeing with the choicest stocks of Cedar squared & soe come directly hither.

9. At y^r return to Carolina from Barbadoes you are to take what order you can with Mr West that a ship loadeing of square stocks of Cedar be readye for you against your returne thither from Providence.

10. In all the stays you shall at any time make at Ashley River, we w^d have you make what discoveryes you can in the Rivers & Countries thereabouts, wherein we have writ to the Governor & Council to be assisting to you.

Your very loving Friends

ASHLEY.	G. CARTERET,
CRAVEN,	P. COLLETON,

Whitehall, 2^d January, 1671–2.

In Lockes hand.   Col: En. B'k 20, p. 74.   _Rivers,_ 363.

---

[1] Capt. Wm. Jeffereys of the William & Ralph at London, Jan. 13, 167½, bound for Charles Town, arrived there before April 19, 1672, with the Dec'r and Jan'y letters.

The Council Journals.

At a meeting of the Grand Councell at Charles Towne this 6th January 167$\frac{1}{2}$ sitting &c. The Governor capt Godfrey Mr Bull Mr Owen, Mr Hughes, Capt Gray Mr Mathews Mr Portman & Mr Marshall. Capt. Mathias Halsted Commander of the Lords Proprietors Shipp Blessing having this day brought before the Grand Councill the account of his voyage from this Port to New Yorke pursuant to a former order of the Grand Councill of the 18th day of August last which said accounts the said Capt. Halsted pretending diverse excuses from time to time had delayed and deferred to bring in from the 13th day of December last being the day of his arrivall in this Port till this day upon perusal of which the Grand Councill remitting some particulars in the said account to be altered by the said Capt. Halsted that soe a misunderstanding may not be created between the Lords Proprietors and the people, the said Capt. Halsted declining to rectify the errors in the said account fell into abusive and reproachful language & undecent behavour to & before the Grand Councill in contempt of the honour of the Lords Proprietors and the present Government of this Province wherefore it is ordered by the Grand Councill that the said Capt. Halsted be forthwith committed to the Marshalls custody there to remaine till the said Capt. Halsted gives in security for his good behaviour. Ordered that Capt. John Godfrey, Capt. Thomas Gray, M^r Wm Owen, Mr Christopher Portman Mr Ralph Marshall and Mr Joseph Dalton doe examine an account this day brought in by Capt. Mathias Halsted and make report thereof to the Grand Councill upon Saturday next.

At a meeting &c this 10th day of January 167$\frac{1}{2}$ sitting &c. The Governor, Godfrey, Owen, Gray, Mathews Portman Marshall. For as much as John Radcliffe, yeoman, Servant to John Foster one of the inhabitants of this Collony hath for some time past remained in Irons in the Marshalls custody by his committment upon suspicion for running away from his said Masters service and relinquishing his allegance to our Soveraigne Lord the King and his fidelity and submission to the Lords Proprietors and endeavouring to persuade and lead William Davys and Richard Bardiner [page 253] two of his fellow servants along with him to the Spanish habitations with the Spaniards there to

26

conspire and procure the ruine of this hopefull settlement and
all his majestys subjects therein And for as much as noe prosecution is hitherto had or made against him for the same Upon
serious consideration thereof had by the 'Grand Councill It is
ordered (nemine contra dicente) that the said John Radcliffe be
and is discharged from his confinement paying his fees and
charges to the Indians who pursued him & brought him back
to this place (that is to say) to Capt. Thomas Gray the sum of
One pound twelve shillings and sixpence, to Thomas Thompson,
Marshall for attendance and diet foure pounds twelve shillings,
to Joseph Dalton, secretary three shillings and sıx pence in the
whole amounting to Six pounds ánd eight shillings sterling.

And it is further ordered by the Grand Councill that if the
said John Foster his Master doe satisfie and pay the said severall
sums to the persons afore mentioned that then the said John
Radcliffe shall enter into his said Masters service and serve his
said Master the terme of one and twenty months over and above
his contracted time of servitude (that is to say) five for soe much
time already neglected in his said masters service and Sixteene
months for the said sum of six pounds and eight shillings disbursed by his said master as aforesaid But if the said John
Foster doe deny the payment of the said severall sums amounting to 6£. 8s: as aforesaid then the said John Radcliffe shall
forthwith serve the said terme of Sixteene months to the said
Capt. Thomas Gray, Joseph Dalton and Thomas Thompson
dividing the said terme of sixteene months according to their
severall proportions &c.   C. J., page 24.

At a meeting &c this 13th day of January 167½ sitting &c The
Governor, Godfrey, Owen, Gray, Mathews, Portman, Marshall,
Hughes.   Upon consideration this day had of the better safety
and defence of this province and the severall persons now or
hereafter to inhabitt the same It is Ordered by the Grand Councill
that capt. Jno Godfrey Capt. Thomas Gray and Mr. Maurice
Mathews doe goe and view Wando River and the severall
Creeks thereon and there marke such place or places as they shall
thinke most convenient for the situation of a Towne or Townes
and their report thereof to returne to the Grand Councill with
all convenient speed And it is further ordered and ordeyned by
the Grand Councill that noe person or persons upon any pretence whatsoever doe hereafter run out or marke any lands on

Wandoe River aforesaid or in any creeks or branches thereof until such report be returned by the said Capt. Godfrey Capt. Thomas Gray and Mr. Maurice Mathews as aforesaid.

At a meeting &c this 15 day of January 167½ sitting &c (*same except Gray*). Upon hearing the matter of the petition of Thomas Badgard against James Deheart both parties having submitted themselves to abide by the judgment of the Grand Councill and because there are some matters which are not yett fully ascertained therefore it is given unto the said Thomas Badgard untill the 22ⁿᵈ instant January to bring in his accounts and in the mean time the Councill will advise.

Mʳ WEST. 15 JAN. 7½.

We being not yet come to a full resolution about the ordering of our joynt Plantation upon the publique stock, farther than that you should goe on to cleare the ground, and plant provisions Where you first began   I have sent this bearer Mʳ Man to be hereafter either imployed in our publique Plantation under you (if we shall agree to carry that on with more hands) or else to be an overseer in my owne private Plantation which I intend to have. In the mean time I would have you take him into your care, and give him accommodation upon my account, and if at any time you want any help, for the oversight of our servants in any part of theire worke his assistance may not be unusefull to you

I am Your very affecᵃᵗᵉ Friend

Exeter House 15° Jan: 7½.   ASHLEY.

In Lockes handwriting.   [*S. P.* Bdle. 48, No. 55, p. 106.]

LORD ASHLEY TO MAURICE MATHEWS.

Mʳ Mathews,

The bearer hereof Mʳ Man,[1] is one whom I have sent over with a designe to imploy there; and tis not unlikely he may be an assistant to you in the management of that Plantation   I designe to have theire upon my owne private account, the care

---

[1] Miles Man, he returned to England June, 1673. Other letter by this ship, the William & Ralph, p. 362.

and government whereof I intend to intrust to you as my cheif overseer. I would therefore have him goe with you when you take up the Colony for me I writt to you of in my other letter sent by this ship and I desire you would consider togeather about the soile, situation and other conveniencys of the land to be taken up for me. To prepare him against the comeing of my servants and stock you will doe well to make him acquainted with your ways of planting and husbandry

I am Your very affec^{ate} Friend

Exeter House 15. Jan. 7½.   ASHLEY.

In Locke's hand.   [S. P. Bdle. 48, No. 55, p. 107.]

JOSEPH DALTON TO LORD ASHLEY.

My Lord

Your Lo^{ps} acceptance of some stammerings formerly from me has wafted the oblation of my humble thankfullness before yor Lordships this time and has encouraged me to present a further essay of our Affaires in this place, not out of any affection other than the pure motions of my duty to your Ld^p: I shall observe the approbation of our Age to forgett prolix Apoligies when higher concernements are to appear upon the Stage: but because the subject of our discourses flow from the hopes of this Country we (now by experience having some competent knowledge of it) shall therefore if your Lords please glance upon its nature and properties which I must confess I did not dare to attempt before this time.

Our Winter will not allow Sugar Canes or Cotton to grow here for any thing of a Comodity for during the winter that is to say from November till February we have severall small frosts We had Ice one day in this Month a full inch thick in Vessels of fresh water though not at all discoverable in any well or River but by the hardness and hoariness of the ground in the morning; And some brushes of such weather we may expect till mid February. yett I have English pease now growing which have withstood the greatest severity of our Winter without any prejudice soe farr as I can yett perceive. Though we be denyd of some Southerne produces at that time yett it is excellent for English Graine, and will afford us the convenient husbandry of wheat, which without frost has been utterly lost:

The Comodities then which will be certaine and profittable in this place will be Wine Oyle Silk Indicoe Tobacco Hemp Flax and some say Ginger.[1] I have seen very good Roots of it and have digged some such from my owne planting, which Barbadians say are as good and faire as they have seen, and I am convinct that we may produce sufficient for our owne uses but I dare not write it a profittable comoditie till further tryall:

As for Indicoe wee can assure ourselves of two if not three Cropps or cuttings a yeare, and as the Barbados Planters doe

---

[1] Cotton and indigo seed were sent in 1669 to be planted "sheltered from ye N W. winde," page 125; were tried 1670, and till Sept. "corn, cotton and tobacco did well," but "all things were blasted in Octr," and March, 1671, West fears "this is not a cotton Country;" the Barbadoes planters said otherwise, and one "Indico, tobacco and cotton to be our main comodities;" in April ginger and indigo were lost by drought, but in Sept. "cotton grows freely, indigo as good as need be, tobacco does well," page 332. 1672, the Prop'rs sent 1 bbl. rice for seed? and wrote Halsted "to get the way of making tobacco, indigo, cotton &c." and he expects "a considerable quantity of ginger, indigo and tobacco fit for the market of England in 3 years;" "indigo like to be a comodity," and 1673-5 tobacco was so. Ash says, 1679, "tobacco grows well and indigo is good," and Wilson, 1682, "cotton of the Cypress and Malta sort grows well &c." 1683, the Prop'rs granted 800 acres to Arthur Middleton, Esq., for experim'ts with oil and cotton. Act 1687, *2 Stat.*, 37, fixes prices of corn, peas, tobacco, &c. Rice tried 1685 and planted 1688, *Drayton*, 115, soon became a staple, *Rivers*, 172. 1691, "we are encoraged wth several new rich comodities as silck, cotton, rice and indigo wch are naturally produced here," *Ibid*, 428, 241. Act 1691 patented an improved engine to husk rice, *2 Stat.*, 63, and Acts 1694-5 encouraged making wine, indigo, &c., and gave bounties "on various comodities the growth of this province." 169$\frac{8}{9}$, "the great improvem't, &c., is wholly owing to the industry, &c., of the inhabitants; they" tried "cotton wool, ginger, indigo &c but finding them not to answer are now set a making pitch &c and planting rice," *Rivers*, 445. Oldmixon says, 1706, "the principal commodities are provisions &c corn, pease &c cotton, silk &c." and Purry, 1731, "Flax and cotton thrive admirably," "rice orders" were current 1719 and rice a great staple, and the bounty acts soon made indigo so. Gov. Glen says, 1737-40, "rice, corn and indigo plenty," and Miss Lucas tells, 1740, "the pains I have taken to bring the indigo, ginger and cotton to perfection." Act 1744 gave bounties on cotton, indigo, ginger, &c., cotton 3d., and indigo 1s. In 1747, 7 bags cotton, 50,000 bbls. rice and 134,000 lbs. of indigo were exported, *Glen;* cotton was exported 1754, *Drayton*, 127, and 1775 rice and indigo were staples, and "a cotton patch no unusual spectacle."

affirme it is as likely as any they have seen in Barbados Wee
cannot question the growth of a good sort of Tobacco with us
which it may be will surpass the fame of Virginia but that which
I humbly conceive is most worthy our thoughts and most agreeable with this Climate and soyle is Wine Oyle and Silke which
without all per adventure may be propagated to great perfection
and profitt, and which the· land seems to promise by fostering
soe many old Vines and Mulberryes for want of better and indeed
I harbour very high thoughts of the more inward part of the
Country as I shall presently acquaint yor Lo^p.   By the report of
some discoveries made up Wandoo River compared with the
relation of the Southerne and Northerne Indians, we are satisfied that the place whereon we are settled, Edista, Cambohee,
St Helena and those places neare us bordering upon the Sea are
all broken lands and Islands apart from the body of the maine
and the further we goe up our Rivers we finde the land to be
much better and inclining to Hills and Stones and the growth of
better Timber The Indians say the Maine is very Hillie and
Mountainous: There is a river next St Helena to the Southwards
called by the Indians Westoe bou signifying the enemies River
a sort of Indians at enmity with ours which runns in fresh water
into the Maine backwards of us beyond the reach of their travills
which if an outlett can be found answerable to the vast length it
is reported to be off when discovered may prove of great advantage to this settlement But of all those places that I have seen
or heard of I cannot finde any to exceed this for security and
which will entertaine a very great number of people with very
good land, Though the further up the River the better yett we
hope yor Lo^p: will not condemne us for seating Charles towne
soe neer the rivers mouth it being advised for our better safety:
If we had settled up in the Country we had laid a way to have
ourselves blockt in and to have our releif intercepted having noe
fort to comand the absence of our Enemies and preserve the
Channel from such troubles.

    Wee cannot reasonably beleeve that the world is now asleep
in that the Spaniard has forgott his sullenness there fore as it has
been the practise of the most skillful settlers so it will become us
to erect townes of safety as well as of Trade to wich purpose
there is a place between Ashley River and Wandoo river about
six hundred acres left vacant for a towne and fort by the direc-

tion of the old Governoᵣ Coll Sayle for that it comands both the
rivers:[1] It is not above a Mile over between River and river with
a bold landing free from any Marsh soe as many ships as can
may ride before the Towne at once and as many ships as can
come into the River under the protection of the fort if one
should be there: It is as it were a Key to open and shutt this
settlemt into safety or danger: Charles Towne indeed can very
well defend itselfe and thats all, but that like an Iron gate shutts
up all the Townes that are or may be in those Rivers: besides it
has a full view of the Sea being but a league or a few Miles from
the mouth of the river and noe Ships can come upon the coast
but may be seen from thence and may receive the benefitt of a
Pilott from that Towne: It is the only Sanctuary of refuge in
the Country being the very center of our Settlements and gives
incouragement to all those rivers equally upon any Alarum to
be there secured for the settlemts being thick round about it it
cannot be surprised, it is likewise the most convenient for building and launching of ships as large as can come into this harbour: It must of necessity be very healthy being free from any
noisome vapors and all the Sumer long refreshed with continued
coole breathings from the sea which up in the Country men are
not soe fully sensible of; It will encourage anything of a fishing
trade that may be found out here: I must confess it will not be
a Towne for Planters to live in for the land is but scanty for
large Plantations and it may be the land is not alltogether soe rich
as in some other places of the Country: Yett it is very answerable for Merchants and tradesmen their gardens and Orchyards
and most convenient to entertaine the stores of the Country into
safeguard and to expedite navigation with less expense of time
then in any other place with us.

My Lord I doe not here endeavour to thinke that this Towne
will be the only Towne of Trade on those rivers the most profittable settlemts in this Country, but that a Granary or Nursery
may be here planted sufficiente to maintaine a larger and better
under taking nor yett is my fancy roveing after any other then

---

[1] New Charlestown, established 1670. Capt. Coming, Mr. Hughes,
Mr. Norris, Mr. Murrell, Lt. Donne, H. Carteret, Jackson, Norton, Hurst,
& others lived at or near it 1671, it was laid out & built on 1672, and declared the port town 1679. It shut safely enough 1861–65.

the apprehensions of a substantiall trade by which nations are
made famous and if the rule be true that causes doe worke
according to the nature of the subject I am confident we
may be putt into a way not much inferior to places of the greatest
emineacy among the English.   If the Porch be so beau-
tifull what must the Temple be? if the broken land be good
certainly the maine much more and herein I am persuaded the
rather to beleeve first from the return of Dr Woodward which
though imperfect yett gave the assurance thereof: 2dly from the
Indians who came from those parts whose furniture were Mul-
berrie Cakes and dies of divers sorts as well as variety of skinns:
It is true that some of us have taken up the scent of better land
and are very ready and earnest to follow the discovery but it
hath hitherto been suppressed and confined to those three Rivers,
least too much variety cause surfetting as too often it hath done
and great expectations have been thereby imbittered in the end.
Yo^r Ld^p may please to comand a cessacon of remote discoveries
but what may be pursuant to the Ld^s Prop^r Order for we now
having gott a secure footing when it pleases God those rivers are
well peopled: The land lyes before the Ld^s Prop^r to be disposed
of at pleasure.   It may be dangerous to follow the fancies of
roveing heads which the English have sufficiently experienced
and then I humbly propose that your Ld^{ps} may send a laborious
and skillfull Engineer or Surveyo^r generall[1] to us who may as well
modellize and sett us to rights as be employed in such services,
and though my instructions doe not load me to tax mens persons
or to judge their crimes, yett justice to the Country prompts
me not to forgett the trouble Capt. Sullivan hath putt this country into by his ignorance whose ill fate is to profess much, to performe noething.   I am sensible yor Ld^p eares have been filled
with reports of him which I could heartily wish he had never
given any such occasions.   I suppose this may be the reason
why some have the thought it hardly agreeable with the Countries advantage to maintaine a Surveyor Generall which I never
yett could be convinced of: I doe confess were it the Surveyor

[1] The first Surveyor of Carolina, M. Robert Vanquillin de la Prairie,
appointed May 23, 1663, page 5, was made Sur. Gen. of New Jersey Feb.
10, 1664; stayed there 1671, and 1669 Capt. O'Sullivan got the Carolina office.

Generall office to doe noe more than Capt. Sullivan has done I should be of their oppinions but my thoughts are otherwise directed when I consider first, the lands in this Country lyes soe irregular that they must be squared by some skillfull Artist to your Ld^p directions, 2^{ndly} such an Officer will satisfye all men in the bounds of their lands and soe prevent suits and differences, 3dly he will strengthen and beautify the Country with those noble contrivances and that even ness proscribed by your Ld^p desired by all men, lastly and which I conceive to be a part of his duty to discover and examine all places about us or where the Ld^s Prop^r shall direct and designe them for such settlemts as may be most agreeable with their contrivances by which meanes people when they doe arrive may be satisfied without much trouble or expense of time a thing too much in use in these parts and a ready way to create a disestime of the Country.

All sorts of people are encouraged to come to us in a number of people it is very likely some of them are but slenderly furnished with provisions yett coming in the spring if places be ready for them to sett downe in they may be soe industrious as to reape new provisions before their old store be spent and though not sufficient till the next cropp yett so much charge is saved them but on the other hand if men must seeke out their owne places; being strangers some time will be spent before they can convince themselves where to sit downe.

The Collony looses the work of soe many men for soe long time besides soe much provisions spent idley which one man I meane a Surveyor Generall with two or three to assist him may save by disposeing of such places at leisure time thus in part it is evident how advantageous such an Officer may be to the Country and what loss it hath and may sustaine for want of him Capt Sullivan could never be gott to doe any such thing for in truth he cannot and this is the true reason why yor Lo^p have not received a draught of our Rivers and way of Settlement.

I should now pass a Sede ad Salutem populi but that to yor Lo^{ps} were to show the Sun with a Candle I shall therefore only say Quum augentur justi extatur populus Quum autem dominatur unprobus suspirat populus Pro; 29: 2:

By our records it appears that 337 men [71 women?] 62 children or persons under 16 years of age is the full number of persons who have arrived in this Country in and since the first fleet out of England to this day whereof 43 men 2 woomen 3 Children are dead and 16 absent soe as there now remaines 268 [278?] men able to beare armes 69 woomen 59 Children or persons under 16 yeares of age.[1]

Though hitherto we have laboured under the want of provisions yett I am very hopefull that this Cropp may afford something of a Store among us by which we may be in a condition to sett forward in the husbandry of Vines and Olive Trees which I judge to be the only profittable comodities wee can follow and most agreeable with our Climate Wee have indeed plenty of diverse sorts of grapes here[2] some very pleasant and large but being prest the thickness of their outward skinn yeilds a kind of harshness which gives us reason to feare (though we intend to make tryall of them) that they will hardly ever be reclaymed or with very great difficulty. We must therefore recomend to yo[r] Lo[p] to furnish us with the Plants of good Vines and Olives with some persons who know the true husbandry of them herein yo[r] Lo[p] need not doubt the diversities of Vines for I doe verily beleeve we have ground suitable to all their varietie. Your Lo[p] may further be pleased to add Almonds and Date stones agreeing with the place as well as any where.

Wee have been something at a loss in the practise of Palatinates out of England and Wales where some questions have arisen in whose name Originall and Judiciall Writts and Indictments of Treason and Felony should be made and in such Writts and Indictments contra cujus pacem should be supposed and though some satisfaction has been given notwith standing the Statutes 27 Hen: 8: ca: 24: and that wee can multiply reasons and some presidents to maintaine that jura regalia in this Province ought to be exercised in the Ld[s] Prop[r] names: Yett yo[r] Lo[p] direction will remove all scruples herein Qui observat preceptum non experitur rem matam: Our Generall Letters bearing soe large a sweep I shall not add furthur but that as your

---

[1] 125 at Ashly river, page 178, 2 from Virginia, 2 from Bermuda, and 15 sailors, 1670; 42 on John & Thos. and 64 on Carolina from Barbadoes, Feb. 167⁰⁄₁; about 50 with Yeamans, July, 1671; 96 on the Blessing, from England, Aug., 1671; 30 on her and 20 on Phœnix from New York, 20 from Barbadoes, on the Charles?

[2] Ash says, 1680, "vines of divers sorts bearing both Black and Gray Grapes, grow climbing their highest Trees." *Car.* 2, page 65.

Lo^p has been pleased to entertaine favourable thoughts concerning me I shall endeavour to demeane myselfe answerable to what yor Lo^p shall require and though I must thinke some will endeavour to slight me into want of Knowledge and experience yett my Integrity dillegence and Study shall allwayes manifest me

Yo^r Lo^p most faithfull humble servt

Jos. Dalton.

Charlestowne upon Ashley River January 20th 1671.

Addressed: To the Right Hono^ble Anthony Ld Ashley at Exeter House in the Strand.   London.   present.

Endorsed: January 20 1672 Joseph Dalton to Lord Ashley.

5¼ *p. with seal.*   [*S. P.*, Bdle. 48, No. 87.]

THE COUNCIL JOURNALS.

At a meeting &c this 20th day of January 167½ &c The Governor, Godfrey, Owen, Gray, Mathews, Portman, Marshall, Hughes. This day being appoynted for the tryall of some persons namely James Willoughby and Thomas Munkister upon an indictment and arraignement for running away from this Collony contrary to an Act of Parliament in this Province on that behalfe made and provided And for as much as the Grand Councill is convened in the number of seven persons besides the Governor as aforesaid among whom there are but two Deputies there being only three Deputies in the Province and now the third having been absent for some time and it is not knowne where he is[1] and the Juries for the said tryall appearing the question is whether upon this exigency it may be warrantable for such of the Grand Councill as are now present to proceed in the said tryall. Affirmants: Mr Ralph Marshall, Mr Henry Hughes, Mr Christ^r Portman, Mr Maurice Mathews, Capt: Thomas Gray, Capt: John Godfrey, the Governor. Negants, M^r Wm Owen.

At a meeting &c this 22nd day of January 167½ sitting &c

---

[1] Godfrey and Owen; the third, Bull, was away from Jan. 6 to Feb. 10, 167½. Yeamans sat Dec. 23, 1671; he must then have gone on the Blessing to Barbadoes and returned with his commission as Governor April, 1672. See *Rivers*, 108.

(*same*) upon the motion of Capt: Thomas Badgard day is further given till tomorrow that is to say the 23rd instant January at
which time It is Ordered by the Grand Councill that the issue
upon the petition of the said Thomas Badyard against James
Dehaert shall be heard and determined peremptorily.

At a meeting &c this 23rd day of January 167½ sitting &c
(*the same*) upon hearing the petition and complaint of Capt.
Thomas Badgard for himselfe and Wm Dernal[1] of New Yorke
merchants Freighters of the good Ship Charles now rideing at
anchor in Ashley River against James Deheart husband of the
said Ship for Jacques Caseau and Balthazar Deheart of New
Yorke owners thereof and of the said James Dehearts answer
thereunto And upon serious consideration thereof had by the
Grand Councill and the several evidences on both sides sworne
and examined, the parties aforesaid having submitted themselves
to the judgment and determination of the Grand Councill It is
resolved and ordered by the Grand Councill that the said James
Deheart as he is husband of the Ship shall forthwith pay or cause
to be paid for and on behalfe of ·the said owners to the said
Thomas Badgard the sum of £37 9s: & 4d: sterl: in full satisfaction of all damages charges and expenses sustained by the said
Thomas Badgard for or by reason of all or any disability of the
said Ship or impediment thereupon from the prosecution of his
voyage from the 23d[2] day of January in the year of our Lord 1671
to this day with all his costs & charges to this suit.

At a Meeting &c this 10th day of February 167½ sitting &c
The Governor, Godfrey, Bull, Owen, Mathews, Portman, Marshall, Hughes. Upon consideration this day of the Scarcty of
provisions now growing in this Collony, which will require a more
frugall disposition of the provisions now remaining in the Lords
Proprietors stores &c. *Rivers*, 377.

At a meeting &c this 14th day of February 167½ sitting &c
Governor, Godfrey, Bull, Owen, Gray, Hughes, Marshall, Mathews. Upon the motion of the Inhabitants of James Towne It is

---

[1] Wm. Dervall, merch't, of New York, 1670–75, writes from Boston
Sep. 20, 1673: New York taken, all his father-in-law's (Duke of York's
auditor) state and his seized as prize, &c.

[2] Mistake for Dec. 23? The Charles had perhaps brought passengers
from Barbadoes, page 386, and was to return for more, page 389.

ordered that the Savanoe nere the said Towne be wholly reserved for the use of the Inhabitants in the said Towne.[1]

At a meeting &c this 17th day of February 167½ sitting &c The Governor, Godfrey, Bull, Owen, Gray, Mathews, Portman Hughes & Marshall.

Upon the motion of M[r] John Foster It is ordered that two warrants be issued out to the Surveyor Generall (that is to say) one warrant for the laying out of one Towne lott in James Towne and tenn acres of land neare the same for Coll. Simon Lambart[2] & one Towne lott and tenn acres of land in and neare James Towne for M[r] Jacob Scantleberry both of Barbadoes &c [pages 30, 54]. For as much as Thomas Hart, Yeoman, being an evill member &c. *Rivers*, 378.

At a meeting &c this 21st day of February 167½ sitting &c (*the same*) Mr Henry Hughes came this day before the Grand Councill & voluntarily surrendred up the one halfe of his land nere a place upon Ashley River known by the name of Oyster Poynt to be imployed in and towards enlarging of a Towne and Common of pasture there intended to be erected.[3] Mr John Coming and Affera his wife came likewise before the Grand Councill & freely gave up one halfe of their land nere the said place for the use aforesaid.

At a Meeting &c this 16th day of March 167½ sitting &c (*the same*) In a plea of Debt 14l. 8s. & 9d. sterling this day to be Owen, defendant. The defendant having pleaded in Bar to the

---

[1] A narrow savana 250 yds. N. W. of Jamestown, extending westward.

[2] An eminent planter of Barbadoes; member of the Assembly 1665, Speaker 1670, and of the Council 1674-76, &c. He was Comm'r for St. Kitts 1668, and Ld. Willoughby wrote: "so Col. Lambert must perform it himself &c a man of good reason and at a bowl of punch I dare turn him loose to any Monsieur in the Indies."

[3] In pursuance of the Prop'rs' wishes, page 361. His land lay S. W. of the crossing of Broad and Meeting streets, the "Market Place" or "Armory ground." *I. no. 4,* page 169. Coming's was 133 acres on Coming's creek from Ashley to Cooper river, between Beaufain and Calhoun streets, left by his will, 1694, to his wife, Affra; she, Dec. 10, 1698, gave to the church 17 acres between St. Philip's and Coming streets, and the part west of Coming (afterwards 'Harleston' village), under her will, 23d December, 1698, passed to her nephew, "John Harleston of Dublin gent.," and his descendants. *Dalcho,* 34.

tryed between Capt: George Thompson[1] petitioner & Mr Wm
said action that the said petitioner hath not subscribed his religion [page 114] The question is put whether the same plea is sufficient to barr the said Thomson from his action And it is resolved
(nemine contra dicente) that the said defendants plea is not sufficient to barr the said Thompson from his said action &c.   See
the Record Booke of Pleadings.   *C. J.*, page 30.

CAROLINA MEMORANDA.—*In Locke's Hand.*[2]

Act of Parliament for the Pamy[t] of the Lds P[rs] $7\frac{1}{2}$.

S. Bull. 70 Persons from Barbados and New Yorke come to
settle and other to view the country.   The New Yorke people
planted on a circle 8 miles from Charles towne nearer the mouth
of Ashley river.   The rivers generally run through marshes
which are not unhealthy.   Great numbers inclined to come from
New Yorke because of their taxes and hard winter they are rich
and industrious willing to settle in towns.   The air agrees better with Northerne then Southern comers.   Severall people
ready to remove from Bermudos when this crop is in if they can
have passage.   All animosity composed and all in health.
Cooper river full of herrings about 70 miles from the mouth
divides and goes beyond the division 30 miles.   Great plenty of
fish and foule in the freshes the land good and high up Cooper
river.   Westo Boo a great river running above the heads of
Ashley and Cooper riv[r].   S. Bull chosen cassica of Ettowan [3]

----

[1] Page 53.   A Barbadoes planter; came to Carolina $167\frac{0}{1}$, and settled
at Ickerbee; was of Parliam't 1672 & 1674; provost marshal $167\frac{3}{4}$, and
$167\frac{4}{5}$ in the Council.   Book of Pleadings and Journal to 19 April are
lost.   Gov. West proves Sayles will 10 April.   *Rivers*, 384.

[2] These letters are all to Lord Ashley from Carolina, except Halsted's
and Colleton's from Barbadoes, about March, $167\frac{1}{2}$; all are missing but
Dalton's, at page 376; Bull's, Dalton's, Cole's and Owen's are about
Jan. 20, $167\frac{1}{2}$, page 383; West's and the Council's about Feb. 14, $167\frac{1}{2}$,
page 384, sent on the Blessing, which sailed for Barbadoes about Jan.
20, $167\frac{1}{2}$, or Charles, which was in Ashley river Jan. 23d, and later went
to Barbadoes? page 389.

[3] The Ettiwan Indians were seated on and about Daniel's Island,
Westoboo, or Westo river, is the Savannah, 2 *Stat.*, 24.

and the reasons of their choise C. Foster ship cast away.   A
Role of tobaco sent, prefered to the best Virginia.   In hopes of
Indigo, Ginger Yames Potatoes.

J. Dalton. Ice once an inch thick in vessells of water but noe
where else.[1]   Commodityes wine oyle silke indigo Tobaco Hemp
Flax and perhaps Ginger.   Westoe Bou to a great river to ye
Southward of Sᵗ Helena.   The farther up into the country ye
better land.   The point between Ashley and Cooper river proposed for a towne and fort.   Desires a skilfull surveyor.   O Sullivan unable 268 men 69 women and 59 children in the plantacen.   This crop is hoped will yeild them a store.   Desire good
sorts of Vines and olives to plant as also Almands and Dates Q
in whose names writts &c are to run.

R. Cole.[2]   Good masts of 30 inches diameter.   Desires respit
of yᵗ part of his debt wᶜʰ is to be paid this Aug: till the next.

J. West. The pʳˢ plantacen whilst he was governor managed
carefully by Godfrey till he withdrew to Sʳ P. Colleton The Produce of the Pʳˢ plantacen last yeare 200 bush: Corne and pease
wᶜʰ will not hold out till next crop very little rain in 12 month.
40 acres cleare soe much for these hands some of the servants
time neare out.   Desires yᵗ ye servants hereafter sent may be
husbandmen or trades man the last that were sent being bad,
bought 4 barrells of beef for 1200ˡᵇ sugar whereof 866 charged
by bill on Mʳ T. Colleton the rest paid in Carolina.   Provisions
like to be scarce before ye next crop 2 acres per head to be
planted with provisions by order of Councill.   Sʳ J. Yeamans
ingrosses the provisions put on board the blessing 1000 foot
square timber 2620 pipe staves.   if another ship were ready to
take them in the people would pay their debts in pipe staves
Capᵗ Halsted hath converted to his own and the ships use ⅓ of
ye 150ˡᵇ besides the credit he got therefore the Councill abated
him ⅓ of ye freight he took in goods at new Yorke under freight.
Cattle thrive very well at litle charge.   Desires Rugs and course

---

[1] "Snow having been seen but twice in ten years from its first being
settled by the English." *Ash., 1680, 2 Car.,* 63.

[2] Carp'r of the Carolina, 1669; settled a plant'n 1670, and returned
1671, with serv'ts and stock; was of parliam't 1672, and appraiser 1674
Robert Cole died 1697 (wife Joane), and Robert Cole, 1708–32 (wife
Mary), may have been descendants.

blankets called cutts at the George Inne in Holburne and course canvas to make beds to preserve health in ye cold winter. A list of medecins to be sent.

Desires another Governor. Cossoes to pay a dear skin monthly as an acknowledgm^t or else to loose our amitie. The Emperor Cotachico at Charles town with 100 Indians who says Woodward[1] is got to Roanoak near Virginia. They invite our people to their country to see it but not thought convenient to doe soe The ships to be employed to Carolina should be of great burden but little charge in saileing.

W. Owen. 600 people resolved to come from New York industrious people. Q whether tobaco from Carolina to England before some time custome free This the Virginians hearken after. Ginger growes well but its cure because of the winter difficult. Indico like to be a commodity. Indians brought back two runwaye servants.[2] Q How many make a Councill. The land and timber is in the freshes of Wando river better then in the salts navigable 20 leagues extreamly windeing and marshey whilest the salts continue but after bold and bluff. Edisto much commended by ye Indians, who think themselves mighty safe by our neighbourhood.

Councill. C. Halsted took in men and goods at ⅔ freight at New York wch ¼ therefore the councill have abated he brought but 101^lb 00^s 11^d instead of 150^lb ½ months difference in ye account of the view of Capt Halsteds voiage to New York with exceptions to ye account severall places in the freshes of Wando fit for towns Oyster poynt a fit place for a port town and thence to plant up the river Wando. No other rivers to be planted till Ashley and Wando are. Desire ½ charge of Fortification to be allowed by ye Lds P. stores of provisions and other things to be continued. people with their goods to be transported from New York at ⅓ freight A ship 3 times as big as the blesseing sailed at ye same charge A savana about James towne to be allowed the people. ⅕ of ye depth to front on rivers cannot always be observed. Desire commoditie for Indian trade to purchase land. Desire all draughts not approved by ye Councill to be suppressd.

---

[1] Cotachico, pages 186, 191, 201. Woodward, page 338.

[2] Willoughby and Munkister, page 383; Halsted's acc't, page 373.

Sullivan. The 20[lb] taken up in Bermudos and charged hither by bill was to procure provissions for his servants to spare the P[ies] stores. The saying it was for ye passengers was a mistake of his clerk. Desire the Lds P[ers] order that the planters lands may be surveyed and be paid. A copy of his petition to ye Grand Councill to ye same purpose sent.

Halsted.[1] He hath received the dispatches for ye Bahamas Promises a carefull observacen of his instructions. Went up Cooper river about 80 miles Ashley river navigable for ships not above 2 leagues above the town. Complains of rude usage from West Godfrey Bull and Gray. New York men planted on James town on Ashley river have erected a town. Hopes to goe loaded from Barbadoes to Carolina with people of quality their servants and provisions. Denys at Barbados port charges and security But promises to act northing injurious to the governm[t] They who had promised to goe in the Charles to Carolina upon the Blessings comeing will goe in her and noe other way. Severall comeing from Londonderry and Virginia he hath cautioned ye masters of the ship to carry none that have not 8 months provisions with them The same course he took at New York. Carrys none from Barbados without tickets.

Halsted. Coming a good sailer but ambitious, undertaking company keeper. hath rec[d] my Ld Shaftesburys letter of 16 Dec:[2]

Mr. T. Colleton. Drawn two bills each for 78[lb] 10[s] one payable to Ed Barton and ye other to Paul Alestree and sent inclosed Cap[t] Halsted rec[t] for 150[l] 7[s] being paid for ye exchange, promisses Halsted his assistance.

Endorsed : Abstract of letters, Carolina, 71.

[*S. P.*, Bdle. 48, No. 84.][3]

---

[1] To Ld. Ashly, from Barbadoes, March, 167½? Dispatches, page 372, by Capt. Jeffreys, who, perhaps, touched at Barbadoes. The Charles was at Carolina Jan. 23, and now at Barbadoes?

[2] Page 364, *A. & W. I.*, 746 has Halsted and Colleton letters "to Ld. Shaftesbury," he was so created 23 April, 1672; Locke wrote and they were received later, but written about March, 167½.

[3] Bill of Lading, shipped, &c., by Rich'd Kingdon for acct. the Lords Prop'rs of Carolina, in the good ship William & Ralph, Wm. Jeffreys master, now in river Thames, and by God's grace bound for Charles

27

THE COUNCIL JOURNALS.

Sir John Yeamans Barrt. pursuant to the Lords Proprietors Commission to him directed dated the 26th day of December 1670 & 1. was proclaimed Governour of all this Territory or part of the Province of Carolina that lyes to the Southward and Westward of Cape Carterett this 19th day of Aprill 1672.[1]

At a meeting of the Governour and the Lords Proprietors Deputies at Charles Towne the said 19th day of Aprill 1672 sitting and present: The Governor Capt. Jno Godfrey Coll. Joseph West Capt. Thos Gray Mr Maurice Mathews Mr Wm Owen. Upon consideration this day had by the Governour & the Lords Proprietors Deputies of the better management of the affairs of this Province & a regard being had to the conveniency of the Freemen now assembled together in this Towne It is advised that a proclamation be issued out to dissolve all Parliaments & Parliamentary Conventions heretofore had or made in this Province And that a summons likewise be proclaimed requiring all the freeholders in this Province to come before the Grand Councill at Charles Towne tomorrow being the 20th day of Aprill instant & there to elect a new Parliament &c.

At which time that is to say the 20th day of Aprill 1672 pursuant to the tenor of the said Proclamation &c *Rivers*, 378, came the Freemen &c at Charles Towne and having then made their election presented to the Governor & the Lords Proprietors Deputies the members of the Parliament hereafter mentioned viz[t] M[r] Stephen Bull Capt. Flor: O'Sullivan M[r] John Culpeper, M[r] John Robinson, M[r] Christo. Portman, M[r] Ralph Marshall, M[r] John Mauericke, M[r] John Pinckard Capt: Robert Donne M[r] Amos Jefford M[r] Richard Conant, M[r] Peter Herne, M[r] Richard

---

Towne, in Ashley river, 42 punc: pease, 31½ bbl. flower, 1 bbl. rice, 1 box boks, 2 bbl. powder, 12 Gun Carriages, 6 drums, &c., to Mr. Jos. West, of Charles Towne, &c. London, 13 Jan. 1671, Wm. Jefferies. *Endorsed:* Charles Towne, April 23, 1672. Rec'd of Capt. Wm. Jefferies, &c. Jos. West. *Rivers*, 382.

[1] Capt. Jeffreys brought the Dec. and Jan. letters, pages 359, 375, this comm'n, page 330, Culpeper's, page 361, Mathews' and Gray's deputations. He left London after Jan. 13, 167½, and reached Carolina April 19, 1672? He perhaps touched at Barbadoes, left the Bahama dispatches, page 389, and brought Yeamans with him.

Chapman[1] Mr John Yeamans Mr Timothy Biggs[2] Mr James Jones[3] Mr Edward Mathews Mr Samuell West Mr Richard Cole Mr Henry Hughes.

And the said Parliament &c then and there out of themselves did elect five persons namely Mr Ste. Bull, Mr Christo: Portman, Mr Richard Conant, Mr Ralph Marshall & Mr John Robinson & them presented to the Lords Prop^{rs} Deputies[4] to be members of the Grand Councill according to the Lords Propr^s directions on that behalfe.

At a meeting of the Grand Councill at Charles Towne this 23rd day of Aprill 1672 sitting &c The Governor, capt: Joseph West, capt: Thomas Gray, capt: John Godfrey Mr Maurice Mathews, M^r Wm Owen Mr Stephen Bull Mr Christo. Portman Mr Richard Conant Mr Ralph Marshall & Mr John Robinson Upon consideration this day had of the better settling of this Province according to the Lords Proprietors Directions It is advised & resolved by the Grand Councell that warrants be forthwith issued out to the Surveyor Generall for the laying out of three Colonies or Squares of twelve thousand acres (that is to say) one Collony or Square of twelve thousand acres about Charles Towne another about James Towne and a third upon a place knowne at present by the name of the Oyster Poynt.

Upon debate this day had in the Grand Councill for that some

---

[1] Conant and Chapman were from N. York; also perhaps Hearn, 1673, viewer of staves for Jamestown; 1683, Com'r Pub. Acc'ts. His estate left by will, 18 Dec., 1688, to his wife, Jean, and 7 children, was sold under Act 169$\frac{4}{5}$ by James Witter and Jon'n Drake. Edith Hearn, 1698, Jno Hearn, 1708, John, Peter and Eliz. Hearn, 1723, and Capt. Edw. Hyrne, mem. Assembly 1716, were perhaps descendants.

[2] Was in Carolina March, 167$\frac{1}{2}$, and had lands 1672–73. He went to Albemarle, and, 1676, was Lord Craven's deputy there. In 1679 he claimed as Collector, but was ejected by Culpeper. 1683, he was Sur. Gen'l, but, 1684, went to England for redress. He m'd the widow of Geo. Ketchmaid, of Albemarle. 1683, Mary Biggs was granted 3,333 acres there.

[3] Land owner 1671, in Parliam't 1672, & Surveyor 1673–93; July 25, 1681, he & Elizabeth, his wife, had "80 acres on S. side of Jamestown creek," and grant 300 acres 1691.

[4] The deputies were Yeamans for Ld. Berkley, palatine, Godfrey Ld. Craven's, West Sir G. Carteret's, Owen Sir P. Colleton's, Mathews Ld. Ashley's, and Gray Duke Albemarle's.

of the Inhabitants of this Province have fallen certain parcells of Cedar Timber upon lands in the Province nott yett taken up by any person and carried the same away to be transported from hence The question was putt If any Cedar Timber being fallen on the Lords Proprietors lands be seized whether the persons from whom such timber shall be taken by such seizure shall be satisfied and paid for their labour in that seizure or noe   And it is resolved (nemine contra dicente) that such person shall receive reasonable satisfaction for such their labour.

JOHN LOCKE TO CAPT. KINGDON.

Exeter House, Apr. 29, 72.

Cap' Kingden,[1]

There is to be within this day or two a meeting of ye Lds. Prop^{es} of Carolina Ag^t wch time my Lord desires there may be a perfect state of y^{eir} accounts some of them presseing hard for it & if it should faile to be there it would discompose their affairs.   I desire you when you come next this way to bring my 20^{lb} with you & if I be not in ye way pray pay it to Mr Stringer or Mr Jones.

I am S^r Y^r most humble servant

J. LOCKE.

Addressed : For Capt Kingden at the Excise office in B   Street.

Endorsed : Mr Locke Lett^r the 29th of Aprill about Carolina business, 1672.

[*S. P.*, Bdle. 48, No. 88.]

THE COUNCIL JOURNALS.

At a meeting &c this 11th day of May 1672 sitting &c (*same*) Upon the motion of M^r Wm Owen it is orderd that a Jury be instructed to appeare upon Thursday next at the new dwelling house of said Wm Owen by Seaven of the clock in the morning of the same day to   the boundary line of the said Wm. Owen's land according to the warrant or order of the late Governour and Councill on that behalf dated the 9th day of June 1671.

---

[1] Capt. Rich. Kingdon, page 389. Stringer was Ld. Ashley's secretary, page 210. Jones ('P. J.,' page 329), the Prop'rs treasurer, page 236.

At a meeting &c 16th day of May 1672 sitting &c (*all but Conant & Marshall*) Upon consideration this day had of the better reducing the settlement of this Province to the Rules of the Lords Proprietors instructions and for disposing and preserving of an orderly method therein to the sattisfaction of all men as much as may be and for the prevention of differences and inconveniences which hereafter may happen for want of the knowledge of the true bounds and limitts of lands And for as much as divers persons have taken up severall quantitys of land in this Province which said lands have not yett been surveyed or bounded as they ought to be thereby impeding the propagation of a regular settlement It is therefore advised & it is this day ordered by the Grand Councill that all and every person and persons possessed of any lands not surveyed & fully bounded as aforesaid doe forthwith take out warrants for their lands so as the same may be surveyed &c within three months &c. For the avoiding all abuses or injurious dealings by or to any persons who have or hereafter shall intend to depart and transport themselves from this Province It is Ordered by the Grand Councill that noe man or single woman shall have a tickett from the Governour to depart and be transported from this Province unless his or her name have been sett up in the Secretarys Office one and twenty dayes[1] and that in that time noe person hath under written him or her unless such person whose name is so sett up and cannot stay the said time of one and twenty days shall give in such good security as the Secretary shall like &c. Resolved that Mr Stephen Bull be commissioned Master of the Ordinance & Captain of the Fort at Charles Towne.

At a meeting &c this 1st day of June 1672 &c present (*all*) Upon consideration of what may conduce to the better safety of this Settlement It is resolved that the Governour doe live in Towne. That Mr Wm Owen Mr Stephen Bull & Ralph Marshall prepare these following particulars to be proposed to the Parliament at their next sitting. 1st An Act for the uniforme building of Charles Towne. 2nd For the building of a bridge on the Southward part of Charles Towne.[2] 3rd An additional

---

[1] Page 369. Such notices appear in the Gazettes, 1732, 40, &c.

[2] Town, page 361; the bridge was from its S. W. point to the first land opposite, the S. E. point of Prop'rs plan'n, page 371.

Act against fugitive persons or absents without lycence.   4ᵗʰ An Act against selling or disposeing of arms or ammunitions to the Indians.

At a meeting &c this 4ᵗʰ day of June 1672 sitting *&c (all)* Upon consideration had of the complaynt this day brought in by Mʳˢ Affera Coming[1] against her servants namely John Chambers[2] Phillip Onill and Michael Lovell for their disobedience to her in refusing to observe her lawful commands & more especially against the said Phillip Onill for threatening to overset the Boate wherein she was or words to that effect, and giving the provisions allowed him and his fellow servants to the Doggs and threatening to run away to the Indians & divers other gross abuses & destructive practices which being sufficiently proved It is ordered by the Grand Councill that the said Phillip Onill be forthwith tyed to the tree and there receive one and twenty lashes upon his naked back and that the others be advised for time to come to render more dutifull obedience to the lawful commands of their said Mistresse upon paine of condigne punishment.[3]   *C. J.*, 35.

---

[1] "A lady of eminent piety and liberality;" benefactress of the Church in Carolina, *Dalcho*, 34; daughter of John Harleston, of Mollyns Co., Essex, gent. (of a family long seated at South Ockenden, Essex), and Elizabeth, his wife.   Her father's "inventorie" shows the furniture of her early home at Mollyns, from " the seller, the parlour, the Inner parlour, the hall, the kitchen, the larder, ye great Chamber, the hall chamber, the painted chamber, the nurserie, the buttrie chambʳ, the back chambʳ the gallerie " to "the garretts."   Her family removed to Ireland, where Mrs. Harleston had estates, *power atty.* 1659.   Mrs. Coming's letters after her husband's death, 1694, to her sister Ann and sister-in-law Eliz. Harleston, in Dublin, give glimpses of early Carolina life; that of March 6, 169⅞, describes " ye Country full of trouble and sicknesse " (near as " distressful" as her own), "ye small pox &c followed by an Earthquake and ye burning of ye towne &c and ye great loss of cattle &c from ye hard winter."   She died at Comingtee? early in 1699.

[2] He was one of Gray's Barbadoes servants, 167⁰⁄₁, and had land at Ickerby, 1674.   Lovell had, 1681, grant of lot 65 in Charlestown.

[3] Mike Lovell so took this advice to heart (some think) that on his mistress endowing the church, he gave his mite (lot 65) to the Huguenots, *Chn. Year B'k*, 1885, page 302.   But this romance was spoiled by his deed of it to Arthur Middleton, Esq., 1684, and the true story told by that of Ralph Izard, Esq., & Mary his wife, exe'x of Arthur Middle-

At a meeting &c this 8th day of June 1672 sitting &c (*all but Conant*) Mr Thomas Norris Anthony Churne and Samuell Lucas came this day before the Grand Councill, & made oath that they were privie to the contract between Richard Deyos and Christopher Edwards, his servant, and that the said Christopher Edwards was to serve the said Richard Deyos the terme of two yeares in this Province, to commence from the time of his arrivall there and ended the 17th day of March last past.[1] The said Christopher Edwards is thereupon reputed a Freeman and his liberty granted him to take warrants for the land due him in the Province aforesaid. Upon request of Coll. Joseph West It is ordered that twenty men from the Lords Proprietors Debtors in this Province (That is to say) from Mr John Coming one man Mr Richard Cole two men Mr Joseph Dalton one man Hugh Carterett & George Beadon one man John Faulconer one man Originall Jackson one man Mr Amos Jefford one man Mr Christo Portman one man M^r Wm Owen one man Capt. George Thompson one man Mr Edward Mathews one man Mr John Meaurick two men Mr Samuel West one man and Thomas Thompson one man doe goe with Coll. West upon Monday next come a fortnight in order to the procureing of a loading of Cedar Timber for the said Lords Proprietors Ship Blessing or any other of their Ships that may sooner arrive.

At a meeting &c 18th day of June 1672 sitting &c (*all*) The Grand Councill taking into their serious consideration how the inhabitants of this Province may be reduced into the best posture for the defence &c *Rivers*, 379, 381, two great Guns be mounted at New Towne &c. a Publick alarm may be given by firing two of the greatest gunns at Charles Towne Upon which alarm all &c who are able to beare arms doe dispose themselves in the manner following. The severall families of Mr Maurice Mathews, Mr Stephen Bull, Mr Nicholas Carterett and Mr Henry

---

ton, Esq., dec'd, reciting the "grant 6 march 1681 to Michael Loveinge, sawyer," of lot 65 in Charlestown, his sale 24 9ber, 1684, to Arthur Middleton, Esq., whose will 27 April, 168$\frac{4}{5}$, devised it to "his dearly beloved wife Mary Middleton;" she married Ralph Izard, Esq., and they convey, 5 May, 1687, to James Nicholas "for ye commonality of ye ffrench Church in Charlestowne." *Sec. Off. B'k*, 1704–8, page 250.

[1] Fixing arrival at Carolina 17 March, 1670, page 165. *Rivers*, 94.

Brayne residing in Ickerby Plantation[1] being about seven men
M[r] John Gardner one, George Canty[2] two, M[r] Amos Jefford five,
M[r] Thos Ingram one, Capt. Florence O. Sullivan two, Capt:
George Thompson two &c. repaire to the said Amos Jeffords
upper plantation to the Westward of the said Thos Ingram and
remaine under the command of M[r] Maurice Mathews and Capt:
Florence O'Sullivan his assistant in order to the defence of that
passage &c.   And the severall families of Capt: John Godfrey
about twelve M[r] Edward Mathews foure Coll. Joseph West five
M[r] Clutterbuck one, M[r] Hughes one to repaire to the plantation
now in the possession of the said Capt: John Godfrey & there to
remaine under the command of the said capt. Godfrey and
Henry Hughes his Lieutenant the better to maintain the leading
path there &c. and that all other the inhabitants of Colony of
Charles Towne (except the negroes in the Governours plantation
who are there left to defend the same being an outward place)
repaire to Charles Towne &c.   And that all the inhabitants on
the other part of the River called the Oyster Poynt doe repaire
to the plantation there now in the possession of Hugh Carteret,[3]
cooper, and being soe embodyed doe march forward to the plantation now in the possession of M[r] Thos Norris or M[r] W[m] Morill
which may be thought most safe under the command of M[r] Robert Donne &c and that all the inhabitants in and about New
Towne doe repaire to New Towne aforesaid & there remaine
under the command of M[r] Richard Conant &c   And that upon

----

[1]Accabee; Peronneau's point on Ashley river and the parts opposite
were then so called by the Indians living thereabouts; the name is now
limited to the east side.   Jefford's plan'n was on Ashley river at the
creek below "Bullfield."   Godfrey's was Sir P. Colleton's plan'n, page
371.   The Governor's at Wappoo, page 337.

[2] From Barbadoes 1669, held lands Ashley river 1671, 80; his will *1682*,
'*92, p. 59*, names wife Eliz'h, d'rs Mary Smericke, Cath: Manely, son
Wm. Canty, &c.   Capt. Wm. Canty, Geo. Canty & Capt. Jno. Canty,
members Assembly 1696, 1703, 1706, were perhaps his sons.   His family,
noted in Carolina wars, is extant.

[3] Or Cartwright; came from Barbadoes 1669, was a partner of Beadon's, of Owen's Parliam't 1670, ensign 1672 and lieut. 1674; he held
land & town lots 1671–90, and died 169$\frac{2}{3}$; his will, 21 Feb., 1687, mentions wife Anne, sons Hugh, Richard and Robert.   Richard left will, 5
March, 17$\frac{15}{8}$, & sons Hugh, Richard, Robert and Daniel (whose dau.,
Mary, m'd Hon. Rawlins Lowndes, 1751).

the appearance of any Top Sayle Vessell one Great Gunn be fired at Charles Towne &c.[1]

To Sir J. Yeamans. *20° Jun: 72.*

Exeter House 20th June 1672.

By the last account that came hither from Carolina I finde that you were not received there with such generall sattisfaction nor soe forwardly admitted to the Government we intended you as perhapps was imagined.   I am sorry to finde any differences at all among you the causes whereof I shall not enquire into.   But shall advise you as my friend not to make use of the Government we have put into your hands to revenge yourselfe on any who have spoke their apprehentions with that Freedom, which must be allowed men in a Country wherein they are not designed to be oppressed And where they may justly expect equall justice and protection.   I have too great vallew for your condition and ability not to desire the continuance of a right understanding betweene us; & therefore I must take the liberty to deale freely with you in a matter wherein we are both concerned and tell you plainly that I cannot avoid thinking that the suspitions of those men who have expressed some feare of your management of the Government had some ground; since your too forward Grasping at the Government when you came first thither and your endeavours since to diminish the authority of our particular Deputys who are our representatives and invested there with all our Power hath given us even at this distance some umbrage. Tis in your power to sett all right, I know you have dexterity enough to doe it.   You are now upon foundations of a larger extent then are usuall, and perhaps then in other places you have met with and if you will but suite the management of your Government to them and direct it wholy to the impartiall pros-

---

[1] By virtue of a war't formerly directed to Mr. John Culpeper, Surveyor General under the hand of the hon'ble Sr. John Yeamans, Baronet, Governor of this Province, & directed from the said Culpeper to me, I have measured & laid out to Mr. John Comings 133 acres of land as above plat doth represent the shape & formes with the B & B & marked trees as is represented and also the Quantity or thereabouts situated & being at the Oyster point, 18 June, '72, & exam'd by me, John Yeamans, Sur. *Book G,* No. 3, page 462.   The plat extends from "Ettiwan or Cooper river" to Ashley river (or 'Acabe'?).

perity of the whole plantation and all the planters in it you will
remove the Jelosies which I must tell you some of the Plantation
have conceived of you you will oblige the Lords Proprietors and
reape all those advantages which are sure to attend him who is
the greatest and most considerable man in a thriveing plantation,
and who hath contributed much to the advancement thereof.
For my owne part I assure you that haveing sett my mind on
carrying on this plantation and engaged my word that the people
shall live safe there under the Protection of a faire and equall
Government upon confidence whereof most of the planters have
come thither I shall thinke myselfe extremely injured by any
one who shall put such an affront on me as to make those who
trusted me be deceived and I am resolved at any rate rigourously
to require satisfaction of any one who by any undue proceeding
shall discompose the quiet of the settlement.   On the other side
I shall be as ready to acknowledge to any one what ever kindness they shall doe or assistance they shall give to this Plantation
I the more frankly make this declaration to you Sir John because
you have already contributed much and are like to doe more to
the growth and increase of this place where you have a considerable and growing interest which ought to make you have
the same concernment for itt that I have.   I returne you my
thanks for the forward inclination you have shewn to Carolina
and tell you more over that you have it in your hand by endeavoring the Publick good of it to make me your Friend as
much and as long as you please.

I am Your very affec^{ate} friend [1]

To Sir John Yeamans.   SHAFTESBURY.

[*S. P.*, Bdle. 48, No. 55, page 108.]

To Mr MAURICE MATHEWS *20 June 72.*

Exeter House the 20th June 72.

In x^{ber} last I writt to you [p. 362] and sent you my deputation
[p. 362n.] whereby you may be assured that I believe you an honest, active and steddy man haveing putt into your hands all the
power and share in the Government I should have myselfe
were I in Carolina in the management whereof I doubt not but

---

[1] This last line is in Locke's handwriting.

you will be carefull   In our Fundamentall Constitutions Temporary Laws and in Instructions you will finde the compasse you are to steere by, we have therein designed nothing but the quiet safety and prosperity of the people and if I am not deceived have better provided for it then ever was done in any other plantation.   You are therefore obstinately to stick to those Rules and oppose all deviation from it since by our Frame noe bodys power noe not of any of the Proprietors themselves were they there, is soe great as to be able to hurt the meanest man in the Country if our Deputys have but honesty and resolution enough to keepe things tight to those rules wherein theire owne welfare and security with that of the whole plantation is soe carefully provided for, and by the observance whereof the settlement is sure to stand prosperous and lasting.   The Distinction of the Governor from the rest of our Deputys is a thing rather of order then of overruling power and he hath noe more freedom thereby then any one of the Councell to swerve from those rules which I expect as my Deputy you should exactly follow, and in soe doeing you will finde your selfe always supported by me, and you shall not faile to receive all those encouragements a good and usefull man may expect.

I desire you to choose out for me a commodious Signiory to plant on when I am sattisfied of your choice I intend to stock it and to lay out a good deale of money in making a Plantation for myselfe the ordering whereof I intend to committ to your care   I am glad you have behaved yourselfe soe well towards the Indians that they have chosen you there Cassica you did well to ask leave of the Governor and Councell before you accepted it in your management of it   pray be careful to use them justly and kindly, and by none but faire ways endeavour to unite them with us   But if you answer my expectation in the management of my affairs and dischargeing of the trust committed to you I shall be able to make you a more considerable Cassique then any of the Indians there.

I am Your very affec^{ate} friend

SHAFTESBURY.

To Mr Maurice Mathews.   *The superscription in Locke's hand.*

[*S. P.*, Bdle. 48, No. 55, page 110.]

To Mr T. GRAY.   *20 June 72.*

June 20th 1672.

I thanke you for your letter to me of 24th of January last[1] by which I finde that you have done us two considerable services, the one in subduing our injurious neighbours the Cussoo Indians the other in the discoverys you have made up Ashley River, and Cooper River for soe the Lords Proprietors have named that which you call Wando.

You have laid the beginnings of your being knowne to me in a way which will oblidge me to remember you with kindness. The service you have done the Plantation and the Civill account you have given me of it will deserve my regard and I shall be very ready on all occasions to give encouragement to sober and active men which is the Character your actions have given of you   I desire you to continue on your endeavours for the good of a place which I will take care shall not ill reward you and be assured that I desire the continuance of your correspondence with me and am

Your very affectionate friend

SHAFTESBURY.

[*S. P.* Bdle. 48, No: 55, page 111.]

———

To Mr WEST AND THE REST OF THE COUNSELL.   *20 June 72.*

Exeter House this 20th. June 1672.

Your late management of the affairs of the Plantation have binn with soe much prudence that I cannot but returne you my particular thanks and tell you that whilst you continue to be carefull of the common good of the place which is your owne interest you shall always have me ready to countenance and assist you in it and to study the good of those men who shall endeavour to signalize themselves that way to keepe to the rules of our Establishment it hath binn necessary for us to take the Government out of Mr Wests hands in which it hath thriven

---

[1] Missing.   The superscription of this is in Locke's hand.

very well to put it into that only Landgraves which is upon the place   But I am very sorry to finde that Sir John Yeamans is not a man soe acceptable to the whole plantation as I could wish   I know how hard it is for Jealousy to be removed and Factions united when once begunn though amongst men (as it often happens) otherwise discreet and worthy.   That therefore this may not prejudice the affairs of our Plantation and the animosity that may arise from hence, disturb the quiet which is necessary to an infant settlement   Wee shall endeavour to finde out as soone as wee cann a man to be Governor who besides other qualifications fitt for that imployment may alsoe have this necessary one of being indifferent to the whole plantation disinterested from all divisions in it and a man not suspected or disgusted by any of the Planters.   This though I have a very great respect for Sir John and noe other exception to him I see will be unavoidable for us to doe to preserve that unity and good understanding in the Plantation that is necessary.   In the meane time I recommend it to your care (whose prudence and integrity we already have had experience of) to keepe unbiassed to those rules you will finde in our Fundamentall Constitutions Temporary Laws and Instructions and particularly our Deputys are to remember that they represent our Persons and therefore they ought not to diminish our right by making themselves but Cyphers and submitting too much to the will of any Governor whatsoever   nay if Sir Peter Colleton himselfe or any of the Lords Prop^rs should come upon the place our Deputys ought to maintaine our authority and share in the Government according to the Fundamentall Constitutions which we have to that purpose put into their hands.   Haveing binn soe carefull to balance one anothers power to prevent the ingroseing it into any one hand that the Palatine himselfe and soe his Deputy the Governor hath but his limited proportion of it suited to the dispatch of affairs beyond which we never intended nor are our deputys to suffer it to extend.   This I am sure whilst you keepe to those rules we have established the Plantation will thrive and every one in it, if it be not his owne faulte be in a prosperous and safe condition   I recommend therefore your owne good and interest to your owne care wherein I am sure to stand by you.   I very much applaud your faire dealing with us in respect of our Stores and debt   this

regard to our concernments will encourage us to take all manner
of care of you   I thinke my selfe particularly obliged by it and
am   Your very affectionate friend

SHAFTESBURY.

[*S. P.* Bdle. 48, No. 55, page 112.]

———

To Mr JOSEPH WEST.   *20 June 72.*

Exeter House June the 20th 1672.

I am extremely well sattisfyde with the faire and punctuall accompt you have sent us of our Stores and plantations both publicke and private; and the concernements thereof and you have
answered all the expectation we could have of an honest, sober
and prudent man What opinion this hath gained you with us in
Gennerall you will see by our Publick letter and for my owne
parte your management of our affairs hath soe well pleased me
that besides that marke of our respect we have given you in a
Cassique ship, I shall be ready on all occasions to consider you
as a person to whom we principally owe the settlement of that
plantation which I hope will come to something in the farther
carrying on of which I still rely very much on your steddy care
and endeavours to keepe the Course of things regularly on in
that Channel we have chalked out to you This you by having
the disposall of our stores and being one of our Deputys will
have as much power to doe as if you were still possest of the
Government which not any dislike of you but the Frame of our
Constitution tooke out of your hands.   I perceive that all the
people are not soe well sattisfied that it is placed in Sir John's.
Whatever cause there is of any jealousy we will provide the best
we cann against all inconveniencys that may happen at this distance and we expect from you our Deputys that are our representatives upon the place that you thinke not your authoritys to
preserve things in the right way then we should have if we who
depute you were there ourselves whatsoever you shall doe in
pursuance of our Constitutions Laws and Instructions and of
the Common good of the Plantation you may be sure we will
maintaine and support you in I desire you therefore to keepe
closely and resolutely to that wherein neither cann the Plantation

suffer nor you be borne downe. As to the wants that you mention to be supply'd and that are necessary to the better carrying
on both the setlement and our private plantation care shall be
taken in it with all convenient speed I thanke you for the constant information you have sent me of our affairs which I desire
you to continue by every oppertunity for I repose much confidence in you and am

Your very loving friend

SHAFTESBURY.

[S. P. Bdle., 48, No. 55, page 113.]

CAROLINA TEMPORARY LAWS.

21 June, 1672.

Since ye paucity of Nobility will not permitt ye fundamentall
Constitutions presently to be put in practise, It is necessary for
ye supply of that defect, that some temporary Laws should in
the meane time be made for ye better ordering of affairs, till by
a sufficient number of Inhabitants of all degrees ye Governm^t
of Carolina can be administered according to ye forme established
in ye fundamental Constitutions We ye Lords Prop^{rs} of Carolina,
upon due consideration have agreed to these following.

1. The Palatine shall name the Governor, and each of ye
Lords Proprieto^{rs} shall name a Deputy, who wth ye Govern^r & an
equall number of others chosen by ye Parliam^t, shall continue to
be the Councell^{rs} till ye Lords Propriet^{rs} shall either order a new
choice, or ye Country be so peopled as to be capeable of ye
Governm^t according to ye fundamentall Constitutions, and as
there shall be Landgraves & Cassiques created by the Lords
Prop^{rs}, soe many of the eldest in age of them that are present in
Carolina, as shall be equall to ye number of ye L^{ds} Prop^{rs}
Deputys, shall be alsoe of ye Councell, that soe ye Nobillity may
have a share in ye Govern^t and the whole Administration may
still come as neere ye forme designed, as the Circumstances of
the growing plantation will permitt.

2. The other Seaven Propriet^{rs} shall respectively nominate
theise following Officers, viz:

The Admirall, The Marshall of the Admiralty. The Chamberlaine, The Register of Births, Burials & Marriages. The

Chancellor, The Secretary.[1] The Constable, The Military Officers. The Cheife Justice, The Register of Wrightings. The
High Steward, The Surveyor. The Treasurer, The Receiver.

And upon the vacancy of any of theise Officers, the Governo[r]
& Councell in Carolina, shall substitute others till that Propriet[rs]
pleasure can be knowne in whose nomination it is.

3. The Govern[r] together wth the Lords Propriet[rs] Deputys, the
Landgraves & Cassiques that are Councellors, and the Councell[rs] chosen by the Parliam[t] shall be the Grand Councell, and
shall have all the power and authority of the Grand Councell and
other Courts till they come to be erected. The Quorum of the
Councell shall be the Govern[r] & Sixe Councell[rs], whereof three
at least shall be Deputys of Proprietors.

4. If it happen that any of the Lords Prop[rs] Deputys shall by
death, or departure out of Carolina, or any otherwise cease to
be Deputy before ye Lords, Prop[rs], respectively shall have deputed others in their roome; That the number of Deputys may
always be kept full, the eldest of the Councellors chosen by the
Parliam[t] shall be to all intents and purposes Deputy of that
Prop[r] whose former Deputacon is by death or otherwise determined till ye s[d] Prop[r], his heir or Successor shall make another
Deputy. And when it shall happen that one or more of the
Councellors chosen by the Parliam[t], shall by this meanes come
to be Deputys of Prop[rs], new Councello[rs] shall be chosen by the
Parliam[t] at its next Session to fill up their places in Councell,
Provided always that if the Propriet[rs] whose vacant place is thus
supplyede shall make some other person his Deputy, then he
who by eldership came to be his Deputy shall be Councell[r] as he

---

[1] Sir George Carterett, Knight & Barronett vice Chamberlaine of his
majesties household, one of his majesties most honourable Privy Councellors of the Kingdome of England and Ireland and Chancellor of Carolina. To Joseph Dalton, Gent: sendeth Greeting: Whereas by our
Temporary laws it belongs to the Chancellor to choose and Commission
the Secretary of the Province of Carolina I out of the confidence I have
of the prudence integrity and ability of you Joseph Dalton doe hereby
constitute and appoint you the said Joseph Dalton Secretary for the said
Province And doe hereby authorize you to doe and execute all those
things that belong to the Office of Secretary. Witness my hand & seale
this 24th day of June A. D. 1672.   G. CARTERET.   This is a
true copy of the Originall examined.   Jos DALTON Secretary.
  Coun. Jour., 58.

was before, and he that was last chosen into the Councell by the Parliam⁺ shall cease to be a Councell⁺, if there be more of those chosen by the Parliam⁺ then there be Deputys of Proprietors.

5. The Parliament shall consist of ye Governo⁺, ye Deputys of the Lords Proprietors, the Nobillity and twenty chosen by the freehoulders, and shall have power to make Laws to be ratti-fyd as in ye fundamentall Constitutions is Provided. And shall be assembled as often and in the same manner as in ye funda-mentall Constitutions is provided concerning Parliaments.

6. All Acts, that shall be made by the Parliam⁺ before our Government of Carolina come to be administered according to our fundamentall Constitutions, shall all cease & determine at ye end of ye first Session of Parliament that shall be called, chosen, and shall sitt according to ye Articles concerning Parliaments established in the fundamentall Constitutions.

7. Soe much of the fundamentall Constitutions as shall be capeable of being put in practise, shall be ye rule of proceeding. Signed & sealed, this 21ˢᵗ of June 1672.

SHAFTESBURY,   G. CARTERET,

CRAVEN,   P. COLLETON.

[*Col. En. B'k*, No. 20, p. 87.] *Rivers*, p. 354.

AGRARIAN LAWS OR INSTRUCTIONS from the Lords Proprie-tors to the Governor and Council of Carolina. 21 June. 1672. 23 Articles. *Signed* Shaftesbury, Craven, H. Cornbury, G. Carteret, Jo. Berkeley, P. Colleton.

[*Col. En. B'k*, Vol. 20, p. 83.] *Rivers*, 355, 359.

To Mʳ JOSEPH WEST. 25ᵗʰ *June*. 72.

Exeter House June 25ᵗʰ 1672.

To shew you the respect and kindnesse I have for you I have made you register for the Province of Carolina¹ wʰich power peculiarly belonged to me as Chiefe Justice and you are (by ver-

---

¹ Commission from Anthony, Earl of Shaftesbury, Chief Justice of Carolina, to Joseph West, appointing him Register of all writings and contracts, with power to execute all things belonging to said office, June 24, 1672. *Col. En. B'k* 20, p. 89. *A. & W. I.*, § 868.

tue of this authority) to register not onely the Titles of the
Lords Proprietors but of all Deeds amongst yourselves noe
Deed being good that is not registered. I desire you to be
kinde to Mr Man who lately I sent you and write me word how
fitt he is for a second Overseer on any Plantation I shall setle.

Pray send an accompt by the next conveyance what Stock of
Catle you have on our Plantation, what servants and when theire
times expire. What Land you have planted? and with what?
Alsoe what the Plantation with the appurtenances is worth were
it to be sould.

I would alsoe desire your care in the choice of a Signiory for
me either on Ashley or Cooper River in a place of the greatest
pleasantness and advantage for health and profitt which must be
where there is high Ground, neare a navigable River and if it
be above the tydes flowing tis the better.

I am Your affec^{ate} friend

SHAFTESBURY.

[*S. P.* Bdle. 48, No. 55, p. 115.][1]

———

THE COUNCIL JOURNALS.

At a meeting &c 29th day of June 1672 sitting &c (*all but
Portman & Owen*) William Barry being this day &c *Rivers*,
381.

At a meeting &c this 2nd day of July 1672 sitting &c The
Governour capt. Thos Gray Mr Maurice Mathews M^r Wm Owen
capt. John Godfrey, capt. Stephen Bull, Mr Ralph Marshall, M^r
Richard Conant. In order to the better defence it is resolved
that a party of thirty men be dispatched to the Southward against
the Westoes who are said to lurke there with an intent to march
secretly to this place.

At a meeting &c this VIst day of July 1672 sitting &c The
Governour, capt. Thos Gray Major John Godfrey M^r Wm Owen,
capt. John Robinson Mr Richard Conant Mr Christo^r Portman
Mr Ralph Marshall. For as much as some former apprehensions
of the approaches of the Westoes have occasioned such constant

———

[1] Lds. Prop'rs to Gov'r & Council.   26 June, 1672, write " y^t therewth
their printed fundamental Constitutions (of march 1.) are sent," and that
letter with ye said Constitutions was received here the 8 day of Feb'y
followinge. *Rivers*, 420.

and diligent watches among the people the continuation whereof may not only hazard their healthes but will prove altogether destructive to their improvements And for as much as nothing appears but that the said watches may be eased It is therefore advised and resolved by the Grand Councill that halfe of the severall guards be drawne off presently and be dismissed till tomorrow morning at which time they are to appeare at the Guards and continue there till monday morning and if no further cause be given to the contrary then to be wholly discharged.

At a meeting &c this 9th day of July 1672 sitting &c (*all but West*) upon consideration &c *Rivers*, 382. It is ordered &c that the said inhabitants be forthwith disposed into six companies besides the Governour's life guard &c it is advised that Commissions be made & directed to Lieut: Coll. John Godfrey, Sergeant Major Thomas Gray, capt. Maurice Mathews capt John Robinson,[1] capt. Richard Conant, capt Florence O'Sullivan & Capt. R. Donne & such other inferior officers &c.

THE COUNCIL JOURNALS.[2]

Att a Meeting of the Grand Councill at Charles Towne this xxii day of July 1672 sitting & present: The Governor, Maj: Thomas Gray Lt. Col: John Godfrey, capt: Maurice Mathews, Col. Joseph West, Mr William Owen, capt. Stephen Bull, capt. Richard Conant, Lieut. Christo^r Portman, Ensigne Ralph Marshall & Capt. John Robinson. ffor as much as the Smith's worke (having not been regulated heretofore) is delayed & done at such unreasonable rates that many Inhabitants of this province are altogether disappoynted in getting their Armes fixed & in good order to the great danger of the safety of this set-

[1] Perhaps Ld. Ashley's deputy at the Bahamas May, 1671. He came to Carolina and held land there 1671; was a captain 1672, and in April chosen to Parliam't and the Council. He sat till June, 1673, but engaged in the Culpeper riots, fled to Barbadoes? and was attainted.

[2] These Council Journals, 22 July, 1672, to Nov. 10, 1674, and June 12, 1675, on original pages 35 to 67, were lately found in Sec'ty's office, Columbia, in "Grant Book, warrants, 1672–1694." They were known to Hewet and perhaps Ramsey, but not to Mr. Rivers nor the commission which collected the Journals 1851. They have never been printed, and abstracts only are here given, neither the very words nor all the words of the original.

tlem[t] if any occasion be offered It is therefore Resolved that Lt
Col. Jno Godfrey, Maj: Thos Gray & capt. Mau: Mathews doe
consider & assess reasonable paym[t] for the same &c.

Mr Thos Hurt[1] came this day before the Grand Councill &
surrendered up two acres of land nere Charles Town E[wd] of capt:
Sayle's land w[ch] he holds in right of his wife Mary Hurt form[ly]
called Mary Gorge for part of s[d] Towne & the G[d] Counc[ll] grant
two acres belonging to s[d] Town situate nere Charles Town &
S[wd] of Hugh Carterett's 2 acre lott &c.

The persons hereunder named came this day before the Grand
Councill & for the better Modell of Charles Towne according to
the annext Schedule did surrender all their lands in the s[d] Towne
& agreed to possess only the same lotts as hereinafter is'ment[d]:

Thomas Ingram takes only one lott 58 M[r] Samuel West only one lott
31. M[r] William Owen 2 lotts 32 & 23, capt: Maurice Mathews & capt:
Stephen Bull for capt: Henry Brane one lott 30, Lieut. Henry Hughes
one lott 3 M[r] John Coming one lott 29, capt, fflorence O'Sullivan four
lotts 5, 6, 26 & 27 M[r] Samuell West for John Williamson one lott 7 M[r]
Ralph Marshall one lott 8 Capt. Stephen Bull two lotts 25 & 24 The
Grand Councill for capt. Joseph Bayley one lott 9, Sir John Yeamans
one lott 22, Coll° Joseph West for Richard Deyos one lott 19, M[r] Thomas
Turpin one lott 33, [Precilla Burke] Maj: Thomas Gray one lott 10, M[r]
John Yeamans & M[r] Timothy Biggs for M[r] John ffoster one lott 11,
Richard Batten one lott 13, Henry Wood one lott 15, George Beadon
two lotts 40 & 20, Ensign Hugh Carterett one lott 18 capt. George
Thompson bought of W[m] Kennis two lotts 16 & 17 M[r] Joseph Dalton &
M[r] Ralph Marshall for capt. Nathaniel Sayle two lotts 59 & 60, M[r]
Thomas Hurt for his wife one lott 61, Coll: West for the L[ds] Proprietors
five lotts 50, 51, 52, 53 & 62, Capt. Maurice Mathews two lotts 37 & 54
M[r] Richard Chapman for M[r] Mitchaell Smith one lott 38 M[r] Thomas
Thompson one lott 55, capt. Gyles Hall one lott 12, Lt Coll. Jno God-
frey for M[r] Thomas and M[r] James Smith two lotts 43 & 57 Richard Cole
one lott 42 M[r] Joseph Dalton one lott 44, M[r] John Pinkerd one lott 36,
Joseph Pendarvis one lott 45, M[r] John Mavericke one lott 43, Philip
Comerton one lott —, M[r] Christopher Portman one lott 4, Ensign Henry
Prettye one lott 56, M[r] Timothy Biggs one lott 34, M[r] Charles Miller one
lott 46, M[r] John Culpeper one lott 35, capt. John Robinson one lott 47,
Ensign John Boone one lott 2, M[r] Edward Mathews one lott 1. See
Dalcho, 17, *who adds* Precilla Burke lot 28.

---

[1] Or Hurst? came to Carolina 1671, was viewer of tobacco 1675 and
1676, had lands on Charleston neck, sold, 1678, to Tothill. Ingram,
came in 1669; was of Owen's Parliam't 1670, and had lands at Ickerby.

Order^d that Capt Richd Conant doe seize the Indian known by the name of Alarum Caseca's brother with his gun & all the powder & gun locks wch shall be found in his custody & him & them take to be brought before the G^d Councill at the next sitting. Order^d that upon any Alarum Capt Maurice Mathews & his Company doe repair to Mr Amos Jeffords plant^n, cap^t fflorence O'Sullivan & his company doe remaine at his now dwelling house,[1] Capt John Robinson & his company doe repaire to Lt Col: John Godfrey's plant^n & Maj: Thos Gray's company doe repaire to the Lords Proprietor's plant^n now in the posses^n of Coll: Joseph West. B'k 1672, 94, p. 36.

Att a Meeting &c this xxvii day of July 1672 sitting &c (*All above except Robinson*)[2] For the speedy ordering of the Bridge on the S^{wd} part of Charles Towne accord^g to the act in that case made &c [page 393] Maj: Thos Gray having consented to the Agreem^t &c It is Resolved &c that he be the undertaker to build that part of the bridge appoynted by the s^d act to be builded at the public charge of the pres^t Inhabitants of this Province And order^d that s^d Maj. Gray for the doeing the same shall have 5½ days worke from every man now in the Province (except such p'sons as are engaged to build any other part of s^d bridge) every man to provide himself & his servants provisions & tools during that time &c. Resolved that Col: West & Lt Col. Godfrey do examine the difference betw^n cap^t fflorence

---

[1] Near and N. W. of Charlestown. For others, pages 396, 412.

[2] Carolina. By the Governor, by and with the advice and consent of the Council. You are forthwith to admeasure and lay out for a town on the Oyster Point, all that point of land there formerly allotted for the same, adding thereto one hundred and fifty acres of land, or so much thereof as you shall find to be proportionable for the said one hundred and fifty acres in the breadth of land formerly marked to be laid out for Mr. Henry Hughes, Mr. John Coming, and Affra, his now wife; and James Robinson, estimated to seven hundred acres, and contained between the lands then allotted to be laid out for Mr. Richard Cole, to the North, and a marked Tree, formerly designed to direct the boundary line of the said Town to the South. And a certificate, fully specifying the situation, bounds and quantity thereof, you are to return to us with all convenient speed. And for so doing, this shall be your sufficient warrant. Given under my hand at Charles Town this seven and twentieth day of July 1672.   JOHN YEAMANS.

To John Culpepper Surveyor General. *Dalcho*, page 19.

O'Sullivan & Rich⁴ Crossley & make such orders as they shall find equitable in that case.

Forasmuch as Wᵐ Argent is now overtaken by some distemper produced by his long idleness & that some suitable remidy may be provided for the same It is advised that Lt Col: Jno Godfrey &c take sᵈ Argent into his plantⁿ to observe such order as sᵈ Lt Col. Godfrey shall give for his recovery & attend during one month &c Mʳ Ralph Marshall having moved for a warᵗ for the land belonging to Jonathan Barker & capᵗ Stephen Bull also claiming a right thereto an injunction ordered &c.¹ *Ibid*, 37.

Att a Meeting &c this iijᵈ day of August 1672 setting &c (*The same*) upon motion of Mʳ Thos Lane ordered that 200 acres upon the Seaman's land be reserved for 6 months next ensuing for sᵈ Lane having engaged to transport 20 persons upon his accᵗ to this province before that time In like manner 200 acres be reserved for Mʳˢ Jane ffookes having engaged for 10 persons.

Mʳ Jnᵒ Norton & Lt. Originall Jackson² came &c and entered into an agreemᵗ that 50 acres by him lately purchased of Jnᵒ ffaulconer³ be &c to uses following: ½ on Ashly river wᵗʰ buildings & improvmᵗˢ to sᵈ Jno Norton his heirs &c and ½ boundᵍ on Wandoe river in sᵈ O Jackson &c and sᵈ Norton pay sᵈ Jackson £12 in 2 months & crops of corn, tobacco & other prophets together wᵗʰ prophets of their other business since their arrivall in this province accordᵍ to their copartnership viz: since 17ᵗʰ of ffebr'y 167⁰/₁ half to each & sᵈ Origⁿ Jackson will give the house he now lives in to sᵈ Jnᵒ Norton before 1 Jan'y next &c.

Att a Meeting &c this 17ᵗʰ day of August 1672 sitting &c

---

¹ Came to Carolina 1669, and of Owen's parliam't, 1670; this claim indicates that he had died or left the province.

² Came from Barbadoes, 167⁰/₁; was Robert's legatee, and held lands near Charlestown, 1672 and 1680, on E. side Ashley river, above Bees ferry; 1692, 500 acres near Stoney Point, Berkley Co., of John Faulconer, dec'd, granted Hannah English, widow.

³ Or Reginald? Jackson, came from Barbadoes 17 Feb., 167⁰/₁, in partnership with Norton, but dissolved 1673; he held lands on Cooper river, below Clement's ferry; 168⁰/₁ he and Meliscent, his wife (was she Millicent Howe, page 135), "being excited with a pious zeal," gave lands to the Church. *Dalcho*, 26. He died 168-.

The Governor, Godfrey, Mathews, West, Bull, Marshall, Portman & Conant.

Forasmuch as there hath been a certain parcell of land at James Town form[ly] designed to be settled by some of the Seamen arriving in the ship Carolina in the first fleet w[ch] hath since remained altogether unsettled to the great prejudice &c on motion of M[r] Robert Gibbs[1] ordered that 90 acres thereof be laid out to him w[d] of cap[t] Thos Jenner for nine people already arrived on his acc[t] & that 60 acres more adjoining be reserved & allotted to him in case he transports 6 people more on his own acc[t] to settle the same in 4 months.

Att a Meeting &c this xxiiij[th] day of August 1672 sitting &c The Governor, Gray, Godfrey, West, Bull, Marshall, Portman & Robinson.

Forasmuch as divers persons in this Province have of their own accords presumed to Retaile strong drinke thereby promoting distress idleness & quarrelling to the great Scandal of Christianity &c the Grand Council orders &c.

Forasmuch as Brian Fitz Patrick hath departed this province with an intent to go to the Spaniards & intelligence is given that he as yett hath gott no further then S[t] Helena It is advised that M[r] Henry Woodward & M[r] James Needham[2] be dispatched to S[t] Helena in order to the taking s[d] Bryan Fitzpatrick & bringing him back but in case of opposition soe as they cannot take & securely bring him alive then to maim, destroy or kill him as they shall find best to agree with their owne safety.[3] *Ibid,* 39.

Att a Meeting &c this viiii day of Sept[r] 1672 sitting &c The Gov[r], Gray, Godfrey, Mathews, Owen, Bull, Marshall, Conant & Robinson.

Forasmuch as inform[n] is given by divers Indians that some Spaniards are at S[t] Helena p'paring to march towards this place

---

[1] Governor of S. Carolina 1710, p. 88. Capt. Jenner, p. 277.

[2] From Barbadoes? He had land and goods at Charlestown, Oct., 1671, but was away and may have gone with Woodward to Virginia. He was, perhaps, the 'heroic Englishman' killed by Indians at Enoe, 1673. Hewett, 1 *Car.*, p. 62.

[3] Concessions of ye Lords Proprietors of Carolina to certain persons in Ireland, &c., 31 August, 1672. *In Locke's handwriting. Col. En. B'k* 20, p. 90. *Rivers,* 365.

It is therefore ordered that Lt. Col. John Godfrey be forthw[th] commis[d] to take into care two & fifty men now raised for that purpose & wth them to march toward S[t] Helena af[sd] wth ample instruccons to inquire concerning that matter.

Forasmuch as M[r] John Coming hath form[ly] made a surrender to the G[d] Counc[ll] of half his land upon the Oyster poynt for the erecting of a Towne there designed to be w[ch] s[d] surrender [p. 385] being by way of instruccon & exemplary for the other Inhabitants there to doe the like & forasmuch as the s[d] Inhabitants have altogether refused the same   It is therefore upon the motion of s[d] John Coming ordered that s[d] surrender from henceforth be null & void & that s[d] half of his land surrendered as af[sd] be returned to him againe &c.[1]

For as &c divers comp[ts] to the G[d] Counc[ll] of Thos Archcraft, smith, having undertaken to fitt up such defective arms as should be brought to him & hath for a long time had many Armes in his custody & willfully neglects to fitt them to the great detrim[t] of the safety of this Province &c ordered on comp[t] any member of the G[d] Counc[ll] issue a war[t] to commit s[d] smith to prison &c.

Att a Meeting &c this —— day of —— 1672 sitting &c The Gov[r], Gray, Godfrey, Mathews, West, Conant, Bull, Portman & Marshall.

ffor as &c divers prisoners have been a long time bound over to appear at the Sessions to be holden for this Province & cannot be discharged for want thereof And for as &c divers matters have lately happened ag[t] the peace of the L[ds] Prop[rs] as is said That a Just inquiry & determin[n] may be made upon the same It is ordered that a Sessions of the peace & Goale delivery be holden for this Province before the G[d] Counc[ll] upon the 5 day of October next ensuing.   Comp[ts] of great prejudice &c to the inhabitants of the Colony of Charles Towne that convenient paths or highways have not heretofore been laid out in the most usuall places of concourse to & from the s[d] Towne [page 323] It is therefore

---

[1] Sir Tho. Lynch, Gov. Jamaica, to Capt. Jno. Wentworth, Gov: New Providence. Jamaica, Sept. 8, 1672, * * wishes they were all well settled at Carolina or here, considering they can never in those islands be convenient, safe or rich, &c.   Told them formerly (his letter 16 March last?) that 3 ships were fitted out at the Havana to destroy them and Carolina, and that 'the Norths' and 'your shoals saved you.' &c. *A. & W. I.,* 921, 916.

advised that a war[t] be issued to the Surveyor Gen[ll] requiring him to cause to be laid out path or highway from the Governor's now dwelling house to the s[d] Towne & one path from Cap[t] Geo: Thompson's plan'n (late belonging to Thos Holton) to Charles Towne & a path from Lt Col. John Godfrey's now dwelling house to the s[d] Towne[1] each path to be   foot broad & to run as much upon the out side lines of lands as may be so as the lands on each side of such path may beare equal part thereof & also avoiding all marshes or watry grounds if convent[ly] it may be so done & the Surveyor dispatch the same before the 5th day of Oct[r] next.

Att a Meeting &c this Eighth day of Octo: 1672 sitting &c The Gov[r], Gray, Godfrey, Mathews, West, Owen, Bull, Conant Portman & Marshall.

For &c Rich[d] Nicklin & Jn[o] Rivers being now prisoners as they have been sentenced to death for continuing to run away from this Province accord[g] to a verdict of a Jury on the Act of Parliam[t] &c & as it is considered &c that the death of the s[d] persons may not only lesser the strength of the province but perhaps may not altogether be a matter so well approved on abroad &c ordered that s[d] prisoners be allowed opportunity of submission & to plead for mercy.

Att a Meeting &c this xviii day of Octo: 1672 sitting &c. The Gov[r], Godfrey, West, Owen, Bull, Portman, Conant & Robinson.

Vpon cons[n] had of the inform[n] given in ag[t] Lt. Col. Jno. Godfrey for taking away the value of 30[s] ster: from the person of W[m] Loe & on motion & request of s[d] Lt. Col. Godfrey Ordered that a Special Session of Goal Delivery be holden before the G[d] Counc[ll] at Charlestowne upon the 24th Octo: inst: to hear & determine the same & that a special venire be issued out mentioning the names of the Jurors, for that the s[d] Lt. Col: Godfrey doth except ag[t] the nomination of them by the present Marshall.[2]

Vpon motion of Cap[t] Mathias Halsted ordered that a Speciall Court of Admiralty be then & there also holden before the G[d]

---

[1] Holton's was beyond Ickerby, north of the town, the Governor's south, at Wappoo, and Sir P. Colleton's S. W.

[2] Thos. Thomson? he was so Jan. 167½, p. 374, but March, 167¾, Capt. Geo. Thompson was Provost Marshal.

Counc[ll] to try the accons betw[n] the s[d] Lt Col: Jno Godfrey, P[m] & the s[d] Mathias Halsted Defd[t], upon damage of certain goods consigned to s[d] Lt Col: Godfrey from Barbadoes.[1]

Carolina.   To the hon[ble] Sir John Yeamans, Govern[r] of this Province & the rest of the worthy members of the Grand Coun- cill the humble petit[n] of Rich[d] Nicklin & Jno Rivers &c do acknowledge their transgres[ns] &c & beg mercy &c.   [*Reprieved.*]

For &c as W[m] Argent hath one son named Peter Argent aged about 4 (?) years whome he is not able to keep &c   Ordered that s[d] Peter Argent be bound to Cap[t] Thos Gray as an appren- tice &c.

Att a Meeting &c this xxiiij day of Octo: 1672 sitting &c. The Gov[r], West, Gray, Owen, Bull, Robinson, Conant, Portman, Marshall.

Pet[n] of Lt Col: Jno Godfrey that the Country be sum'oned to make enquiry &c.   [*acquitted*]   *B'k* 1672, 94, p. 42.

————

To Sir Thomas Linch [2] Governor of Jamaica   Oct. 29, 72.

Exeter House 29° October, 72.
Sir,
His Majestie hath ben pleased to bestow on me with some other partners A Propriety in some Islands not lying far from Jamaica.   I am now upon making myself a Plantation and in- tend to throw away some money in making some experiments there.   Amongst other things I designe to try whether Cocao trees and your peper will grow there which some are apt to thinke will not beare the Clymate of these Islands and grow to bearing in a soyle not soe rich and moyst as grows in Jamaica. However I am resolved to make the triall, and to that purpose

———

[1] The Blessing had lately arrived, she was at Barbadoes bound for Carolina March, 167½, but had apparently not arrived June 8th, p. 395. She may have gone to the Bahamas and then to Carolina?

[2] Col. Lynch, afterwards Sir Thos., appointed Lt.-Gov. and Com'r in Chief of Jamaica to succeed Sir Tho. Modyford, Sep. 23, 1670, and Governor 5 Jan., 1671.   His com'n was revoked Nov. 4, 1674, John Ld. Vaughan having been appointed.   He writes Sec'ty Slingesby: "Jamaica Oct 9, 1672,   *   another letter from Gov'r of New Providence should have sent them no com'n, for thinks ill of that settlem't, &c.; nor would he do anything to interfere with the Lords Proprietors of Carolina, but their present necessities may excuse him."   *A. & W. I.*, 943.

must be beholding to you not only for plants and nutts fitt to set but also for directions in the ordring of them and the peper Trees whereof I desire some seed. I should not trouble you on so slight an occasion did I not take you to bee my friend to that degree that you would be ready to imploy your care to satisfye my curiosity though in things of noe great moment. I know you may command the best sort of Cocoa trees in Jamaica and my experience in planting hath informed mee that there is great difference amongst plants and seeds of the same kinde of vege- table. I doubt not but you will by this bearer furnish mee with the best sorts and the most likely to endure (in the lesse agree- able soyle of my plantation) the hardshipps of a colder climate.

I am Sir Your very affec^{ate} friend and servant

SHAFTESBURY.

[*S. P.*, Bdle. 48, No. 55, p. 118.]

THE COUNCIL JOURNALS.

Att a Meeting &c this xxxi^{yth} day of Octo: 1672 sitting &c the Governor Col: West Lt Col. Godfrey Mr Owen & cap^t Bull.

Pet^n of Thos Witty ag^t Capt fflorence O'Sullivan. Ordered that Lt Col. Godfrey & Mr Ralph Marshall hear & determine the difference.

Att a Meeting &c this xxi^{yth} day of November 1672 sitting &c The Govr, West, Godfrey, Gray, Mathews, Owen, Portman & Marshall.

On motion of Mr Jno ffoster relating to an order of the Counc^ll 10 Jan: 1671 [page 373] concern^g Jno Radcliffe his ser- vant &c paym^{ts} made &c Order^d he be returned into his Masters service there to abide &c.

For &c as the scantlings of the bridge on the S^{wd} part of Charlestowne accord^g to the Act of parliam^t made &c have not yet been agreed upon Resolved that Col: West, Col. Godfrey, Capt Bull & Capt Robinson calling to their assistance Mr Jno Simpson on Munday next ninth Decr inst: by nine of the clock in the morning at s^d Col: West's now dwelling house [1] for settling of the scantlings & that they return a draught of their inspect^n to the Govr by Thursday next 12th Dec^r. *B'k, 1672–94*, p. 43.

---

[1] The Lords Proprietors plantation near the bridge foot.

To Sir Peter Colleton in Barbadoes.

Exeter House 27th November 1672.

Yours of the 30th of September last I have received and am glad to find that the tobacco of Carolina gives it soe good a reputation amongst you I was always confident and am dayly more and more confirmed that it will prove the most flourishing plantation that was ever setled in America if it be not overlaid and strangled in its infancy by those into whose hands we committ it. For though I am willing to believe all that you say of Sir John Yeamans and to have as good an opinion of him as may be yet I must deale freely with you and tell you I cannot forsee what advantage wee shall receive from all those able parts you mention if he proceeds as he hath begunn and continue to buy up the peoples provisions at rates not very conscionable on the one hand and on the other sett all things there soe as to increase and continue our expense without any regard of stop or returne, which the people before he came thither had ingenuity enough to consider and were beginning to provide for. But hee noe sooner gott the Government into his hands but he turned it all quite another way. And whereas the people just before had made an act for repayment of their debts and theire Addresses to us all looked that way since he came in we cann hear of nothing but wants and suplys. We must build a house for the Governor and we must make provission for the entertainment of the Council and the Reception of Strangers soe that if to take care of One what ever becomes of us or the people, if to convert all things to his present private profitt be the marke of able parts Sir John is without doubt a very judicious man. Notwithstanding all this my dissattisfaction in him ceases as soone as he ceases to discompose our affaires but you must give me leave to profess to you that unlesse theise things be cured, and I finde that care of us and the plantation be in earnest minded I shall not have patience quietly to sitt still and look on whilst the Collony is destroyed and should it fall by his perverse and indirect management the Indignation of haveing a design of soe faire hopes and soe great consequence on which I had sett my minde ruined by his covetousnesse or ambition will make me endeavour to reach him and require sattisfaction in the remotest parts of the world For in this which is my Darling and wherein I am entrusted alsoe by others I cannot suffer myselfe and them to be injured by any-body without great resentment which I have discoursed thus plainly to you because I take you to be a friend to us both, and I desire to be soe to Sir John Yeamans as soone as by an easye turne of himselfe and his taking care of our and the publicke concernment there he shall give me occasion.[1]

Our other Plantation in New Providence promises not only a remote advantage by a flourishing settlement there, but a present bennefitt by a trade we have established thither for their supply according to the designe we were upon before you left England. What termes we have brought it to you will finde in the Wright-ings, herewith sent you wherein disposeing onely of those Roy-altys which are ours we leave them perfectly a free trade in all their owne Marchandize and assure them we never intend to set up any thing like a Comp^a over them.   All the Proprietors except my Lord Craven (who putts in his share for the Govr) have subscribed their £200 a piece as Collonel Thornburgh[2] hath for you.   What other partners we have taken in you will see by the Articles who haveing laid down their money upon my having tould them that you had promist me at your goeing out of England to pay your part (as it is done) and to doe all things else that I should in this case have now desired of me to procure your hand and seale to those Articles which the Lords Proprietors have entered in with them.   To this purpose I have herewith sent you the Articles which all the Lords Proprietors there have executed and there only wants your confirmation to compleat the assurance.   I know I shall not need to say I desire it where both your word and interest ingadge you to it   I take this for granted and only desire you to take what care you can that this trade which I am very chary of and upon which depends the good and setlement of those Islands be not disturbed by any people from Barbadoes.

The notice you have sent me of the ships I thank you for but

---

[1] This letter shows Ld. Shaftesbury's deep interest in the settlem't, of which he was indeed the founder and leading spirit. 1707, Gov. Holden, of Bahamas, writes: South Carolina's "powerfulness arises from the timely supplies sent thither on its first settlem^t by the Lords Proprietors who are devotedly attached to it, the late Earl of Shaftesbury in partic-ular." *His. Col.*, 2, page 215.

[2] Col. Edward Thornburgh, agent for Barbadoes in England?

the person you mention in your letter to be directed to me to give me more full information of that matter being not yet come I cann say nothing more about it.   I am

Your very affec^{ate} friend

SHAFTESBURY.

[S. P., Bdle. 48, No. 55, page 120.]

————

THE COUNCIL JOURNALS.

Att a Meeting &c this viith day of December 1672 sitting &c The Govr, West, Godfrey, Mathews, Owen, Bull, Conant, Marshall. Upon hearing the Comp^t of Wm Kennis'[1] ag^t Jos. Pendarvis &c that s^d Pendarvis build a house &c on s^d Kennis' land by 1st Jan: next.   For the better regulating of the meetings of the Councill it is resolved that the Councill doe from henceforth meet at Charles Towne (unless some other place be appoynted) once every month upon a Saturday, this day being the first & so every Monthly Saturday.

Att a Meeting &c xiith day of December 1672 sitting &c   The Govr, Gray, West, Godfrey, Mathews, Owen Portman, Bull, Marshall, Robinson, Conant.   Comp^t Ag^t Thos Archcraft, smith &c.[2]

Att a Meeting &c xxviijth day of Jan'y 167$\frac{2}{3}$ sitting &c (*the same*)   For &c as Christo^r ffield serv^t to Mr Jno Maverick came &c complains his master would not maintain him &c Capt: O'Sullivan may maintain him &c   Upon comp^t of Col: Jos: West ag^t Robert Lewis[3] for taking one bushel of corne from s^d

---

[1] Came from England 1669, of Owen's parliam't 1670, and lot owner, Charlestown, 1672, his fate is unknown. Pendarvis came, 1671, from Barbadoes? had lands on Ashley river, 1671, '75, and lived, 1686, on east side next above Carteret. He was mem. Assembly 1692, and J. P. 1693, died 1694? His son? Jos. Pendarvis' will, 1719, mentions brothers in law Sam: West and R'd Butler, sons Joseph, &c.

[2] Villars House, Jan. 1, 167$\frac{2}{3}$, Dr. Benj. Worsley to Sir T. Lynch. 'The Ld Chancellor on perusal of his letter and papers from the Inhabitants of New Providence, commanded him to give him thanks in his Lordship's name and those of the Lds Prop^{rr} of Carolina for his great humanity to the Govr and poor inhabitants, and to inform him that a vessel was ready to set sail with all manner of provision for them, &c.' A. & W. I., 1015.

[3] 1707 Adm'r of Jno. Murrell, of Wando river, dec'd.

Col: West's serv^ts ordered he do pay s^d Col: West or his order 2 bushels of Indian corn before 1st Oct^r.

For &c as it hath been proved that Capt fflorence O'Sullivan hath malitiously given out divers unjust & reproachfull speeches ag^t the Governm^t &c but more specially ag^t Mr Wm Owen one of the L^ds Prop^rs Deputies to the great dishonour of the s^d Lords Prop^rs & for the s^d O'Sullivan's continuall & contemptious misdemeanors this day before the board ordered that s^d fflorence O'Sullivan be committed to the Marshalls custody till he make submission to the board & give security for his good behavior & appearance at the Genl Sessions to be holden for the Province.

Att a Meeting &c xv^th *day of ffebruary 1672 sitting &c (the same)*

For &c as many of the Inhabitants of this Province have arrived here slenderly accomodated wth provisions depending too much upon some speedy supplies thereof from their corn &c or other places wch hath hitherto been frustrated from want of ships[1] by means whereof they are reduced to extraordinary great wants, to the great hinderance of their improvem^ts wch the Govern^r & G^d Counc^ll consider^s & how much the promising & forward growth of this settlm^t may be impeded thereby have taken care to provide a cargoe to send to Virginia to supply that default It is therefore resolved &c that the sloop Endeauo^r Mr Joseph Harris comd^r now riding at anchor in Ashly River be forthw^th dispatched to Virginia wth the s^d cargoe from thence to bring such provisions as shall be putt on board her &c allowing s^d Jos: Harris 30^li ster: per month for freight of the s^d sloop And for &c as Lt Col: Godfrey hath provided 4 bbls of rum valued 12£ 8^s, one bbl sugar 5 & hath singly undertaken for £50 for the freight &c in all 80£ 12 And Sir John Yeamans Govr, Coll. Jos. West, Lt Col: Jno. Godfrey Maj: Tho. Gray cp^t Mau: Mathews Mr Wm Owen, cap^t Step: Bull, Mr Christ^r Portman, cap^t Jno. Robinson cap^t Richd Conant agree that they will severally put into stock 10£ ster: to advance the sum of £100 for s^d Adventure & freight as well as hazard of losse & gaine &c the produce of s^d cargoe equally shared among said Adventurers on the arrivall of the sloop at Ashly river &c.

Att a Meeting &c February xxiiij^th *167⅔ sitting &c* The

---

[1] Caused by the 'Dutch Warr.' See *Hewit*, p. 65.

Govr, Gray, Godfrey, Mathews, West, Owen, Robinson, Conant, Marshall.

For &c as the Indians have a long time practiced the killing & stealing of hoggs in this settlem^t to the great damage of the Inhabitants thereof Resolved that Maj. Thos Gray doe take that party of men raised under his command for that expedit^n & doe inquire after the s^d Indians & take as many as he can find to be proceeded against as their offence may deserve. Resolved that Lt Col: Jno Godfrey & cap^t Mau: Mathews be comis'^{d} to follow & take the bodyes of Richd Batten & Wm Loe who on Satterday 22^d ffeb'y run away from the settlem^t & have stolen a negroe belonging to cap^t Nathl: Sayle & divers other goods &c Resolved that a Special Sessions of Goal Delivery be holden at Charles Towne upon Satterday next for the tryal of all of some Malefactors now in custody.

Att a meeting &c March 4th 167$\frac{2}{3}$ sitting &c (*all above & Portman*) For &c as ye G^d Coun^{ll} having this day rec'd credible inform^n that divers Indians lurking about James Towne have latcly destroyed several hoggs there Resolved that Lt Coll. Godfrey & cap^t Richd Conant doe forthwth enquire apprehend & take those Indians whome they have reason to suspect &c to be brought before the G^d Counc^{ll} at Charles Towne the 6th inst. March. P. 47. Resolved that a Special sessions of Goal Delivery be holden at Charles Towne ye 6th of March ins^t to trye some Malefactors now in Custody. Capt Mau: Mathews reports that he has marked 12000 acres of Land for my Lord Ashley on the first bluff bank upon the first Indian plant^n on the right hand on the Western branch of the North river com'ly called ye Mulberry tree[1] & alsoe a seinorie wth the land about for about 3 or 4 miles above the passable tree that lyes over Ashly River,[2] both wch the G^d Counc^{ll} have resolved be reserved till further orders. On mot^n of Maj: Thos Gray liberty is granted him to take 1000 acres for cap^t Abel Gay[3] & to be reserved &c 12 months. *B'k* 1672, 94, p. 46.

---

[1] Marked "Mulberry" on Sieur S. map 1680? later of the Colletons, and then Gov. Broughton's seat; now called "Mulberry Castle."

[2] Ashley Barony, on W. side Ashley river below Bossu creek, extending up the river and west to Edisto. The "passable tree" was probably above Bossu creek. See *Woodward*, 1674.

[3] Had 100 acres in St. Andrew's Parish, Barbadoes, 1679.

"Plott of the Lords Prop[rs] plant: 44½ acres land." 18 by 14 in: scale (*2 ch: to 1 in:*) 66 foot a chain, *shewing star palisade, buildings within and gardens in front.* B. & B. *East* "Along the great marsh of Ashly River" *the N E point* "the bridge foot where the landing now is" *then on N. irregularly* "Along the Creek & Small marsh sides" *past* "the old Landing" *and* "the tree that Lyes over the marsh" *to N W. corner thence on W. and S. lines* "to the Railes (*and road*) along the Rail side" *till* "here we leave the railes" *and* "along the point of wood" *5 chains to* the "great marsh side" *again.*

Inscribed: Carolina. This plott Represents the shape & forme of the Cleare plantable Land belonging to the Lords proprietors of this province wherein Colo. Joseph West now Liveth which at Request of the said Colo. Joseph West I have measured & surveyed & find it to containe fforty foure Acres & one half of Land or neare thereabouts, scituate and being neere Charlestowne In the aforesaid province butting & bounding as by the plott appears, performed March 7th 167⅔ & certified ℔ *John Culpeper.* (*S. P.*, 48, No. 72.)

The Council Journals.

At a Meeting &c March 10th 167⅔ present: The Govern[r] Godfrey, Gray, Mathews, Owen, Bull, Conant.

For &c as Rich[d] Batten & W[m] Loe have been arraigned & found guilty upon the Act of Parliam[t] ag[t] running away & for felony & judgm[t] of death passed upon them this day to be done & the s[d] prisoners having wth extraordinary penitency expressed their acknowledgm[t] & deep sense of their criminality wth their utter detestation of the like &c and upon the warmest solicitations of Margaret Lady Yeamans[1] & the rest of the Ladyes & Gentlewomen of this Country It is Resolved that the Execution of the s[d] persons be suspended &c.

At a meeting &c March xxii[th] 167⅔ present: The Govern[r], West, Godfrey, Mathews, Owen, Bull, Conant, Robinson, Portman, Marshall.

For the prevent[n] of differences that sometimes happen from the marking of lands not laid out Resolved &c any person who &c mark any lands &c shall enter the same in the Surveyor Gen[lls] office who is hereby ordered to receive the same & further

---

[1] Sir John's 2d wife? She survived him and married James Moore.

29

that this ord^r be forthwth published. For &c as fflorence O'Sullivan is this day brought before the G^d Counc^{ll} for uttering of divers seditious words &c he remaine in the Marsh^{lls} custody till he give good security for his good behavior & appearance at the next Genl sessions to be holden for this Province.

At a meeting &c March xxixth 1673 present: The Goven^r, West, Godfrey, Mathews, Owen, Marshall, Portman & Conant, Upon mot^n of Lt Col: Godfrey liberty is granted him to plant one acre of public land neare Charles Town lying E^{wd} of ye land of Thos Hurt.   For &c as it is thought fit that the Indian prisoner now brought in be kept in prison till the Indians who brought him doe come to witness ag^t him as they have undertaken and for as much as by reason of the great scarcety of provisions none appeare to spare any in order to ye maint^{ce} of ye Indian &c Resolved that the mainten^{ce} of Nationall prisoners ought to be allowed by ye L^{ds} Prop^{rs} cap^t Mau: Mathews as he is Deputy to ye Rt Honble Anthony earl of Shaftesbury one of the L^{ds} Prop^{rs} doth promise to give maint^{ce} to ye s^d Indian.

At a Meeting &c May xth 1673 present: The Govr, West, Godfrey, Gray, Owen, Bull, Robinson, Conant, Portman, Marshall.

Lt Col: Jno Godfrey & cap^t Mathias Halsted having this day person^{ly} appeared &c requested the Counc^{ll} to sett a value on 2 bbls of Molasses wch s^d Halsted was obliged to pay by a judgm^t at a Court holden at Charles Towne the xxiiijth October 1672 &c [page 413].[1]

P. 51.   It is Resolved that all persons setting up their names in the Secretarys office in order to their departure from this port & exceed the time of six weekes shall not have a Tickett granted them till their names be sett up againe & remaine accord^g to the act &c [page 369].

———

SIR P. COLLETON TO JOHN LOCKE.

Barbados this 28th of may, 1673.

My deare frend

I have been long expecting to hear newes from you from Newingland, & my lord Willoughby & I had projects of taking

———

[1] The Blessing had gone to Barbadoes and back since Oct., 1672. She sailed for England via Bermuda May or June, 1673.

Carolina in our way & viziting of you there, but it hath pleased
God to dispose things otherwise, he is dead you I understand in
imploym¹ in England, & I lyed by the legg wᵗʰ an ofice here,¹
untill his majesty please to release mee, Our frends in Carolina
sing the same song they did from the begining, a very healthy,
a very pleasant & fertill country, but great want of victuall,
cloathes, & tools, & I am of opinion the 2 last ought to be sent
them, one suply more of that kind would bee enough, victuall
they will be sufficiently furnishd wᵗʰ this year never to want more,
& if wee should omit the other two wee may run a hazzard of
loozing all the mony we have been out, for after Barbados had
been setled 6 years, the people who were then upwards of 600
men were leaving of it in a humour, & you see what this Island
is come to, & no doubt if wee hould our ground but Carolina
will excell all other English plantations, severall men of considerable estats will ingage from hence as soon as there is peace &
shipping is to be had, I have sent all the letters I have received
to my lord who I doubt not but will comunicate them to you, I
send to Coll: Thornburgh by this conveyance a box of Carolina
China root to bee devided between yourselfe & a cozen of mine
that is a dragster, they tell me here they are the right sort, &
they may bee so for any thing I know, I find I am your partner
in the Bahama trade wᶜʰ will turne to accomp¹ if you meddle not
wᵗʰ planting, but if you plant otherwise then for provision for
your factor you will have your whole stock drowned in a plantation & bee never the better for it, planting is my trade & I
thinke I may without vanity say I understand it as well as most
men, & I am sure I am not deceived in this particuler, if other
men will plant there, I mean the Bahamas hinder them not they
improve our province, but I would neither have you nor my
lord² ingadge in it, I can give reasons I am sure will sattisfye
you, I was in hopes to have sent you a jarr of this Islands tar by

---

¹ Wm., Lord Willoughby of Parham (brother and successor to Francis Ld. Willoughby). Governor of Barbadoes and the Carribees 1667,
1673; died at Barbadoes April 10, 1673. In his illness he put the government in the Council and appointed Sir P. Colleton President and
Deputy Governor. Locke was about the same time appointed Secretary
of Presentations. Thus Carolina missed three distinguished visitors.

² "My Lord" is Shaftesbury. Compare his letter, page 413.

this conveyance but it shall come by the next wth what other raritys wee have, in the mean time I desire you to beeleeve that I am most sincerely

your faithfull frend & serv[t]

M[r] Lock.   [*not signed.*]

Addressed: To John Locke Esq[r] att little Exeter house in the Strand   London.

Endorsed by Locke.   S[r] Peter Colleton to J. L.   28° May, 73.

[2 pages with seal. *S. P.*, Bdle. 48, No. 90.]

THE COUNCIL JOURNALS.

At a meeting &c June 25, 1673 present: The Govern[r], West, Godfrey, Mathews, Owen, Bull, Conant, Marshall. Upon motion of Jane Gray wife of Thos Gray &c considering her great necessity Ordered that she be allowed the greiter kettle & necessary wearing apparell, her childrens cloths 3 pewter dishes 6 plates &c all her provis[ns] aboard the sloop seized for the delinquency of her Husband & others.[1]

At a meeting &c June 25, 1673 present: (*same except Bull & Conant*) For &c as John Mauericke came &c and took oath that 300 ft of cedar boards &c really belong to him form[ly] lent to Jno Robinson one of the Delinquents. Ordered that he receive the same &c.

CAPT. WEST TO JOHN LOCKE, ESQ.

Sir.

Allthough I have writt severall times to you both by way of Barbads and Virginia and by M[r] Portman who latly went from hence by way of Bermuda, in the ship Blessing yett I could not omitt this opportunity to present you with this my humble service, and to intreat your assistance by importuning the Earle of Shafs Bury to hasten a ship from England with more People and supplyes of Cloathing, and Toole &c for the people are not able to subsist long without they are supply[d] by the Lords Prop: and there is nothing but the L[ds] Prop[rs] assistance can preserve the

---

[1] Culpeper, Gray, Robinson and Pinkard had engaged in disturbances and fled the province. Gray was trying to remove his family and goods in the sloop.

settlem^t from falling which in time I am confident will come to something, and if timely supplyed will answer every man's expectations of it and for the advantage of healthfullness and pleasantness, I beleeve noe plantation settled by the English in America doth afford the like, and if wee ware but once stocked with cattle, that we might fall upon English Husbandry it would quickly be a very plentiful place, I suppose before this you have heard of our extream wants of provisions this year, which now God be praised we have almost overcome, for about a month hence we shall have corne enough of our owne groweth; and hope we shall never fear wanting Indian corne againe, for this want will doe much good in the country, by teaching people to be better Husbands, and more industrious for the future, and not depend any more upon supplys. But I being straightened for want of time I shall refer you to the Report of the Barer Mr Miles Man who I hope will truly informe you of all things here, nothing else. I am

Sir: yor most humble servant to command

JOSEPH WEST.

Charles Town nere Ashly river June 28th '73.

Addressed: To John Locke Esqre at Littell Exeter House In the Strand   present   London.

Endorsed by Locke: Carolina Jos: West to J. L.   28 June '73.

[*S. P.*, Bdle. 48, No. 91.]

———

THE COUNCIL JOURNALS.

At a meeting &c July the iiij 1673 present: The Govern^r, West, Godfrey, Mathews, Owen, Bull, Marshall. Ordered that a Special Session of Goal Delivery be held at Charles Towne before the G^d Councill upon tuesday next to try the felonies of Saml Lucas^1 & Thos La: ford & that Juries be summoned for that purpose.

At a meeting &c July the xiith 1673 present: (*the same*) For as much as John Culpeper Surveyor Gen^{ll} hath run away from

---

^{1} Came in the Carolina from Barbadoes 1669, and testifies to time of arrival 1672. James Lucas was an Indian trader 1710.

this settlem^t so that divers persons are extraordin^y injured having none to lay out their lands &c Ordered that Mr Stephen Bull, Mr Jno Yeamans^1 & Stephen Wheelwright be com^d Surveyors during pleasure & that they doe attend the G^d Coun^{ll} next saturday.

At a meeting &c July the 24th 1673 present: (*same but Owen*) The Grand Councill grants liberty to mrs Jane Gray to receive &c from aboard the late seized sloop.   Capt. Step: Bull sworn Surveyor Mr Jno Yeamans do: Step: Wheelwright do:

P. 52.   *At a meeting &c* July the 29th 1673 present: The Govern^r, Lt Col. Godfrey, capt Mathews, Mr Owen, capt. Bull, Mr Mathews.   Ordered that the war^{ts} form^{ly} directed to the Surveyor Gen^{ll} &c be executed by the Surveyors at present appointed, by direct^n from the Secretary.

At a meeting &c august 2^d 1673 present: The Govern^r, Col. West, Lt. Col. Godfrey, capt: Mathews, Mr Owen, Mr Marshall, Mr Richd Ditty,^{2} Mr Saml West.   Upon consid^n had of the better defence of this province Resolved that Lt Col. Godfrey & capt: Mathews consider & assess rates of Smith work &c.

At a meeting &c august 9th 1673 present: (*the same*)   Mr Wm Murrell^3 & Mr Richd Berrey came & made oath that the damage by them viewd done to Euan Jones his corne in Charlestowne &c is 1½ bu^s &c.

---

^{1} Came from Barbadoes? 1671, was chosen to Parliam't 1672, was Surveyor 1673, and of the Council 1674–1675.   Wheelwright came on the Carolina, 1669, from England with Capt. O'Sullivan.

^{2} In Council 1673–74.   Capt. R. Goldsborough, James river, Va., 1662, writes: 'left Jamaica bare of ships stores.   Rich: Ditty has accepted bills and been very ready to serve H M.'

^{3} Came from Barbadoes 1671, had lands on Charlestown Neck 1672 and 1678 sold 74 acres to Jno. Tothill.   Had lands at Wando, 1680, '90 (1679 Wm. & Jno. Murrell had lands in St. Michaels, Barbadoes).   1707 Wm. & Jno. Murrell & Ro. Lewis were adm'rs of Jno. Murrell, of Wando, dec'd, for his wife Elizabeth & children.   Euan Jones was probably John (called Owen, page 187) Jones, Sir Jno. Yeamans' agent.

LORD SHAFTESBURY TO [STEPHEN] BULL.[1]

Exeter House Aug: 13, 1673.

He has behaved so well as a planter in the country & in the government as Shaftesbury's Deputy, though for unavoidable reasons he bestowed his deputation on Mr Mathew's, yet to let him know it was not through disesteem he has got Lord Cornbury to choose Bull his deputy. Cannot but take especial notice of his acquaintance among and interest with the Indians, however it may be discountenanced by some there, looks on as very wisely done and very agreeable to our design which is to get and continue the friendship and assistance of the Indians and make them useful without force or injury. Should be very glad that all the tribes of Indians round about had each an Englishman for their Cassique.

[S. P., Bdle. 48, No. 55, page 136.] *Abstract A. & W. I.*, § 1127.

THE COUNCIL JOURNALS.

At a meeting &c August 30th 1673 present: (*the same*) For &c as Richd Nicklin came & complains that he had already served Col: Joseph West two years wch was his contract time of servitude &c [2] ordered that he serve one year more &c.

At a meeting &c Sept: 3^d 1673 present: (*same except West*) upon consid^n had of the murther committed by a certaine nation of Indians called Westoes, their continuall Alarums & publick declaration of an intended invasion in & upon this settlem^t It is ordered &c that a party of men be raised under command of Lt

---

[1] P. 192. This letter is not in the MS. from Public Record Office. Stephen Bull, Esq., settled 167½ Ashley Hall, which till lately remained in his male line. It descended, 1707, to his eldest son, Gov. Wm. Bull, and 1751 to *his* son Gov. Wm. Bull, who, 1790, left 'my plant'n on Ashly river 1150 acres, where my Grandfather lived, died and lies buried, where my Father and all his children were born I wish to remain in the possession of his posterity' to his nephew, Hon. Wm. Bull (of the Council 1775), whose only son, Lt.-Gov. Wm. Stephen Bull, left it, 1818, to his only son Col. Wm. I. Bull (whose family are the only male line of the first Gov. Bull).

[2] Hence he must have come on the Blessing, Aug., 1671. His extra year was for running away, see p. 412.

Col. Jno Godfrey & capt. Mau^e Mathews jointly & be expedited
to marche against the s^d Indians to kill & destroy them or otherwise subject them in peace.   Resolved & advised that all Horses
be taken up & that 1^{lb} of powder & 2^{lbs} of shott for every man
10^{lbs} of lead & such things are absolutely necessary for to fitt the
people in the s^d expedit^n out of the Lords Prop^{rs} store.

At a meeting &c Septr 16, 1673, present: (*the above & Conant*).

Upon debate the Resolut^n of 3 Sept. 1673 is put, affiants: the
Govenor, Lt Col: Godfrey, capt. Mathews, Mr Owen Mr Marshall, capt. Conant, Mr Ditty, Negant, Col. Jos: West.   For
&c as of late divers obstanite & evil disposed persons have run
away from this settlem^t Resolved forthwth a party of men under
command of Lt. Col. Godfrey be dispatched to follow & take
the s^d persons &c.

At a meeting &c Octo^r 4th 1673 present: (*the same*)

The time having lapsed by intervening accidents, upon a new
motion the question was putt whether the design of going ag^t
the Westoes be prosecuted accord^g to the former resolut^n.   Aff^{ts}
The Govern^r, Lt Col. Godfrey Mr Owen, Mr Marshall, Mr Ditty
Negants, Col West, capt Mathews.

At a meeting &c Octo^r the 7th 1673 pres^t (*same except Conant*)

For &c as the improvem^t as well as the safety of this settlem^t
consists in the knowledge of the lands & inhabitants contigious
to this place & for &c as it is advised that the present Warr of the
Westoes will be most effectually accomplished by the assistants
of the Esaugh Indians[1] who are well acquainted wth the Westoes
habitacons & have promised all the help they can afford Resolved that cap^t Mau^e Mathews [p. 54*] Mr Wm Owen, Mr Jos:
Dalton & Mr Jno Boone be imployd to the s^d Esaugh Indians
there to treat & agree wth the s^d Indians as they shall find most
convenient for the better accomplish^g the s^d warr & for the discovery of those parts of this country.   And for the better
knowledge of the maritime parts It is advised that Coll. Jos.
West & Lt Col. Jno Godfrey doe undertake the same soe farr as
the same be not S^{wd} of Westoe: bou.

---

[1] "Easaws 150 men" east of and below "Catawbas 120 men," on
heads of Wateree, *old map;* lower were the Waxaws; Logan, 183,
names them as allies.

At a meeting &c Decem^r 22th 1673 present: The Govern^r West, Godfrey, Mathews, Owen, Marshall, Conant, Ditty & S. West.

Resolved forthw^th that the Ketch late belonging to Thos. Gray & others be valued & appraised by Mr Jno Simpson, Mr Robt Taprill, Richd Cole & Thos Buttler or any 3 &c they returne their judg^t &c of her in the condicon they now find her within 3 days &c [p. 424].

For &c as the Ketch late belonging to Thos Gray &c for want of due repair^n now remains altogether useless &c Resolved that Coll. West, the L^ds Prop^rs agent may repair, fitt out & load the s^d Ketch wth what conven^t speed he may to be designed to Barbadoes saving always the intentions that the s^d Ketch, as well as other estates of the s^d Thos Gray & Partners shall be disposed of for satisf^n of their creditors & that s^d Ketch doe bear the name & be called the Fellowship of Carolina.

At a meeting &c Jan'y the 29th 1673 present: (*the same*).

Mem: Jno Norton p^r came &c doth acknow^ge to owe Lt Coll: Jno Godfrey 7000^lbs of good muscovado sugar to be paid in Barbadoes &c 4000^lbs on arrivall of any shipps now bound from Ashly river to Barb^s &c.

[P. 55*] *At a meeting &c* ffeby 2^d 1673 present: (*same*).

This day capt. Mau: Mathews, Mr Wm Owen, Mr Jos: Dalton & Mr Jno Boone having returned safe from Esaugh gave an account of their journey to the Grand Councill.[1]

Upon consid^n of the comp^t reported by certain neighbouring Indians & enquiry being made Ordered that Thos Holton,[2] Jno Sullivan, & Jno Pinke doe deliver the goods they have taken from s^d Indians & make full satisfaction &c besides other goods of 20^s for their trespass to be paid at Ickabee tomorrow & if they fayle capt: Mathews, Mr Owen & Mr Marshall doe

[1] They were appointed Oct. 7; but went and returned between Dec. 22 and Jan. 29, unless the journal errs in noting Owens and Mathews present in Council on those days.

[2] Of Barbadoes; settled at Ickerbe, 167$\frac{0}{1}$, and 1675–85 near "Clear Spring, died 1704; Long Island granted him 1696, went to his only son, Tho. Holton, of C. T., who sold 172$\frac{0}{1}$, Q. 3, 28; died before 1736, and left dau. Mary. Jno Sullivan, of Ashley river, sold land, 1685, to Chr. Smith, wit: Tho. Holton, Ra. Marshall. He died 169$\frac{2}{3}$; his wife, Rachel, admin'd Jan. 15.

award a war^t of distress for seizure of s^d goods to be delivered to s^d injured Indians.

At a meeting &c March 7th 1673 present: The Governor, West, Godfrey, Mathews, Owen & Marshall. For &c as in the infancy of this Settlem^t the attendance of Jurors for the tryal of accons betw^n party & party seem to be very burthensome to the people as well impeding the progress of their husbandry as occasioning losses by Indians & vermine during absence wch have moved them to desire a speedier admin^n of Justice   It is therefore advised & resolved &c that any person henceforth having cause of complaint bring a petition to the Secretary's office whereupon the Secretary is to endorse a sumons requiring both the parties to such comp^t to appear wth their evidences before the G^d Coun^{ll} at their next sitting after to make appeare the meritt of the cause when if both parties submit to be tryed by the Court a finall Judgm^t shall thereupon be given, this to continue till further Orders. Resolved that a publication be issued out that all persons who justly have any debt or demand upon the estates of Thos Gray, Jno Robinson, Jno Culpeper & Jno pinkerd do appear before the G^d Coun^{ll} at Charles towne the 4th April next then & there to make the same fully appear. Upon consid^n of the acc^t of fees of Geo. Thompson Prov^t mars^{ll} in appraism^t of the estates of Thos Gray, Jno Robinson, Jno Culpeper & Jno pinkard & other services &c^1 [page 56*] Ordered he be allowed 5l &c.

Charlestowne March 28th 1674 present: The Governor, West, Godfrey, Mathews, Owen, Marshall, Conant, S. West. Jno pinkerd being one of the persons attainted by the act of parliam^t in that behalf & is now arrived in this port Ordered that he be taken into strict custody by the Prov^t mar^{ll} & kept in irons till further order. upon mot^n of M^r Ra: Marshall ordered that he may mark out 100 acres for Agnes Shepherd to be reserved 2 years if in that time she doe arrive or send some one to plant upon it. Upon consid^n of acc^t of charge of Mr Jos: Dalton Sec'ty in appraism^t of estates of Thos Gray &c ordered that he have 5l. ster: of s^d estates.^{2}

---

^{1} Here the book is reversed, and pages 73, 68 & 56 follow.

^{2} Commission from the Lords Proprietors of Carolina to Joseph West, Governor of that part that lyes between Cape Carteret on the north side

ARTICLES BETWEEN THE LORDS PROPRIETORS.

Articles Indented of seaven parts made and concluded the sixth day of May in the yeare of our Lord one thousand six hundred and seaventy and foure.   And in the six and Twentieth yeare of the raigne of our souveraigne Lord Charles the second by the grace of God of England Scotland France and Ireland King defender of the Faith &c.   Between the right hono^ble Christopher duke of Albemarle of the first part   The right hono^ble William Earle of Craven of the second part   The right hono^ble Anthoney Earle of Shaftesbury of the third part   The right hono^ble Henry Lord Viscount Cornebury of the fowerth part   The right hono^ble John Lord Barkeley of the fifth part, the right Hono^ble Sir George Cartarett of Westminster Knight and Baronett of the sixth part and Sir Peter Colleton of St Martins in the feilds in the Countie of Middx Baronett of the seaventh part.

Whereas the before mentioned persons being the Lords and Proprietors of the Province or Plantation comonly called Carolina in America   And haveing taken into their consideration how absolutely requisite it is to supply the said place with clothing and other necessarys untill the inhabitants thereof by the product of vendible Comodities shall bee enabled to draw a Trade of Merchants to themselves for their supply therein and being also sensible that if some speedy care be not taken of the said plantation it will be utterly ruined and forsaken and all former charge as well as further exportation be quite lost   And whereas the said Proprietors have resolved that supply to the

---

and five miles beyond Ashley River on the south side and so westward to the South Sea, and to the Council. Granting power to let, set, convey and assure lands with consent of his Council and under conditions set forth in his instructions. To execute all powers and authorities in relation to government with power in case of sickness or absence to appoint a deputy, &c april 25, 1674.

Identical with the Commission ante p. 330 but with this addition: All former commissions granted to Sir John Yeamans to be Governor are hereby revoked and made void. *Signed by* Craven, Shaftesbury, Cornbury, Berkeley & G. Carteret (*Col. En. B'k*, 20, pages 91, 92). Another copy *with mem:* "The aforesaid is a true copy of the original Commission examined this 29th April 1675 Jos. Dalton Sec^ry."   *A. & W. I.*, 1265, 1266.

value of seaven hundred pounds at the least shall bee yearely
raised expended and disbursed for the benefitt of the said Plantation in manner and forme hereafter mentioned and expressed
concerning the same.   Now therefore these presents witnesse
and the said Christopher duke of Albemarle, William Earle of
Craven, Anthony Earle of Shaftesbury, Henry Lord Viscount
Cornebury, John Lord Barkeley, Sr George Cartarett and Sir
Peter Colleton doe for themselves their Executors and Adminis-
trators and not one for another severally covenant and agree to
and with each other and they the said Lords Proprietors of the
said Plantation within tenn days next after the date hereof shall
and will severally and respectively pay or caused to be paid to
Peter Jones of St Clements Dane in the said countie of Middlesex gent or such other treasurer as the Major part of them, the
said Proprietors shall appoint the full sume of one Hundred
pounds of lawfull English money and in like manner shall and
will from time to time dureing the space of seaven yeares to be
reckoned from the date hereof yearly and every yeare pay or
cause to be paid unto their said treasurer for the time being the
Annuall sume of one Hundred Pounds of like lawfull money of
England on or before the feast day of the Annunciation of the
blessed Virgin Mary which shall be in every yeare   And that
the said sume of seaven hundred pounds to be advanced as
aforesaid and the said sume of seaven hundred pounds yearely
to be paid as aforesaid together with all returns and effects in
which they are or shall be jointly concerned to be received from
the said plantacon by the said Proprietors dureing the said seaven
yeares shall be applyed in the first place for the dischargeing the
present debts oweing by the said Proprietors upon the account
of the said Plantacon and from thenceforth to be yearely laid out
in fitt and convenient Comodities to be sent unto the said Province for the better carrying on the plantacon there unless they
the said Proprietors that have paid their full share of the said
money unto that time respectively shall unanimously at any time
or times otherwise order and determine concerning the same   Provided allwaies That they do not in any one yeare disburse lesse
then seaven hundred pounds value for the supply of the said Plantacon   Provided alsoe that the said Annuall supply to be trans-
mitted unto the said Plantacon as aforesaid shall be managed by
an Agent for that purpose to be chosen by the major part of the

said Proprietors that shall have duely paid their share as aforesaid according to such direccons as he shall on that behalfe
receive from them   And that neither the Governor nor Councill of the said place shall anywaies intermeddle therein   And
it is further Covenanted and severally agreed by and betweene
all the said Proprietors parties to these presents That all such
sume and sumes of money that they or any of them shall respectively advance and lay out as aforesaid shall be severally and
respectively reimbursed unto them or such of them as shall have
paid the same together with interest after the rate of eight pounds
in the hundred for a yeare out of the proffitts and proceed of the
said plantacon soe soone as the proceed and Improvements
thereof will admitt of the same (regard being alwaies had in the
first place to the supply of the said plantacon) and that the said
interest shall be stated every six Monthes and use upon use
reckones for the same at eight pounds p. cent as aforesaid
untill the payment thereof or untill by such use they shall have
respectively received treble, the principal money which they are
or shall be out as aforesaid which shall first happen And that
such of the said Proprietors as shall have advanced and paid the
said sumes of money shall untill they be reimbursed the same as
aforesaid have full power and authority in such way and manner
as on that behalfe shall be agreed amongst them to nominate,
constitute make and appoint all Langraves and Cassiques and
all other officiers in the said province and also to receive all debts
rents proffitts and emoluments alreddy arisen and growne due or
that shall hereafter arise or grow due from the said plantacon and
to do all other things in the management and government thereof
which by their patent or by the fundamental constitutions or
Temporary or Agrarian Laws the Lords Proprietors or any of
them or the Palatines Court may or [any of them might]¹ do and
in particular to nominate make and appoint a new Proprietor in
the room and place of Sʳ William Barkley² that the person soe to

---

¹ The words in brackets have a pen stroke thro' them.

² Sir Wm. Berkeley devised his proprietorship to Dame Frances, his
wife. In 1681 Jno. Archdale agreed for it (for his son Thomas), and
was admitted a proprietor, *His. Soc.*, I, page 106, *I Stat.*, 16. Sir Wm.
had not paid his share, and 1683 the Prop'rs treated with Col. Ludwell
and his wife, Lady Berkeley, for it, and April 10, 1684, took deed to

be nominated by the major part of such of the said proprietors as at the time of the said nomination shall have contributed their full share toward the said seaven hundred pounds a yeare shall in all regards be reckoned and esteemed a proprietor and shall forthwith by all the parties to these presents as well such as shall not as such as shall then have contributed as aforesaid to the said Annuall Charge be legally constituted and made (as Councell on that behalfe shall advise) a lawfull proprietor of that plantacon in as large and ample manner as the said Sr William Barkley was and might have had and enjoyed the same And it is further covenanted and severally agreed by and betweene all the said parties to these Presents that if any of them the said Proprietors shall at any time hereafter faile to pay in his proporcon of the said money to be advanced or yearely to be paid and expended as aforesaid dureing the said seaven yeares aforesaid that then and in every such case the said other proprietors parties to these presents shall and will by an equall dividend amongst them from time to time advance and make up the share of him or them so failing as aforesaid And that the person or persons soe making default and faileing as aforesaid from thence forward shall loose and be divested (and from such time do and doth hereby divest him and themselves) of and from all power right and share in the Government or Management and unto the proffitts or emoluments of the said plantacon or any part thereof untill the residue of the said Proprietors who shall then carry on the said plantacon and pay in their money as aforesaid shall be fully reimbursed all such money as from the time of the said default they shall either pay or advance as aforesaid at the rates interest improvement and proporcon as aforesaid And that from thenceforth the said proprietors and undertakers who shall then pay and advance the said money for the said plantacon as aforesaid shall have the only Government of the said place and the only power and authority to nominate, constitute and appoint Landgraves

Thomas Amy, who acted as proprietor till Sep. 29, 1697, when they gave him Southwell's escheated share (Ld. Clarendon's), he to reconvey the other to Wm. Thornburgh, who thereupon also acted as proprietor, *Ib.*, 108–17, and June 29, 1705, the Prop'rs reciting Amy's trust, sold to Jno. Archdale, who, 1708, settled it on his dau. Mary, wife of Jno. Dawson, and on Amy's death the legal estate came to his co-heiresses, Ann Trott and Eliz. Moore. *3 Browne's P. C.*, 449.

Cassiques and officiers as aforesaid and to receive the debts rents proffitts and emoluments of the said plantacon as aforesaid and wholly to exclude the said defaulters from the same untill they shall have received and shall be reimbursed such sume and sumes of money as they the said proprietors contributory to the said charge shall paye and advance as aforesaid with the interest and improve thereof as aforesaid & so from time to time successively as often as any default shall be made as aforesaid the remayning proprietors that continue to send the said annuall sume shall be reimbursed as aforesaid and from and after their receiving their said money with the interest and improve thereof as aforesaid the said proprietors that shall have soe made default shall be againe admitted unto their former interest in the said plantacon anything herein conteyned to the contrary notwithstanding In Witness whereof the parties abovesaid to these presents have sett their hands and seales the day and yeare above written.

Signed by the Duke of Albemarle in presence of J. Baynes & Ant: Bowes, Earl of Craven in presence Wm Jones & Ra: Marshall,[1] Earl of Shaftesbury in presence of John Locke & Tho. Stringer, Lord Visct. Cornbury in presence Garrett Cotter & Will. Parham, Ld Berkeley in presence Philip Frowde & James Worrall & Sir Geo. Carteret in presence John Locke & Rich: Davey. Sir Peter Colleton has not signed. *Parchment.* [*S. P.*, Bdle. 48, No. 93.] *A. & W. I.*, 1270.

The Proprietors to the Governor and Council at Ashley River.

Whitehall 18th May, 1674.

Gentlemen:

"Wee have herewith sent a Patent to Mr West to be Landgrave and a Comission to be Governor[2] who hath all along by his care, fidellity and prudence in the management of our affaires to our generall satisfaction recommended himself to us as the fit-

---

[1] Of Westminster, gent., Com'r of Aids 1677, 1696, and not he of Carolina, page 277. John Locke, the Philosopher; Stringer, Ld. S.'s Secretary, page 210. Froude (Sir Philip's son) was a clerk of Secretary Slingesby.

[2] Page 431 Act for payment of Ld. Proprs. debts pp. 53, 386.

test man there for this trust.   This we cannot forbare plainely to
say, though wee have a great Regard to Sir John Yeamans, as a
considerable man that hath come and setled amongst us when
Mr West had formerly the management of afaires things were
then puting into such a posture (as appears by the Act of Parliament made att the latter end of his Government, which we herewith
send you confirmed) That wee had some encouragement to send
suplies to men who took into their consideration how wee might
be reimbursed as well as they could which was all wee expected
but immediately with Sir Johns asumeing the Government the
face of things alltered the first newes was of severall proposalls for
the increaseing our charge, the same still hath ever since continued on, and in your verry last Dispatches a Scheme sent to us
of wayes of suplying youe which would presently require the disbursement of severall thousand pounds and all this without the least
mention of any thought how wee might be repaid either our past
debts which allready amounts to severall thousand pounds or be
better answered for the future: But instead thereof complaints
made and reproaches insinuated as if wee had dealt ill and unjustly
with you, because wee would not continue to feed and cloath you
on without expectation or demand of any Returns this we must let
you know put a stop to our supplies more than the Dutch Warr
For wee thought it time to give of a charge which was like to
have no end and the Country was not worth the haveing at that
rate for it must be a bad soyle that would not mainetaine industrious people or we must be verry silly that would mainetaine the
idle but wee have no suspition att all of the barrenness or any other
ill qualities of the Country which some of us are soe well assured
of that at theire own private charge they are going to setle a plantation at Edistow without expecting a farthing assistance from us.
That Sir John Yeamans management has brought things to this
pass wee are well satisfied, which yett wee cannot charge upon
his mistake, the Caracter which wee have received of him and
his long acquaintance with Barbados and the world gives us other
thoughts of him and perhaps it would very well have served his
purpose if wee had Supplyed you and he reaped the profits
of your labour att his own Rates and our own plantation
soe ordered that in Reputation people and Improvement itt
might arive att no other pitch then to be Subservient in ℔vis-
ions and Timb^r to the Interest of Barbados.   Consider at what

Rates Sir John bought your poore planters provitions in theire necessity, and how industrious and usefull to you the generallity of the people that came from Barbados have been and then tell us whether wee have not reson to be of this minde For wee would not have those that went from hence (whom we are Still willing to encourage) bee any longer misled and the people that have come to you from New York and the Northward, have by their planting and way of living amongst you fully Satisfied us that they are Friends to and doe in earnest meane and desire the Settlement and prosperity of our Province, being therefore willing to give all reasonable encouragement to honest and industrious men, we have sent another supply of Cloathes for cloathes and tools and have entered into engagement one to another to Send yearly to youe whereby our stores shall never want necessaries for the use of the industrious planters to be had at moderate Rates, by those that will pay for them, yett wee do not intend any more carelessly to throw away our stock and charges upon the Idle For though wee the Lords Proprietors have tyed one another by covenant that none Shall be behinde others in the Charge of carrying on this plantation Yett wee are all agreed not to make any more desperate Debts amongst you though wee intend to be at charge in procureing vines olives or any other usefull plants or commodities fit for the Climate out of any part of the World and men Skilled in the management of them And therefore if you intend to have suplyes for the future you will doe well to consider how you will pay us, in what comodities you can best do it and how the Trade of those Comodities you can best procure may bee soe managed as to turn to account for in our trade with you we ayme not att the profit of merchants but the incouragement of landlords.   In your letters you have been frequent in the mention of a Stock of Cattle, but not having paid us for tools and clothes, how do you think that we should be at so far a greater charge in cattle? You say it will enable you to pay your Debts, but do you not think if wee bring cattle thither wee who doe not want ground can not keep them & make the profit of our charge and venture as well as others especially it being our designe to have Planters there and not Graziers for if our Intentions were to stock Carolina att that Rate, we could doe better by Baylife and Servants of our own, who would be more observant of our orders than

30

you have been, plant in Townes where we direct Take up noe more lands than what they had use for nor by a scattered Settlement and large Tracts of ground taken up not like to bee planted these many years, exclude others from coming neare them and yet complaine for want of Neighbours, We rest, your very affectionate friends,

CRAVEN, SHAFTESBURY, G. CARTERET.[1]

[*Col. En. B'k*, 20, p. 93.]   *Rivers*, 332.[2]

———

LORDS PROPRIETORS OF CAROLINA to Joseph West, agent in Carolina. Let Dr. Henry Woddard, the bearer, have out of the stores what he desires to the value of 9l. there being so much remaining due to him of the 100l. formerly promised to him. *Signed in Locke's hand :*   CRAVEN,
            SHAFTESBURY,   G. CARTERETT.

Whitehall May 22 1674.

[*Col. Ent. Bk.* 20, p. 97.]   *A. & W.*, 1282.

———

LORDS PROPRIETOR'S INSTRUCTIONS.

To Joseph West our agent at Ashley River, in eight articles. Find by his acco[t] Sir John Yeamans owes 100l. and upwards & M[r] Foster above 30l. they are both responsible men so know not why they should not pay. Dr. Woodard has a bill for 9l. upon the stores to which amount he may draw, and Thos. Butler of Carolina 14l. &c. To get in the remainder of the debts

———

[1] The signatures are in Locke's handwriting.

[2] Henry Lord Viscount Cornbury, one of the absolute Lords Proprietors of Carolina. To Stephen Bull, Gent: Greeting: Whereas each of the Lords Proprietors has a power to make a Deputy to be his representative in Parliament and in the Grand Council and to have and exercise other powers and rights in the absence of the Deputators out of Carolina, as by our fundamental Constitutions and instructions more fully doth appeare, I, out of the trust and confidence I have in the wisdome, prudence and integrity of you Stephen Bull, do hereby constitute and appoint you, the said Stephen Bull, my Deputy in Carolina, with power to act as in our fundamental Constitutions, temporary laws and instructions is or by further instructions hereafter shall be provided. Witness my hand & seale this nineteenth day of May, 1674. H. Cornbury. This is a true copy of the originall examined. Jos. Dalton, Secretary. *Coun. Journal ; same Col. En. B'k* 20, p. 101, dated May 11.

& pay himself 40l. per annum for the time past & for the time to come 100l. per annum, till their Lordships are in a condition to make a better settlement upon him. Send a bill upon Henry Hughes for 10l. lent his wife by their Lordships in England. To discourse with Andrew Percivall, Governor of the plantation upon Edisto River, how to be reimbursed for the present supply and about settling a plantation in a signiory of 12,000 acres for the Lords Proprietors. To sell the sloop he has seized for debts. To receive from Mr. Percivall the supply now sent by the Edisto dogger and dispose of the things to the best of his discretion. [May? 1674.] *Signed in Locke's hand.*

CRAVEN, SHAFTESBURY, G. CARTERT.

[*Col. Ent. Bk.* 20, p. 96.] *Abstract A. & W. I.,* 1294.

INSTRUCTIONS TO oʳ GOVERNʳ & COUNCILL of our Plantacon at Ashley River in Carolina   23 May 1674.

1. You are upon all occasions to afford all Countenance, help & assistance to oʳ plantacon in Loch Island.

2. You are to affix ye publique seal[1] to all such Grants as Mʳ Andrew Percivall, Governʳ[2] of that plantacon shall send to you, signed by his hand, with advice from him specifying ye Grants he desires to have sealed.   CRAVEN, SHAFTEBURY,

Whitehall, 23ᵈ May 1674.   G. CARTERET.

Mem: by Locke: Mʳ Andrew Percivall had a copy of ye Fundamentall Constitutions signed and sealed with him.

[Col. En. Bk. 20, p. 97.] Rivers, 388.

INSTRUCTIONS TO Mʳ ANDREW PERCIVALL, *23 May, 1674.*

1. Yoᵘ are to grant Land to none that comes to setle under yoʳ Government, but upon condition they setle in Towneships, and

---

[1] This seal was probably sent by Percivall. It was not, I think, the Great seal; the first grants are in 167⅘, p. 286.

[2] "John Lord Berkley & the rest of the Lᵈˢ Prop of Carolina. To oʳ trusty & well beloved Andrew Percivall, Governʳ of the plantation to be settled on both sides Edisto or Ashipow River &c." to convey lands, execute all powers &c and in case of his death power to the householders to choose a Governor, May 20, 1674. *Signed:* Shaftesbury, Cornbury, Berkeley, G. Carteret. [*Col. Ent. Bk.* 20, p. 99.] *Rivers*, 388. Locke island was Edisto island. *Ch. Yr. Bk.* 1886, p. 248. *Rivers*, 121

take up land according to ye draught herewth delivered yo^u, vizt
To each house built in ye said Towne, & forme fifty acres home
lott, as in ye draught, viz: five acres for a house & garden, ten
acres in ye Comon Cow pasture, and thirty five in a peece be-
yound ye Comon.   And an out lott containing 300 more in one
peece in ye same Collony &c.   *Rivers,* 387.

2. Yo^u are to take care that store of Provizzions are planted.

3. Yo^u are to keep faire Correspondance wth ye Neighbour
Indians to ye utmost of yor power.

4. Yo^u are to deliver to Mr Joseph West all ye Goods now sent
in ye Edistoh Dogger & consigned to y^u for ye use & supply of
o^r people at Ashley & Cooper River.

SHAFTESBURY   CRAVEN

Whitehall, 23^d May 1674.   G. CARTERET.

[Col. En. Bk. 20, p. 93.]   Rivers,387.

INSTRUCTIONS FOR Mr ANDREW PERCIVALL.[1]   23 May, 1674.

Mr Andrew Percivall

1. You are to take charge of the Cargo on board the Edisto
Dogger[2] and to sayle with all possible speed to Bermudoes.

2. God sending you safe to Bermudoes you are to store your
selfe with Indian Corne for six months and other necessarys fitt
for the plantation of Carolina viz: Hogs, poultry, potatoes,
Orange trees &c.   And to consider what things you may have
there either for profit or pleasure, which you may send for from
thence when you are better setled.

3. You are to enquire the price of Catle at Bermudoes and

---

[1] Ld. Shaftesbury's kinsman. He reached St Giles before Oct., 1674;
was made Register and Duke Albemarle's deputy, 1675, and June 10,
1680, Secretary of the Province. He was deputy till displaced, 1685;
the Propr's gave him 1000 acres, but, 1693, complain of his "refractory
humor."   In 1694, leaving his estates, Weston hall, Black Robins,
Brickil, &c., to Col. Broughton's care, he went to England. His will,
Feb. 10, 1695, "of Westminster, Esq:" mentions his wife, Essex, sons,
Andrew and James, dau. Mary, cousin, Samuel Percivall.   1703, his
widow managed the Carolina estates; by 1713 Andrew Percivall, of the
Inner Temple, Esq., did so.

[2] Dutch fishing boat build and rig, 2 masts, with square or lug sails forward and spanker aft. John Coming commanded her.

what number of Cattle fit to be transported is to be had there, that soe you may consider whether it be best to furnish yourselfe with cattle from thence or from Maryland for you are not without farther order to trade either with New Yorke or Virginia.

4. At Bermudoes you are to Informe yourself in the way of planting and useing Cassatha for bread and Drinke which I am informed growes in Virginia, and alsoe in all the Husbandry of Bermudoes applicable to Carolina.

5. If you see it convenient you may carry with you some grown Cattle from Bermudoes to Carolina for a present supplye of the family with Milke.

6. You are to enquire concerning the loading hence of Oranges from Bermudoes and to consider whether the best Cargo for my vessell returneing be not partly Cedar from Edisto and partly Oranges from Bermudoes.

7. You are to settle a Correspondence in Bermudoes with a fitt man and one of good reputation.

8. You are to consider what Orange flower water Rose water, hony or any other Rarities are to be had there and at what rates cheapest.

9. You are to make noe longer stay at Bermudoes then what is necessary for the taking in your supplyes which being done you are to saile directly to Edisto River and there choose a convenient place to settle in upon Lock Island where you may have a bould landing and marke out as soone as you can conveniently 2½ Miles on either sid your settlement in a straite line and 4½ miles back from the River being for my first Signiory.

10. You are not to suffer any one to take up any plantation on Lock Island with Directions from me, but if any come they are to settle in Townships upon the opposite shore and not scatteringly as they have done at Ashley River.

11. Haveing chosen the place you are forthwith to build 2 Houses one for your selfe, and stores and such as you thinke convenient to lodge there with you, the other for a common lodgeing Roome for the servants and after those two you are to build a third for Corne and other products of the Country as you shall see occasion.

12. As soone as you have any hands free from building you are to set them a worke in planting provisions. If there be any cleare ground fit for it or in cleareing grounds for provisions

and you are to fence in that ground soe as may preserve it from Hogs or Catle.

13. You are to endeavour to make Irish potatoes grow and to have a sufficient stock of them to supply your necessity if your other provisions should faile they serveing in Ireland both boyled, roasted and baked on such occasions.

14. You are to make your provisions chiefely of Indian Corne but in the meane tyme to trye English graine and to sow your English wheat where lyes a bed of clay which preserves the mould moister in drye wheather.

15. As soone you have unloaden the shipe you are immediately to send her away either to Bermoodoes or Maryland for cattle where they are most conveniently to be had. And you are to have a Regard that some of them be milch Cows for the present supplye of the Familye My Intention being to have 300 or 400 head of Cattle upon the place as soon as I cann.

16. The vessell being returned to your settlement with a freight of cattle you are imediately to send her away to Bermudoes laden with the stocks of the best Cedar onely leaveing room for ⅕ Freight of Bermudoes Oranges if that be a convenient season, which being taken in you are to order the master to saile directly hither.

17. If you find it not convenient to touch at Bermudoes for ⅕ Freight in Oranges or other things, you are to send her away from Carolina directly hither full loaden with stock of Cedar or any other Freight you shall judge more convenient and to this purpose while she is upon this trip for cattle you are to imploy a fit number of hands in cuteing and squareing of Cedar to load her.

18. You are to send me word what will be the most convenient season of the yeare for the sending home of my vessell hereafter, soe that she may make in Bermudoes the most profitable freight of Oranges if that will turne to accompt. And to consider whether packing Oranges in drye chests will not preserve them better then greene. If soe then whether it will be best for the future to prepare chests in Carolina of drye Tymber for that purpose and to make tryall what sort of Tymber doth best.

19. You are to endeavour to begin a Trade with the Spaniards for Negroes, Clothes or other Commodyties they want wherein

you are to take speciall care that it be soe managed that they get noe Intelligence of our strength, condition or place of settlement.   In order to which you are to get some Trusty Indian by whome D[r] Woddard is to write to Don Pedro Melinza[1] and to let him know that the person from whome he is imployed is of all the English Nobility the most affectionate to the Spaniards and that he desires to have a Commerce with them for the accommodation on both sides setled in some convenient place about or beyond Porte Royall soe as to give Jealousy to neither side and with as much secrecy and by as few persons as he pleases and that soe managed it might be very advantageous both to him and me.

20. You are to send me an accompt from tyme to tyme of the Country, the properties of the soyle what progress you have made in every of the above Articles and what else you propose to be don or are goeing upon.

21. You are to take up a Signiory for me in Lock Island and get it setled according unto the usuall forme of the Lords Proprietors grants of land in Carolina.

22. You are to understand that at present you are noe way under the Government of the plantation at Ashley River, the Commission to the Governor of that plantation not extendeing soe far south and you therefore have liberty to trade as you thinke fit with the Natives or any other theire Laws haveing noe influence upon you.

23. If any people from Ashley River applie to you for Cloathes or Tooles I am willing they should be supplied in theire necessity out of my stores when you find you have to spare at 25 per cent profit for ready pay either in money, provisions or other Commodities that you judge may turne to accompt here or if they want these in labor but you are by noe means to give them any credit or make any Debts amongst them.

24. If any come to you either from Ashley River or any other place and are willing to be entertained as Leetmen, you are to receive them upon condition they be first my servants for 2 yeares at the end whereof respectively they shall have the Tearmes of my Leetmen which are as follows.

Every original Leetman shall have from me when the tyme of servant is out, a house in a Towne appointed and set out by me

---

[1] Governor of St. Augustine? page 173.

with 60 acres of land belonging to it to be as it were coppyhold
of Inheritance to him his heires or posterity with Common for 3
or 4 Cows and also shall have at the end of his tyme of being
servant 2. Cows 2. sows, 15 bushells of Corne, he to pay ½
yearly of the value of the land to be let and ⅓ calvd till I have
received 3 yearlings for every Cow he hath had of me and the
same proportion of Sow pigs att two months old. His posterity
is to setle and dwell on my Land, and I am to setle theire children when they marry in a liveing of at least 10 Acres.

25. You are to take care that every of the servants that goe
now with you or Leetmen that you shall hereafter entertaine enter
themselves according to the 25th of the Fundamental Constitutions and you are to carry a Register booke to that purpose.

26. If any comes there as planters and bring an years provision with them they are to be received upon condition they will
plant in Townships according to the draught you have with you
wherein every one of the house shall have 35 Acres belonging to
it. The Home Lotts of 50 Acres a peece to be set out presently
according to the draught, and the remaineing parte of theire
shares set out in the same Colony when ever they will pay 1
penny the Acre rent for it provided they take up the whole or
what part of theire remayneing parte within 16 years after theire
respective grants, after which tyme they shall have noe farther
clayme.

27. You are to send me word what Trees fit for masts and to
what bignesse and length you have any there and at what Distance
from Water carriage and to send me Samples of the timber of
your Mast Trees, and of any Dying Drugs or any sorte of Tymber
or Wood that is finely grained or sented that you thinke may be
fit for Cabinets and such other fine Workes.

28. You are to send me the soundings at the entrance of
Edisto River at low water and carefully to searche out the Deepest parte of the Channell and send me a draught of it.

29. You are by every opportunity from tyme to tyme to give
me advise of the state of my affaires there.

30. You are to send me a scheme of the Trade of Pipe Staves
and how it may be best managed and informe me whether this
way of imploying our Tymber and Labour will turne to accounte.

31. You are to cleare and plant the Towne plot first.

32. If you have no fraight for any vessell from Carolina nor

any probabillity to load her at Bermudas you are to send her to Maryland in Virginia to take in fraight there and soe come hither.

33. You are to discourse and consult with Mr West about the Plantation at Ashley River and about a way how a trade may be setled that the supplys we send may not be throwne away but we may be paid in Commodyties that will reimburse us I would have you in this subject informe him that wee doe not see what can become of the poore people there that have noe stocks unlesse they will become leetmen to some that are able to support and supplye them which the Lords Proprietors are resolved not to doe if they doe not find a way and shew them how they may have returnes for the Commodyties they send for though they are engadged to one another to lay out money upon the place yet it is but to one another to pay their equall proportions but have noe engadgement to furnish them with necessarys unpaid for but that they intend to ley out their money in procuring skilfull men and fitt materialls for the Emprouvm^t of the Country in Wine, Silke, Oyle &c And that to this purpose Mr West should consider where to take up 12000 acres for a Plantation for the Lords Proprietors where Leetmen may be enterteined and setled those experiments they intend to be at the Charge of may be made. And that if he will remove to Edistoh he shall be Governor of both places for the condition of the people and way of planting at Ashley River will be a hinderance to Townes and the Comeing of Rich men thither That to this purpose he should dispose the poorer sort who are not able well to subsist of themselves to apply themselves to those who are able better to provide for them and become Leetmen which will be a very comfortable liveing as he may see by the conditions I propose to mind.

SHAFTESBURY.

Exeter House 23° May 1674.
Instructions for Mr Andrew Percevall.

[*S. P. Bdle.*, 48, No. 55, page 127.]

INSTRUCTIONS FOR Mr HENRY WODDARD.

1. You are to treat with the Indians of Edisto for the Island and buy it of them and make a Friendship with them.
2. You are to setle a Trade with the Indians for Furs and

other Comodities that are either for the Supplye of the Plantation or advantageous for Trade.

3. You are to consider whether it be best to make a peace
with the Westoes or Cussitaws which are a more powerfull
Nation said to have pearle and silver and by whose Assistance
the Westoes may be rooted out, but noe peace is to be made
with either of them without Including our Neighbour Indians
who are at amity with us.[1]

4. You are in management of the trade and treaty of the
Indians alwayes to have the consent and Direccon of Mr Percivall my principall Agent.

5. You are to consider what other Comodities besides these
we already know are to be had from any of the Indians which
may be profitable unto us.

6. You are to have $\frac{1}{5}$ of the profit of Indian Trade.

7. Haveing consulted Mr Percivall you are to writ a letter to
Don Pedro Melinza about setling a Trade betweene mee and the
Spaniards which if by your care and industry it succeed well I
purpose shall bee an occasion of my farther kindnesse to you.

SHAFTESBURY.

Exeter House the 23rd May 1674.   Ex^d

[*S. P.*, Bdle. 48, No. 55, page 134.]

LORD SHAFTESBURY TO JOSEPH WEST.

Exeter House 23^d May 1674.
Mr West,

Though by the great tracts of land taken up upon Ashley
River, whereby there is little convenience left to those who would
come thither, and that smale care was taken by the people there
to set apart for me a comodious Siginory who had designed to
come and plant amongst them.   I am driven to seeke out some
other new place to setle in yet I am soe much a friend to your
plantation at Ashley River, that I have at last with much labor

---

[1]Order for trade with the Westoes & Cussatoes Indians, 10 April 1677.
Whereas ye discovery of ye Country of ye Westoes & ye Cussatoes two
powerful & warlike nations, hath bine made at ye charge of ye Earle of
Shaftesbury, &c., and by the Industry & hazard of Dr Henry Woodward, and a strict peace & amity made Betweene those said Nations
and our people in o^r province of Corolina, &c. *Rivers*, 389.

got the rest of the Lords to agree to lay out more money there, but in this agreement amongst ourselves I did not intend, nor can I advise them to be at any farther charge in supplies till you can send us from thence rationall proposalls how we may be payd in Comodyties produced there, which at the Markets, they must be carryed to, shall really reimburse us; A scheme of such a trade when you have drawn and sent us, we shall be ready to send you such things as you want and at more reasonable rates then you can have them from Merchants, but we cannot afford to give them away.   I have nevertheless ventured to persuade the rest of the Lords to send you A present supplye of cloathes and as many tooles as could be got ready by my Dogger which hath stayd severall Dayes on purpose after she was ready to saile.   You must use your best discretion in the disposeing of them, for you are the man in the Plantation whome I most rely on as one who will take care to bring it to some thing, and put things into such a Method that the people may be supplyed, and we not lose by it.   What Opinion I have of you you will find by the Patent and Com^{con} [page 430 n] I have procured for you, and you will receive from Mr Percivall, with whome I would have you hold a friendly Communication and be assisting to each other in the support and carrying on of both the Plantations From him you will understand that the Lords Proprietors designe in laying out theire money for the future will be to get the best Improvem^t for this Climat from all parts of the world and men experienced in the right Managm^t of them.   And it is in the Signiory we would have you take up for us where we would be at the charge to make the First Tryalls, and have a stock of Catle ready, which We Intend to bring on, whereby Wee could Offer encouragm^t to rich men, to come amongst us, who might be sure there from us to have catle at a certaine and cheap rate, and advice, and assistance in the planting of Such things, which Wee upon tryall at our cost have Found Successfull, and which we shall be ready to Comunicate.   I would have your Dispatches concerneing these matters come to me from you and Mr Percivall Joyntly:

    Exa^r Your very affectionate Friend

                                            SHAFTESBURY.

        [S. P., Bdle. 48, No. 55, page 142.]

LORD SHAFTESBURY TO MAU. MATHEWS.

Exeter House 23° May 74.

Mr Mathews,

I am sorry you came not into England that I might have discoursed with you at large touching my private concerns in Carolina and made you understand fully my Designe in planting there and instructed you in all the particulars how I would have it managed which cannot well be done by writing to one at a distance Tis not therefore out of any dislike to you that I have imployed another from hence, who hath a Relacon to my Family to manage a plantacon I am setling there and which you could not well attend at that distance from Ashley River I intend to sit down My thoughts were to have planted on Ashley River but the people tooke soe litle care to allow or provide me any accommodacon neare them having taken up for themselves all the best conveniences on that river and left me not a tolerable Place to plant on nearer then two Miles from the Water that I am forced to seeke out in another place and resolve to take me up a Signiory at Edisto River, In the meane time I cease not to be a friend to your Plantacon, who without prejudice to themselves might have used me with more respect, and in particular I continue my Deputacon and kindnesse to you.

Exad   SHAFTESBURY.

[*S. P.*, Bdle. 48, No. 55, page 144.]

LORD SHAFTESBURY TO JOSEPH WEST.

Exeter House 30° May 74.

Mr West,

There are, (as I understand) in the plantation at Ashley River one John Barley and Henry Pretty, whose Friends here in England are very desirous they should come over. If they are in Debt to the Lds Proprs let that be noe hindrance to theire comeing, but send me a State of theire accounts with us, and if they come I will be answerable for it to the Lords Proprs, but it is not enough that you permit them to come away, but I would have you if you finde either of them averse to it to endeavour to persuade them, And be as instant with them as you can, especially Mr Barley whose Father is a Gent of a very considerable estate and till of late knew not what was become of this his Son, who it seems transported himselfe into our Country without the knowledge of his Father or Friends, The inclosed Letters will give you a more particular Account of these persons, which having reade pray seale and deliver to them. Mr Dalton also as I am told desires to come home, let his accounts with us be stated, and let him give his own Security for it there, and then let him come when he pleases.

Exa: I am Your very affec^ate friend

SHAFTESBURY.

[*S. P.* Bdle. 48, No: 55, page 145.]

LORD SHAFTESBURY TO JOHN BORLEY.[1]

Exeter House May 30 1674.

Mr Barley,

Your Father (without whose consent you went to Carolina) haveing found that you are there, hath made application to me that you might come home againe, till I heard it from your friends here, I knew neither your name nor Condicon nor of any such person in our plantation, And cannot but wonder that you whose Father was of soe considerable Estate and able to doe soe well for you should Transport your Selfe into another Country upon such Tearmes as you did without acquainting some of your Friends or at least makeing your Selfe known to me or some of the Ld^s P^rs. What ever your reasons were of goeing I must acquaint you your Father, whose heire you are is very earnest that you should returne, which I have promised him and therefore desire you upon receipt of this you prepare your Selfe to come into England.

Exa: I am your very affec^ate Friend

SHAFTESBURY.

[*S. P.*, Bdle. 48, No. 55, page 146.]

LORD SHAFTESBURY TO HENRY PRETTY.

Exeter House 30° May 1674.

Mr Pretty,

Your Relations here who are my Friends have acquainted me that is of great Concernment to you that you should by the

---

[1] He had come on the Carolina 1669 with Wm Owen, p. 135.

First Oppertunity come into England, and that you suffer inconveniences in your Estate here if you doe not soe.   They have
also promised me that when you are here you shall be at Liberty
to returne to Carolina if you please.   I thinke you will not doe
well not to comply with theire desires, you may be assured I
should not be willing to drawe away soe considerable a planter
out of my Country, but I cannot forbeare to presse you to give
your Friends this Satisfaction wherein I find not that they propose anything to themselves but your advantage and the Setlem[t]
of your Affairs.

Exa: I am Your very affectionate friend

SHAFTESBURY.

[*S. P.*, Bdle. 48, No. 55, page 147.]

THE COUNCIL JOURNALS.

Charlestowne may xxx[th] *1674 present:* The Governor, Coll:
Joseph West, Lt. Coll: John Godfrey, capt: Mau: Mathews, M[r]
W[m] Owen, capt: Rich: Conant, M[r] Ralph Marshall.   For the
better intelligence of & to any ship that hereafter may happen
upon this coast Resolved that a Great gun be mounted in some
conven[t] place near the Rivers Mouth w[ch] wth one charge of powder at a time shall be committed to the charge of capt: fflorence
O'Sullivan to be fired upon the appearance of any Shipp or
Shipps & that the s[d] Gun be conveyed to the s[d] place upon tuesday next   cause a permit for w[ch] purpose.   The Governor hath
promised the assistance of 6 men, Col. West, Lt Col. Godfrey
& capt. Mathews each one &c   For as &c John Pinkerd by an
order of Council dated 27 March last was commit[d] into the Prov:
Mars[lls] custody Resolved that he be inlarged giving good security to appear at the next Gen[l] Sessions of the peace &c then &
there to answer all matters &c.[1]   *1672, 92,* p. 56.

TEMPORARY AGRARIAN LAWS.   21 June 1674.

Agreed upon by the Lords Proprietors of Carolina in 23 sections.   "Since ye whole foundation of ye Government is setled

---

[1] "Ben. Wych's Bill" for writing West's patent to be Landgrave and
his Commission, for writing an Act of Parliament for Carolina, &c., *so
endorsed by Locke.*   (*S. P.*, 48, No. 94.)   *A. & W. I.*, 1296.

upon a right and equall distribution of Land and the orderly takeing of it up is of great moment to ye welfare of ye Province &c.'' *Signed and sealed by*

SHAFTESBURY,   CRAVEN,   H. CORNBURY,
J. BERKELEY,   G. CARTERET,   P. COLLETON.

(*Col. En. Bk.*, 20, pages 83, 86.)   *Rivers*, 355.

THE COUNCIL JOURNALS.

*Charlestowne 25*th *July 1674 present:* (*the same*) upon hearing petn of Jno pinkard agt Thos Archcraft both parties being present & submitting their cause &c to the judgmt of the Gd Councill Ordered that said Thos Archcraft pay 17£ in full &c.

For as &c it is credibly informed that the Indian Stonoe Casseca hath endeavored to confederate certaine other Indians to murder some of the English nation & to rise in Rebellion agt this Settemt Resolved that capt. Mau: Mathews doe require & command nine men of the Inhabits of this Settlemt to attend him in this expedn to take the sd Indian & him cause to be brought to Charlestowne to answer to these things but if any opposition happen the sd capt. Mathews is to use his discretn in the managmt thereof for the securiy of himself & the sd party of men whether by killing & destroying the sd Indian & his confederates or otherwise.[1]

*Augt. 3*d *1674. present ut supra.* [P. 57*] And forasmuch as it is credibly informed that the Kussoe Indians have secretly murdered 3 Englishmen and as these Indians have noe certaine abode Resolved that Capt. Mau: Mathews, Mr Wm Owen, capt Richd Conant & Mr Ra: Marshall doe inquire where the sd Indians now are & if any probability can be had that these Indians may be taken then to raise a party of men as they shall think convent under command of the sd capt Conant or any other parties under other commanders to use all meanes to come up with the sd Indians wheresoever to take or destroy all or any of them, the whole matter being left to their advisemt.

*Charlestowne August xiii*th *1674 present:* Coll. Joseph West, Lt. Coll. John Godfrey, Capt Mau: Mathews, Mr Wm Owen, Capt Richd Conant, Mr Ra: Marshall Mr Saml West. At a meeting

-----

[1] 1674, July 29, "Mem: of having sent Mr Locke a copy of the Fundamental Constitutions." *Col. En. Bk.*, 20, fly leaf.

of the Councill this day for the establishing of affairs after the
decease of S[r] John Yeomans late Govern[r] of this province[1] the
Councill (nemine contra dicente) have & doth nominate Coll.
Joseph West to be Governor of this province to all intents &
purposes as fully & amply as the L[ds] Prop[rs] by their commission
to the s[d] S[r] Jno Yeomans bearing date xxvi[th] day of Decem[r]
1670 & 1.   And forasmuch as there is a defect of 2 Deputies viz:
the duke of Albemarle Deputy [p. 58*] & S[r] Geo. Carterets Deputy accord[g] to the L[ds] Prop[rs] instruc[ns] on that behalf the 2 Eldest
of the Councill viz. cap[t] Rich[d] Conant is admitted as S[r] Geo.
Carteret's deputy & M[r] Ralph Marshall the Duke of Albemarles
deputy until the pleasure of the s[d] Deput[ors] be signified to the
contrary.   [Page 367.]

   Charlestowne August 16th 1674 present: The Govern[r], Godfrey,
Mathews, Owen, Bull, Conant, Marshall, S. West.   Resolved
that the ffreeholders of this Settlem[t] be sumoned to appear at
Charlestowne upon Thursday next in the morning then & there
to elect a Parliam[t] & that the then Parliam[t] doe choose six persons to be councellors accord[g] to ye L[ds] Prop[rs] instruc[ns].

   August xx[th] 1674 present : (same less Bull & S. West) The
parliam[t] being this day chosen did elect 6 persons namely Cap[t]
Christo[r] Portman, Cap[t] Geo. Thompson, M[r] Jno ffallock & M[r]
Samuel West, M[r] Jno Yeomans, & M[r] Jos. Dalton to be of the
Councill to act & doe accord[g] to the L[ds] Prop[rs] Directions in that
behalf.   1672, 92.

————

   "CAROLINA, DISCOVERIES ACROSS THE MOUNTAINS by Maj[r]
General Wood 1674."[2]   Ft. Henry Aug 22 1674.   Maj: Gen.

---

   [1] He was in Council Aug. 3, and must have died soon after in Carolina
and not at Barbadoes, as Hewet says, see page 52 n.

   [2] So endorsed by Locke, but not about Carolina except Gabriel
Arthur's tales of going ag't the Spaniards and seeing the steeple where
hung the bell Needham spoke of, &c., and again to Port Royal to cut
off a town of Indians who lived near the English; so they marched over
the mountains, and in six days came upon the head of Port Royal river.
At a house they crept up to Gabriel, heard one say pox take such masters that they will not allow a servant a bit of meat upon Christmas Day,
&c.   From the Indian town one Englishman ran for his life, the Tomahittans let him pass but made great slaughter upon the Indians, and
about sunrise hearing many guns fired by the English they hurried away
and in less than 14 days arrived at the Tomahittans.

Abr^m Wood to his friend Jno Richards in London. Discoveries in the mountains S and W. of Virginia mentions Tomahitan and Occhoneche Indians also Sarah and Totero "under the foot of the mountains" &c never heard anything since he employed James Needham who passed from Aeno an Indian town two days journey beyond Occhoneeche in safety &c 25 Feb. 1674 news that Needham was certainly killed &c "so died this heroic Englishman &c which had ventured where never any Englishman trod." (*S. P.* 48, No. 94 MS. *Abs. A. & W. I.* 1347, 647.)

THE COUNCIL JOURNALS.

Septr vth 1674 present: The Govern^r, Godfrey, Mathews, Owen, Bull, Marshall, Conant, falock, S West, Yeomans & Dalton. Resolved that a Genl Sessions of the peace & Goal Delivery for this province be held at Charlestowne upon the first tuesday of Octob^r next &c

[P. 59*] *October 3^d 1674 present:* (*the same*)
Mem: that James Donaghoe,[1] p^r aged 30 years or thereabouts Hannah ffogartie wife of Edmond ffogartie p^r aged 35 yeares &c being persons of an honest fame & repute came &c took oath upon the Holy Evangelists &c did declare they were present & did hear Mathew Dowling late of Charlestowne p^r dec'd some time before his decease & in his perfect mind & memory (as these dep^{ts} doe conceive) declare that he did make & ordain Capt fflorence O'Sullivan to be his heir &c Resolved that the printed coppy of the ffundamental Constitutions lately sent [p. 439] by the L^{ds} Prop^{rs} be read at the present meeting of the parliam^t.[2]

---

[1] From Barbadoes, held lands at Ickerbe 1671, 76, and near Canty, 1685, 1704, on 13 mile run, both he and Fogartie left descendants.

[2] Afterw'ds ye L^{ds} Prop^{rs} did send new Instruc'ns dated 10 May, 1671, seeming in one article to direct to some fundamental Constitutions wch had not before been scene, and in a letter dated 16th of 7^{ber} y^t their L^{dsps} are pleased to write, that the fundam^l Consti^{ns} were the termes upon wch the people had settled in their Countrey, and that therefore the people had reason to expect ye L^{ds} Prop^{rs} should (as they did resolve to do) make them good to them and at y^t time ye fundam^{ll} Constit^{ns} dated 1 March, 1669, were not sent hither or knowne to be made wch further appears by another lett^r to ye Govr and Councill here dated 26th June,

*November ij*ᵈ *1674 present:* The Governᵣ, Mᵣ Wᵐ Owen, Cpt
Ste. Bull, Mᵣ Samˡ West, Mᵣ Jno ffalock, Mᵣ Jno Yeomans.
Mathew Smallwood, planter, being examinᵈ as to some matters
of misdemeanor formˡʸ committed ordered that he be comitᵈ to
the custody of Prov: Marsˡˡ till he find security for good behavior.

*November 10*ᵗʰ *1674 present:* The Governᵣ, Godfrey, Mathews,
Owen, Bull, Conant, Capt Geo: Thompson, Mᵣ Jno ffalock, Mᵣ
Jno Yeomans. Upon report of Capᵗ Mau: Mathews this day
made &c that an Indian is supposed to have been privately killed
by some of the English   Resolved that Capᵗ Mathews Mᵣ Wᵐ
Owen & Mᵣ Chrᵣ Portman some time this week meet at Capᵗ
Mathews his now dwelling house & make diligent enquiry into
the whole matter & doe make report thereof to the Gᵈ Council
wᵗʰ all convenᵗ speed.   1672, 92.

————

LORDS PROPRIETORS TO LORD SHAFTESBURY.

Whitehall 20 Nov 74.

My Lord

We have here inclosed sent yr Loᵖ an extract of the letters
[p. 256] we lately received from Carolina wherein yr Loᵖ will
finde the present state of the plantation.[1]   The progresse where
of since its first setlemt with all the errors and miscarriages in
the managemt of it all along being as we believe well setled in
your thoughts, we thinke ourselves obleiged as well in acknowledgment of your Loᵖ particular care and pains in it hitherto
as also in pursuance of our designe of carrying on this plantation to acquaint you with the present condicon of it, and desire

————

1672, in wᶜʰ their Lordships write yᵗ therewᵗʰ their printed fundamˡˡ Constitⁿˢ, wᶜʰ are those dated ye 1 March, are sent, and that lettᵣ with ye
said Constitⁿˢ were received here 8ᵗʰ Febʸ followinge & then ye sᵈ
Constⁿˢ are first declared by their Lᵈᵖˢ an authentique coppey. About
Febʸ 167⅔ the Gov: Col. Jos: West did propose to the Councell,
in the name of the Lᵈˢ Propᵣˢ, a booke of fundamˡˡ Constitⁿˢ, &c., dated
1 March, 1669, to be subscribed by all men, p. 162. *Rivers*, 420.

[1] This letter is in Locke's hand, but with autograph signatures. The
extracts from 18 letters, 1670, are given, p. 256.

your advice what course is now to be taken to avoid those inconveniencys we have formerly ran into, to set as narrow bounds
as may be to our future expenses and yet order it soe that all our
former charges may not be lost by a totall desertion and ruin of
the setlemt at Ashley river. We have reason to think they will
no longer need nor expect any supplys of provisions from
abroad but we see not well how they can subsist unless we furnish them with clothes and tools and armes till the products of
their labour draw trade to them, only we would consider how it
may be best managed soe as to be bought here and sent thither
at the cheapest rates and how be disposed of there so as we may
be the soonest reimbursed. We think they may be able now
they are got before hand in provisions to make us considerable
returnes in tobaco which they speak of as equall to your Spanish
and in a little time there may be considerable quantitys of Indigo and cotton produced the growth of both which they very
much commend. They desire the Custom on their Tobaco may
for some time be taken off by his M^{at} But we thinke this for
many reasons soe difficult to obteyn that we have noe thoughts to
move in it. We are very much importuned by that idle fellow
Halsted who used us soe ill to mak an end with him we desire
your Lo^{ps} advice what we shall doe in that particular and in the
whole managemt of our joynt concernes in Carolina we rest

My Ld Your Lo^{ps} humble servants

C. CRAVEN

G. CARTERET   JO BERKELEY.

Addressed: For the Righ ho^{ble} the Earle of Shaftesbury at St
Giles.

Endorsed, in Ld Shaftesbury's hand: Carolina the Lord Proprietors to me November 20th 1674.

[*S. P.*, Bdle. 48, No. 95.][1]

---

[1] Lords Proprietors, of Carolina, commission to John Richards, Treasurer & Agent in matters relating to their joint carrying on that Plantation, with authority to receive debts due upon that account, and
particularly to take the acco'ts of their late Treasurer and Agent, Peter
Jones, deceased, and receive from his ex'ors or adm'ors all books and
papers belonging to the Lords Prop'rs, with the salary of 2ol. per annum,
Dec. 4, 1674. *Signed*, Shaftesbury, Jo. Berkeley, Craven, G. Carteret.
(*Col. En. B'k* 20, p. 102), *A. & W. I.*, 1402.

THE COUNCIL JOURNALS.

December 5th 1674 Present: The Governour, Capt Maurice Mathews, M[r] Wm Owen, capt Richard Conant, capt. Stephen Bull, M[r] Ralph Marshall, M[r] John Fallock, M[r] Samuel West, M[r] John Yeamans, M[r] Joseph Dalton. Upon the motion of Capt. Christopher Portman for a small portion of vacant land lying to the Westward of his planting lott neere Charles Towne. It is ordered that a warrant doe issue out for the same to his use.

December 26th 1674. Present. The Governour, Lieut: Coll: John Godfrey, Mathews, Owen, Bull, Conant, Marshall, Fallock, Yeamans, Dalton. Joseph Dalton Gent: having this day assigned & surrendered his planting lott next Ickaby into the hands of the Grand Councill for the better settling of more people about Charles Towne the Grand Councill doth grant the same to Anthony Churne & John Chambers equally before the 25th march next and which of them doe not settle his part before that time shall forfeit the same &c. The G[d] Councill considering the poor condition of John Pinkerd &c order that one cross cut saw, one muskett and one fowling peace in the Gov'rs custody, one bed stead &c in Oliver Spencers[1] be delivered to him requireing the same for the pres[t] relief of himself and family. *C. J.*, 46.

WOODWARDS WESTO DISCOVERY.

Carolina: Dec[br] 31: 1674

Right Hono[bl]

Haveing received notice at Charles Towne from M[r] Percyvall y[t] strange Indians were arrived at y[r] L[dshps] Plantation,[2] Imme-

---

[1] Came, 1671, from Barbadoes? 1685, 95, of C. T., blacksmith, left descendants. 1720, Oliver & Rebecca Spencer, Jos. & Sarah Spencer, Christ Church *Register.*

[2] Ashley barony, or St. Giles (the old Kussoe Indian settlem't, hence called "Cussoo" or "Cussoe house"), 12,000 acres " on the south side of the head of Ashley river," from the 2d Creek above "Middleton Place" to Bacon's Bridge, and west to Edisto, granted 18 March, 167$\frac{4}{5}$ to L'd Shaftesbury, and by his grandson, L'd Ashley, conveyed 20 July, 1698, to his brother, Hon. Maurice Ashley, and by him, 2 Aug., 1717, to Sam'l Wragg, Esq., who 6 April, 1720 sold to Alex. Skene, Esq., 3,000 acres. *D. p. 317.* St. Gyles plantacon Cussoe. To all menner of People, &c., know ye that wee, the Cassiques naturell Born Hears & Sole owners & proprietors of great & lesser Cussoe, lying on the River of Kyewah, the

diately I went up in ye yawle, were I found according to my former conjecture in all probability that they were ye Westoes not understanding ought of their speech, resolving nevertheless (they having first bartered their truck) to venture up into ye maine wth them they seeming very unwilling to stay ye night yet very desireous y^t I should goe along wth them. The tenth of Oct^ber being Saturday in ye afternoon I accordingly set forth, ye weather raw and drizzling, they being ten of them and my selfe in Company. we travelled ye remaining part of y^t afternoon West & by North thorough y^r L^dships land towards ye head of Ashley River, passing divers tracks of excellent oake and Hickery land, wth divers spatious Savanas, seeming to ye best of my judgment good Pastorage, as we travelled this day I saw (as divers other times likewise in my journey) were these Indians had drawne uppon trees (the barke being hewed away) ye effigies of a bever, a man, on horseback & guns, Intimating thereby as I suppose, their desire for freindship, & comerse wth us, ye weather continuing wett wee tooke up our quarters,[2] haveing steered exactly by Compass from St Giles Plantation according to ye forenamed Course. the Indians being diligent in makeing two barke, covered Hutts, to shelter us from ye injury of ye weather, this night as well as ye afternoone proved tedious, having had soe large a vacation from my travels, ye diet before almost naturalized now seemed unpleasant, & the ground altogether was uneasy for lodginge soe soon as ye day appeared wee set forth steering West & by South, after wee had passed ye head of Ashley River I found ye land indifferently good, in ye afternoon wee entered

River of Stonoe, & the freshes of the River of Edistah, doe for us ourselves, our subjects & vassals, grant, &c., whole part & parcell called great & lesser Cussoe unto the Right Honble Anthony Earl of Shaftesbury, Lord Baron Ashly of Wimborne St. Gyles, Lord Cooper of Pawlet, &c., 10 March, 1675. *Marks of* The Great Cassiq , &c., an Indian Captain, a hill Captain, &c. *Witness:* John Smyth, Jacob Waight, James Palmer, David Maybanke, *marks of* John Walker, Jas. Clurs, Henry Clement. *Sec: office, B'k 1683, 90 p. 10, Mills Ap. A., Rivers, 124,* mistakes, name, place, grantee, and purpose.

[1] Their origin and race are unknown, their tongue was so to the Savanas and Woodward (who knew the coast indians and Cusitaws), even their name seems given by enemies. In defeat they joined the Muscogees, but seem not of them, nor of the Euchees.

[2] N. W. of Bacon's bridge, near heads Long & Westo Savanas

a large tracke of Pines, which continued untill we came wth in two
or three miles of y^t part of Ædistaw River were wee crossed over.
The land seemeth fertyl along ye banks of this River, whose head
they report to bee about four score mile up in ye main from ye
part wee passed, being then twenty mile or something more distant from were divideing himselfe he makes ye pleasant plant^n of
Ædistawe. here killing a large buck wee tooke up our rendea-
vouze wth two mile of ye river,[1] glad of ye opportunity of lying
in two of their hunting hutts. Uppon Monday morning four of
ye company went to give notice of our comeing wee following
steered West S. West, ye land Piny except along ye skirts
of small rivulets, many of which wee passed this day, ye
weather all over cast, this evening wee provided shelter,
ye night proveing extreame wett wee supped wth two fatt Turkeys to helpe out wth our parcht corne flower broth, the following
day proveing as bad as ye night, wee forsooke not ye benefitt of
our hutts[2] uppon Wedensday morneing wee sett forth nothing at
all varying our former course this day wee had a sight of Ædistaw River bearing north west by north of us ye soyle very prom-
iseing, & in some places excellently tymbered in ye afternoon
wee shott a fatt doe which proportionably divideing amongst
them, was carried along by them for our better comons at night
quartering along ye sides of a pleasant run,[3] Thursday wee tooke
our journey dew West passing many large pastorable Savanas
the other land promising very well. this day wee shott two
Bucks ye best of both wth a fatt Turkey wee carried along wth us,
for our better accomodation at night.[4] ffryday wee traveled
West & by South haveing towards three the afternoon a sight
of ye mountaines, which bore northwest of us, passing ye head
of Port Royall river over a tree, were ye river intricately runs
through large vallies of excellent land.[5] At ye begining of ye

---

[1] Rounded the heads of Jacks and Horse Savanas, crossed Edisto about
Sullivan's ferry and camped?

[2] On Round O road, west of Scull creek? (or at its head?). Edisto is
hardly visible from either. His description better suits a more northern
route than his stated course.

[3] Creek south of Parker's bay, above the Walterboro road?

[4] Camped at or near Big Salkahatchie river?

[5] Hills in Barnwell? Crossed the river about Crooked creek?

adjoyning Hills, along whose banks in a mighty thicke wood wee tooke up our Quarters, the ensuing day wee went over many fattigous hills, ye land especially ye vallies being excellent good, our course West a little Southwardly in the afternoon wee mett two Indians wth their fowling peeces, sent by their cheife to congratulate my arrivale into their parts who himselfe awaited my comeing wth diuers others at ye Westoe River, the ridge of hills through which ye river runs then being in sight bore West and by North ye banks of this river seeme like white chalky cliffs and are at least one hundred foot perpendicular opposite to which banks uppon a sandy poynt were two or three hutts under whose shelter was their cheife wth divers others in his company the two Indians wee met had a canoe ready to pass us ouer, were soe soon as wee landed, I was carried to ye Cap^ts hutt, who courteously entertained mee wth a good repast of those things they counte rarietys amonge them the river here being very deep wth a silent curent trended North & by West & South and by East nearest, soe soone as ye raine ceased wee sett upp ye fertyle banks of this spatious river, haveing paddled about a league upp wee came in sight of ye Westoe towne, alias ye Hickauhaugau which stands uppon a poynt[1] of ye river (which is undoubtedly ye river May) uppon ye Westerne side soe y^t ye river encompasseth two-thirds thereof when we came wth in [sight] of the towne I fired my fowling peece & pistol wch was answered with a hollow & imediately thereuppon they gave mee a vollew of fifty or sixty small arms. here was a concourse of some hundred of Indians, drest up in their anticke fighting garbe Through ye midst of whom being conducted to their cheiftaines house ye which not being capable to containe ye crowd y^t came to see me, ye smaller fry got up & uncouvered the top of ye house to satisfy their curiosity. Ye cheife of ye Indians made long speeches intimateing their own strength (& as I judged their desire of freindship wth us) this night first haveing oyled my eyes and joynts with beares oyl,[2] they presented mee divers

---

[1] I cannot locate it. Perhaps Hago:slago bluff near Brier creek where the old trading path came, or Matthews bluff higher up. *Map Ch. Y'r B'k* 1883, p. 376, puts Westo a little higher.

[2] "Bears there are in great numbers of whose fat they make an Oyl which is of great virtue &c which I observed the Indians daily used." *Ash., 1680, 2 Car.,* 75.

deare skins setting before me sufficient of their food to satisfy at least half a dozen of their owne appetites. here takeing my first nights repose, ye next day I veiwed ye Towne which is built in a confused maner, consisting of many long houses whose sides and tops are both artifitially done wth barke upon ye tops of most whereof fastened to ye ends of long poles hang ye locks of haire of Indians that they have slaine. ye inland side of ye towne being duble Pallisadoed, & y^t part which fronts ye river haveing only a single one. under whose steep banks seldom ly less then one hundred faire canoes ready uppon all occasions. they are well provided with arms, amunition, tradeing cloath & other trade from ye northward for which at set times of ye year they truck drest deare skins furrs & young Indian Slaves. In ten daies time y^t I tarried here I viewed ye adjacent part of ye Country, they are Seated uppon a most fruitfull soyl, ye earth is intermingled wth a sparkling substance like Antimony,[1] finding severall flakes of Isinglass in ye paths, ye soales of my Indian shooes in which I travelled glistened like sylver, ye clay of which their pots & pipes are made is intermingled wth ye like substance ye wood land is abounding wth various sorts of very large straite timber. Eight daies journey from ye towne ye River hath it first falls West. N. West were it divides it selfe into three branches, amongst which dividing branches inhabit ye Cowatoe and Chorakae[2] Indians w^{tn} whom they are at continual warrs. forty miles distant from the towne northward they say lye ye head of Ædistaw river being a great meer or lake. two days before my departure arrived two Savana Indians[3] living as they

---

[1] Like gold, page 316. Mica scales which name Silver Bluff.

[2] Savannah, called "River of the Caouitas," a Muscogee tribe settled on the Salwege 1674–91, but retired to the Ocmulgee, and in 1715 to the Chattahoochee. 1540, DeSoto marched 7 days from Cusitachique to Chelaqui; Moore went to the Cherokees 1690, and 1693 they sent to complain of the Esaus, Coosas and Savannas. Act 1691 stops trade "S. of the Westoe river on the Sea coaste and of the now Savana towns on the same river inland," and calls in goods from "the Yemassees &c or the Cussetas or Kaweeta Indians &c or the Attoho, Kolegey or Cheraque Indians." 2 Stat., 66.

[3] Great raiders and wanderers; their then towns were near the Gulf west of Apallachicola river. This seems their first visit to the Westos. By 1680 they had pushed to the Westo river, "and the Westoes the more

said twenty days journey West Southwardly from them. there was none here y^t understood them but by signes they intreated freindship of ye Westoes showeing y^t ye Cussetaws, Checsaws & Chiokees[1] were intended to come downe and fight ye Westoes.[2] at which news they expeditiously repaired their pallisadoes, keeping watch all night. in the time of my abode here they gave me a young, Indian boy taken from ye falls of y^t River. the Savana Indians brought Spanish beeds & other trade as presents makeing signes y^t they had comerce wth white people like unto mee, whom were not good. these they civilly treated & dismissed before my departure ten of them prepared to accompany mee in my journey home returning by ye same ways y^t I came, killing much game wth two large she beares uppon ye way through much rain ye fresshes being mightly encreased ye 5th of nov^{br} wee our selfes carrying our trade upon barke logs swam over Ædistaw River & ye 6th of y^t Instant in safety I

---

cruel of the two were at last forced quite out of the Province And the Savanas continued good friends &c of the English," *Arch.* 1708, they had 3 towns (near Sand Bar Ferry) and 150 men; but in 1715 retired to the Creeks.

[1] The copyist has "Chaesaws and Chiskers," and *A. & W. I.*, 1422, "Cheesaws and Chiskews." The Cusitaws, pages 186, 191, lived about the heads of Oconee and Salwege, and ranged down and across the Savanna where perhaps Woodward met them. Map, 1700, shows "Cusattee" on west side of Salwege, and at its junction with Savanna huge mounds and terraces exist called the Cutisachique of DeSoto. The Chicasaws lived below Muscle Shoals on Tennessee, and the Keyokees above.

[2] A ranging people, great warriors and slave raiders, called man eaters. From their town they raided the coast Indians for slaves and warred on all others. They "ruinated St Helena &c 1670, and 1672-73, harrassed the English also." July, 1677, "ye inland Indians called ye Westoes who of late are observed very forward to find out ye way and strength of this Settlem't" are warned off. April, 1680, the Gov'r held a talk at Capt. Walley's with Westo chiefs, but June 1 "the Westoes &c have of late contrary to their league and amitie made with the Governor, killed taken &c some of our neighbour indians." War followed, and the Westoes "had well nigh ruined this hopeful settlem't" but for the invading Savannas (and Yemassees?), who, 1681, destroyed them. 1715, the "Westas 15 men" were settled with the Muscogee tribes on the Ocmulgee (above Macon), and, 1716, retired with them beyond the Chattahoochee. Map 1716 shews 'Westos' on its W. bank.

arrived at yor Hon^{rs} Plantation at ye Head of Ashley River, for good reasons I permitted them not to enter y^r Plantation, but very well satisfyed dispatcht them homewards y^t evening, whom I againe expect in March wth deare skins, furrs & younge slaves.

In this relation as in all things else I am

y^o L^{oshipps} ffaithfull Servant

HENRY WOODWARD.

Discovery.   A ffaithful relation of my Westoe voiage begun from ye head of Ashley River the tenth of Oct^r & finished ye sixth of Nou^{br} ffollowing.

Endorsed by Locke :   Carolina   H. Woodward   To the E. of Shaftesbury 31. Dec. *74.*

[*S. P.*, Bdle. 48, No. 96.]

"CAROLINA [1674?]

TWO PAPERS OF MEM: by Locke so marked.   One of weights and measures, the other lists of places, the soil, vegitables, animals and inhabitants; under this last "kind to their women, dye their deer skins of excellent colours 1536.   Kill servants to wait on them in the other world 1553," &c.

[*S. P.* 48, No. 83], *A. & W. I,*, 1429.

AN ACCOUNT OF WHAT MASTS a ship of 300 tons may bring from Carolina to London and what they may be worth here.   10 masts of 76 feet long and 29 inches diameter at 24l. each and other masts from 72 to 60 feet long and 24 to 13 in^s diam^r also 155 spears [spars?] of 55 feet long and 7 to 9 in^s diam^r Pipe staves, cedar plank, knees &c to fill up the ship.   £826 10s. *Ibid,* 1430.

[1]MEM: OF PROVISIONS required for 48 men 3 months outward bound allowing 50 beef days with pudding and peas, 20 days for pork and peas and 20 days stock fish with oil or butter   Also mem: of provisions for 30 men in the country and for 8 seamen for 3 months, with prices.   *Ib.,* 1431.

THE COUNCIL JOURNALS.

February 9th 1674. Present. The Governor, Godfrey, Mathews, Owen, Bull, Fallock, Marshall, Dalton.

The Grand Council having this day advised upon the erecting

of a new fortification about Charles Towne It is resolved that
Capt. Stephen Bull be present at the Councill upon Friday next
with his surveying instruments to run the line of the said fortification as shall then be advised.

February 15th *1674. Present.* The Governor, Godfrey, Mathews, Owen, Marshall, capt. George Thompson, Dalton &
Bull. Upon hearing of the matter of the Complaint of Abel
Aldridge against James Moore attorney of Margaret Lady Yeamans[1] adm'x of Sir Jno. Yeamans, dec'd, it appears by the
accounts between the said parties now produced before the
Grand Councill that the said Sir Jno Yeamans in his life time
was indebted to the said Abel Aldridge the sum of 48 s: 6d. ster.
which said sum the said James Moore hath (before the Grand
Councill) undertaken to pay the said Abel Aldridge.[2]

April 26, 1675 present. The Governour, Lieut. Coll Jno
Godfrey, Capt. Maurice Mathews, M[r] Wm Owen, capt Richard

---

[1] She later married Mr. Moore. 1694, "Dame Margaret Moore, wife
of said Jas. Moore, &c." "1700 ye Hon. Jas. Moore and Margaret my
wife sell &c." "Jas. Moore, gent:" came from Barbadoes, 1674; was
in the Council, 1677, and 168¾, in Gov. Morton's. 1690, with his friend,
Col. Mathews; he "journied over the Apalathean mountn's for inland
discovery and indian trade," and fought the Cherokees. He was in
Assembly, 1692; in Council, 1694-6; Receiver, and 1698 "a gent" of a
good estate in this Country, Secretary of the Province and Sir Jno Colleton's deputy." In 1699–1700, he was Att'y Gen'l, Chief-Justice and
Governor. He beseiged St. Augustine and conquered the Apallachians.
1702, he was reappointed Rec'r Gen'l and Sir John's deputy, and served
till his death, 1706. His will, 1 Nov. 1703, names (tis said) children
James (Gen. agt. the Tuscaroras & Yemassees & Gov'r, 1719), Roger,
Maurice (Col. 1715), Nath'l, Anne (m'd Da. Davis, Esq.), Mary, Marg't
(m'd Ben. Schencking, Esq.), & Rebecca.

[2] Jno. Ld. Berkley, pallatine, and the rest of the Lords and absolute
Prop'rs of the Province of Carolina, do hereby grant unto John Coming,
Mariner, a plan'n containing 133 acres English measure, and now in the
posses'n of the said John Coming, situate upon the Oyster point and
Bounding upon Ashley River to the West thereof and Cooper River als.
Ittuan River towards the east, as appears by the plat, &c. Given under
the Great Seale appointed for that purpose at Charlestowne, 17 April,
1675. *Joseph West, Ste. Bull, John Godfrey, Mau: Mathews, Richard
Conant, Will: Owen.* Registered in the Register's Office, 15 June, 1675,
pr. *Joseph West Reg'r. B'k G* 3, p. 462. This grant is in the form, p.
122. Later that granting "hawking, hunting &c." and reserving "all
mines & miniralls & quarryes of gems" was used. *Rivers*, 404.

Conant, Capt. Stephen Bull, Mr John Yeamans, Mr Samuel West, Capt. George Thompson, Mr Joseph Dalton.

In order to the better defence of this Province it is advised & resolved that the people now inhabiting here be divided into three Companies the first under the Governors immediate command the second under Lieut: Coll. John Godfrey and the third under Capt: Maurice Mathews and that a generall muster be had at Charles Towne upon Whitson Tuesday next & that the severall Companies vizt Lieut. Coll. Godfreys Company doe meet and exercise upon May day next and the Governours and Capt: Mathews Companies doe meet upon the Satturday following that the said Companies may be the better fitted for the said Generall Muster.

Resolved that forty pounds of Powder be delivered to the Master of Ordinance for the Scaleing of the Great Gunns mounted at Charles Towne upon Saturday the 8th of May next. For as much as the Governor hath this day signified his occasion to be absent from the settlement for some time[1] It is resolved that Lieut: Coll. Jno Godfrey dureing this time shall and may act and doe as the Pallatines Deputy to all intents and purposes. *C. J.*, 49.

LORD SHAFTESBURY TO ANDREW PERCIVALL.

Exeter House 9. June 1675.

Mr Percivall,

There come now in my Dogger[2] Jacob Waite and too or three other familys of those who are called Quakers These are but the Harbengers of a greater Number that intend to follow. Tis theire purpose to take up a whole Colony for themselves and theire Friends, here they promised me to build a towne of 30 Houses. I have writ to the Governor and Councell about them and directed them to set them out 12000 acres. I would have you be very kind to them and give them all the assistance you can in the choice of a Place, or anything else that may conduce

---

[1] Where he went and for how long is unknown; he was present again June 12; the journals between are missing.

[2] The Edisto, capt. Coming. Jacob Wayt had 764 acres at Ashley River, 1676, on "Wait's Creek," N. of "Middleton Place," still so called, and 1686 lot 27. Abr'm Waight, of Assembly 1695, was his son?

to theire convenient settlement For they are people I have a great Regard to and am obliged to care of

    Exa :   I am your very affectionate friend

SHAFTESBURY.

    To Mr Percivall at St Giles Plantacon on Ashley River in Carolina.

[S. P., Bdle. 48, No. 55, p. 151.]

To the Governor and Councell in Carolina.

Exeter House 9. June 1675.

    The Bearer hereof Jacob Waite with some others of his perswasion are come to setle in your neighbourhood, They are people I have had transactions with here and am concerned to have a perticular care of myselfe and doe therefore recommend them to yours. At theire Arrivall pray let them be accommodated with what conveniencys the place affords, and theire reception and usage be such as may encourage them to invite over the rest of theire friends here, who intend in a considerable Number to follow them upon the accompt they shall receive from them, as soone after theire arrivall as they shall desire pray set them out a whole Colony of 12000 Acres in such convenient place as you and they shall pitch on, where they have undertaken to me That they and theire Friends who intend to follow them will within five years build a Towne of Thirty Houses. You are therefore to grant them in theire owne Name or whose Names they shall desire a Colony of 12000 Acres, on condition that within five yeares they build a Towne of Thirty houses and 100 inhabitants at the least to each of which houses must belong as a home lot three score Acres inseparably for ever which Threescore Acres belonging to each house They are to have each householder as he comes immediately in his possession.

    Exam'd: I am your very affectionate friend

SHAFTESBURY.

To the Governor & Councell in Carolina.

[S. P., Bdle 48, No: 55, p. 152.]

Ld Shaftesbury to Mau: Mathews.

Exeter House 9° June 1675.

Mr Mathews,

    I take very kindly the care you have expressed and the service you have don mee in my perticular affairs in Carolina and shall upon all Occasions let you see how sensible I am of it. For you may assure yourselfe that by promoting and stickening to my Interest there you have fastened yourselfe to a man who never casts of or neglects anyone that does soe. And though my Designe to setle at Edistoh forced me to put the affairs of my Privat Plantacon into other hands then yours and to commit the oversight of them to one whome I had discoursed it with here.[1] Yet now by a disapointment of that Intencon, I have planted in your Neighbourhood I am not out of hopes that you may be serviceable and helpeing to me in the carrying on of that Plantacon I am soe well assured of your honesty, ability and perteculer affection to mee, that I promise myselfe you will afford M[r] Percivall all the assistance in my affaires that he shall desire of you within your power. And my Setlement on Ashley River pleases me something the better, that it hath at hand an old Planter my Friend and Trustee in my other concerns there ready to promote and take care of it on all occasions. The pains you shall bestow at any time upon that or any other businesse of mine will not be lost labour to you for you are to remember that

I am Your very sincere Friend

Exam[d]   SHAFTESBURY.

To M[r] Maurice Mathews at Charles Towne in Carolina.

[*S. P.* Bdle. 48, No. 55, p. 153.]

———

To THE GOVERNOR & COUNCELL at Charles Towne Carolina.

Exeter House 10th June. 75.

You cannot be ignorant of the particular care I have taken of you and your Setlem[t] ever since you first sate downe upon Ashley River. And how the rest of the Lords Proprietors have been perswaded by the hopes I had that theire expenses would not be endless to be out a greater Summe of Money in carrying on that Plantacon and sending you supplyes then they at first designed or could have imagined.

---

[1] Mr. Percivall. Commission from Anthony, Earl of Shaftesbury, Chief Justice of Carolina, to Andrew Percivall, Gent: appointing him Register of Berkley county and the parts adjoining, during pleasure, until by the increase of people the parts adjoining shall be divided into other counties and need a distinct registry to be erected in them, June 10, 1675. (*Col. En. B'k 20*, p. 103.) *A. & W. I.*, 582.

The last yeare when theire Expectacon of returnes grew weary, haveing received from you neither any begining of paym^t nor any faire or probable Proposalls how they may in tyme be reimbursed   I got them to consent to a new Method of supplying you, and to enter into Articles for a constant and regular supplye, Some parte whereof you then received by my Dogger. It was expected that when wee had put the continuance of sending you necessarys for the future, into soe setled an Order, you at least would have considered of some way of makeing returns to us, and given us some such acc^t that wee might have seene, that you had taken it into your thoughts.   But when instead thereof there was noe such scheme of paym^t proposed and you the Governor and our Agent did not soe much as pay yourself out of it but all tended to an Enlargem^t of your Demands and our Expenses The rest of the Lords Proprietors were at a stand and grew very backward to bury any more money amongst people who tooke soe litle care to satisfie them, that they intended never to live of themselves   This dissatisfaction of theirs, and the little leisure I have had since I came to Towne to debate the Matter with them hath made my ship return to you without any cargo on the L^{ds} P^{rs} account   I hope Sir Peter Colleton will be here in some time who I believe will join with mee, and I promise myselfe that he and I together shall be able to prevaile with the rest of the Lords Proprietors for a farther supplye.   If you will be but soe much Friends to yourselves as to consider and lay downe any rationall way that may satisfie us, that you mean to pay for those things are sent you and not give us any longer just cause to apprehend that by the Expence of 9 or £10000 we have purchased nothing but the charge of maintaineing on 5 or 600 people who expect to live upon us.   And I make this faire proposall to you that if you and the people there undertake to pay what is owing from us to Coll. West and cleare those debts which have been contracted by yourselves and charged upon us in Carolina or elsewhere I doubt not but to prevaile with the rest of the L^{ds} Prop^{rs} to forgive you all the debts you owe us, and for a part of satisfaction to Coll. West to throw in our private plantacon too, that he hath hitherto, managed for us and therewith put an End to our Bargain with him as our Store-keeper or Agent.   And for the Governor We shall expect that he should be without any charge to us.   All scores being

thus even'd Wee will take care that Noe body shall want Supplyes for the future who will pay for them at moderat rates.
Thus you see Wee expect noe other Improvem[t] of that great
Summe, wee have been out, but that the Planters there should
wholly share the benefit of it amongst themselves, soe We may
at the rate of £9 or £10000. put an End to our Expences.

But I must here tell you how ill I take that treatment my
Agent M[r] Andrew Percivall hath received from you. You know
I designed my Plantacon at Edisto and not neare you, and have
agreed with the Lords Prop[rs] not to be under your Governm[t] or
Jurisdiction, nor to be controuled by you in my dealeing or
trade with any of the Indians for you cannot thinke me soe mad
to venture soe considerable an Estate under your Governm[t]
unlesse the Gov[r] were richer. For it is as bad as a state of Warr
for men that are in want to have the makeing Laws over Men
that have Estates. Therefore I must desire you to let me and
my people alone. I am at a distance from you, and if you
disease me will goe farther   And I have given Orders to M[r]
Percivall in all things to shew all faire kindness and respect to
you, but to observe none of your Commands For I am resolved
to be independent from your Governm[t] for some yeares untill
you are become capable of puting our Excellent Modell in some
measure in practice by haveing more men of Estates come
amongst you. I beseech you doe not discourage nor disoblige
the best friend you have in the World for that I am sure I am
and ever will be

Your very affectionate friend

Exam'd.   SHAFTESBURY.

To the Governor and Councell at Charles Towne Carolina.

[S. P., Bdle. 48, No. 55, page 154.]

TO THE GOVERNOR AND COUNCELL at Ashley River Carolina.

Exeter House 11th June 75.

The Bearer hereof M[r] Seth Sethell[1] being a person of a con-

---

[1] Made Gov'r. of Albemarle Feb. 167$\frac{8}{9}$ but "taken by the Turks and
and carried into Angier." He reached Albemarle 1683 but in 1688 was
deposed and banished. He went to S. Carolina 1690 and owning L'd.
Clarendon's share, held the government as sole Proprietor there till 169$\frac{1}{2}$
when he was recalled. He died 169$\frac{3}{4}$ at Albemarle ? where his will was
proved Feb'y. N. C., 283,293. Rivers, 159.

siderable estate here in England hath an Intencon to come and plant in Carolina and to take up a Mannour of 12,000 Acres, which he doubts not to plant in a short tyme with people which he shall carry over from hence. I think I need not use many words to persuade you to use him kindly and take care of his Accommodacon your own Interest as well as Civility will dispose you to it. Since nothing can be more advantageous to the Country Nor soe much contribute to the growth and posperity of the Plantacon as that men of Estate should come to setle amongst you Pray therefore set him out a Mannour of 12,000 Acres on condition that within five years he build in it a Towne of at least Thirty Houses and have at least Six score people upon it, which houses are to be built, and people to be brought on it, at least one fifth part every year of the said five. Pray treat this Gentleman as my Friend and One whome I would have to receive all incouragem^t to be a planter that the Country can afford. I am Your very affectionate friend

Ex^d SHAFTESBURY.

To the Governor and Councell at Ashley River Carolina.

[*S. P.*, Bdle. 48, No. 55, p. 156]

THE COUNCIL JOURNALS.

June 12th, 1675, present: The Governor, Godfrey, Mathews, Owen, Marshall, Thompson, Yeomans, cpt Rob: Donne, Dalton. Jno Boon Gent:[1] makes demand for a grant of 100 acres at the Watring place now in poss^n of Wm Owen gent: claiming the primary right & forasmuch as s^d Owen's land there is not yet run out by wch the right cannot appeare Ordered that s^d Owen do cause his land to be run out & marked & produce the plat thereof

---

[1] Perhaps "Mr Boone arrived by way of Virginia at N. York from London Dec. 1669." Lt. Boone was in Carolina 1672, com'r to the Esaws 1673, interpreter 1677, and 1683 com'r Indian affairs and in the Council till 1686, when he was removed "for correspondence with pirates." 1694 "Sarah Boone, widow & adm'x of Thos. Boone, late of London, mcht, dec'd, appoints her son, Jos. Boone, to receive, &c., of Maj. Jno. Boone, late of London now of S. Carolina." His will 8 Nov. 1706 names wife Elizabeth, children Thomas, Theophilus, Susana, Sarah, and Mary Boone. He died 1711, his seat " Boon hall " went to his son Tho: Boone, J. P., 1749, to gdson Jno. Boone and to ggson Tho. Boone 1811. *1 Rich: 348.*

or the report of the Surveyor at the next monthly sitting &c else s^d Jno Boon have the grant thereof.

———

To THE GOVERNOR AND COUNCELL at Ashley River. Carolina.

Exeter House June 14. 75.

Mr John Smith[1] who brings you this brings with him also his wife and a family and a considerable estate with an entention to plant amongst you.   how much the setlement of such a man in Carolina will adde to the reputation and trade of the Country and benefit those who are already there I need not tell you nor perswad of you on that account to be very civill to Mr Smith and thereby incourage him and others llke him to be your neighbours. I doubt not but that the consideration of your owne Interest and the respect due to strangers of his condition will make you forward to bid him Welcome but besides this I must recommend him to you as my particular friend whom I would be glad that by the accommodacon and good office he receives from you should find it was of advantage to him to be soe I beleive he intends to take up a Mann^r which I desire may be set out to him in some commodious place, to any Number of Acres prescribed for Man^{rs} in our Fundamentall Constitutions provided he people it at the proportion of 10 men for every 1000 acres within 5 yeares and bring over at least one fifth part of the said Number every year till the full Number be compleated pray take care that whilst my Interest is laid out in bringing over to you men of Estate which will be greate supporte and improvem^t of the Plantaⁿ that you give them such treatm^t as may answere there and my expectacon & may not bring in question either my credit or y^r discretion if you doe what becomes you in this point I doubt not but to see very speedily a very popular and thriving Country.

I am your very affect^e Friend

Exam^d   SHAFTESBURY.

[S. P., Bdle 48, No. 55, p. 157.]

———

[1] "Of Booshoee, esq:" in council 1677, deputy 1680, 82, and cassique. Died 1682, adm'n to Mary his wife May 26.   She married Dec. 6, 1682, Arthur Middleton, Esq.

THE COUNCIL JOURNALS.

Sept[r] 4th 1675 present: The Govern[r], Mathews, Owen, Conant,[1] Bull, S. West, Yeomans, cpt Ro: Donne M[r] Jos: Dalton.

Upon address made by Jn[o] Morgan p[r] for a certaine parcell of land in a place called Thomas his Island[2] Ordered that W[m] Thomas, gent: or his attys doe cause the land already marked for him on s[d] Island to be run out before 6 months or Jn[o] Morgan have his grant not withstand[g] the caveat entered by Col. Jno Godfrey atty of s[d] W[m] Thomas.

Sept[r] 9th 1675 present: The Govern[r], Mathews, Owen, Bull, Marshall, Donne, Yeamans, Dalton.

The G[d] Councill having considered & advised upon the proposall made [P. 63*] by the R[t] Hon[ble] Anthony Earl of Shaftesbury one of the Lords & absolute Prop[rs] of this province to the Inhabitants of this settlm[t] for the settling of all acc[ts] betw[n] the L[ds] Prop[rs] & the people here by his Lord[pps] letter 10th June 1675 [p. 467] And as it is by the Councill hereby accepted and embraced as a great favour from their Lordships Resolved that all care be taken to make paym[t] to Jos: West, Landgrave & Governor accord[g] to s[d] proposall & to that end that Rob[t] Browne, merch[t], Jno Simpson, carp[r], James Moore, gent: & Thos Butler, carp[r], being independ[t] persons & not indebted to the L[ds] Prop[rs] meet at the L[ds] Prop[rs] plan[n] where the Govern[r] now resides on tuesday next in the morning then & there to view Inventorie & faithfully appraise s[d] plan[n] with its appurt[ces] & stock & the same return w[th]in 3 days &c.

Sept[r] xi[th] 1675 present: (the same, less Marshall)

Upon further treaty betw[n] the Govern[r] & Councill to the mak-

---

[1] From N. York; settled and commanded at Jamestown; was captain, of parliam't, and in the Council, 1672 to 1674, and then Sir G. Carteret's deputy to 1676, and April 10, 1677, was com'd Ld. Clarendon's till 168$\frac{2}{3}$, then ass't judge, and May 27, 1691, Clerk of Crown & Peace, and 1692–5 sat in the council; was living 11 Dec., 1696; but 3 Jan., 170$\frac{3}{4}$, Tho. Rowe, of London, gent., residuary legatee of Rich. Conant, late of S. C., merch't, recites his death, leaving lands, &c., and Wm. Elliott, of Ashley river, sole ex'or.

[2] Daniel's Island. A Wm. Thomas was of the Council of Antigua, 1671. Jno. Morgan, late of this province, planter, dec'd 1701; left a wife and dau., Mary Morgan, Jas. Boswood her guardian.

ing of full paym^t of what is due from the L^{ds} Prop^{rs} to the Governor accord^g to the R^t Honble the Earl of Shaftesbury's letter 10 June 1675 & the Councill accord^g to their former Resol^n made 9th inst: Septr having tendered the L^{ds} Prop^{rs} plant^n whereon the Govern^r now dwells in part of s^d paym^t &c all wch the Govern^r is now pleased to refuse as conceiving it not to be intended by s^d letter.   Resolved that a parliam^t be sumoned to meet at Charles Towne upon Satterday next come a fortnight.

Septr 14 1675, present: (the above and Mr S. West).   Jno Holmes p^r being brought before G^d Coun^{ll} for his unlawfull killing & destroying of 2 piggs &c belonging to the Govern^r & upon examin^n hath confes^d ordered into the marshalls custody till he give security &c.

Octr 2^d 1675 present: The Govern^r, Godfrey, Mathews, Owen, Bull, Conant, S. West, Ro: Donne, Dalton.

Lt Col: Godfrey having brought into Court the Coppy of Sr John Yeamans last will & testam$^{t\,1}$ certified by Sr Jon^n Atkins Govr of Barbadoes &c 15 June 1675 &c wch s^d will wth the certificate being viewed & considered on by the Court is allowed to be firme & good.   Upon motion by John Smith merch^t liberty is granted him to take up 670 acres above the proport^n now due him Soe that he hath soe many persons upon his acc^t to settle thereon as will make up the right thereof accord^g to the L^{ds} Prop^{rs} concessions within 2 years next.

Octr vii. 1675 present: The Govern^r? Godfrey, Mathews, Owen, Bull, cpt Christ^r Portman, S. West, Dalton.

For as &c the Govern^r hath thought fit to disist from apprais^g the L^{ds} Prop^{rs} plant'n accord^g to a former Resol^n ye 9 Sept. last Resol^d to wait the L^{ds} Prop^{rs} further pleasure therein & advised how the Govern^r may receive satisf^n for what is due &c upon wch treaty he has agreed to receive 200£ ster: in Barbadoes or the value in Muscovado sugar at xii &c per hund^d in part paym^t of

---

[1] Dec 13, 1674 copy of last will of Sir Jno Yeamans Kt & Bart. proved by Sir Wm Yeamans Bart. sone and sole ex'or of said will Letter of atty to Col. Jos. West Gov'r 14 Sep. 1675. In the name &c I Sr John Yeamans Bart. being ready to Imbarque myself in ye Province of Carolina &c my deare wife Lady Margarett Yeamans in full of dower £30 per ann: the house where I now dwell, 45 acres &c. 21st May, 1671. *witness Will. Browne, Thos Bampfield, Nich: Carteret.*

his Salary &c and also agreed betw^n the Govr & Coun^{ll} that what tobaccos shall be raised for paym^t of s^d 200 the hazards of the sea to Barbadoes shall be equally borne by the Govr & the people &c.

Octr 16, 1675 present: The Govern^r, Lt Col: Godfrey, capt Mathews, Mr Owen, capt: Bull, capt Ro: Donne, Mr Yeamans, Mr Marshall, Mr Dalton.

Andrew percivall gent: came this day &c & produced a Deputation of his Grace Christi^o Duke of Albemarle one of the L^{ds} Prop^{rs} dated 9 June 1675 constituting him Deputy[1] who is accordingly admitted & Mr Ralph Marshall being the preceding Deputy accord^g to the rule in the temp^y laws doth now take his former place as Councellor for the people. Resol^d that Jacob Wayte may take a parcel of land to the S^{wd} of his &c.

November ii, 1675 present: The Govern^r, Godfrey, Owen, Percivall, Conant, S. West, Donne, Yeamans, Dalton.

For &c divers conferences have been had betw^n the Govr & Coun^{ll} for paym^s of what is due Resolved that what tobacco shall be brought to the L^{ds} Prop^{rs} storehouse at Charles Town the Govern^r will receive & give a receipt. And John Hooper[2] & Thos Hurt p^{rs} are appointed viewers of Tobacco.

Decr X. 1675 present: The Govern^r, Godfrey, Mathews, Owen, Percivall, Bull, Portman, Donne, Dalton.

Upon motion of Mr And^w Percivall on behalf of Anthony earl of Shaftesbury one of the L^{ds} Prop^{rs} &c   Resolved that s^d A. Percevall may take up & build upon the 2 & 50 lott as is specif^d in the modell form^{ly} sett out for the regular building of Charles Town being one of the lotts reserved for the L^{ds} Prop^{rs} & ffor

---

[1] The Deputies now were, Gov. West, the Palatine L'd Berkley's; Mathews, L'd Shaftesburys; Owen, Sir P. Colletons; Godfrey, L'd Cravens; Bull, L'd Cornburys; Conant, Sir G. Carteret's; & Percivall, Duke Albemarles. Councillors, Marshall, Portman, Yeamans, Dalton, S. West & Donne. June, 1673, Capts. Gray and Robinson left, and Aug. 2, R. Ditty & S. West became Councillors; Aug., 1674, Bull, Conant & Marshall became Deputies and Portman, Thompson, Fallock, S. West, Yeamans & Dalton, Councillors. June, 1675, Donne succeeded Fallock & now Marshall took Thompson's place.

[2] Had grant 240 acres Ashley river above Cuppein creek 1675; lived there 1680. It was regranted Abr'm Waight 1696.

(as is conceived) this will be a princip[ll] means to lead on the Regular building &c (P. 66*) M[r] John Boon the English Interpreter & cap[t] Titus the Indian Interpreter came this day voluntarily before the G[d] Counc[ll] & did declare that the Indian prisoners w[ch] the Sowee & other neighbour Indians have lately taken are Enemies to the s[d] Indians who are in Amity wth the English & that the s[d] Indian prisoners are willing to worke in this country or to be transported from hence, upon w[ch] it is conceived that the s[d] Indian prisoners may be transported by any who have or shall purchase them.[1] [p. 367.]

January viii 1675 present: The Governor, Godfrey, Owen, Bull, Percivall, Conant, S. West, Yeamans, Donne.

Upon a suit betw[n] James Sayle marin[r] by Jos: West, Landgrave his atty Plaintf & Josias pitt, plan[r] def[t], Def[t] excepts ag[t] the suffic[y] of the Govern[rs] letter of Att'y whereupon the Question is put whether the Govern[rs] authority now shewed unto the Court be suffic[t] to prosecute the suit & it is voted in the negative.   Resolved that s[d] Josias pitt give security &c for any damage to the estate of James Sayle or the heirs of Nathaniel Sayle in this province.

January xv, 1675 present: The Govern[r], Godfrey, Mathews,

---

[1]An abstract of the records of all grants of lands that have been made in the Province of South Carolina, from the first establishment of the Colony, specifying the names of the grantees, the time when each grant was made, the quantity of acres, and the quit rents, if any reserved thereon, and expressing the situation and location of each grant to 31st October, 1765. *The following are abstracted* for 1674 and 1675:

Persons names to whom granted.	Number of Acres.	In what County Parish or Township, or on what River or Creek situated	Date of Grant.
Lady Marg. Yeamans..	1070	On Yeaman's Creek.	9 February 1674.
Anthony earl of Shaftesbury............	12000	On Ashley River....	18 March 1675.
Joseph Pendarvis.. ..	137	....	1 January 1675.
Mathew English and John Morgan.. . ..	140	On Wandoe River..	....
John Smyth......... ..	1800	On Ashley River....	25 November 1675.
John Hooper and Wm Cason...............	240	....	20 November 1675.

(*Col. En. B'k 23*, p. 1.)   *A. & W. I.*, ⅔ 717.

Percivall, Owens, Conant, Bull, Portman, Donne, Yeamans, Marshall, Dalton.

Upon cons'n of better security &c of the public stock of gun powder from suddane accidents of fire or otherwise Advised that 2^{bbls} be lodged at Lt Col: Godfrey's house 1^{bbl} at Capt Mau: Mathews his house 1^{bbl} at Jos: Daltons house & the remainder in the Govern^{rs} custody. Capt Mau: Mathews having set forth that some of the neighbor Indians have requested him to direct them to settle a Town &c for &c as in time the same may be of great use to this settlm^t. Resolved that he (being willing to undergoe the trouble) doe instruct the s^d Indians & settle them in a towne in some convenient place not injuring the English settlm^{ts} & w^n done make report thereof to the G^d Councill.[1]

[*Bk.* 1672, 94.]

---

[1] 1671. 1686 Lists of names of Landgraves, Cassiques and Deputies in Carolina, by whom nominated, and date of nomination, viz. Names of Landgraves: John Locke, Sir John Yeamans, James Carteret, James Colleton, Edmund Andros, Joseph West, Thomas Colleton, Joseph Morton, Daniel Axtell and Richard Kyrle and John Price. Names of Cassiques: Capt. Henry Wilkinson, Major Thos. Rowe, John Gibs, Thomas Amy, John Smith and John Monke, by nomination of the Duke of Albemarle. Names of Deputies and by whom nominated: T. Gray and Andrew Percivall by the Duke of Albemarle, Stephen Bull by Lord Cornbury, John Godfrey by Earle of Craven, Maurice Mathews and Joseph West Register of writings, by Earl of Shaftesbury, Sir John Yeamans by Lord Berkeley, Joseph West and Joseph Dalton, secretary, by Sir G. Carteret, and William Owen by Sir Peter Colleton. *Mostly in Locke's hand.* *Col. En. Bk.* 20, p. 80. *A. & W. I.,* 721.

NOTES.

Pages 119, 165.   Bermuda, arrived "Jan. 12, 1670 The ship 'Caroline' (wherein came Sir John Youman in his expedition for Port Royall) captain Henrie Braine Comander thereof, sailed from these Islands the 26ᵗʰ of Ffebruarie vppon the expedition aforesaid, whereof Capt William Sayle went Comander in cheefe therevnto called and made choice of for the manadgeing the said honble expedition By the Right Honble Proprietor (Resident in England) Agents Sir John Youmans Captain Joseph West &c Since their arrivall in these Islands as aforesaid." *Lefroy's Bermuda* I., page 737.

Page 119.   Capt. Wm. Sayle was in the Bermuda Council 1630, Sheriff 1638–40, Governor 1641–42 and again 1643–45; 'was wholly guided by the ministers' 'tho' himselfe not a member (his wife being).'   1646, he and Rev. Wm. Goulding went messengers to Parliament, page 3.   *Ibid.*

Page 250.   Mrs. Margery Saile was presented Oct., 1647, "for absenting herself from frequenting the ordinances of God."   She went to Eleuthera, but returned to Bermuda; arrived "march 1657 The 'John' from Eluthera with Capt W. Saile, his wife, 3 children & 13 other passengers."   Oct., 1658, Margery Saile releases Capt. Wm. James for damages to property of "my husband Capt. W. Saile at Eluthera."   *Ibid.*

Page 280.   Bermuda, arrived "July 16, 1670, the sloop 'Three Brothers;'" she sailed thence "Sept 7, 1670."   *Ibid.*

Pages 279, 281.   Bermuda, arrived "Feb. 16, 1671 The vessel 'Blessing' from Jamaica For Carolina carrying with him Richard Hanke (a Quaker) his wife, 9 children & one negro man."   Bermuda, March 15, 167⁰₁, Gov'r & Council write "after reading yʳ genˡ letter we sent Mʳ Sampson Bond a copy of yʳ order for his dismission.   The next Council Table he sent a petition &c In answer &c that yʳ order be put in execution &c there being seuerall shipps in Harbor fit for acomodation som bound for old England and New &c and one vessell for Carolina to Ashlie river &c send another minister over to supply Mʳ Bonds place that wee may have more peace in the Countrie."   *Ibid*, 692.

Page 390.   Bermuda, "1672 a Ketch, was spoken with on the south Coast of the islands March 22ᵈ 'That was sent out of England by the Lords Proprietors of Carolina, Bound for the same Port, having in her two Indian Princes.'"   *Ibid*, 740.   The Wm. & Ralph, page 372? or the Blessing?   Perhaps the Cassique's sons taken to Barbadoes on the Carolina, entertained by Colleton, page 249.

INDEX.

132, 165, 176, 181, 192, 256, 258, 275, 277, 287, 291, 295, 307, 310, 330, 373-4, 376, 387, 395, 428-9, 430-1, 438, 449, 475;' in par't, 452; of Council, 167,' 182,' 204, 214, 224, 248, 253-5, 340, 357, 359, 370, 473;' at, 453, 456, 462-3, 469, 471-5; com'n to, 181, 261, 404, 408,' 475;' Letters from, 182, 225, 245, 250, 258, 281, 347-8, 376, 383, 386; to, 310; his death, 182.'

Damages, 104; suit, 414, 426, 475.
Dangers, great, 25-6, 40, 157, 160.
Daniels island, 371,'386.'
Danson, Mr. Jno. & Mary (*misp't Dawson*), 434.'
Darkenwell, Nath'l, 136, 137, 292;' Sampson, 136. 137, 292.'
'Darling,' Carolina, Lord Ashly's, 416.
Data island, 341.'
Dates, 382, 387.
Davenport, Humphrey, 88.
Davey, Richard, 435.
Davis, Capt. Wm., letter to, 27; Wm. 253, 271, 274,' 373; David 274;' David and Ann, 463.'
Daughters, 97, 98, 166.
Dawho river, 67.'
Dawson, Jno., 134; tanner, 329.
Day, Mr., linen draper, 208.
D'Arsens, Jean de Wernhaut, 177.'
Dead eyes, 139, 140; 'dead lift,' 286.
Deals, 144, 147; merchants, 328.
Deaths, 180, 193, 197, 222, 250, 257, 272, 299, 309, 351, 382; registered, 112; vac'ys by, 40, 47.
Debates, 304; free, 111.
Debt, plea, 385; debtors, *Lords Prop'rs.*
Declarat'ns, 5, 13, 17, 18, 32, 46, 293.
Deeds, recording, &c., 34, 84, 112, 406, 433.
Deep sea lines, 139, 144.
Deer, 24, 77, 188, 211, 308, 334; great, 201, 309;' skins, 21, 166, 168-70, 388, 462.
Defence, colony, 37-8, 40, 346, 395, 406-7, 464; from Indians, 90, 179, 194, 374.
Defendants, 385-6, 414, 474.
Deheart, James, 375, 384; Balthazar, 384.
De Gomara, Fran'o Lopez, 265.
De Laet, Jan., 265.

Delaval, Thos , Esq., 271.'
De Lyon, M. Gov. Gaudeloupe, 125.'
Demesne lands, 98.
Democracy, numerous avoided, 93.
Denizens, 38, 103.
Deputations, 107, 132, 349, 390, 398, 404, 448, 473; to be Palatine, 162.
Deputators, 107, 452.
Deputies, 249, 264, 272, 302, 305, 337, 341,' 390-1. powers, &c., 36. 101-2, 107, 110-11, 118. 120-3, 128-9. 322-4, 330, 349, 361-2, 397 399, 401-5, 419; appointment, 107, 367, 403-5, 431, 452; only 3 in Ca., 337, 352, 354, 357, 383. 452; lists, 475;' *1669* 132;' *1670*, 204;' *1671*,330,' 352,' *1672*, 391;' *1674*, 452; *1675*, 473; names, 192,' 196,' 204,' 229.' 231,' 290, 291,' 302, 340.' 362-3. 365, 391 ' 419.' 452.' 473;' *Bowman, Bull Conant. Donne Godfrey, Gray, Foster. Marshall, Mathews O'Sullivan. Owen, Percival, S a y l e, Scrivener, West.*
Deputy Gov'r. 32, 34, 36, 48, 49, 119 330; Bar., 12.' 423.'
Dernal or Derval, William, 384, 384.'
Descent, 94, 97. 219.
Deserted people, towns, &c., 90, 165, 175.
Design, Ca., 4, 6, 10, 15, 20, 59, 87, 154, 176, 200-1, 203, 206, 216 218-9 232. 243, 252, 261. 291. 310 314. 416-7, 448, 466; only to plant. 205, 327; security, 197; against Westos, 427-8.
De Soto, Ferdinando, 186,' 191,' 461.'
Devine, a, 349. *See Minister.*
Devonshire, 231.'
Deyas, Rich'd, 140, 143,' 292,' 300, 395, 408.'
Devil's Elbow, the, 341.'
Diamonds, like, 182.
Dickenson, Mr. John, 29, 30.
Dickes, Mr. Thos., 29.
Dignities, 37, 40, 95, 96, 97, 173.
Dill (fennel), 335.
Dimmocke, Elizabeth, 134.
Directions, 286, 304, 321-2, 330, 337, 381, 391, 452; planting, 343, 415, 440.

Disbrow, Maj. Gen. Jno., 117.'
Discoverers Park (Bull's island?), 77.
Discoveries, 29, 58, 78, 81, 188, 211, 335-6, 452-3; First, 87, 164, 190, 220, 266, 282-3; Hiltons, 18, 25, 62, 254; Pt. Royal, 57-9, 61-2, 67, 215; Chufytachique, 186, 189, 191, 225, 245; intended, 334, 351, 362, 372, 378, 380; Westo, 456, 462-3; m'ts, 452-3.
Description Ca., 89, 265, 458; inlets, 70-3, 80, 323, 333.
Dishes, 139, 144, 145, 424.
Dispatches, 102, 351, 371-2, 389, 436, 447; Bahama, 322, 352, 390.
Dissentions, 13, 35, 102, 117, 240, 285,' 290-1, 293-4, 303, 337-8, 346, 397, 424; dissenters, 113.
Distempers, 180, 197, 235, 257, 276, 309, 410.
Distribution stores, &c., 249, 264, 272, 350, 365.
Distress order, 430.
Districts, 36, 37.
Ditch, trench, 21, 173, 343.
Ditty, Mr. Rich'd, 426-29, 473, 473.'
Divisions, 36-7, 40, 94; lands, f, 48, 84-5, 253, 323.
Doctors, 191, 248, 259, 299, 349; Indian, 201.
Doctrine, 113, 198, 338.
Doe, Edward, 331; Doe (deer), 458.
Dogger, 439, 440,' 447, 464, 467.
Dogs, 394.
Dogwood, 333, 354.
Domestic or internal affairs, 104.
Dominion, 12-14, 51, 118, 307.
Donne, Capt. Robt., f, 134, 136,' 167, 289,' 290, 340; in parl't, 390; captain, 396, 407; counc'r, 167,' 175, 204, 473;' deputy, 290;' in coun'l, 277, 287, 289, 291, 295, 469, 471-5; his character, 224, 248, 261; death, 290;' Jane, his wife, 290.'
Donohoe, Jas., f, 271,' 302,' 340, 453.'
Dorril, or Darrel, Mr. Jno., 160-1, 189, 208, 322, 351; letters from, 160; to, 207.
Doves, 308; dove house, 20.
Dowden, Mr. Jos., f, 302,' 338-9, 359, 371; Mr. Thos., 30, 54, 271, 283.
Dower, 472.'
Dowling, Mathew, 453.
Downs, the, 133-4, 137, 142-3, 156.

Dragster, a, 423.
Drake, Sir Francis, 265; Mr. Jonathan, 391.'
Drakes (guns), 310, 318.'
Drains, 104.
Drawers, 132, 146.
Draughts, 339, 361, 388; coasts and rivers, f, 253, 258, 339, 350, 354, 381; Edisto, set't, 440, 444; arms for judic'y, 353.
Dress, mean, 287.
Drifts, iron, 141.
Drink, 211, 411, 441; act. ag't retailing, 358.
Driver (tool), 140.
Drought, 89, 333-4, 347, 349, 354, 377.'
Drum (fish), 336.
Drummond, Wm. Gov. Albemarle, 50, 55, 57; letter to 166.
Drums, 147, 169, 350, 353, 390.
Dropsy, 235.
Dual Governm'ts in S. Ca., address, i, xx.
Dublin, 385,' 394.'
Duch grass, 275.
Duck, cloth, 24, 138; ducks, 308, 335.
Dudley, Lord, *see Ashly*, 186, 220, 222; Sir Robert, 265.
Dunlop, Rev. Wm., 177.'
Dunnage, 144.
Durham, county Palatine, 93.
Dutch, 91, 355; War, 419, 436; boat, 440.'
Duties, 48; port, 351.
Dyes, 319, 380; dying drugs, 444.

Earth, 168, 218, 261; Earthquake, 394.'
East Greenwich, manor, 47.
East cheap, little, 328.
Eding's plant'n, Edisto, 62.
Edisto, 19, 26, 28, 62, 65, 75, 388, 436, 445; famed, 65, 76, 388; Indians, 23, 79, 170, 187, 199, 223, 250, 263, 334; town, 62, 64-5, 74; casiques, 19, 26, 65, 68; queen, 65; N. inlet and directions, 19, 20, 23-4, 61-2, 64, 66-7; S. ditto, 67-71, 353-4, 444; Lat. and name, 70-1, 266; Island, 62,' 458, 466, 468; *see Lock Island;* River, 334,' 353-4, 439,' 441, 448; freshes, 334'-5,' 353, 456-8, 460-1, 464; Gov. 439.
Edisto, ship, 231,' 439-42, 444-5, 447, 463,' 467.

3, 408, 410–12, 420–1, 456, 469,
473; roads and bridges, 409,
412, 415; quarantine, 410; provis'ns, 130, 341, 366, 384, 387,
419; drink, 411; *re* smiths work,
407, 412, 418, 426; L'ds debts,
355, 362, 395, 471–3; entries &
tickets, 369, 393, 422; letters,
368, 373; defence and war,
341–2, 345 6, 374, 395–6, 406,
409, 411, 420, 427–29, 450–1,
462, 464, 475; transporting Indians, 474; Council meetings,
and oath, 331, 416, 418; suspend'g members, 175, 294; calling sessions, 412–13, 420, 424,
453; judgm'ts & decrees, 356–
7, 359, 373–4, 384, 419, 429, 451,
475; modelling actions, 346,
430; *re* prisoners and serv'ts,
344, 395, 413, 415, 422, 424, 427,
430, 454, 474; hearing causes,
332, 340, 345–6, 356–7, 359, 375,
384–5, 453, 463, 472; criminal,
356, 373, 383, 394, 454, 472; addresses to, 359, 368, 389, 414,
421; by, 281, 287; com'ns by,
393, 407, 426; constit'ns read
in, 162,' 454.'
Grand juries, 109; model, 119, 120.
Grande river, 23–4, 62, 81. *See N.
Edisto.*
Grants, 29, 34, 40, 42 (*a*) 45, 102, 115,
121, 284, 294; method, 17, 34,
45, 47, 98, 122, 439; form, 47,
93, 122, 463'; warrants, 47, 407,'
409;' record and index, 47, 48;
Book for, 185, 225, 245, 286;
Seal for, 40; made, 51, 332;'
420, 439–40, 457, 463,' 469; list
of, 474;' Ca., 3,' 5–9, 11, 14–5,
17, 93, 102, 219; Bah., 207.
Granville county, 341.'
Grapes, 24, 382; vines, 74, 126.
Grapnel, 139, 144.
Grass, 63, 65, 76–7, 238, 275, 354.
Gratis, passage, 182, 245, 258, 285.
Gravesend, 133, 146, 150, 233, 350.
Gray, George, 141.
Gray, Capt. Thos., f, 222, 222,' 229,
234–5, 247, 251–3, 257–9, 262,
271, 274, 302,' 331, 334, 338,
339'–40,' 341, 346, 356–7, 368–
70, 373–5, 389, 394,' 407–9, 414,
419–20, 430, comend'd, 349–51;
Capt., 342, 345; in Coun'l, 222,'
331; suspended, 354; deputy,
390–1, 473'–5;' at Coun'l, 331,
340–1, 344–6, 356–7, 359, 368–

70, 373–4, 383–5, 390–5, 406–7,
409–15, 418–22; rioted & fled,
222,' 424, 429; letter from, 353;
to, 400; his ketch, 424,' 426,
429, 439; Jane, his wife and
ch'n, 424, 426.
Graziers, 437; grazing, 41.
Great or Chief Officers, 93–4, 100–1;
elec'n of, 155, 159, 403–4. *See
Palatine, Ch. Justice, Chanc'r,
Constable, High Steward,
Treasurer, Chamberlain, Ad-
miral.*
Great seal, 9; *see Seal;* blast, 272,
butts, 149.
Greenesmith, Jno., 30.
Grenville, Sir Richard, 265; his
heirs 7, 16.
Grey, Mathew, 30.
Gridiron, 139.
Grievances, 293; pet'n, 49, 109.
Griffin, John, 271,' 359.
Grig, Will. (Willgress?), 88.
Grindstone, 149.
Groves, 64, 71, 77, 308.
Grouse (ruffed), 308.'
Guinea corn, 333.
Gt. Pa? Indians; *see St. Pa.*, 334.
Guardians, 107; Guard, 22, 407.
Gubbs, Thos., 135.
Gulf, Fla., 161, 227; mexico, 266,
460.
Gunner, 141; stores, 138.
Guns, for Carolina, war't, &c., 31,
49, 50, 93, 150; Providence,
372; great, 137–8, 147; mount-
ed, 120, 179, 250, 257, 395, 450,
464; scaling, 187, 195, 464;
Indians frighted by, 187, 195,
203, 249–50, 258–9, 262–3; sig-
nal, 131,' 397, 450; small, 216,
224, 237, 248, 261–2, 318; *small
arms,* 19, 71, 80, 130, 166,' 168,
199, 224, 226, 239, 457.
Gunsmith, 246, 264; tools, 353.
Gust, sudden, 22, 59; gale, 62.
Guy, Col. Richard, 240.

Haberdine, Fish, 146.
Habitations, 66, 113, 325, 428.
Habits, 105; dress, 166, 287.
Hacket, Mr. Robert, 29.
Hadlutt, Mr. Benj., 30, 53–4, 255,
283.
Hadock, Mary, 328.
Hafts, 150.
Hago=Slago, bluff, 459.'
Hair of slain Indians, 460.
Halsted, Lawrence, 29.

36

Shell fish, 24; heaps, 63-4, 77.
Shepherd, Agnes, 430; James, 142.
Sheriffs, 12, 88,′ 100, 108, 177.′
Ship affairs, 248, 260; build'g, 379;
  carriages, 93, 310; chandler,
  wright, 329; masters, 125, 129,
  169, 175, 242, 333, 336, 370, 389;
  stores, 143, 233, 245-6, 263,
  426.′
Shipping, 103, 150, 201-2, 241, 256.
Ships, 3, 4, 32-3, 74-5, 117, 119,′
  158-9, 160, 171, 180, 211, 223,
  252, 256, 279-80, 349, 351, 397,
  450, 476; H. M., 14,′ 91;′ Ld.
  Prop'rs, 124-5, 127, 176, 208,
  231; wanted, 83, 89, 91, 193,
  224, 353, 364, 387-8, 419; gratis,
  182, 245, 258; another, 157, 215-
  6, 222-4, 230-1, 251, 257, 261,
  263-4, 387; of force, 184, 225,
  245, 258; burden, 73, 182, 263,
  308, 388, 462; entries, 369-70;
  lade, 38, 129-30; at Pt. town,
  344, 361; on skids, 210, 251,
  263, 308; by banks, 353, 379;
  arrive, 167, 293, 297, 417; sail,
  242, 295, 345,′ 424, 429; lost, 4,
  14,′ 20, 25, 28, 52,′ 59, 116,
  119,′ 156, 226, 263, 278, 387;
  Span'h, 19, 174, 187, 195, 201,
  218, 227, 245, 249-50, 261-2.
  v. Vessels, dogger, frigate, fly-
  boat, ketch, pink, pinnace, 4,′
  sloop, & Adventure, Albemarle, Blessing, Carolina,
  Charles, Coventry, Edisto, Fellowship, Hope, John, John &
  Thomas, Phœnix, Pt. Royal,
  Rebecca, Three Brothers, Wm.
  & Ralph.
Ships' companies, 10, 57, 61, 63, 65,
  69, 74, 77, 141-3, 241, 251, 254,
  261-2, 278, 331, 335.
Shirley, Sir Anthony, 265; John,
  253.
Shirts, 132, 146, 169, 246, 259, 264.
Shoals, 22-3, 59-61, 68-9, 70-1, 73,
  80, 167, 412.
Shoes, 132, 147, 234, 246-7, 259,
  262, 264.
Shore, 4, 18-20, 22-4, 62-3, 67-8, 74-
  5, 77, 165-70, 174-5, 179, 195,
  199, 205, 226, 238-9, 278, 308.
Shot, 31, 33, 38, 50, 194, 321, 428;
  bird, fowling, 130; musket, 138,
  147; small, 147, 179; moulds,
  93, 147; round, 138.
Shovels, 148; fire, 139.
Showers, 348.   Shrouds, 139.

Sickly, 24, 79, 201, 223; sickness,
  125, 235, 272, 299, 309, 347,
  350, 353, 394, 431.
Signs, 165, 168, 198, 201, 227, 238,
  461.
Signet, 6, 55-6; office, 7, 55-6.
Silk, 14, 15, 41, 127-8, 176, 321,
  377-8, 387, 445; worms, 321.
Silver, 48, 115, 220, 316, 446, 460;
  mines, 48, 327.
Silver Bluff, 186,′ 191,′ 460.′
Simons, Mr. Henry, 131,′ 176,
  177,′ 204;′ Frances, his wife,
  177.′
Simpson, John, 415, 429, 471.
Sinkler, Robert, 30.
Sizzard? 150.
Skene, Alexander, Esq., 456.′
Skif, 238.   Skirmish, 183.
Skids 210, 251, 263, 308.
Skins, 66, 74, 128, 138, 147, 194, 224,
  380, 462.
Sky, 308.
Slaves, 42-5, 52, 115; Indian, 166,
  460, 462; raiders, 460′-1.′
Slingesby, Henry, Esq., 435.′ 414.′
Sloop, 58-9, 74-5, 347, 353; see
  Ships, Shallop, Bermuda do.
  Gray's, 424,′ 426, 439.
Slop seller, 328.
Small arms, 351, 353, 459; pox,
  394.′
Smallwood, Math'w, 135, 136,′ 454;
  Math'w, Jr., and Mary, 136.′
Smericke, Mary, 396.′
Smiths, 144, 305, 328 412, 418;
  work, 407, 426; tools, 147, 350.
Smith, Abraham, 135; Mr. Christo-
  to'r, 429;′ Elizabeth, 134; Mr.
  James, 368, 408; Mr. Michael,
  368,408; Mr. Paul, 134, 136,′
  275,′307; in council, 167,′176,
  181, 204, 287, 289, 291, 295;
  acc't of, 247, 259, 277;′ Samuel,
  29; Mr. Thos., f, 134, 176, 204,′
  277,′ 408; & Co., 340;? Gov.,
  &c., 136.′ 177;′ William, 328.
Smyth, Mr. Jno., 457, 470, 472, 474;′
  Casique, 470,′ 474;′ his wife
  Mary and family, 470.
Snakes, 309.
Snares (of drums) 350. Snaths, 148.
Snow, 272, 275, 387.′
Socage, free and common, 47, 122.
Sockets, 141.
Soil, 8, 24, 74, 82, 126, 250, 266, 414,
  436, 462; rich, 63-5, 76, 81, 218,
  250, 332, 354, 458, 460.
Soldiers, 38, 40, 116, 131; Span.,